D0223354

The Child as Thinker
Second Edition

This second edition of *The Child as Thinker* has been thoroughly revised and updated to provide an informed and accessible overview of the varied and extensive literature on children's cognition. Both theory and research data are critically examined and educational implications are discussed.

After a brief discussion of the nature and subject of cognition, Sara Meadows reviews children's thinking in detail. She discusses the ways children remember and organise information in general, the acquisition of skills such as reading, writing and arithmetic, and the development of more complex reasoning as children grow to maturity. As well as studies that typically describe a generalised child, the book also reviews some of the main areas relevant to individual differences in normal cognitive development, and critically examines three major models of cognitive development. In outlining the work of Piaget, information-processing accounts and neo-Vygotskian theories, she also evaluates their different explanations of cognitive development and their implications for education. Finally, the book examines biological and social factors that may be involved in normal and suboptimal cognitive development.

Sara Meadows provides an important review of the crucial issues involved in understanding cognitive development and of the new data and models that have emerged in the last few years. This book brings together areas and approaches that have hitherto been independent, and examines their strengths and weaknesses. *The Child as Thinker* will be required reading for all students of cognitive development and psychology.

Sara Meadows is a Senior Lecturer in Education at the University of Bristol. As a psychologist she uses the concepts and the methods of developmental psychology as a way of understanding what children are experiencing at home and at school and the ways in which they grow up as learners. Much of her current research is with the Avon Longitudinal Study of Parents and Children (ALSPAC), also known as the 'Children of the 90s' study.

The Child as Thinker
Second Edition

The Development and Acquisition of Cognition in Childhood

Sara Meadows

Routledge
Taylor & Francis Group

LONDON AND NEW YORK

First edition published 1993

Second edition published 2006 by Routledge,
27 Church Road, Hove, East Sussex, BN3 2FA

Simultaneously published in the USA and Canada
by Routledge
270 Madison Avenue, New York, NY 10016

Routledge is an imprint of the Taylor & Francis Group, an informa business

© 1993, 2006 Routledge

Typeset in Times by Garfield Morgan, Mumbles, Swansea
Printed and bound in Great Britain by TJ International Ltd, Padstow, Cornwall
Cover design by Anú Design

The publisher makes no representation, express or implied, with regard to
the accuracy of the information contained in this book and cannot accept any
legal responsibility or liability for any errors or omissions that may be made.

This publication has been produced with paper manufactured to strict
environmental standards and with pulp derived from sustainable forests.

British Library Cataloguing in Publication Data
A catalogue record for this book is available from the British Library

Library of Congress Cataloging in Publication Data
Meadows, Sara.
    The child as thinker : the development and acquisition of cognition in
childhood / Sara Meadows. – 2nd ed.
       p. cm.
    Includes bibliographical references and indexes.
    ISBN 1-84169-511-4 (hardcover) – ISBN 1-84169-512-2 (softcover)
    1. Cognition in children. 2. Human information processing in children.
I. Title.
BF723.C5M383 2005
155.4'13–dc22

                                                          2005027572

ISBN13: 978-1-84169-511-2 (hbk)
ISBN13: 978-1-84169-512-9 (pbk)

ISBN10: 1-84169-511-4 (hbk)
ISBN10: 1-84169-512-2 (pbk)

Dedication

With gratitude to all those who made contributions to the development of my cognition during my childhood: and to all those who have allowed me to examine the development of cognition in other children: and with love to the star of this book.

Contents

List of figures

List of tables

Chapter 1

Introduction

The study of cognitive development in childhood is one of the major areas of child psychology. The aim of this book is to provide an informed and accessible overview of the area that will give the reader useful descriptions of what children do as thinkers and begin to show how we could explain why their cognition develops. Currently there are a number of interesting shifts in what cognitive development is thought to be, and this book is intended to review the field and, as far as possible, suggest what answers to the issues involved might be like. There is relevant research in a wide range of disciplines. These have tended to be isolated from each other, and I am convinced that workers in each field need to be better informed about each other's progress. Recent work has generated new data and new explanatory models that I want to juxtapose, and has shown that some of the assumptions we have left unquestioned need to be re-examined. I hope to give students who are new to the field of cognitive development a sense of what is going on, to allow researchers who are more dug into it to access the relevant research flowering outside their own areas, and to fork over and refresh the general compost heap: which may all, finally, help us to grow children's cognition better than we do at present.

Here, in the first chapter, I will present, briefly, some of the issues that will surface for closer examination elsewhere. The first is fundamental for how we describe cognition; it is the question of what 'cognition' is. This may seem to be capable of a clear answer, but in fact there are a number of problems in the background, stretching right back to psychology's unresolved tension between its two definitions as 'the science of mental life' and 'the science of behaviour'. At one level cognition is what people can be observed to do when they have to think, learn, remember, understand, judge, use concepts and so forth; at another it is the system behind these different abilities. Researchers tend to focus on one level rather than another, just as they differ on whether they attend to the formal properties of a cognitive system or to the material it is made of, when seeking to explain why it works as it does. Sometimes this is because different researchers are using different allied disciplines; the user of the latest neurophysiological research is probably not dealing with quite the same question about cognition as the users of the latest advances in artificial intelligence or in educational programmes. I am going to argue that there would be more progress in the study of cognitive development if practitioners who differed in their focus on the subject nevertheless took into account the illumination that other focuses provided. The study of reading processes in childhood and adulthood is a shining example of the advances that arise when different disciplines, in this case experimental cognitive psychology, developmental psychology and cognitive neurophysiology, are brought together intelligently.

Another uncertainty stretching back to the early days of psychology is about what the limits of cognition are in the sense of what is not 'cognitive'. Virtually every human action involves some thinking, learning, use of concepts, and so forth, and is therefore cognitive. The traditional division of psychology's subject-matter was into 'affective' (or emotional), 'conative' (or motivational) and 'cognitive' (or intellectual). The problem with this division is that it underplays the links between cognition, emotion and motivation, and they have been largely neglected in research, which, as I show later, is regrettable. Nor does it easily accommodate the social dimension of behaviour, and here another problematic issue about cognitive development is relevant: is it a matter of each individual constructing his or her own individual cognitive system, or are cognitive systems constructed within and by social interaction? Again, much of the literature tends to focus on either individual or social without giving the other adequate consideration, and many of the descriptive studies do not help with the problem because they seek to describe a generalised child and do not examine the variation between individuals with different powers of construction or different experience of social interaction. The theoretical models that make individual construction pre-eminent tend to focus on very general abstract cognitive processes instantiated in behaviour on problems that are not part of the usual educational curriculum, such as conservation, or solving the problems of the Tower of Hanoi. The social constructivist theories are more likely to look at cognition in socially valued areas, such as school achievement or becoming a skilled craft worker. It might be that these are in important ways different sorts of cognition, and so might have different origins and development; but as they operate in the same individual and very probably with pretty much the same brain cells, it seems a pity to treat them separately.

One way of putting this sort of problem about cognition is to question whether it is general – a matter of a few processes that dominate cognitive behaviour in all disciplines and all domains – or whether it is 'domain-specific', with each area of subject-matter having its own specialised ways of thinking. Again, it must be both, but we need to say how the two work together in development. A parallel debate to this one is concerned with whether there are universal cognitive processes that are the same for every normal individual, or at least a level of description where universals may be used, or whether there may not be more than one normal way of solving the same problem. The two very important developmental versions of this are whether the successful solution processes of children might differ from the successful solution processes of adults, and whether there might not be distinctly different pathways from early childhood to adulthood for different individuals or groups. I argue that some attention to the possibility of differences between individuals in their cognition may illuminate both what cognition is and how it gets to be as it is, and would clarify how individual construction and social construction are balanced.

A whole set of even more unresolved issues arise about the parallel question of what 'development' is. These interact with the problems of the nature and limits of 'cognition' that I have just mentioned; if these are difficulties when we look at completed cognition in adults, they are much more delicate when we look at cognitive development in childhood, because in childhood we have to explain both development and stability. Even when we have a stable state of language, cognition or intelligence, it may be the result of dynamic processes that maintain that stability within a permanent process of change. Development is not just about how X becomes Y or gives rise to Y, but about how X maintains itself as X. As I discuss in Chapter 3, there are theoretical accounts of both development and stability (e.g. Fischer and Bidell 1998; Gottlieb et al. 1998; Lerner 1998; Magnusson and Stattan 1998; Overton 1998; Valsiner 1998b; Oyama et al. 2001), which need to be brought to bear on descriptions of the ways in which children behave.

The introduction is not the place to discuss these difficult issues. They will be implicit (occasionally explicit) in my description of 'the child as thinker', and are more fully addressed in the later part of the book, in which I look at accounts of 'cognitive development' and what pushes, pulls and mauls it. I hope readers will read the descriptive chapters to get a reasonably firm sense of what has to be explained, but be able to enjoy a bit of uncertainty about what sorts of explanation might work. Years of immersion in the field have taught me that very little indeed is at the level of scientific certainty that we would like, but there are enough fairly firm tussocks in the marsh of our ignorance to keep us from getting wet much above the knees.

There are, I think, three good reasons for studying the development and acquisition of cognition in childhood. First, it is there, interesting in itself. Second, understanding it is going to make a major contribution to understanding human cognition: as J. M. Baldwin (1895) said, 'the study of children is often the only means of testing the truth of our mental analyses'. Third, understanding it should illuminate our activities as formal and informal educators of children; I think we can already draw ideas from the field about how to facilitate their cognitive development, and about what could impede it, even though we are some way from a rigorous understanding.

The plan of the book is as follows. It begins with description of cognition in childhood (Chapter 2), with a review of what children's thinking is like in a number of different areas, beginning with the generally applicable cognitive skills of talking, reading, writing and arithmetic and the ways that children remember and organise information in general, and going on to areas such as drawing, spatial reasoning and ideas about socio-economic systems. This long chapter addresses the 'what' of cognitive development in childhood: what do children do when they remember, draw maps, act as naïve psychologists or physicists, or whatever; what changes and what remains the same as they grow to maturity? Developmental principles begin to appear here, and get some discussion in terms of how well they could account for children's cognitive behaviour.

The studies reviewed in Chapter 2 typically seek to describe a generalised child: they say '5-year-olds do this, 10-year-olds do that'; variation among children of the same age or stage is rarely focused on, and may be explicitly consigned to the separate study of 'individual differences'. I think that this is unfortunate, for reasons developed throughout the rest of the book, and therefore Chapter 3 reviews some of the main areas relevant to individual differences in normal cognitive development. As it happens, much of the work on intelligence, creativity and cognitive style has been assertively non-developmental, insisting that many of these individual differences are to a major extent innate; my discussion of them focuses on how this has impoverished the research and how it could be enriched by a developmental perspective.

Having discussed the 'what' of cognitive development, I move towards the 'how': what drives, leads, or produces change in cognition over childhood. Chapter 4 reviews the three major current models of cognitive development. Here Piaget's work, information-processing accounts, and neo-Vygotskian theories are outlined and evaluated. It is in this section that I present theorists' accounts of the principles behind cognitive development, and discuss them in terms of their adequacy as models of the development described in Chapter 2. Each has a different set of answers to the question of how cognitive development occurs, and different descriptions of its causes and of the role of education. I use some examples of children's thinking to illustrate their goodness-of-fit with the data and suggest their achievements and inadequacies.

Chapter 5 examines some of the areas in mainstream psychology that might contribute to our understanding of the 'what' and 'how' of cognitive development. The first part is predominantly biological and medical, drawing on research on genetics, brain development and the effects of environmental problems for what they can tell us about both normal and suboptimal cognitive development. The second part looks at social influences on cognitive development, focusing first on demographic variations in cognitive achievement and then on the effect of social interaction in the family and in school on how well cognitive development proceeds.

The final chapter raises some of the pervasive problems and omissions of the field, and indicates where I think progress is likely.

Note to second edition

Users of the first edition of this book suggested that it should be expanded to include discussion of cognition in infancy and the development of spoken language. I have added some description of language development to Chapter 2, I now include it in my discussion of debates about the causes of cognitive development, and there are many more items on it in the References. I have not added much on infancy research. My reason is that this deserves a book in itself. The field is full of interesting but conflicting data and interpretation, and as an outsider I did not feel well placed to discern what was the best account of it. It would also add to what is already a long book. No-one identified parts of the first edition that could be cut out, and so each has been retained and revised. There are a lot of indications of cross-references, as similar points are made or related issues raised in different chapters. I have tried not to repeat myself, though as many topics were related or had been addressed from different angles it was not possible to provide a simple linear structure to the material. I have tried to prune as well as add, and to rethink more than either, but have retained most of the older references. The balance has shifted a little towards more on cognition in its biological and social setting, and less on purely cognitive accounts, reflecting the opening up of new research areas and my own preferences.

Chapter 2

Descriptive studies of children's cognitive skills and knowledge

This chapter contains reviews of some of the knowledge and the cognitive skills that children develop and acquire during the years of childhood, including talking, reading, writing, arithmetical computation, remembering, reasoning, drawing, metacognition, categorising into concepts, and their ideas about music, persons, socio-economic systems, science, stories, maps, and so on. I provide here only a brief outline of each topic with references to the material from which my outline is derived; readers must consult these references to get anything like a comprehensive picture. I have not attempted to integrate the separate bodies of research that have produced the descriptions I summarise here, nor to go beyond description to explanation. Nor have I dealt with every skill or area of knowledge that has appeared in the literature. The selection of material has necessarily been dependent on what I came across: doubtless there have been many brilliant studies that I simply failed to notice, and some I failed to understand, which are therefore not dealt with here.

I would not want to draw a strong distinction between skills and knowledge, being persuaded by the evidence that they are so interdependent as to be inextricable. However, there is some difference in the descriptions of children's behaviour in this section that maps on to the skills–knowledge distinction. In some areas what is described is what children *do*, and these areas are on the whole more skill-like (reading, writing, reasoning, and so forth), while in other areas the description is of what children *say* about a topic, and here the focus is perhaps knowledge (of people, socio-economic systems, music, etc.). There are some intermediate areas, metacognition for example, where the interplay between skill and knowledge is most conspicuous. Many would argue that knowing enough about your cognitive skills to apply them consciously, deliberately and flexibly is a major part of cognitive development, perhaps *the* major part so far as cognition acquired through formal education is concerned. How far knowledge about one's 'declarative' knowledge (of persons, countries, sub-atomic particles, or whatever) affects either that knowledge or one's 'procedural' knowledge (skills such as remembering, understanding and reasoning) is not clear; but certainly differences in the efficiency of such cognitive procedures will affect one's access to and use of one's knowledge. An ability to remember information or to recognise that there is a contradiction between two 'facts' will no doubt be necessary for using knowledge satisfactorily. Some aspects of the procedural knowledge–declarative knowledge distinction are discussed later in this book. The distinction functions here only as the reason why the contents of this section are presented in the order that follows: roughly, 'mainly about skills' before 'mainly about content'. This structure separates some areas that would ideally be linked, and deals with some topics several times, from somewhat different angles. Readers will find that the text does contain cross-references, but it would be advisable to use the index too. It is essential, rather than advisable, that readers should not believe that any section contains all that is to be said about its subject! The References section includes a number of review articles that will give a supplementary overview to mine and start the reader on more extensive study, as well as original books and papers. I have referenced what I say rather thoroughly, with the intention that readers should have no excuse not to follow up ideas or experiments rather than rely on my review.

2.1 Language development

Being language users, and more specifically highly educated literate adults, those reading this book, and I myself writing it, may be inclined to think that human language is the pinnacle of achievement for our species and for each of us as an individual. We delight in what we can do with language, with what we can see it do in the utterances or writings of other people. We may find its development in the child especially amazing; find it wonderful how fast children learn to use language to communicate, describe, argue, analyse, persuade, inform, and deceive. Language seems a more special, uniquely human ability, than any other; it has often been said to be the defining attribute of *Homo sapiens*. While sharing the delight and the admiration, I am going to argue that we need to be cautious about the specialness of language.

Much of the literature on children's language development deals with it as a phenomenon separate from other human activities. In the first edition of this book, I omitted discussion of it for this reason; if the language development specialists dealt with language as different from the rest of children's cognition, then a book on children's cognition that was already in danger of being far too long could refer its readers to other sources for an account of something that specialists thought was separate. Since then, readers have asked for language development to be added to the book, and the theory around language development has itself shifted towards more links between language and the rest of children's cognition. This has given me more incentive to look (selectively) at the enormous amount of literature on child language and provide a brief review of its development. It also increases the scope for addressing the difficult question of the relationship between language and cognition.

Classic pictures of children's language development centred on the quite brief period between the first recognisable word (early in the second year of life) and the child using language fluently (by something like age three). They also centred on language production, especially on the production of grammatical sentences. The dominant theoretical accounts of language development for many years were models that gave the child an innate ability to develop language given minimal exposure to other people's language use, models that were heavily nativist; these had developed in reaction to earlier models in which the child was a passive recipient of parental conditioning to use language as the parents did. The nature–nurture polarity flourished, just as it did in theories of intelligence (Chapter 3). A tremendous amount of interesting research and theorising was done, but it was unhelpfully influenced by a set of presuppositions: that the crucial period during which language developed was 13 to 36 months; that word production and grammar rules were the most important part of the phenomenon; that language could be separated from its context in the child's experience and the child's cognition; that nativism was capable of explaining it. I shall be arguing that none of these presuppositions are helpful to understanding language development and its place in the child's life. Emphasising throughout the importance of the time before and after the classic two year period, I shall look at language perception as well as production, place language development in its social and cognitive context, and try to specify what about language development might be 'native' and how its 'native' predispositions and constraints affect development. Language development is, of course, something we need to relate to the development of cognition, notably of reading, both when the two proceed well and when there are difficulties with each (Snowling 2004), and readers should cross-reference this section with the next.

2.1.1 Language perception

The age at which attention to language and ability to discriminate between language and other sounds, and within the sounds of language arise, has been shifted further and further back in the child's life by successive research studies. It now appears that the foetus's sensitivity to sounds heard through the wall of the mother's womb is sufficient for it to be able to discriminate between her voice and another woman's, between different types of music, and between different languages if they have different stress patterns, the abilities that have been noted in newborn babies (Jusczyk *et al.* 1993; Pinker 1994; Bloom 1998; Nazzi *et al.* 1998; Karmiloff and Karmiloff-Smith 2001). Infants of course hear speech around them and addressed to them after birth; here too they have opportunities to learn about the sounds of language. In many cultures, infants are spoken to by their mothers or other caretakers as their daily routines are carried out, or for fun. The adults' language is often given exaggerated stress patterns and intonation, a clearer child-specific 'melody' that catches children's attention and highlights all sorts of useful information for the language learner. It is also accompanied by exaggerated facial expressions, gestures and actions; the semantic content is restricted to the here and now, and to what the child is doing or appears to be attending to; vocabulary is simplified at the 'level of appropriateness'; syntax is simple, sentences are brief and frequently they are repeated; and much of what the adult says involves extensions and expansions of the child's own contributions, contemporaneous comment on ongoing activities, questions to which the adult already knows the answer, and prompts and modelling of discourse (e.g. Baumwell *et al.* 1997). These are also features that may be especially useful for language development, and I will return to them later after discussing sound patterns.

Very young babies selectively attend to the speech they can hear, and show discriminations between certain of its features. One particularly interesting discrimination is between consonant sounds. Speech sounds depend on a combination of body movements shaping the sound wave more or less simultaneously (Pinker (1994: 170–172) provides an accessible description). Vowels vary somewhat freely in exactly how a particular speaker produces and hears them (as in local dialects). Adults perceive the consonants of their language categorically: /b/ and /p/, for example, differ only in terms of whether they are pronounced with 'voicing', vibration of the vocal cords; other variation in the production of each is irrelevant to whether it is categorised as /b/ or /p/. Babies as young as a few months display categorical perception of such consonant contrasts too (e.g. Eimas *et al.* 1971; Streeter 1976; Jusczyk *et al.* 1993) even if the community they are growing up in does not use this contrast. People who have not used the consonant contrast gradually lose the ability to hear it readily, and adults have difficulty in deliberately producing the consonants differently. This is part of what makes learning a new language difficult. Initial categorical consonant discrimination is probably a result of wired-in sensitivities in the brain's sound perception, shared with some other species (Aslin *et al.* 1983, 1998), with the brain's sensitivity altered by experience of the native language.

Although speech may come out as a cascade of speech sounds without obvious breaks in the acoustics of the signal, we do not process it as an uninterrupted stream, but as a succession of larger units such as words, phrases, clauses and sentences. This requires us to recognise what to chunk together and what to separate. Sounds that occur together frequently may be processed together; the juxtaposition of sounds that do not occur together within a word may signal a break between words in the speech stream. Stress patterns may also give clues: for example in English a word is more likely to begin with a stressed syllable that is followed by a weak syllable (TIger) than the reverse (girAFFE), so the detection of a stressed syllable suggests there may be a new word. Babies are using these sorts of information before their first birthday. With accumulating experience of their own language, of course, they become better and better at doing it. It will be several years, however, before phrases that almost always operate as a unit (for example 'How do you do?') become capable of deconstruction into the constituent words (Peters 1983). Analysing units down to basic sounds (phonemes) is going to be almost essential for reading (see pp. 31–33, 39–44, and Snowling 2004) but is very difficult for people who are not experienced with a writing system that uses grapheme–phoneme correspondences (Ferreiro 1999; Castro-Caldas *et al.* 1998; Shu *et al.* 2003), perhaps because their brains have not learned to do this.

2.1.2 Producing words

Almost all babies go through the same sequence of producing vocal sounds. The earliest, of course, are inarticulate cries, grunts, gasps, and murmurs, which may unintentionally signal their emotional states. It is some time after birth before the infants' vocal apparatus has developed to the adult state. Initially, the baby's larynx is high up in the throat engaging the nasal passage, so that the infant breathes through the nose and is able to drink and breathe at the same time (very useful to someone whose waking hours contain a lot of suckling). By about three months of age the larynx has descended in the throat, the pharynx has opened up and there is scope for the tongue movements that are necessary to produce the full variety of vowel sounds. Babies begin to play with sounds, producing a larger and larger range and seeming sometimes to try out systematic contrasts of sounds based on different positioning of their speech organs. This vocal activity is not produced more in social than in solitary situations; it appears to be for its own sake rather than involved in any attempt to communicate. Around seven or eight months babies start to combine vowels and consonants, producing the ba-ba, ma-ma, da-da sorts of sounds (canonical babbling) that many languages use as names for things relevant to babies because they are babbled in much the same way across languages. A baby randomly producing a babbling noise which is also a name for a significant person in the native language may get a great deal of reward from its adults, who believe, or act as if they believed, that the baby is now addressing them by name. This sort of social reward has been shown to increase not specific noises in babble but the general amount of babble and the proportion of it that is produced as a social activity rather than a solitary one (Karmiloff and Karmiloff-Smith 2001). A wide range of sounds are produced in babbling initially, but by about ten months of age the range is narrowing to include mainly those sounds that the baby hears produced by other people.

The stable sequence and timing of speech sound production to the babbling stage in virtually all children suggests that a high degree of genetic programming and maturation is involved. However, experience is also necessary. Congenitally deaf children start to babble vocally but commonly give it up, presumably because they have not been able to hear themselves (Bishop and Mogford 1993). If their parents are fluent or native users of a sign language and sign to the baby, the baby will babble manually, probably at a slightly younger age that a hearing baby starts to babble vocally, perhaps because the muscular control needed for signing is easier for the baby than the muscular control needed to articulate speech. Signs may be invented as well as imitated (Goldin-Meadow and Mylander 1998).

From around the first birthday, infants both babble and produce what we could call words, that is sounds that are consistently linked to a particular event or object and might be performing at least some of the same functions as an adult's word would be. My daughter's first 'word' of this sort was /wow/, which we first noticed when she looked at a dog (in her father's talk to her a 'bow-wow') running round in a local wood. We will never know what exactly 'wow' meant to her at this stage, whether it was an imitation of the dog's noise or of her father's comment, or truly referred to the creature or something about it, or was even the sort of superlative that 'WOW!' is to an adult; but in that it was uniquely linked with a particular sight (dogs running about) and was a derivative of an adult's conventional word it was pretty typical of first words. The 'first words' follow from a period where the baby has shown understanding of words in adults' speech, has built up a receptive vocabulary of twenty to fifty words, and may have produced idiosyncratic words (some of which go unrecognised by anyone else). Early words are commonly phonologically simplified; indeed, the same sound may be produced in different contexts as different words – /da/ could mean dog, or duck, or daddy, depending on which of these interesting creatures was present, and be unambiguous in context. By the child's second birthday, productive vocabularies will probably be upwards of fifty words, perhaps into the hundreds. Most early words are names of familiar people, objects, animals, food, toys, body parts and functions, and social routines, or social phrases such as 'bye-bye', but verbs, adverbs and expletives ('uh-oh') also appear early (e.g. Murachver *et al.* 1996; Tardif 1996; Bloom 1998; Woodward and Markman 1998). Children also invent words, often for fun, often when they do not know the conventional word for what they want to express – the equivalent of adult words like 'thingummy' or 'kinda'.

2.1.2.1 Early word use

Early words typically serve a range of functions for the child (Woodward and Markman 1998). Michael Halliday's young son used his early words to satisfy his own wants, to regulate others' behaviour, to establish or maintain interpersonal contact and eventually to talk about himself, to find out about the world, to pretend, and to inform others (Halliday 1975). As children get older a single utterance can have multiple functions, indeed as in speech act theory (Grice 1975) it may have an ostensible function and a far more important implicit one, which the listener may or may not catch and act on, and even for very young children the intended function is not always simple. Adults may frequently name things that the child sees; children may copy them and simply name objects – it becomes a game for some child–adult pairs (Bruner 1983) – but often what could appear to simply be a referential comment is actually a 'proto-imperative', uttered because the child wants what it is talking about. Only an unwise adult would think that the small child is disinterestedly naming the ice-cream, rather than trying to bring about the desired outcome of getting some to eat. Children very quickly learn that words are powerful ways of controlling other people, fortunately for the adults who would like to use words to control the child.

Using words as names is an important cognitive achievement (McShane 1980; Woodward and Markman 1998). A telling example of this comes from the autobiography of Helen Keller, who having become blind and deaf at the age of eight months had words finger-spelled to her by her governess, Anne Sullivan, from the age of 6. Anne Sullivan tried to spell out on Helen's fingers 'everything we do all day long, although she has no idea yet what the spelling means'. Helen quickly imitated the finger-spellings but made no connection between them and the objects they symbolised. The insight came in an incident that has become famous.

> They had been wrestling with the words M-U-G and W-A-T-E-R, recorded Helen, and she persisted in confusing the two. Later they went for a walk by the well-house. Someone was pumping water. Annie placed Helen's hand under the spout and 'as the cool stream gushed over one hand, she [Annie] spelled into the other the word water, first slowly then rapidly. I stood still, my whole attention fixed upon the motion of her fingers. Suddenly I felt a misty consciousness as of something forgotten – a thrill of returning thought; and somehow the mystery of language was revealed to me. I knew then that W-A-T-E-R meant the wonderful cool something that was flowing over my hand . . . I left the well-house eager to learn. Everything had a name, and each name gave birth to a new thought. As we returned to the house every object that I touched seemed to quiver with life.'

> Annie Sullivan wrote 'She has learned that everything has a name and that the manual alphabet is the key to everything she wants to know . . . She has flitted from object to object, asking the name of everything.'

> (Lash 1980: pp. 57–58)

2.1.2.2 Mistakes with names

The mistakes young children make with their early words, and the apparent constraints on their vocabulary development, have been of great interest to researchers (Bloom 1998). One phenomenon that has been intensively studied is the child's over-generalisation or under-generalisation of new words. Toddlers often use a word to embody a whole event or need – 'ice-cream' to mean something like 'I can see a source of ice-creams and I want one right now'. They may also apply them to categories of objects or events or feelings that are too wide or too narrow – all furry animals are referred to as 'cat', or only one's own individual Mowzer receives that name and other cats are barred from it. Clark and Clark (1977) suggested that 'over-extensions' resulted from the child picking out one or two salient features, for example furriness or having four legs, and so over-extending the word to objects such as dogs that have these characteristics but are not actually cats. By adding more salient characteristics of cats – purrs, sits on laps, scratches – the category is gradually narrowed to exclude other categories and a new label is acquired for the differentiated out category. Eventually a superordinate label – animals – is developed. An alternative explanation credits the child with more competence. This child knows that cats and dogs are different but does not have the appropriate vocabulary to differentiate them in speech (like an adult who knows that her teenage child has various devices for storing music downloaded from the internet but does not know their names). Unless the whole topic is to be excluded from conversation entirely, until the right words are learned speakers without the crucial vocabulary will have to resort to using what words they have, and people with more adequate vocabularies may underestimate how much they know but cannot talk about fluently. In any case, the child may not simply be labelling; he or she may be comparing, joking or using language meta-phorically, or just saying something vaguely appropriate to fill in a conversational turn.

Furthermore, the words the child has will be dependent on the words the adult feels are appropriate for the child. Adults talking to young children tend to use words that are at Rosch's basic level of category differentiation (Rosch 1978, 1981; and see pp. 151–152), neither more specific nor more general. The adult is likely to reckon that 'plant' is a bit too general, 'rose' a bit too specific, 'flower' about right, for a small child; and 'flower' needs to be contrasted with 'tree', 'grass' and 'fruit' because the child is expected to do different things with each. If the adult has a particular interest (or recognises the child's interest) and encourages it in the child this will make a notable contribution to the child's vocabulary and cognition; Chi and Koeske (1983)'s dinosaur expert is a nice example. There are numerous studies relating vocabulary content and rate of growth to the topics adults talk about with the child: almost invariably, if the adult and child converse about a subject more than average, the child's vocabulary in that area will be larger and more usable than average (Woodward and Markman 1998; Bloom 2000; Hoff and Naigles 2002). This may contribute to the child's thought in this area (e.g. pp. 176, 185–186, 191).

2.1.2.3 Constraints on learning new words

There are probably, however, certain constraints on how children react to new words. In the early years of language learning, children seem to expect that an object that they already know under one name will not be what is referred to if a new word is produced; that a novel word will apply to an object for which the child does not already have a name (Gelman and Williams 1998). Bilingual children do learn two different labels for the same object, one for each language, but they store and use them rather separately during their early talk (Woodward and Markman 1998; Bishop and Mogford 1993). Children also assume that a novel word uttered in the presence of a novel object applies to the whole of that object, not just to a part or a feature of it; new words referring to objects that already have names are taken as applying to something specific about the object. Further, when children have just learned a new word as the name of a new object and are then asked to find another object that would have the same name, they will choose an object from the same taxonomic category rather than an object from a different category that has an attribute in common; for example, if they have just learned to call Batman a Superhero they would rather say Spiderman is a Superhero than that a bat is.

Constraints on what a child expects a new word to mean may also derive from adults' talk to children. From infancy onwards, parents often label the thing a child is already attending to – 'That's a doggie'. Or they may draw the child's attention to something by gesturing and labelling it – 'Look at the doggie'. Establishing joint attention between oneself and the other person is one of the most important achievements of infancy (and one of the salient problems of autistic children). Most young children monitor their parents' attention even while they are themselves engaged with some other object or activity, and react to new words accordingly (Messer 1994; Nelson 1996). Parents also may talk about both cognitive and old/new contrasts – 'You're not BIG, you're LITTLE', 'That's not NICE, that's DIRTY'. Differences in parents' use of such talk, and of labelling objects in picture books, are associated with differences in the rate of language development (Gelman and Williams 1998; Woodward and Markman 1998).

Other constraints in children's learning of new words show use of purely linguistic information to understand the novel word. For example, if children are shown a doll from a group of dolls and told 'That's Zav', when asked to give the experimenter 'Zav' they will only pick up that particular doll. But if they are shown the doll and told 'That's a Zav', they will then, when asked to give the experimenter 'a Zav', hand over any one of the group of dolls. They can also use the presence of the indefinite article 'a' as a signal that what is being talked about is a single countable object rather than an uncountable or amorphous mass object, such as water or porridge, or use the presence of the suffix 'ing' to distinguish a verb from a noun. As researchers in Slobin *et al.* (1996) pointed out, it may be very useful to pay attention to the ends of words, where there may be markers of tense, number, or agency. This is even more true in languages like Italian, which make more use of endings to convey meaning than English does.

The question of whether there are constraints on children's language development is linked to the question of whether language follows or precedes thought. This has been dealt with philosophically as well as psychologically (e.g. Fodor 1976; Bloom 2000) and will crop up in other areas of this book, notably my discussion of Piaget and Vygotsky in Chapter 4. An interesting piece of empirical work was recently published in *Nature* (Hespos and Spelke 2004; Bloom 2004). In Korean, tightly-fitting and loose-fitting connections between objects are categorised differently and different verbs are used. Korean speakers readily learn to class a mixed set of tightly-fitting objects together and to separate them from loosely-fitting objects. The English language does not mark the distinction: English speakers find it much harder, and feel it is an arbitrary basis for classification. Hespos and Spelke (2004) investigated babies' use of the tightly-fitting/loosely-fitting contrast by means of a habituation technique. They found that four-month-old American babies who would begin to show use of English a year or so later were just as able to use the contrast as babies who would grow up to speak Korean, which strongly suggests that babies can make the cognitive contrast between tightly-fitting and loosely-fitting pre-language, although if they acquire a language that does not mark it their ability to use it will decrease. What is presumably happening here is that babies can notice a range of contrasts and classify objects according to them: which of these contrasts they become able to express and work with is influenced by the language they learn and the contrasts and categories it employs or omits. The question of why fit mattered enough to be marked in Korean, and did not matter enough to be easily marked in English, I leave to linguists.

Constraints such as language features or cognitive distinctions are not applied rigidly or all the time, and some are detectable earlier than others (Golinkoff and Hirsh-Pasek 1994; Gelman and Williams 1998; Lidz and Gleitman 2004), but they operate often enough to help the child acquire new vocabulary quickly and manageably. They are an example of the intertwining of children's language development and their cognitive development, with influence going in both directions between cognition and language.

2.1.2.4 The growth of vocabulary

The initial growth of children's vocabulary is fairly gradual, say three new words a week. The rate of word acquisition increases, with some children suddenly increasing the rate at which they acquire new words as much as twenty-fold. These children show a marked vocabulary spurt, while others progress more steadily (Ganger and Brent 2004). As more words that sound alike or have related meanings enter the vocabulary, the child is forced to make finer distinctions in producing and using them; if you only have one word starting with /m/, or one word to express motion, you do not have to choose between words or pronounce them more accurately, but once you have other words beginning with /m/, or 'walk' as well as 'run', your communication needs to be more differentiated. At this point children are often inclined, like Helen Keller, to ask the name of every object they see, an incessant 'What's that? What's that?' that the parent may be maddened by or indulge enthusiastically (Wells 1985; Baumwell *et al.* 1997; Huttenlocher 1998; Woodward and Markman 1998; Bloom 2000). Children also develop the insight that it is not only objects that have names; attributes, events and actions have words to describe them too (McShane 1980). This too increase the growth of the lexicon. In almost every respect this is an incomparably important step forward for the child, making all sorts of new language behaviour possible. But being able to do more does make it more necessary than before to select what to do, and to store and then retrieve language information efficiently. As well as semantic storage, there is interesting evidence of very young children using phonological information in their memory for words, perhaps something that could be related to the pleasure they have shown, ever since they were babbling, in playing with the sounds of language (Dowker 1989). Phonological awareness has turned out to be one of the important skills useful for learning to read (see pp. 40–42).

2.1.3 Combining words

The enormous creativity of human language stems not so much from vocabulary as from the possibilities that it offers of new combinations of vocabulary items to say things that have never been said before. Word combinations are rule-governed. There are rules about combining units of meaning smaller than words into words (for example 'talked' combines 'talk' and the past tense morpheme 'ed', 'handbags' combines the morphemes 'hand', 'bag' and 's'); rules about combining words into grammatical phrases, clauses and sentences; rules for combining sentences into more extended speech (or text: these may be slightly different, typically more elaborate). These rules differ from language to language but some theorists argue that there is a 'deep structure' common to all languages that children have innately accessible to them as they come to grips with combining words (Chomsky 1968, 1986 and Pinker 1994). I will return to these nativist theories later; for the moment I want to provide some examples of children's early development of grammatical (morpho-syntactic) rules.

Infants are sensitive to some aspects of grammar. For example they notice word order, a crucial grammatical device in English, showing an ability to detect simple differences in the order of words in short utterances, and by age two discriminating between the paired sentences 'Big Bird is flexing Cookie Monster', which implies Big Bird is doing something to a passive Cookie Monster, and 'Big Bird is flexing with Cookie Monster', matching only the latter to a video where the two characters are both active (Marcus 1993; Hirsh-Pasek and Golinkoff 1996). This shows sensitivity to grammar way before the children are producing utterances with grammatical structure themselves, let alone such complex grammar as the *Sesame Street* sentences. Parental emphasis and systematic contrasting may help with both understanding and producing grammatical utterances. Some syntax is more difficult for both children and adults; passive sentence structure, for example, which is rare in normal talk to children, continues to confuse them for years past the point at which they can deal with simple declarative sentences and questions.

Children's earliest word combinations juxtapose words – 'allgone milk', 'Mummy shoe' – omitting articles, prepositions, adverbs, etc. The words are sometimes in different orders to serve different functions; the young child's strong interest in who is doing something, where something is, who is in possession of or owns something, for example, may lead to particular emphasis and different word order. Some of the juxtaposed words are not single morphemes ('wossat?', 'allgone', for example) having been taken on unanalysed from adult speech. Roger Brown's pioneering study of the language development of Adam, Eve and Sarah (Brown 1973) suggested that grammatical morphemes appeared in the children's speech in a consistent order. First they expressed continuing action by adding the present progressive morpheme 'ing' – 'Baby crying'. Next they expressed location by using 'in' or 'on'. Third they added plural morphemes, fourth irregular past tenses such as 'came' or 'went', next 's' to express possession. Subsequent studies support this general order, though of course some children differ from it to some degree. What is especially interesting about it is the picture it reveals of what young children are thinking about, what they want to comment on: commentary on current action, location of objects and people, possession, are not just of linguistic interest but social and cognitive and emotional too.

Children famously make errors with some of these morpheme combinations – they talk about 'mouses' or 'foots' or say 'wented' or 'helded'. They often do this after a period of saying mice, feet, went and held. It seems that they have learned a general rule about how to form plural nouns and past tense verbs which they apply to irregular nouns and verbs, sometimes while continuing to use the correct irregular versions that they have picked up from adult speech (Brooks *et al.* 1999; Karmiloff and Karmiloff-Smith 2001; Maratsos 1998). As both the correct irregular form and the over-generalised regular form express what the child means quite intelligibly, and as locating the correct form within the communicative setting may just be too much processing, the mistake has been quite resistant to adults' attempts to correct it.

It's also worth pointing out, reminded by Karmiloff and Karmiloff-Smith (2001), that although the rules about adding 's' for a plural and 'ed' for a past look simple, this is because we are using written language in which that is indeed what you should normally do. The spoken sounds are not so consistent; the plural morpheme added to 'cat' in speech is not the same as that added to 'dog', and that added on to 'horse' sounds different again. Even adults may be confused with some of these. I will discuss the importance and the difficulty of getting spoken word and spelled word to correspond consistently when talking about children learning to read (pp. 34–36).

Children's word combinations also, of course, combine independent words. Frequently there is a useful 'pivot' word, such as 'more', 'where' or 'my', to which many other words can be added (Maratsos 1998). Typically the utterance includes the words that are crucial for meaning and omits grammatical morphemes such as 'the' or 'a' that may not convey so much extra information to the listener. This sort of child speech used to be described as 'telegraphic', but the term is in some ways misleading. The child is not trying to minimise the number of words, as in a telegram where you had to pay per word; rather, the demands of producing what is meant may occupy too much cognitive space to allow the grammatical markers that refine meaning but may not be necessary for communication.

2.1.4 Language acquisition devices

There has been debate for decades about what are the grammatical rules of children's early word combinations (Karmiloff and Karmiloff-Smith 2001). Nativist theorists such as Chomsky and Pinker argue that even these early utterances exemplify the universal grammatical rules of human language (Chomsky 1976, Pinker 1994), universal rules that are not obvious in the language that is overtly produced or processed, but lie at a 'deep structure' level of competence that produces the 'surface structure' of observable language performance. Chomsky's position was that as almost all children develop language fast and in very much the same way, despite the impoverished, incomplete and inaccurate language that they hear, there are compelling arguments for saying that the child is born with an innate set of tacit grammatical understandings that push language development on to competence, and need only minimal exposure to other people's language to trigger development and specify the details of the particular language the child is learning.

Even if we accept these assumptions and also accept Chomsky's model of what adult grammatical understanding is like (and not all linguistics theorists do), even in its own terms this theory has some problems. It focuses on grammar and under-emphasises other aspects of language, such as its sound patterns, its meaning and its social context; these sorts of information may help support the child's learning of grammatical relations. It does not incorporate much of the detailed descriptive data that we have accumulated on children's early utterances. It does not account for how the child maps innate universal grammar on to the particular grammar of their mother tongue. And its basic assumptions are shaky. Language development begins well before the period that the Chomskyan model focuses on, and continues after it. It is more individual and wobbly than he supposed. And the language addressed to children is, as we shall see, specialised in ways that we would expect to make it easier to learn.

Various theorists have suggested that there are mutually supportive relationships between syntax and other aspects of language such that development in one area may support or 'bootstrap' development in another (Hoff and Naigles 2002). Sound patterns – in particular patterns of rhythm and stress – carry grammatical information. Prosody can be quite a good clue to both meaning and syntax. We insert emphasis and pauses in to what we say in ways that signal what's important and where the sentence and clause boundaries are. The Prologue to the artisans' play in the last act of *A Midsummer Night's Dream* is an example of how important this is. It has been argued that this gives usable support to the child's syntactic analysis (Kemler-Nelson *et al.* 1989; Morgan and Demuth 1996), even if it would not give completely reliable information all the time. Similarly, Pinker (1994) suggests that there is reciprocal support between learning about syntax and learning about semantics, 'semantic bootstrapping', where the child's knowledge of many nouns and semantic representation of what a sentence means combine with innately specified syntactic knowledge and support from parents' child-directed speech to allow the child to derive precise syntactic understanding. The child maps the actions and objects that he or she sees on to the syntactic string that is being uttered, and inferring meaning from the event and the utterance also derives information about the grammatical expressions that are being used. For example, seeing a boy chase a dog and hearing 'The boy is chasing the dog', the child would be able to note that the agent or subject of the sentence comes first, that a current action is expressed in a verb phrase with the morpheme 'ing', that the object of the sentence comes last. When a moment later the child hears 'Now the dog is chasing the boy' and maps that on to what can be seen, there is a further opportunity to match semantics and syntax.

Pinker may not be giving quite enough acknowledgement to the fact that events can be described in different ways. The dog is chasing the boy, but also the boy is running away from the dog. Landau and Gleitman (1985) point out that the different accounts not only embody different emphases, they use subtly different syntax. The verb 'chase' requires a direct object, the thing you are chasing; the verb 'run away' has an indirect object introduced by the word 'from'. The sentence 'The boy is running away the dog' is incorrect, and the sentence 'The dog is chasing' feels incomplete. Parental input seems to highlight differences such as these. The mother Landau and Gleitman studied used the verb 'look' as an imperative and the verb 'see' only in questions, highlighting a semantic difference syntactically.

The bootstrapping account implies, I think, that the process would be helped by the expansion and recasting of children's imperfect utterances that parents quite often do for their children, rather than by the correction, which seems to have a much less positive effect. It also implies that children will find it more difficult to process sentences where the grammatical structure does not map so neatly on to the semantics, for example passives such as 'The boy is being chased by the dog', or in discussion of absent (past, future, counterfactual, hypothetical or imaginary) events; as indeed they do. Parents tend to avoid passives with young children, and to take a more 'as if' playful attitude to discussion of the absent.

2.1.5 Language acquisition principles

In contrast to the nativist accounts of language development, which focus on inferred competence with universal grammatical deep structure, various researchers have proposed principles that are operating in children's processing of observable language as children begin to develop grammar. Slobin *et al.* (1996) and Gelman and Williams (1998) analyse not children's underlying competence (as Chomsky did) but their actual performance and what they attend to in the language they hear. Taking their attention first, besides the sensitivity to prosody and the constraints that I have already described, in English they preferentially attend to the ends of words (which may have morphological information about number and tense) and to the beginning of the utterance – an attention pattern reminiscent of the onset–rime distinction that is part of phonological awareness and contributes to reading development (p. 41). Turning to storage principles, frequency and regularity are noted and stored; this resembles the rule found in most information-processing accounts of cognitive development (pp. 283–284), and also reinforces the idea that quantity of language exposure may be important, as I discuss below (pp. 24, 27–28). Children notice and store together scraps of speech that share a common part but come attached to a variety of other parts – tense and number morphemes are a core example, but there are instances of similar analyses in reading and spelling by analogy (see pp. 32–33, 41–42) and in play with language. Using these attention, storage and analysis principles, children discover what the grammar of their native tongue marks out and what it doesn't – for example, a French- or German-speaking child has to learn that nouns have gender markings, whereas an English-speaking child does not. Language principles operate alongside cognitive and strategic principles. For example, Slobin suggests that children will seek to express their perspective on the scene they are talking about; if they want to emphasise that it is a car they are pushing across the garden with a stick they will say 'push CAR', while if they want to emphasise their own agency they will say 'ME push'. Basic principles such as these guide children as they get through their early language development, though Slobin has not fully specified what they are and how they combine and succeed each other.

Bates and MacWhinney (1989) suggest that there is competition between the cues provided by different language features, with different balances between features in different languages (for example word order is very important in English and morphological marking is less important, while in Italian word order is used mainly to express the speaker's perspective and meaning depends on morphological markers at the end of words). Children have to balance cues of stress, intonation, rhythm, morphological marking, and word order with pragmatic clues outside the utterance itself. English children learn to place much weight on word order and hence may misunderstand passives. However, a passive that has an obvious pragmatic clue in it, such as 'The girl was bitten by the dog', will be interpreted correctly at a time when a passive without a commonsense clue will not – children are very likely to interpret 'The cat was bitten by the dog' as saying that the cat did the biting. During development, cues vary in strength and when a new cue becomes prominent it may be over-used (comparably with the over-generalisation of regular plurals, perhaps). Bates and MacWhinney suggest that such competition between cues continues even in adults' language; searching out the grammatical rules that have produced the language that has been heard using specialised language-relevant principles is done by adults as well as children.

Other theorists, for example Elena Lieven, Julian Pine, and Michael Tomasello (Lieven et al. 2003; Theakston et al. 2004; Tomasello 1992, 1997, 1998, 2000; Cameron-Faulkner et al. 2003) think that children slowly construct grammar. These theorists place more emphasis on the concreteness of children's early language, and the occurrence of strings of words that look like grammatically constructed phrases but are more likely learned as unanalysed chunks; the child may often use 'slot-and-frame' or 'fill the blank' structures that step by step are just a little more complex than the pivot word structures that began word combinations. More complex structures may be developed for particular verbs but never used for others – for example, the child may be able to add three slots, donor, recipient and gift, to the verb 'give', but not at that time combine any other verb with three grammatical slots. Children can become fluent producers of language using these sorts of slots, but they are skilled users of specific structures rather than possessors of an abstract or generalised grammar. What they have really learned is where to place words within certain familiar recurring patterns; progress towards an adult abstract grammar is piecemeal and gradual. Again, analogies with children's development as writers come to mind (pp. 63–67).

Thus, where nativists programme language learners with a set of language-specific knowledge about grammatical stuctures such as subject and object, active and passive, present and past, universal in languages though expressed differently, other theorists programme language learners with fundamental processing mechanisms specialised for language but enabling the child to discover structure in the language that he or she hears and begins to produce. Grammatical categories such as subject, verb or object emerge from the regularities and pragmatic emphases of the language children are using via their interest in what to emphasise about an event. The child or adult is not given linguistic understanding by evolution, but is actively engaged in discovering or constructing it. One important point is that children may use a different balance of strategies as they develop their language skills: Hoff and Naigles (2002), for example, present evidence suggesting that lexical richness and syntactic complexity may become important in acquiring new vocabulary at a point when pragmatic and social cues have been used for some time, and Lidz and Gleitman (2004) suggest that learning verbs may differ in some ways from learning nouns. What predicts development of language may well change as the child's skills increase. For these theorists, language development is returned from linguistics to psychology, and could therefore be re-embedded in the social and cognitive context.

2.1.6 Language acquisition support systems

The support system for children's syntactic development has also been suggested to be outside language itself. Just as much of children's vocabulary growth comes from picking up the words that adults use, possibly their interaction with adults can be used to learn about syntax. Bruner is the pioneer of work on the language acquisition support system that children grow up with (Bruner 1976, 1983). Early joint attention, turn-taking, looking at picture books and naming objects, routine talk and nursery rhymes, all figure heavily in the interaction of Western middle class babies and toddlers with their parents (but may be harder for other parents, e.g. Evans *et al.* (1999), Hart and Risley (1999), Johnson-Glenberg and Chapman (2004)). They could facilitate vocabulary growth, semantic representation systems, and inferences about grammatical structure without the innate understanding of such rules that the nativist theorists propose, especially perhaps if they are accompanied by the specialised sort of language that became famous as 'motherese' but is better called 'child-directed speech' (CDS) because it is not just mothers who do it, but also fathers, teachers, and even older siblings. In this sort of language, as used to young children, there are various syntactic, semantic and pragmatic modifications that cumulatively provide the young child with a good model to learn from, perhaps such a good model that no Chomskyan innate knowledge of language is required (Moerk 1989; Huttenlocher 1998; Bloom 1998). Among the many adjustments are attention getters and holders, such as a frequent use of the child's name, a high pitch or exaggerated intonation, and many gestures and touches; restriction of semantic content, for example by talking more than usual about the 'here and now', or by running commentary on the child's activity; selection of vocabulary, such as using 'baby names' such as 'tummy' and choosing from several possible labels the one best known to the child, 'dog' rather than 'Pekinese'; syntactic restriction to comparatively brief and simple sentences without, for example, passives or subordinate clauses, but with lots of repetitions; a specialised strategy of discourse, high on expansions and extensions of the child's own utterances, high on contemporaneous comment on ongoing activities, and high on questions, directions, prompts and modelling of discourse, and produced more slowly than language to adults. This sort of language is a relatively consistent, organised, simplified and redundant set of utterances.

Western middle-class parents are quite likely to use CDS to their young children, and to do so often in the context of books and stories. Their language is closely contingent on the child's current stage of cognitive and linguistic development, and it directs the child's attention on the development of a structured linguistic representation of reality. Two points have to be made about why CDS is used. It is evoked by the child as well as provided by the parent. As Wells says:

> for most of the time the relatively finely tuned modelling of meanings and forms that the frequency data reveal occurs incidentally, as adults carry on conversations with their children for quite other purposes – to control the child's behaviour in the interests of his safety and their joint well-being, to share in and extend his interests, to maintain and enrich their interpersonal relationship and so on. Success in achieving these aims requires that the majority of the adults' contributions be pitched at a level of complexity that is not too far beyond the child's linguistic ability. However, this is achieved quite spontaneously by most adults under the control of feedback from the child's comprehension and production and does not require deliberate attention. The tuning that occurs is thus as much a response to, as a determinant of, the sequence

in the child's learning . . . It appears, therefore, that the influence of the input on the child's learning is enabling rather than determining. Once the child has the prerequisite cognitive understanding of the distinction which is encoded by a particular linguistic category, frequent appropriately contextualized occurrences of the category in the speech that is addressed to the child provide opportunities for him to make the connection between linguistic category and non-linguistic experience.

(Wells 1985: 380–381)

Further, CDS or any other use of language is presented to the child because of the rules and beliefs that the culture and the language impose. Parental interaction with children is based on beliefs about what children are like, how they should learn, and for what purposes and by what methods they should be socialised. These beliefs reflect the culture and the status of the family within it. Ervin-Tripp and Strage describe four styles of interaction with children found in different cultural environments. These are:

(1) ignoring them conversationally until they are older, (2) challenging them to participate, modelling what to say, and praising success, (3) accommodating to them by simplification and a special style of speech, and (4) helping them speak by prompts and questions.

(Ervin-Tripp and Strage 1985: 75)

Child-contingent language, as it stars in the language development literature, is characterised by (3) and (4): (2) is what the working-class black children of Trackton (Heath 1983; see also Akhtar, Jipson, & Callanan, 2001) grow up with; (1) seems mainly to occur in certain small-scale traditional societies (Ochs and Schieffelin 1983), though it is an extreme of the prescription traditional in Europe that 'children should be seen and not heard'. Children grow up into normally competent language users apropos their culture even in groups that rarely or never use the sort of CDS that I have described, so it clearly is not *necessary* for language development. Children are able and willing to learn from whatever language they encounter, to seek out meaning and knowledge actively as well as to imitate the parent's behaviour. They may have other interactional and conversational partners, such as siblings or older children who are their caretakers, and are likely to have developed language that differentiates between partners of different skills and status (Dunn 1988; Dunn and Kendrick 1982; Heath 1983; Shatz and Gelman 1973, 1977; Bloom 1998; Huttenlocher 1998).

Research on the relationship between parental input and child output finds mixed effects. Vocabulary, topic understanding and social routines do seem in many instances to be related to amount of parental input in that specific area: Meins and her colleagues (Meins 1998; Meins and

Fernyhough 1999, and pp. 207–208), for example, link mothers' mental state talk and children's ability to talk about minds. Specific effects on syntax have proved more elusive (Hoff-Ginsberg 1986, 1990; Bloom 1998; Maratsos 1998). Farrar (1990), for example, found that when mothers reformulated children's utterance, maintaining the semantic topic, this was associated with the child's subsequent use of plural 's' and progressive 'ing' morphemes, but not with past tense 'ed' morphemes or use of 'a' and 'the'; and plain corrections had no apparent effect. This, plus cultural differences in CDS, suggest that children's learning to produce correct syntax may not be entirely dependent on parental input. There is an example of this in the literature with some slightly worrying implications (McNeill 1966):

Child: Nobody don't like me.
Mother: No, say 'nobody likes me'.
Child: Nobody don't like me.
            [eight repetitions of this dialogue]
Mother: No, now listen carefully; say 'nobody likes me'
Child: Oh! Nobody don't LIKES me.

However, it is clear that conversational exchanges between the child and more expert language users who are to some degree familiar with the child's language and interests can play a positive role in language development. In the first place, they are likely to direct the child's attention to language as something useful, as a source of information, a means of expression and a way of communicating with others. They may make using language in social interaction seem a rewarding activity. Sooner or later, children who do not use language fluently in these ways, or who avoid language, will be at a disadvantage socially and educationally. Conversation with adults allows children to practise taking turns, listening as well as speaking, and other social routines, all socially-valued skills. More specifically, its requirements may help improve the intelligibility of the child's pronunciation, and make children practise reformulating utterances that have not been understood as they desired, conversations with interlocutors who do not know the child quite so well being particularly helpful here (Robinson and Robinson 1981, 1982). Adult corrections of children's speech may help, though if they get in the way of making the exchange effective and enjoyable they could be counterproductive. 'Child-contingent' speech might be a better term than 'child-directed' speech, both because of the inadequacy of correction as a teaching model and because it is so important to acknowledge the activity of the child as a language learner.

   There are different 'routes into language'. These appear in various forms in the literature. Moerk (1989) lists three major processes in the early acquisition of language, processes applicable also in cognitive development.

The first is 'rote learning' which includes overt and covert repetitions and simple imitations. The second is 'pattern abstraction', involving the perception of rhythmic and melodic patterns, semantic and cognitive patterns, and syntactic structures. The third is rule learning. Moerk suggests that young children rarely or never have rules as part of their declarative knowledge, that though they could be inferred from the procedures that produce acceptable language, they rarely are. Heath (1983, 1986) describes the language learning of Trackton children, growing up in a rich language environment that goes on regardless of them, as involving first rote repetition, then repetition with variations, then participation. The Trackton child must select for himself or herself what to practise from the 'noisy' 'multiple-channelled stream of stimuli' that is the linguistic and social context (Heath 1986, 2004), while in 'motherese' the more skilled adult partner focuses the child's attention. Lock *et al.* (1989) suggest that imitation and analysis are dual processes in language acquisition: each might be enhanced or hindered by the communication strategies for assimilating, analysing, evaluating and using both the language and its related cognitive skills. Some children may prefer, some adults facilitate imitation (Bates *et al.* 1988); others may focus on analysis (Bijou 1989, Lieven 1982, Bloom 1998).

Katherine Nelson (1973, 1981, 1985) and other researchers (see Lock *et al.* 1989, Lieven *et al.* 1992, Pine 1992) have reported apparent differences in children's strategy for using language as they learn to talk. Some children are 'referential', using language to talk about things in an analytic way, while others are 'expressive', using many more unanalysed social formulas in language meant mainly for social interaction. Whether these are two ends of a continuum or two separate categories is not clear; nor is it clear whether these styles originate in a preference of the children or in the behaviour and language use of their culture and their interlocutors. Lock *et al.* (1989) suggest the latter: 'it is not that infants develop differently by the exercise and practice of their individual skills; those skills, and the infants themselves, are constructed differently via socially-constitutive interaction'.

In the end, it would seem that any combination of these 'routes into language' results in a broadly similar sequence of language development (Wells 1985) and broadly similar levels of language competence. But the emphasis is on 'broadly': there may well be differences that seem small in themselves but have far-reaching effects. Children who have very little experience of using language tend to develop it very much less fluently than those who are engaged in talk more often (Wells 1985; Hart and Risley 1995; Meadows 1996; Heath 2004). Differences in orientation to literacy (see pp. 30–56) are an example of a language difference with long-term developmental significance. The meeting of home language and the school is another (see pp. 24–25 and Meadows (1996)).

2.1.7 Children with specific language impairment

Some children have problems with language because they are suffering from hearing loss or structural abnormalities of their articulatory organs, some because they have lacked exposure to input language for social reasons (pp. 37–42). Some, however, do not have obvious causes for their language problems, and these are said to be suffering 'specific language impairment' (SLI). Their difficulties vary in type, but for a substantial proportion their most obvious difficulties are with the rule-like aspects of language, for example phonology and syntax (Bates 1997; Leonard 1998; Bishop 2004). Bishop (1997; Viding *et al.* (2004)) argued that some children with SLI have got stuck on the immature strategies of analysing words at the level of the syllable or phrases as unanalysed chunks, rather than moving on to analyse words at sub-syllable levels, or phrases as separate re-usable words, and so have only cumbersome attack skills for new words and an inefficient way of storing and retrieving familiar ones. For example, such children might know that the words 'dogs' and 'cats' each refer to more than one animal of the same type, but not appreciate that English has a general rule of adding a plural morpheme to mark number. The representations of language that underlie their behaviour may not work very well, which means they use up more processing capacity and are more likely to break down when the language system is heavily burdened with other tasks. Reading is often fraught with difficulties for children with SLI (Snowling 2004; Carroll and Snowling 2004; Hatcher *et al.* 2004).

There have been enormous improvements in the techniques that are available for looking at brain activity as people do different cognitive tasks, and these cast increasing light on the problems of children with SLI. They do not usually have obvious evidence of gross brain abnormalities (if they did, they might have been diagnosed differently), but it does seem possible that there are subtle differences in areas relevant to language functioning (Bishop 2004; Leonard 1998), both comparing children with SLI and normal language users, and in comparisons between young children who are developing phonological awareness at different rates. Worse phonological awareness in young children seems to be associated with less asymmetry favouring Wernicke's area, a region critical for language comprehension. This might be a result of subtle genetic differences such that brain development is not quite set up for language development right from the beginning, so that the connections that are made in the brain are unusually arranged even pre-natally. This explanation would fit in with the tendency for children with SLI to have parents and siblings with language impairments, and with the fact that SLI is not as easily recovered from as localised brain damage. Viding *et al.* (2004) recently reported on their study of language development in a large population sample of twins aged two to four, which showed that there is a strong environmental effect on both normal language development and the incidence of specific language impairment, but also considerable heritability, 49 per cent heritability for being in the bottom 5 per cent of the language ability distribution. Karen Thorpe and her colleagues (Thorpe *et al.* 2003; Rutter *et al.* 2003) have shown, however, that twins' language development is subtly different from singletons' because each individual twin receives less language than a singleton, even though the total for both twins is increased over a single child's. This is important evidence for the effect of quantity of parent input, and a warning against generalising from twins to singleton children. Alternatively, the neurological differences might arise post-natally as a result of abnormal language input. If the child does not, for some reason, receive or attend to social interaction and parental communication, the areas of brain that are waiting for this input may not receive enough of it to have evidence to activate the left hemisphere brain mechanisms that analyse phonological or grammatical structure. Sometimes the areas crucial for phonological processing may be partly turned over to other tasks; deaf children who have learned to communicate with signs, for example, seem to use language areas of the brain for analysis of sign movements rather than the sounds they cannot hear and do not need to analyse.

2.1.8 Recapitulation: speech and language development

I have argued that, contrary to the strongest claims of the nativists, language learning obeys general laws of cognitive and motor development and thus need not depend on a unique human module. Like everything else that we do, it stems from and is shaped by both biological and social influences.

> Human language is unique because humans have: (1) more cortical processing areas biased to code distributional and combinational features of auditory input [than other species]; (2) a sensorimotor system capable of complex vocal imitation; (3) a long period of immaturity; (4) caretakers who focus attention on useful environmental features, shape and reward useful actions, and protect the child from adverse results of sensorimotor experimentation; and (5) a powerful drive for task mastery. [. . .]
>
> Words, concepts and sentences might simply emerge from social reinforcement of children's attempts to imitate and to generalize from experience.
>
> (Leonard 2003: p. 127)

Human infants and children growing up under reasonably favourable conditions are deeply curious, extremely interested in understanding, categorising and generalising what they experience. They seek out contrast and notice equivalence. They observe and they imitate. They have brains that allow and expect these sorts of behaviour. They use these proclivities when they are attending to other people's vocal behaviour and when they are producing their own. Their caretakers are strongly interested in them acquiring the language of their community and using it in socially approved ways. Over the first year of life and during the preschool years they gradually build up linguistic procedures that are at first implicit but later may become explicit and capable of articulation and discussion (Karmiloff-Smith 1992; Karmiloff and Karmiloff-Smith 2001). Brain development is the basis of language learning (Bishop 2004).

Infants have learned things about sounds even before they are born. They discriminate their mother's voice from other women's; they recognise rhythmic stress patterns in foreign languages and distinguish between those that differ from their mother tongue. They are able to perceive contrasts and confuse equivalent sounds within the first couple of months after birth (Kuhl et al. 1997). Their parents are likely to address them in 'baby talk' that emphasises relevant language features. Often infants prefer this sort of talk (and singing, see section 2.9). They selectively attend to it. Their brains carry out the categorical perception of consonants, which is probably part of the 'givens' of the mammalian auditory system and is complemented by a tendency to confuse even quite different sounds that all fall within the same phoneme category. By the time babies babble and produce their first words they experiment with sounds as well as attending to their parents' talk. They apply their evolved powers of selective attention and learning from reinforcement to the language input they are given, and derive information about statistical probabilities of sounds from it (Saffran et al. 1996). Computer simulations fed adult language can do this to form clusters of words with similar uses, both semantically and syntactically (Seidenberg 1997; Leonard 2003). The redundant repetitive and child-contingent language that children are exposed to may make it possible for them to categorise language units (sounds, morphemes and words) too.

It seems that the 'phonological loop' that is a constituent of working memory in adults is operational in language-learning children too (Baddeley et al. 1998; Alloway et al. 2004): I discuss working memory below (pp. 86–87). Children's propensity to imitate speech sounds may enable the phonological loop to hold the sound in working memory while a long-term representation of it, and of its meaning and associations, is laid down in long-term memory. The human brain develops functional lateralisation and cortical maps including expanded detail of the ranges used in speech discrimination through gestation to the post-natal period. The synapses in the brain are modifiable by experience, with pruning of synapses continuing throughout childhood and adolescence. If infants are hearing-impaired and do not have this early exposure to sound, there may be a shrinkage in their cortical maps and hearing loss that cannot be remediated later (Yoshinaga-Itano et al. 1998); the areas of brain normally used to process spoken language may instead be turned over to processing sign language if they are exposed to signing.

Language is a complex auditory cognitive and motor skill. The brain must be involved via the auditory cortex with its maps representing word sounds, the motor cortex controlling the mouth, throat, lungs, etc., and also through brain areas that link them or are involved in imitation. These areas mature gradually and on different timescales, but it could be that the vocabulary burst in the second half of the second year depends on them reaching a certain level of development and on activity in each beginning to become synchronised with the others through the development of joined-up circuits. Experience interacts with the preset biases that suggest what features of input should be given most attention or preferentially stored to produce a modified map; for example, there is a preset bias to map and discriminate sound contrasts, but which ones feature in the fully developed map depends on which were meaningful in the language the child hears. Children's brains select speech sounds for special attention, categorise them in terms of equivalence and contrast, discriminate and cluster them at successive levels of meaning, and sustain imitation and play with sounds and words (Bishop 2004). All this takes place in a rich social context where more expert language users celebrate and facilitate children's developing language, and where language itself is a powerful cognitive and social tool (Bloom 1998; Hoff and Naigles 2002). Children's own productions become in many respects more and more imitative of their parents' input, even as they launch into new topics and produce sentences that no-one has produced before. They become successful vocal imitators (and may get a lot of social reinforcement for this) and skilled social collaborators. Their language also becomes important in their cognition, the core medium for their expression of their knowledge and the tool used in much of their processing. Cross-cultural diversity in language may be reflected in cross-cultural differences in cognition (Majid *et al.* 2004).

2.2 Reading

Reading is an unavoidable requirement of our education system and of much of our daily life outside education, a source of information and entertainment, a way into new worlds, a tool of many professions and occupations, one of the means we have to deepen our understanding and our empathy. It is regarded as one of the most significant of the cognitive skills that children are expected to achieve (e.g. Chall *et al.* 1990; Olson and Torrance 1991; Adams *et al.* 1998; Ruddell and Unrau 2004b; Snowling 2004) and it is at the focus of educational initiatives from preschool to adolescence. It is a cognitive skill and also a social one, in the sense of being socially required, as a contributor to social interaction and social experience, and as a source of information that builds up our understanding of the social world. I will discuss it as cognition first, moving on to some discussion of its social nature (pp. 36–38, 55–56).

2.2.1 Linking meaning and sound and text: skilled readers' reading skills

When we seek to describe the acquisition of reading skills, we have to remember, as Vellutino and his colleagues point out (Vellutino *et al.* 2004: 3), that written words are encoded (symbolised) representations (in visual form) of spoken words. Spoken words, in their turn, are encoded representations (this time in sound form) of environmental experiences and entities. Additionally words may be encoded representations of concepts that do not have a straightforward concrete existence, for example justice, unicorns, dinosaurs, obsolescence; and of course there are words that are functional bits of language rather than being representational in any obvious way (e.g. 'of course', 'rather', and 'than'). Thus reading written words is an activity involving links between the real world, conceptual worlds, and language structure, complicated by changes in sensory modality between sound and vision and in time scale from near-simultaneous to more or less sequential. To succeed in reading, readers have to call on language knowledge, both general and domain-specific world knowledge, knowledge about text, and long-term and working memory, as well as visual and auditory processing. No wonder it is, as Uta Frith says, 'a complex and astonishing accomplishment' (Frith 1980a). Systematic research combining different methods and calling on different theories has linked with practice in very fruitful ways; we know far more about how to facilitate children's reading development, and why things work, than we did a few years ago or than we do in most other areas. Because reading involves an enormous range of cognitive skills and knowledge that also contribute to other cognition and could seem very abstract, illustrating how they contribute to the development of reading shows how powerful, important, and vulnerable they may be.

When we read we look at written symbols of spoken words that refer to meaningful objects, events and concepts, some of them concrete, some hypothetical, some linguistic, some real, some imaginary, some metaphorical, all of them represented in speech sounds. Necessarily the cognitive processing we have to do will involve visual processes, auditory processes, and short-term and long-term memory processes, among others. The purposes for which we read may require us to achieve exact pronunciation of the words, access to their deepest meanings, comparison with other texts; or we may only need to get the gist without worrying about implications, inferences, or sounds. Clearly this is not a simple activity, though it may feel simple, perhaps, for the very skilled. Skilled readers with years of experience have read most of the words they encounter many times over.

The links between, say, the letter string 'cat' and its sound and its referent are so over-learned they are automatic and fast. Only under very adverse conditions – too short a time, too little light, minute print, really distorted handwriting, poor motivation, tiredness, very difficult text – will skilled readers misread a word in the sense of not understanding it. They will probably not make a conscious analysis of words beyond the initial rapid recognition, and they will have difficulties spotting minor errors in spelling because they go from what is on the page to what is meant so easily. Skilled readers rarely have to do more than scan the page, and they may well understand what is written there without having to process much of it consciously. It seems that skilled readers have three distinct 'routes' into extracting meaning from a written word (Marshall 1987a, 1987b). These are a 'phonic' route, a 'direct' route and a 'lexical' route. In the 'phonic' route the phonological representation of written units smaller than words (letters, syllables, morphemes) is conjured up prior to accessing meaning, so that for example a word might be spelled out as '|k| |a| |t|' means 'cat' means 'a small furry purring animal'. In the 'direct' route the pronunciation is assigned directly to the whole word, and in the 'lexical' route meaning is attached directly to the written word before its pronunciation is arrived at. I understand the meaning of 'flaccid', for example, but would have to check its pronunciation (to 'rhyme' with accident rather than with acid). In Ellis's 1984 model (Figure 2.1) of reading English skilled readers normally go straight down the inner right-hand side.

If skilled readers meet a new word, then they have to do something a little different. This may involve going down the outer right-hand side of Ellis's model and round to the outer left, i.e. compiling the sound of the word from its constituent units, recognising it as a word that is familiar as a heard word, though never before seen, using the links between spoken words and meaning. (This is necessarily hard to illustrate in text; but if we have watched international football matches on television before we read about them in the newspapers we may perhaps process foreign players' names in this way.) Skilled readers faced with a new word may also divide it into units that they know in other words with analogous spellings. The word 'dispauper', for example, breaks down quite easily into three pronounceable syllables or two morphemes, and the latter analysis suggests its meaning: to deprive of the privileges of a pauper, for example, to disqualify from suing without payment of fees: an early piece of evidence (1631) for the existence of a legal aid system under threat, perhaps! If the unfamiliar word is phonemically irregular, however, the reader may not be able to do much more than guess at a pronunciation and will have no access to meaning other than the context or resource to a dictionary.

Ellis (1984) suggests that skilled readers have met most of the words they have to read many times and know their meaning and pronunciation very well. Visual recognition of such words at once activates their meaning in a

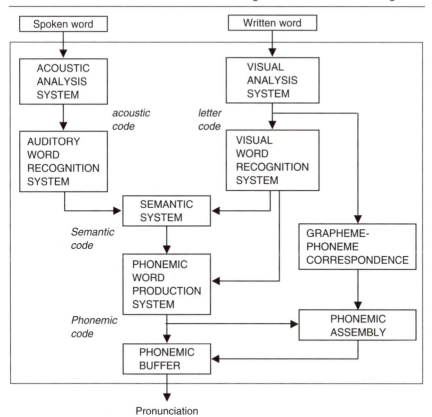

Figure 2.1 A model for both the direct and the phonically mediated recognition, comprehension and naming of written words. Adapted from Ellis (1984: 33).

semantic representation system, and their pronunciation can be retrieved from the phonemic word production system either directly from the semantic system or through one-to-one correspondences between units in the visual word recognition system and units in the phonemic word production system (Figure 2.1). If the word encountered has not been seen before, its component letters have to be identified. The letter sequence may be close enough to a familiar word to be accepted as a version of it, particularly perhaps if it is being read from material where misprints are likely. If it is not close enough, it may be possible to guess it from the context or to use familiar letter sequences to assemble a possible pronunciation.

Thus skilled readers mainly get by perfectly well using the direct route, recognising whole familiar over-learned words. Occasionally they may use the phonic route, sounding out an unfamiliar word's individual sounds and compiling an auditory representation of a word they have heard before, thus accessing meaning. More often, perhaps, they will analyse their unfamiliar word using analogies with familiar words; this can give access both to sound and to the meaning of unfamiliar words, which would not reveal as much meaning under a purely phonic analysis. Sometimes the sound of the word will not be used in reading at all, though it can be compiled if required. A bookish child, by the age of eleven I had understood the word 'mirage' in my solitary reading for several years and used it in writing; but I still remember the humiliation when I first used it in speech and mispronounced it as 'mire age', to the great amusement of my little friends.

Being able to read a sentence or a longer passage involves much more than the sum of reading each individual word. Knowledge about language becomes more important at this level, though it has been helpful even at the single word level (as in reading 'dispauper'). Readers use their knowledge of syntax (for example word order or inflections) and of story scenarios and the real world.

Winograd (1972), commenting on attempts to program computers to interpret English correctly, emphasises the amount of world knowledge that we bring to bear on tasks like finding the referents of pronouns in sentences such as 'The city council refused to allow the protesters to hold a demonstration in the main square because they advocated violence' or 'The city council refused to allow the protesters to hold a demonstration in the main square because they feared violence'. This sort of processing for deep implicit levels of meaning has implications for other levels of reading. Skilled readers who are reading aloud, for example, give their sentences appropriate emphasis, intonation and phrasing, even if the sentence is long and even if getting to the end of it requires turning over a page. The eyes run ahead of the voice so that the interpretation of the sentence can run ahead of having to express that interpretation. Skilled musicians reading and performing music manage the same feat. *Hearing* what is being read does not seem to be necessary for understanding its meaning except when subtle meanings or minor linguistic anomalies and changes have to be detected (Baddeley and Lewis 1981). I will return to the ways children read extended text after I have described their reading of single words (pp. 50–55).

2.2.2 Linking meaning and sound and text: children's problems

Children at the beginning of learning to read clearly do not have a large store of over-learned words where they can link written symbol, auditory symbol, and referent instantaneously. Nor do they have a large store of words analogous to each other. Nor do they have much practice in breaking down words into their constituent parts. This is in fact particularly difficult in English, where the relationship between grapheme and phoneme is inconsistent in many words. Some other languages, for example Italian and Finnish (Silven *et al.* 2004), do have a nearly unambiguous relationship between how a word is spelled and how it is pronounced, and children find it somewhat easier to learn to read and spell in these languages. While this is the case for many English words also, there are others that break the normal correspondences between grapheme and phoneme. Stubbs (1980) goes into these in some detail, and Gelb (1963) provides a very useful history of different writing systems. For our present purposes, there are several important points to be made. It is somewhat easier to learn symbol–sound correspondences that are consistent; children learning to read Italian are less likely to have problems than children learning English (Harris and Hatano 1999). Hence there is some usefulness in regularised alphabets such as the initial teaching alphabet (Downing 1979). However, spelling reforms like such alphabets do not provide a totally unproblematic solution. If later reading has to be done with the conventional alphabet and spelling system, then the reader has to transfer the skills that were developed for a simplified situation to more complex material; not necessarily an easy task. The regularised alphabet does not allow for regional pronunciation differences, so that the same symbol would be associated with different vowels in, say, Yorkshire and Sussex: we know that children who use a dialect in which English words are pronounced differently have more difficulty reading texts in 'School English' (Charity *et al.* 2004). Another problem would arise with homophones, that is, words where the same sound stands for two or more different meanings; these sound the same but are spelled in different ways so that the spelling can show the reader which of their meanings may be intended. There are no fewer than twelve such words in the preceding sentence (only four of them put in deliberately!); 'would', 'where', 'for', 'two', 'or', 'more', 'but', 'in', 'so', 'their', 'which', and 'be' could not be distinguished, if sound and spelling correspondence were regularised, from 'wood', 'wear', 'four', 'to', 'too', 'awe', 'ore', 'maw', 'butt', 'inn', 'sew', 'sow', 'there', 'witch', and 'bee', except by syntactic rules and lexical probabilities. Readers would probably in the end be certain what was meant, but losing the visual distinction means that an additional cue to meaning is lost. Most important, the conventional English spelling system contains, and the regularised alphabets' spelling systems do not, a great deal of lexical and syntactic meaning that is of great use to the reader. For example, conventional spelling indicates the plural of many words by adding an 's' to the singular form: for example 'cats', 'cows', 'horses'. The way in which the 's' is sounded, however, is slightly different for each of these: in 'cats' it is |s|, in 'cows' it is more like |z|, and in 'horses' something like |iz|. If the words were spelled phonetically with a regularised alphabet the morpheme indicating the plural would be different in each case and the syntactic regularity would be obscured (Kemp and Bryant 2003). Similar problems would arise at the lexical and etymological level. 'Sign' and 'signature' or 'bomb' and 'bombardment' look similar because their meanings are related; regularised spelling would obscure such relations. It would also disguise the origins of the many words that English has borrowed from other languages, preserving the spelling even if the pronunciation is somewhat mangled. All in all, it is very plausible that, as Stubbs (1980) argued, the English spelling system is extremely informative for a native speaker who knows its phonological and morphological rules and something of its history: that is, it is better suited to adult fluent readers than to children learning to read.

2.2.3 Learning to read in a literate environment

What do beginning readers do, then? Can we describe common strategies or common stages in becoming able to read? Normally, children begin to learn to read having already learned to use spoken language. They have a heard or spoken vocabulary of hundreds of words; they may have played with sounds as nursery rhymes do and as some babies and children do spontaneously as they first learn to articulate. Both vocabulary size and knowledge of nursery rhymes predict the ease with which children learn to read – in both cases the children with the most limited knowledge are the most likely to have reading difficulties (Burgess et al. 2002; Dickinson and Sprague 2002; Dowker 1989; Hart and Risley 1995; Whitehurst and Lonigan 2002; Williams and Rask 2003). Children are often, of course, read to, and this too is associated with literacy development (e.g. Heath 1983, 1986; Bus and vanIJzendoorn 1995; Pellegrini et al. 1995; Pellegrini et al. 1997b).

Hall (1987) reviews the evidence on 'the emergence of literacy'. He compares it with the development of spoken language and its use, which he sees as a matter of child construction within parent facilitation, not parent instruction (pp. 22–26). In the development of spoken language, speaking and listening are used for non-linguistic ends (including developing meaning and understanding the world, and participating in social interaction). He argues that literacy, like spoken and heard language, is used to create meanings and to allow communication between people. Many early experiences relevant to literacy are embedded in a social interaction, for example discussion of a shopping list (Tizard and Hughes 1984; Pellegrini et al. 1995; Pellegrini et al. 1997b; Senechal and LeFevre 2002; Williams and Rask 2003; Haney and Hill 2004). Such interaction carries information about literacy – for example that writing can be used to organise information and plan events, that it can be stored and amended, that it can be translated by reading into spoken language incidentally to the social purpose of feeding the family. Hall suggests that it may be more powerful, intellectually, therefore, than 'purer' literacy activities such as reading storybooks. Possibly, he argues, the child could learn about literacy as 'naturally' as he or she learns to talk and to listen.

Children growing up in literate cultures are likely to have a great deal of text around them in the form of 'environmental print': shop signs, advertisements, slogans on T-shirts as well as books, newspapers and letters. Many young children show much interest in this print and make good use of it. Hall argues that such use is an intrinsic part of becoming literate. It develops along with experience of being read to, which is known to show a high correlation with learning to read well (Heath 1983, 1986; Wells 1985; Burgess *et al.* 2002; Senechal and LeFevre 2002; Williams and Rask 2003; Haney and Hill 2004; Gregg *et al.* in press). Parents reading stories may discuss such text-based concepts as 'word' and 'letter' as well as modelling reading behaviour. Stories also provide experience with 'literary language' and with settings beyond the child's daily life; again these can be discussed, and children can reflect on text and experience. The whole constellation of seeing text, being read to, using written and spoken language, and discussion with more expert users, may lead to 'emergent' literacy well before reading and writing are formally taught in school. Hall argues that formal teaching must respect the knowledge and understanding that learners already have, and the variety of uses literacy may be put to.

Language knowledge and book knowledge contribute to the process of learning to read. Skilled readers know that the text is the main source of information; that it has a direction; that gaps between text units separate words (or, on a larger scale, paragraphs and chapters); that it is made up from a limited number of symbols, the alphabet and punctuation marks (the latter are a comparatively modern invention and are generally taught much later in the school years). Knowledge of these sorts of conventions, and of the alphabet, generally comes from having used books, particularly from having seen them while being read to, and are further predictors of reading progress. Children who have had less opportunity to learn them have ground to make up when they begin to have formal reading lessons (Senechal and LeFevre 2002; Williams and Rask 2003; Haney and Hill 2004); they have also had less opportunity, perhaps, to learn that reading gives you access to interesting information and enjoyable stories, and thus may be less motivated to work at learning to read (Francis 1982).

These may be very important parts of learning to read. In the socially representative sample of children whom Gordon Wells studied in his research on language development (e.g. Wells 1981b, 1985; Senechal and LeFevre 2002; Williams and Rask 2003; Haney and Hill 2004) there were significant positive correlations between parents' and children's interest in literacy, particularly the frequency with which stories were read to the child, during the preschool years, and the child's progress in learning to read. The same relation holds in a population study of 14,000 children studied in the Avon Longitudinal Study of Parents and Children (ALSPAC). Even when all sorts of other possible influential variables were allowed for, the amount that parents read to the child or taught education-relevant things, how often the public library was used, and the number of books the child owned, made independent contributions to the child's reading readiness at school entry (Gregg *et al.* 2004). Children who learn to read early and easily (Clark 1976) have generally acquired very early a good understanding of what reading is about in general, and about such specific aspects as that you go along the lines from top left to bottom right, that the message is in the text though the pictures may provide clues, what things called 'words' and 'sentences' are, and so forth (Elley 1989; Rice 1989; Rice and Woodsmall 1988; Tunmer *et al.* 1988). Precocious talkers may not be especially likely to learn to read early; instruction by parents, parents' reading to children, and, especially, the child's engagement in being read to, are better predictors of early reading (Crain-Thoreson and Dale 1992; Silven *et al.* 2004).

2.2.4 Children's reading skills

Since 'reading' involves visual processing of a visible text, I will start my discussion of children's reading skills with visual processes. Unless the amount of text we have to deal with is very small (ten or twelve letters or spaces), we have to move our eyes over the text. This is not normally problematic; the saccadic eye movements which produce rapid changes in fixation that relocate targets from the periphery to more sensitive foveal vision are functional, within limits, at birth, and babies three months old can manage fairly smooth eye movements following a moving object or along an informative shape. They can also discriminate between shapes like *b* and *d* (Banks and Salapatek 1983). The *uses* to which visual processes are put may well change as development proceeds, but the basic capacities are functional very early. Nor does there seem to be much evidence for there normally being a general visual processing problem even in poor readers (Beech and Colley 1987; Bryant and Bradley 1985; Vellutino *et al.* 2004) except the inexperience that is the result of their reading less; that is, they do not read worse because they cannot distinguish letters, they distinguish letters worse because they read less.

In the earliest stages of 'reading', most words that the child can read are in fact probably dealt with by recognising either their shape or their standard sequence of letters; many children are taught very early to recognise their names, for example, and the environment has many emphasised written patterns such as 'STOP' or 'EXIT'. Throughout later stages of learning to read, the presence of a particular letter or combination of letters that distinguishes a particular common word may be taken as a sign that the present word is the known one, even if the other letters in it are not quite right. There are many examples in *Winnie-the-Pooh* (Milne 1926). Pooh receives Piglet's urgent message-in-a-bottle requesting rescue from a rising flood, but misreads the written word 'Piglit' as his own name because it begins with 'P'. Consequently he misinterprets the message as a personal message to himself, and it is only when it is taken to Christopher Robin, who is a more advanced reader, that it can be acted on appropriately (though it is Pooh who invents the rescue method). Similar errors are documented in the research literature. Bryant and Bradley (1980, 1985) found children who could read certain words whose spelling was irregular but whose shape was distinctive (such as 'school' or 'light') very well, but if they were asked to spell these words they could not. Conversely, there were words that could be spelled correctly but not read, even when produced for reading in the child's own handwriting. *These* were phonetically regular words such as 'bun' and 'mat'; children did better at reading them after a brief training in reading words phonologically letter by letter. There would seem to be quite strong evidence here for a discrepancy between a phonological spelling strategy and a reading strategy that chunked letters into complete familiar words or familiar parts of words (pp. 45–46).

Commonly children begin reading by building up a sight vocabulary, words they recognise at sight without analysing them much and often from only partial cues. Typically these include interesting often-used words such as their own name or the distinctive logo of some interesting place or product (commercial companies exploit this ruthlessly). Early reading schemes sometimes restrict themselves to a simple and repetitive vocabulary to enable children to build up sight vocabulary. As I argued earlier, fluent adult readers read using their sight vocabulary, and new words enter it as they become familiar. Sight vocabulary is a useful basis for learning to read. Its problem is that it only works when the word that is met is already visually familiar. What can you do when you meet a new word?

If children are to extend their sight vocabulary there are really only two ways to do this. One is by rote memory, which is shown by the experience of children learning the logographic writing system, Kanji, in Japan to be extremely slow. Japanese learners of Kanji go on acquiring new word symbols into adulthood, though they have mastered other writing systems that use a simple correspondence between written symbols and the pronunciation of spoken syllables in the very early years of school or even before (Oakhill and Garnham 1988). The other method, potentially faster and more generalisable, is to analyse the constituent parts of words in terms of sounds. Knowing that spoken words are made up of sounds, and written words are made up of letters, and having a writing system with a fairly simple correspondence between letters or groups of letters and the sounds they represent, enables the reader meeting an unfamiliar written word to make a good guess at how it should be pronounced, and then to recognise it and access its meaning from the way it sounds. To do this the child has to recognise letters or letter groups and know what sounds are associated with each. As we saw earlier (pp. 34–36), English has grapheme–phoneme correspondences that are not 'fairly simple' but distinctly complicated, so even this first step may be problematic. Further, the sounds of individual letters (or of subgroups of letters) have to be 'blended' to produce the word as a whole. Analysis of 'dog' into |d|, |o|, |g|, has to be followed by blending into the single-syllable word, not into the trisyllable 'duh-o-guh'. Unfortunately young children have great difficulty in analysing sounds at phoneme level; children who are particularly poor at phonemic awareness tests in preschool and the reception class are especially likely to have difficulty learning to read (Bryant and Bradley 1985; Ellis and Large 1987, 1988; Silven *et al.* 2004; Vellutino *et al.* 2004). Even better readers may rarely use phonic attack skills until they have developed a degree of competence in the use of visual contextual cues. In the study by Francis (1982) her quicker readers used 'sounding out' unfamiliar words largely to supplement an analysis of graphemes and context that was not quite adequate for succeeding in reading the word. Grapheme–phoneme correspondence rules may not be equally used (or useful) to all readers. It seems possible, for example, that some children may use phonological rules when spelling but not when reading (e.g. Bryant and Bradley, 1980, 1985; Cataldo and Ellis 1988; Vellutino *et al.* 2004). Adult readers may read unfamiliar words using analogy with known ones rather than sounding them out letter by letter (Oakhill and Garnham 1988 and pp. 31–34 above). Nevertheless, phonic strategies combine with visual and contextual ones to extend reading. Realising the possibility of letter–sound correspondences seems to be one of the crucial insights of learning to read.

The beginning reader, unlike the expert, does not have much in the way of word analogies to use, and would have difficulties using a dictionary, full of more unfamiliar words and organised according to an alphabet principle that is not very accessible to a novice. Guessing from the text is a possibility, though it is discouraged in much reading out loud where the child is expected to get each word right; asking an expert works if there is a willing expert to hand, but again may be discouraged in much school practice lest children become too dependent on help from others, and may in any case involve delay and loss of face. The child needs his or her own 'word attack' skills. The main ones taught to beginning readers involve analysing and reconstituting words at sub-unit levels – phonemes, morphemes, syllables, or onset and rime. All of these involve phonological skills and mastering the alphabetic code, and these have turned out to be powerful predictors of success or difficulty in learning to read in a number of different languages (de Jong and van der Leij 1999; Lonigan *et al.* 2000; Silven *et al.* 2004; Vellutino *et al.* 2004; Wagner *et al.* 1994, 1997). Children whose spoken language is poorly represented by standard spellings may have particular difficulties in learning to read (Charity *et al.* 2004).

2.2.4.1 Phonological skills

There are a number of related phonological skills including phonological awareness, which refers to the understanding that spoken words consist of individual speech sounds (phonemes) and combinations of speech sounds (syllables, onset–rime units); representing speech sounds systematically and discriminatingly, which is important in speaking and listening as well as in reading; phonological decoding, that is the application of letter–sound correspondence rules; spelling ability; and verbal working memory (Vellutino *et al.* 2004). These have been extensively researched, and although there is disagreement over details there is an agreed general picture of poor phonological processes being very damaging to a child's chances of finding it unproblematic to learn to read, crucially in English and to some extent even in languages with a more regular relation between written symbol and sound, such as German or Finnish (Wimmer *et al.* 1994; Silven *et al.* 2004), or based on characters (Ho and Bryant 1997; Ho *et al.* 2002). Children who are very poor phonological processors before learning to read begins are likely to have difficulties; training that improves phonological processing improves reading. These paired findings, that poor phonological processing precedes reading, and that remedying it improves reading too, show that the poor phonological processing of poor readers is a cause, not a consequence, of their reading difficulties. Poor readers probably tend to have limited vocabularies, low enjoyment of reading, and low levels of educational success as consequences of their poor reading; poor phonological skills, in contrast, precede poor reading even though they may also be made even worse by it.

Phonemic analysis is quite hard to learn, and young children and illiterate adults find it almost impossible to segment words correctly into phonemes, though relatively easy to segment them into syllables (Liberman *et al.* 1977; Castro-Caldas *et al.* 1998), or, as recent research has shown, into onset and rime (e.g. c-at, thr-ead) (Goswami and Bryant 1990; Goswami 1991; Hansen and Bowey 1992; Marmurek and Rinaldo 1992; Masterson *et al.* 1992; Naslund and Schneider 1991; Thorstad 1991; Silven *et al.* 2004). Experience of playing with contrasting sounds, as in nursery rhymes and as in many of the 'poems' and monologues young children often create for themselves (Bryant and Bradley 1985; Bryant *et al.* 1989, 1990; Chukovsky 1976; Dowker 1989; Kirtley *et al.* 1989; Stuart 1990), and as in babies' babbling (pp. 10–11), looks like a facilitator of phonemic awareness and later learning to read.

Experience of reading also facilitates the child's awareness of both letter–sound and letter-group–sound correspondences. Becoming able to 'sound out' words successfully is one of the important breakthroughs in the early stages of reading. Sounding-out reduces dependence on recognising the visual patterns of words (and hence is particularly useful for the less distinctive patterns of words like 'bun' and 'leg') and supplements the reader's knowledge of likely meaning. It also makes it possible to read regularly formed non-words, such as 'vib', which readers without phonic skills typically refuse to read (Campbell and Butterworth 1985; Vellutino *et al.* 2004). A reciprocal relation develops between phonological awareness and orthographic awareness, for example that 'at' sounds the same in a number of words – 'rat', 'fat', 'mat' – but if followed by an e represents the different sounds of 'rate', 'fate', 'mate'. However, because of the irregularities of letter–sound relationships, the existence of homophones, and the problem of blending separate phonemes into a word, as well as the example I have just given, reading based on grapheme–phoneme correspondence alone will not work well. Something more is needed.

2.2.4.2 Children with reading problems

Corroborative evidence on the roles of different ways of reading comes from studies of 'dyslexic' readers (Vellutino *et al.* 2004). These are people who have problems learning to read that cannot be accounted for by general intellectual impairment, specific sensory impairments, lack of education or emotional or motivational problems. Their reading attainment is much lower than would be expected from their age and IQ. Poor readers tend to have problems in other school subjects (these might well require reading, of course). They are regarded by their teachers as more anti-social, inattentive, clumsy and anxious, and as having parents who were not very interested in the child's education (remember this is the teachers' view of the parents, and not necessarily true; even if true, we would need to ask why they were less interested). They are more likely to be boys than girls. They are likely to attend schools with a high proportion of children from poor housing, with parents of non-UK cultural groups, and with parents in manual occupations (Rodgers 1983; Chall *et al.* 1990; Snow *et al.* 1991; Heath 2004; Stanovich 2004). Some of these differences may be causes of their poor reading; many might, rather, be consequences of it. This direction of causation problem complicates what we can draw from the research literature (Ellis and Large 1987; Vellutino *et al.* 2004). Studies that compare poor readers with normal readers of the same age and find they differ on some diagnostic task cannot differentiate between three possibilities. The first is that the diagnostic task does indeed measure a cause of the reading difficulty, for example that the reading difficulty is caused by poor short-term memory, or poor phonological awareness, or poor shape recognition skills. The second possibility is that, on the contrary, poor performance on the diagnostic task is caused by not having learned to read; if the shapes or sounds to be recognised or remembered or analysed are graphemes and phonemes the good reader is likely to have had more experience with them than the poor one, and the greater experience may be the cause of the difference. Thirdly, poor test performance and poor reading may have the same underlying cause, such as neurological immaturity; the underlying deficit causes two problematic areas of performance but these two areas may not affect each other.

We can reach clearer conclusions on the causes of reading retardation if we combine research designs to decide between these possibilities. As well as comparing poor readers with normal readers of the same age, we can compare them with a control group matched for reading age and IQ but younger, that is reading at a level appropriate for their age. These controls will have the same absolute level of reading skills as poor readers, and their use and experience of reading will thus differ from the poor readers less than would the same-age controls. If the reading age controls differ from the poor readers on some measure, the difference is less likely to be due to differences in experience and more likely to be related to the cause of the poor reading. However, lack of difference on a measure does not mean that it is irrelevant to the cause of the reading problem in the older children: they may be suffering from a development lag in some process, remaining in an immature state that the younger children will grow out of. Longitudinal studies help here. The first measures are taken before the children have started to learn to read. Poor performance on a measure at this stage cannot be due to the effects of failing to learn to read, and should therefore, if it does predict later reading performance, show possible causes of reading failure. Longitudinal studies, however, are expensive and in this case have to be done on a large scale because severe reading retardation is quite rare and there would be only a few children likely to become very retarded readers in any sample chosen before reading began. They cannot rule out the possibility that the diagnostic difference found does not itself cause the reading problem but is another symptom of some underlying cause.

The best way out of the problem of interpreting the causes behind correlations such as those between poor reading and poor scores on other tests is to do training studies. If training memory, visual skills or whatever improves performance on the criterion task *and* on reading, this is quite strong evidence that initial deficits in the trained skill contributed to the reading problem. It may also show what might be a useful remedial programme for poor readers, though not all deficits may be amenable to remediation.

Given these caveats about research problems, what can we say about the causes of reading retardation? It seems probable, first, that poor readers are the tail of a normal distribution, showing deficits on skills that work better in better readers, rather than a special group whose reading processes are different in kind from those of better readers (Ellis and Large 1988; Rodgers 1983; Hulme 1987; Vellutino et al. 2004). Typically difficulty in learning to read is not due to visual problems such as abnormal eye movements or abnormal lateralisation of visual function, though a small minority of poor readers may indeed have these problems and be helped if they are remediated. Slower processing of visual information presented for a brief period of time may be a sign of an underlying neurological problem that also causes difficulties with normal reading (Eden and Zeffiro 1998), but is unlikely to be the cause of reading retardation itself; in normal reading, after all, the material to be read can be looked at for as long as the reader wishes. While poor readers do sometimes show visual processing deficits compared with good readers, this seems to be confounded by differences in the familiarity of the symbols, by the involvement of verbal mediation in naming and remembering letters, and no doubt by motivational factors. Difficulties in holding material in the correct order in working memory may contribute to reading retardation (Gathercole and Pickering 2000a, 2000b; Swanson 2003). Differences in long-term memory have received less attention from researchers but may contribute to reading problems, as they would complicate use of the gist of the text to sort out the difficult word.

Research findings suggest that the clearest difficulty shown by retarded readers is in their word recognition skills. Awareness of speech sounds is now known to be closely related to learning to read. Here, the evidence comes from studies involving the whole range of designs discussed earlier. Various tests of phonological awareness such as the ability to segment words into the correct number of phonemes predict later reading ability (e.g. Liberman *et al.* 1977; Silven *et al.* 2004). Bryant and Bradley showed that the ability of four-year-olds to categorise sounds predicted their reading three or more years later (Bradley and Bryant 1983) and that training on sound categorisation plus letter–sound correspondences, spread over two years, produced a significant advance in reading compared with control groups. Phonological awareness is obviously necessary for the development of phonic skills, and it seems that retarded readers have particular difficulty in using phonic rules, for example an inability to read nonwords, that is, letter strings that are pronounceable but happen not to be meaningful words. Schatschneider *et al.* (2004) used multiple measures of reading-related skills in kindergarten and found that levels of phonological awareness, letter sound knowledge, and naming speed predicted reading two years later while measures of perceptual skills and oral language did not. Swanson (2003) and Cain *et al.* (2004) found in older children that working memory predicted reading comprehension after word reading, vocabulary and verbal skills had been controlled for. The skills of reading change their balance as reading develops.

2.2.4.3 Genetic basis of dyslexia

It has long been assumed that dyslexia is associated with constitutional factors, and recent advances in technologies of examining brain function (Chapter 5) have allowed us to begin evaluating this assumption. Tasks involving reading and phonological processing are associated with increased levels of activation in the left temporal and parietal areas in normal readers, and more bilateral activation in dyslexics (p. 346; Vellutino *et al.* 2004), suggesting that there may be some subtle anatomical and functional differences in the brain. Emerging research suggests that these differences in brain functioning may be modifiable. Experimental interventions involving intensive training of phonological skills have raised both the level of left-hemisphere activity and the word reading accuracy of poor readers, which implies that experience may be essential in constituting the neural networks that are involved in reading (Shaywitz *et al.* 2004). As our knowledge of brain development would lead us to expect (Chapter 5), genetic influences combine with environmental ones in complex ways in the development of reading skills and reading problems (Fisher and DeFries 2002; Grigorenko 2001). Monozygotic twins are more likely to share their twin's dyslexia than dizygotic twins are; dyslexic children commonly have at least one parent with reading problems. Recent research has identified specific genes associated with dyslexia, though not all these identifications have been replicated by other researchers. Even in these studies, however, there is strong evidence for environmental effects from less reading going on in the home or fewer books available where the parents have reading difficulties of their own. Current work on a major British cohort (Gregg *et al.* 2004) shows that if there are low levels of reading, of books owned and of use of the public library system during the preschool years, the child is likely to be functioning at a low level of reading readiness at school entry. (Such children are also more likely to have behaviour problems at age four, implying that reading is good for your behaviour as well as for your cognition.)

2.2.4.4 Spelling

Standardised spelling is a comparatively recent invention – Shakespeare, for example, spelled his own surname in several different ways on the documents that have survived to us. Its rules vary from culture to culture and language to language, are in many cases arbitrary and capricious (Chliounaki and Bryant 2002), and may take a long time to learn. In some languages there is an alphabetic orthography with words and sounds represented by sequences of letters, but, as I discussed when describing how children learn to read, such systems typically have many inconsistencies and irregularities. Some languages do not represent phonemes systematically, rather they represent morphemes with little attention to the words' sound. Many languages incorporate words adopted from other languages with different spelling rules and different orthographies, with transliteration difficulties leading to inconsistent spellings ('Peking' was changed to 'Beijing', for example, after a change in transliteration rules). Some languages combine all these idiosyncrasies. Additionally, punctuation (another recent invention) is at least as 'arbitrary and capricious' and also has to be mastered if the user is to be regarded as literate.

Although much English spelling teaching centres on the phonological structure of the words, like most European spelling systems English also uses morphemic information. Different sounds at the ends of the words 'cats', 'dogs' and 'horses' are spelled the same because the words have the same morphemic structure (plurals). The same sounds at the ends of the words 'missed' and 'fist' are spelled differently because the first is a regular past tense and the second isn't. The representation for the past tense morpheme in regular past tenses in English is 'ed' ('kissed', 'hugged', 'cried', 'parted'), so this at the end of a word is (relatively) consistent in signalling an important morpheme; where that morpheme is not present, the different spelling shows it is not. Children learning to spell (or talk, pp. 16–18) have to realise that spelling represents morphemes as well as phonemes, and have to choose the right spelling if there is a difference between what a morpheme-based rule would generate and what a phoneme-based one would suggest. This is not straightforward. If I happened to burn the toast yesterday and want to say so in a simple sentence with 'burn' as the verb, or I want to describe the toast with an adjective derived from 'burn', do I use 'burned' or 'burnt'? Does it matter? How do children do it?

Recent research (Bryant *et al.* 1999; Ferreiro 1999; Nunes *et al.* 1997; Totereau *et al.* 1998; Juel and Minden-Cupp 2000) shows that children typically start by spelling past tense or plural morphemes phonetically. For example, in English this may mean adding a 't' or 'd' to the end of the present tense: in French, where the plural ending is often silent, the children do not add any grammatical marker to the singular word. After two or three years children learn about the regular morphemic ending and add it not only to the past tense or plural where it is appropriate but to the words that sound the same but are not based on the same morpheme; for example an English child who used to write 'next' correctly might assimilate it to the 'ed' ending rule and spell it 'necsed'. Something very similar happens with the apostrophe, which children (and greengrocers) often add to plurals ('buy our fresh tomatoe's') as well as using it to indicate possession ('Anne's cat') or omitted letters ('can't'; or as in my Victorian copy of *Alice in Wonderland*, 'ca'n't') (Bryant *et al.* 1997, Truss 2003). They appear to think that the new, morphemic, spelling pattern is just an alternative to the old phonetic one, and so overgeneralise it; but feedback from teachers, parents and other pedants may lead them to learn the rule and restrict the use of their new spelling (or, in the case of the greengrocers and the apostrophes, it may not).

As Chliounaki and Bryant (2002) point out, the sequence of adopting and using a simple rule, seeing that it does not fit all cases and simply extending it to cover the exceptions too, thus receiving new feedback, and then eventually using this feedback and accumulated experience to construct a new rule (which also appears in children's spoken language development) is a familiar Piagetian one, also prominent in information-processing models (Chapter 4). It is not necessarily incompatible with a more Vygotskian sequence where experts' explicit teaching of the rules plays a part. Within either sequence, however, children are clearly likely to actively produce their own ideas about spelling and use their experience of reading and writing to converge on the 'correct' spellings.

2.2.4.5 Learning to read Chinese

I have discussed how children learn to read in English, which uses an alphabetic writing system that has many lapses of phoneme–grapheme correspondence, in part because English has enriched itself from other languages for so long. Learning to read might be somewhat different in other languages (Silven *et al.* 2004). Recently, much more work has been published on children learning to read Chinese, which has a profoundly different writing system. This work highlights differences but also many similarities in how children learn to read using different writing systems (Chan and Nunes 1998; Ho and Bryant 1997a, 1997b; Harris and Hatano 1999; McBride-Chang 1996, 1999; McBride-Chang and Kail 2002; McBride-Chang and Ho 2000; Shu *et al.* 2003, McBride-Chang *et al.* 2004).

The basic units of Chinese are characters, which represent morphemes rather than sounds. There are about 200 radicals in written Chinese; these represent basic meanings. They are combined with other radicals or with phonetic components to make compound characters. If words are related in meaning, they may share characters; thus the character for wood is repeated several times in the character for forest. (The nearest example I have thought of for similar character construction used by English speakers is in mathematical writing, where for example = and < are combined to make the sign for 'less than or equal to', = and > for 'more than or equal to', = and / for 'not equal to', and so forth.) The pronunciation of a character may be quite different in two different local 'dialects' of Chinese, for example Cantonese and Mandarin, although the character represents the same meaning. The majority of modern Chinese characters also contain a phonetic component that gives information about the pronunciation of the character; there are about 800 of these. Characters with the same phonetic component often, but not always, have the same pronunciation. The radicals and phonetic components of characters also have subcomponents that do not have either meanings or pronunciations themselves but serve as building blocks of the major components; there are about 650 of these. Some Chinese compound characters are produced with the same tonal pattern as their phonetic constituent, others with a different tone (Shu *et al.* 2003). Chinese is analytical, tonal and non-inflected, a stark contrast to English which is synthetic, atonal and inflected.

Given these complexities, it is not surprising that learning to read Chinese is not easy (though we should remember that nor is learning to read English). McBride-Chang and Kail (2002) examined the predictors of reading acquisition in young children in the US and in Hong Kong. The American children, kindergarteners and first graders aged five to seven, were just starting to learn to read English. The Hong Kong children, kindergarteners aged three to six, were native Cantonese speakers, learning to read in Cantonese, Mandarin and English. Thus comparisons between alphabetic and character writing systems, and between first-language and second-language reading were possible. The children completed a battery of tasks assessing their reading skill, processing speed, phonological awareness (at the syllable level because this is the level it functions at in Chinese), naming and visual-spatial skill; Chinese children did most tasks in both English and Chinese, the American children only in English. Their basic vocabulary in their mother tongue was measured as an estimate of general ability. As would be expected, within each culture older children did better on all tests than younger ones; the oldest Hong Kong children, who were an average of two months younger than the youngest American children but had had more years of formal education in reading and were more likely to be bilingual, outscored the Americans on six of the eight tests, the American children scoring higher only on a task involving speeded naming of English numbers. When the scores were fitted to models predicting reading in the children's native languages, the patterns were identical in English and Chinese. Reading, both words and characters, was associated with phonological awareness much more strongly than with naming or visual processing; age-related change in processing speed was strongly associated with naming, phonological awareness and visual processing abilities. What is more, almost the same pattern emerged for the Chinese children in their learning to read English. This suggests that phonological awareness is important in the very earliest stages of learning to read in character-based orthographies as well as in alphabet-based ones; that visual processing is not a predictor of reading independently of general cognitive skills; and that increases in processing speed affect reading indirectly because of their effect on such skills as phonological awareness, visual processing and naming. It may be the case that Chinese–English bilingualism facilitated the children's ability to manipulate speech sounds and hence had benefits for their phonological awareness at the syllable level; and that skills have reciprocal effects on each other as each improves (Wagner *et al.* 1994, 1997); McBride-Chang *et al.* (2004) suggest that training in the Pinyin system of writing may help phonological awareness.

Ho and Bryant (1997), Chan and Siegel (2001) and Shu *et al.* (2000) showed that high-frequency characters were easier for young readers to pronounce than phonetically regular ones, but that awareness of the information in the phonetic component of the character was helpful to some children and these children were making more progress in reading. The errors made by good readers were more phonetic-related than those of poor readers of the same age. Good readers were better at naming pseudo-characters, and older readers were better than younger, less skilled ones. Pronunciation of regular compound characters is easier than pronunciation of irregular characters or tone-different characters. Pronunciation of tone-different characters by young readers is dependent on their familiarity; high-frequency tone-different characters are read as well as regular characters, and low-frequency tone-different characters are hard to read (Ho and Bryant 1997). Repeated exposure to characters seemed to be the major factor behind children's ability to pronounce them, though better readers did pick up and use clues to pronunciation. This was true also for children learning new compound characters, where the presence of a known phonetic character made the compound easier to learn than one where the phonetic component was unknown. The researchers also compared children who had spoken the Cantonese dialect of Chinese but were learning to read the Mandarin dialect, which is differently pronounced, with children who had grown up speaking Mandarin; not surprisingly, the Cantonese speakers were less able to use phonetic information to learn Mandarin pronunciations of the characters they were learning to read.

As I described, Chinese characters have semantic constituents as well as phonetic ones. The radicals of characters provide obvious information about meaning in about half of the characters that Chinese school children are required to learn to read and some information about meaning in a further 30 per cent (Shu *et al.* 2003). Children who can recognise radicals have an additional clue to the meaning of a compound character. Shu and Anderson (1997) and Chan and Nunes (1998) showed that children used this information throughout the primary school years and could use semantic components to specify the meanings of characters, particularly when the semantic components were familiar and the words conceptually easy.

It is too early to synthesise the emerging research evidence on how children learn to read Chinese. It does seem, however, that Chinese children find it easier to read familiar characters, just as English children start reading by recognising a few familiar words. Where Chinese characters do give clues to pronunciation, or where phonological analogies are possible, Chinese children as young as six can use them to read characters, just like children reading English words; but fewer Chinese characters than English words allow this, and phonological awareness contributes mainly at the level of syllables rather than that of phonemes. Written Chinese characters also have some orderly semantic structure, and this also young children can access and use to identify meaning. However, the advantage that Chinese children have in reading characters where they can use phonological or semantic regularities is smaller than the advantage that they gain from reading a familiar rather than an unfamiliar character; which implies that for Chinese children, just as for English ones, there is no easy way round repeated practice if they are to become skilled readers.

2.2.5 Recapitulation

The cognitive psychology studies of reading single words and the research on children learning to read and retarded readers all suggest, then, that there are several ways of decoding a written word into its meaning.

Beginning readers, and skilled readers reading familiar words, probably rely heavily on sight vocabulary, going directly from visual image to meaning without necessarily needing the sound of the word. Linking sight and sound is, however, necessary for expanding the sight vocabulary and dealing with unfamiliar words. Sensitivity to sounds and an ability to make and use grapheme–phoneme correspondences are important here. However, the research summarised in the last few lines has centred on reading isolated words or small units of text. As we saw in discussing models of reading earlier, skilled readers probably use both sight vocabulary and phonic analysis within a more contextual way of reading. In text comprehension the information given in a text is integrated with the reader's prior knowledge of the topic, which may itself have been gathered, of course, from earlier encounters with text. Beginning readers lack both general knowledge about topics and knowledge about the general characteristics of text.

These may be very important parts of learning to read. In socially representative samples of children (e.g. Wells 1981b, 1985; Gregg *et al.* 2004) there were significant positive correlations between parents' and children's interest in literacy, particularly the frequency with which stories were read to the child, during the preschool years, and the child's progress in learning to read. Children who learn to read early and easily (Clark 1976) have generally acquired very early a good understanding of what reading is about in general, and about such specific aspects as that you go along the lines from top left to bottom right, that the message is in the text though the pictures may provide clues, what things called 'words' and 'sentences' are, and so forth (Elley 1989; Rice 1989; Rice and Woodsmall 1988; Tunmer *et al.* 1988; Silven *et al.* 2004).

2.2.6 Reading longer texts

This very brief account of what experimental cognitive psychology is suggesting about reading processes does not do justice to the field's achievements. It does, however, make the point that 'reading' includes many different activities at different perceptual, linguistic and cognitive levels, and that these may well operate in different ways as the reader tackles different tasks. In some ways it may be misleading to call all instances of 'reading' by the same name. What we do when we recognise 'cereals' in a supermarket is probably simpler than what we do when we see it in a newspaper article on the government's farming policy, and that 'reading' might be different from meeting the same string of letters in a scientific article or a poem. My next concern therefore is with the cognitive skills necessary for comprehending text. These include (Oakhill and Garnham 1988; Hayes 2004) decoding words, applying grammatical knowledge, applying semantic knowledge, using schemas and world knowledge, making inferences, applying genre conventions, identifying the gist, and inferring the writer's intentions and point of view.

Some examples may help to embody these cognitive processes. Even apparently simple and straightforward texts may require readers to import knowledge from the outside world if they are to make sense of what is written. The sentences I quoted earlier from Winograd (1972) about the city council refusing protesters permission to hold a demonstration because 'they advocated [or feared] violence' is an example: the two different verbs imply different referents for 'they', but only a reader who knew that city councils rarely advocate violence, but more often fear it, could get the referents right. Similar inferences may be needed to sort out connections between sentences, or to discover what their full implications are. Consider the following sentences:

> Tybalt hated Romeo. He loved Juliet and felt that the young man's love for her was outrageous. The feud between the Capulet and Montague families ended in tragedy.

Only some knowledge of the whole story makes clear which is the 'he' and which 'the young man' talked about in the second sentence, or indeed whether the love felt for Juliet is cousinly or passionate. If the passage ended after Juliet the 'he' would be completely ambiguous; spoken, an unstressed 'he' would mean Tybalt and an emphasised one Romeo, but the written text does not present such cues. The relevance of the third sentence has to be assumed unless the reader knows that Tybalt and Juliet were members of the Capulet family and Romeo a Montague.

Some inferences are *necessary* parts of understanding a text. Oakhill and Garnham (1988: 21–2) quote a children's story:

> Jane was invited to Jack's birthday party.
> She wondered if he would like a kite.
> She went to her room and shook her piggy bank.
> It made no sound.
> Jane frowned.

This only makes sense in the light of knowledge about birthday parties, birthday presents, buying things with money, saving money in piggy banks, and so forth. Without it Jane's musings and her actions would be completely incomprehensible. However readers with the relevant knowledge seem often to make necessary inferences as they read without much difficulty, and often with so little awareness that they are inferring information rather than simply reading it that they later believe the implied information had actually been explicitly presented (Paris 1978; Paris and Lindauer 1978; RAND Reading Study Group 2004; Ruddell and Unrau 2004). Similarly there may be inferences that *elaborate* the text. If we read 'Mary cut into the pudding' we have, from linguistic necessity, to infer that she used some instrument to do so. Readers probably make inferences about possible referents and possible implications by using the knowledge that they have accumulated into 'scripts' (pp. 159–161), though exactly how this is done we do not know. Obviously children may have problems with inferences because they do not have the necessary information.

Text also involves links that integrate its various parts. 'Scripts' integrate large sections: adjacent sentences will be linked by *anaphoric* devices such as pronouns (such as the 'he' in the second sentence of the 'Romeo and Juliet' example given above) or noun phrases beginning with 'the' (such as 'the young man' in the same sentence). These sorts of expressions take their meaning from other parts of the text and do not stand alone. They are very common in written text, and children often have problems with them (Anderson 2004; Cote and Goldman 2004; Spiro 2004; Many *et al.* 2004; Oakhill and Garnham 1988; Ruddell and Unrau 2004b). Work by Annette Karmiloff-Smith (1986, 1988, 1992; Karmiloff and Karmiloff-Smith 2001) suggests that they also use them in an immature way when talking and narrating stories.

2.2.6.1 Understanding the structure of a text

Readers may approach a text with an idea in mind about its overall structure. Even children as young as four use their world knowledge to understand stories, and have 'story grammars' in the sense that they have 'scripts' of familiar events in their lives (Mandler and Johnson 1977; Wimmer 1980; Tizard *et al.* 1982, 1984; Anderson 2004; and see pp. 159–163). Four-year-olds' narration about a set of pictures is primarily descriptive but if the pictures tell a story, the narration includes details derived from their understanding of the story (Poulsen *et al.* 1979). Although their initial retelling of stories contains mainly surface events, probing with 'why' questions elicits many inferences about the characters' motives and intentions (see also the section on 'children's theories of mind'). This is particularly the case if the story is a familiar, interesting and profound one. In an innovative nursery school curriculum, Christianne Hayward introduced serial readings of books such as *Watership Down* by Richard Adams; she linked it with activities such as puppet rabbits and a 'burrow' for imaginative play, and materials based on the story for early mathematics work. Children who had had this experience were able to produce elaborate and sophisticated retellings of the text, as is shown by this verbatim example of part of one four-year-old's retelling, using a book of pictures from the film of *Watership Down* (see also Hayward 1982).

> And they were chewing the rope so that the ahh boat or something could move out, and by the time that they come they were, they just

finished off so that . . . and they were all ready in the boat except for the one that was chewing the rope and then he, and then the boat nearly rushed off, and he gave a great big leap so that he could get on the boat, and he just about finished ahh, didn't get in the boat. And then General Woundwart nearly went in the water. And then they were all in the boat sailing off and Kehaar flew and they got across the water, and then they rested and they fell asleep. And then Fiver, Fiver said there was something going wrong again. And then they find Hazel to talk to Woundwart and then they're trying to get in the burrow where there's Bigwig and Hazel [before the relevant frame] and then they found it [before the relevant frame]. And then Bigwig finds something, some mud to cover him over with [predicts] and they're about to get in, and they were chewing the rope so that the dog could get out. And ahh, ahh except for the cat and then General Woundwart finds the little one and as he was walking, Bigwig jumped and bit him and they fighted and the dog was chasing one of the rabbits and that looks like they're killing each other [pointing]. And the dog's coming and he [points to Woundwart], and he scratched him just there, like that [points to own face above eye] and then they were both all scratched and then the dog was coming to get the rabbits and was going to eat it and he did. He got the rabbit in his mouth. And General Woundwart is covered in blood, he is, even his teeth. I still can see he hasn't got an eye there 'cause something pulled his eye out before. Bigwig doesn't die.

(Meadows and Cashdan 1988)

As they grow into older and more experienced readers children also become more able to identify the more important and less important ideas in a text (e.g. Brown *et al.* 1983; Yussen *et al.* 1980), using the sorts of strategies that turn up in their writing too (Cote and Goldman 2004). Even the youngest children are likely to remember more important points than unimportant ones, but picking them out explicitly or even rating them as 'very important' or 'very unimportant' is hard even for children of ten to twelve. This might make it harder to study texts effectively: we do know that children's efforts may be inappropriately directed in memory tasks. Increasing knowledge of texts and of the world, and better metacognition, will both be involved in the developmental advance that children make.

The comprehension of written text, then, involves a wide range of cognitive skills, including word recognition, use of syntactic knowledge for processing sentences and larger units of text, inferences derived from the text and from world knowledge external to it. It will also involve decisions derived from knowledge about the nature and purposes of a text, such as the likely characters and motives of fictional personages or the relative importance of items of information in a factual text, and understanding the understanding and intentions of the writer (Hayes 2004). It will perhaps be necessary not just to comprehend the text but to monitor one's compre-hension, that is, to check whether the text is being understood, to be aware of breakdowns in understanding and to take some appropriate action to remedy them – metacognitive skills, see pp. 132–135. Very many of these comprehension skills are deployed simultaneously, so it is necessary for some of them to become automatic as otherwise the cognitive overload would result in failure to comprehend. One of the reasons why beginning readers may decode a text into recognised spoken words but fail to under-stand it is that they cannot manage to decode and to comprehend simul-taneously, and slow effortful decoding leads to the forgetting of earlier text and its information. Children may in any case have difficulty in integrating bits of text into a consistent whole (e.g. Garner 1987; Markman 1979; Robinson and Robinson 1983). In her work Markman assessed children's ability to spot ambiguities and omissions in instructions about how to play a game, and logical inconsistences in texts. Even ten-year-olds quite often judged that texts that had gross internal contradictions, like the one that follows, were perfectly satisfactory.

Ants
Everywhere they go they put out a special chemical from their bodies. They cannot see this chemical, but it has a special odor. An ant must have a nose in order to smell this chemical odor. Another thing about ants is they do not have a nose. Ants cannot smell this odor. Ants can always find their way home by smelling this odor to follow the trail.
(Markman 1979)

Obviously failure to recognise that there has been a comprehension break-down means that it is impossible to take appropriate action to correct it. Forewarning children about possible problems means that they are more likely to recognise them (Markman 1979); however, problems such as incomplete instructions and unfamiliar vocabulary, for which the criteria for comprehensibility are explicit, are easier to detect than internal incon-sistencies like those in the 'ants' passage, where each word and individual sentence would pass comprehensibility tests. Older children do better than younger ones, and good readers better than poor ones (Baker 1984). No doubt further experience of texts as a result of having done more reading is a contributor to this development, but explicit instruction has also been shown to be helpful in various research studies (e.g. Garner 1987; Marton *et al.* 1992; Masterson *et al.* 1992; RAND Reading Study Group 2004; Cote and Goldman 2004).

Having detected a problem, the next question is of course what to do about it. Possible strategies include ignoring the uncomprehended words or passages; waiting to see if the meaning becomes clearer later; guessing, the guess being confirmed or disconfirmed later; re-reading the immediate problem passage or the larger part of the text in which it occurs; seeking outside help, from peer, teacher, dictionary or another text; or combinations of these. Which of these strategies the reader uses will depend, among other things, on task requirements and the available resources; casual reading is likely to use the simpler strategies at the beginning of the list, while detailed mastery of difficult text requires much more re-reading, analysis and comparison of different sources. Which strategy is used will also depend on the characteristics of the reader, and, in the case of very young readers, on how they are being taught to read. Experience of reading, how expert one is at it, will affect one's strategies for coping with comprehension. Even the most novice reader will, however, have used skills somewhat like these in trying to understand spoken language, and the language they hear when being read to. The most obvious skill that is more applicable to written language than to spoken language is re-reading, both because spoken words are much more ephemeral and because requests for the repeating of an uncomprehending utterance would often produce, in normal discourse, a rephrasing of what was said, not a verbatim repetition. Guessing, ignoring and seeking outside help are, however, well-practised strategies, and children have little difficulty in applying them.

However well children understand the structure of the text, however good their metacognition is, they will not be able to comprehend what they read unless they have an adequate working memory. Working memory serves as a buffer for the parts of the text that have been read most recently, and for information from more distant parts of the text and from long-term memory that needs to be integrated with the current text. Its central executive is necessary for the planning and monitoring of reading, information flow, and comprehension. Verbal resources and therefore verbal skills are perhaps particularly important (Nation *et al.* 1999; Vellutino *et al.* 2004). Cain *et al.* (2004) recently showed that sentence-span and digit-span measures of working memory predicted variance in the reading comprehension of children aged eight to eleven after control for word reading ability, vocabulary and verbal ability. Performance at the very basic level of word recogntion contributed to reading comprehension, but so did higher level skills such as inference making and comprehension monitoring, which involved strategic cognition beyond the comparative simplicity of word recognition and basic working memory. Reading comprehension required word-level and verbal skills, working memory, knowledge of text structure, and skills of inference and metacognition.

2.2.7 Reading and the social world

I promised at the beginning of this chapter to return to the question of reading's relationship to social experience. I am going to do this only briefly. Ever since the beginnings of literacy, parents, teachers and other authorities have developed texts to socialise children (Applebee 1978; Tucker 1981; Steedman 1982; Zipes 1983) as well as to entertain them. Children often play out the story they have been read, in social pretend play. My three-year-old daughter was very enthusiastic about pretending to be Sleeping Beauty and Snow White: both roles involved her lying on the floor with eyes tight shut and a smug smile on her face while her role-play partner had to do all the other parts, finally 'waking her' with a kiss. This irritated me into providing an intensive course of stories with more feminist themes, such as Molly Whuppie the giant-killer and various clever girls who outsmart the male baddies, such as Leeson (1993), with much the same effect as making 'sensible' clothes for her Barbie dolls. Experience of stories is documented in many autobiographies as shaping people's sense of them-selves, of other people, and of the social world, across different cultures (Miller *et al.* 1997). The children in Christianne Hayward's *Watership Down* experiment (Hayward 1982, and pp. 52–53) used their understanding of the group of rabbits to consider the nature of leadership and the attributes of leaders: Bigwig is the strongest rabbit and Fiver the visionary, but Hazel is the leader – why?

As well as the relationships between parents and children where their attachment enriches and is enriched by sharing a bedtime story (e.g. Heath 1982, 1986; Scarborough and Dobrich 1994; Bus and vanIJzendoorn 1995), children's friendships affect how they approach literacy tasks and may be affected by the friends' shared interest in reading. Sharing out roles in pretend play, or identifying with the characters of a story, can be contri-butors to the life of the peer group. Experiences such as these are part of forming one's view of oneself and of forming affiliative relationships with other people; these affiliations and attachments in turn shape one's expo-sure to further activities and experiences, including more experiences with literacy. Peer conversations about books and stories are often characterised by language that focuses on literacy matters and cognitive processes, and this language facilitates understanding literacy (Pellegrini *et al.* 1995, 1997a, 1997b) as well as understanding other people. The social and emotional ties you have with your reading partners and with the books you read may interact – we read something because it is admired by someone we like, or even revise our rating of a person because unexpectedly they like or dislike a particular author or text. The recent rise of book groups is an interesting phenomenon extending this into adult life.

2.3 Writing

Like reading, writing is an activity that integrates many different processes – physical, linguistic, cognitive, even social and affective – in different ways according to the writer's age, experience and purposes. Scardamalia (1981) lists the interdependent skills involved, among them the physical production of text through handwriting or typing; spelling and punctuation (these may be avoided through dictation, which delegates them to someone else, but involves other skills); considerations of content, word choice, syntax and textual connections (which must be at least minimally included); and considerations of overall purpose, intended effect, organisation, clarity and euphony (which may be optional or subjective). Each of these skills is itself of course highly complex; each shows developmental change in what is done and in what is expected. Some writing skills, but not all, are intensively taught; some remain the area of expertise of comparatively few writers. Two aspects of writing, its nature as a physical skill and the 'ecology' of its use, I will only mention briefly, concentrating my discussion on the cognitive skills of writing, and I have already talked about spelling (pp. 45–46).

2.3.1 Making written symbols

Writing involves the use of fine muscle movements in varied but co-ordinated patterns, with visual monitoring, at a speed (in experienced writers) far faster than the brain can send messages to the hand and receive feedback, though more slowly than thinking or speaking. The human hand is an extraordinarily intricate and delicate mechanism, controlled by a large number of muscles. During writing, movements in fingers, wrists, arms and shoulders, plus movements of the eyes (and perhaps head) for monitoring writing, have to be co-ordinated. These muscle movements have to be small, quick and precise, and because the speed of transmission of neural control messages along the length of the arm is relatively slow, the brain cannot wait for one movement to be completed before the next is begun. Even at this level the brain must plan ahead to get the hand in the right position at the right place at the right time (Thomassen and Teuling 1983).

To do this, we write not in single letters but in larger units. As an example, compare the ease of writing 'written backwards' with the difficulty of writing 'sdrawkcab nettirw' and note where the pauses and breaks in writing came. 'Units' may occur over longer strings than single words: we pause more between clauses than within them, for example. 'Over-uniting' may produce errors; I planned the first sentence of the last paragraph, 'Writing involves the use of fine muscle movements' etc. as it is now printed, but wrote 'final' instead of 'fine', conflating 'fine' with the sound at the end of 'muscle' rather than making a semantic error. Motor skills of the highly complex sort involved in writing fluently are acquired mainly through practice. Children's fine motor co-ordination continues to develop throughout childhood (Laszlo and Bairstow 1985) and maturation may limit the neatness of their handwriting. Nineteenth-century pedagogy did successfully force several generations of children to write (and sew) neatly, as witness surviving copybooks and samplers sewn by what now seem remarkably young girls. However, accounts in biographies and novels testify to the pains of being made to conform to strict standards of neatness, and casual observation today will show that a high proportion of people never really learn to write neatly!

Given a piece of paper and a pencil, a child in the second year of life will enjoy making marks on the paper. Initially these line and dot scribbles are probably not unsuccessful attempts to write or draw, rather they are successful attempts to make marks on the paper where there were no marks before. 'Writing' usually follows attempts at drawing representations of objects. Vygotsky (1978b) points out that writing is a second-order symbol system: the letters stand for the spoken word, which itself stands for the object (see also Vellutino *et al.* (2004) for a relation of this point to reading). Drawings and idiosyncratic pictographs are, like spoken words, in a first-order symbolic relation to the object they represent. Such an account of writing's symbolic relations implies that writing will develop after drawing has begun (pp. 139–140): writing is a special sort of drawing that represents language. As children experience written language by being read to (or reading for themselves), they learn that 'writing' consists of particular sorts of patterns arranged on the page in particular orientations; in English, horizontal lines from left to right of the twenty-six letters of the alphabet (Adi-Japha and Freeman 2001). Young children may 'write' in a scribble or string of letters running horizontally across the page, or accompanying a picture as an adult might produce a caption. Kamler and Kilarr (1983: 187–189; see also Meadows 1986: 89–91) provide a fascinating observation of a child just under five as she composes a 'story' to accompany a picture. She writes horizontal 'words' using a limited set of letters. Her first word is written at the top of the page, the second nearly at the bottom, the third, fourth and fifth words are fitted in between them, and the sixth is a late addition at the bottom of the page. She composes in bursts, and reads what she has written from top to bottom of the page. Thus when she first wrote it, 'Kioe' at the bottom of her page was her second word and meant 'sat', but when she next rereads from top to bottom it is the third word and means 'mat'. She completely fails to be consistent in her matching of written word to thought-of word. Kamler and Kilarr comment that the child may be making her 'random clusters of letters' first, and only later attributing meaning to them, like the child artists who seem to decide what their drawing represents after they have produced it. The demands of making the movements and marks that produce the written words are themselves considerable and may make coherent composition virtually impossible. Smith (1982) advocates writing practice that is free from demands for correctness in spelling, punctuation or composition, demands that may distract from establishing automatic motor patterns. It is important to point out that children do not normally write letters untidily or

incorrectly because of inadequate visual processing, but because of production difficulties: letters have to be precisely formed in direction, size,
joins, spaces and so forth, and the motor control needed for this is very
considerable. Practice gives a fluent production system, but children who
lack one make the sort of errors and attempt the sort of solutions that they
do in drawings (p. 141). There is a complex interaction of the purely motor
and the cognitive skills in the apparently simple making of written symbols.

2.3.2 The environment of writing

Writing is embedded in a social context, and can serve a variety of purposes. Where a reader is essentially concerned with extracting meaning
from a pre-existing text, with or without increase in enjoyment or knowledge, a writer may have any of a wider range of purposes, for example to
inform, to entertain, to persuade, to criticise, to record, to express something personally felt, and so forth (Many et al. 2004). This list is obviously
similar to one listing the functions of spoken language: recording is the
major exception, as generally it is better done by writing than by speaking,
and indeed some theorists suggest that writing was invented largely for
record-keeping purposes (records of property and liability for taxes,
regrettably; Goody 1977; Goody and Watt 1968). Children's spoken
language will have been used for most of these functions by the end of the
pre-school years (pp. 10–12), but they may not have experienced all these
functions expressed in writing. Although most adults write sometimes,
studies of the 'ecology' of writing (e.g. Griffiths and Wells 1983) show that
the main functions of writing at home are in response to social or mnemonic requirements: domestic messages, family letters and shopping lists.
When adults do write to express themselves, to tell stories or to record their
own experience they mostly do so privately or at least away from the
interruptions of pre-school children, who will thus have little writing
activity to observe that involves anything other than notes of information
or domestic letters. Adult literacy is positively correlated with children's
literacy (Wells 1981b, 1985; Gregg et al. 2004), perhaps because the children
of literate parents have both more opportunities to observe literacy and
more formal and informal teaching from their parents. Tizard and Hughes
(1984) describe some mothers teaching their daughters to write, sometimes
as a session of letter forming or copying words, sometimes as part of an
activity such as writing a letter to grandparents. The latter is probably a
fairly common real-life experience for quite a lot of children. Parents may
encourage (or require) children to write letters to grandparents or to people
who have given presents or hospitality; thus there is a real social purpose to
writing. Examples from young children are often conventional rather than
expressive, apart from some tear-stained letters home from children in
boarding schools that have failed to censor their pupils' productions. The

child 'learns that letters can be a means of reporting and interpreting experience, a device for exchanging information, and a method of maintaining social interaction among friends' (Collerson 1983: 92).

2.3.3 Composition skills

Writing is not simply written-down speaking. Stubbs (1980) points out that the relationship between written and spoken language differs for different writing systems, different authorial purposes, and different cultures, but one consistent difference is that the written text has to convey its meaning more independently of paralinguistic context than spoken language has to do. The writer must construct the text without the assistance of signals from the recipient about whether the meaning is being understood, whether more or less information is needed, whether jokes are being appreciated or persuasive arguments are having the desired effect. The reader has to get meaning from the text in the absence of many of the signals that accompany spoken language: cues from the speaker's 'body language', pitch, intonation, speed of speaking, facial expression and so forth are not available in conventional written text, though devices of punctuation and typography may be used to make up for some of this loss. Writers and readers interact much more distantly than speakers and listeners. Writers cannot, alas, monitor their readers' understanding. If they wish to be effective, they must therefore plan, compose and review their writing more carefully than most speakers need to do, lest problems in their choices of words and syntax and the overall organisation and clarity of the text, or adverse reactions by the readers to the writer's purpose and assumptions, should prevent satisfactory communication. The text must create its own paralinguistic context, so the writer must assess what knowledge can safely be assumed and what information must be incorporated into the text. The writer must also assess what is the best order for pieces of text and present each piece unambiguously and explicitly. It may be easier for the reader to go back and read text again than it is for the listener to recall speech in order to re-examine it, but the writer cannot adjust content, order or emphasis, as the speaker can, in response to the reader's cues of understanding or failure to understand. Writers need to appreciate some of the conventions that differ between spoken and written language. In short, effective written language normally needs careful thought in the composing.

Given this need, and given the high importance placed on being able to compose effectively (at least at the level of writing applications for jobs), it is not surprising that a considerable amount of research has been done on composition. One interesting model, co-ordinating writing and reading, is presented by Hayes (2004) (Figure 2.2). Although the core of the model is the cognition involved, Hayes emphasises the social and affective nature of writing:

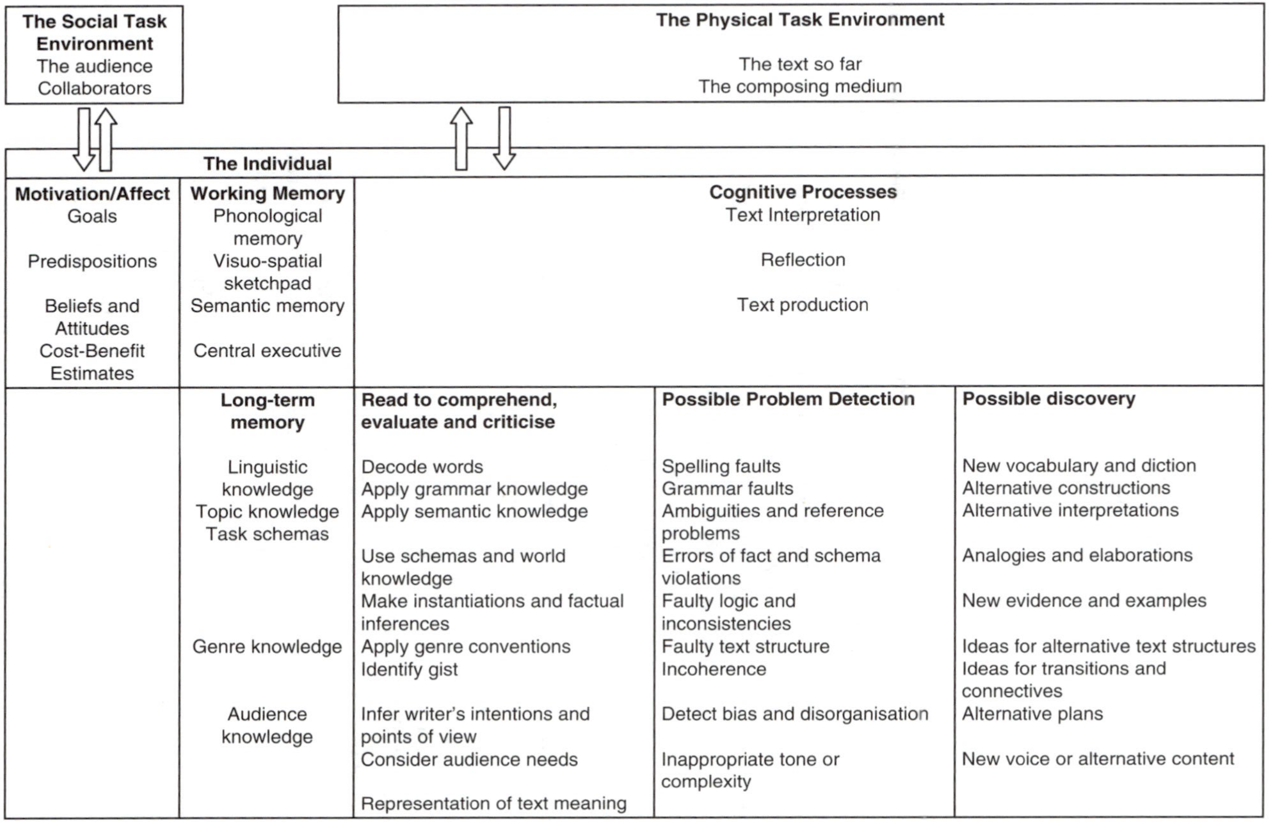

The Social Task Environment
The audience
Collaborators

The Physical Task Environment
The text so far
The composing medium

The Individual

Motivation/Affect
Goals
Predispositions
Beliefs and Attitudes
Cost-Benefit Estimates

Working Memory
Phonological memory
Visuo-spatial sketchpad
Semantic memory
Central executive

Cognitive Processes
Text Interpretation
Reflection
Text production

Long-term memory	Read to comprehend, evaluate and criticise	Possible Problem Detection	Possible discovery
Linguistic knowledge	Decode words	Spelling faults	New vocabulary and diction
Topic knowledge	Apply grammar knowledge	Grammar faults	Alternative constructions
Task schemas	Apply semantic knowledge	Ambiguities and reference problems	Alternative interpretations
	Use schemas and world knowledge	Errors of fact and schema violations	Analogies and elaborations
	Make instantiations and factual inferences	Faulty logic and inconsistencies	New evidence and examples
Genre knowledge	Apply genre conventions	Faulty text structure	Ideas for alternative text structures
	Identify gist	Incoherence	Ideas for transitions and connectives
	Infer writer's intentions and points of view	Detect bias and disorganisation	Alternative plans
Audience knowledge	Consider audience needs	Inappropriate tone or complexity	New voice or alternative content
	Representation of text meaning		

Figure 2.2 Model of cognition involved in writing and critical reading. Adapted from Hayes (2004: 1403–1415).

> Writing is primarily a social activity. We write mostly to communicate with other humans. But the act of writing is not social just because of its communicative purpose. It is also social because it is a social artifact that is carried out in a social setting. What we write, how we write, and who we write to is shaped by social convention and our history of social interaction. Our schools and our friends require us to write. We write differently to a familiar audience than to an audience of strangers. The genres in which we write were invented by other writers, and the phrases we write often reflect phrases earlier writers have written. Thus, our culture provides the words, images and forms from which we fashion text.
>
> (Hayes 2004: 1404)

Hayes suggests that working memory is at the core of the writing process (p. 86). A representation of the semantic content that the writer wants is retrieved from long-term memory (which stores writers' knowledge of language, tasks, topics, genres and audience) and stored in working memory. The articulatory component of working memory is then used to store a syntactic form that expresses this semantic content. When all the semantic content is expressed, or when the articulatory capacity of working memory is full, the sentence is produced, evaluated and revised as necessary. Word choice was affected by both semantic and syntactic considerations. Demands on working memory limit the amount that is produced, but skilled writers can produce words in larger units, and thus longer sentences, than less skilled ones. Skilled writers appear to produce clauses of seven to eleven words when generating a sentence, composing mainly from left to right, rereading the sentence so far before adding words at the end of the sentence.

The primary cognitive functions that working memory serves in Hayes's model of writing are text interpretation, reflection and text production. These need to be co-ordinated. Text interpretation, based on reading, listening and scanning graphics, produces internal representations of the input. Reflection operates on these to produce further representations. Text production uses internal representations of the topic and the task and produces written and spoken output (and graphic output if this is appropriate). These processes are very similar to those used in reading comprehension (pp. 50–55), and it is argued that successful writing involves an alternation between composing and critical reading (pp. 63–64).

Given the complexities of writing as seen in this and other models, it is not surprising that inexperienced writers may have difficulties with it. Martlew (1983) reviews some of the errors that poor or inexperienced writers make: they write as they speak, leaving their writing dependent on a context that the reader may not share; they plan poorly, if at all, and prepare themselves for writing too briefly to be able to produce clearly organised text; they rarely review or criticise what they have produced, and what review and self-criticism occur almost never lead to improving the text. Some of these inadequacies no doubt arise because the whole task of considering the adequacy of the text *plus* spelling correctly *plus* writing neatly *plus* producing the right amount to satisfy the teacher overwhelms young writers. Some, however, probably stem from their uncertainty about what to do in composition, and how to do it. Frederiksen and Dominic suggest that important cognitive resources 'include the writer's knowledge, the already established strategies and procedures for constructing a meaning and expressing it, and the general characteristics of their cognitive systems such as processing capacity and both the automaticity and efficiency of component processes' (Frederiksen and Dominic 1981: 4).

Very young writers often find problems simply in generating content. They frequently produce the equivalent of one utterance on the subject, and then stop, claiming that that is all they can think of to say. Bereiter and Scardamalia (1982) demonstrate that devices of various sorts increase the amount produced. Instructions to produce a large amount, the opportunity to speak or to dictate the text instead of having to write it, instructions to continue composing leaving aside questions of difficult spelling, the provision of simple prompts such as 'on the other hand' or 'also', all increase both the number of words and the number of ideas expressed, as well as the children's satisfaction with their writing. On their own, children have clearly not really reached the limits of what was available on the subject. They welcome prompts and appreciate their effects. Learning to provide prompts for yourself is part of the development of writing skills.

Although not generating enough material is a problem in writing, the optimum solution is not simply to generate more irrespective of its quality, truth, relevance, suitability and so forth. It is preferable that the writer should think what to say, stay on topic, produce a coherent and intelligible whole without hesitation, deviation or repetition, and keep it appropriate to the audience and purpose. To do all this involves co-ordinating searches of memory for useful material with the various physical, linguistic and cognitive processes that I mentioned earlier. This may be comparatively straightforward when writers are recounting personal experiences or dealing with routine scripts and stories. It becomes more problematic when the task is one of making a critical examination of a subject. Scardamalia and Bereiter (Bereiter and Scardamalia 1982, 1987; Scardamalia 1981; Scardamalia and Bereiter 1983, 1986) suggest that the predominant and 'natural' strategy is what they call 'knowledge-telling'. It is 'natural' because it uses skills developed in normal language competence and learned through ordinary social experience, but it does not go beyond them. It starts with the writer constructing a mental representation of a writing task, identifying topic and genre. The writer has some relevant knowledge on the topic (Piaget's theory, say) and on what the genre (an exam question calling for 'evaluation') involves (a tabulation of positive and negative points). The mental representation of topic and genre calls up from memory an item of content, for example the experiments that assessed children's understanding of conservation. As this is relevant to the topic and to the demands of the genre it is expressed in language suitable for the essay, for example 'Piaget did experiments on conservation where he asked children if spacing out a line of counters changed the number of counters and young children said the number did change. However Margaret Donaldson did the experiment with a naughty teddy messing the line up and her children said the number was still the same.' This then serves as a probe for a further search of memory so perhaps an account of other variations on the conservation situation is produced. This alternation of finding a relevant idea and expressing it continues until a sufficient quantity of text has been constructed, or memory yields no more material, or time runs out. The results of each probing of memory are juxtaposed like beads on a string, independent of each other. One of Scardamalia and Bereiter's students, aged 12, summarised it thus:

> I have a whole bunch of ideas and write down until my supply of ideas is exhausted. Then I might try to think of more ideas up to the point when you can't get any more ideas that are worth putting down on paper and then I would end it.
>
> (Bereiter and Scardamalia 1987: 9)

The 'knowledge-telling' strategy for composition is comparatively rapid and automatic, and it does not involve much reflection on what is produced; knowledge-telling does guarantee a fairly easy generating of text that is on topic and does fulfil the minimum demands of the genre, and it usually leads to a quantity of text sufficiently large to satisfy task requirements. It fits, in fact, many novice writers' needs and beliefs about what writing involves. However, it lacks goal-related planning and significant revision, and the pouring forth of what is known is only minimally adjusted to the precise demands of the task or to the characteristics of the reader. The text is not interconnected but made up of unrelated passages produced one after the other without reference forward or, more particularly, back. It may therefore contain repetitions and contradictions; there is evidence from reading comprehension studies (Brown *et al.* 1983; Markman 1979, 1981) that children seem to have difficulties in spotting such problems in other people's writing as well as in their own. Knowledge-telling followed by rigorous revision and ruthless discarding of weak material, or knowledge-telling sustained by a vivid and detailed script and set of characters, are perfectly respectable techniques of composing. However, inexperienced writers are very unlikely to do such revision: they normally limit themselves to proof-reading, word choice and checking the 'mechanics' of spelling, punctuation and grammar (e.g. Nold 1981; Brown *et al.* 1983).

Knowledge-telling is a serviceable strategy, and may persist because of that, as it is conspicuously difficult to give up strategies and theories that work well within limits in favour of a more complex strategy or theory that has greater potential but also higher 'running costs' (Brown *et al.* 1983; Karmiloff-Smith and Inhelder 1974/5; Van Geert 1991). Scardamalia and Bereiter (1986 and Bereiter and Scardamalia 1987) describe another writing strategy that is distinctly more complex and distinctly rarer. In it knowledge-telling is a subordinate process within a far more radical questioning and reorganisation of both content and genre. Memory search is not simply a matter of taking whatever item comes next, but involves personal elaboration of the connections and implications of items and thus the construction of reformulated representations of what is known: a heuristic search of memory (Newell and Simon 1972), not just a mechanical probing of it. Similarly the writing task itself is represented in a more complex way, with explicit considerations of the goals involved, the probable effect of the text on the expected reader, and so forth. Content and topic can influence each other: for example, if a passage seems unclear, the effort to achieve clarity may be translated into a need to examine whether the ideas to be expressed have really been fully understood; or thinking of a new item of content may change the direction of the argument or the possible conclusions to be drawn. This strategy is therefore called 'knowledge transforming'. It involves far more integration of procedures for composing, monitoring and revising, consideration of the text in terms of its overall structure, gist, and goals as well as at the microlevels of spelling and so forth, and, especially, far less automatic production of text and more self-regulation. It is harder work, more problematic, but also more rewarding. It is also, perhaps, an important means to better thinking, not just better writing (Scardamalia and Bereiter 1986; Palincsar and Brown 1984) – at least *some* authors have occasionally felt that they only knew what they thought when they read what they'd written! Hayes (2004) offers one description of the sorts of cognitive processes that are involved; his diagrams of reading to comprehend or to evaluate text set out more fully the activities that writers must combine.

Bereiter and Scardamalia present a variety of material in their description of writing strategies, but asking writers to think aloud as they write is one of their central methods. They found that young and inexperienced writers 'rehearse' their text as they think aloud, repeating out loud (with trivial variations) what they are about to write down. Good writers are more verbose and provide more commentary on their activity and more attempts at clarifying and solving problems, so that much less of what they say is part of their eventual text. Similarly the written revisions of inexpert writers tend to remain at the level of addition and rephrasing, while experts may make revisions that transform the essay and the information that it contains. Training programmes designed to improve children's planning and revision of their text have had some success, both in the research by Bereiter and Scardamalia (Bereiter and Scardamalia 1982, 1987; Scardamalia and Bereiter 1983), and in 'real world' programmes such as the National Writing Project and the National Literacy Strategy in British classrooms (Czierniewska 1992; Henn 1987; Morgan 1989; Styles 1989; Many *et al.* 2004). It is of some relevance to the models of cognitive development discussed elsewhere in this book that while Bereiter and Scardamalia insist on the individual nature of writing and are interested mainly in the internal processes of the autonomous writer, the National Writing Project has made very successful use of collaboration (both between teacher and pupil(s) and between peers), thus using a more socially based approach to developing writing, as Hayes (2004) suggests.

There are several interesting descriptions of child writers working on an extended text (for example Steedman 1982; Many *et al.* 2004). These young writers combine, with varying degrees of success and satisfaction, the tasks of planning, research, composition, revision and collaboration – even those who were supposed to be working alone borrowed ideas, material and text from fellow pupils. They differ in the levels of their skills, both as compared with other individuals and within their own abilities, being for example better at research than at presentation. Strategies of knowledge transformation, shown in skim-reading, genre-switching, note-taking, brainstorming, reflection, and drafting, were there even in some of Many *et al.*'s eleven-year-olds, though not all of them approached their writing task in a reflective, recursive way.

One issue that needs some comment is the nature of the relationship between oral speech and writing, which I raise above. It has been believed for a long time that the 'autonomous text' (as in, for example, a scientific essay) is the highest point in the shift from speech in context to the expression of facts in such a way that there is an exact correspondence between text and meaning and no ambiguity, and no need for implicit inference between writer and reader remains (e.g. Olson 1977; Olson and Torrance 1991). Bereiter and Scardamalia, by focusing on the genre of short expository essays and by rejecting the value of exercises focusing on improving awareness of the audience, seem to be using this view of the best text being the most autonomous. But it is questionable whether text can ever be substantially autonomous, for even the purest scientific text has to be related to the alternative ways of making the same statements, such as graphs, formulae or reworded text, and to the replicatable phenomena of the experiments described, and exists in the context of other texts on the same subject that it questions, refutes, amplifies, extends or otherwise revises. Even here, but more obviously in the texts of the humanities literature, there is the phenomenon of 'intertextuality' (Kristeva 1986), the implicit or explicit presence of other, antecedent, texts in the present text. Except perhaps in the case of text produced by a writer who has never before encountered any text whatever – if such a production could be found, let alone made – any text must be a response, reply, reflection, remembrance of earlier texts. Readers need to share the earlier texts to some degree if they are to understand the present one; shared knowledge of earlier texts is as necessary for understanding written language as shared knowledge of earlier dialogue is for understanding oral language. Shared, intersubjective discussion of texts may be essential to understanding them and to producing better ones.

This seems to be one of the main pedagogic assumptions now embodied in the National Curriculum. It is assumed that all children should, by the age of eleven,

> begin to revise and redraft in discussion with the teacher, other adults, or other children in the class, paying attention to meaning and clarity
> (DES 1990: 12)

and this emphasis on discussion and revision and on the context of reading and writing pervades the Key Stages. Redrafting partnered by discussion seems likely to facilitate not only the production of a clearer or more elegant or more copious text but also the clarification of thought that 'knowledge-transforming' writing produces. An educational ambience that encourages revision and successive improvements rather than perpetuating the demoralising myth that writing involves producing a single perfect draft is desirable. Calkins (1983) describes various classroom strategies directed to this end, and see also various papers in Ruddell and Unrau (2004b).

2.4 Arithmetic

Having discussed the development of reading and writing, I want now to look at 'the third R', children's arithmetic. A considerable amount of work has been done on children's understanding and use of mathematics in recent years, as psychologists have increasingly focused their attention on cognitive skills that are related to school learning. Neurobiologists are also beginning to identify the brain areas that are involved in mathematical operations. A 'psychology of mathematics' is emerging. It includes fine-grained task analyses, but goes beyond defining what knowledge is necessary for success on a task to examine the cognitive processes and knowledge that must go on in the student's mind (or brain), whether or not the task is successfully tackled. There is thus a growing body of work on students' incorrect strategies (e.g. Brown and Burton (1978) on 'buggy algorithms'), and some on individual differences in solution strategies (Siegler 1988). Mayer (1985) provides introductions to the field and its educational implications: among useful collections of papers are books edited by Brainerd (1982), Ginsburg (1983) and Lesh and Landau (1983), Donlan (1998) and a review chapter by

Ginsburg *et al.* (1998). I will discuss here some aspects of early number concepts and their role in children's handling of addition, subtraction and multiplication, how children represent mathematical problems, and some of the cognitive processes that make up competence in the use of written mathematical symbols. Throughout I will try to bring together task analytic approaches, ecological work on children's spontaneous mathematics (since there is beginning to be documentation (e.g. Carraher *et al.* 1985; Towse and Saxton 1997) of what mathematical goals children set for themselves, both in school and outside it), and considerations of mathematical language (see also Davidson 1987).

2.4.1 The basics of number

One basic and very early aspect of using numbers is knowing number words, their names. Almost all human languages have number words, though some are limited to the equivalent of 'one', 'two' and 'many' and some have developed concepts like 'the square root of minus one'. Observations of preschool children at home and in settings such as playgroups show that they quite frequently encounter number words and number word sequences in nursery rhymes, songs, conversation and games (see, for example, Tizard and Hughes 1984; Davie *et al.* 1984). Saxe *et al.* (1987) (pp. 384–385), document the number-related activities of two-year-olds and four-year-olds in Brooklyn; more than 70 per cent of these children engaged in such activities as counting toys, reading number books, playing games and so on at least three times a week, and both mothers and children showed a high level of enthusiasm for number play. Most had invented their own number activities, but television and commercial games that taught number or used it in the course of some other activity were also used. Thus adults often make use of opportunities to use numbers. Parents may deliberately teach their children to 'count' in the senses both of reciting number words and of applying those words in finding out how many objects there are. As Saxe *et al.* (1987) describe in an analysis of the levels of the goals involved in number activity, the former is conceptually much simpler and appears earlier in development. Many two-year-olds use number words in a consistent order in what appears to be a form of denotative reference, saying 'one, two, four' and so forth while gesturing in a sweeping way at a set of objects, but they show little evidence that they are counting in the sense of linking words to the corresponding objects, or that they are using the last word they say as a representation of the number in the array. Young children's number lists do not always use the conventional number sequence: they often are idiosyncratic, with an initial conventional and correct sequence such as 'one, two, three' followed by an unconventional portion – 'five, eight, nine, eleven' – that is used consistently, and a final non-stable portion that varies from occasion to occasion. However, knowing number words is one useful component of later mathematics. Such number lists gradually develop towards the correct form; Fuson and Hall (1983) showed that a majority of children can count to twenty or so by the time they are five, and most can count to one hundred by the age of six given moderate practice in school.

Languages vary in both the quantity and the regularity of number words. In Chinese-derived languages number words are very systematic, with both the number of tens and the number of units made explicit in the names for two-digit numbers (thus the Japanese for twenty-one is *ni-juu-ichi* or two-ten one, and for forty-four *shi-juu-shi*, or four-ten four; Korean fraction words name both part and whole). It seems likely that this very clear labelling of the base-10 components of a number helps children to understand number and compute more effectively (Towse and Saxton 1997; Zhang and Zhou 2003; Zhou and Wang 2004). In English numbers are regularly structured from the teens onwards, with a units part, a 'decades' part and a hundreds or thousands part as appropriate. The number names up to the teens have to be learned more or less by rote, as do the names of the decades; the rest can be generated by rule. Children's learning of number names seems to be initially by rote. It is usually after they have learned to recite the sequence to beyond twenty that they realise there is a repetition of 'something-one, something-two' and so on, and after they have grasped the sequence to one hundred that they can really generate numbers iteratively *ad infinitum* (Siegler and Robinson 1982). Many children find this exciting and set themselves the number goal of counting to some enormous figure, like the four-year-old who could not leave the playground to take part in a research project because she was 'very busy counting to a million', and seemed to be only marginally discouraged that it was taking a very long time. Understanding infinity (and zero, negative numbers, fractions, etc.) comes of course later still, though we may underestimate what children can do here (Siegal 1991).

Knowing the number words is not, as Piaget (1952) pointed out, the most important part of number concepts. An essential early component is discriminating between sets of different sizes. There is more than one way of doing this, and it may not be necessary to count.

It may be possible to discriminate easily between sets of different sizes either if the numerosities are very different or if the sets are very small. Rather a diverse range of other species (non-human primates, dolphins, lions and salamanders, for example) seem to be able to discriminate sets that only differ in numerosity, which suggests that the roots for the human number sense come from far back in evolutionary history, and that it is a basic, evolved, capacity of the human brain, possibly located in the horizontal segment of the bilateral parietal sulcus (Dehaene *et al.* 2003, 2004; Feigenson *et al.* 2004). Adults can produce the cardinal number for small sets (up to four) and very well learned larger sets (such as the configurations on playing cards and dominoes) very quickly and without observable counting. This capacity may be what has been called 'subitising'. It is possible that young children can also subitise small sets of two or three items, possibly even as neonates, though babies' abilities here remain controversial (Antell and Keating 1983; Starkey 1992; Starkey and Cooper 1980; Strauss and Curtis 1981; Wynn 1998; Feigenson *et al.* 2004). It is, however, hard to define what even adults' subitising consists of, given the problems of distinguishing between pattern recognition and very rapid covert counting (see e.g. Fuson and Hall 1983: 59–61; Gelman and Gallistel 1978: 64–68, 219–225). Thus it is not at present clear what role subitising plays in the development of counting. Feigenson *et al.* (2004) suggest that we have two core systems of number, which are largely innate and evolved. One represents the approximate numerical magnitude of large sets, and can discriminate between large number sets in terms of the ratio between them (something like 'some' versus 'lots more'). The other provides a numerically accurate representation of small sets; up to about three or four for babies and chimpanzees, perhaps slightly larger for human adults. Numerical reasoning is easy if it can use these systems. If we have to get the exact numerosity of a larger set, or work fluently with number representations of, for example, fractions, square roots, or negative numbers, we have to invest years in learning the number systems our cultures have developed. As we will see, children have difficulties with this.

As I said earlier, number words have to be matched to countable objects if the child is to 'count', that is, to be able to answer questions involving 'how many'. Using a number word to represent a single set is level 2 in the hierarchy of number goals described by Saxe *et al.* (1987). It requires an understanding that correspondence between number word and object in a count can lead to the identification of 'how many' objects are present. The analyses pioneered by Gelman and Gallistel (1978) show how complex an activity this is. Accurate counting requires that each and every object must be tagged with one and only one number word, with the words in the right order. To do this, objects and words have to be kept in step, and objects have to be accurately divided into 'already counted' and 'not yet counted' groups, with this division being continually updated in step with the counting. Children often use pointing or touching or moving objects to help themselves do this; rhythms in the counting or orderliness in the array may also help. There is quite a lot of evidence that children's counting (Fuson and Hall 1983; Wynn 1992; Sophian 1998) does mainly allocate one number to one object; it is less clear whether they regard this as a necessary principle of counting. Unsystematic organisation of what to count next leaves a real possibility of double counting or skipping items, and the rate at which number names are generated may get out of step with the touching of objects. Smaller sets make successful counting more likely for young children because there is less scope for these errors to arise.

By age four, children also appreciate that counting is related to addition and subtraction, and that spatial rearrangement of a single *small* set does not change its number (Gelman and Gallistel 1978). However, appreciating that you would get the same cardinal number for any correct count of the objects in any order is a rather later achievement, as Piaget pointed out long ago, and both Fuson *et al.* 1982 and Saxe *et al.* 1987 show that even four-year-olds have a shaky grasp of this principle. It is of course an achievement that depends on accurate counting: if your procedure for counting is imperfect, you might get a different numerosity each time and not realise the source of the variation. Detecting counting errors, and avoiding them by the use of more systematic counting strategies, may form a major part of the development of three- to five-year-olds (Saxe *et al.* 1987; Wynn 1992; Sophian 1998).

Although there are possible comparisons of numbers implicit in producing strings of number names and in counting a single set of objects, once there are two or more sets there are inevitably comparisons of numerosity to be made. Terminology such as 'more', 'less', 'fewer', 'same', 'equal', 'greater than', and so on, becomes involved. Siegel (1978) reviews studies of children's problems with these terms. One source of confusion is that comparatives are correlated in the natural world: in comparing sets of the same objects, for example, the longer line does quite often have more in, the taller heap does contain more objects. Sorting out the dimensions of the comparisons, deciding that 'less' is not a synonym for 'more' (Donaldson and Balfour 1981), and sorting out exactly which entities are being compared (Siegel *et al.* 1978) seem to be among the harder preliminaries to making a comparison.

Ecological studies suggest however that activities at this level are common in the day-to-day lives of children (e.g. Saxe *et al.* 1987; Saxe 1988). As well as the discussions of, 'who's got more?' and, 'is it fair?', that are prevalent in later childhood, preschoolers are frequently involved in activities such as setting the table with equal quantities of plates, glasses, knives and so forth. Efforts to do tasks like this are a bit laborious to begin with. Commonly, if four-year-olds are asked to put out as many plates and glasses as there are children they will count all the plates, then count all the children, recount the plates and unsystematically add or subtract plates until the right number is arrived at, then work out the number of glasses in the same trial and error way. A six-year-old is much more likely to use the streamlined strategy of counting the people and then counting out that many plates and glasses from sets that do not need to be counted further.

In many tasks, a number of different strategies will reach the final goal though they may vary in their cost-effectiveness. Perceptual strategies may give quite successful results for comparing quantities. If numbers are small, or if there is a big difference between the sets to be compared, or if an approximate answer will do, relative judgements work quite well, and young children use them quite readily (Bryant 1974; Sophian 1988, 1998; Feigenson *et al.* 2004). Relative judgements work less well with exact comparisons between larger sets or sets nearer in size, and do not work at all, of course, on number symbols: 71 is not obviously larger than 48. New strategies therefore have to be developed, and the old ones relegated to the tasks for which they are adequate. One possible strategy is matching each item in one set with an item from the other: if a set has one or more items left over after this procedure it has more items. The evidence reviewed by Fuson and Hall (1983) suggests that if children have perceptual cues like touching, moving and linking with drawn-in lines (techniques that also help with counting, as I described above), they can use matching to establish relative numerosity by the age of about six. If matching is perceptually harder, fewer children use it (Brainerd 1979). One-to-one correspondence remains a useful strategy in some tasks.

Another possible strategy for establishing relative numerosities is of course counting. If the cardinal numbers of two sets are the same, they are equal in quantity; if not, the *order* of the cardinal numbers in the sequence of number words shows which set has more and which fewer items in it – at least to someone who knows the number sequence and that if number *a* comes before number *b* then number *a* is smaller than number *b*. This is level 4 of the hierarchy in Saxe *et al.* (1987), an arithmetical function of a high order. Exactly how children make these judgements is still controversial (Fuson and Hall 1983: 93–98; Siegler and Robinson 1982: 267–286). They are probably easier to make if the smaller number is very small and the gap between the numbers is large (Feigenson *et al.* 2004). Siegler and Robinson suggest that young children do not view numbers as a scale with even intervals but categorise the number sequence into smallest, small, medium and big numbers. Preschoolers judge nine to be a big number in all contexts: adults judge it to be a big number in the context of one to ten but not in the context of one to a million. Adults, however, have difficulty in appreciating the very large or very small numbers involved in such things as geological time, sub-atomic physics, and the number of cells in the brain. Number, indeed, turns out to be a more complex and sometimes problematic subject than common sense suggests (Butterworth 1999).

Counting may be of two separate sets existing simultaneously, or of one set before and after a transformation. In the classic number conservation test, both comparisons are involved. It is a well-replicated finding that children who have counted both sets before the transformation, and agreed that they are equivalent, will deny the same equivalence when one set of counters is spread out, even though they may count again and reach the same numbers. Nevertheless, counting does help in conservation of number tasks (Klahr and Wallace 1976; Siegler 1981). It is presumably *not* used as the best cue to numerosity in conservation when the child has a strong perceptual strategy and a low level of confidence in his or her own ability to count accurately. A conviction that spatial extent is a good cue to numerosity, and the knowledge that your counting techniques are shaky, would both make counting do badly in a cost–benefit analysis. As we have seen elsewhere, children (and adults) find it difficult to give up a 'good enough' strategy in favour of a perfectionist one (Karmiloff-Smith and Inhelder 1974/5; Siegler 1988).

I have discussed using numbers to find the numerosity of a set or the relative sizes of several sets. Numbers can also be used to describe relative positions within a set. Children do learn ordinal words such as second, third, twentieth, but some time after they have learned the conventional counting sequence, and probably the ordinal number sequence becomes systematic and iterative through school practice. Using the ordinal words to refer to the correct items of an ordered set indicating the third, fifth or whatever item is also difficult. Putting items in order of size or some other physical quality is something preschool children enjoy doing, though, as Piaget's seriation experiments show, they may stick at comparisons of pairs of objects and not systematically complete an ordered set (Piaget 1952); they may deal with equipment such as nested cups by trying to fit them by brute force, not by taking out the small cup that has been misplaced in a large one and prevents the insertion of a medium-sized cup. How ordinal number development is related to cardinal number development is not known: ordinal number may lag behind because it less frequently occurs in children's everyday activities (though ordinal numbers are used daily in the calendar) or because its vocabulary is acquired later, or for both reasons.

2.4.2 Addition

In contrast to the comparatively small amount of research done on the development of children's ordinal number concepts, there has been a great deal of work on children's strategies for adding numbers. Among useful reviews of this area are Carpenter *et al.* (1982), Carpenter and Moser (1983), Ginsburg (1977), Levine *et al.* (1992), Resnick (1983), Siegler and Robinson (1982), Ginsburg *et al.* (1998), and various papers in Hiebert (1986) and Donlan (1998). Children's most basic strategy is to construct sets of objects or fingers to represent the two numbers to be added, move the two sets together and then count *all* the joint set from one to the total. A more sophisticated (and quicker) strategy is to *count on* from the cardinal number of the first set through the members of the second set to the total number of the combined set. More efficiently still, the child may count on from the larger number through the smaller set to the total: the *counting-on (min)* algorithm. The counting-on (min) strategy requires an understanding of commutativity: that the order of the numbers in an addition or multiplication sum can be changed without affecting the sum;

for example, $2001 + 367 = 367 + 2001$, or indeed $2001 + 367 = 2000 + 300 + 60 + 7 + 1$.

Reaction time evidence (Groen and Parkman 1972) suggests that in their first year of school children use the counting-on (min) algorithm, as it took longer to reach the correct answer if the minimum addend was two than if the minimum addend was one, and so on. The mean response times for $1 + 6$ and $6 + 1$ were identical and over a second shorter than the mean response times for $3 + 4$ and $4 + 3$, for example. Children's verbalisations also often mention counting-on from the larger number (Ginsburg 1977). The main sums that were exceptions to the reaction time pattern were 'double' sums such as $1 + 1$ and $4 + 4$. These were particularly easy. It may be that these short solution times reflected a fourth strategy for coping with addition, that is, the memorisation of number facts. Ashcraft and Fierman (1982) suggest that there is a transition from counting strategies in addition to retrieving number facts from memory, for their samples at about the third grade (ten years old). Resnick (1983) also suggests that adults do most of their addition and subtraction by using mental short cuts such as using memorised number facts with little or no overt counting; professional calculators and savant calculators may use these strategies especially expertly (Smith 1983; Hermelin 2001). Siegler (1986, 1988, 2005) points out that it may be most useful to have a number of different strategies to call on to solve addition problems. What is needed is not a single 'hierarchy' of strategies that children are assumed to pass through in sequence, discarding each as they grasp the next, but analysis of what range of strategies a problem-solver uses, how they are brought to bear on different problems or on different occasions, and why there is variation. He reports a study of overt strategy use by preschoolers which found that there was a correlation of 0.91 between error rate and use of overt counting strategies such as reciting number words aloud or putting up fingers. Thus these young children were more likely to use an overt strategy on the harder problems, while on the easier ones they more often answered without having shown any sign of counting. Using overt counting strategies increased the children's chance of getting the right answer on almost all the sums. It was much slower than remembering the relevant number fact, so only counting on difficult problems, not on easy ones, saved time overall.

Siegler (1986, 1987, 2005) suggests that the child's information-processing system contains number facts (or pseudo-facts) amounting to a distribution of associations linking problems and answers: a very well learned fact, such as '$2 + 1 = 3$', a very strong association at the right answer, '3', and very low associations with other possible answers; a less well learned sum (for example $18 + 23$) will have a flatter and wider distribution of answers so that none would reach a high confidence criterion but several might reach a low one. The system sets a confidence criterion for accepting a number fact as stateable and a limit on how many searches for number facts will be made. On each search, if there is a strongly associated answer, this will be put forward as the solution; if not, another search may be made. If the preset number of searches has been made without retrieving a satisfactory answer, the child has to try another strategy, perhaps imagining the sum mentally or using fingers, or counting, or both; or editing the sum, for example decomposing and recomposing the numbers into ones where the relevant facts are known (for example 18 + 23 can be turned into 18 + 2 + 23 – 2). Adults do this often: so, particularly, do professional arithmetic calculators (Smith 1983) and savant calculators (Hermelin 2001). Siegler suggests that distributions are built up as a result of accumulated practice: children associate whatever answer they state with the problem to which they state it. Correct answers probably receive reinforcement from outside the child and so become somewhat more strongly associated, but errors may also become linked with the problem they have seemed to answer, and thus receive an increase in associative strength that may make them hard to get rid of. Siegler suggests that this sort of model may underlie much non-arithmetical problem-solving, for example reading or spelling. It is worth noting first that children who do not carry out enough searches may fail to find the right answer, and second that the system could set a lower confidence criterion if the required answer were an estimate rather than precise.

2.4.3 Subtraction

A similar variety of strategies for doing simple subtraction is described by Carpenter and Moser (1983), Ginsburg *et al.* (1998) and Rittle-Johnson and Siegler (1998). A strategy involving concrete objects is *separating from*: making a set of the larger numerosity, separating the smaller number off from it spatially, and counting the remainder. This is an enactment of phrasings such as '5 take away 3', which various researchers and educators (e.g. Conroy 1984; Coleman 1982) found to be the preferred and easiest phrasing for children. There is a parallel counting strategy called *counting down from*; the child counts backwards, starting with the larger number, for as many number words (in sequence) as the given smaller number. The remainder is the correct answer. Other strategies include starting with the smaller number and *counting up* until the larger one is reached, noting how many names have been added as that is the answer. Again, children by the age of eight or so seem to combine strategies to use the minimum of counting, so that if the sum is '8 – 2' they will count down from 8 but if the sum is '8 – 6' they will count up from 6, in each case using the quickest strategy. As in the case of addition, using number facts supersedes these counting strategies to a considerable extent.

A new set of problems arise as children become required to do more complex addition and subtraction with multi-digit numbers, and they will have to use procedures that require an understanding of place value (the 3 in '13' does not mean the same quantity as the 3 in '31'), which many children find difficult (Fuson 1990; Fuson and Briars 1990; Fuson and Kwon 1992; Hiebert and Wearne 1992, 1996). Although *counting-on, counting-down-from* and the other strategies continue to be capable of giving the right answer, they become cumbersome and thus slow and inaccurate. Imagine using a counting strategy to solve 10,543 – 6,975, for example. Number facts that will solve the problem in one step will also be less likely to be usable, though the regularity of the number name system may help (Geary *et al.* 1996). One strategy is using 'derived facts', for example the solution to 14 – 8 may be found as follows: '7 and 7 is 14; 8 is one more than 7; so the answer is 6' (Carpenter 1986: 116–117). Decomposition into 'hundreds, tens and units' and the computation of each of these using number facts or counting strategies makes up a useful procedure for the addition and subtraction of large numbers, but it is far from unproblematic (e.g. Brown and Burton 1978; Resnick 1983). 'Buggy' procedures seem often to arise from one's learning of procedures without understanding them (Davis 1986; Hiebert and Lefevre 1986; Hiebert 1988), that is, there is a dislocation between conceptual and procedural knowledge. One aspect of the complication of later arithmetic is that it may involve competence with written mathematical symbols and with representing the structure of problems, topics that I will discuss later.

2.4.4 Multiplication

To rehearse what we have seen about children becoming more skilled and knowledgeable about solving arithmetical problems of addition and subtraction: over time they develop and use a variety of procedures for calculating their answer, they learn to select procedures strategically, they develop and draw on conceptual knowledge to evaluate their solutions and generate new procedures, and they learn to operate more effectively within information-processing constraints such as working memory (Bull and Johnston 1997; Dixon and Moore 1996; Ginsburg *et al.* 1998; Little and Widaman 1995; McLean and Hitch 1999; Nunes and Bryant 1995; Shrage and Siegler 1998). Although there is less research than on addition and subtraction, the same seems to be true of children learning about multiplication (Ginsburg *et al.* 1998; Lemaire and Siegler 1995; Mabbott and Bisanz 2003; Nunes and Bryant 1995). Direct retrieval from memory of the number fact ($4 \times 5 = 20$) is the most efficient strategy and the one that learning your tables enables you to use, but there are back-up ways of calculating the answers to multiplication problems, such as repeated addition (e.g. 4×5 is solved by adding $5 + 5 + 5 + 5$). The size of the numbers involved and frequency of exposure to the answer to the multiplication sum seems to be a likely predictor of relative success; for example, multiplication calculations involving 2 or 5 tend to be done faster and more accurately than calculations involving 7, and children (and adults) more often count in groups of 2 or 5 than of 7. As children become more experienced with multiplication problems, their use of the number facts that they have increasingly overlearned becomes their preferred strategy and there is less need for strategies such as repeated addition (Mabbott and Bisanz 2003; Nunes and Bryant 1995). Expert calculators (Smith 1983) typically use combinations of strategies to solve complex multiplication problems; for example if you have to calculate 29 × 32 it may be easier to work out 30 × 32 and then subtract the additional 32.

2.4.5 Division (etc.)

It is not surprising that children's general multiplication skills improve as they get older, nor that schooling is very important in this development; the same is true for other areas of arithmetic. There may be some subtle differences between simpler and more complex arithmetic, however; more variation in performance associated with the characteristics of the particular problem, more variety in strategy, more children who seem to have discrepancies between their competence with different ways of solving the problem (Ginsburg *et al.* 1998; Mabbott and Bisanz 2003). The working memory model (Bull and Espy 2005; p. 86) is clearly relevant.

Understanding arithmetic involving concepts such as fractions, proportions, ratios, and division tends to be harder than understanding whole numbers. Children may have problems with calculations involving these concepts and procedures for years after teaching about arithmetic has begun. In the early stages of formal teaching about fractions and division, the problems often involve analogies and implicit or explicit notions of sharing; for example, the child is asked to divide a cake or a pizza or a box of chocolates fairly between several individuals. This 'partitive' division involves dividing a quantity into equal subcollections for a known number of recipients. Children are sometimes able to do this by the beginning of the school years (Frydman and Bryant 1988; Spinillo and Bryant 1991; Singer-Freeman and Goswami 2001), possibly because of their experience in ensuring 'fair shares' between friends; halves are easier to understand than other fractions, and even four-year-olds manage to make a correct analogy between two of four slices of pizza and four of eight slices. Dividing discontinuous quantities and understanding the implications for the resultant fractions can be harder than subdividing continuous quantities (Singer-Freeman and Goswami 2001) if the task is assessed by whether the child understands that 'half a pizza equals half a box of chocolates'.

In 'quotitive' division, the given quantity has to be divided into sub-quantities whose size is specified but the number of subquantities has to be discovered. Although this is not computationally more difficult than partitive division, children find it harder to understand. For example, Correa *et al.* (1998) argue that when sharing, children need only be concerned with fairness and the equality of the shares. A full understanding of division involves grasping the relationships between the original number, the number of parts it is split into, and the number or quantity in each part; the greater the number of parts, the smaller the size of each part; the larger the original number, the larger the parts will be if the number of parts is constant. Children under the age at which such concepts are part of the school curriculum showed some success at this, possibly because they linked division with repeated subtraction, just as multiplication can be done by repeated addition; but understanding all of this probably requires formal instruction. Fraction names that explicitly refer to part–whole relations may aid calculation (Paik and Mix 2003). Calculations with fractions are often done in ways that suggest a complete failure to understand the problem. Carpenter (1986) quotes the answers given to the problem '*Estimate* the answer to $^{12}/_{13} + ^{7}/_8$. You will not have time to solve the problem using paper and pencil.' Over half of thirteen-year-olds chose 19 or 21 as the best estimate of the sum of these two fractions, and almost as many seventeen-year-olds made the same error as chose the correct answer, 2. It should have been obvious that the sum of two fractions each slightly less than 1 would be nearly 2, but these teenagers simply added the numbers that were numerators or denominators of the fractions without thinking how their answer made conceptual sense.

Reasoning about probabilities, another area of cognitive development pioneered by Piaget and Inhelder (1975), is another area where children make systematic mistakes. A common task is to present the child with two sets each made up of objects of two colours, a 'winning' colour and a 'losing' colour. Either the ratio of 'winners' to 'losers' or the total number of objects (and hence the numbers of 'winners' and 'losers') differs in the two sets. The child is asked to choose the set where they would be more likely to get a winning colour. The young child's strategy will probably be to choose the set with the largest number of 'winners', even if it also contains a large number of 'losers' and so gives a worse chance of winning than a small set with fewer 'winners' but also fewer 'losers', though even preschool children can be seen to try to take the total number of objects into account as well as the number of 'winners' (Acredolo *et al.* 1989). By about eight to nine years of age, children are likely to use the correct proportional principle on this task. There are, however, differences between tasks. Falk and Wilkening (1998) asked children to make a second set that would give a 'fair chance' of winning as compared with a model set. Uncertainty about the proportional principle was prolonged, with even thirteen-year-olds regressing to simpler strategies on difficult problems. Very probably adults would have made similar mistakes, as probability is another concept where the answer is by no means always obvious and we are by no means always completely correct in our reasoning (see

Butterworth (1998) and Haddon (2003) for examples). Understanding that mixing entities, such as liquids of different colour intensity or temperatures, will produce an averaged entity somewhere between the originals is also a late developer (Jager and Wilkening 2001).

2.4.6 Procedural and declarative knowledge in arithmetic

Carpenter (1986) and Rittle-Johnson and Siegler (1998) argue that it is important to examine the relationship between knowledge of step-by-step procedures and rich knowledge of a network of concepts, capable of more flexible access and use. Children enter schools, as we have seen, with considerable experience of arithmetic and highly developed informal arithmetical systems. By holding up fingers or pointing out objects, or mentally, they can directly model quantities named in a problem (if they are small quantities), perform actions on these models that reflect arithmetical manipulations, and enumerate sets to get the answers to problems. Thus they can cope with problems such as 'Sally has 5 candies. She bought 8 more candies. How many candies does she have altogether?' or 'Sally had 13 candies. She ate 5 of them. How many candies does she have left?', though a non-canonical form such as 'Sally had some candies. She ate 5 of them. Now she has 8 candies left. How many candies did she have to start with?' is harder to solve, no doubt because of the difficulty of modelling the unknown initial quantity, or because the solution requires reversing the sequence of actions described in the problem. This procedural knowledge in young children uses semantically accurate representations of the problems, but lacks the flexibility of older children's behaviour. With a richer conceptual base, more practised and efficient procedures, and better links between concepts and varied procedures that can be used to check up on each other, much greater flexibility and efficiency become possible.

The relationship between conceptual and procedural knowledge in arithmetic is likely to be complex. A number of different emphases can be found in the literature: Riley *et al.* (1983) characterise procedural advances as stemming very largely from advances in the representation of concepts and problems, while Carpenter (1986) points out that more advanced procedures may be constructed not only because they reduce the demands of cognitive processing but also because they represent knowledge more fully (see also Chapter 4, on mechanisms of cognitive development as described by information-processing theorists). Children do often invent arithmetical procedures that reduce information-processing demands; however, some of these are inefficient because they give the wrong answer (as in the subtraction 'bugs' mentioned above) and others because they depend too much on the availability of outside help (as in relying on a calculator or a clever neighbour). Conceptual knowledge is often local before it can be broadly applied, and initially there may be a limited range of linked procedures and representations of problems. With increases in both conceptual and procedural knowledge, children will become better able to recognise that 'this is another problem of this sort, which usually worked with this procedure', a recognition (or problem representation) that seems to be important in understanding mathematical and scientific problems. A lack of links between conceptual and procedural understanding, such as may arise in an educational programme that emphasises one at the expense of the other, can lead to superficial analysis of problems with consequent gross errors, as in the study of adolescents estimating the sum of two fractions cited earlier (Carpenter 1986).

2.4.7 Mathematical representations

Similar problems arise in coping with alternative forms of writing arithmetical problems equations. Learning the formal code of arithmetic is part of the whole endeavour. Hiebert (1988) proposes a model for the development of competence within written mathematical symbols. Competent use involves *connecting symbols with referents*; for example, 75 could be represented with seven ten-unit Dienes blocks and five single-unit blocks, while ÷ represents partitioning an initial unit into a number of smaller equal groups. Both numbers and actions can be more or less helpfully represented, as the work mentioned above illustrates. As in all such translations, different symbol systems have different advantages and disadvantages. Dienes blocks are cumbersome but make it quite clear that the 7 represents seven large items, while the written 75 makes the difference between large and single units far less obvious. Children do indeed have difficulty in grasping the principle of place notations, and hence have problems in the second aspect of competent use of written mathematical systems, which is *developing symbol manipulation procedures*. They may learn by manipulating the referents of the symbols first and then paralleling this action with action on the symbols. To use Dienes blocks again as an example, blocks representing 75.1 and 12.84 can easily be added together by combining blocks of the same size, and in the same position relative to the decimal point. To do the same with written symbols involves the rule 'line up the decimal points', size no longer being transparently mirrored in symbols. Manipulations of symbols have to preserve what is true in the referent world; as said earlier, procedural knowledge is best backed up by conceptual understanding, lest mistakes like the fraction 'addition' ones arise.

Children first apply written symbols to comparatively simple referents, such as small numbers and concrete objects. However, symbol manipulation rules can be analysed and elaborated so that they apply to new or more complex tasks. These more complex tasks may be much more easily performed using written symbols than concrete objects or other non-written symbol systems, as the example of what it would be like to solve five-figure subtraction tasks using a counting-down strategy will have made clear. Similarly, understanding the use of regrouping or recomposition of numbers, discovered in addition sums such as '43 + 29', may be applied to subtractions. The history of mathematics includes many examples of inventions of new ways of representing quantities and actions that allow a dramatic extension of the possibilities of computation: the algorithm for long division, the slide rule, logarithms and computer programs, to name parts of just one progression. There is a move away from attention to the concrete referents and towards reflection on the symbols and rules themselves, and on the consistency of the results produced by these different procedures, not just on whether what they produce is true in the concrete world ultimately referred to, as this is less easily checked, and in some advanced mathematics is unknowable except through its symbolisations. High-level mathematics can manipulate even imaginary entities (for example, the square root of -1) to useful effect. James Hiebert quotes the physicist and mathematician Henri Poincaré: 'It is by separating itself from reality that [the symbol system] has acquired this perfect purity. The power of mathematics lies in this purity, this abstraction from particular situations', and the philosopher and mathematician Alfred Whitehead: 'By the aid of symbolism, we can make transitions in reasoning mechanically by the eye, which otherwise would call upon the higher faculties of the brain' (Hiebert 1988: 341). Thus the third aspect of competent use of written mathematical symbols is *analysing and elaborating symbol manipulation rules*. This includes extending a simple algorithm to deal with more complex problems; for example, a child might learn to manipulate written symbols to add small numbers (which he or she can also efficiently add by using concrete objects) and extend the written procedure to larger numbers where the concrete objects would be more cumbersome. The realisation that the written addition algorithm can be used for *any* numbers demonstrates its power and the usefulness of analysing and elaborating techniques for manipulating symbols. Similarly, a subtraction procedure might be developed from an addition one, or vice versa. The relationship between procedures becomes increasingly important; for example, two different addition procedures should produce the same answer! Consistency is an important feature of mathematics: rules that are extended to new contexts must not contradict rules that apply to the old familiar context.

Mathematical procedures, like other cognitive procedures, may develop because they are analysed and reflected on, but they also have to be run efficiently, and becoming automatic and routinised may be the means to maximum efficiency under normal circumstances. Automatic procedures need less mental effort so that cognitive working space is freed for other processes. Much school mathematics aims at routinisation of procedures, for example acquiring a large stock of 'number facts' such as '5 × 7' in the primary school. Increasing use of electronic calculators may make such knowledge less useful (except of course as a check on whether the machine has worked properly). It is worth noting that the amount of time spent on school mathematics appears to underlie both cultural and gender differences in achievement (e.g. Raymond and Benbow 1986; Song and Ginsburg 1987; Stevenson *et al.* 1986; Stigler *et al.* 1987).

The final aspect of competence with written mathematical symbols described by Hiebert (1988) is building more abstract symbol systems, either by mapping a familiar symbol system on to new, more abstract, referents and rules, or by creating symbols of the patterns and consistencies between earlier symbol systems. Again, this is very much a feature of creative high-level mathematics, but it is in some ways similar to Hiebert's first process, when the meaning of concrete referents is transferred to a first system of written symbols; here meaning is transferred from one symbol system to another, and through a chain of related symbol systems contact can ultimately be made with the concrete world.

Studies of children's early use of written mathematical symbols suggest that they are interested in producing written symbols and do so quite successfully. Hughes (1983) gave five- to seven-year-olds the task of showing on paper how many bricks there were on the table. They found this easy, drawing the objects or an equivalent number of tallies or writing the appropriate conventional number. They were then asked to show what happened when a few more bricks were added or subtracted. Most just drew the final number of bricks. There were a few attempts to represent initial number, final number and what had been added on or subtracted, for example by showing hands adding bricks or putting bricks away in the box, or the ingenious if slow strategy of drawing a line of British soldiers marching from left to right to represent added bricks, and a line of Japanese soldiers marching from right to left to represent subtracted ones. Not one of the seventy-two children tested used the conventional operator symbols of + and –, although they were using them regularly in their arithmetic lessons, and although, as shown in further work by Hughes, even younger children could use these symbols in a number-guessing game.

Work by Thomas Carpenter and his colleagues (Carpenter 1986; Carpenter and Moser 1983; Carpenter *et al.* 1982) suggests that many children in the early years of school may manipulate written number problems with little or no connection of them to the world of real objects. Instruction that refers to concrete situations and actions that children have experienced and understand well is particularly helpful. Children are able to develop procedures for manipulating symbols (Hiebert's second level of processes), recognising that these procedures parallel procedures they have already used on concrete referents, but instruction that does not highlight this recognition may lead to symbol manipulation that lacks understanding and hence cannot lead either to insightful use or to elaborated procedures.

Written mathematics must not lose its attention to what the symbols mean until the aspirant mathematician has progressed far through the stages Hiebert describes (Davis 1986; Gelman and Meck 1986; Ginsberg *et al.* 1998), and even then translation from one symbol system to another or to concrete referents, as appropriate, may still be a useful aid. It will be essential in coping with algebraic story problems such as 'If one man digs a ditch in three days, how many days would two men take to dig the same ditch?', which can easily be misrepresented (Mayer 1982a, 1982b). Children need to understand the 'reality context' of the calculation, its mathematical structure and the appropriate representations and algorithms, and to relate all these, if they are to work successfully. This is an important field for collaboration between psychologists, mathematicians and educators (see e.g. Davis (1986), Hiebert (1988), Mayer (1986), Ginsburg *et al.* (1998)). Studies of mathematics learning outside school will also be illuminating (Saxe 1988; Saxe *et al.* 1987), as will examination of what happens in classrooms (Brissenden 1988; Desforges and Cockburn 1987; Mellin-Olsen 1987).

2.4.8 Children's mathematics: not a summation but an estimate

Similar themes will have emerged from the different areas of arithmetic and mathematical problem-solving that I have discussed. Children begin their formal learning about mathematics with an extensive range of knowledge, some of it apparently rooted in infancy, some associated with playing number games and parental teaching. This knowledge continues to grow and becomes reorganised as it accumulates. Their initial procedures work with simple or small-scale problems, but are comparatively inefficient with more complex ones and larger numbers; procedures become smoother and more efficient with practice. They use a range of procedures from very early on, becoming more strategic in fitting procedure to problem. Their representations of quantities and procedures shift from iconic towards using the conventional symbol systems of mathematics, so that eventually they become able to deal with unknown quantities (as in algebra or estimation) or even non-existent ones (the square root of minus 1, for example). Information-processing accounts of cognitive development are obviously useful in modelling how this happens (see Chapter 9), and so is the working memory model discussed in section 2.5.

Bull and Espy (2005) examine working memory, executive functioning and children's mathematics. They argue that the ability to hold information in working memory, to manipulate it and to update it, is of crucial importance for all arithmetic and becomes more and more so as the complexity of the problems increases. Children have to select the relevant information from the problem they are tackling; they have to retrieve relevant information from their long-term memory to support their short-term storage;

they have to inhibit irrelevant information; everything has to be integrated and updated as the calculation proceeds. Children also have to shift attention between procedures and part solutions on complex tasks. Working memory involving both the 'slave systems' of the phonological loop and the visuo-spatial scratch pad and the central executive control system will be heavily involved in all this. It could become overloaded, resulting in difficulty in completing the task successfully; individual children with weaknesses in a slave system or in the central executive will show characteristic errors on particular maths tasks.

A lot can be done to reduce demands on working memory. If children can use external representations, this reduces memory load. Frequent revision of number facts and computational procedures makes retrieving and using them more efficient. Presenting the task in a logical order also makes information processing more efficient than when attention and memory space have to be used to rearrange the premises and represent the calculation in a form that can be used efficiently. Children who prefer to use their visuo-spatial sketchpad may find visually-presented problems easier than verbal ones, and children with weaker visuo-spatial sketchpad systems may find them harder. Diagnosing such relative strengths and weaknesses may be possible at quite an early age, and curricula or even remedial programmes could be devised to help children who might otherwise have problems (Bull and Johnston 1997; Bull and Scerif 2001; Gathercole and Pickering 2000a, 2000b).

2.5 Memory

It is obvious that remembering of some sort is necessary for virtually any human cognitive activity. Whatever stimulus or whatever problem we encounter, we are likely to deal with it using some comparison with situations met earlier in our experience. Even a novel situation must evoke some review of our memory if we are to be able to say 'I've never seen one of those before'. It is hard to believe in the possibility of an intelligent organism that does not store, recall and use at least some of the information it has encountered. All the major models of cognitive development discussed in Chapter 4 include memory processes, conspicuous in the information-processing model that underpins much of the work that I discuss in this section but implicated also in Piaget's model of assimilation and accommodation. Almost all cognition – perhaps all – involves some sort of memory. Conversely, the use of memory is rarely an isolated intellectual skill of 'pure' remembering. It is affected by people's language skills, knowledge, judgements and inferences, for example, as well as by various cultural influences. Early memory researchers found it necessary to concentrate on memory for meaningless materials such as nonsense syllables because this was the only way to control for differences in other aspects of subjects' cognition.

Experimental cognitive psychology, research on amnesia, and neuro-science research all show that distinctions need to be drawn between different types of memory. Among these distinctions are those between non-declarative and declarative memory (or implicit and explicit memory); then, within declarative memory, between semantic (or generalised) and episodic and autobiographical. There are different memory stores and a range of memory processes. Different theorists define, assess and divide these differently. They do not all develop in exactly the same way. They do not function independently of each other, or develop independently. Memory development, therefore, is likely to be both important and multifaceted.

Even though memory development is a well-established and successful field, exactly what it is that develops in memory development is still debated (Schneider and Bjorklund 1998; Schneider 2002; Cowan 1997; Tulving 2002; Murphy *et al.* 2003; Nelson and Fivush 2004). There have been four main suggestions about what develops in the improvement of children's memory from infancy to adulthood. They are, first, an improvement in basic capacities such as memory size or the speed of simple memory processes; second, development in memory strategies, which might for example diversify and be used more often, more effectively, more deliberately, or with more flexibility; third, changes in children's knowledge about their own memory such that they can regulate their remembering more appropriately; and, fourth, an increase in the amount of knowledge other than about memory available, which could make remembering related information easier and mean that fewer situations are completely unfamiliar. Finally, there has been much interest in autobiographical memory. Obviously there could be developmental changes in more than one of these areas. I will examine them in turn, after first setting up a simple model of what memory is, focusing on working memory but extending beyond it.

2.5.1 Developmental changes in basic memory processes and capacities?

There are various accounts of the basic structure and processes of memory (derived mainly from work on adults), but the distinction between sensory store, short-term memory, and long-term memory (e.g. Atkinson and Shiffrin 1968) provided the classic framework. Their memory system would look something like Figure 2.3.

Information enters the system through the sensory register, and persists there for a short time after the end of stimulation, but much never passes beyond it. If it proceeds, information then enters the short-term store and, perhaps, passes thence to the long-term memory store. At each point of entry some information may be lost, in part because both sensory register

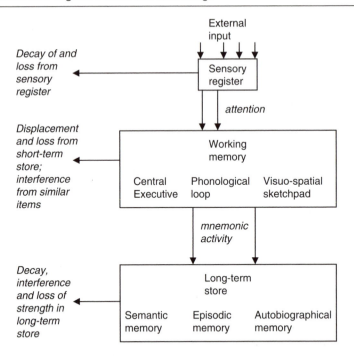

Figure 2.3 The multi-store model of memory. Adapted from Atkinson and Shiffrin (1968).

and short-term store are believed to be limited in size and in how durable the information they contain is, and all three stores need time to execute basic processes. The stores use various control processes on the information they contain. For example, rehearsal, or repeating items to be remembered over and over again, is an important control process in the short-term store where its use stops material being lost. The examination of associated information and inference contribute to the storage and recall of information in long-term memory, because such examination is associated with the semantically based processing of information which produces a more durable and accessible memory trace. Control processes affect whether information is lost or transferred from one store to another. They also affect the organisation of information within each store, and thus are important in affecting functional capacity, since better organisation and ready transfer can transcend the stores' limitations of size and processing speed.

The working memory model developed first by Baddeley and Hitch (1974) has since shown itself to be a more precise and differentiated model of the processing parts of memory (e.g. Baddeley 1986, 1996, 1999, 2000), and to have very interesting implications for developmental psychology and education (e.g. Gathercole *et al.* 2004; Gathercole and Pickering 2000a,

2000b; and see the index for various examples of working memory and areas of children's cognitive development). Working memory has a central executive (CE) and two (or possibly more) 'slave systems', notably the phonological loop (PL) and the visuo-spatial sketchpad (VSSP). More recently an episodic buffer has been added to the model; this is a multi-dimensional representation system that integrates temporary representations from other cognitive systems, including from parts of working memory. The CE regulates attention, action and problem-solving; it controls the slave systems, allocates resources between them, and mediates the relation between working memory's short-term storage and long-term memory. The PL is specialised for dealing with language-based information; it contains a passive phonological short-term store and an active phonological rehearsal mechanism. In rehearsal decaying representations are refreshed and inputs that can be recoded into phonological form can gain access to the phonological store. This is obviously important for language processing and for reading. The VSSP stores material in terms of its visual or spatial features; some of this information may be recoded phonologically and stored in the PL.

There is a considerable amount of both experimental and neuropsychological evidence for this model, and the basic structures appear to be up and running in children at the beginning of the school years (e.g. Gathercole 1999; Gathercole et al. 2004) or slightly earlier (Alloway et al. 2004).

The sensory register is the entry point to the memory system. If young children could not take in as much sensory information as older ones, or if they could not take in certain sorts of sensory information, or if they took in sensory information more slowly, or if it was lost faster, the sensory store could be a cause of developmental differences in memory. Not much is known about the sensory store in infancy, though research on perception suggests that babies are capable of perceiving information very much like adults do (for details see papers in Haith and Campos (1983), Rovee-Collier (1997), Schneider and Bjorklund (1998), Gathercole (1998), Cowan (1997), Schneider (2002)). There is evidence that the capacity of the sensory store does not change in childhood (Morrison et al. 1974). Children probably can take as much information into the sensory register as adults can, but their attentional orienting improves during the school years (Rueda et al. 2004, Schul et al. 2003), becoming faster, more accurate and more efficient. Differences in the sort of sensory information they can take in are also unlikely to account for children's poorer memory performance; adults would be more likely to suffer from poorer sensory acuity (they would be worse on very high-pitched auditory stimulation, for example), though children's inhabiting of an adult-sized world might reduce their access to some sensory information that is, for example, literally 'over their heads'. Children may possibly be somewhat slower in forming a sensory representation of what they see, although there is some controversy about this (Hoving et al. 1978;

Anderson 1989a, 1992; Nettelbeck and Wilson 1985, 2004). This lower speed of taking in information might restrict learning and memory, given that the phonological loop has a limited capacity in terms of time. We do not know why children are slower, or why the speed of representation increases. There is some association with IQ, though there is disagreement about exactly what. Anderson's model of intelligence and cognitive development (Anderson 1992 and pp. 223–227) sees speed of information processing as the non-developing core of intelligence. Nettelbeck and his colleagues see it as subject to developmental change (Nettelbeck and Vita 1992; Wilson and Nettelbeck 1986; Wilson et al. 1992; Nettelbeck and Wilson 2004). Schneider and Bjorklund (1998) suggest that perhaps children take longer to transfer information from the sensory register to the short-term store, either because they make less or less effective use of strategy or focused attention (Schul et al. 2003) or because slower processing leads to more information being lost.

The next possible source of developmental changes is the short-term store, the working memory core. Here information from the immediate environment (via the sensory register) and information from past environmental encounters (via retrieval from the long-term store) are combined by the central executive as required for the current problem-solving situation: here is the consciously accessible 'working memory' part of the cognitive system. As in the sensory register, development could be due to changes in speed or capacity or to how they are used. Some theorists, for example Pascual-Leone (1970), believe that children's capacity is more restricted than adults', that because their working memory or 'M-space' is smaller they are subject to severe limitations in their information-processing. A task might require more information-processing capacity than is available, and in this case the child would fail on it. As children grow older their M-space grows with them so that they become able to operate more programmes or processes at one time. Thus their cognitive performance is markedly improved. However, it is not clear how we can distinguish between growth in M-space and development in processing. As we shall see, it is clearly the case both that people's repertoires of cognitive processes and strategies increase with age and that the members of the cognitive repertoire may become slicker, more automatic and more efficient, thus taking up less of the resources of working memory, in effect increasing its functional size (Gathercole et al. 2004). Children's performance on any task will be a function of the cognitive processing used, the demands that processing makes on M-space and the size of M-space itself. We know the first two of these develop with age: attempts to use performance to measure M-space have to hold processing and processing demands constant if they are to distinguish between changes in the size of M-space and changes in the way a stable-sized M-space is used, for example by simply recalling an over-learned fact. Gathercole et al. (2004) see a 'sizable' increase in the rate of rehearsal in the phonological loop, and an increased use of phonological recoding of visually-presented material. Only very precise experimental analysis of tasks, of learner activities, and of the interdependencies between strategies and processing can clarify the relative importance of capacity and its use.

At present, researchers differ in their views about developmental changes in short-term memory capacity (Cowan 1997; Schneider and Bjorklund 1998; Schneider 2002): it seems a reasonable guess that structural changes are less important than usage changes, that development is due not simply to an increase in the total size of working memory but to an increase in the proportion of working memory that is free from the demands of basic operations and so can be used for more complex information processes and storage. Case takes this view (Case 1985; and pp. 285–289). Cowan (1997) and Schul et al. (2003) point to speed of processing and focused attention. These would seem to be very basic nervous system properties, and it is noteworthy that prenatal exposure to pollution can damage the nervous system and be detrimental to short-term memory and sustained attention (Jacobson et al. 1992; and pp. 357–361).

Capacity changes in long-term memory are not thought to be a source of cognitive development, as for all practical purposes long-term memory seems to have no effective size limitations, at least until extreme old age when the deterioration of the senile brain might result in literal holes in its structure as well as metaphorical holes in its memory (Mayes 1988; Squire 1987). However, control processes in both short-term and long-term stores are very convincing candidates for developmental change. As the research emphasis has been on strategic control of memory, most of these developments will be discussed in the next section. Recognition, which is not structural capacity but is not strategic either, will be dealt with here, however. Infants show an ability to recognise objects remarkably early, as their habituation to repeated events and their preference for particular faces and voices show (e.g. Fagan and Singer 1983; Kagan et al. 1978; Mehler et al. 1978; Papousek 1967; Wetherford and Cohen 1973; Cowan 1997; Schneider 2002; p. 28). Infants' rate of habituation and capacity for sustained attention may be among the best predictors of their intelligence, incidentally (Anderson 1989a; Bornstein and Sigman 1986; Fagan and Singer 1983; Rose et al. 1988; McCall and Carriger 1993; Rose and Feldman 1995, 1997; Slater 1995; Dougherty and Haith 1997). Infants who attend to and recognise objects and events about them, particularly if they don't sleep much during the day, are presumably giving themselves many more opportunities to learn about all sorts of aspects of the world!

The main development of recognition is not in the ability to do it at all but in the complexity and reportability of what is taken in and later recognised. Young infants recognise simple or very salient stimuli over surprisingly long periods of time (Bachevalier and Miskin 1984; Rovee-Collier and Hayne 1987; Rovee-Collier 1997; Schneider and Bjorklund

1998; Bauer *et al.* 2002; Nelson and Fivush 2004): older ones remember more information about the stimulus and can therefore discriminate smaller differences between the familiar stimulus and the novel one, and do so over a longer period of time. Children's implicit memory, involving unaware recognition, is good at very young ages; for example they show perceptual priming, recognising a fragmented picture at a less complete stage if they earlier saw it built up from fragments, and may show conceptual priming, being more likely to mention a typical example of a category in their recall of items from a category if they had been presented with it earlier, though there seems to be less priming if the previously presented item is an atypical example of the category to be recalled (Schneider 2002). Similarly, pre-school children recognise pictures of simple objects about as well as adults but do less well on recognising pictures of complex scenes, where adults can make more use of their interpretations of the meaning of the scene and are more likely to examine it thoroughly (Nelson 1971, Nelson and Kosslyn 1976, Newcombe *et al.* 1977, Ackerman 1997); that is, strategies can make a marked difference to performance. Children's recollection is significantly improved by scaffolding from adults.

To summarise, the basic structure of memory is not thought to change during childhood, though possibly the size of working memory stores may increase. Basic speed of processing may be developmentally stable (Anderson 1989a, 1992). Recognition and learning too seem to be basic processes that are present from very early in life and are refined by experience rather than changing radically (Bachevalier and Mishkin 1984; Rose 1981). Gathercole and Pickering (2000a, 2000b) link differences in working memory with differences in cognitive performance, including reading (Alloway *et al.* 2004; and see p. 87). However, the use of structure and processes often involves strategies. We will now discuss what develops in this area.

2.5.2 Developmental changes in memory strategies?

There is a great deal of evidence now that there are marked changes in the use of deliberate memory strategies as children grow older, changes so marked that some researchers have seen this as the major developmental shift in memory (and in other cognitive areas; see e.g. Baron (1978), Brown *et al.* (1983), Schneider and Pressley (1989), Siegler (1986), Cowan (1997), Schneider and Bjorklund (1998), Schneider (2002), Schneider *et al.* (2004)). Strategies are deliberate controlled mental or behavioural activities used so as to enhance memory performance by improving the encoding, the storage or the retrieval of information. A variety of memory strategies are discussed in the psychological literature (e.g. Pressley *et al.* 1985; Schneider and Bjorklund 1998). A sophisticated learner will know about a number of strategies, for example the following: single item repetition, that is, repeating material over and over, one item at a time; cumulative rehearsal, repeating material over and over in a cumulative fashion, rehearsing new items along with old ones; meaningful organisation, looking for and remembering meaningful relationships between items such as common categories or syntactical rules such as 'they're all opposites'; imagery elaboration, making up a memorable image in which the items to be learned interact, such as a scene in which a tiger in a boat eats a bun; verbal elaboration, making up a sentence or story including the to-be-remembered items such as 'The tiger in the boat is eating a bun'; differential allocation of effort, for example deciding which items are most important and studying those most, or putting more effort into studying material that has not yet been memorised; and complex combinations of these. Professional mnemonists (see e.g. Luria 1969, Ericsson *et al.* 1980) can perform extraordinary feats of memorisation as a result of bringing such techniques to a high degree of expertise. Retrieval, too, may be strategic (Ackerman 1997). Children under seven or so are rarely seen to use memorisation or retrieval strategies that would be appropriate to memory tasks. There is little spontaneous use, for example, of the simple and quite effective technique of rehearsal. Where older children and adults would repeat such material as a telephone number or the words they have to speak in a play over and over to themselves, under the age of about seven there is little rehearsal, and what there is rudimentary and inefficient, for example repetition of isolated items or only part of what is required. Older children and adults are more likely to rehearse several items and to adapt their rehearsal strategy to the particular demands of the task, for example giving more rehearsal time to items they have not yet remembered adequately and less to material that has already been memorised. Subtle improvements such as this contribute to a steady improvement in memory performance over childhood.

A similar result is found with the organisation of material. It is frequently helpful to the learner to reorganise material into categories and rehearse categorised material as such, using the information about what categories were included to summon up and recognise the actual instances involved: if we notice that four words in the list were animals, for example, we can use 'animal names' as a cue to help us remember whether 'cat', 'pig', 'fly' and so forth were in the list. Young children are less likely to divide a list according to stable and helpful categories, or to search categories systematically. They are also less likely to use helpful elaboration techniques. These create a connection between the items to be learned by, for example, juxtaposing them in a vivid visual or verbal image, or associating them with an already learned string of items or some other memorable structure such as rhyme or a tune. 'One, two, buckle my shoe' does this job for number words (or alternatively for the items that rhyme with the overlearned number list). These strategies too are rarely spontaneously used until quite late in childhood, and are more often found in schooled than unschooled cultures

(Ackerman 1997; Cowan 1997; Hasselhorn 1992; Moely 1977; Pressley *et al.* 1985a; Rogoff 1990; Schneider and Pressley 1989).

Why do young children rarely show a use of memory strategies? One explanation would be in terms of a 'mediational deficiency', that young children do not rehearse, organise or elaborate because they cannot effectively regulate their behaviour through internal mental processes mediating between the task stimulus and the response. This explanation suggests that the deficit is irremediable, that training could not produce the radical shift of behaviour that is required. It is thus effectively countered by the considerable amount of evidence that children can be taught to use memory strategies such as rehearsal, categorisation and cue-based search (e.g. Kail 1990; Lange and Pierce 1992; Pressley *et al.* 1985b; Cowan 1997; Schneider and Bjorklund 1998; Schneider 2002; Schneider *et al.* 2004 for reviews). Even children as young as six or seven have shown themselves perfectly able to use the mnemonic strategy they had been trained in while the experimenter required them to use it. So inability to use mediating strategies of rehearsal, categorisation, cue use and so forth is clearly not their main problem. However, strategy use is sometimes not so effective in the hands of trained young children as it is for older children who are better memorisers, a utilisation deficit (e.g. Flavell *et al.* 1966; Miller and Seier 1994; Schneider *et al.* 2004) and they may not continue to use the strategy later, when not explicitly instructed to use it, a production deficit (e.g. Hagen *et al.* 1973; Keeney *et al.* 1967; Bjorklund and Miller 1997; O'Sullivan *et al.* 1996). The pre-school subjects of Lange and Pierce (1992) showed an increase in strategic activity even as late as three days after training, though improvement in memory achievement was less marked. The most likely explanation for both the failure to produce strategic memorising behaviour initially and the failure to continue to employ a useful strategy after the instruction has ended, or to transfer its use to a new task, lies in the child's poor knowledge about memory problems and how to transcend them. For a full discussion of this, the role of 'metamemory' in memory development, see the next section.

Two points remain to be made about memory strategies *per se*, however. First, they typically show further development in how effectively they are used for some years after their first appearance. These developments include more complete and polished performance of the different components of a memory strategy. For example, Pressley and Levin (1980) showed that although both six-year-olds and eleven-year-olds could be taught to generate and use an elaborative imagery strategy to memorise words, the six-year-olds had to be reminded to think back to the images they had thought up earlier when they were trying to recall the words; the eleven-year-olds did this without being reminded. Development also includes an improvement in fitting the strategy to the task (Schneider and Bjorklund 1998); for example Naus *et al.* (1977) found that eleven-year-olds remembered more items in a list than eight-year-olds even when all of them used rehearsal, because the younger children over-rehearsed the first items in the list while the older ones continually changed the items they rehearsed, thus learning more items well enough to recall them. This sort of strategy adaptation may be one cause of a related development; younger children may find the adoption of a strategy provided by the experimenter is more helpful than using a strategy they have devised for themselves, because their own strategy is not maximally efficient, while older children who can devise particularly helpful strategies may find the experimenter's less effective for them than their own (e.g. Siegler 1986: 237). Familiarity with the material to be remembered will also affect strategy use: helpful clustering of well-known material, such as the names of classmates, may be used where there is no sign of clustering of less familiar material (e.g. Bjorklund and Zeman 1982; Hasselhorn 1992; Marmurek and Rinaldo 1992; Schneider and Bjorklund 1998). This of course means that an apparent failure to use a strategy on one material does not mean that the child is incapable of using the strategy on any material.

The second point about memory strategies is that although they are rarely seen in the performance of young children it is very evident that young children can and do remember. Improvements in the use of strategies probably account for many of the developmental changes in memory performance during the school years, but babies' and preschoolers' memories may be impressively accurate. Rovee-Collier and Hayne (1987) investigated three-month-olds' recollection of mobiles suspended over their cots, for example, and found that they remembered how to move the toy for as long as eight days. My own daughter at the age of sixteen months remembered the actions that went with a nursery rhyme she had last heard two weeks earlier. Forbes (1988) reports on his slightly older child's feats of recollection. We do not know how these children remembered; presumably they did not consciously and deliberately set out to memorise, but behaviour such as repeatedly requesting recitations or namings may facilitate recollection – rehearsal with the parent as the stand-in who does the work for the child!

2.5.3 Developments in knowledge about memory: 'metamemory'?

'Metamemory' is one of the major components of 'metacognition'; it was in fact the first metacognitive area studied (Flavell 1971; and see pp. 132–135). It is one's knowledge of memory, that is one's awareness of what memory behaviour is happening at the moment, and one's knowledge about task difficulties, one's own skills, abilities and deficits, and strategies that will enable one to perform a task satisfactorily, just as metacognition in general is such awareness and knowledge of a range of cognitive procedures. It is assumed that someone with mature metamemory will recognise when a task requires deliberate memorisation and that there is a range of mnemonic techniques suitable to different tasks, that there are individual differences in memory skills and variation within individuals on how well they remember in different situations, and that monitoring memory will often be useful in the performance of memory strategies. A mature memoriser will know about the value of a strategy, the range of tasks it applies to, and how best to execute it appropriately. It is assumed that such metamemory knowledge is associated with better memory performance (Schneider 1985; Schneider and Bjorklund 1998; Schneider 2002; O'Sullivan *et al.* 1996) and that young children's worse performance is associated with their less complete metamemory.

It is not clear whether 'metacognition' and 'metamemory' are really unitary things; in particular the relationship between knowledge and action has not been clearly conceptualised (Robinson 1983). It seems fairly clear that one could have relevant knowledge and not be able to put it into action, or one could act appropriately without being able to give an account of one's understanding. Given this complexity, it is perhaps not surprising that Schneider and his colleagues (Schneider and Pressley 1989; Schneider 1985; Schneider and Bjorklund 1998; Schneider 2002; Schneider *et al.* 2004) find that the relationship between metamemory and memory behaviour varies. It is more likely that there will be a positive relationship for young children when memory monitoring and the recall or recognition of small quantities of information are concerned, and there is at best a weak relationship when more demanding tasks involving a combination of complex strategies are employed. Older children show closer relationships between metamemory and memory, but these are still task-related, with more positive links when memory monitoring is considered and weaker ones when metamemory knowledge is linked to recall tasks. Metamemory knowledge predicts how well children transfer a taught strategy to another task and their use of elaborative and organisational strategies.

This intricate pattern of results suggests several important points. First, it is not easy to measure 'metamemory', and a variety of assessment methods may be needed. In particular, children may have less to say about their metamemory when they are asked before a memory test than they can report having just done the test, with a very recent experience to reflect on and describe. Similarly they may show more knowledge about performance on a real task than on a hypothetical one (Thorpe 1988). Second, we need a more complete theory of how and why metamemory and memory behaviour affect each other at different ages and in different tasks. Children's knowledge about memory clearly increases as they go through the school years. They know more statable facts about memory and they know more memory strategies. Particularly during the early stages of development, some of this knowledge may be only loosely related to the monitoring and regulation of memory activities, which only become linked to factual knowledge late in childhood. This dislocation of knowledge and action characterises the early stages of many skills. It is an interesting area for training studies. In the memory area, training that combines facts and procedures relevant to memory is maximally effective if it involves explicit use of children's metamemory activities. Thus Whittaker (1983) suggested that showing children that their memory was significantly improved by their use of mnemonics increased the extent and effectiveness of their mnemonic behaviour, and children who attributed their success to a particular mnemonic technique were more likely to use the same strategy in a different appropriate situation. Continued use of mnemonics is more likely if the demonstrated improvement is large, as if the mnemonics have to be seen to be cost-effective. Here knowledge of specific strategies and specific tasks may be involved, that is, knowledge of when and where the strategy can be used, its usefulness on a task compared with the usefulness of other approaches, how the strategy may be modified to suit task demands, whether it is suitable in the general task context, and so forth. (A consideration of the social context may be relevant here, for example using a calculator to get the result of multiplying 9 by 7 may not be acceptable in a school curriculum that expects children to 'learn their tables', and reciting the multiplication table from the beginning may not serve in a school that expects 'number facts' to be well learned and instantly retrievable.)

Children's metamemory knowledge about tasks develops during the school years but begins earlier (Brown *et al.* 1983; Wellman 1983, 1985b; Schneider and Bjorklund 1998; Cowan 1997; Schneider 2002; O'Sullivan *et al.* 1996; Pappas *et al.* 2003). Preschool children know that, all other things being equal, familiar lists are more memorable than unfamiliar, and long lists are harder than short ones. They do not appreciate that a homogeneous set of items that show a consistent relationship may be very easy to learn irrespective of its length, thus they predict that a short paired associate list where there are arbitrary pairings will be easier to learn than a longer paired associate list where all the pairs are common antonyms. By the age of nine or ten children (like adults) judge that the antonym list is easier to learn, and if asked to generate a list that will be 'easy to remember' invent one with highly related items. Preschool children know about the rapid decay of short-term memory, so that they will advise that one should use a telephone number directly after looking it up and not stop and do something irrelevant to telephoning; they tend to agree with adults that recognition is easier than recall. It is not until the age of about ten that they say it is harder to remember word for word than to paraphrase and 'tell you in my own words'. These results suggest that although children have achieved some understanding of the demands of memorising by the time they enter school, they can gauge task demands accurately only after considerable further experience of memorising. Young children frequently overestimate their memory capacity (Cavanaugh and Perlmutter 1982;

Schneider 2002); being over-confident about remembering would probably reduce the amount of special effort to remember, while a realistic appraisal of the difficulty of remembering would show that extra effort or time was needed for success. Failure on a memory task is peculiarly hard to judge. One may know that one has not remembered everything one meant to get at the supermarket but feel that only one item has been forgotten; back home with the list one initially forgot to take out to the shops one all too often finds that several items have been listed and then forgotten without the list as an *aide-mémoire*. Over-confident children may do badly on memory tasks but not notice their deficit. Unlike shoppers, young children may only rarely have their failure made visible to them, as adults probably take much of the responsibility for remembering things. A child who goes to school, on the other hand, is having to live in two 'microsystems' (Bronfenbrenner and Morris 1998), 'at home' and 'at school', which will involve both relatively spontaneous reporting of school events at home and vice versa, and the deliberate carriage of information from one to the other. No longer can one caretaking adult take all the responsibility for the child's remembering: it is only the child who inhabits both microsystems and knows all their details. The school microsystem, what's more, requires the child to memorise larger and larger quantities of information, for more formal testing, and may model mnemonic strategies and even, occasionally, discuss them.

Teaching memory strategies for a specific task has been effective in improving performance on that task (see Brown *et al.* (1983) for a review and Chapter 6). Other researchers have shown that providing explicit information on the usefulness of the strategy increases generalisation to similar tasks, and children who have learned to make their own evaluations of their strategy use may perform even better (Pressley *et al.* 1985a; Pappas *et al.* 2003). However, although training improves performance, most children's performance improves without training as they move through the school years. They know more about memory and they remember better, but the extent of any causal relationship remains unclear.

2.5.4 Developmental changes in knowledge?

It is so obvious that children acquire more knowledge as they grow older that many psychologists have shown little interest in knowledge growth (Chi and Ceci 1987; Schneider 2002; Schneider and Bjorklund 1998). However, what we remember and how we remember are inextricably tied in with our relevant knowledge. Once information has progressed beyond short-term memory it becomes mixed up to some degree with information we have acquired at other times. It is (generally) much easier to remember information if we already have related information. Older children's greater quantity of stored information might account for much of their remembering better than younger children. Chi's elegant experiments with chess players illustrate this particularly neatly (Chi 1978). She compared children (average age ten) with adults on two tasks: immediate recall of a string of digits, and immediate recall of stimuli placed within an eight-by-eight array. The adults performed better than children on the digit list, as expected; but the children remembered more about the stimuli in the eight-by eight-array. This unusual finding of better performance by children is explained by the fact that the children were experienced chess players and the adults were not, and the 'stimuli placed within an eight-by-eight array' were chess pieces in a mid-game position on a chessboard. This array was meaningful and thus memorable to a chess player, meaningless and difficult to someone ignorant about chess. It is worth noting that chess players did not find the array easier to remember if the pieces were put on at random, but only if they were in positions that they could legitimately have reached in the course of a genuine game.

Familiar and meaningful information can be processed faster, allowing use of mnemonic strategies that are not evident in the handling of unfamiliar material. There will also be associations between the familiarity of material and the sort of memory errors that are made. In familiar material, errors often consist of substituting one plausible element for another related to it, or drawing inferences that go beyond the information that has been given (Myles-Worsley *et al.* 1986). Memory for information that is familiar and meaningful can use reconstruction and inference rather than the rote learning and recall of every detail. Experience and familiarity both highlight the salient points and so make understanding and remembering easier, and aid recall through allowing association, inference and other active reconstruction processes. It seems that there may be an interaction between knowledge of the material to be remembered, the strategies that can be used, and the capacity of short-term memory (Huttenlocher and Burke 1976; Kobasigawa 1977; Schneider and Bjorklund 1998). Well-known information may need fewer attentional resources in short-term memory, and thus leave more mental working space for other items or for demanding strategies. Children, who know most pieces of information less well, have to use up more resources on remembering each piece and would thus both remember fewer items and be less able to work through a complex memory strategy. Strategies may first be used effectively on comparatively familiar material (e.g. Bjorklund and Zeman 1982; Chi and Ceci 1987). Practice with using strategies might lead to their becoming automatic and using fewer resources, and then being applicable to content that is less familiar and more demanding.

Thus some of the development of children's memory must be associated with increases in their knowledge base. General knowledge, the information already stored in long-term memory, facilitates the remembering of new information in several different ways: guiding strategic memorisation, providing structure, aiding and checking inference, reducing the demands made on working memory, thus facilitating deeper and strategic information-processing. There may be some minor costs, however, particularly in the form of more errors in recall due to implied information being inferred and so judged to have been explicitly presented. Prior knowledge can interfere with memory as well as help it. Sir Frederick Bartlett, one of the British pioneers of memory research, asked subjects to retell a strange little folk-tale about how some North American Indians encountered a party of ghosts (Bartlett 1932). The successive retellings gradually Anglicised the story, losing or changing details that had significant meaning in the Indian mythology but had none to Cambridge minds. The children's party game in which a whispered message is passed from one person to another round a circle of players illustrates the same phenomenon. Memory is normally holistic and inferential, and while in most cases this is advantageous it can contribute to errors and distortions of information.

2.5.5 Summary

This review of what develops in memory development has been long and perhaps not memorable. I will therefore recapitulate some of the conclusions that are being drawn at present, before moving on to infantile amnesia and autobiographical memory.

First, it seems unlikely that the structure or the capacity of children's memory stores changes with development to any developmentally significant extent, though the efficiency with which memory capacity is used increases as cognitive operations are executed more quickly, more effectively and more automatically. There may well be differences between individuals in the speed or capacities of their memories, as shown in such measures as digit span and speed of habituation. Second, there certainly are developmental changes in the use of memory strategies, with a major increase in the frequency and the efficiency of their use over the school years (though younger children are sometimes strategic in well-understood tasks such as hide-and-seek games, and adolescents and adults will quite often fail to use strategies). Third, children acquire knowledge relevant to their memory performance in two ways: they come to know more about themselves, tasks and possible memory strategies, and they acquire more knowledge about things other than memory, which lends more meaning to what they have to remember and so improves encoding and recall.

Integrating these different areas of memory development is hampered by a lack of empirical data on how they interact in development. As my discussion of whether memory capacity develops will have indicated, it is hard to tease different components apart (see e.g. Hasselhorn (1992), Marmurek and Rinaldo (1992), Naslund and Schneider (1991), Schneider and Bjorklund (1998), Tulving (2002)). Age by age, rather than memory component by memory component, the picture would look something like the following: The basic brain structures of memory have developed to something much like the mature form by the age of five at the latest. Babies and young children are learning an enormous amount during this period, they can remember some quite complex events over quite long periods of time, their implicit memory is good; but they show little use of explicit strategic memory outside a few well-learned contexts such as hide-and-seek games and nursery rhyme repetition. They provide incorrect answers to many questions about memory and the variables that affect it, for example tending to be wildly optimistic about what they will remember. They are not good at monitoring memory performance and so may remain unaware of failure to learn or to remember.

During primary school, more memory strategies and more awareness of memory develop, as does the knowledge base. Children are more likely to use effective input and retrieval strategies and to judge their performance more accurately. They have more information at their command and so can reconstruct memory actively as well as retrieving it passively. The cultures they live in, and in particular the schooling they take part in, require them to remember and provide mnemonic techniques. These sorts of development continue through adolescence into adulthood, though few adults reach the highest levels of memory skill.

2.5.6 Memory for events in childhood

Two consistent phenomena crop up in the literature on memory for events in childhood. First, most people's 'earliest memory' dates from their fourth year of life, or later: it is rare to remember anything about the period of one's life before one's third birthday, and there are comparatively thin recollections of the period from three to five. This is the phenomenon that Freud (1973, 1977) called 'infantile amnesia', and attributed either to repression of the unacceptable sexual and aggressive impulses of early childhood, that is, to a later blocking of memories with too strong an emotional tone, or to an initial failure to create a fully formed narrative memory for an event and a later difficulty in translating the fragments of incoherent early memories into a form reportable by the grown-up person (Pillemer and White 1989), explanations that I will look at a little later. Second, young children have great difficulty in answering questions such as 'What did you do at school today?', despite their rapid learning over the preschool years of immense quantities of material such as names of objects, nursery rhymes, and even generalised 'scripts' of events such as what one does in school (Fivush 1984, 1987; Fivush et al. 1992).

The traditional account of infantile amnesia is challenged by a sizeable number of research studies. The competing theories of (1) emotional blockage, (2) failure to encode the data to be memorised, (3) failure to translate material remembered earlier into a form that is retrievable later and (4) the effects of brain maturation (Bachevalier 1992), are reviewed by Pillemer and White (1989), Howe and Courage (1993), Bauer (1997), Bauer *et al.* (2000) and Nelson and Fivush (2004). The emotional blockage theory seems the least likely of the four (though perhaps relevant to the minority engaged in Freudian psychoanalysis), given findings which suggest that the emotions that accompany memories of early childhood are very similar to those accompanying memories of other periods of life (Davis 1987; Kihlstrom and Harackiewicz 1982; Pillemer *et al.* 1988; Nelson and Fivush 2004). Failure to encode data to be memorised remains one possible source of childhood difficulties in remembering, but this is not a total failure. Anecdote and careful observation of children's spontaneous conversation and behaviour document many instances of data being registered, retained for some time, and recalled. My own daughter, for example, recalled at the age of twenty months a unique sight from two months earlier. She had first visited my sister's house just before she was eighteen months old, and had seen there balloons hanging from the curtain rail in the sitting-room (it was my sister's birthday). We next visited the house nine weeks later. When she re-entered the sitting-room through the French windows to the garden, Anne looked up at the curtain rail and said 'balloon'. No one had mentioned those balloons to her at any time in the intervening period, and she had not played with them during the birthday party. Her 'balloon' and look upwards demonstrated a memory for an earlier feature of the room. Eisenberg (1985), Farrar and Goodman (1992), Fivush *et al.* (1987), Forbes (1988), Nelson (1988), Perlmutter (1980), and Nelson and Fivush (2004) similarly report excellent memory appearing in young children's everyday talk. Nelson (1989a) documents a two-year-old using bedtime monologues to construct a memory and an understanding of her day's activities. Specific cues from adults may elicit more information, as may relevant non-verbal context (Morton 1990; Wilkinson 1988; Bauer 2002). Adults who are familiar with the child's life are able to confirm the accuracy of the child's reports, but such prior knowledge is often essential if the people, places, events and so forth implied in the child's 'loose and disorganised' narrative are to be identified correctly (Eisenberg 1985).

The whole process of communicating what one remembers may become quite emotionally fraught. My daughter and I had a long conversation when she was three and a half trying to select the videotape she wanted to watch. She initially listed the following distinctive features: 'he's in the snow, there's a monster, there's a robber lady'. I considered these cues, and offered *The Snow Queen* which has snow, robbers and some odd if not monstrous characters; this was turned down. So were *Toad's Winter Sports* (snow, wicked weasels who steal Toad's snow goggles) and *The Snowman* (snow but no other relevant features). These were very firmly rejected, and a further cue offered: 'the robber lady steals some bananas'. I am afraid my reaction was 'we haven't got a tape like that, you've got it mixed up', and her reaction to this insult was so strong that to re-establish good relations we had to look at every tape in her collection and identify what was in it. This exhaustive search produced what she wanted. We had a tape on which two Charlie Chaplin films were recorded: *The Gold Rush* (he's in the snow, there's a monster in the shape of wicked prospectors in enveloping furs threatening the little tramp's life), and *Modern Times* (the waif or 'robber lady' steals bananas to feed her orphaned sibs). Anne's memories of the tape were correct, but her expression of them was fragmentary and her headings were not accessible to an adult, who was in any case operating on the assumption that the headings might be slightly wrong, an assumption probably all too commonly made by adults.

As we know that young children often have difficulty constructing a narrative about material that is in front of them, it could be argued that this problematic construction of narrative may handicap them in their accounts of remembered material, even if they actually have a well-formed memory of it. Young children can re-enact a game learned two weeks earlier better than they can describe it in words (Morton 1990; Smith *et al.* 1987; Bauer *et al.* 2000), and there is evidence of toddlers showing associations between places they knew much earlier and the events or activities they had gone through there. However, verbal memories of pre-verbal baby experiences seem to be both anecdotal and concerned with repeated experiences and so, perhaps, with general knowledge rather than specific event memories (Pillemer and White 1989; Haden *et al.* 1997). Nelson (1986) suggests that children have difficulties with memory for individual episodes because they automatically build up 'general event representations' (GERs) in which repetitions of the same type of event are fused into a generalised schema or script (pp. 159–162). Having a rapidly formed and accurate general script of 'what you do in school', the child has, Nelson supposes, little or no access to the specifics of 'what you did in school today', and with increasing time since a particular event, the GER built up from the repeated invariants will increasingly dominate the specific and idiosyncratic parts of the particular experience (Myles-Worsley *et al.* 1986; Murachver *et al.* 1996; Haden *et al.* 1997; Powell and Thomson 1996). The experience of recalling something verbally may well influence future recall of that event; possibly as GER builds up.

Certainly, events whose uniqueness is very marked do seem to be remembered more specifically and more accurately than any particular instance of a routine event, but part of the difference is due to the sort of question asked. Open-ended questions are harder to answer than direct questions about specific parts of events; indeed, when adults search their memories for information on 'what they did yesterday afternoon' they are likely to attempt several direct probes (Morton (1990: 6) provides an example). It seems likely that young children's recollections of specific events are more often expressed in conversation with other people than in monologue, particularly during episodes when an adult is trying to elicit recall narratives from the child. (We could link this to language development (pp. 7–30), Vygotskian theory (pp. 295–312), and family contributions to cognitive development (pp. 374–388).) It has been argued (Pillemer and White 1989; Haden *et al.* 1997; Nelson and Fivush 2004) that this conversational memory builds up a socially addressible memory system that is added to the less communicable and predominantly non-verbal, affective and image-based memory existing from birth. This 'social memory system' is what is used when an intentional, purposeful search of memory and a narrative-like recall are required, and thus is what is typically needed to answer a researcher's request for verbal recall of an earlier event. If it is not operational until the age of three to five, little from before that age will be recalled except events that are non-verbal, affective and image-based (of which my own earliest memory, of the look of a new pair of socks and of pride in them, would be an example; they were red, white and blue socks, at Coronation time). When we remember such events or images as adults, they may become overlaid with information from later memories and later-developed skills: my image of my Coronation socks, for example, is something I can describe verbally in ways that I certainly did not command at the time, and this description and the image of other, later, socks tend to intrude on the memory.

Several researchers (e.g. Pillemer and White 1989; Haden *et al.* 1997; Bauer 2002; Nelson and Fivush 2004; Murachver *et al.* 1996; Powell and Thomson 1996) argue that language, and especially socially constructed language, is the basis of the later memory system that builds up over the primary school years. This is heavily influenced by the social and culturally influenced parenting practices that surround the child; providing event information prior to the event leads to better recall and better integration of the particular event into a GER (Sutherland *et al.* 2003). Another development is an increasing ability to provide one's own memory probes, perhaps through the use of increasingly elaborated scripts: Murphy *et al.* (2003) link explicit memory development with increases in strategic processing and in the knowledge base. The social sharing of memory experiences both teaches what must be included when you recount a past experience and establishes it as a rewarding activity: Mummy asks what you did at the childminder's today while she was at work, and is interested in discussing why one of the other children cried and what was done about this. It might be expected that a memory system so dependent on language and on the understanding of 'scripts' and narrative would develop rapidly from about three onwards, and so might account for the developmental changes in memory for events in childhood. The social setting of remembering may be important for the content and the style of what is remembered; hence individual differences in autobiographical memory (Conway and Rubin 1993; Haden 1998; Haden *et al.* 2001; Han *et al.* 1998; Miller *et al.* 1997; Reese 2002; Wiley *et al.* 1998; Wang 2004). Adults' discussion of salient events seems to shape children's recollection of them (Fivush 1997) and may feed into children's self-concepts (pp. 187–191). The immaturity of the very young child's self-concept may contribute to the sparseness of their early autobiographical memories, and autobiographical memories will contribute to the development of the self-concept (Howe and Courage 1993, 1997; Reese 2002; Dweck 1999).

Nelson and Fivush (2004) have recently published a theory of the development of autobiographical memory which includes many of the themes I have indicated above. Defining it as 'an explicit memory of an event that occurred at a specific time and place in one's personal past' (Nelson and Fivush 2004: 486) their model emphasises its many different interrelated components, and the contribution to it of basic memory systems, of complex spoken language (or other representational systems), of use of narrative, of talk with parents and others, of understanding of time, especially of past time, of self-representation and of theory of mind. As each of these develops over a long period of years, autobiographical memory emerges gradually over childhood (and is subject to reinterpretation throughout life). They argue that whereas for many species generalised event representations are important for anticipating and predicting the environment, autobiographical memory is unique to humans and is crucial for defining self in relation to time and in relation to others – hence its psychological and social importance, especially in individualistic cultures (Wang 2004). Many parents work hard to support their children's emergent autobiographical memory; contradiction of one's own developed autobiography by significant others is puzzling and irritating; loss of autobiographical memory in the very old is extremely distressing to them and to those who care for them. Autobiographical memories of specific events:

> allow individuals to create a shared past with others from which an individual personal past emerges. The human ability to create a shared past allows each individual to enter a community, or culture, in which individuals share a perspective on the kinds of events that make a life and shape a self [. . .] In some cultures, and to some extent in all, these functions may be served by shared cultural narratives, whereas in others (such as the contemporary western culture), more may depend on the individual's self-definition and self story.
>
> (Nelson and Fivush 2004)

If an individual's autobiographical memory, or a social group's, is different from that of the majority culture, the discrepancy may endanger their participation in the wider culture, as in the ethnographical studies of Heath (1983, 1986, 1989, 2004). It may be that children's autobiographical memories differ according to their social experience: Howe *et al.* (2004), for example, find socio-economic status (SES) differences in the true and false memories of children, though not the differences between maltreated and nonmaltreated children that they had expected. Autobiographical memory is inextricably social, cultural, historic, related to one's self-concept, and emotionally loaded.

2.6 Children's reasoning

There is an enormous literature on 'reasoning' in general and on children's reasoning in particular. Exactly what 'reasoning' is taken to be varies (DeLoache *et al.* 1998a; Goswami 1998; Leighton and Sternberg 2004). 'Going beyond the information given' (Bruner 1957) or 'searching through a problem space' (Newell and Simon 1972) are wide definitions, while other writers centre their attention on, for example, induction of a rule from an initial set of assertions (Wason and Johnson-Laird 1972) or deduction from an initial general and abstract rule to the particular case (Holyoak and Nisbett 1988). Galotti (1989) proposes a definition that takes the middle ground – reasoning is:

> mental activity that consists of transforming given information (called the set of premises) in order to reach conclusions. This activity must be focused on at least one goal (but may be focused on more than one). The activity must not be inconsistent with systems of logic when all of the premises are fully specified, although there may not always be an applicable system of logic to govern specific instances of reasoning. The activity may or may not be self-contained; that is, people may implicitly or explicitly add to, subtract from, or otherwise modify any or all of the premises supplied. When original premises are modified, the final conclusions must be consistent with the modified premises. The activity may, but need not, involve the breaking of mental set. The conclusions may, but need not, be startling or nonobvious at the outset of the activity. The conclusion may, but need not, be deductively valid.
>
> (Galotti 1989: 333)

This definition would include solving syllogisms, assessing probabilities, doing analogical reasoning tasks, and similar laboratory or psychometric problems; it would also include many more 'everyday' tasks such as evaluating arguments, testing hypotheses, and deciding between the balance of merits of two different soap powders, places to go on holiday, or economic policies. (It excludes one-step mental processes such as simple memory retrieval, 'gut reactions' or flashes of insight.)

Galotti is very much interested in the relationship between 'formal reasoning' and 'everyday reasoning'. Formal reasoning is typical of certain domains and problems, for example logic; all the premises are supplied and must be taken as read, there is only one correct answer, there are rules about how to move from premises to answer, it is inexorable and dispassionate (see Smith *et al.* (1992) and various papers in Leighton and Sternberg (2004) on the psychological reality of rules of reasoning). Such reasoning seems to be a somewhat artificial and abstract activity (cf. Braine and Rumain 1983; DeLoache *et al.* 1998a; Leighton and Sternberg 2004) and adults frequently make mistakes in formal reasoning assessments (Johnson-Laird 2004; Leighton 2004; Markovits 2004). On the other hand, 'everyday reasoning' uses less specified information, can reach a more open-ended range of goals, and is typically far more embedded in one's normal context of interests and values. Developmentally, everyday reasoning seems to emerge much earlier than formal reasoning (DeLoache *et al.* 1998a; Moshman 1998; Markovits 2004). 'Good' reasoning, however, has commonly been supposed to approximate as closely as possible to the rules of formal reasoning.

2.6.1 Reasoning within the rules of formal logic

Braine and Rumain (1983) and Moshman (1998) summarise a substantial amount of work on the psychology of logic. There are different sorts of logical problems (and different systems of logic), but among those most commonly discussed by psychologists are tasks where the subject is required to reason from given information to come to a logically correct solution. For example, in a traditional syllogism you are presented with two statements that have to be taken as true, such as 'If it rains, then the grass gets wet', and 'It is raining'. The task is to judge what follows from these initial statements (the premises), for example whether combining the information that 'If it rains the grass gets wet' and 'It is raining' means that, necessarily, 'The grass is wet'. Solving classic syllogisms involves accepting and combining the given information to infer either a certain answer or that there is no certain answer. In the conditional reasoning task devised originally by Wason (1977), the task is to use available evidence to test the truth of the initial rule. In his classic task, the subject was told that the rule was 'If a card (in a given set) has a vowel on one side, there must be an even number on the other'. The subject was asked to test this rule by turning over their choice from a set of four cards that showed a vowel, a consonant, an even number or an odd number. Subjects commonly turned over the vowel card (which would support the rule but not test it if it had an even number, but could allow them to disconfirm it if it had an odd number) but less often the odd number card (which could allow them to disconfirm the rule, by having a vowel on the reverse). Verbal problems can be used, for example 'if a person exercises a lot, then s/he will be in good shape' or 'if a person takes out a library book, s/he must have a library card'; the last example, which involves social rules and obligations about what ought to be done, is called 'deontic'. Children may possibly reason better on deontic problems, or they may only find it easier to justify their reasoning (Evans 2002; Klaczynski *et al.* 2004; Markovits and Barrouillet 2002). Another commonly-used reasoning task involves rules with quantities; if 'all cats purr' and 'Mowzer is a cat', then, necessarily, it is true that 'Mowzer purrs'; if 'some cats bite' and 'Mowzer is a cat', then she may bite, but we cannot be certain about it (she does, as it happens, but only after being provoked). Tasks such as these have been the staples of formal logic for centuries; there is not, however, a consensus about their logical structure, or how best to represent them, or the psychological processes involved. Chapters in Leighton and Sternberg (2004) discuss some of these issues and provide further references to sources.

There appears (Braine and Rumain 1983; Moshman 1998; Goswami 1998; Pillow 2002; Markovits 2004) to be a considerable resemblance between the reasoning of children just entering school and the reasoning of older children and adults; Markovits suggests, tongue in cheek, that very young children may be 'more logical' than adolescents and adults. Even very young children find some logical problems very easy, and those that they find hard tend to be solved incorrectly or inefficiently even by adults. Children and adults make the same sort of errors. Premises are often inadvertently altered, for example 'All A are B' is taken as meaning that A and B are identical, so that 'All B are A'; world knowledge is allowed to intrude, sometimes helpfully, sometimes damagingly; negative premises, such as 'No B are A', are dealt with less successfully than positive ones; some of the possible interpretations of a premise, and some of the ways of combining premises, may not be thought of, particularly if to do so would mean allowing contradiction of one's initial beliefs. Reasoning is subject to a 'confirmation bias' (Wason 1977), and reasoners are often over-confident about the reliability and validity of their judgements, a failing that may be associated with their tendency to draw firm incorrect conclusions to logical problems that have no deductively valid conclusion (Baron 1985, 1988; Pillow 2002; Johnson-Laird 2004). Despite these general similarities between young children and older people, at least in schooled cultures, skill in formal reasoning increases over the school years. Young children are more likely to use 'pragmatic processing' (Bucci 1978; Goswami 1998) in reasoning about logical problems, that is, to determine meaning using facts they knew previously about the domain rather than restricting their interpretation to the words used in the premises. Thus they may reason more accurately on fantasy-content problems than on problems where they know about the domain (Hawkins *et al.* 1984; Harris and Nunez 1996). Children's limited knowledge base may, on the other hand, sometimes mean they stick to the premises better than adults, if the adults know that the premises are not really as straightforward as the problem suggests, and import alternative information into the problem (Evans and Feeney 2004). Their reasoning may be correct on one task, but sometimes they do not carry it forward to new tasks or combine it with new information when they usefully could (Goswami 1998; Moshman 1998; Markovits 2004). They are also more likely to define terms within the problem incorrectly, for example misunderstanding 'some', 'more', and 'less' (as Piaget pointed out long ago). It is a real problem in solving logic problems that the common conversational meaning of some terms is not what is meant in the context of formal logic; for example the logical 'some' means 'at least some, and maybe all', whereas in common speech 'some' is taken as excluding 'all'. In a substantial number of studies (Markovits 2004; Moshman 1998), it has been shown that children are likely to take 'If A, then B' as also meaning 'If B, then A', the biconditionality problem in syllogisms (Russell 1978, 1982): this may have to do with the tendency of permission statements to be biconditional – 'If you don't eat your cabbage, you won't have any pudding' does tend to imply (in parenting with a reasonable amount of justice and foresight) that when you can claim 'I did eat my cabbage' the pudding will be dished out to you, even though the logical structure does not promise it. Working memory overload, and less useful representations of the information, may also be crucial in reasoning correctly (Johnson-Laird 2004; Klaczynski et al. 2004). Finally, children need to be able to assess their knowledge, to recognise how reliable their inferences are, and to differentiate them from their guesses (Pillow 2002).

One of the debates about the nature of logical reasoning and the usefulness of formal logic as a representation of human induction and deduction centres on how reasoning functions within our day-to-day social world or our environment of evolutionary adaptedness. The argument (Cummins 2004) is that reasoning will be strong when it is pragmatically useful to get it right; for example to detect life-threatening regularities such as an association between a novel food and food poisoning, or in reasoning involving 'permission schemas' where what is important is to comply with powerful others and avoid breaking their rules, or to detect cheats. Inductive reasoning (from particular instances to a general rule that goes beyond the particular instances) is particularly fast and strong if the association between the instances is such that our survival or welfare is involved; the child who has bitten into an apple and found half a maggot in it may quickly infer that apples are likely to contain maggots and inspect any further ones that are offered with extreme suspicion. Evolution, it is suggested, has equipped us with an exquisite sensitivity to whether we are getting our rights and others not getting more than theirs; thus versions of logical problems involving social permission rules, such as variants of Wason's selection task where the rules to be tested concern whether a drinker in a bar is of statutory drinking age (Evans and Feeney 2004), or whether a child has disobeyed her mother's rule that she must put her coat on if she is going to play outdoors (Harris and Nunez 1996), are very much easier than arbitrary abstract rules. We may not have a cognitive mechanism as specialised as the cheat-detecting one that the evolutionary psychologists suggest (Evans and Feeney 2004), but the social situation of the reasoning problem, and the verbal form in which it is posed, are likely to influence the reasoning of both children and adults.

Moshman (1998) reads the field with a somewhat different emphasis. He recognises that there is evidence of quite young children reasoning systematically, but argues that they may not be doing so intentionally and may lack the 'metalogic' or epistemic understanding that adults and adolescents may show; they may not, for example, understand logical necessity or be able to reason in a valid way when they know the given premises are incorrect. This position resembles that of Piaget and some of his followers (Piaget 1983; Russell 1982, 1988; Goswami 1998; Pillow 2002; Smith 1996, 1997, 2002; Markovits 2004). Recognising when something is necessarily so is certainly an important part of cognition, and children's knowledge about the certainty of their knowledge develops through the primary school years (Pillow 2002; Samuels and McDonald 2002). Both being certain that something is necessarily so, and recognising that one cannot be certain in a particular situation, are likely to require complex processing and knowledge, which could be expected to develop gradually, although logical necessity is itself an all-or-none thing. Young children may find it difficult to recognise that something is logically inconsistent (Ruffman 1999). Children may also develop an increased awareness that there may be not one possible solution to a given problem but more than one, or no valid solution at all (Acredolo and Horobin 1987; Braine and Rumain 1983; Johnson-Laird et al. 1986; DeLoache et al. 1998a; Moshman 1998). The apparent shift from effective but unbased reasoning in children to potentially logic-based reasoning in adolescence may perhaps be because of a developmental trend towards more exhaustive processing and the avoidance of premature conclusions, or perhaps because of increasing recognition of multiple possibilities and ambiguity. Developmental increases in working memory or short-term storage space (Case 1985; Gilhooly 2004) might underlie these improvements, if indeed these increases actually happen (see p. 89). So might changes in the representation of the problem information (Markovits 2004): these are still very much debated (Leighton and Sternberg 2004). As the cross-cultural evidence suggests that literacy or schooling, or both, may be necessary for competence in formal reasoning problems (Laboratory of Comparative Human Cognition 1983; Olson and Torrance 1983; Goswami 2002), the goals and comprehension skills of the reasoner may be very important. A number of school programmes have sought to teach reasoning, with some success (Coles and Robinson 1989; Resnick 1987b; Nickerson 2004; and p. 419).

2.6.2 Children's causal and scientific reasoning

Goswami (1998), Gelman (2004) and Hickling and Wellman (2001) argue that human infants and children are equipped with an innate bias to attend to causation. They appear to draw inferences about the causes of events they see, to discriminate between self-caused and other-caused movement, to categorise living things that are agents as different from inanimate objects. Their early concepts tend to be guided by and to include information about causal relations. A bias towards considering causes is evident in their early questions – their focus on 'why' and 'how' implies this – and it leads to an extensive body of knowledge about physical causes. By the beginning of the school years, it follows basic causal principles, for example that causes precede effects rather than following effects, that they covary with their effects – the effect regularly and predictably appears after the cause and does not appear without it, and the cause and the effect are close, or at least linked, in time and space. Given information about a cause, they can infer its effects, and like adults they find this easier than working out the probable cause of a given effect (Johnson-Laird 2004). This focus on understanding cause builds up into what has been called a 'naïve physics', a coherent set of notions about how objects behave; if this gives rise to the formation and testing of hypotheses by observation and experiment, it becomes the basis for a physics that is scientific rather than naïve.

Experimental scientific method involves the control of variables to assess their effects and identify which ones play a causal role in an effect, which are necessary for it, which sufficient, which irrelevant. This is a step beyond the naïve observation of associations, and it is far more difficult to carry through systematically. An extensive body of research (e.g. Koslowski and Maqueda 1993; Kuhn 1993, 2002; Ruffman *et al.* 1993; Samuels and McDonald 2002) shows that young children have a shaky grasp of the relationship between hypothesis and evidence, fail to co-ordinate multiple variables, find it hard to keep in mind more than one hypothesis at a time, do not readily hold one variable constant while testing others, do not test their hypotheses by seeking to disconfirm them, often stop short at identifying one cause when several need to be identified as relevant, and rarely succeed in co-ordinating and differentiating their theories and their evidence. While they are unsystematic in their research they have difficulty making progress towards valid conclusions. Some of their difficulty can be put down to memory overloads, and rectified by helping with record-keeping, but some of it is associated with lack of system, some with hanging on too long to a disproved theory and difficulties with negative evidence. They may also not have a rich enough knowledge base to find and develop good analogies. Such problems are not totally unlike those faced (and not always overcome) by professional scientists (Kuhn 1962; Kuhn *et al.* 1995); but professional scientists (one hopes) have more grasp of how to do hypothetico-deductive thinking, more ability and willingness to treat their preferred hypothesis as a 'what if' that has to be systematically investigated, and more access to the metacognition necessary to control it effectively.

There has been considerable interest in the conceptual systems that untutored people bring to bear on scientific problems. These are often referred to as 'naïve' or 'intuitive' conceptions. Linn (1986) summarises some of the findings. She suggests that untutored reasoners have constructed a view of natural phenomena from personal experience guided by the use of analogies. For example, they predict that the weight of an object will affect the amount of water it displaces, justifying this (incorrect) prediction by pointing out the importance of weight for momentum, pressure and so forth. Like people did before Galileo, they believe that heavier objects fall faster, their understanding of movement in space may be pre-Newtonian, or even Aristotelian (Caramazza *et al.* 1981; McCloskey *et al.* 1980), and these beliefs are no easier to modify in the individual than they were in the history of science (di Sessa 1982, 1983).

Intuitive conceptions also arise in the biological sciences (Carey 1985; Inagaki and Hatano 2004; Gelman 2003, 2004) and social sciences (Voss 1989). Here too experts and novices may represent domains differently and use different strategies. Analysis is the first step in problem-solving, as the major factors of the problem must be correctly identified if a successful solution is to be found. How the problem is represented also affects the evaluation of the solution: experts generate more high-level abstract solutions than novices, and also consider what sub-problems their solution would solve and which points would need to be considered if the abstract solution were to work. Experts thus do more to provide arguments for and against components of their problem analysis and their problem solution: evaluation, confirmation and disconfirmation are an intrinsic part of the problem-solving process.

2.6.3 Children's analogical reasoning

Scientific problems and formal logic tasks need to be represented in our cognitive systems, and we may seek to link them to existing representations. It has been suggested (e.g. Bryant 1974; Crisafi and Brown 1986; Siegler 1989b; Sternberg 1985; Vosniadou and Ortony 1989; DeLoache *et al.* 1998a; Goswami 1991a, 1992, 1996, 1998, 2002) that the use of analogy is both the core of intelligent cognition and one of the most important mechanisms of cognitive development. Analogical reasoning is seen as critical in bringing existing knowledge and skills to bear on new information and tasks, as central to the processes of learning and transfer and to the construction of mental models. It facilitates cognitive development by allowing poorly understood situations to be reconceptualised in terms of better understood ones, both in the course of cognitive development and in the course of any novice's becoming expert in a domain. Using analogies appropriately is thus believed to be definitively intelligent. It is also a skill whose development in the child has been studied with somewhat different conclusions being drawn.

There is debate about exactly what 'analogy' is and is not. Most researchers agree that it is a 'fuzzy concept' (De Jong 1989; DeLoache *et al.* 1998a, 1998b), but it would seem that essentially it involves a correspondence between two things (or subject areas) that are alike not so much in their surface elements, attributes, properties and effects as in the relations between two or more of these. The familiar examples from so many tests of intelligence and reasoning illustrate the classic Aristotelian type: 'cat is to kitten as dog is to (puppy, kid, collar)'. Metaphors (Glucksberg and Keysar 1990; and see pp. 115–120 on metaphor and p. 120 on transfer) may use analogy to offer the possibility of understanding one thing in terms of another: 'Shall I compare thee to a summer's day?'; No, because you are more lovely, yes, because your beauty is vulnerable to time and rough weather just as the day's is, but it can, like the day's, be immortalised by a poet's praise. Similarly, in the somewhat outdated analogy that compares atomic structure to the solar system, the relationship between sun and planets in the forces acting between them and in size and movement relative to each other is transferred to the atomic nucleus and the electrons: enormously different in scale but taken as similar in their relations. Analogy may also be used in problem-solving tasks (e.g. Johnson-Laird and Wason 1977), where a solution worked out for one problem can be extrapolated to another where the relational structure is the same. The classic example is Duncker's radiation problem: the patient has an inoperable malignant tumour which could be destroyed by massive radiation focused on it, but healthy tissue around it should not be damaged. The analogous problem involves getting attacking forces to an enemy citadel whose approach roads are defended against major (but not minor) forces; this is done by splitting up the army and sending parties of soldiers too small to set off the defences along each of the roads that converge on the fortress. Similarly, the tumour deep in the body can be attacked by converging many narrow and weak rays on it so that only there at the tumour is the radiation strong enough to destroy tissue. Duncker gave the castle example before the tumour test, and subjects who had previously solved (or even just heard) how to besiege the castle were better at discovering how to attack the tumour. More recent research (Goswami 1991a, 1996; Pauen and Wilkening 1997; Singer-Freeman and Goswami 2001) also shows such a 'priming effect'.

Much of cognition and learning depends on identifying the relevant knowledge that the learner already has in existing memory so that this knowledge can be used as a starting point for learning what is new. Having no starting point, or an unnecessarily distant one, or a starting point from which one sets off in the wrong direction, will hamper learning and reasoning; so will an unwillingness to deal with a starting point from which the end-point is not obviously within reach. Finding, using and evaluating analogies may therefore be one of the most important aspects of successful cognition. At least three sorts of processes are involved: finding an appropriate source domain to provide the basic analogy; mapping some of the information we have about the source domain on to the elements of the target domain; and producing from the success or otherwise of this new mapping a new representation of the target domain (which may in its turn have implications for how the source domain is represented in future). Various papers in Vosniadou and Ortony (1989) present models of the stages of analogical reasoning. Rumelhart (1989), for example, discusses how the 'parallel distributed processing' mechanism, which he believes the human mind to be, would cope with reasoning by similarity and analogy. Anderson and Thompson (1989) and Gentner (1989) present 'structure-mapping' computer simulations of the mapping stage and less thoroughly instantiated accounts of the other stages. Johnson-Laird (1989) argues that analogies vary more than the purely 'structure-mapping' models allow, and in particular that the computational models cannot account for profound and creative analogies. He insists that analogies cannot rest entirely in structural relationships; rather, matters of fact and meaning must also be taken into account. These semantic considerations will be crucial at the point when the relationships that could be mapped from source to target have to be evaluated. Thus the more knowledge individuals have of the source and target domains the more likely they are to find and use appropriate analogies. Knowledge may be an essential prerequisite for creativity and expertise (see pp. 253–260), and for the intelligent use of analogies (Halford 1993). This is an important point for developmental studies of analogical reasoning and I will return to it later.

Researchers from a number of theoretical backgrounds have studied children's analogical reasoning; Goswami (1991a, 1996, 1998, 2002), Singer-Freeman and Goswami (2001) and DeLoache et al. (1998a and b) provide very useful reviews. A large number of studies, including Piaget's work and experiments by various Piagetians, suggested that pre-adolescents were unable to reason by analogy because it was only during adolescence that an ability to recognise and reason about 'higher order' relations was developed. Thus nine-year-olds were unable to solve analogies such as 'Bird is to air as fish is to?', while twelve-year-olds and fifteen-year-olds were quite successful (Levinson and Carpenter 1974). However, Levinson and Carpenter also demonstrated both that the younger children could solve what they called 'quasi-analogies' such as 'A bird uses air, a fish uses?' and that there was a transfer effect in that children who were given quasi-analogies first and true analogies second solved more of these analogies at all ages. Thus, making the relevant relation between the elements and the nature of the analogical exercise improved performance significantly. Research by Brown and Goswami and their colleagues (Crisafi and Brown 1986; Goswami and Brown 1990b; Singer-Freeman and Goswami 2001) has shown that young children may use analogy to solve problems particularly well if a causal principle that they understand is involved. Children as young as three or four could solve problems such as 'instant coffee granules is to mug of coffee as soap powder is to soapy water', or 'half circle is to half rectangle as quarter circle is to quarter rectangle' (Goswami 1991a, 1996; Singer-Freeman and Goswami 2001). Again, there was positive transfer if the child had previously solved analogous problems, and performance was enhanced if the principles common to the problems were highlighted by explicit discussion, or if children had to recount the story in which a problem was solved to another person before they went on to a new problem that could be solved analogically. This work shows that children can solve classical analogies and problem-solving analogies well before adolescence, if they understand the nature of the task and the relations on which the analogies are based. Even when children import information, what they insert is often principled and sometimes sensible (Gelman 2004; Hickling and Wellman 2001; Gopnik and Schulz 2004). Because children can work wih analogies, analogical reasoning tasks can be used to assess their understanding of the relationships that the analogies are based on: for example, Singer-Freeman and Goswami (2001) use an analogical reasoning task to investigate children's proportional reasoning and Pauen and Wilkening (1997) to investigate a physics task.

Children can reason analogically even when the target and source are not obviously similar perceptually. This success is contrary to the long-held theory that young children are 'perceptually bound'. It was for a long time assumed that transfer and analogy occurred most readily when the perceptual characteristics – shape, colour, size and so forth – are identical in the situations involved, and that such perceptual identity was a *sine qua non* for young children. Gentner (1988, 1989) suggested that 'surface' similarity, that is, similarity based on perceptually similar attributes, is the basis for young children's analogical solution strategies, and is superseded by 'relational' similarity in which surface appearance is no longer important and higher-order relations are preferred. (This would no doubt be analogous to the characteristic-to-defining shift in children's use of the properties of concept members that Keil (1989) suggested.) Among Gentner's evidence for this use of perceptual similarity were two studies (Gentner and Toupin 1986). In one children who were told a story about animals such as a chipmunk, a robin and a horse were more willing to transfer the story to perceptually similar animals such as squirrel, bluebird and zebra than to dissimilar ones (elephant, shark and cricket). In another, children preferred attribute-based similes such as 'soap-suds are like whipped cream' to relational ones, such as 'a cloud is like a sponge'.

Brown (1989) argues that physical similarity of stimuli, problem and situations is indeed an important criterion for whether children consider them to be alike, either as members of a concept or as material for analogies and metaphors, but it is also important for adults. Given the right circumstances, children too can override perceptual similarity and go beyond it. She proposes that children rely on appearance as a fall-back option, for use mainly when there is no other basis for them to use. That is, children are not perceptually bound, but, like adults, they organise their experience on the basis of appearance if they have no other theory about how it should be organised. Lacking knowledge, they are forced back on surface perceptual similarities, and may fail to transfer an appropriate solution from one situation to another because it does not look sufficiently similar. Lack of knowledge may prevent them finding relational similarities or even noticing ones that are presented unless they are strongly highlighted by discussion, repetition or other emphasis. The traditional ways of investigating children's analogical reasoning did not contain these facilitating conditions, the experimenter never giving any indication that transfer might be appropriate. Children are faced with what might well be a 'now for something completely different' experience, and so treat each test as a new one. This may be a problem that spreads beyond analogy-finding. Karmiloff-Smith (1988) suggests that children may treat successive instances in her block-balancing task as being independent problems, working out how to balance each successive block *de novo*. Such behaviour would make transfer and analogy-finding much less likely, but it may be quite sensible for beginning learners, who do not have enough experience and knowledge to link successive experiences appropriately, to proceed instance by instance rather than by carrying through one solution too optimistically to the next problem. Children's willingness to make analogies when they know the course and target domains and when they understand the relational principles involved makes a telling contrast with their failure on abstracted artificial tasks. Perhaps a certain amount of knowledge is required before any deliberate use of similar content or structure can contribute to analogical reasoning.

I will point out here, parenthetically, that an interesting case has been made that an innate drive for 'coherence' and a high-level cognitive mechanism for producing it are at the heart of human cognition, and that 'autism' is caused by a failure to develop the latter. Uta Frith (1990; see also Frith and Frith 2003; Hill and Frith 2003) has argued that the central cause of autism is a physiologically based inability to see and develop coherence between different but analogous events and rules. The autistic person cannot 'see the wood for the trees', each of which is uncontrollably novel, mysterious and demanding. This handicap leads to characteristic behaviours such as the compulsive ordering of objects into rigid patterns, facility in analysing complex shapes into the components and failure in synthesising them into a reassembly, repetitive and stereotyped language that does not develop into the normal give and take and implicitness of conversation, absence of pretend play, and a failure to develop a 'theory of mind' (see the last section of this chapter). A full consideration of autism and of Frith's account of it is outside the scope of this volume, but this view does provide an interesting sidelight on analogy in normal cognition, suggesting that it is indeed central and has effects on many different cognitive areas.

Reviewing the literature on the development of analogical reasoning, then, it would seem that even preschool children can display analogical reasoning in both Aristotelian analogies and in story problems if they understand the sort of relations on which the analogies are based (Brown 1989; Goswami 1991a, 1996), though they may not display it unless given hints or instructions that highlight the underlying relations. Older children and adults are more likely to show analogical reasoning even without supportive conditions, though as both the classic and the modern problem-solving literature show, they may need hints to succeed in analogy tasks (e.g. Holyoak and Nisbett 1988; Johnson-Laird and Wason 1977; Goswami 1991a, 1996). This difference in the facility of analogical reasoning might be associated with differences in the development of the conceptual bases of source and target domains (Vosniadou and Ortony 1989; Singer-Freeman and Goswami 2001), or to differences in metacognitive skills which mean that young children cannot yet consciously reflect on the nature of analogy or analogical reasoning strategies (Goswami 1991a). These two possibilities are not mutually exclusive, and neither is adequately documented. They need to be linked to the points made at the beginning of this section about the successive processes involved in using analogies. Limitations of working memory should probably also be considered.

The developmental literature and the traditional test paradigms centre on understanding (or even perhaps merely recognising) an analogical relation set up by the tester, and have much less to do with finding an appropriate source domain for a particular target domain, let alone creating new domain representations or evaluating analogies. They do not go far beyond the 'structure-mapping' focus that Johnson-Laird (1989) criticises. To elucidate the development of this wider range of analogical reasoning it may be necessary to search the literature on language development for instances of child-generated analogies, and for the ways in which adults present ana-logies to help children structure new information, as in the 'links' and 'world links' that mothers present to their two-year-olds (Meadows and Mills 1987; Mills and Funnell 1983; Chapter 5 this volume).

2.6.4 Children's use of metaphors

Metaphorical language (such as 'Anne is a flowerbud') has been of interest to philosophers, students of rhetoric and of literature, and psychologists from Aristotle onwards. Exactly how it works is still a matter of debate. A topic ('Anne') is linked with a vehicle (a 'flowerbud') by an implicit unstated relation (the ground), so that the statement is literally false but figuratively true. Aristotle concentrated on metaphor as an implicit comparison between the topic and the vehicle that conveyed some sort of esoteric poetic or rhetorical truth through the analogy it set up. Another view is that the vehicle is simply an ornamental substitute for literal language, such as 'Anne is young and beautiful and will be still more beautiful when she grows up'. A richer description is that the topic and the vehicle interact so that each acquires some of the constellation of meaning of the other: Anne's youth, tenderness, vulnerability and potential unfolding are emphasised, and flowerbuds become more associated with brightness, liveliness and freshness, and with the need for protection. Metaphor allows the reinterpretation of topic and vehicle in terms of each other, thus extending their meaning. This is the view of metaphor that I find most useful. It involves the use of some perceptible similarity between topic and vehicle (a sentence like 'Anne is a tin of baked beans' might be a metaphor if the child was particularly cylindrical in shape or ate nothing else, perhaps, but is otherwise anomalous), and they must belong to different conventional categories ('Anne is a pretty baby' is not a metaphor but a literal (if bald) statement). Many metaphors have become absorbed into language (or 'frozen') so that their non-literal origins are no longer obvious: the sentence 'Anne is sweet' is not literally true, though we have no difficulty in perceiving its intended meaning as directly as if it were. Metaphors must also be distinguished from other non-literal sorts of language such as sarcasm and hyperbole ('Anne is the most beautiful thing in the world') and analysts of language have traditionally distinguished them from similes ('Anne is like a flowerbud') where the fact that a comparison is being made is explicitly indicated.

The remarks I have just made about the characteristics of metaphor should suggest that they are not linguistically or psychologically altogether straightforward. I want to draw two points from this before I describe the literature on children's use of metaphors. The first is to raise the question of why we use metaphors if they are so complex and so problematic. While they can have a number of simple functions such as avoiding undue repetition ('Anne is a flowerbud, a treasure, a peach, an enchantress, a honey, an angel') three major functions suggest themselves. They may allow the expression of ideas that the speaker could not otherwise express because his or her language lacks suitable terms. English uses temperature-linked terms ('hot-blooded', 'a cold fish', 'a sunny temperament') to describe personality traits, for example, and wine buffs have imported phrases from other semantic areas to describe the nuances of their gustatory experiences. This function is obviously an interesting one developmentally since children, comparatively lacking in specialist literal terminology, might resort to metaphor to express their meaning (we will examine this possibility later). A second major function of metaphors is their communicative compactness:

all the applicable characteristics of the vehicle are implied through the naming of the vehicle itself and do not have to be listed. Conversely, of course, a metaphor may suggest the application of inappropriate characteristics and so be misleading or disturbing or incomprehensible. One example from the research literature, 'hair is like spaghetti' (Billow 1975, 1981) seems to me to run into this problem (besides being a simile, not a metaphor). The third important function of metaphors that I want to raise is perhaps a consequence of their usefulness for expressing the inexpressible and for conveying meaning compactly. This function is the use of metaphorical models drawn from one domain to facilitate our understanding of another: we have tried to understand brains in terms of computers, for example (see Chapter 4 this volume, and Boden (1987)), or to understand the polity in terms of a body ('the head of state', 'communism/Fascism/ materialism/liberalism/political apathy is a cancer in the body politic'). Such metaphorical 'mental models' as these are widespread and may be our normal way of getting a grasp on highly complex subject-matter (Johnson-Laird 1983; see my discussion of analogy elsewhere in this chapter). They can of course get us into trouble if we breach the applicability of the vehicle by transferring its inappropriate qualities to the topic, or if we forget that it is a metaphor that is involved, not a literal description. It may be necessary to look at what we understand to be the limits and the strengths of a particular metaphor as well as of metaphor in general. What is and what is not a metaphor may also be ill-defined and disagreements may arise. These may be particularly acute when children's use of metaphor is being discussed.

Even preschool children produce utterances that look like metaphors or similes (see e.g. Billow (1981), Gentner and Markman (1997), Woodward and Markman (1998)). Piaget (1962) recorded his daughter Jacqueline, aged between three and four, saying that a winding river 'is like a snake' and a caddis worm in its stone coat in a stream 'is an insect in its cage'. He did not believe that utterances like these are true metaphors, however. Essentially this was because he believed that such young children think in 'pre-concepts' based on symbolic images and action schemas and not in terms of true concepts 'defined by the objective qualities of the objects themselves'. Metaphor involves a deliberate violation of concept boundaries; as Piagetian young children lack the concepts they cannot violate them and produce true metaphor. Recent work (see pp. 156–164) suggests both that young children do have an ability to classify items into conceptual groupings with clear boundaries based on similarity and contrast, and that not all concepts fit the classic type that Piaget centres on. Thus his dismissal of early 'proto-metaphorical' utterances is not sound: very young children are able to construct systematic classes and thus may be able to make comparisons across class boundaries in the awareness that they are metaphorical. It could be argued that what changes is not the possibility of metaphor but the knowledge on which metaphor is based (Palermo 1989). Thus in a well-understood domain even four-year-olds may understand metaphor correctly (Johnson and Pascual-Leone 1989; Waggoner and Palermo 1989).

It may, however, be difficult to distinguish between metaphor and more literal comparisons (Mandler 1983; Vosniadou 1987; Goswami 1995; Gentner and Markman 1997). My daughter aged not quite two watched her tights being put on, the flaccid pale pink woolly length swelling out as her leg went down it, grinned with delight and said 'Pink balloon'. Should she be credited with a metaphor or only with a sharp bit of observation? A child (or indeed an adult) may use a term not normally applied to an object to pick out a perceptual similarity without necessarily intending a metaphor, as in some of the 'overextensions' discussed in the literature on early language development, or as in pretend play (Lillard 2001, 2002; Taylor 1999; Taylor et al. 2004) where objects are renamed in terms that suit their role in the 'pretend': a chair is renamed 'my castle', is used as a castle and in a sense 'becomes' a castle. Metaphor requires a marking of perceptual similarity between objects from different conventional categories in a non-literal comparison (Vosniadou 1987: 874). Its development is probably associated with the development of classification skills and of symbolic play. Evidence from children's spontaneous productions needs to be supplemented by their response to production tasks and comprehension problems.

In one study, Vosniadou and Ortony (1983) asked children aged three to six to choose between pairs of statements in a comparison task ('A is like X') or a categorisation task ('A is the same kind of thing as X'). In the categorisation task the pair contained a metaphor and a literal statement, such as 'Rain is the same kind of thing as tears' and 'Rain is the same kind of thing as snow'. Children over four selected 'Rain is the same kind of thing as snow' as the better alternative significantly above chance level. In the comparison task they chose the best of all three pairings of a metaphorical statement (e.g. 'Rain is like tears'), a literal statement ('Rain is like snow') and an anomalous statement ('Rain is like a chair'). Even three-year-old children chose this last nonsensical statement least, and there was no preference for literal or metaphorical statements as comparisons. These results (since replicated several times) suggest that an early distinction was made between comparisons that made no sense and comparisons that picked up similarity, and that by the age of four literal and non-literal similarity were beginning to be distinguished as possible bases for comparison and categorisation. Vosniadou regards this latter distinction as analogous to the appearance–reality distinction investigated by Flavell and his colleagues (Flavell 1986, 1988, 1998, 1999, 2001; Flavell et al. 1986, 1995, 1997, 1999; and pp. 201–203).

Tests of children's comprehension have produced conflicting results: success by preschool children in work by Gardner (1974), Gentner (1977;

Gentner and Markman 1997), and Waggoner and Palermo (1989), or even babies (Marks *et al.* 1987), failure by children younger than fourteen (Winner *et al.* 1976). One source of the differences was the use of different tasks. Gardner's young subjects were asked to match adjectives to items from the same domain, for example 'quiet' and 'loud' to sounds differing in volume, and also to other domains such as colours and faces, where sound words might be used metaphorically (grey is a 'quiet' colour, scarlet a 'loud' one). Winner *et al.* asked for paraphrase or explanation of sentences such as 'The prison guard was a hard rock', or 'Summer's blood is ripe black-berries'. The differences between such tasks makes comparison of results difficult, though it does make conspicuous something that some of the literature fails to emphasise, to wit that since metaphor can involve a wide range of language forms, concepts and comparisons, its successful use may not be an all-or-none affair but rather something that is achieved over a period of years. Failure to comprehend a metaphor may arise because of a failure to realise that an implicit comparison and not a literal one is intended, as in James Thurber's recollection of:

> the enchanted private world of my early boyhood . . . In this world, businessmen who phoned their wives to say that they were tied up at the office sat roped to their swivel chairs, and probably gagged, unable to move or speak, except somehow, miraculously, to telephones . . . then there was the man who left town under a cloud. Sometimes I saw him all wrapped up in the cloud, and invisible . . . At other times it floated, about the size of a sofa, three or four feet above his head, following him wherever he went . . . There were many other wonderful figures in the secret, surrealist landscapes of my youth: the old lady who was always up in the air, the husband who did not seem to be able to put his foot down, the man who lost his head during a fire but was still able to run out of the house yelling, the young lady who was, in reality, a soiled dove.
>
> (Thurber 1953: 23–4)

Another source of failure would be to fail to see the similarity between the metaphorical vehicle and the topic (this is my problem with 'summer's blood is ripe blackberries', where colour, function, location and every other perceptual and conceptual characteristic seem incongruent). Finally, if the comprehension test involves explanation or paraphrase the subject may understand the metaphor but be unable to produce an adequate verbal account (Palermo (1989) discusses this). Tasks and materials appropriate to the child's linguistic powers and knowledge level are needed if metaphorical competence is to be correctly diagnosed.

Recent work has established that very young children show understanding of some metaphors (Mandler 1983; Ortony 1988; Vosniadou 1987; Gentner and Markman 1997; Woodward and Markman 1998), mainly those where topic and vehicle come from fields the child already knows about as distinct domains; children's ability to understand metaphorical language improves considerably during the primary school years. Vosniadou (1987) discusses the variables that affect the comprehension of metaphor. These include the linguistic input, the available context and the child's knowledge base, metacognitive abilities and linguistic skills. Knowledge and understanding interact. A metaphor cannot be properly understood if the relevant conceptual areas are not known about. Which attributes of a vehicle are transferred to the topic may obey some basic conceptual constraints (Carey and Gelman 1991; Keil 1979; Markman 1990). For example, Vosniadou and Ortony told children stories containing an analogy from a more familiar to a less familiar domain; in one story the white blood cells (the topic) fighting an infection were compared to soldiers (the vehicle). The children correctly concluded that the white blood cells kill germs but not that they wear uniforms or use guns; but they also attributed human emotions to the blood cells, supposing that they thought the germs were bad and felt frightened while fighting them (Vosniadou 1987: 881). They were not willing to attribute blood cell characteristics to human soldiers, an asymmetry of attribution that Susan Carey also found in children's generalisations about biological characteristics (Carey 1985).

Finally, it has been argued, as I said earlier, that we can usefully employ metaphors drawn from a well-understood area to understand a newer, less familiar, one (Goswami 1991; Johnson-Laird 1983). Knowledge acquisition may require the use of metaphor and analogy, using the existing model of one subject to understand another subject, 'Knowing that they are not quite the same things but slowly figuring out the full range of their differences' (Vosniadou 1987: 882). A conscious and sceptical use of metaphor and analogy may be one of the sources of cognitive development. It may be crucial to my next topic, transfer.

2.6.5 Transfer

When we first learn or develop a skill it is often closely tied to the original situation we used it in, and we may have difficulty using the skill in a different situation. At least one child has been able to add large numbers correctly and easily when the sums concerned her pocket money, but has been seen to have much more difficulty when the same numbers were involved in ordinary content-free two-digit addition sums (Siegler 1986). Or a new task may require a new composite skill in which older skills and knowledge have to be recombined in novel ways. As Brown *et al.* (1983: 142) say, development consists in part of going from the context-dependent state where resources are welded to the original learning situation to a relatively context-independent state where the learner extends the ways in which initially highly constrained knowledge and procedures are used.

How do we make this move? How do we transfer knowledge from the situation where we first learned it to other relevant situations? What are the cognitive processes involved in bringing the results of past experience to bear on our present tasks? How do we learn to learn? Do individuals differ in their ability to transfer knowledge appropriately? Questions such as these, on the nature of 'transfer', are a crucial part of the study of the development and acquisition of cognition, and have enormous educational importance.

Gick and Holyoak (1997) provide a useful review of the cognitive psychology of transfer. The classic study of transfer compares the performance of a test task by people with prior experience of a related task and people who have no such prior experience. If the group with related experience do better than the no-experience control group, it is said that there is 'positive transfer' from the prior task to the related test task. If they do worse, there is 'negative transfer'; the knowledge they have of the prior task has interfered with their performance of the test task. In a related type of study, people may be tested for the effect of earlier learning on tasks that are related to their earlier experience in different ways, highly similar or more distantly analogous, for example. In this sort of study it may be possible to identify what was learned about the first task and what inferences are carried forward to the new one, and thus to address questions of how general or how specific transfer is and to diagnose what has gone wrong in cases of negative transfer or failure to transfer.

'Transfer' concerns the use of prior knowledge in new situations; thus we need to consider how knowledge and situations are represented. As I discuss elsewhere in this chapter, there are considerable theoretical complexities about how we represent the knowledge we have learned. However, for our present purposes it is useful to adopt the information-processing approach (e.g. Anderson 1983; Holland et al. 1986) and assume that knowledge of concepts and procedures is represented as clusters or networks of 'production rules', for example, 'if something is a furry animal which barks, then it is probably a dog', and 'if something is a dog then it should be approached cautiously as it may bite'. We can apply, or transfer, such rules to new possible instances. Small children's vocabulary learning provides many examples (see e.g. Mervis (1987), L. Bloom (1998), P. Bloom (2000), and pp. 16–17). Gick and Holyoak (1987) suggest that 'overgeneralisation' and 'undergeneralisation' are transfer mistakes; for example a small child whose rule was 'if something is small and has a tail, then it is called "doggie"' would overgeneralise to a cat, 'a sort of negative transfer', and fail to transfer (or undergeneralise) to a large dog such as a Great Dane. This analysis suggests that failure to transfer may be due to having an inappropriate restriction in the initial rule (in this example dogs are labelled as 'small', which is not always the case), and negative transfer may be due to lack of appropriate restrictions that would show that there should be no transfer to the new instance (in this case an extra condition that would differentiate dogs from other furry animals; 'barks' might be such a condition). Both the existence of such rules and their strength will be relevant to how they are involved in transfer.

We talked initially of transfer to 'related' or 'similar' tasks or situations. The notion of 'similarity' needs some unpacking (pp. 149–151). Sharing common features and having few different ones is part of the core of 'similarity', and the degree to which two tasks share features, the degree to which they are perceived as the same, will affect the likelihood that transfer will be attempted. If the transfer task bears a close resemblance to the prior task, it will be more likely that the prior task is remembered when the transfer task is attempted. When learning to drive a car I may comparatively often remember earlier road safety lessons but will rarely think of learning to play tennis. Shared features may, however, be causally related to the desired outcomes or goals to a greater or lesser degree. Attention to the actions of other road users is causally related to the desired outcome of safety for both pedestrians and drivers, and there may be positive transfer here from one to the other. However, the advice to make yourself highly visible by wearing light-coloured clothing, armbands of reflective material and so forth, though valuable for pedestrians and cyclists, is less appropriate for drivers. A straight transfer here would only have a positive effect on performance (safety) when the driver was outside the car, though transfer of the abstract principle to make sure that the vehicle was visible would be appropriate.

'Similarity' is not just a matter of shared features, then, but involves consideration of which shared features are relevant to the prior task and to the transfer task, and in what ways. This obviously can involve calling on general knowledge or expertise. Novices in physics tasks, for example, treat problems as similar on the basis of shared features such as all involving levers or inclined planes, where experts make use of the underlying structural similarities that determine how the problems are best solved (Chi *et al.* 1980; Pauen and Wilkening 1996). The context of the tasks will also affect transfer, as in the case of the child calculating her pocket money correctly but getting more abstract sums wrong.

Gick and Holyoak (1987) summarise the relationship between similarity and transfer thus:

> The amount of transfer depends on the similarity between the two situations . . . the direction of the transfer depends on the similarity of the two responses . . .
>
> When two situations are perceived as unrelated, no transfer occurs regardless of response similarity. When the situations are perceived as

similar or identical, transfer occurs; the greater the similarity of the situations, the greater the absolute magnitude of transfer. If transfer occurs, it becomes increasingly negative as the appropriate responses become objectively more dissimilar. If the required transfer response is highly similar to the training response (many shared structural components and few distinctive ones), transfer is positive. But as the response appropriate to the transfer task becomes less similar (few shared components and many distinctive ones), overall transfer shifts to the negative side. The structural dissimilarities cause the training response, evoked by strong perceived similarity, to interfere with the new response that must be acquired for the transfer task.

(Gick and Holyoak 1987: 18–19)

This account implicates memory in the possibility of transfer. Prior experience has to be remembered for there to be any possibility of transfer. Thus, representation of both initial task and transfer task is important; encoding of the initial task in a way that emphasises its structure rather than superficial idiosyncratic features may be crucial. Presenting a range of varying examples for prior learning may make transfer easier than if only one prior example has been learned. Later, how the transfer task evokes earlier learning may be important: if you are unable to relate it to relevant earlier tasks, positive transfer will be less likely.

The extensive experimental literature on memory and learning provides Gick and Holyoak (1987) with useful data on transfer. Thorough learning of the prior task makes positive transfer to similar tasks more likely than a slighter degree of initial learning does, particularly if the thorough learning involves familiarisation with the rules governing the tasks. Understanding the rules may also lead to the acquisition of general abstract problem-solving strategies so that there is positive transfer to new tasks that require new responses too. Kendler and Kendler (1975), for example, gave children a learning task in which objects that were either large or small and either black or white were associated with a reward on the basis of either size or colour. Once the child had learned that, for example, black objects were always rewarded and white ones never, and size was irrelevant, the reward pattern was changed. Some children were given a 'reversal shift', so that white objects were now associated with the reward, never having been rewarded before: other children got a 'non-reversal shift', so that size became the discriminating variable for reward and colour was now irre-levant. Children over the age of about seven who had generalised a rule rather than reacting to each individual case found the 'reversal shift' much easier. Younger children showed less positive transfer to the new task, and made more errors based on their old learning: thus they did better on the 'non-reversal shift' where their old response still gave them a success rate of about 50 per cent. Zelazo (2003, 2004) reports on a similar difficulty that three-year-olds had in shifting from an old rule to a new one, even when prompted.

Learning and transfer of rules that are based on the important structural features of a task, not on trivial surface characteristics, will be easier if the learner encounters a range of examples with a common structure and different irrelevant characteristics. Initially variety in examples may be confusing, but if enough moderately varying examples are given the learner can increasingly infer the general principles that underlie them and transfer them to a wider range of examples. It may be best if initial examples are similar and represent typical instances of the concept or procedure, and more variable examples are given later. Including an abstract rule with the examples may also be helpful in facilitating transfer, as this too will make it more likely that enough is learned about the structure of the initial task for it to be identifiable and usable later (Resnick 1987a, 1987b; Chapter 6).

Whether past experience gives rise to better performance in the present task will depend on whether that prior experience is thought of, and seen as relevant, at the right moment. This is more likely to happen if the goals of the new task and the old ones are seen as the same, and as capable of being brought about by the same processes. If the goal of the original task is too specialised, there may be no transfer to new tasks that appear to have different goals. School-based skills, for example, are all too often not used outside school because they are not connected to any clear goal other than 'getting school work done', and therefore won't be thought of as potentially useful when a more practical task is at hand outside school. It may thus be helpful to make it clear what sort of range of uses a particular skill or piece of knowledge may have, just as clarifying the effectiveness of an activity such as strategic memorising makes it more likely that young children will continue to use it (see p. 96). Here too knowledge of results may be important.

Ann Brown and her colleagues (Brown *et al.* 1983; Campione *et al.* 1982; Ferrara *et al.* 1986) see 'transfer' as an inseparable component of learning, and as crucial in the assessment of cognitive status. They argue very strongly against the 'static' assessment of cognition, which seeks only to estimate a person's current independent cognitive achievements. One way to supplement this and discover useful information about a person's potential cognitive status is to assess, additionally, what can be achieved with the support of a more skilled person, which is what Vygotsky saw as the upper end of the 'zone of proximal development' (pp. 308–310). Another way we will be concerned with here is to assess how the person's present cognitive skills are transferred to new situations. Some individuals may manage little or no transfer of their skills and others a great deal, and though static assessment might have suggested they were equally competent, Brown *et al.* would argue that the latter, the ready transferrers, are in a much more favourable position cognitively: they have 'learned to learn'. The psychologist is also better off, as what is being assessed is not the hodgepodge of declarative and procedural knowledge resulting from a long, complex and unknowable history of acquisition and development, but cognitive processes in action. These may be far more illuminating about the nature of cognition and the nature of effective instruction (Siegler 2005).

In a series of experiments Brown and her colleagues have found that although groups who are different in age or ability may perform at similar levels in initial 'baseline' testing, after equal training older or more able subjects perform at a higher level than younger or less able ones; that is, they have got more benefit out of the same training input. Weak students were reluctant to transfer what they had been taught to related, novel, situations, and would transfer only to highly similar tasks. They seemed to require more explicit instructions and to learn to cope only with the particular task they had been trained on, not to take the risk of 'going beyond the information given' as stronger students would do. Brown and her colleagues argue that students should be assessed using measures of learning and transfer that focus on general rules and principles, for three reasons: first, rules and principles that have some generality within the guided instruction programme will resemble normal school learning and hence will predict students' probable school progress better than conventional intelligence tests can do; second, because measures of how well students have learned general rules and principles will diagnose their strengths and weaknesses more accurately; and third, because this improvement in diagnosis and prediction will make it easier to provide appropriate remedies where better learning and transfer are needed (Brown and Campione 1986; Ferrara *et al.* 1986; see also DeLoache *et al.* 1998; Siegler 2005). Their experimental work supports this argument. Ferrara *et al.*, for example, found that children of higher IQ needed fewer prompts to reach learning criteria and needed less assistance in transferring their learning to somewhat dissimilar tasks, that is, they learned more readily and more flexibly. Older children, similarly, did better than younger ones. Learning and transfer were still related when age and IQ were partialled out, and also occurred to similar degrees on two parallel sets of tasks, one where what had to be discovered was the rule governing a series of letters (such as NGOHPIQJ–) and the other involving a matrix completion task. Less able students showed less transfer and needed help with transfer on more similar tasks than abler students did.

It has been argued that an individual's ability to respond to instruction with learning and a flexible transfer of that learning to new tasks is a better index of future progress than static tests of general ability or initial competence. 'Readiness' to learn, too, can be measured not simply by seeing what skills a child already can deploy, but by examining how these skills can be used or modified on the job. Ferrara's doctoral dissertation (Brown

1988) reports research that documents this assertion in children's early mathematical learning. Mathematics is a discipline in which a rich knowledge base exists and becomes perhaps increasingly important as a person's expertise increases (see Smith 1983), while tests of deductive reasoning, as used in earlier research, involve minimal prior knowledge. However, although mathematical knowledge is relevant to children's potential performance, their propensity to transfer is still extremely important in predicting their capacity to profit from instruction, and learning and transfer efficiency are the most sensitive predictors of growth in mathematical understanding.

The data from all the experiments converge on the conclusion that if the goal is to distinguish students who are likely to do well within some area from those likely to experience difficulties, estimates of their initial response to instruction and of their ability to make use of newly acquired resources are powerful tools. They also indicate that the most diagnostic indicator is transfer performance. Ensuring that new skills have been learned, even to some constant criterion across students, is no guarantee that those skills will be useful subsequently. If we want to monitor progress through a domain, it is essential that we constantly check to see if 'acquired' skills can be used flexibly, or whether they remain 'welded' or 'inert', triggered only by a relatively complete instantiation of the context in which they were learned.

Brown and her colleagues (Brown and Campione 1988) emphasise the role of metacognitive processes underlying individual differences in learning and transfer (p. 132). They believe that students who are good at transfer are inclined to plan problem-solving approaches, seek additional information, search for and use analogies, check their reasoning, monitor their progress, engage in efficient 'fix-up' strategies when getting off track, and so forth. Poorer performers generate solutions more quickly but try them out less systematically, and when working on a new problem they are less likely to refer back to prior problems. What seems to be involved is a difference in the array of general self-regulatory skills, skills that are 'weak' in the sense that they do not guarantee success as a more specific skill might do, but can be applied to a wide range of tasks.

2.7 Problem-solving

William James, in *The Principles of Psychology* (1890), elegantly defines solving a problem as a search that occurs when the means to an end do not occur simultaneously with the establishment of the end; that is, problem-solving is what you do when you work towards a goal but do not have a routine way to get there, or when an obstacle such as lack of skill or of knowledge interferes with a previously possible solution. It might be thought of as a general skill, or studied as it is embodied in people's attempts to find a solution to a specific problem. It is thus an important cognitive activity, at least for those who do not live in a perfectly predictable world. It has been seen as critical to education, especially in mathematics and the physical sciences but also as both an index of how well a pupil has learned and an aid to learning, since active engagement in solving a problem has been regarded as providing better understanding than more passive learning would. Rather similar things have been said about reasoning (DeLoache *et al.* 1998a and b; Siegler 2005; Section 2.6): much of what I said there is relevant here too, though problem-solving need not be logical, or, indeed, verbal. There is a considerable literature on problem-solving. It is clear that many cognitive processes are involved, for example those usually considered as memory, perception, transfer, analogical reasoning, deduction and so forth; thus 'problem-solving' is in some ways a microcosm of cognition. In particular, as we shall see, there may be a complex interaction between strategy and declarative knowledge, whose effect may be that problem-solving is more effective in some domains than in others; and a case can be made for the importance of social interaction as the key to improvement in children's problem-solving skills (Garton 2004).

Much work on problem-solving has involved tasks like the Tower of Hanoi, in which a graduated set of discs has to be transferred from one peg to another so that they end up in the same order; during the transfer only one disc can be moved at a time, and at no time may a larger disc be placed upon a smaller one. A simple version of this task would use five discs and three pegs. More complex versions with more discs and more pegs require progressively longer solutions. Tasks like this have a clearly defined goal state and the problem as given contains all the necessary information: analysis of the problem-solver's performance looks at the successive steps taken towards the goal.

Only a limited range of possible actions are appropriate, and the problem itself strongly suggests what these are (for example, it would clearly not be appropriate to seek to solve it by converting the discs into wheels for a vehicle to run from one peg to another, since only one may be moved at a time and they are of different sizes, among other reasons). The problem-solver is thus likely to provide comparatively easily analysed sequences of steps to the solution, including some systematic enough to be regarded as evidence of strategy use. One strategy frequently used by adults for well-defined problems is means–end analysis, selecting moves that reduce the difference between the goal state and the current state, if necessary by setting up sub-goals. Less expert problem-solvers may have less sophisticated strategies: for example at sixteen months old my daughter often successfully stacked graduated rings, largest first, on a peg, but her 'strategy' was simply to put the nearest ring on the peg first and this only led to a successful solution because her normal 'strategy' for getting the rings off the peg involved upending the peg and moving it in a linear motion from left to right, thus tipping the rings off one after another in a line which often left the largest nearest to hand and the smallest further away. More complex problems may provide a less definite structure, such that the constraints on what can be done, what information is relevant, and even exactly what the goal is may have to be assumed or worked out during the problem-solving. More exploratory activity may be necessary (Vandenberg 1990; Siegler 2005) and problem-solving will therefore involve much more interpretation and more use of knowledge not given in the problem. Interpretation and possession of relevant knowledge may be crucial, since the solution that is proposed may depend on how the problem is represented. There is obviously a source of developmental differences here, if what the individual knows about the problem and the problem area is important, and if younger individuals know less than older ones, just as with finding analogies (see pp. 110–115).

Another area of developmental differences is the degree of planfulness shown by the problem-solver. My daughter, in the last example, had only the crudest of plans for getting the rings on and off the peg, and the plan was inflexible. The extent to which the effects of the moves made in solving the problem are monitored may also be important, as may be limitations in memory capacity. It is harder to solve problems that require thinking many moves ahead or backtracking, for example.

Information-processing analyses of problem-solving suggest four main points (Voss 1989; DeLoache et al. 1998a and b; Siegler 2005). First, problem-solving involves a wide variety of different cognitive processes, depending on the nature of the problem, the individual's experience with the subject-matter, and other factors such as practical constraints. Second, one crucial aspect is the way in which the problem is understood. The information in the problem statement must be comprehended and a reasonable representation of the problem must be constructed. This involves analysis of what sort of problem this is, which pieces of information have what degree of importance, how the problem resembles or differs from problems met previously, and so forth. Third, skill in dealing with problems involves the gradual build-up of both content-based factual knowledge and procedural knowledge useful to particular sorts of problems: it is thus not quickly acquired. Fourth, the most effective problem-solvers in a domain have typically developed highly abstract knowledge structures that powerfully organise their declarative knowledge and their handling of problem-solving strategies (Chi et al. 1980, 1983; 1989, Karmiloff-Smith 1992; Case 1998; Klahr and MacWhinney 1998; DeLoache et al. 1998a and b; Garton 2004; Siegler 2005). Expert chess players, for example, use their extensive experience of specific configurations of pieces in selecting and evaluating moves, and they are able to keep very large amounts of information in memory, by 'chunking', which overcomes working memory's limitations, or by rapid accurate access to their long-term memory stores (Chase and Simon 1973).

It is clear that even young children are capable of systematic attempts to solve problems, though their 'strategies' may be crude and relatively ineffective (e.g. Karmiloff-Smith and Inhelder 1974/5), or in some cases may not be put into action because a more expert person is present to do the work (Caplan and Hale 1989; Meadows and Cashdan 1988). Garton (2004) argues the importance of social interaction as the key to problem-solving. Children may even show hypothetico-deductive reasoning, controlling variables and experimenting like mature scientists, if they have external help with record keeping, contrary to Piaget's original findings (Inhelder and Piaget 1958; Braine and Rumain 1983; Brown et al. 1983; Pillow 2002). Conversely, some older children and adults are often poor problem-solvers, making invalid inferences and reasoning well only in familiar contexts (e.g. Wason and Johnson-Laird 1972; Leighton and Sternberg 2004). Thus it is not the case that young children are worse problem-solvers than adults because the former lack even the rudiments of the cognitive skills that the latter can apply regardless of problem-based constraints: rather children have cognitive processes that may be less fluent and may be applied in fewer contexts. Their problem-solving does seem to be more disrupted by increases in the complexity of a task, which might reflect the limitations in processing capacity hypothesised by some information-processing theorists (pp. 283–293). Children, and novices, may also be less practised than adults at the metacognitive activities that are helpful in problem-solving. They are less successful than adults at identifying the more and less important facts in a passage of prose (Brown 1994; Brown and Day 1983; Brown et al. 1984). As compared with experts they tend to rely on superficial features of the problem, not representing it in ways that use the essential information required to develop a solution, and spending an inadequate amount of time in planning how to attack the problem (Spilich et al. 1979; Chi et al. 1980; Larkin et al. 1980; Larkin 1983; Kuhn 1993; Kuhn et al. 1995). This makes for a more piecemeal approach: where experts apply relevant information and procedures in a co-ordinated way, novices are more likely to have to backtrack, or to set up sub-goals, and generally produce a less planned performance.

Improvement in planning involves improvement in recognising which features of the problem to consider, and hence in having a more helpful representation of the problem. It thus is inextricably confounded with the role of subject-matter knowledge. Experts' problem-solving in physics will resemble novices' if the expert is given a problem from an area outside his or her area of expertise, or if the novice is familiar with the type of problem (Voss 1989; Carey 1991; Gelman 1991; Case 1998; Klahr and MacWhinney 1998; DeLoache et al. 1998a and b). Nevertheless, experts and novices differ in how they organise the problem area. Novices sort problems mainly on surface features: experts are more likely to sort, and to understand their reading, in relation to more abstract laws and principles. Part of becoming 'expert', therefore, is developing a structured abstract knowledge of the area of expertise, a conceptual system adequate for solving its problems (Karmiloff-Smith 1992). Having two different representations, for example gestural ones that are more advanced than verbal representations, may facilitate development (Pine *et al.* 2004).

My discussion of problem-solving has emphasised that it requires both good representation of the problem, which involves the use of knowledge that may be specific to that domain (and indeed to that particular type of problem), and problem-solving strategies and procedures, which will also vary in how generally they can be applied. There is debate about whether there are general problem-solving strategies that can usefully be taught, or whether how problem-solving should be done is specific to particular subject domains. There clearly are strategies that can be applied in many different situations, for example analysing a problem into a sequence of sub-problems, seeking to reduce the difference between the present situation and the goal state, systematic testing of variables, finding analogies, and so forth, as well as less general strategies applicable only to a limited range of problems, for example methods for transferring unknown quantities from one side of an algebraic equation to the other without invalidating the equation. Both types of strategy are necessary, though to varying degrees for problems that differ in, for example, the degree to which they are well defined or to which they require the use of information from the domain beyond the problem. While problem-solving strategies can be taught (e.g. Brown 1994; Brown *et al.* 1983; Resnick 1987b; Voss 1989; Smith *et al.* 2000; Lawson 2003; Venville 2003; Georghiades 2004a, 2004b; Nickerson 2004; and Chapter 6), it seems to be crucial that they should be taught in those contexts where they are useful. Transfer of learning can be difficult and analogies may be misleading (Gentner 1977; Gentner and Gentner 1983; Case 1998; Klahr and MacWhinney 1998; DeLoache *et al.* 1998a and b; and see pp. 110, 120), because of the crucial role of the knowledge base required for the effective solution of problems. Good performance in solving problems of all sorts and at all levels requires an adequate knowledge base (and in many cases this means a substantial one). This base must be integrated with knowing how to use such knowledge in both strategies that are widely applicable and strategies that are specific to a particular problem. Thus a considerable amount of learning from relevant experience lies behind problem-solving ability.

Children meet 'problem-solving' situations both in psychologists' experimental set-ups and in their daily lives. In the real world other people often mediate between the child and the problem, and conversations can provide evidence of the child's reasoning (Hickling and Wellman 2001). Parents often adjust the task for their child so as to make it more likely that it will be solved successfully: Vygotskian theory does a great deal to elucidate this (see Rogoff (1998) and Chapter 4). Sometimes the other person may be an active collaborator on the task; Garton (2004) examines this thoroughly. She points out the importance of a fine-grained analysis of the social interaction in which the problem-solving is embedded.

The participants in a problem-solving collaboration may differ in what they bring to the task. Levels of expertise have been a focus of attention, partly because of the argument between Piagetian theorists and Vygotskian theorists about the role of teaching in cognitive development (see Chapter 4). The social dynamics of the partnership affects the outcome (Azmitia 1988; DeLoache *et al.* 1998a and b; Rogoff 1998; Garton 2004), but on the whole in most research studies the less expert problem-solver is more likely to move towards the more expert individuals' ideas than the reverse. Piagetian theory, which emphasises the role of intra-individual debate, interprets this as the less expert individuals recognising the superiority of the other's solution and adopting it as their own if they think of their partner as rather like themselves; though if the partner is an adult the authority relation may be too salient for the learner to fully adopt the better solution or way of thinking. In Vygotskian theory, learners are less insistent on pulling themselves up by their own bootstraps, and show more willing-ness to learn ideas and skills slightly more advanced than their own. Both bodies of theory would predict that explanation of the better solution may be an important contribution to whether it is engaged with by both partners, and indeed this is important. Collaborative problem-solving in which participants have to explain what the other person thought seems to produce particular advances in solutions; something similar seems to be the case in discussions in theory of mind tests (see pp. 110–115).

The social situation of problem-solving, and the social skills of the problem-solver, may affect its success. Bonino and Cattelino (1999) assessed children's level of 'cognitive flexibility', their ability to suppress their initial preferred response and consider another person's viewpoint. The children were given a task that needed co-operation if it was to be completed successfully. Children who showed a high level of cognitive flexibility were better able to take turns and to work co-operatively with their partners rather than competing with them. Garton (2004) reviews a number of studies comparing children who differ in their sociability or friendliness. Children who are good friends with their partner may find it easier to co-ordinate their plans and actions, to explain what they want to do, and to resolve conflicts. More sociable children benefit from the opportunity to discuss the problem and communicate their ideas; less sociable children may work in parallel and depend on themselves for new ideas rather than profiting from their partner's. Again, overt discussion of why a partner's solution works, or why the partners may have thought it would succeed when it didn't, seems to be an important part of making progress.

2.8 Metacognition

'Metacognition refers to one's knowledge and control of the domain of cognition' (Brown *et al.* 1983: 106); 'metacognition refers to cognitions about cognitions or the executive decision-making process in which the individual must both carry out cognitive operations and oversee his or her progress' (Meichenbaum *et al.* 1985: 4–5). It involves many basic 'on line' metacognitive processes, including: analysing and defining the character of the problem at hand; reflecting upon one's own knowledge (and lack of knowledge) that may be required to solve the problem; devising a plan for attacking the problem; checking and monitoring how the plan helps in the problem-solving; revising the plan (and perhaps the analysis of the problem) in the light of this monitoring; checking any solution reached; and, generally, orchestrating cognitive processes in relation to the cognitive contents and objectives involved, in the service of whatever is one's goal. It includes a range of somewhat diverse psychological contents. Among them would be: awareness of present cognitive and cognitive–emotional states, for example that one has understood, that one had forgotten some necessary information or that one was finding this all rather easy, at the present moment; knowledge about the particular task and its difficulties, and of one's own skills in general and in relation to this task; regulation of the execution of cognitive processes such as those listed earlier in this paragraph; and, importantly, linking the present metacognitive episode with others in the past, so building up a coherent model of oneself as a cognitive person, which is likely to have a significant influence on one's approach to future occasions in which metacognition is involved. One possible constituent linking cognition, emotion and personality here is attribution of credit or blame for success or failure between one's own skill, one's effort, task variables and extraneous conditions (Bandura 1995, 1997; Dweck 1999; Thompson 2004).

In the early 1980s metacognition took a prominent place in discussion of cognition and cognitive development. This was surely in part the result of the growth of information-processing work, where many theorists gave a central status to metacognitive or executive processes (pp. 279–295). Sternberg's work on intelligence, for example (Sternberg 1985, 1990; Sternberg and Kaufman 1998; and pp. 227–231), identified 'metacomponents', a number of key, fast acting, decision processes, as an important part of all knowledge acquisition and problem-solving. Case (1985) suggests that one of the three basic types of cognitive building blocks is 'executive schemes', which choose and monitor strategies and deal with their results. The later Piagetian model, too, emphasises cognitive development's roots in what could be called 'metacognition': both Piaget's account of the role of contradiction between schemes of thought and of conflict between different judgements by peers with different viewpoints, and his work on 'reflective abstraction', a sort of pondering about cognition (pp. 267–268), suggest that awareness and control of thought are important contributors to its development. Research on metacognition has looked at its role in memory (e.g. Kreutzer *et al.* 1975; Brown *et al.* 1983; Goswami 1998), reading (e.g. Meyers and Paris 1978), reasoning (e.g. Moshman 1998), communication (e.g. Markman 1977; Robinson 1983), intelligence (e.g. Veenman *et al.* 2004), giftedness (e.g. Alexander *et al.* 1995), consciousness (Zelazo 2004), mathematical problem solving (Pappas *et al.* 2003) and other areas (see Kuhn (2003) for a review). Some discussion of its role in these areas appears in the sections of this book that take them as their central topic. Here, I will focus mainly on some issues common to most metacognition.

The first is the nature of metacognitive experience, the awareness children have of their own cognitive processes. When do children know that they don't know something? What effect does such an experience have? When do they begin to have a notion of themselves as persons with particular cognitive abilities? Where does relevant experience come from? It is clear that even very young children have an awareness of an intended outcome and of whether it is achieved or not: their pleasure or frustration can be very visible (e.g. see Dunn 1988; Kagan 1984; Goswami 1998). Such awareness obviously does not always bring with it awareness of exactly what is wrong, nor is it always a lasting awareness. Similarly in later thought, children might be expected to be aware that there is a contradiction without knowing what to do about it, and without being able to take appropriate action (Piaget, 1978a, 1978b; Zelazo 2004). However, Piaget's position was that such awareness of an incipient or unsolved problem was unsettling for you, whether it was a contradiction between two of your own ideas or a conflict between one of yours and one of a peer's, and this 'disequilibrium' acted as a pressure towards advances in cognitive development. This is not always a trouble-free progress, since diagnosing that there is a problem is only the first step in the long path to solving it.

An experiment by Karmiloff-Smith and Inhelder (1974/5) illustrates the usefulness of having a theory, which requires a high level of metacognitive activity, in progressing towards a solution to a problem. They gave children aged from four to nine the problem of balancing blocks of wood on a narrow bar. Some were simple uniform slabs that balanced at the geometric centre; some had a less regular shape, with a conspicuous bar on one end; others had a heavy weight hidden in one end of an apparently uniform block. The children's simplest strategy was to use physical trial and error, nudging the blocks and rectifying any tilt until they found the balancing point; this was slow but successful for all blocks in the end. This purely 'suck it and see' strategy was, however, supplanted by simple theories that worked for some blocks and not for others. One such was to put the block with its geometric centre over the bar, which was successful for uniform blocks but not for those with an uneven distribution of weight. The latter were dealt with by nudging or by an alternative simple theory, so that the child operated two juxtaposed theories without co-ordinating them. Constructing a higher level procedure, which integrated the simpler theories and left no exceptions, was slow and costly in that it gave rise, while being developed, to more errors than its predecessors had done. Simple theories worked perfectly, though with a limited range of blocks; those blocks the theory couldn't cover were set aside as 'impossible to balance', until there was an intolerably large number of exceptions. Kuhn (1962) and other philosophers of science have observed that advance in scientific theory often is achieved in a similarly slow and painful way. Instances that cannot be dealt with by a theory are discounted or hived off; at best the theory is tinkered with to cover them, thus losing its coherence as it is stretched and patched to fit. Only with reluctance is it given up in favour of a new and better theory, perhaps when the results of metacognitive monitoring are too salient to be ignored any longer.

For scientists, and for children developing metacognitive awareness, disagreement with peers has been suggested as a source of metacognitive conflict and hence metacognitive advance. Conflict with peers was one of the few social factors behind cognitive development that Piaget focused on (Piaget 1983). Experiments by Genevans such as Doise and his colleagues (e.g. Doise 1985; Doise and Mugny 1984; elsewhere in this volume) address this area. Garton (2004) argues the importance of social interaction as the key to metacognition. Social interaction within the group of pupils, and metacognitive analysis skills, are features of some of the successful attempts to teach scientific thinking (e.g. Brown 1994; Adey and Shayer 1993; Adey et al. 2002; Smith et al. 2000; Lawson 2003; Venville et al. 2003, Georghiades 2004a, 2004b; Nickerson 2004).

Cultural input may influence children's metacognition. Li (2004), for example, interviewed Chinese and US preschoolers about 'learning'. US children often talked about ability, task attempting and strategy use, apparently seeing 'learning' as a task, while Chinese children placed more emphasis on diligence, persistence and concentration, 'learning' as a 'process of cultivating personal virtue' (Li 2004: 602). Each group of young children discussed success in learning and failure to learn in ways consistent with their own culture (Li 2003). Li suggests that the Chinese emphasis on learning as a personal moral duty may be part of the underpinnings of Chinese children's higher achievement; European American children who see learning as a task with less personal-moral importance may not invest as much in it.

Developmental research (Kuhn 2003) has shown that even young children have some metacognitive skills and that adults' metacognition sometimes lapses, but that it interacts with knowledge in complex ways. Mills and Keil (2004), for example, investigated children's awareness that their theory was not adequate. They asked children aged five to ten to explain how familiar household objects worked (for example, a toaster). All the children knew how to work these objects, and initially rated themselves positively as being able to explain how the object worked. A sample of adults had shown the same pattern of confidence. Once required to explain the workings of the objects, however, the self-ratings of children over seven (and of adults) fell, suggesting they now recognised that their initial confidence had been illusory. The youngest children did not reduce their self-ratings after the explanation had been given, which is similar to their tendency to believe they have memorised more than they really have, or that they would find it very easy to learn a long list of items (pp. 90–93). They may also have been less aware of the gaps and discrepancies in their accounts of the objects (pp. 54–55). This all suggests that young children need to become more accurate in knowing what they do not know, and some of the programmes for teaching thinking that have been produced (see Chapter 6) do, gently, try to help them to see where they have problems. But their failure to downgrade their view of their understanding might also be protective, as if, if they (or we) felt we should have complete explanations and detailed theories of everything but also knew just how many gaps and confusions there were, the result might be despair. What we normally have is 'folk theories' that work well enough; what we need is to be able to recognise when these are inadequate for our purposes, and how we might seek to improve them, or who we might consult for a better account (Danovitch and Keil 2004). Hilaire Belloc in the gleeful and gruesomely illustrated *Cautionary Verses*, which gave a lot of malicious pleasure to twentieth-century children, included one about an incautious peer, Lord Finchley.

> Lord Finchley tried to mend the electric light
> Himself. It struck him dead: And serve him right!
> It is the business of the wealthy man
> To give employment to the artisan.
> (Belloc 1940: 268–269)

Besides neglecting his social obligations, Lord Finchley perhaps had not distinguished clearly between his knowledge of how to switch the light on and his understanding of how it worked . . . With the beginnings of neuroscience models of metacognition that will allow us to identify the areas of electrical activity in the brain (Frith and Frith 2003; p. 345), we may have scientific as well as socioeconomic reasons to do better than him.

2.9 Children's musical cognition

Research on children's musical cognition presents a sort of microcosm of research on children's cognition in general. It includes an extensive body of work on individual differences in musical ability using psychometric techniques (Shuter-Dyson and Gabriel (1981) review this thoroughly); a body of work on developmental changes in the understanding of the structure of music (see for example Serafine (1988)) which is often heavily Piagetian; information-processing and psychophysical studies (Sloboda 1985; Deutsch 1982; Shuter-Dyson and Gabriel 1968/81); studies of musical taste and preference (see Hargreaves 1986; Macdonald *et al.* 2002; Lamont *et al.* 2002, 2003); and observational studies of children singing, dancing, playing instruments, composing and listening to music (e.g. Moog 1968/76; Hargreaves 1986; Swanwick 1988; Davidson *et al.* 1996). A recent article in *Nature* discusses the links between music, brain plasticity and the origins of emotion (Zatorre 2005). Clearly, music is too heterogeneous and too widespread to be summarised in the space I have available, and interested readers should go to an excellent review by D. J. Hargreaves (1986); Swanwick 1988 is also useful, though more educationally oriented. The existing variety of approaches is hardly surprising, given the heterogeneity of psychology and, more important, the complexity of music, which is obviously open to neurophysiological, psychophysical, cognitive, psychometric, sociological, aesthetic, anthropological and other approaches, all of them legitimate and not one of them comprehensive.

Musical abilities share basic processes, perhaps, with other cognitive skills and with language (Barwick *et al.* 1989; Trehub 2003). Like spoken language, music uses a relatively small number of rules that can generate an infinite number of compositions, and these can be transformed systematically – changed in speed or pitch or harmony or melodically, re-orchestrated, rearranged as another type of music, taken as the basis for a set of variations – without losing their original identity completely, as if there is a 'deep structure' however differently the 'surface structure' embodies it. Another similarity with spoken language is that most people attain basic musical competence in recognising, performing and even composing effortlessly (Patel 2003), just as they learn to speak effortlessly, though musical expertise and high-quality performance are rarer and achieving them is much more effortful. All cultures have music, songs and chants using repetition, rhythm, and specifically musical devices, most produce special types of music for children (Trainor 1996; Trehub 2003), and music is often closely linked to emotion.

Much of the evidence on the preschool years comes from a major study by Moog (1968/76). He carried out 'over 8,000' tests with 'nearly 500 children' and evaluated 'the observations of about 1,000 parents' (the English text was prepared for a music publisher, not a psychological one, and is intended primarily for practising teachers), and recorded examples of the children's own singing. Moog's data show babies from somewhat before the age of six months (prenatally, even, if mothers' experience of their foetuses' kicking is accepted) responding to music with active listening, pleasure and bodily movements, and a little later to indulge in 'musical babbling', sounds of varied and somewhat indeterminate pitch, mostly descending in melody but covering quite a wide range, and not imitations of songs they have heard. More recent studies show a response to the loudest part of a musical piece (Brahms' Lullaby, so probably not very loud) as early as twenty-eight weeks of gestational age, with sustained increased heart rate, suggesting sustained attention, by thirty-three weeks (Kisilevsky et al. 2004); my daughter, at about thirty-five weeks of gestational age, responded to a broadcast of the Last Night of the Proms with something that felt uncommonly like a hornpipe. Sixty per cent of Moog's twelve-month-old babies responded to music with musical babbling or singing of their own. At this age babies also showed definite likes and dislikes for Moog's sample material: they reacted positively to songs and rhythmic words, and also to instrumental music, but disliked non-musical sounds (twenty seconds each of a vacuum cleaner and traffic at a busy crossroads) and tapped-out rhythms. Unlike adults, some of them positively like cacophonous music (one instrument in a quartet playing a semitone higher or lower than the others, or four different melodies in four different keys played simultaneously).

More recent research by Trehub and her colleagues (Trehub 2003; Trainor 1996; Milligan et al. 2003; Bergeson and Trehub 1999) confirms and clarifies infants' interest in music and their early discrimination and preferences. This work also links music to the sounds of speech. Mothers' singing to infants exaggerates musical features such as melody and rhythm compared with when they are singing alone; infants prefer this sort of musical 'motherese' and pick up emotional expression in their mothers' songs – thus lullabies are especially soothing and play-songs especially jolly. What adults perceive as a 'loving' tone to the mother's music is particularly salient to infants. By six months of age, babies can perceive differences in pitch and timing as well as adults can, detect the consistency in a melody that has been changed only in pitch or tempo, and like and dislike the same musical intervals as adults. They remember both tempo and timbre (Trainor et al. 2004). While this could result from the exposure to ambient music they have had since birth (and from earlier than birth, as they hear in the womb and are born able to discriminate between familiar and unfamiliar music as well as familiar and unfamiliar speakers, pp. 8–9) the similarity of preferences across epochs and cultures suggests a brain-based preference and a wide power of discrimination that narrows to just the sort of music the child is exposed to, a development analogous to adults' loss of speech sound discriminations that were available to them in their infant years but were not used by the language they grew up to speak (Trehub 2003).

Between the ages of one and two, more children respond overtly to music, and movement to music in particular becomes important. Babies begin to beat time or clap to music, or to wish to join in musical games such as 'ring a ring of roses', and enjoy this as an important social action (Trevarthen 2002); they spin round to music, make regular stepping movements and eventually carry out dance movements with others. Some children under two are able to co-ordinate their movements with the music for a few bars, or to carry out dance movements with others, and some can manage to sing recognisable songs. Their spontaneous songs commonly contain a melodic phrase that is repeated with slight variations, for example three descending notes repeated at different pitch levels (Hargreaves (1986: 68–77) discusses some examples). They also have versions of standard songs: the earliest versions focus on distinctive words and the correct rhythm and pitch for the song usually come later. Imitating pitch seemed to be particularly hard, the general directions sometimes being followed with reduced intervals, or the imitation being kept up successfully only for a bar or so. Repetitive songs may be performed with the wrong number of repetitions: my daughter could produce a recognisable version of 'Happy Birthday' at eighteen to twenty-four months, but sometimes sang 'Happy birthday to you' only once before she got on to 'Happy birthday dear X' and sometimes seemed to get stuck into an unending repetition of the phrase. Songs with similar phrases may be compounded, or a bit of original melody interpolated, in what Moog calls 'pot-pourri' songs. The child's spontaneous composing of songs is becoming influenced by the standard repertoire, whose songs are more organised and more easily memorised than spontaneous songs. Hargreaves is among those who believe that children first develop a 'topological' grasp of the song, acquiring its global outline with its words and phrases and underlying pulse first, then its surface rhythm and its approximate pitch contours, with stable pitch and stable intervals following later. Early songs are not structureless, but it takes time for them to develop towards standard songs, particularly to move from 'floating' pitch to accurate reproduction of conventional tonal scales.

Moog's data and the subsequent studies reviewed by Hargreaves (1986: Chapter 3) show that by the end of the preschool period children possess many of the basic skills of musical perception and performance. This competence argues against the neo-Piagetian account of musical cognition which bases it on operational thought. Gardner (1973, 1983) has argued that musical intelligence is one of the multiple forms of human intelligence. Children at the beginning of formal schooling will have achieved an elementary understanding of the music of their culture, its basic harmonies, cadences, rhythms, and will be able to learn the culture's songs and compose culturally given motifs into their own independent compositions. Clearly much more musical acculturation and deliberate training occurs during the school years, the children's musical skills (including motor skills) become more fluent, and they develop their musical identities (Macdonald et al. 2002). Hargreaves (1986), Shuter-Dyson and Gabriel (1981) and

Davidson *et al.* (1996) review development in this period. Musical training, and musical experience, affect the development of musical skills such as singing in tune, discriminating pitches and processing melodies: amount of practice is a strong predictor of musical expertise (Radford 1990; Davidson *et al.* 1996; Ericsson 2003). Training and experience also affect preferences for different sorts of music; however more children listen to music than perform it (Boal-Palheiros and Hargreaves 2001). Studies of musical prodigies suggest that they usually come from a background where there is a lot of musical activity (Radford 1990; Borthwick and Davidson 2002; O'Neill 2002; Davidson *et al.* 1996), even that such children may in some cases be fulfilling a parental script.

Music is often very social; whether as performer or audience, it can involve the participation of hundreds or even thousands of people, and the sharing of excitement and emotion (Milligan *et al.* 2003). The availability of recorded music and electronic apparatus for making music has newly enabled it to be private, but for most of our history it has been embedded in the social world. It is used to entertain and to soothe infants (and other 'savage breasts'), and to engage them in turn-taking games; it is linked to dance; it can generate a sense of 'flow' (Csiksentmihalyi *et al.* 1993). Not surprisingly, the psychology of children's musical cognition cannot be reduced to a simple account of what develops and why. A lot more work is needed; let us hope that it is as rewarding as music itself.

2.10 Children's drawings

Children's drawings are often charming, sometimes beautiful. Producing them is fun for the child artist; interpreting them has been a matter of serious concern for the adult, whether therapist seeking to diagnose the child's inner conflicts and emotional states or more dispassionate psychologist wishing to discover how the child represents the world or how he or she combines perception and drawing to produce a picture. My concern here is to outline current psychological ideas about children's drawing processes as a subset of cognitive skills, and I will not discuss the use of drawings to diagnose or ameliorate children's emotional problems. Thomas and Silk (1990) and Golomb (2004) provide useful introductions to psychological theories of children's drawings and their relation to emotional and cognitive development. Karmiloff-Smith (1992) and DeLoache (2002, 2004) discuss children as users of symbolic representations.

The developmental sequence of drawing in childhood seems to be fairly clear. Drawing follows from babies' visual-motor exploration of the space within their reach (Golomb 2004). If the infant making the typical hand and arm movements (vertical stabs, sweeping horizontal arcs, and push out–draw back movements) is holding a crayon or a paintbrush then a visible trace will be left by these movements. The toddler's interest moves from making the movement to making a visible trace of it. During their second year of life children show an increasing interest in making marks on paper, becoming absorbed in making 'scribbles' that are not aimless and uncoordinated movements but are frequently positioned so that a degree of visual balance is achieved. Gradually deliberate shape-making emerges – lines from side to side of the paper come to be supplemented by dots, circles and zig-zags as the child's motor control improves. These earliest scribbles are probably not intended to be representational; the child is strongly interested in the marks that appear on the paper and may vary them or place them systematically, but they are the result of what Arnheim (1956) calls a 'motor impulse', not of an intention to draw a representation of an object or event. Children's first assertions that their drawings represent something tend to be *post hoc* interpretations: a fortuitous squiggle is pointed out as being, say, 'a rabbit', though no intention to draw a rabbit was announced before the drawing was begun. The claim to have done a representational drawing sometimes seems to be opportunist, and indeed even if the intention to draw 'a rabbit' was announced early on, the interpretation of the shape that is actually produced may be very flexible (Freeman 1987). Such changes in interpretation are not of course unknown in adults' doodles or other informal drawings, even when the adult is a considerable artist such as Picasso!

Early representational drawings show characteristic problems in achieving a realistic image. Drawings of human figures, for example (Freeman 1988; Cox 1993), often appear to be based on a simple formula, initially a 'tadpole' figure where a circle with facial features inside it represents the head or head and body, and dangling lines the legs and arms. Such formulaic drawings are perhaps convenient symbols rather than attempts at realistic representations (Barrett and Light 1976). It has to be noted that the culture's conventional representations of objects influence children's drawings from very early on: houses with a central door, four square windows, a gabled roof and a smoking chimney dominate the drawings of people whose own homes look nothing like that.

Children's formulaic drawings have been interpreted as showing how they represent the world mentally, revealing their feelings about and understandings of what they see. Thus the drawer of tadpole figures is accused of having a distorted 'body image'. Norman Freeman (1975, 1980, 1987, 1988, 1995) has argued that this is an unreasonable and unnecessary inference. Task demands may get in the way of expressing what one knows. The child's mental representation has to be accessed, and young children may need prompts more than older ones do, as is the case for many of the other cognitive skills discussed in this chapter. The physical demands of producing a drawing are also formidable and may push unskilled artists into the use of formulaic shapes even when they know better. Drawings have to be constructed step by step, and decisions at earlier stages affect what can be done at later ones. Thomas and Silk (1990) consider the process of constructing a drawing, and note a number of different problems of planning, positioning and alignment. Both perceptual and performance biases may be of influence. For example, young children typically construct their pictures from a limited 'vocabulary' of forms, notably circles and short lines, while more mature drawers often use an outline that continues round the whole shape to be drawn. Fenson (1985) suggests that outlining avoids artificially segmenting objects into simple component shapes and thus the problem of recombining them, and that it may also make it easier to represent objects from more varied perspectives. Manuals teaching drawing to adults (e.g. Edwards 1979) may seem to contradict Fenson's suggestion, in that they often prescribe drawing by putting together simple shapes rather than using outlining, but the 'simple shapes' have to be based on retinal image rather than on conceptualised formulae.

Watching children drawing reveals a number of biases in their approach to deciding how to do a drawing (Goodnow 1977; Golomb 2004). They commonly start drawing near the top of the paper and move from left to right (regardless of the direction of writing in their culture), and such preferences as these may go some way towards explaining such phenomena as why the majority of children in the West start their drawings of people with the head (Freeman 1980; Thomas and Tsalimi 1988; Cox 1993). Freeman also suggests that children may show a tendency towards 'end-anchoring': the end-items in a series are often recalled better and dealt with better than less conspicuously placed intermediate items, hence a preference for drawing heads and legs over mid-body features such as torso and arms, and for eyes and mouth on faces rather than noses. In tadpole figures the body parts are usually produced in the order head, legs, and finally (if at all) arms, which are more often joined on to the head than the legs. If a body is also provided, tadpole drawers add the arms to the larger of the two: if the head is larger than the body it attracts the arms, if it is smaller the arms are, more conventionally and more correctly in anatomical terms, added to the body. Freeman sees this as an instance of children's problems in organising lines on the page, in handling the interaction between what is already on the page and what is still to come. To produce a representational drawing of even moderate complexity, children have to decide in what order they will draw the component parts, position each so that space remains for later parts, and draw each so that it can be joined on to other elements appropriately. They have to represent three-dimensional objects on a two-dimensional space, leading to problems of representing depth and occluded objects (Ghent-Braine et al. 1993; Klaue 1992). They typically run into problems of not leaving enough space, separating elements completely instead of positioning one appropriately inside the boundaries of another, having to distort a late-drawn item because an earlier one occupies the same space, aligning one element with another rather than with the edge of the sheet of paper, and deciding what to do about parts of an object that are actually hidden by other parts. Freeman (1980; 1988), Golomb (2004), and Thomas and Silk (1990) see these sorts of production problems as being a major cause of 'childish' drawings of tadpole people, 'object-centred' and 'transparent' pictures where, for example, a man seen in profile has two eyes, failures of scale (Silk and Thomas 1986, 1988), difficulties with occlusion and with representing what the viewer sees as well as knows (e.g. Crook 1984, 1985; Light and Humphreys 1981), and difficulties over depth and perspective (e.g. Ingram and Butterworth 1989; Willats 1977). The classic explanation has been in terms of cognitive inadequacies such as 'intellectual realism' rather than production difficulties; children are inclined to draw what they know is there, so that in a drawing of a horse and rider facing left the rider's right leg may be drawn in, although it would really be hidden by the horse's body. What children draw rather than leave out is affected by their knowledge of the object or event they are drawing, their interpretation of what aspects of it are important (Golomb (2004) shows that instructions to emphasise a body part, such as 'draw a man holding a flower', lead children to far more sophisticated drawings of the salient body part), and their capacity to handle the demands of presenting the information (Nicholls and Kennedy 1992; Golomb 2004). Failure to recognise particularly the last of these has contributed to an under-estimation of what information young children can represent. It is now suggested that 'inadequacies' in their drawings should not be attributed to conceptual limitations but rather to difficulties of execution or to prefer-ences for doing particular sorts of drawings; it is interesting that savant artists do not seem to share these formulaic preferences and produce far more visually accurate drawings (Selfe 1977, 1983; Hermelin 2001). Again, performance is seen as being constrained by experience: drawing may be another cognitive skill where real developmental changes are ultimately mixed up with practice effects, and where education can play an important role. Golomb (2004) includes an example of this in the artwork of a Chinese girl, daughter of an artist, who from a very early age produced beautiful brush drawings that combine childish exuberance, lively and balanced composition, and mastery of brush strokes, in the tradition of Chinese painting.

2.11 Children's spatial cognition

As in other areas of cognition, there is some disagreement about the child's understanding of the layout and use of the environment, and the sources of whatever competence may be shown. Liben (1981) summarises the con-trasted epistemological positions taken by different theorists: the empiricist view that concepts of space are derived directly from experience with physical space and are to at least some degree isomorphic with it; the nativist view that, on the contrary, innate factors such as the organisation of areas of the brain determine how psychological concepts of space are organised (e.g. O'Keefe and Nadel 1978); and the constructivist view that individuals' activity develops their conceptual grasp of space. As in other areas, Piaget and his colleagues (Piaget and Inhelder 1956; Piaget *et al.* 1960a) made pioneering studies that have had a considerable influence on subsequent work.

A number of conceptual and methodological points need to be made before I describe the evidence on the development of spatial cognition. First, we may have to distinguish here (as elsewhere in cognition) between 'knowing how' and 'knowing that', between what Piaget called 'practical' space and Presson (1987) calls 'primary' space use on the one hand, and 'conceptual' space or 'secondary' space use on the other. The former is the capacity to act and move intelligently in space. It guides one's immediate orientation and action within the spatial world: there is incontrovertible evidence for considerable 'primary' competence in infants, chimpanzees, rats, pigeons and insects, who can in their varying ways reach for objects, avoid bumping into them, navigate from A to B or indeed from A to Z, and generally cope with living in the three dimensions of the revolving Earth. We have 'primary' space use because evolution has induced in us perceptual mechanisms and processes that specify where we are, orient our actions, monitor our movements and help us to predict their effects. These capacities and our early experience quite rapidly build up our sense of near space to form a working spatial memory for orientation and action. Obviously this primary spatial understanding is refined with more experience, and we may sometimes have difficulty in using it appropriately, but it is considerable and useful from early childhood or before.

'Secondary' spatial use involves the symbolic representation of an environment by the construction of a 'map' that can be used when one is absent from the actual environment. Competence at this is necessary for the drawing or reading of (literal) maps, and for tasks like mental rotation and perspective-taking. It is dependent on 'primary' understanding but goes beyond it; it has been thought to be specific to the human species (Presson 1987) but may not be (Suddendorf and Whiten 2001), and develops, as we shall see, over the years of childhood. It is complex and far more open to cultural influence than 'primary' understanding; cultures have developed tools specialised for spatial tasks (pictures, models, diagrams, blueprints, maps) and children have to learn to use these (Karmiloff-Smith 1992).

In examining the development of spatial cognition after infancy, therefore, we are mainly investigating children's mental representations of the environment. Methodological difficulties are likely to arise. The 'representation' called up when one has to draw a sketch map is likely to be different from what is produced by a request to give verbal directions; the former may display knowledge of spatial relations, the latter of a sequence of landmarks. Obviously different productions make different demands: inefficiency at drawing could make a sketch map a poor concrete representation of the mental representation, for example. Such production problems will (as in other areas) be particularly marked in children, who are less likely to be adequate artists or adequate verbalisers, as well as perhaps less able to make an adequate search and analysis of their mental maps. It may be wise to use several investigative techniques. Cousins *et al.* (1983), for example, used photograph recognition to assess knowledge about landmarks and routes and a pointer to assess estimates of direction, and also tested actual routes through the area in question.

Using a model environment, asking the child (for example) to assemble a scale model of his or her classroom or neighbourhood may be a useful technique (Weatherford 1982), but using models will itself be affected by the child's experience of models in general (DeLoache 2000; DeLoache *et al.* 1991, 1998a and b). However, it is likely to present fewer problems for the child than constructing a map by drawing. Matthews (1984, 1987, 1992) investigated children's knowledge of the areas around their homes using recall mapping, large-scale plans or an aerial photograph. Not surprisingly, the first of these techniques produced much less rich recall than the other two.

'Spatial cognition' is a broad term. Among the phenomena that psychologists have investigated are children's search strategies and their location of themselves and objects in space; children's use of landmarks and directions in their route-finding and knowledge of familiar areas (e.g. Cornell *et al.* 1989; Cousins *et al.* 1983; Gauvain and Rogoff 1986; Hart 1979; Matthews 1992); children's maps, both those they construct themselves and the more formal maps that they meet in school (see Anooshian and Young 1981; DeLoache 1987; Matthews 1984, 1992; Presson 1982; Uttal and Wellman 1989; Vasilyeva and Huttenlocher 2004); their use of formal map symbols (e.g. Matthews 1992; Somerville and Bryant 1985; Spencer *et al.* 1989); their understanding of models and pictures (DeLoache 1991, 2000; DeLoache *et al.* 1998b, 2004; Karmiloff-Smith 1992), children's knowledge of distant places, including their cosmological ideas (Siegal *et al.* 2004); and the extent of children's use of their own environment and how well fitted the environment is to such use (e.g. Hart 1979; Moore 1986). Such topics may be very relevant to social and political issues, such as how to provide facilities that will occupy children safely and usefully and so reduce injury and the sort of hanging around on street corners associated with minor delinquency (Coleman 1985; Rutter and Giller 1983), or how to encourage the knowledge and empathy necessary to act sensibly on questions of ecological damage or aid to developing countries, and of course to education. I will not try to cover these diverse areas here, referring the reader to the very useful reviews by Spencer *et al.* (1989) and Matthews (1992) in the first instance.

However, a couple of general points relevant to the acquisition and development of spatial cognition may be derived from the literature. It is clear that spatial cognition involves a complex variety of mental representations and processes, which may have a wide range of applications or be very task-specific. It has been suggested that there is a developmental sequence of spatial frames of reference, with the child's awareness and skills beginning with body image and body co-ordination and moving outwards to the immediate environment and then onwards to more distant spaces. It seems unlikely that any other direction could obtain: for example, that one could know about distant places if one knew nothing at all about near ones, even if directly experienced space was not restricted by the comparative immobility of infancy and the chaperonage supplied to children. However, as Pick and Lockman (1981) point out, although there may be an outward expansion of knowledge of this sort, it is clearly not the case that the more local frame of reference has to be fully mastered before any use or understanding of more distant ones begins. Knowledge and skills even of very close space can continue to be developed throughout life as an individual's tasks demand. One can be a somewhat clumsy person, without a highly sophisticated understanding of one's body's movements, but skilled at activities such as map-reading or orienteering, or vice versa; whether body-centred understanding is useful or a handicap depends on what the task is. Many tasks will require co-ordination of frames of reference, so that replacement of earlier schemes by later ones must be a matter of addition, not of superseding. Cultures differ in the frames of reference that they offer and this will affect the rate and the content of children's development of concepts of space, as Siegal et al. (2004) demonstrate for children's adoption of a heliocentric model of the world in the solar system.

Psychometric studies (e.g. Gardner 1983; Vernon 1972) have suggested that there is a component of intelligence described as 'spatial abilities'. One important 'ability' is 'spatial visualisation', that is, imagining how a pictured object would appear if rotated, inverted or otherwise manipulated, perhaps by mentally manipulating an image in this way. Another is 'spatial orientation', the ability to comprehend the relation between elements in a visual stimulus pattern without being confused by changes in the orientation of the stimulus. These abilities seem to be related to mathematical performance (more closely to geometry than to arithmetical computation, not surprisingly), and are seen as being implicated in sex differences in mathematical and technological performance (Linn and Peterson 1985; Maccoby and Jacklin 1974). It is, however, clear that there is little difference before adolescence, that the difference on some 'spatial understanding' tests is very small, that cross-cultural differences exist, and that girls and boys are often in receipt of different experience of space, boys being allowed to roam further afield and given more manipulative toys, so no conclusion about the innate superiority of one sex could be supported (see e.g. Matthews 1992). There do not seem to be marked sex differences in algorithms for processing spatial information (Carter *et al.* 1983) such as one might suppose would be involved if there were brain-based and unmodifiable sources of the sex differences, rather than differences of practice and exposure.

Majid *et al.* (2004) make the important point that spatial representations are often themselves represented using language. Particularly when communicating to other people about space, but also when solving a spatial problem ourselves, we may well use language to describe, analyse and reason. Thus cross-cultural differences in language about spatial relations may affect our cognition. If we are talking in English about the conventional table setting of cutlery on my kitchen table, we might say 'The fork is to the left of the spoon' (a 'relative' coding) or 'The fork is pointing at the bowl of the spoon' (an intrinsic coding; intrinsic codes often are related to function, for example if we say someone is 'in front of' the television we are likely to mean that they are facing the screen rather than merely between ourselves and the TV screen). We could say with equal truth that 'the fork is to the south-east of the spoon', but this would contravene our normal use of spatial terms – in ordinary English the absolute terminology of 'north' and the other compass points is reserved for talking about larger-scale geographical space, and we may not even be aware of the north–south orientation of our homes. If we spoke Guugu Yunithirr (Australia) we would only ever use absolute terms, and if we spoke Balinese we would prefer them to the relative terms that are also available. Relative terminology involves the position of the speaker as well as of the objects – and the confusion between spatial term and individual viewpoint that is so difficult for children arises. In absolute terminologies, the objects are relative to a fixed point that is independent of the speaker (the North Pole, or thereabouts); but the speaker has to know where the Pole is in order to use the terminology correctly.

Which set of language terms people use most readily to represent spatial relations seems to be associated with what their language makes available to them. (Additionally, rural cultures are more likely to use absolute terminologies than are urban ones; the relevance of north and south may be lessened by the urban environment, except perhaps for gardeners and estate agents, for whom it is of practical interest in terms of when the sun shines where.) The representation dominant in the language is also the representation that dominates when spatial relations are described in gesture. Children's acquisition of spatial language reflects the language of their culture. If that culture uses absolute terms, it may be that children begin to use them at somewhat younger ages than children learning languages more reliant on relative codings use relative terms such as 'left' and 'right' (Majid *et al.* 2004). But the evidence compares different children in the different cultures; we do not have a study of children growing up bilingual in an absolute and a relative language to assess how their spatial language, gesture and problem-solving developed.

The literature on the development of spatial cognition suggests that young children may show more competence than earlier researchers had concluded. A survey by Uttal and Wellman (1989), for example, investigated the development of the ability to acquire integrated knowledge of a space from a map in four- to seven-year-olds. The children memorised which animal lived in each room of a large playhouse from a map, and then navigated a route through the playhouse itself, during which they named the animal that lived in the room they were about to enter or were to the side of. Children aged six or seven did very well on the task, but even four- and five-year-olds succeeded to a degree that allowed the researchers to claim that the children had constructed a representation of the playhouse that captured the two-dimensional layout of spatial relations between the rooms. They were not dependent on a single landmark nor on a succession of points on a route, but had what might be called an 'integrated' or 'survey-like' representation (McNamara 1986). Of course in other situations we may use landmarks and route sequences to find the way (Allen et al. 1979; Cornell et al. 1989). The test did not demand precise information about quantitative aspects of the space and the children did not display such knowledge. Uttal and Wellman call their subjects' map-reading abilities 'impressive'. Similarly, DeLoache and her colleagues initiated a series of experiments (e.g. DeLoache 1987, 1991, 2000, 2004; DeLoache and Burns 1994; DeLoache et al. 1998a and b; Marzolf and DeLoache 1994; Troseth and DeLoache 1998; Robinson et al. 1994; Thomas et al. 1994; Suddendorf 2003) suggesting that young children have difficulties using representations such as photographs, video and models to locate objects in real space. For example (DeLoache 1987), children just past their third birthdays were able to draw on their knowledge of where an object was hidden in a model of a room to find an object hidden in the real room; children aged 2½ could not reliably find the object in the real room using a model but could find it if they saw a photograph of the hiding place. This pattern of findings suggests that the two-year-olds' difficulty with the model, as a source of information about the place it represents, stems from having to treat the model as a representation of another place as well as a real object. Failing to think about a symbolic object (the model) as simultaneously both an object (a miniature room) and a symbol (of the real room), and preoccupied by the former, they did not generalise their experience of where hidden objects were in the model to the task of finding a hidden object in the real room. Their more extensive experience of pictorial representations meant that they were able to generalise appropriately from a photograph to the real world. The almost complete success of the three-year-olds in using the model as a representation suggests a rapid developmental change in 'representational insight' during the second half of the first year. Another study (DeLoache *et al.* 1991) examined what characteristics of the model are associated with better performance on the 'finding a hidden object' task, and found that physical similarity seems to be important. The medium of the representation is also important (DeLoache 1987, 1991, 2000; Marzolf and DeLoache 1994; Suddendorf 2003) and some of the children's errors are due to perseveration (Suddendorf 2003; Sharon and DeLoache 2003). However, young children sometimes have startling difficulties with model objects amounting to a 'perception–action dissociation' and suggesting brain development limits on their cognition. In a recent study (DeLoache *et al.* 2004), children aged between 18 and 30 months were introduced to objects in a playroom. Among them were a slide the child could slide down, a chair they could sit on, a car they could sit in and propel with their feet. After the children had played at least twice with each of these, they were escorted from the room and a miniature slide, chair and car were substituted for the real-size ones. The child was then returned to the room and videotaped while playing with the miniature toys. Almost half of these children made at least one attempt to use the new miniature objects as if they were life-size, for example trying to slide down the miniature slide or to squeeze into the miniature car; this sort of scale error was especially likely in the children aged between twenty to twenty-four months. DeLoache *et al.* (2004) propose that the sight of a miniature replica triggered the child's representation of the category of real-size objects that the replica stands for. This representation of the category includes information on its affordances (Gibson 1979) and hence for the actions that can normally be carried out on category members. The children who make scale errors have activated the normal motor routine and their actions have not been inhibited by the visual information about the scale of the object, although this scale information has allowed them to adjust their movements to the size of the object (for example, by using a precise grip to open the door of the miniature car). These children have experienced a dissociation between their use of visual information for planning their actions and their use of visual information to control their actions.

It appears, then, that some of the difficulties very young children have in using scale models have to do with the models' activation of general schemas of concept and action and the difficulty young children have in inhibiting these. They may, similarly, try to use pictures of objects in the same way as they would use the object (DeLoache 2004). Brain maturation may underlie the rapid decrease in such difficulties between eighteen and thirty months. But using representations in general also involves learning the cultural tools that surround the child, often with the guidance of parents (Szechter and Liben 2004; Callaghan and Rankin 2002; Gauvain 2001; Liben 2003); cultural tools that are becoming more and more complex, flexible and powerful. Children have to use their mental representation of the representation (photograph, map, video or model) which is a representation of the real world. DeLoache speculates that this is a maturational development, and the capacity for such 'metarepresentation' has been linked to the emergence of a 'theory of mind' (see Anderson 1992; Perner 1991a). Spencer *et al.* (1989) agree that young children have difficulty dealing with models and suggest that toy play may improve their understanding. Perhaps each child should have a dolls' house resembling his or her own, or a model of the neighbourhood and the daily-used routes to shops, swings and school? Perhaps parents should desist from encouraging children to stroke the cat pictured in the picture book? As the culture we live in is developing more and more different media of representation and there is an enormous amount of exploitation of cultural symbols, we have both to become 'symbol-minded' and to be aware of how symbols can influence us.

2.12 Children's use of concepts

My concern here is with work on how children develop systems of concepts and how they are organised, with the general issue of conceptual thought in childhood. Work that describes the content of various conceptual areas is dealt with later; the focus here is on structure and process, via philosophical and psychological accounts of conceptual development.

2.12.1 Conceptualising concepts

Children and adults alike, we live in a world dazzlingly rich with unique objects and experiences; as the Chinese proverb says, we never step into the same river twice. But we naturally treat very similar objects, events and experiences as if they were the same, ignoring their uniqueness, because the world would be impossible to cope with if we did not. Without concepts we could not predict, could not remember, could not communicate, could not act appropriately with other people. The world that flows by us has to be generalised and organised if we are to survive.

The argument begins when we try to specify what sort of concepts we have, and how we get them. The notion I used in the previous paragraph was that of similarity. Objects and events are put into categories because they are similar to each other and different from objects and events that belong in different categories. This is the 'classical' theory of category representation: all the instances of a concept share common properties, which are necessary and sufficient for membership of that category. Thus in the world of playing cards, cards belong to the suit or category of hearts because they all bear one or more red heart-shaped symbols and represent a value between the ace and the king. Cards that do not have hearts on do not come into the hearts category, though they may be members of other categories, for example spades, court cards, part of my winning hand, useful bookmarks, etc.

This model of what concepts are has two assumptions that need to be questioned (Lakoff 1987). The first is that since categories are defined by properties that all members share, no members are better examples of the category than others – 'a rose is a rose is a rose', perhaps. Second, since categories are defined by properties that are inherent in each member, they are independent of the peculiarities of categorisers: there exists in the real world a 'true', objective category of red things, for example, and my category of red things is a fairly representative sample of the true category while that of a red–green colour-blind person would be a poorer approximation. Concepts are assumed to be abstract and disembodied, independent of people, eternal, unchangeable, really 'out there' to be discovered, largely by the identification of common properties or similarities. All of this we will question, and limit.

'Similarity' may seem an obvious and straightforward basis for organising concepts, even a natural one, and in many cases it is. However, closer analysis reveals some philosophical and psychological difficulties. In the first place, any two entities could have an infinite number of properties in common. Take, for example, a beetroot and the *Mona Lisa*. Both weigh more than 1 gram and less than 2,000 kilograms; both contain vegetable matter; I am not going to buy either; I thought of them both a moment ago when trying to invent as dissimilar a pair of entities as possible; and so forth. It may not be obvious which attributes of entities are important; and it might be still less obvious to a naïve observer, such as a child, than to an adult experienced at categorising.

Rather than relying on similarity of surface attributes, we may say things are the same because they share an 'essence' or crucial nature that may not be obvious on the surface. 'Essential' characteristics are shared by all members of the category and only by members of that category, and they play a causal role both in conferring identity and in giving rise to the other surface characteristics of members of the category. 'Essentialist' concepts may be emotionally laden. The campaigners for the abolition of slavery used the slogan 'Am I not a man and a brother?' The essence of being a 'man' here is to do with having an immortal soul, or with empathy, of being a 'brother' is both shared humanity and closeness. In another context being a man might be about having the right DNA, being a brother about being the male child of a couple who had other children as well. These examples suggest that 'essence' is a cultural construction, dependent on knowledge base and all sorts of subjective preferences. Nevertheless, as we will discuss, children and adults do use essentialism in their categorisations.

Essentialism is stringent in insisting on a common quality. But there are also many concepts where not all members share all the relevant properties.

Philosophers have amended the classical theory of necessary and sufficient properties and suggested that properties are characteristic of instances, that instances of a concept probably have the relevant properties but sometimes may not. Some instances will have more of the relevant properties and others will have fewer. Take the concept of 'chair', for example. People agree, on the whole, that chairs normally have a seat and back and legs, and can be sat on: some have arms, some cushions; some are made of wood, some of metal; they vary in size and location and comfortableness. There are certain marginally acceptable instances of 'chairs': deckchairs, for example, or stacks of cushions, or car seats, or the coronation chair in Westminster Abbey. Not everything that we could sit on would be categorised as a chair: it would be eccentric to call a bicycle saddle a chair, and a patch of grass would only be a chair in a rather fey poetic context. Concept members may even have 'family resemblances', such that two particular individual members may have no properties at all in common but each has some of the wide variety of properties that characterise the concept. Games are a good example; some games are competitive, but not all (hide and seek versus ring-a-ring-of-roses), some but not all involve skill (chess versus snakes and ladders), some but not all involve vigorous physical activity (tennis versus Consequences), some but not all are fun, or important. Because of such issues, it has been suggested that concepts are probabilistic. We might in principle be able to arrange instances of a category according to gradations in their probableness, better instances having more characteristic properties than worse ones. However, this suggestion of 'linear separability' seems to be too simple a measure of the psychological structure within a concept: the instance with all four relevant properties is not seen as being twice as good as that with two, or four times as good as that with only one. It is also true that in many cases the relevant properties are not independent and so cannot be simply summed: birds have two legs partly because they have wings, for example, and the feathers, light bones, strong breast muscles and so forth are correlated attributes all necessary for flight. Again we need some sort of principle to explain which attributes are most relevant and important; and again it seems possible that which these are will depend on the context. Most people agree, for example, that car seats could be classified as 'chairs', and that the category of 'chairs' belongs within the superordinate category of 'furniture'; but they would not include car seats as instances of furniture (Hampton 1990).

2.12.1.1 Basic-level concepts

Considerations like these suggest that there might be better and worse exemplars of categories and more or less 'basic' categories. Using a combination of similarity within instances of a category and dissimilarity with non-instances and with members of other categories may help. Rosch *et al.*

(1976) call the categorisation level where such similarity and difference are highest the 'basic' level, as they believe it is the core level of the categorisation system. Basic-level categories are relatively easy to recognise, recall and name, using as they do distinctive overall shape and motor interaction, and being at the most general level where a coherent mental image is possible. Classical taxonomic categories, in contrast, involve an 'achievement of the imagination'. This probably does not resolve the problem completely. In order to use both similarity and difference and end up with cohesive categories there have to be some principles that determine what is relevant and important: we will look at possible principles later.

Rosch's model (Rosch et al. 1976) is also a 'prototype' theory of categories. Some category members are 'prototypes' or 'cognitive reference points'. People consistently rate these as best examples, recognise them and judge them to be true category members particularly fast, produce them more often when asked to think of category members, generalise more readily from prototypical member to non-prototypes than the reverse, and so forth (e.g. Rosch 1978). Both prototypes and less prototypical members are equally truly members of the category – penguins and emus are just as much birds as sparrows are – but there are structural distinctions within categories that are as important as the specific defining properties that classical concept theory picked out.

One major work concerned with basic categories looked at words for colours (e.g. Berlin and Kay 1969). They found that although different languages divided colours in different ways, there were basic colour categories with the same 'best instances', and the terms used for them formed a hierarchy. The simplest basic terminology was to name 'black' or 'cool' colours (black, green, blue and grey) in contrast with 'white' or 'warm' colours (red, orange, yellow and white). The third basic colour term was always the equivalent of 'red', differentiated out from the 'warm' category; yellow, green and blue were equally probable as the next distinction. Boundaries between categories varied from speaker to speaker, but the best or 'focal' colours were the same for all speakers, whatever language terms they habitually used. Thus if the language had only one basic word ('bleen') for the range that English describes as 'blue' and 'green', the focal colour in the 'bleen' range would not be a bluey-green or turquoise but either the blue that English speakers regard as a good blue or the green that they see as prototypical green. Neurophysiological sensitivity seems to underlie these particular foci.

In prototype models, instances of a category need not have specific defining properties: the category is represented by examples and new instances are included if they are sufficiently similar to existing members. Unlike the 'classical' and 'probabilistic' theories, this suggests concept learning that could begin with instances whose properties are not clearly defined, as they probably are not for naïve or young learners, but it runs into the same problem of what 'similarity' is, and which ways of being 'similar' are relevant and important.

Characteristics may also differ in their obviousness for different concepts or levels of concepts. Redcurrants are all small, red and globular; fruit, though like redcurrants edible, seed-containing, etc., varies very much in perceptual characteristics. In the case of abstract social concepts such as 'justice' or 'liberty' there is such difficulty in either finding sound defining characteristics or comparing each new and unique case with a prototype that we may do better to regard the concept as being comparable to an elaborate theory that is used to explain examples rather than to match them.

We have seen, then, that focusing on similarity as constituent attributes of concepts leads to a lack of attention to questions about how concepts are structured, in their relations to other concepts but also in the internal organisation of elements and their characteristics within the structure itself. I mentioned earlier, for example, that characteristics may be correlated or variably important; they may also be in particular specified relations to each other. Medin and Wattenmaker (1987) and Murphy and Medin (1985) address this problem.

2.12.1.2 Theory

Medin and Wattenmaker (1987) and Neisser (1987) explicitly argue for the importance of 'theory' in the acquisition and coherence of concepts, and specify that developmentally the 'theory' is unlikely to be one of matching up perceptual characteristics in any simple fashion. They believe that a great deal of the person's accumulated world knowledge is incorporated and used in ways that fit the immediate context. Thus, for example, Medin and Wattenmaker suggest that only rarely will the characteristic 'inflammable' be linked to money, as money is used in other ways in our usual economic theories. A person who has encountered an eccentric and vulgar tycoon who lights his cigars with spills made of banknotes, or has heard it remarked of a teenager that her first wages are burning a hole in her pocket, may make a stronger link between this attribute and instances of money, but it is not likely to become a central part of the normal theory.

This example may already have suggested that perhaps we would be wrong to assume (as the classical work on concepts has done) that concepts are completely static. Barsalou (1987, 1989) has argued that, on the contrary, concepts are to a considerable degree unstable. The local context affects how a concept is represented: we don't normally think of pianos being heavy until we have a furniture-moving context, to give another example of the 'money is inflammable' type, and we regard robins as more typical birds than swans are if we are Americans reporting our own culture's judgement, but swans as more typical birds than robins if we are

Americans reporting the supposed viewpoint of the average Chinese citizen. We can also readily construct *ad hoc* categories to fit the moment's need, for example a category of 'things we must take on our visit to Granny'. Barsalou's view is that concepts have a core of stable context-independent information as well as information dependent on the current context or on recently encountered contexts, in a comparatively loosely organised system. This sort of reconstitutive conceptual system, with particular bits of information or particular criteria in play or not depending on the immediate context, is roughly what the connectionist models of cognition suggest (McClelland *et al.* 1986; Rumelhart and McClelland 1986). Part of what children have to learn is the contexts in which particular concept systems will be useful, and where an alternative might work better (Danovitch and Keil 2004).

Concepts are now largely agreed to be embedded within theories (Johnson *et al.* 2004); so the same issues recur on this higher level. Theories influence which aspects of specific concepts people attend to in a particular task, and constrain decisions about similarity relationships and about patterns of reasoning. Theories, like concepts, may be more or less simple and more or less coherent. Simplicity, or 'parsimony', has often been invoked as a hallmark of the good theory, but there are problems here as there were at the level of attributes of concepts. If two theories are equally accurate in their picture of the same data and relate equally well to other theories, then it is reasonable to prefer the more parsimonious; but what if the simpler theory can only cope with a smaller range of data, or if it is discrepant with wider theories of the world? A belief in extra-sensory perception (ESP), for example, provides a simple explanation for a range of phenomena that we otherwise cannot explain; but it fits rather badly into the wider frameworks of physics and of psychology, which, though imperfect, probably could provide more complex if less exciting accounts of paranormal phenomena. We do not yet understand very well how people develop or choose between theories (we know they will probably have particular difficulty dealing with evidence that negates their theory (Kuhn 1962; Wason 1977; Wason and Johnson-Laird 1972; p. 105)), even if they are professional scientists. It does seem possible, however, that it has been a matter of evolutionary adaptiveness for successful theories to arise from the interaction of an intelligent and purposive organism with the perceptual world (see e.g. Lakoff 1987). The point I want to make here is that theories and concepts are likely to imply causes, relations and usefulnesses to the organism, not just to map attributes, and they are likely to vary according to the context. Developmentally and cross-culturally, this suggests a rather different account of children's concepts from the ones that dominated the field until quite recently, an account that does not so much supplement the traditional view as revalue it (and also highlights the importance of looking at the development of choice between conceptual systems, e.g. Danovitch and Keil (2004)).

2.12.2 The development of concepts

Young children have been seen by many investigators as being rather inept at concept formation and concept use. The classic work of Vygotsky (1962, 1978a) and of Inhelder and Piaget (1964) was taken as showing that they were unable to form stable and coherent sortings of objects that were consistent in their use of defining characteristics. I will give a brief description of some of the evidence that apparently justified this view, before reviewing recent work showing greater competence in categorisation, and discussing this in terms of the shift in our theories about concepts that I outlined in the first part of this section.

In several pieces of research, children were given objects and asked to sort them out into a number of discrete classes. The central material Vygotsky (Vygotsky 1986; Kozulin 1990) used, for example, was a set of wooden blocks that varied in shape, colour, height and area; Inhelder and Piaget (1964) used blocks varying in shape and colour. Typically young children did not appear to pick out blocks of the same shape, colour and so forth in any systematic way. The youngest children seemed to be arranging blocks in patterns that pleased them, rather than classifying them, so making what Piaget and Inhelder called a 'figural collection', or using some diffuse and subjective feeling of 'these go together'. At a slightly later stage a few blocks were picked in succession that were alike on some criterion, for example colour; but before all the blocks of that colour (say red) had been picked out, the child appeared to switch criteria and pick out a few more blocks that were the same shape as the last red block. After a few chosen by shape, and again before the criterion had been applied throughout the set, they might switch a second time, sorting by a new criterion or reverting to colour. Such sorting seemed to involve 'chain complexes' where one object led unsystematically to the next, and the experimenters' interpretation would be that the child had no overall plan for sorting the set.

Later still, one criterion might be applied to all the objects so that they were sorted into mutually exclusive groups on the basis of, for example, being the same colour. But there is no abstract rule and the child would not construct groups on the basis of other criteria such as shape, either as an alternative sorting or as subclasses within the different colours. Making a co-ordinated use of the less salient criteria of height and area to sort the Vygotsky blocks, ignoring shape and colour, was quite a late achievement. So is the proper use of negative evidence (Kuhn 1962; Wason 1977; Wason and Johnson-Laird 1972). In Vygotsky's work, pre-adolescents who might appear to be grouping objects using truly conceptual reasoning (for example sorting by colour), when faced with the revelation that two objects that had been put together because they were the same colour actually belonged to different categories, would react only by tinkering with these objects' place in the sorting, not seeing that this evidence disconfirmed their hypothesis that colour was the correct basis for sorting. Vygotsky said such behaviour involved the use of 'pseudoconcepts', apparently rule-governed and often labelled exactly as true concepts would be, but not properly formed, not properly understood and problematic in various ways, not least in the possibility that they are talked about and used parrot-fashion.

Pseudoconcepts have their developmental place, Vygotsky argued, because children who use them, even though they do not understand them, will get positive responses from adults who see the child behaving as they themselves would do and assume that the child's understanding is as advanced as his or her behaviour. The child becomes aware of his or her cognitive operations only after the practice of these operations is 'endorsed' by others: human cognition is a social construction. Adult and child may act alike and talk alike but have different underlying types of concept and conceptual reasoning. The child, being a language learner, develops conceptual complexes that are to a considerable degree predetermined by the meaning particular words already have in the language of adults. Because children need to function and communicate adequately, they seek to understand and to talk as adults do, taking on ready-made meanings without necessarily understanding their conceptual basis.

Children's ability to form and use concepts, it was concluded on the basis of findings like these, was rudimentary until somewhere around school age. Since about 1970 this sort of conclusion has come under an increasingly intense and successful attack in many areas of cognition (as much of the rest of this book shows). In the case of children's concepts, a major contribution was made by work on language development and by changes in theories of the nature of human concepts. If children in their second year could understand and use verbal labels for concepts like 'dog' and 'fruit' in ways that resembled adult usage (though the resemblance was not exact), they were showing some ability to acquire and use concepts in their everyday lives. As cognitive psychology started to examine real-world concepts instead of the tightly defined artificial material that had dominated the field, so theories of concepts that did not go beyond clearly defined necessary and sufficient attributes became more obviously inadequate. Rosch's work on basic-level categories suggests that basic-level categorisation may be easier than superordinate or subordinate categorisations, and early negative conclusions about children's categorisation capacities might have relied too heavily on tasks requiring superordinate-level categorisation (Rosch *et al.* 1976). Instead of looking at attribute-based sorting of objects with low ecological relevance (neither salient in the child's experience nor easily related to other objects that might have been salient), investigators looked at a wider range of behaviour and material. As a result they found competences in young children that had not been obvious in the classic experiments.

Sugarman (1981, 1983), for example, gave children aged between twelve and thirty-six months a number of tasks involving two groups of small identical objects. She looked at the sequence in which objects were manipulated and the way they were arranged in space. At twelve months the children manipulated items from the same group, selecting them sequentially, though they did not make separate spatial arrangements of groups. Older children did arrange the groups separately, picking out one group by eighteen months and by thirty to thirty-six months being able to shift from group to group while they sorted. More recently (Fivush 1987; Mandler 2004a) Jean Mandler and Robyn Fivush made a similar analysis of what fourteen- and twenty-month-old infants did with objects that were not identical but were groupable in terms of whether they were used when eating or when washing. Here too infants touched objects from the same group sequentially, more than half of even the younger group touching at least three of the four objects from one group sequentially. None of this can be taken as suggesting that infants can categorise like adults, but these and similar studies (see Clark 1983; Gelman and Baillargeon 1983; Smith 1989b; Hespos and Spelke 2004) do show classification in infants; infants are also quite demonstrably capable of recognising a new instance of an important and familiar category, such as feeding bottles, and treating it as similar to previous encountered instances.

I mentioned earlier that categories can be formed at a variety of levels of specificity and inclusiveness and that it seemed to be useful to think of there being 'basic-level' categories (Rosch and Lloyd 1978; Rosch et al. 1976; p. 151). Rosch has argued that basic-level categories are early developers, and basic-level object names do seem to be predominant among children's early words (Clark 1983; Mervis 1987; Rosch et al. 1976; p. 14). Roger Brown (1958) describes the actions that typically accompany early labelling: flowers are smelled, balls bounced, pussy-cats stroked. Actions as well as labels differentiate between categories. The basic level for parents' labelling, like that for colours, has the shortest names, is used earliest and most frequently, feels 'natural', and involves distinctive actions. Although adults' talk to young children tends to present basic-level labels, the child does not necessarily pick up what are the relevant criteria or what other instances are members of the same category (Mandler 2004). They may attend in particular to criteria of shape and function, though adult labels in conjunction with concrete examples will eventually be helpful in the development of adult-type categories.

Children's over-extensions (pp. 13–14) often apply a basic-level term to instances that are actually from an adjacent class, usually one with similarities of appearance, and a member of the same superordinate category (for example, cats somewhat resemble dogs in appearance and both are animals). This sort of usage might be taken as implying that the user 'knows', in some sense, that there is a relationship between the two basic-level categories via the superordinate category; or it might be attributable to the child's sense of the social obligations of discourse, so that he or she uses an over-extension when the correct label is not available but some sort of label is required. Once an appropriate label is available (either the correct basic-level label or a high-level general one such as 'thingummy') there will be fewer over-extensions. Young children certainly feel a strong desire to communicate, and this is one of the strongest determinants of language use and development. In so far as basic-level categories really do both pick out correlated attributes that take similar values within categories and differentiate instances from other categories, that is, as they break down the world into really useful units, they will facilitate both the child's communication and his or her understanding and use of information (Waxman and Hatch 1992).

How do children abstract common features from the instances they encounter? One theory (Clark 1973) was the semantic feature hypothesis. This assumed that meanings or concepts break down into combinations of perceptual (and conceptual) units. Children beginning to use words only have parts of the full adult meaning available. The development of meaning involves adding further conceptual units until the child's meaning matches the adult meaning. Thus the theory predicts that children will produce over-extensions (as they do); that if two words share several semantic features the child may confuse them in both comprehension and production (as they do 'more' and 'less', for example); that if one word adds extra semantic features to another it will be learned later ('boy' should and does precede 'brother'); that children should learn more general semantic features earlier than specific ones and that they will learn combinations of features word by word, not necessarily realising how they apply to related words.

Clark (1983) criticises her 1973 theory. It does not deal with the question raised very early in this section of what semantic features, what attributes, will be salient or decisive. Children seem to prefer contrastive features, those that mark within-category similarities and between-category differences, as if they assumed that the meanings of different words are contrasted. Nor do children always simply add more attributes or semantic features in their development of a concept; there are, for example, examples of initial 'under-extensions' where 'dog' applies first only to the family's pet but is eventually extended to other canines that lack his particular characteristics of appearance and behaviour. More interestingly, perhaps, there is evidence of conceptual reorganisation where features are reshuffled and reweighted as knowledge grows (see e.g. Carey (1985), Gelman (2003), Johnson et al. (2004) and other sections in this chapter). Finally, the semantic feature theory relies too heavily on linguistic evidence, in part because it is emphasising the verbal attributes of concepts, and does not take sufficient account either of the non-linguistic strategies that children use in their communication and language comprehension or of the embedding of conceptual material in their non-linguistic lives.

2.12.3 Using concepts in the real world

My discussion of concepts so far has led to emphasising the place of particular concepts within the person's wider knowledge of the world and how it works. General world knowledge and theories of what is relevant and important to the present particular case seem to influence both the structure and the use of concepts. A similar picture arises from studies of biological classification, both folk classification and the scientific classifications deriving from Linnaeus (Lakoff 1987). Psychological discriminability seems to be an important component of our categorisation of the natural world. Ultimately such a view as this leaves cognitive psychologists and philosophers with the impossibly formidable task of describing not just isolatable concepts such as 'furniture', 'peace', 'triangle', and so forth, but entire knowledge systems in more or less flexible use. Fortunately a more manageable task arises for developmental psychology: to examine the possibility that children's concepts arise in considerable part from their direct experience of the working of their own worlds. In particular, there is the more precise hypothesis that children quickly build up mental representations of familiar daily routines (as procedural knowledge) and that analysis of these routines leads (sometimes quite slowly) to formal conceptual achievements such as categorisation into hierarchical concept systems (as declarative knowledge).

2.12.3.1 Scripts and general event representations

A major body of work on this problem was done by Katherine Nelson and her colleagues (Nelson 1986) under the banner of 'general event representation'. They have been concerned with children's generalised representations of 'events' and how such representations develop and interact with other aspects of cognition. An 'event' normally involves people in purposeful activities, acting on objects and interacting with other people in order to achieve a particular result. Events are organised around goals and given conventional labels and conventional boundaries. The event 'grocery shopping', for example, has the goal of buying the groceries that the household needs, and typically includes activities such as writing shopping lists, getting to the grocers', buying the groceries, bringing them home and unpacking them into the appropriate cupboards, but probably does not include menu planning or eating the groceries that have been bought. Representation of the event 'getting married' might include the ceremony itself and the planning beforehand, but would probably not include at least the earlier stages of the courtship, or specificities of 'being married' beyond the generalised 'live happily ever after'; infrequently experienced events may have different sorts of detail and less realism than those that have been gone through daily.

Events, like scripts (Schank and Abelson 1977), normally have a temporal sequence that may be a matter of convention or of logical or pragmatic necessity, and may be more or less strong and specific. In the 'getting undressed' script, for example, there has to be an invariant temporal sequence of taking socks off after shoes, if both are worn; but the script may not specify whether socks should come off before or after trousers, or, more probably, different people's scripts may specify different orders, and doing things in what would be one's own 'wrong order' (trousers off but socks still on, for example) may seem endearingly comic or disturbingly dangerous (as in the dispute (Swift 1985) between Lilliput, where the 'script', and indeed the law, specified that breakfast boiled eggs should be broken at the small end, and its neighbour Blefuscu, where 'Big Endians' prevailed). Event representations also enshrine causal sequences ('We needed some bread so we went to the baker's') and specify actors, activities and props. These allow of alternative specifications: we would go to a baker's for bread, cake, pies, etc., but perhaps not before zip fasteners, electric light bulbs, melons or a daily newspaper. Nelson suggests that experience of these alternative 'slot fillers' leads to categorisation: if two items are alternative props or actors (or, no doubt, activities) at a particular point in a script then they are likely to be seen as in the same category. Similarly, if the script makes two items co-occur, they may be categorised together: a possible source of children's thematic categories.

Many of young children's daily experiences are highly routinised: new instances of the event can be incorporated without changing the general expectation of how the routine goes, but marked deviation from the routine causes distress even in infancy (Dunn 1988; Mandler 1983). Adults clearly teach infants and children to take part in routines ('peekaboo', for example, or 'reading' picture books (Bruner 1983), or going to see Granny), and children learn the script by acting in it. By the time children come to use language, they have accumulated a great deal of event knowledge from their daily experiences, and much of their early language use is associated with routines of feeding, playing and so forth. Being able to use language to construct knowledge may be very dependent on being able to relate it to prior experience, including experience that is provided by other people and given a social structure by them. Routines enable children to learn the meanings of words (which mark and comment on the sequence of events) and to engage in a discourse with adults that is more extended than they can manage alone (e.g. Tizard and Hughes 1984, and pp. 380–382). Within routines they can show advanced skills such as giving informative answers to questions, talking about objects and events that are not present, making causal inferences and so forth. Representations of routine events give children good opportunities of attaching meaning to the routine's constituents and also of comparing this routine with other ones, because the general event representation carries performance and frees the child's attention from maintaining the current activity.

Nelson (1986) suggests that event representations could be the 'basic building blocks' of cognitive development; that from late in their first year children work with generalised event representations (GERs) of whole meaningful events, especially routinised interactions with familiar adults, to come to understand social relations and object categories in the world, and to support their language development (pp. 100–104). The coherent structure of familiar event representations facilitates cognitive processes such as categorisation, analysis of patterns and of cause–effect relations, analysis and synthesis of attributes, specification of what is optional and what is obligatory, and so forth. Using an event representation in a familiar situation to guide both verbal and non-verbal action (and interaction with other people) allows children to make sounder predictions and to organise their own actions and verbalisations more appropriately than would be possible without a GER. As well as helping smooth performance in a routine, GERs support high-level cognitive functions such as making and carrying out plans, using logical relationships, extending reality into fantasy, making inferences and so forth. Social and physical knowledge are not so clearly separated as in adult analysis, as objects take part of their meaning from the social interactions and events they are used in, and social interactions often involve or refer to physical props.

2.12.4 Socialised knowledge

As I said at the beginning of this section, we are throughout our lives faced with the problem of achieving some sort of stability in the face of a continuously changing reality. Event representations involve a lifelike picture of elements and relations changing over time and with different details on different occasions. They are generalised and have a structured organisation, but are also specific to particular times, places and persons through the possibility of inserting equivalent specific items as 'fillers' in particular points in the script. They help the child (and the adult) to predict what is likely to happen, to understand what has happened, and to get a grasp on the changing reality of the present. A person who has no available event representation will have fewer cognitive and emotional resources free to deal with the demands of the moment, and may be overwhelmed by the chaos of existence (as, perhaps, in autism; see e.g. Frith (1990), Frith and Frith (2003), Hill and Frith (2003), Hobson (2002), Lewis (1987), Rutter (1983a)). Young children seem to use routine as an aid to cognitive stability, and their participation as actors in adult-led routines contributes to their cognitive development.

This implies that children's concepts develop within the child's experience of other people's concept systems. They gradually learn that different sorts of specialists have different and differently organised knowledge (Danovitch and Keil 2004). These other concept systems may accelerate or impede their development; children may be forced, nudged or encouraged towards adopting received ideas. I will mention briefly here another aspect of Vygotsky's work on concepts as an example. He was very interested in the impact of educational processes on the child's cognition (pp. 401–406). He therefore compared the development of concepts that the child learned in school with those spontaneously developed through everyday activity. The former were 'scientific' in the sense that they were formal, logical and decontextualised; the latter were experientially rich but unsystematic and very much embedded in context. In terms of the coherence and rigour of the concepts, the taught 'scientific' ones were more advanced than the 'everyday' ones, and the children had more reflective control of them; but they lacked the rich base of experience and the connection with other concepts that the everyday concepts had. The two types of concept interacted in development:

> In working its slow way upwards, an everyday concept clears the path for a scientific concept in its downward development. It creates a series of structures necessary for the evolution of a concept's more primitive, elementary aspects, which give it body and vitality. Scientific concepts, in turn, supply structures for the upward development of the child's spontaneous concepts towards consciousness and deliberate use.
>
> (Vygotsky 1986: 194)

For example, the systematic learning of scientific concepts in one field could translate into increased abstraction, awareness and control of thought in other fields, though it will not do so automatically (Johnson *et al.* 2004, and Chapter 6).

2.12.5 Recapitulation: the growth and organisation of children's knowledge

Studies of the organisation of knowledge have moved from an almost exclusive focus on attribute similarities within artificial categories to a recognition that we more probably organise our knowledge in many different and more multidimensional ways, as I have indicated above. This gives us a different basis for evaluating young children's knowledge systems. Instead of stigmatising them as immature, inadequate and inferior to adults' ways of understanding the world, recent researchers have been impressed by how much adults and children share in their conceptual systems (Mandler 1983; Carey and Gelman 1991; Johnson *et al.* 2004). I will suggest some general points here, while discussion of what children think about within particular areas of cognition may be found, subject by subject, throughout this chapter.

Clearly there are infinitely many different ways of organising what is known, and many of them will be useful; many actually are used. It used to be claimed that children had no capacity at all to use conceptual systems (such as taxonomic classifications), which were the dominant feature of adults' conceptualisation; it now seems that children do show conceptual structures very like adults', and adults have not given up some 'childlike' conceptual structures (though, as Johnson *et al.* (2004) show, amount of knowledge is a more important predictor than age). Infants show categorical perception in certain domains (hue, speech sounds, faces) very early indeed, for example (see Harris 1983a), and adults can use thematic bases for categories as well as attribute-based ones. Probably learning to use language influences how older children organise their knowledge; indeed, it seems unlikely that it should not, but it has been hard to establish specific effects in children (but see Luria (1976) and Cole (1990) for discussion of the effects of becoming literate). It is still an unresolved question whether language changes the representation of concepts that the toddler already has, or whether it is 'merely' facilitating their expression and use (Hespos and Spelke 2004). It certainly does mark out new and better specified information for the child and allows discussion of concept with other people (at least in so far as they share the same language and concepts and relate them similarly). There is much debate about whether children's concepts are 'incommensurable' with adults', or whether there is merely a gradual elaboration and tidying-up of their concepts as they grow older (Carey and Gelman 1991). It may be that it is this sort of minor change in flexibility of use and a growth in the amount of information acquired that characterises conceptual development from the preschool years into later childhood. Where children are knowledgeable and encouraged to discuss their knowledge they seem to have concepts very like those of adults. Chi and Koeske (1983) provide a detailed description of a four-year-old's dinosaur knowledge; Keil (in Mandler 1983: 470) provides an example of a five-year-old who thought rocks were alive, the adult-type reasons for his belief being that 'they could have babies (pebbles), grow (perhaps into boulders), and die, as evidenced by their just lying around and being still'. These are perfectly sound criteria for distinguishing the animate from the inanimate (pp. 166–167); the child's answer is wrong (and charming) because his evidence is poor, not because his concept has a childish structure or his reasoning is poor.

Although the quality of reasoning in children's concepts may be like adults', it can be more limited in the content it applies to: Johnson *et al.* (2004) found 'dinosaur expert' children had theories that were constrained to highly familiar dinosaurs, and not well linked to their more general biological theories. It seems that much of the change in thinking over the school years comes from the acquisition of more and more declarative and procedural knowledge, the development of metacognition, an improvement in the accessibility of knowledge, and increased familiarity with a wider range of cognitive and social domains. There is in recent literature an increased interest in domain-specific knowledge, and a recognition that there may be marked discrepancies in understanding between different domains. Thus students may succeed on a contextualised version of a logical task but not on an abstract version with exactly the same structure (Wason and Johnson-Laird 1972), or an adolescent may combine high creative achievement as a mathematician with immature social skills and political awareness. Even if highly abstract concepts are available, both children and adults may in any case prefer more pragmatic thinking and rely on familiar knowledge and procedures.

Thus the current state of opinion seems to be that Piaget was right when he insisted that knowledge and thinking are based on processes that are 'functional invariants' throughout life, but wrong or at least over-simplifying when he described qualitatively different structures of knowledge at different ages. Later conceptual structures are bigger, more flexible and more easily accessed and reflected on than earlier ones, but not unambiguously different in their organisation and certainly not generalised into a uniform level of competence across different ages. Our concepts are embedded in our theories, and differences in world knowledge interact with differences in levels of explanation (Johnson *et al.* 2004). Throughout our lives we use event representations, attribute and functional similarities, contiguities and contingencies, sequences and co-occurrences, inferences, and taxonomic classifications to organise our world knowledge, choosing our representation of our knowledge to fit a particular domain, context or task. Developmental changes seem to be a matter of differentiation, elaboration and perhaps integration of knowledge systems rather than qualitative changes in the whole basis of conceptualisation (though there are clearly microlevel changes in limited areas; see sections elsewhere in this chapter). Conceptual development is heavily dependent on experience, and in many domains on instruction, though certainly we go 'beyond the information given'.

2.13 Children's concepts of this, that, and the other

As well as the research on concepts in general that I have described earlier, there are many studies that focus on children's concepts of a particular area. Such areas range from conception (e.g. Goldman and Goldman 1982) to death (e.g. Gartley and Bernasconi 1967; Lansdown and Benjamin 1985; Lazar and Torney-Purta 1991; Orbach *et al.* 1985; Speece and Brent 1984; Stambrook and Parker 1987; Bering and Bjorklund 2004); from dinosaurs (Chi and Koeske 1983; Chi *et al.* 1989; Johnson *et al.* 2004) to the threat of nuclear war (Tizard 1986). A substantial proportion of studies of children's concepts of X content themselves with getting age differences in children's answers to leading questions, with attempts at explanation of developmental change being comparatively rare, and many studies do not consider variations in the answers given that might be associated with the respondents' experience, sample peculiarities, or the form of question being asked. As interviewing children in depth about X can be time-consuming, samples are often small and dubiously representative of 'children in general'.

The major information-gathering technique is the obvious one of asking children to say what they know about X, commonly by using the 'Piagetian' clinical interview of core questions and auxiliary probes intended to explicate the child's line of reasoning. This technique is seen by its users as being sensitive and flexible; by its critics as unstandardised, overly verbal and generally unscientific. Piaget's initial account of why he introduced his *méthode clinique* (Piaget 1929) was that the rigid form of question used in a standardised test might raise the issue in a way that was foreign to the child's conception and thus produce a 'romancing' answer. For example, the question 'what makes the sun move?' would be anomalous and hard to answer for a child who imagined the sun was a living being that moved of its own accord, or indeed for a child who knew that the earth moves round the sun. Varying the questions according to the way the child has appeared to understand earlier questions may elicit a 'truer' picture of the child's concepts. Alternatively, however, such varying of questions may evoke confused responses; children may respond to the repeated questions of an older interviewer with self-corrections elicited by the social structure of the clinical interview, not by their attempt to clarify their account of their concept (see e.g. Rose and Blank (1974) and Siegal (1991) for how easily this can happen even in a conceptually clear situation). Broughton (1978, 1982) argues that variation in the content of questions will produce only variation in the content of answers, not in the form of reasoning those answers reveal. I find myself dubious about this argument; surely the content (which he admits will be affected by the question) may make the reasoning look like one thing rather than another, or even be one thing rather than another. Probe questions may offer or close off opportunities for displaying understanding that other questions might have revealed differently. Indeed, understanding may develop during the course of the interview for children who are open to revising their ideas in public, who can say 'Ah. I never thought of it that way before: that would mean . . .' Microgenetic research methods deliberately capitalise on this by examining change in answers as the subject learns the task and reflects on it (Siegler 2005).

Categorising children's answers may involve the use of 'stage' models imported from other sources (frequently Piagetian) and of dubious validity, or the use of categories derived from the present field of data and available as a lengthy coding manual available from the authors on request, but not clearly self-evident from the examples given in the published text. Such categorisations may well be entirely justified, but they risk suppressing real individualities in children's concepts to fit them into a rigidly differentiated system, and they tend to work against explanation of how children come to move, as they get older, from one category of answer to another.

Methodologically, the solution is, no doubt, the alternation of flexible clinical interviews with more precisely standardised test methods and experiments, and of categorisation analyses with analyses that allow more continuity in development. Above all, what is needed is a resistance to simplifying development into claims that young children do not and cannot use particular sorts of categories, which older children use to the exclusion of more immature forms, when the data really show wide variation in the use of all sorts of categories at all ages. There may be such variation within an individual's performance; variation between individuals might usefully be examined in terms of the contribution of their experience or other cognitive skills to their concept systems. Finally, studies that extend their investigation of a focal area to other related areas would be welcome, so that we could begin to examine links between distinct but linked topics.

The reader will probably not be surprised to learn that although there are many studies of children's concepts of this, that, and the other, comparatively few are going to receive further attention here. To some extent my selection of topics and studies reflects the methodological points I have just made or recent progress in the area, but my subjective feeling that the area studied is conceptually important has also determined my choice. Limits had to be drawn somewhere, and readers have to put up with a writer's limitations!

2.13.1 Childhood animism

Some of Piaget's early work (Piaget 1929, 1930) showed children attributing animate characteristics, such as independent movement or causal intentions, to inanimate objects, such as bicycles or the moon. Laurendeau and Pinard (1970) and Carey (1985) similarly found young children saying that objects such as cars, fire, the wind, televisions and rocks rolling down hills were alive. Not all young children fail to make a distinction between animate and inanimate objects. Shields and Duveen (1982), for example, asked nursery-school children which of a farmer, a cow, a tractor and a tree could eat, sleep, move by itself, talk, feel angry, and so forth. The children's answers drew a clear distinction between the tractor and the tree, which could not do any of these things, and the farmer and the cow, which could. (There was some disagreement over whether cows could talk or have emotions, but children who said they could maintained they talked to other cows or the farmer, extending the meaning of 'talk', but not applying this extension to the firmly inanimate tractor and tree.) Bullock (1985) found three-year-olds making this distinction, though inconsistently; by the age of five, judgements were adult-type. Similar studies reviewed by Gelman and Spelke (1981: 48–51) and Gelman and Opfer (2002) suggest that children as young as two may make some adult-type distinctions between animate and inanimate objects if the objects are well known to them and if the questions asked are relatively straightforward. Arterberry and Bornstein (2001) find the rudiments of the distinction in babies. Some of Piaget's animistic answers may have stemmed, it is argued, from asking problematic questions such as 'Does the sun know where it is moving?'. The animate–inanimate distinction may be fundamental to the ontological aspects of semantic development, and has been argued to be an evolutionarily given cognitive module (Fodor 1983; Leslie 1994; Cosmides and Tooby 1994; Pinker 1997).

The beginnings of a distinction between animate and inanimate objects, and between people and other animate objects, seems to be discernible in very young children (Arterberry and Bornstein 2001; Carey and Gelman 1991; Gelman 1990, 2003; Gelman and Kremer 1991; Gelman and Spelke 1981; Gelman and Opfer 2002; Inagaki and Hatano 2004). It is not entirely clear what the distinction is based on and we do not know how it is built up in the early years of life. No doubt one source of the distinction is differences in the ways persons act on the child and react to his or her actions, compared with the actions and reactions of objects. Such differences would be a better basis for distinguishing the truly animate from the truly inanimate than what children are directly told, given the extensive anthropomorphism to be found in young children's literature, replete as it is with talking animals, toys, trains and so forth. Carey (1985) attributes children's animism to their lack of knowledge of biology. She suggests that only the basic biological functions are good criteria for distinguishing a unified category of 'living things' from 'non-living things'. Children who do not know about biological functions can only apply their general knowledge of people when they try to distinguish between 'living' and 'non-living', and so will be unlikely to have a coherent concept of 'living things'. If their rudimentary 'living things' category is internally heterogeneous, they will be more likely to include objects that are not actually alive. They might be said to have what is essentially a 'family resemblance' concept rather than a 'defining characteristic' one. For example, the very conspicuous movement of cars and clouds may resemble that of animals enough for them also to be said to be alive. Developmental change might then be largely a matter of elaboration of the knowledge base, and sorting out the factual information from the metaphorical and fictional (rivers that run, trains and rabbits that talk, thunder that is the gods' anger). These changes may of course amount to a substantial restructuring (Johnson et al. 1992, 2004; Carey and Gelman 1991; Venville 2004) and may differ between cultures (Astuti et al. 2004).

2.13.2 Children's concepts of bodies

One obvious but important component of the development of children's concepts of their bodies is an increase in knowledge. Slaughter and Heron (2004) suggest that we develop from earliest infancy a sensori-motor body knowledge that is responsible for on-line control of our own bodies and perception of other people's movements; as we see bodies we develop a visuo-spatial knowledge of body structure; and as we learn language we accumulate vocabulary and language-based concepts of what bodies are like, what they can do, and how we use them. Very young children just beginning to talk learn to point to their hands, toes, faces, tummies and so forth, and grazed knees that produce an ooze of blood are also discussed with interest. By the time they start school most know that their bodies contain brain, bones, blood and a heart (Carey 1985; Eiser 1985; Eiser and Patterson 1983). Adults often have poor knowledge about their own bodies and make errors in locating organs when asked to draw them on an outline body; children's degree of informedness does them no discredit. A study by C. Porter of 144 American schoolchildren aged six to ten (Eiser 1985: 21) found they were, admirably, able to draw organs with accuracy and to scale, and to name, among other body parts, adenoids, bone marrow, cerebellum, cerebrum and cortex, optic nerve, pancreas, pores, schlera and tooth-root.

The naming of body parts can be economically investigated by distributing drawings of bodies to whole classes of children to be filled in or annotated appropriately. Questions about how children's knowledge of their bodies is organised, and what its sources are, and how it is constrained, are harder to provide answers for. As children got older the involvement of body parts increased beyond the periphery; for example, eating involves mouth and teeth for the youngest children, but stomach, bladder and the rest of the digestive system for older children (Eiser and Patterson 1983). By about the age of nine children were beginning to show awareness of some of the transformations occurring within the body, for example the digestive process and the circulation of nutrients round the body in the blood. Knowledge of reproduction has been seen to lag behind other areas of understanding, but is also known to be correlated with children's exposure to sex education (Goldman and Goldman 1982).

Knowledge about the anatomy of bodies can be related to knowledge about their functions, about species and about the properties of living organisms (Carey 1985, 1987; Carey and Gelman 1991; Johnson et al. 1992, 2004; Keil 1979, 1981b, 1989; Gelman 2003; Astuti et al. 2004). Carey claims that an 'intuitive biology' emerges from the young child's essentially psychological understanding. Early accounts of biological functions and organs are in terms of human activities and intentions: activities such as eating, breathing and sleeping are conceptually the same sort of phenomena as playing or bathing. The concept of eating includes information about table manners and about what food appears at what meal as well as the facts that food is put into the mouth (not some other orifice), that it is swallowed, that after eating one's stomach feels fuller, and so on. Eating is explained in terms of intentions: people eat because it is dinner-time or because they want to grow strong. Mature biological theories discriminate between intention and function, between biology and psychology, and have both far more integrated data and more principled explanations, Carey suggests.

She has a variety of different pieces of evidence supporting her claim for the emergence of an intuitive biology from a human-centred psychology (Carey 1985, 1987). One piece shows how people extrapolate information about a particular species to other species. Subjects from four years old to adult were taught about an internal organ that was new to them. At all ages those who had learned that humans had, for example, a spleen inferred that other mammals were very likely to have one too, birds, bugs and worms progressively less likely, and that flowers, the sun, clouds, vehicles and tools couldn't be assumed to have one. However, the pattern with which a new organ was 'projected' on to other species differed for children under ten and older people. Adults and older children who had learned that people had spleens or that dogs had spleens were equally willing to propose that the other species had them too. Younger children would only extrapolate human organs to other species, not non-human ones to either humans or other species. Four-year-olds who were taught that humans had a spleen projected it to other mammals, birds and bugs at a rate above 50 per cent; those taught that a dog had a spleen projected it to other species at about a 25 per cent rate, those taught that a bee had a spleen at below 15 per cent, even if the comparison animal was another insect. Carey suggests (1985: 150) that only if new knowledge can be integrated into a child's knowledge of humans and human activities will the four-year-olds project it sensibly to other animals. By age ten, people are only one mammal among many with respect to biological properties, and there is no longer an asymmetry of projection from people and from dog. However, projection from bees remains low.

A second body of evidence that young children structure their knowledge of biological properties such as eating and sleeping in terms of human behaviour is in the asymmetry of their attributing such functions between species. As with the possession of a spleen, young children are much more willing to attribute people-like biological functions to animals similar to people, under-attributing functions such as breathing and eating to animals such as bugs and worms. Older children may make similar judgements, but they do so by deductive inferences from category membership or from reasoning about knowledge of biological functions. Thus they can say that worms breathe because they are animals and all animals breathe, or because all living creatures need to burn oxygen for energy and must therefore be able to obtain oxygen from the air. Their knowledge is both greater and more precisely and usefully organised. In particular it involves much more understanding of biological functioning, with a move away from the 'one organ one function' model of the young child. Older children have more awareness of how different organs function together to solve the basic problems of living that confront all organisms. Older children and adults also find it easier to make correct inferences about possible new instances of a concept (Johnson et al. 2004). Processes such as death, growth, reproduction, eating and so forth are initially seen in terms of the behaviour of the person, without much knowledge of the mechanisms that mediate between inputs (such as eating too much) and outputs (such as getting fat). Later development may bring about an understanding of the cause and effect relationships here, though the success of the slimming industry suggests that for many people this understanding is incomplete and easily obscured.

In a study of children's concepts of the mind and the brain (Johnson and Wellman 1982), children between five and eleven, and a group of adults, were asked to judge whether the brain was involved in each of a number of activities. All the children could say where the brain was, and all agreed with adults that it was needed for mental acts such as thinking and remembering. However, there was an age change in the recognition that the brain was involved in sensori-motor acts or involuntary movements such as sneezing. The youngest children denied that the brain was involved in, say, walking: you just need feet. Adults too are susceptible to the mistake of believing that brains are essentially for thinking with, and underestimating how much of the brain is busy controlling all sorts of non-cognitive body functions.

We have used different models of the brain with different implications (pp. 321–324, 326–327, 340, 341–343). One common current one is the 'brain as container' model – we talk about memory stores, or of intellectual 'capacity', or of having it 'in mind' to do something, we think of brain transplants as conveying thoughts and memories to the recipient. We also talk of brains as doing things. The idea of brains doing things, that the brain is essential for general mental processes such as thinking or remembering, is apparent in young children, and seems not to require the brain-as-container metaphor (Johnson and Wellman 1982; Johnson 1988, 1990; Gottfried et al. 1999; Watson et al. 1998). Young children are happy to say that brains are important for mental activity such as thinking or remembering specific things, but may not believe that brains contain thoughts or memories; thus if a brain was transplanted from a kangaroo to a monkey the animal that had the brain could 'think about things' and the animal with no brain could not (though preschoolers were somewhat uncertain about this effect of having no brain), but the monkey would not 'think about hopping' rather than 'think about swinging from trees' as a result of having a kangaroo's brain. Adults, and children aged nine upwards, were likely to say that the brain transplant would result in the recipient animal having the thoughts and memories of the donor, rather than arguing that the animal would continue to have the sorts of thoughts it had always had despite now having a brain from a different species.

Gottfried *et al.* (1999) interpet this pattern of results in terms of the young children holding an 'essentialist' conceptualisation of what makes an animal a particular sort of animal; the category membership of the animal, although normally accompanied by possession of the right sorts of organs, behaviour, thoughts and memories of that sort of animal, is not changed if some of these are changed because category membership is defined by some sort of 'essence' of being a cat, or a raccoon, or a kangaroo, or a monkey (cf. Keil 1987, 1989, 1992). As children get older, though, they learn more about the interdependence of brain and body, and mind and brain (Johnson and Wellman 1982), and the 'brain-as-container' metaphor becomes more salient.

I think there is some room for debate about the adequacy of the idea that a brain transplant would lead to a mind transplant, however rich a frisson it has provided for horror films and stories. The descriptions of brains that are emerging from cognitive neuroscience (Chapter 5) would not, I think, encourage the idea that a skunk that has had a rabbit's brain transplanted into it would remember being a baby rabbit rather than a baby skunk, or that a horse with a cow's brain would 'think about giving milk' rather than 'think about running fast'. The researchers did not ask questions that might have produced interesting debate, for example whether a chicken that received a duck's brain would be able to swim and dive, or whether a rat that received a mole's brain would be able to see and smell like a rat or like a mole. Nevertheless, we seem to have a developmental shift here from early incoherence through a period of consistent attribution of it being difficult to change an animal's identity or characteristics by changing body parts, even including the brain, to a view that the transplanted brain would retain its original characteristic thoughts and memories, which the researchers say is characteristic of adults.

2.13.3 Children's concepts of health and illness

Eiser (1985: 15) claims that 'there is beginning to be considerable evidence that children's beliefs about these issues [the causes and prevention of illness, and their definitions of health and behaviours they think important in maintaining health] develop in a systematic predictable sequence'. She bases this claim very largely on the work of Bibace and Walsh (1981), who describe neo-Piagetian stages in children's concepts of health and illness. They interviewed twenty-four children at each of the three age levels of four, seven and eleven, using questions such as 'what does it mean to be healthy?', 'were you ever sick?', 'how did you get sick?', 'how did you get better?', 'what makes colds go away?', 'what is a heart attack?', 'why do people get heart attacks?', 'what are germs?', 'what do they look like?', 'can you draw germs?', 'where do they come from?'.

In the 'prelogical' stage of the youngest children, the main cause of illness was contagion, though God and certain other external causes were cited ('How do people get colds?' 'From trees'). In the 'concrete-logical' stage (seven to ten) illness arose through contamination by physical contact with the illness, more elaborately by swallowing or inhaling it. In the 'formal-logical' stage illness was seen as caused by specific malfunctioning or non-functioning of an internal organ or process, with psychological and physiological functions ultimately interacting.

Similarly, Brewster (1982) found that young children believed that illness was the result of human action and children from seven to ten that it was caused by 'germs', while only children over eleven acknowledged that ill-nesses were the result of interaction between several factors, different for each specific illness. Kister and Patterson (1980) also found lack of differ-entiation between different illnesses: young children judged that a cold, toothache and a scraped knee could all be explained by contagion (or even immanent justice). Eiser et al. (1983) describe children's ideas about health. Being energetic, taking exercise and eating good food were increasingly frequently mentioned between six and eleven years of age, and were the main components of descriptions of 'health' throughout this age range.

It is not entirely clear that these findings represent children's concepts of health and illness completely fairly (see Harbeck and Peterson 1992; Siegal 1988, 1991; Au et al. 1993; Hejmadi et al. 2004). The work stemming from a neo-Piagetian 'cognitive developmental' approach focuses very much on cognition without examining social or cultural influences; it seems very likely that phenomena like the young child's tendency to say that illness is caused by wrong-doing owes something to parental invocations of illness as a consequence of not doing what you're told – 'if you don't eat up your dinner/wrap up warm/wear your boots, you'll get ill'. Neo-Piagetian ana-lyses of such data, focusing on cognitive structures characteristic of discrete stages, will run into the same problems that have brought Piaget's own stage model under question (see Gelman and Baillargeon 1983; Mandler 1983; pp. 268–273). In particular they will fail to account for transition from one stage to another and to acknowledge the existence of individual differences that may be associated with different experiences and cultures. Further, the interview technique used may be insensitive to the understand-ing of young children, so underestimating their competence. Siegal (1988, 1991; Hejmadi et al. 2004), for example, investigated children's understand-ing of contamination and contagion. In one study children were asked to judge other people's (a puppet's or another child's) account of why they got a cold or toothache or a scraped knee. Even four-year-olds showed a good substantial knowledge of contagion and contamination: they knew that contagion was a good explanation for a cold and a poor one for a scraped knee, and believed that milk into which a foreign body such as a cockroach or a dirty comb had fallen was no longer really safe to drink. (Contamination is also a concept with social and sometimes religious connotations. Hejmadi *et al.* (2004) found that Hindu children showed more sensitivity to contamination than American ones, though both cultures recognised and disliked contamination from very early ages.)

Further research using ingenious techniques such as these, or examining children's scripts (Eiser 1988; Eiser and Eiser 1987), may uncover more understanding in young children and more variation at a particular age than Bibace and Walsh (1981) found. In particular, it is essential that alternative theories of why cognition develops about health and illness should be considered, both for the improvement of accounts of cognitive development and for the improvement of the care of chronically sick children who need explanations of their illness to allay their fears and increase their co-operation with treatment (Eiser and Eiser 1987).

2.13.4 Children's concepts of death

Having looked at studies of children's concepts of life, and health, I will briefly survey the literature on children's concepts of death. The literature is predominantly descriptive and the findings described are not entirely consistent – not surprisingly, given that there is variation in method and samples. However, the general picture emerging is that the idea that death is final, inevitable and universal is not expressed until somewhere around the age of eight or nine (Gartley and Bernasconi 1967; Lansdown and Benjamin 1985; Lazar and Torney-Purta 1991; Speece and Brent 1984; Stambrook and Parker 1987; Cuddy-Casey and Orvaschel 1997; Slaughter and Lyons 2003; Bering and Bjorklund 2004). Children may deny that they themselves will ever die, or say that a dead person would return to life if only the correct measures were taken, or that life continues on a reduced, less active level – 'she is not dead, but sleepeth', to use a phrase that I remember hearing in Sunday School. Alternatively it is claimed that such young children 'know about but deny' the fact of universal irreversible and inevitable death, an obviously untestable hypothesis.

Slightly older children may recognise that death is inevitable and universal, but believe that unless an external agent or event is involved death only happens to the old. (No doubt some parental input intended to reassure them contributes to this.) Death may also be personified, not surprisingly given the long cultural tradition of doing just this. By about the age of nine, the account of death starting to predominate is of an internal biological process operating according to natural laws, universal and final and meaning the complete cessation of body functions, and thus not like sleep or a temporary separation.

There are of course cultural ideas about death and the possibility of an afterlife. Bering and Bjorklund (2004) asked children and adults whether a baby mouse that had just been killed by an alligator would have biological functions (would need to eat or drink, would grow up to be an old mouse), psychobiological functions (be thirsty, hungry, sleepy), perceptual functions (hear, taste, smell, see), desires (wish he didn't have a brother, hope to get better at maths), emotions (scared of the alligator, love his mom) and epistemic states (believe he's smarter than his brother, believe his mom is the best in the world, know he's not alive). Almost all respondents of all ages agreed that the biological functions ceased at the mouse's death. Half the kindergarten children, and virtually all in the older groups, also agreed that the mouse would no longer have psychobiological feelings of hunger and thirst, or perceptions. There was more variation in ideas about the mouse's desires, emotions and thoughts, with almost all kindergarten children and two-thirds of adults saying that the dead mouse still loves his mom. Bering and Bjorklund (2004) suggest that there is an increasing acknowledgement of biological cessation with an increasing and perhaps compensatory belief in spiritual continuation emerging. I find it striking that so many subjects – the majority of adults! – said that the dead mouse still had positive emotions. This might be a biconditionality error, if it was supposed that the bereaved mother mouse still had positive emotions about her dead child, or these people may perhaps be subscribing to the common sentimental version of a life after death purged of all negative feelings. It might be interesting to see what they would have said about the afterlife of a thoroughly evil and unrepentant baby mouse; or what they would say if they came from a religious perspective that expects eternal damnation for most people; or what they would say if they came from a more secular society than southern Florida.

This sequence of ideas derives from studies of Western schoolchildren in the twentieth century who probably have not experienced the death of a close relative. They are thus limited to a particular historico-cultural experience, or, rather, lack of experience. There are four reasons for caution about drawing from these results any strong conclusions about children's ability to understand death. The first I have mentioned already: there is variation even in these studies of comparatively similar samples in what is understood about death – at what age, for example, its finality is understood. The second is that death is an emotive subject, where even for adults a mature understanding can coexist with feelings and ideas that deny the irreversibility and the universality of death. For example, a bereaved person may find it impossible to accept that someone loved is dead and cannot be retrieved, or a healthy adult may be unwilling to consider what should happen to his or her possessions and responsibilities in the event of his or her death, and may therefore not make a will or other such plans. The third reason is that emotion, and anxiety in particular, may distort the account people give of what death is. An interesting study by Orbach *et al.* (1985) showed that anxiety impeded young children's expression of their ideas about death.

The fourth reason for caution, which needs rather more discussion, is that most child respondents in the research literature have little or no experience of death except in emotionally distant contexts. They may have seen real human deaths reported on the television news, or experienced the death of pet animals, but the loss of a close family member or close friend is unlikely to be within their experience. This would not have been the case for such children in the nineteenth century or earlier, when infant and child mortality was much higher, and when far more people died in their own homes rather than away in hospitals, hospices and so forth; nor would it be the case today for many children in the Third World. It appears that children who have suffered a death in the family may express far more adult feelings and ideas about this loss than children with no such experience, that the age of the child need not limit their understanding so severely as the literature on 'inexperienced' children would suggest. Eiser (1985) describes studies of children's reactions to the death of a sibling, and Mandell *et al.* (1983) and Burns *et al.* (1986) describe the responses of children who had lost a baby brother or sister through sudden infant death syndrome. Children who had suffered such a sudden and traumatic change in their family showed grief similar to adults' in its content and duration, even when they themselves were as young as two. A therapeutic group described by Krasner and Beinart (1989) showed an understanding of death far in advance of the children's ages (four to seven), and expressions of anger, sadness and resolution of feelings echoing those described in adults, for example by Parkes (1972). The expression of their ideas and feelings in their group meetings seemed to ameliorate the behaviour problems that had followed the death of their baby sibling, problems that seem typically to increase following a death in the family (Burns *et al.* 1986; Eiser 1985; Mandell *et al.* 1983). Experience thus seems to advance understanding, and discussion of death with young children is possible and may be helpful.

2.13.5 *Children's understanding of emotions*

Understanding emotions is an important part of our understanding of ourselves and other persons. As 'natural psychologists' we use concepts of internal emotions to explain many actions: 'he kissed his mother because he loved her', 'he ran away because he was frightened, not because he wanted to play chase', and so forth. We not only explain actions, we seek to predict, control and use them. We thus need to have at least a pragmatic grasp of what emotions are commonly associated with what situations, and of how emotions are typically expressed in postures, movements, facial expressions and tones of voice. We may, as Darwin proposed, have both an innate repertoire of emotional expressions – ways of looking pleased or unhappy that are extremely similar not just in different cultures but in different species – and an innate ability to recognise these expressions (Darwin 1872), but we are also expected to learn cultural rules about what emotional expression is acceptable or admirable, to turn the evolutionarily universal quivering lip of distress to the stiff upper lip of English manhood at its traditional public school finest. Understanding emotions is thus an important part of children's 'theory of mind' (see section 2.13.10), part of their socialisation, part of their moral development (Meadows 1986; Nunner-Winkler and Sodian 1988; Nucci 2002a) and part of their mental health. This is particularly the case if we presume that it is better to be aware of one's emotions and able to modulate them to some degree than to lack insight and control. We also have reason to believe that emotion and cognition intertwine in development (Attili 1989; Harris 1990); the effects of emotion on cognitive development are briefly discussed in Chapter 6.

There is a rapid increase in understanding of emotions over the period of infancy (Campos *et al.* 1983). By the end of the first year babies are well able to recognise whether a familiar adult is showing a positive or negative emotion and to begin to identify what has caused the emotion. Dunn (1988) convincingly demonstrates that early in the second year children move from reacting passively to another person's emotions to actively seeking to change them, providing comfort to someone who is distressed or distressing someone who has annoyed them. In doing this they show that they know it is possible to change emotional states, and that often they appreciate what has caused and what can change an emotion. Some may have quite a large repertoire of emotion-altering techniques that they can apply to others, for example trying several different ways to comfort an unhappy younger sibling. Parental handling of emotions is one of the variables behind individual differences in this (Dunn 1988, 1995; Dunn *et al.* 1987, 1995; Brown and Dunn 1996; Cutting and Dunn 1999; Dunn and Hughes 2001b; Meins and Fernyhough 1999; Cicchetti 2002; Cole *et al.* 2004). It seems that some parents, who demonstrate concern and who act to comfort the distressed, explaining what distress has occurred and why it is appropriate to comfort, tend to have children who as toddlers show more understanding of other people's views and feelings and respond more helpfully to someone else's distress (Light 1979; Zahn-Waxler *et al.* 1979).

Preschool children who are abused by their parents, however, are more likely to react to another child's distress with hostility or with distress and fear of their own, and less likely to show active concern (Main and George 1985; Cicchetti 2002). This is not because they do not understand that distressing another child or acting aggressively are serious offences, as they distinguish them quite clearly from minor breaches of convention (Smetana *et al.* 1984). It may perhaps be that abused children have learned less well to inhibit their own aggression, or perhaps they become so disturbed by the other person's distress that they are no longer able to act in a comforting way and even act aggressively in order to get rid of the person whose distress is disturbing them; or perhaps, having seen their parents react to their own distress in non-comforting ways, they have learned to act in the same way themselves, though not yet to assert that causing distress is in the victim's good, or that 'it hurts me more than it hurts you'. The psychoanalyst Alice Miller (Miller 1985, 1987, 1990) argues that denial of the truth of one's own emotions and of other people's is one of the components of abusive parenting and one of the main causes of social psychopathology.

As children grow older, they become increasingly able to show a diversity of emotions and to react to them in others. Harris (1989, 1990; see also Gnepp and Klayman 1992) argues that they may show complex emotional reactions, for example ambivalence, as toddlers, long before they are aware that emotions may be mixed. Typically, children under about six will assert that only one emotion can be felt at one time. For example, Harris (1983c) presented six-year-olds and ten-year-olds with stories in which the protagonist might be expected to feel conflicting emotions, for example when a lost pet dog is eventually found, injured. The younger children typically said that the child who owned the dog would feel entirely happy, because the dog was found, or entirely sad, because it was injured, but not both happy and sad. Ten-year-olds acknowledged that the protagonists in such stories would experience both feelings at the same time. Similar age differences were found when children were questioned about their own experiences. Eight-year-olds who had just started at boarding school admitted to mixed feelings about the whole experience, but attributed their feelings of pleasure and excitement to the new opportunities of school and their negative feelings to their separation from home and their parents, that is, to two different aspects of being at boarding school. Thirteen-year-olds said they had mixed feelings about one single aspect of school that they could appraise from two different viewpoints, being simultaneously excited about their new lessons and worried about whether they would be able to cope with them (Harris and Lipian 1989). Harris (1990) suggests that this developmental shift occurs because there are two ways of appraising situations that arouse emotion. The first develops early, and translates fairly automatically into behaviour. A situation that has been associated with pleasure in the past evokes pleasure the next time it is encountered; a situation that has been associated with lack of pleasure evokes distress. A situation associated with both pleasure and lack of pleasure evokes ambivalent reactions, as in the 'ambivalently attached' infant (Ainsworth *et al.* 1978; Bretherton 1985; Goldberg 2000) who seeks reunion with the mother but immediately rejects contact with her. This would seem to be a fairly simple conditioning process, which does not involve awareness of the emotions aroused, just an automatic reaction to the situation.

The second type of appraisal of emotions develops much more slowly. It involves appraisal not just of the situation that evokes emotion but of the emotion evoked. This makes it possible for a child to identify his or her own emotional reaction to a situation, to predict what emotion a particular situation would arouse, and to think of situations that would elicit a particular emotion. This appraisal can be more exhaustive or less so. The child examines the situation for aspects that are known to be associated with emotion. Typically, young children end this examination when one such aspect is found and the emotion identified (Gnepp *et al.* 1987). Thus, in a situation such as receiving a present that is not what one hoped for, a young child might find 'I'm pleased when I get a present' and report pleasure, not going on to 'I'm disappointed that it isn't what I wanted' and the sadness that would result, and so denying that any negative emotion would be felt. Older children are more likely to examine the situation and its possible emotional consequences more exhaustively, and so acknowledge the possibility of ambivalent emotions. Some adults, acknowledging the ambiguity of everything, may be able to emphasise some emotions more than others and so use them to enhance their own self-esteem or effectiveness; a useful form of emotion regulation.

Harris is suggesting that early emotional responses are pretty well automatic and not monitored by the child, but that children monitor their emotional responses to an increasing degree as they grow up. They also become increasingly subject to the display rules that their culture prescribes for the expression of emotion: 'big boys don't cry', 'say "thank you" to Granny for the nice present (even though it's not what you want)'. A study by Cole (1986) found girls as young as four obeying these social display rules, in that they smiled when the experimenter presented them with a disappointing gift, though not when they examined their gift and experienced their disappointment alone. (Boys at this age did not attempt this masking strategy at all; girls were visibly disappointed or disgusted but smiled bravely.) Questioned by another experimenter, the little girls admitted they had been disappointed (and eagerly swapped the disappointing gift for a more attractive one); when asked whether the first experimenter would know what they felt, they focused on what they had told the experimenter, not on their own facial expressions, nor did they mention having deliberately controlled their own expression of their emotion. These children said that someone else in the same situation would show the real emotion, even if they had a good reason to dissemble. McDowell *et al.* (2000) link this to emotional reactivity and social competence. Older children (see Harris 1990; Harris and Gross 1988; Harris *et al.* 1986) realise that real and apparent emotion may not coincide and that an observer may be deceived by the displayed emotion, taking it as real. Six-year-olds understood this if they understood why the protagonist was concerned to hide real emotion; ten-year-olds did not seem to need so much explicit information about motives.

This development in understanding that real and displayed emotions can be discrepant, and that observers and experiencers of emotions may differ in their understanding of the experiencer's emotional state if there is a discrepancy, Harris (1990) attributes to the child's awareness of two conflicting sorts of information. The child is aware of his or her own real emotions, but under social pressure to display a more acceptable emotion may do so and mislead observers, who attribute to the child an emotion different from the real one. The child may feel, for example, disappointment at an unattractive gift, but smile so convincingly that the donor says 'I'm so glad you really like it!' This could alert the child to the possibility of misleading others by displaying a more positive emotion than is really felt, and, as we said earlier, children will have been exhorted to do this. Gnepp and Hess (1986) report that children's understanding of display rules in this sort of pro-social situation was more sophisticated than their understanding of how to falsify emotional displays for self-serving ends such as concealing one's guilt or embarrassment. However, Harris (1990) mentions a study of emotionally disturbed children where egocentric and self-serving displays were better understood than pro-social ones.

Harris (1990: 209–210) sketches a very interesting and important picture of how the changes in children's understanding of emotion come about, drawing parallels with several other areas of development. He suggests that the task facing the child is to develop a representation of his or her behaviour that acknowledges how it is differentiated, in the case of emotions differentiated across socially constructed situations. His preferred metaphor is one of 'amplification'. Children spontaneously produce behaviour that varies (with some appropriateness) from situation to situation, but this variation goes unnoticed unless it is amplified by some environmental correlate. For emotional displays one major correlate would be the social consequences of the emotion; these include other people's reactions and, perhaps especially, their comments on the emotion (see also Dunn (1988)). If the child shows ambivalence, for example, the mixed emotional display makes other people respond to both its components, thus encouraging the child to recognise that more than one emotion is involved. Similarly, the feedback following emotional behaviour that successfully follows a display rule alerts children to the discrepancy between the emotion they are expressing and the one they feel. Thus children who are subjected, as Miller (1987) describes, to a regime in which they are only allowed to display socially prescribed emotions, even in situations that evoke negative ones, and where the displayed emotions are said to be the true ones and the real ones are denied, would be likely to grow up with a distorted understanding of emotion, and indeed distorted emotions. Other strategies for controlling emotion (Harris 1989) may be healthier. I discuss links between social input, cognition and emotional state later (Chapter 5).

2.13.6 Children's moral reasoning

The nature of morality and its relationships with our biology and our society have been debated by philosophers for millennia, and by psychologists for centuries. Their not necessarily compatible musings sometimes include consideration of the evolutionary usefulness of moral reasoning and action, sometimes examine the effect of social pressures and sanctions, and sometimes focus on the internal organisation of the reasoning involved. Judgement and action both need to be considered, and discrepancies between these may be especially important in our complex social world. All these issues are relevant to children's development as moral persons, but in total they amount to far more than I can address at this point, particularly as the issues remain profoundly unresolved. I am going to restrict my discussion to three main points: the adequacy of the cognitive-developmental model developed by Piaget and Kohlberg; children's views on the relations between convention and morality; and the importance of emotion in moral action. For a general review of moral development I recommend Turiel (1998) and Nucci (2002c).

The field of moral development has been dominated by a model of morality that emphasised its rationality and to some degree separated it from emotional content. This model began with Piaget (1932) and was developed by Kohlberg (1984). It involved a succession of stages of moral reasoning in which notions of justice and rights were central. Development started from early stages in which children's self-interest and their knowledge of social norms dominated their choice of what was 'right' or 'wrong' and their justifications of their choice, and gradually reached later stages in which principles of moral justice replaced self-interest and convention as the core of moral reasoning. The developmental forces include changes in relationships with parents and peers (especially for Piaget), and an intrinsic drive for coherence and commitment to a key moral principle (Kohlberg). Both researchers used stories about moral dilemmas as a major way to elicit evidence, though Piaget's account also uses charming examples of his own children's response to their moral dilemmas and of children playing games like marbles.

Critics of this approach have debated its methods: does discussion of fictional dilemmas reflect real-life moral reasoning, can children remember all the quite complex information in the stories, is the categorisation of children's answers reliable, can children express their reasoning fluently, are the stages really so clear-cut, so coherent, and so sequential? They have disagreed with its depiction of young children as amoral and of many adults as falling far below the final stages of Kohlberg's sequence; questioned whether people show consistent levels of reasoning across topics or occasions; identified lapses between reasoning and action; and disputed whether valuing justice and respect for human life above all else was the only tenable highest stage of moral reasoning (Emler 1998; Gilligan 1982; Nucci 2002a, 2002c, 2004; Turiel 1998).

Some of these issues have been developed in more recent work. One of the most important of these new areas has been children's recognition of the moral and the conventional as related, but not identical, domains.

Table 2.1 Nucci (2002c: 306–307) shows Kohlberg's stages in parallel with the characteristics of children's moral reasoning and understanding of convention. Turiel (1983, 1998) and Smetana *et al.* (1984) demonstrated that children as young as three differentiate between convention and morality, seeing convention as contextually dependent and agreed-upon social rules, and morality as less arbitrary, less avoidable, and appealing to universal moral principles. Thus they would agree that although one should participate in 'show and tell' at one's nursery school this was merely because not participating and not abiding by the nursery's conventions would upset social expectations, and it might be quite permissible to keep out of 'show and tell' in 'another country' or 'another planet'; but they would assert that to wreak unprovoked harm on someone would be wrong everywhere, regardless of whether it had been specifically prohibited. Compliance with convention comes to be seen as a good thing if it increases social harmony but as problematic if the conventional norms transgress a principle of moral authority or fairness. This may be a matter of debate, because whereas the link between breaking a moral rule (for example, by deliberately shooting someone) and harm to someone is typically immediate and obvious, the link between a social rule (the right to bear arms) and harm to other people (as indexed by the homicide rate) is less immediate, and much more arguable. In this sort of predicament, individuals have different views, and may have to choose between conventional and post-conventional (principled) moral reasoning; Emler (1998, 1999) finds this choice to be linked to political affiliation, with more left-wing people tending to appeal to moral principles and more right-wing people tending to appeal to social convention or outside authority. Readers may wish to interpret this bias pattern in terms of their own political preferences.

Another area of debate has been over the possibility that different groups have different bases for their moral reasoning. Following critiques of Kohlberg's model after his suggestion that women were less likely to reach higher stages of moral development than men, Gilligan (1982) suggested that the problem was Kohlberg's prioritising of justice as the core principle of moral judgement. She proposed compassion as an alternative, and linked a feminine preference for compassion to socialisation into sex roles. More recent studies (Jaffee and Hyde 2000; Lapsley and Narvaez 2004) show that both males and females reason about both justice and caring, though with a

Table 2.1 Levels of moral and conventional development in relation to Kohlberg's stages.

Approximate ages	Kohlberg stage	Moral domain	Conceptual domain
5–7 years	Stage 1 Rules are to be obeyed. Avoid physical damage to persons and property. Inability to co-ordinate perspectives of self and of others, thus favouring the self is seen as right.	Recognition of simple obligations such as not to hurt others. However, fairness is largely seen in terms of self-interest.	Conventions are 'reified' as descriptions of empirically observed regularities (e.g. men are supposed not to wear dresses because men are rarely seen in dresses).
8–10 years	Stage 2 Morality as instrumental exchange – 'You scratch my back and I'll scratch yours'. It is morally right to act to meet one's own interests and needs and let others do the same. Rules only followed when in someone's interests.	Fairness is now co-ordinated with conceptions of 'just' reciprocity defined primarily in terms of strict equality with some beginning concerns for equity (taking into account the special needs, situations or contributions of others).	Negation of the conception that conventions are just empirical regularities. Exceptions to conventions taken as evidence that conventions are arbitrary. Mere existence of a norm not a sufficient basis for compliance.
10–12 years	Stage 3 Being good means living up to what is expected by people around you, and by one's role. Fairness is the golden rule. One should be caring of others.	Fairness seen as requiring more than strict equality. Concerns for equity now co-ordinated with reciprocity in structuring moral decisions.	Concrete understanding that rules maintain order. Top-down conception of social authority and rules. Rules may be changed and vary by context.
12–14 years	Stage 3B Moral decisions based on the fairness or harmfulness of actions independent of rules, laws or role expectations. Morality prioritised over convention.	Consolidation of the relations between equity and equality in conceptions of what is fair and caring in social relations.	Conventions are viewed as 'nothing but' social expectations. This undercuts the force of conventional rules. Acts are evaluated independent of rules.

14–17 years	**Stage 4** Morality is as codified in the laws of the governing system. Adherence to law provides an objective basis for the right. Maintaining social system and equal protection from harm are basis for moral order.	Emergence of systematic concepts of social structure. Conventions seen as normative and binding within a social system of fixed roles, and static hierarchical organisation.
17–20 years	**Stage 4B** Morality is relative to systems of laws and norms. No system may lay claim to moral superiority. What is right is a function of what seems most right for the particular individual in the particular situation.	Negation of view that uniform norms serve to maintain social systems. Conventions are 'nothing but' societal standards that have become codified through habitual use. Systems of norms are arbitrary.
Adulthood	**Stage 5** 'Prior to society' perspective. What is moral is values and rights that exist prior to social attachments and contracts. Such values and rights are those that any rational being would want to see reflected in a moral society.	Application of conceptions of fairness and beneficence to reasoning about one's social system. Morality understood to be independent of norms of particular systems. Co-ordination of universal and prescriptive features of morality with incommensurate/intrinsic worth of all persons. Logical extension of moral obligations to treatment of humankind.
		Conventions as uniformities that are functional in co-ordinating social interactions. Shared knowledge of conventions among members of social groups facilitates interaction and operation of the system.

Source: Adapted from Nucci (2002c, pp. 306-307)

small gender bias in orientation. Again, the justice and compassion might be hoped to go together, rather than the one winning out over the other; but here, too, there might be conflicts. Cultural differences are an even more difficult issue. Some theorists emphasise the ways in which individuals' moral reasoning is constrained and constituted by the socially constructed norms that they meet, with cultural emphasis on individuality or on community being one developmentally powerful dimension (e.g. Shweder *et al.* 1990); others see these as superficial differences that conceal universal obligatory moral values. Again, it may be more a matter of what is prioritised than what is possible. Children growing up in a highly collectivised society may think that they should have a set of values that are personal, private and autonomous (Nucci 2002b); children in a highly individualistic society may nevertheless be desperately anxious to espouse the values of the society and so 'belong' to the desired social group (Power 2004; Wren and Mendoza 2004; Keller 2004).

A philosophical tradition that can be traced back to the ancient Greeks insists first that morality is not a self-subsistent entity but a part of the functioning of the individual as a whole that is integrated with the personality system and so linked to social functioning and motivation; second that it involves questions of intention, identity, power and agency; and third that it is linked to other human ideals such as truth and beauty (Blasi 1999, 2004; Nisan 2004). The embedding of moral reasoning within social settings suggests that it will not be free of emotion, and hence that emotion-free accounts of moral development will be missing important issues. Young children recognise the emotional colouring of the situations that involve moral reasoning. In studies by Arsenio and colleagues (1988, 1992), for example, even kindergarten children thought that people who were doing morally good things, or benefiting from them, or witnessing them (helping another person, sharing out a reward fairly) would have positive emotions; those suffering from or observing an unfair act would feel bad (though the younger children thought the victimiser might feel good about their act if it got them what they wanted). Those going against a convention, or witnessing a breach of convention, would feel neither good nor bad about it, though they expected authority figures to be upset. Moral issues are thus associated with emotional outcomes from the beginning, and children's understanding of emotion, for example their difficulties in recognising incompatible emotions, might be an area of relevance to their moral development.

2.13.7 Children's conceptions of intelligence

What children think 'intelligence' is, and how they come to have more or less of it, is obviously relevant to both psychology and education. I will introduce here some of the research in which children have been asked to say what being 'intelligent' or 'smart' means, and what causes it, and then review briefly what this understanding may do to their motivation and self-concept. The causes of intelligence I discuss later (pp. 213–247, 347–401).

Like adults, children in primary school associate intelligence with having a lot of knowledge and doing well in school, and doing well on academic subjects becomes increasingly often mentioned as a defining characteristic during this phase of schooling (Cain and Dweck 1995; Kinlaw and Kurtz-Costes 2003). Young children include social characteristics in their description of 'intelligence', while older children are more likely to differentiate between cognitive strengths and social strengths. Ideas centring on abstract reasoning become more frequent in adolescence (Chen *et al.* 1988). Good performance on cognitive tasks, and high school grades, are seen as specific and fairly precise signs of 'intelligence', and the reason why you would pick someone to be on your team in an academic competition (Droege and Stipek 1993; Stipek *et al.* 1995). Differences in academic performance are taken as signs of difference in 'intelligence' increasingly as school careers wear on; young children (and teachers!) attribute more of the difference in performance to effort, but older pupils are inclined to attribute differential success and failure to differences in ability. Ideas about the self as a learner are obviously relevant here (Burnett 1999; Burnett and Proctor 2002; Dart *et al.* 2000; Chapter 6).

Attributing successful performance to ability, and ability to stable, uncontrollable, internal causes, may be deleterious for cognitive confidence and achievement (Dweck 1999; Pomerantz and Ruble 1997; Pomerantz and Saxon 2001; Thompson 2004). In particular, believing that intelligence is an 'entity' that you have a fixed amount of and cannot improve may lead to anticipation of failure except on tasks that have already been mastered, unwillingness to take up challenges, and consequently to failure on tasks that could actually have been coped with successfully (Dweck 1999). So far as the stability of intelligence is concerned, young children seem to be quite optimistic about how clever they will be in a year's time, but older children seem to believe that their ability will remain stable and so will their class-mates', perhaps with some regression towards the mean in that the very bright student may be thought to be likely to do not quite so well next year and the less bright might up their achievement a little (Stipek *et al.* 1988; Droege and Stipek 1993; Pomerantz and Saxon 2001). Part of what is going on here may be a shift from 'intelligence' as an index of what you can do (which young children would be quite right to expect to get better year by year) to 'intelligence' assessed relative to other people, which need not get consistently better (pp. 231–235).

There are individual differences in whether people believe that intelligence is malleable, that it can be improved, from early childhood onwards, without much evidence of age-related changes in this belief. Children do say that how intelligent you are is to do with what you have done or experienced, but also that you may have been 'born that way' (Pomerantz and Ruble 1997; Pomerantz and Saxon 2001; Heyman and Gelman 2000). Stipek and Gralinski (1996) found that children who believed intelligence was relatively fixed and general also believed that performance was relatively stable, while other children were more sanguine about the usefulness of effort in improving performance. Children who consistently attribute their academic success to their ability plus their effort and their failure to lack of effort (Pomerantz and Saxon 2001; Dweck 1999; Stipek and Gralinski 1996) are more likely to persist on a difficult task than those who have more self-deprecating interpretations of success and failure. This reminds us that cognition cannot always be separated from emotion and motivation (pp. 435–439). Conceptions of one's intelligence are likely to be very salient in the achievement-oriented, competitive, assessment-heavy conditions of the classroom, and, as Dweck (1999) argues, we need first to know how children come to make attributions in more or less helpful ways, and then to act so that as few as possible will come to believe that they cannot become more effective in their use of their intelligence. Dweck's recommendation is praise for success that focuses on how the task was done rather than on how clever the person is – 'I really like the way you concentrated on the critical points' rather than 'you are clever' – and comments on failure that identify what needs to be done better next time, rather than on the inadequacies of this particular child or the difficulties of the task for them. It has to be said that there is not a conclusive body of evidence for this recommendation, but my own experience of trying to operate like this is (reviewers please note) that most learners like it.

2.13.8 Children's concepts of persons

Children have to operate with other people in their daily lives; social isolates may suffer an impaired development (Curtiss 1977; Rutter 1985a, 1985b; Skuse 1984) and knowledge of persons may be a critical deficit in autism (Hobson 1990, 2002; Leslie and Frith 1990; Tager-Flusberg 1992; Hill and Frith 2003; Meltzoff and Decety 2003). As cognition itself has been argued to have evolved to serve social functions (Humphrey 1983) and as social cognition undoubtedly has a neurophysiological basis (Blakemore *et al.* 2004), it is obviously an important topic. Nevertheless, some puzzling paradoxes are emerging from the relevant research.

One stream of research stems from a neo-Piagetian tradition, heavily influenced by his model of cognitive structures that limit understanding and functioning and succeed each other as discrete and coherent stages and by his assertion that children are egocentric, that is, that they are unable to appreciate that other people have knowledge, feelings or views different from their own (pp. 277–278). Often a neo-Piagetian interview technique is used in this tradition of research. Such studies generally paint a rather negative picture of children's understanding of people (Rogers 1978; Shantz 1983; Broughton 1978; Selman 1980; Damon and Hart 1988; Harter 1998). In a typical study, Livesley and Bromley (1973) asked their seven- to fifteen-year-old subjects to write free descriptions of eight persons they knew, including themselves. The younger children's descriptions were predominantly in 'peripheral' and 'external' terms, such as appearance, age and surroundings, rather than inferred or explanatory psychological characteristics. They used interests, abilities, likes and dislikes more frequently in describing themselves than in describing other people. By adolescence, there was some shift towards more abstract descriptions, more qualified with acknowledgement of variation in different settings or at different times, and more in terms of psychological dispositions, though global verdicts and behaviour-based descriptions of other people remained common. Damon and Hart (1988) discuss work by Aboud and Skerry in which child and adult subjects first named characteristics that described the 'self' and then said whether or not the self would still be 'the same person' if a particular characteristic were changed. There was an increase with age in naming psychological characteristics of the self and in saying that one would not be the same person if a psychological characteristic was changed.

These and other similar studies have been taken as showing that young children have a poor understanding of other people and older children a better one. One argument against this is that it is still a debatable issue in the psychology of personality whether abstract descriptions based on generalised psychological dispositions are indeed 'better' than more concrete descriptions (Hampson 1982; Harter 1998). For the moment the critical point to be made is that it may be useful to examine separable facets of 'understanding persons' rather than going for a one-dimensional development.

Damon and Hart (1988) offer a differentiated account of the development of self-understanding. Their model of the 'self' derives from the classic ideas of William James. It incorporates the 'me', the relatively objective material, social and spiritual or psychological characteristics that identify each self as a unique entity, and the 'I', the subjective experiential features such as awareness of oneself as an agent with a unique life history and experience, and continuing over time, distinct from others and capable of awareness of one's own awareness, that is, of self-reflection. They present a model of self-understanding in which seven 'schemes' each progress through four levels, not necessarily in synchrony. The first level, characteristic of early childhood, involves categorical identifications; the second (middle to late childhood), comparative assessments involving consideration of the self as measured against others; the third (early adolescence), interpersonal implications of the self; the fourth (late adolescence) systematic beliefs, principles and plans; these apply mainly to four 'schemes' that are the physical, active, social and psychological selves; the other schemes are the continuity, distinctness and agency of the self. Damon and Hart say that at all ages children have some understanding of their physical, active, social, and psychological selves. Although one may be more salient than another at a particular time (as in the earlier work's account of young children's physical descriptions of the self and older children's psychological ones), this does not mean that one is transformed into the other. Nor do children move neatly from one level to the next on all fronts at once: they are likely to make statements characteristic of several developmental levels at any given time.

Damon and Hart's data derive from 'clinical interviews' of Massachusetts schoolchildren, with smaller studies with children from a fishing village in Puerto Rico, a sample of anorexic girls and a sample of boys with conduct disorders. Some of their examples of material may give a flavour of the work. The following snippets from interviews seem typical (Damon and Hart 1988: 59–69):

Q: How are you different from your mother?
A: 'Cause I play a lot and I read a lot.
Q: Is that what makes you different from your mom?
A: Sure, my Mommy just watches television, cooks or cleans.
Q: And you read.
A: And I write, and I play with my toys.
(Level 1, active self-scheme)

Q: What are you like?
A: I'm bigger than most kids.
Q: Why is that important?
A: I can run faster than everybody.
(Level 2, physical self-scheme)

Q: What kind of person are you?
A: I'm a nice person.
Q: What's nice about you?
A: I'm not selfish. Like if somebody says, they go to the teacher and say, 'I don't have any ice-cream, and I don't have any lunch either, and I can't have any money to buy any fruit. I need that lunch, and the lunch guys won't give me any lunch.' I would say, 'Here, have my money.' I did that to Shannon.
(Level 4, physical self-scheme)

Q: What are you especially proud of about yourself?
A: I'm always learning and growing.
Q: How are you always learning and growing?

A: I try to find out as much as I can about things, all different things, and put it all together so I can really know what's going on. And I'm always getting better and better at it.

Q: Why is that important?

A: That's what's going to make me become the kind of person I want to be, a person on top of things.

(Level 4, psychological self-scheme)

There are slightly different levels for the agency, continuity and distinctness components of the self. Views of agency were elicited by questions such as 'How did you get to be the way you are? How could you have turned out different?' The first level of answers involved external biological, super-natural or social forces: 'I just grew'. At the second level, the person's own wishes or activities had an influence: 'I tried really hard to be like I am now', 'Because I used to do all my homework'. At the third level, com-munication with others was important: 'I learned from my parents. I even learned from my friends, just listening to 'em and talking to 'em.' At the fourth level, personal or moral evaluations of life possibilities influenced a person's actions. The next component of the self-as-subject is its continuity 'from year to year': at Level 1 this is said to rest on stable preferences, behaviour, or characteristics such as name, and at Level 2 on reference to immutable personality characteristics:

Q: How do you know it's always you?

A: 'Cause I still like science, and I still like swimming. And I'd still be doing science.

Q: So you still like the same things, so you know it's always you?

A: Yeah.

(Level 1 example)

Q: How do you know it's always you?

A: I've always been good at baseball.

Q: You've always been good at baseball?

A: Yeah, and I always will be.

(Level 2 example)

Level 3 ideas about self-continuity involve the recognition of self by others, and at Level 4 the self's characteristics are seen as evolving from earlier ones, not as being simply identical with them: 'Well, nothing about me always stays the same, but I am always kind of like I was a while ago, and there is always some connection'. The final aspect of the self-as-subject is its distinctness, expressed in terms of it being different from every other self. This progresses from differences in characteristics such as fingerprints or having shoes with laces, via one-dimensional characteristics such as friendliness to one's unique combination of psychological and physical characteristics at Level 3 and one's unique subjective experiences at Level 4: 'Nobody else sees things or feels the same way about things as I do' (Damon and Hart 1988: 72–3, 76).

Damon and Hart's research provides some fascinating glimpses of children's ideas about themselves and various other matters, including the child as developmental psychologist, perhaps, in their accounts of how they got to be the way they are or might have turned out differently! However, even the representative examples I have presented here suggest some problems with the work. First, are the questions and the prompts used fully appropriate? Questioning in the Piagetian *méthode clinique* is supposed to follow what the child says: in many examples the reader of Damon and Hart's book may have a sense of leading questions shaping the child's answers. Second, how coherently does the elicited material fit into the levels and the separate schemes? The physical, active, social and psychological schemes are not always separable in the data, though they do reflect distinctions drawn by William James and implicated in the more unidimensional models constructed by, for example, Broughton and Selman. Later levels incorporate earlier ones and a child is likely to make statements representative of several different levels: thus the analyst has had to use the modal levels 'to represent a subject's typical performance': 'on average, 61 per cent of the chunks (separable statement plus explanation, clarification or explicit failure to provide one when given an opportunity) were at the modal level' (p. 89). Information on how subjects' statements were spread across levels is not given. Again, it is not entirely clear to an outsider why some of the examples given were classified at different levels: the 'Level 1' child quoted earlier who explains that she or he is the same from year to year ''cause I still like science, and I still like swimming' might be seen as differing from the 'Level 2' child ('I've always been good at baseball') merely in using 'still' rather than 'always', for example. This sort of problem has long been endemic with the complex material elicited in *méthode clinique* interviews.

Thus interview studies often represent children as immature understanders of persons, dominated by notions that they have to grow out of but that might meanwhile be expected to impair their ability to get along with other people. Some stage or level theorists have seen immature concepts as reflected in inadequate social behaviour (such as 'egocentricity'); few of these models explain why children change from one level of understanding to another, a change that would be easier to explain if the later levels of understanding were in some way more useful than the earlier ones. Damon and Hart see comparison between self and others as predominant ('modal') in middle childhood, and see interpersonal relations in early adolescence as modal. Might this reflect the social predicaments of children at these ages, as they are embroiled in first school and getting good grades and then in all the early stages of mating behaviour, the getting dates and going steady that loom large in so many accounts of American adolescence? The development of self-understanding seems likely to be one of the areas of social cognition where social factors go a long way towards determining developmental change.

Stage and level models of children's understanding of persons are undermined by a growing body of evidence that children are very skilled at many sorts of social interaction and may casually express a considerable and conscious understanding of persons. Here, instead of neo-Piagetian studies of the 'cold' cognitions of children interviewed about themselves and other persons, we have detailed and systematic observations of children taking part in the normal daily interactions of their families and other social groups. Among my favourites is the work of Judy Dunn and her colleagues (Dunn 1988, 1993; Dunn and Hughes 2001b; Dunn *et al.* 1995):

> Children develop their powers of communication, understanding and thought, their emotional security and their sense of themselves, within a complex social framework: do they nevertheless fail to grasp the nature of the moods, interests and relationships of others who share that world, or the ground rules of that world, until they are five or seven years old?
>
> (Dunn 1988: 3)

Dunn examined the 'social intelligence' of children as they grow up with siblings and parents. She emphasises the relationships between understanding on the one hand and the children's emotions, relationships and self-interest on the other, considering the children's behaviour and speech in 'the daily dramas of family life in which their powers of social intelligence are revealed and fostered' (p. 11). She observed under-threes in ordinary working-class and middle-class families in and around Cambridge, in their disagreements and confrontations with their mother and their siblings as well as in their co-operation, their comforting and their jokes. Some representative examples give a flavour of the children's social understanding as revealed in their practice.

John (21 months) and his older sister Annie have pushed stools up to the kitchen counter next to the oven, to investigate cooking materials.

Mother to John:	Ah ah! Don't touch please. Hot! [removes child].
John:	[protest noise]
Mother:	Oh I know!
John	[*angrily*]: Annie going there!
Mother to Annie:	Annie come right away. Right away.

(1988: 53)

Jay (30 months) is concerned about his older brother Len, who is crying because his mother scolded him and refused to comfort him after he had bitten Jay.

Jay to Len:	Len. Don't – stop crying, mate. Stop it crying.
Jay to Mother:	Len crying, Mummy! Len crying. Look. Me show you. Len crying.
Jay to Len:	Look, Len. No go on crying (pats Len) . . . [Len still sobs.] Ah Len [Helps Len with Lego bag.] I put it back for Lennie, Hey? . . . [Shows Len a car.] There's this man in here. What's this, Len? What's this, Len? [Len sobs.]
Mother to Len:	Do you want me to smack you?
Len to Mother:	No.
Mother:	Then just stop it, please.
Len to Mother:	I'm trying to [sobs].
Jay to Len	[*still crying*]: Stop crying, Len. Smack your bottom.

(1988: 94–95)

Polly (28 months) intervenes in her older sister's conversation with their mother about the sister's pretend game of shopping at Sainsbury's.

Polly to Sib:	Better get your cheque book.
Sib:	Yes . . .
[Later in pretend game]	
Sib to Mother:	Did I leave my bag there?
Mother to Sib:	You didn't leave your bag at Sainsbury's, did you?
Sib to Mother:	What I want?
Polly to Sib	[*points out mislaid bag*]: No at home!
Mother to Sib:	You left it at home! . . .
Sib to Mother	[*confused about having lost her list and her bag*]: Umm – what did I want then?
Mother to Sib:	What did you want?
Polly	[*triumphantly*]: I got all my shopping list in. I's got my shopping list in my bag.

(1988: 114–115)

Finally, John (now aged 36 months) collaborates with his older sister in a fantasy game about what he is going to do with a bonfire.

John:	I'm going to burn everyone. I'm going to burn Jimmy I am. To burn Jimmy Green. To burn Jimmy Green . . .
Mother to John:	Well, I think you're horrid. Making fires to burn people.

Annie to Mother:	Anyway he needs to burn Jimmy Green. Because he keeps biting him.
Mother to Annie:	He doesn't keep biting him, Annie.
Annie:	Yes he does. [to John] Doesn't he John?
John:	Yes he does! He does bite me! You know he does. He does he does he does!
Mother:	I think the boot's on the other foot!
John:	No! [laughs]
Mother:	Jimmy Green's a nice quiet little boy.
John:	No! [laughs].

(1988: 164–165)

Dunn's observations show children with an excellent practical grasp of others' feelings and intentions, and of general social rules, for example of how relationships within the family can be used:

> by two years old, children are using maternal authority for support in their fights with siblings: they draw their mother's attention to the siblings' misdemeanours, while pointing out that they themselves have not acted in the same way.

(1988: 67)

Similarly, siblings share the amusement and excitement when one or both have done something that has been forbidden, egging each other on in delightful joint wickedness. Dunn sees children as developing social knowledge as family members, whose feelings of attachment, rivalry and affection motivate them to understand people's emotions, intentions and motivations and the social rules that govern their interaction. She further points out how the mother's behaviour carries both implicit and explicit messages about the social rules of the world in which the child is growing up, with many conversations about what was acceptable and what unacceptable behaviour: messages that differ in content in different cultures but are universally learned early in ordinary domestic discourse (Heath 1983; Shweder *et al.* 1990; Rogoff 1998, 2003; Wang 2004). The children had a considerable motivation to learn to cope with their social worlds, and their self-interest drove their understanding on. Cognitive development undoubtedly contributes to their sense of self and their emotions (Parke 1989; Sroufe 1979; Harris 1989), but emotional experiences also fire cognitive development; in Dunn's data, it was in those contexts where children had experienced anger and distress that they later came to reason rather than merely protest, as if their emotion had heightened their attention to and intensified their reflection on their experiences. (Research on children's understanding of emotion and their theory of mind may be mentioned here: see pp. 175–180, 205–212.)

All these features suggest a model of the growth of social under-standing in which development starts from the child's interest in and responsiveness to the behaviour and feelings of others. In the sub-sequent development of social understanding, contributions are made, first, by the intensity of the child's self-concern in the context of family relationships and, second, by the child's participation in the moral discourse of the family. In other words, the model gives weight both to the cognitive changes that lead to the child's developing sense of self and ability to participate in argument, and to the affective significance of the tension between this self-concern and the child's relationships with other family members. In discourse about the social world, both the affective and the cognitive messages are significant.

(Dunn 1988: 186)

In her next sentence, Dunn points out that this model raises more questions than it answers. I will not address these questions here (though see Chapters 4 and 5 for discussion of related issues), but merely point out the dis-crepancy between the sophisticated social skills of Dunn's toddlers and the apparently scrappy ability in understanding of older children in interviews. Obviously children may act appropriately but still be unable to explain the principles behind their actions, just as adults may. There are a number of different senses in which one can be said to 'understand' something, as I have pointed out earlier in this chapter. My present point is that if children fail to display an adult understanding in that epitome of a non-practical situation, the clinical interview, their failure is not explained by attributing to them a global inability to understand arising from pervasive and ineradicable characteristics such as egocentricity or an overly behaviouristic outlook. Rather, *what* the child understands *where* must be mapped, and more specific explanations sought for both failures and successes. Again, this is a message applicable in areas of developmental psychology other than the child's understanding of persons.

2.13.9 Children's understanding of socio-economic systems

Children's development, including their social cognition, has mainly been studied in terms of microsystems such as home or school, or mesosystems such as the relationships of agreement or discrepancy between home and school (Bronfenbrenner 1979). Home and school are of course the settings most immediately relevant to children, but they live also, as we all do, within wider socio-economic worlds that impinge on the child in the more intimate settings where they develop many cognitive skills (e.g. Jordan 2004). Their part in the economic and political system is less prominent than their part in the life of the family, and we may overlook it in ways that disadvantage children (Leach (1979) argues this strongly), but it is nevertheless of potential interest to developmental psychologists. Turiel (1983), Emler (1998) and Nucci (2002a, 2002c) argue that it is reflected in the three general categories of children's social cognition: their concepts of persons or psychological systems (pp. 186–194), their moral judgements of justice, rights and welfare (pp. 180–184), and their concepts of systems of social relations, organisation and institutions.

In our industrialised society children have a comparatively limited amount of economic activity. They are not normally economically productive, as child labour is forbidden by law, though some do work in the home or the family business or illegally in the so-called 'black' economy, and older children may have part-time jobs as baby-sitters, newspaper deliverers, shop assistants and so forth. While low on economic productivity, children may be substantial consumers. Their own direct purchasing power may not be large but they exert a significant influence on the purchases of others. Adults' patterns of expenditure are substantially altered by becoming a parent. As children become able to change adult expenditure by their direct requests as well as by their mere existence, they as well as their parents increasingly become the target of advertisement, and their reaction to advertising has been studied by social scientists as well as by advertisers and market researchers (Lea et al. 1987; Ward et al. 1977; Valkenburg and Cantor 2001). Children can learn to be sophisticated and critical observers of advertising (Ward et al. 1977; Roedder-John 1999; Derbaix and Pecheux 2003; Pine and Nash 2003) but its role in their understanding of the economic world has not been fully examined. (Nor has its role in the child's socio-emotional life (Buijzen and Valkenburg 2003), which is another interesting area.)

Besides studies of children as consumers and producers there have been a number of studies of their understanding of socio-economic institutions such as shops, banks and money, and of pocket money or allowances (Furnham 1999; Furnham and Kirkcaldy 2000). These are concerned to document the succession of ideas that children hold as they develop towards the ideas and attitudes that adults commonly have about the economic systems of society, but also to explain how these changes occur. The social institutions concerned are mostly thought of as social systems that children can observe other people playing roles in, inferring economic laws from their observations of economic activity just as they might infer the laws of physics from watching the physical world, and researchers can be criticised for not asking political questions about the nature of these institutions (Dickinson 1990; Emler and Dickinson 1985; Walkerdine and Lucey 1989). There could indeed be far more research on how children are confronted with socio-political inequalities and constraints, or come to grips with problematic issues such as class, sexism and power.

Most of the studies of children's understanding of socio-economic systems involve questioning children, perhaps inevitably, since children do not normally vote, have bank accounts, or play many of the roles of economic or political persons directly, unless through adults; and adults' perceptions of such roles may determine the child's opportunities and cash (Furnham 1999; Furnham and Kirkcaldy 2000). This poses two problems. First, children's answers to questions such as 'What things, jobs, people are important in a town?' (Furth 1980) are often full of charm but hard to analyse. Many investigators have classified answers into neo-Piagetian stage analyses, although data about the uniformity of 'stage' across contexts or the separation of 'stages' are not usually conclusive, and are often not even presented. Second, children's verbal accounts may or may not reflect their practical understanding. Piaget himself moved from eliciting verbal accounts of 'reality' as observed by the child to examining aspects of reality that lie within the grasp of the child's action. Studies of children as economic actors, perhaps via script elicitation or even role play, might provide information that complements what is gathered from interview questions.

Although economic roles, institutions and laws form an interlocking system, and how children see their interrelations is perhaps the most interesting aspect of their thinking, I will deal with the elements of children's construction of the economic world separately, beginning with children's understanding of shopping. Children get many opportunities to observe shopping, and so might be expected to understand it comparatively well. The youngest children take the central transaction in a shop as a simple exchange, between customer and shopkeeper, of goods and their value in cash (Berti and Bombi 1988; Jahoda 1979, 1984). This is certainly the most visible part of shopping but it is far from the whole. The retail shopkeeper is himself or herself a customer to the wholesaler who supplies the shop with goods; the shop has assistants who exchange their labour for wages, and there are also various running costs such as rent, cleaning and lighting. These components of the shop are less salient to the shopper, but they have significant effects on the cost of the items in the shop. Typically such costs are not visible to children, who seem to have some difficulty in grasping the existence of these components and their effects, let alone their scale. A further source of complexity and confusion is that the passage of money between the customer and shopkeeper may be two-way: the customer gives £1 and receives the chocolate bar and 20p in change. To a small child with little grasp of the monetary values involved, this may look like a ritual, or a profit to the customer who ends up with goods and money, rather than the exchange it is.

At this age children believe that goods were given to the shop (by another shop), not bought by it, and they seem not to be aware of any 'overheads', for example not distinguishing between the shopkeeper and the shop assistants. Even when these last two misconceptions begin to weaken, at around seven to eight, the idea that the price the shop charges the customer is the same as the price the wholesaler charges the shop remains strong. The shopkeeper merely passes on goods at the same price as their original cost: the overheads of the shop, if recognised at all, are met from some external source such as the Mint, social security or the government. It is felt to be unfair, theft or fraud, for the shopkeepers to charge a higher price than they have paid themselves; only at the age of about eleven do children realise that a 'mark up' between wholesale and retail price is necessary if the shopkeeper is to cover expenses and make a living (or a profit). The scale of 'mark ups', the extent of the profit made, probably isn't grasped by children; it is often a surprise to adults!

A similar development occurs in children's understanding of banks (Berti and Bombi 1988; Furth 1980; Jahoda 1979, 1984), though with some delay compared with their understanding of shops. The youngest children, who might have shown a little understanding of profit in the context of shops, showed no idea of it in banks. They viewed banks as being much like money-boxes and borrowing from friends: you get out exactly what you put in; to get more or to pay for a loan would not be fair. Even if they knew about interest they had little idea where it came from, and still thought of the bank in interpersonal terms. Berti and Bombi (1988) report ideas of banks as 'for giving money'; so people who only have a little money go to a bank and:

> they give them a little, then they give them a bit more, and they get to have a lot of money . . . then he gets to have lots of money and he buys lots of furniture, or a house and then other things, like that.
>
> (Berti and Bombi 1988: 19)

and the bank is a place where money can be deposited to be safe from thieves and an equal amount can be withdrawn later if needed. Then came a recognition that banks use the money deposited with them to make loans, and, eventually, that lenders receive interest paid by borrowers. As children move through adolescence they show more appreciation of interest and the bank's use of the money deposited with it. Not all, however, understand the reciprocity of interest in the bank's lending and borrowing, and few appreciate that the bank must charge a higher interest on its loans than it pays on its deposits if it is to pay its own workers, cover its costs and realise a profit. Again, appreciation of what scale banks' profits are on, and what is done with them, is quite possibly unusual in adults.

Why is children's understanding of banks less mature than their understanding of shops? One obvious possibility is that they have far more contact with shops than with banks, many more opportunities to observe and think about shopping activities. Berti and Bombi (1988) suggest that an understanding of banks involves construing money as a type of merchandise, to be bought and sold like other goods. Berti and Bombi present data on children's ideas about the source of money. Even the youngest children knew there was an association between 'work' and 'money', though they might also entertain the idea that you get it from transactions in shops or that it somehow spontaneously generates itself in pockets or wallets (an idea to be found in numerous fairytales). They may also have an idea that one must pay to go to work, for example train drivers have had to buy the train they drive and may also go to work in an office to raise the money to purchase the train. Later, children insist that to get money it is necessary to work, and that the amount of money received is proportionate to the amount of work done. This notion runs up against the realities of social stratification and the existence of rich and poor people (see also Dickinson (1990), Emler and Dickinson (1985)). Young children believe that almost everybody is rich, partly because money is freely given away by banks or shops and also because being 'rich' is defined as having enough money to cover basic needs. As working comes to be seen as the only way to make money, working is also seen as the way to become rich: the poor are poor 'because they don't work' and the rich are those who work the most. The idea becomes differentiated somewhat:

Q: Is every job good for getting rich?
A: No, there are some where you get a little money and some where they give you lots.
Q: Which are the best ones for getting rich?
A: The heaviest ones.
Q: If a man has a heavy job is he sure to get rich?
A: No, sometimes they start wheezing and they can't go on any longer, because when you work you can't stop for a minute, it's not like school where you can stop and finish things at home.
Q: Can you also get very rich doing a heavy job?
A: Yes, it depends on the boss, how much money he gives you, and you can't squabble about it, you have to take the money they give you.

(Berti and Bombi 1988: 72)

Later still children described riches as being associated not with hard work but with qualifications, or with highly responsible jobs, or with inheritance, crime, or political corruption. These children saw becoming rich as much more difficult, and hard work as having a much less powerful influence on riches. They also differentiated income levels much more, no longer regarding an adequate income as being 'riches'. Differentiation may proceed differently for children from different social classes, as Emler and Dickinson (1985) demonstrated. They asked children aged between seven and twelve to estimate the weekly incomes of doctors, teachers, bus drivers and road sweepers, to explain why the incomes differed, and to say whether equality of income would 'be better'. The average estimates given by middle-class children for each job were higher than those of working-class children: doctors were seen as having the highest incomes, followed by teachers, bus drivers and, finally, road sweepers. Middle-class children gave much more differential in the estimates of income than working-class children did, as well as judging incomes to be higher overall.

The children were asked about the 'fairness' of the different amounts they had estimated for each job and of a hypothetical equality of remuneration. There were no significant differences in judgement of fairness by age or by social class, though it was less common for the oldest children or for middle-class ones to say that equality of income would be better. Most of the children justified inequality of income by reference to some form of equity consideration, such as differences in the work or the responsibility involved in the job or the amount of training required for it. Middle-class children were more sophisticated in their justification of inequality, producing more (and more varied) reasons. In Berti and Bombi's study, similarly, middle-class children more often mentioned criteria other than physical fatigue, such as the greater or less utility of the job, or the level of intellectual activity that it demands.

Thus, although most children believed that income differences were justified, middle-class children estimated that the inequalities were larger (though even they underestimated their scale). The absence of age differences argues against this class difference being caused by the fact that middle-class children might develop faster than working-class children, more quickly reaching a complex understanding of social systems. The different estimate levels seem more likely to be due to different information about incomes. Emler and Dickinson argue that social representations of economic inequalities are more detailed, extensive and salient in the middle class, and hence middle-class children have had more opportunity to assimilate their community's shared knowledge and belief about income inequality.

In a study of American six- to twelve-year-olds, Liben et al. (2001) investigated job status and job aspirations in relation to gender stereotyping. Texan children rated 'masculine' jobs as higher status than 'feminine' ones, and were less interested in opposite-sex jobs for themselves when the jobs were familiar. Novel jobs, such as 'chandler' or 'limner', were also rated for status in gender-linked ways, but children were more likely to aspire to a novel job associated with the opposite sex. Gelman et al. (2004), observing mothers and children talking about gender and jobs, found children making more mention of explicit gender stereotyping than the mothers, whose gender stereotyping was more implicit. A similar study looked at African American children's views on race and the workforce (Bigler et al. 2003). Here, too, there seems to be a depressing amount of stereotyping and acceptance of socio-economic inequalities, with lower status children rarely aspiring to higher status jobs.

Exactly what economic knowledge is to be found in what parts of the community, and where it comes from, remains to be investigated. This sort of information may not be readily accessible to young children (Berti 1991). There are some findings of class differences in parents' ideas about pocket money (Furnham 1999; Furnham and Kirkcaldy 2000).

2.13.10 Children's theory of mind

One area of children's concepts and skills that has been considered in some depth is their beliefs about the mental world, their understanding of the processes that variously underlie perception, cognition, intention, emotion, belief and other mental states and activities. Such knowledge must surely have cognitive consequences, and play a role in the development of metacognition; it has also been argued (e.g. Dennett 1979; Humphrey 1983; Hobson 2002) that it is a critical contributor to successful social interaction, where understanding other people's mental states may enhance the possibility of making sense of their behaviour (and of manipulating it). The study of mind has also of course been an important part of philosophy. Many of the questions studied in relation to children, for example the distinction between 'appearance' and 'reality', have a long philosophical history. I cannot discuss all that has been done concerning children's 'philosophy of mind' here; among useful reviews and collections are Astington *et al.* (1988, 2004), Bartsch (2002), Butterworth *et al.* (1991), Estes *et al.* (1989), Perner (1991a), Pillow (1988a), Symons (2004), Wellman (1990), a special issue of the *British Journal of Developmental Psychology* (1991 (1)), Flavell (1998, 1999), Wellman and Cross (2001), and a special issue of *New Ideas in Psychology* (2002 (2)).

As in many other areas of the psychology of cognitive development, one source of ideas about children's understanding of the mind–brain relation has been work about children's concepts of mental events done by Piaget, in this case ideas put forward in two early books, *The Child's Conception of the World* (1929) and *The Child's Conception of Physical Causality* (1930). He suggested that young children were egocentric and animistic and had difficulty discriminating between the physical and the psychological; for example they claimed that their own view was what other people could see, that dreams were external images that could be seen by people other than the dreamer, and that the sun, the wind and other natural objects were alive and conscious and followed them around. Some of the recent work on children's understanding of mental states and processes has been concerned to investigate these Piagetian findings. Wellman and Estes (1986), for example, investigated whether young children distinguished between mental events or objects, such as a dreamed of or imagined dog, and real ones, such as a real dog. They found that even three-year-olds could make a better than chance judgement of which of the 'real' and 'mental' pair could be touched, seen by others, and which existed consistently over time, thus showing they appreciated three of the main criteria necessary for distinguishing between the real and the mental. They also knew that you could dream about or imagine but not really see or touch an object that is physically impossible or non-existent, such as a dog with fiery eyes as big as windmills. Thus the preschool children in this study were not Piagetian 'realists', claiming that dreams and thoughts have a concrete and public existence. They were also making more adult ontological judgements than the children interviewed by Frank Keil (Keil 1981a), perhaps because Keil's subjects were asked about thought contents in general, not about a specific thought-of dog. In other studies children this age believed you could engage in conscious mental activity such as thinking or deciding while you were asleep (Flavell *et al.* 1999); adults would doubt this, though the models of creativity I discuss in Chapter 4 give a role to non-conscious processes in solving puzzles creatively.

Even a mental event that you know is not real may affect your reaction to the real world. Harris *et al.* (1991) asked children to imagine that there was either a monster or a bunny rabbit in a box that they knew was really empty; the pretend being over, they were then asked to put their hand in the box. Children who had just imagined that the box contained a monster were much more reluctant to put their hand in, so they may have believed that their pretence had caused a real monster to be in the box; alternatively they may have been carrying on the pretence (see also Golomb and Galasso (1995), Taylor (1997, 1999), Taylor *et al.* (2004), Rakoczy *et al.* (2004)). The rudiments of the distinction between real and mental events were apparent in three-year-olds, but as children get older, they may make more mature distinctions. Woolley *et al.* (2004) found children who had some concrete grounds for believing in the reality of a novel fantasy person (a 'Candy Witch' who brought candies on Halloween), in that they had received candies 'from the Witch' the year before, were more likely to say she was real, but children who frequently indulged in fantasy said she was real too. Wellman (1985a) suggests that some of the earlier findings of children attributing concrete existence to mental events may have been due to methodological differences, that young children's knowledge may be less accessible and stable than adults' knowledge and easily obscured by the difficulty of giving an adequate verbal explanation. Alternatively a child might use mentalistic language without it being based on an adult-like understanding of mental events. Methodological caution is needed.

John Flavell and his colleagues investigated a basic distinction, between what an object 'looks like' and what it 'really and truly' is. In a typical study children are shown (by sight then by feel) a sponge that looks like a rock (or a candle shaped like an apple or a white shape behind a coloured cellophane filter) (Flavell 1986; Flavell *et al.* 1986). At various points in the procedure they are asked questions like 'When you look at this with your eyes right now, does it look like a rock or does it look like a sponge?' (the appearance question), or 'What is this really and truly – is it really and truly a sponge or is it really and truly a rock?' (the reality question). Adults and older children reply that it looks like a rock but it really and truly is a sponge. They also know that someone who has only seen the sponge would say it was a rock, being deceived by its misleading appearance; thus they appear to have two different 'mental representations' of the object, one of what it 'looks like' and another of what it 'really is'. Children under four tend to give the same answer to questions about appearance and about reality, so that they answer 'rock' or 'sponge' to both questions. Flavell (1988) interprets this as an inability to realise that the same object can be represented in different, seemingly contradictory, ways. Astington and Gopnik (1988) show that this refusal to manage different representations can be retrospective. Their three-year-old subjects saw the sponge 'rock' and said it was 'a rock'; after feeling it, what they said was 'it is a sponge', 'it looks like a sponge' (a 'realist' error) and 'I thought it was a sponge when I first saw it'. They therefore deny the change in their own mental state, even though they may say that another person who hasn't felt the sponge may believe it to be a rock. The error occurs over different objects and pairings of modalities, for example a candle shaped like an apple or a white cardboard shape shown with a coloured cellophane filter, and has been resistant (so far) to training (Flavell 1988). But when the question is asked in the context of trying to deceive someone, or when the child is asked what the ambiguous object could be used for, children are much more likely to give an adult answer (Rice *et al.* 1997; Peskin and Ardino 2003; Sapp *et al.* 2000).

These complex findings on the appearance–reality distinction have been related to children's judgements of other people's views, both literally and in the sense of their wider mental states (Butterworth *et al.* 1991; Astington and Gopnik 1988; Moore *et al.* 1990; Perner 1991a; Wellman 1990; Wellman *et al.* 2001). Piaget's suggestion that young children were 'ego-centric' in such judgements (Piaget and Inhelder 1956) has spawned much research. Piaget and Inhelder asked what view could be seen from various points around a three-dimensional array of mountains. Their youngest subjects tended to choose a picture showing their own view irrespective of whether the viewpoint currently in question was their own or not. More recent studies, however, have shown the 'egocentric' error to be less common than Piaget described it and to be attributable in some degree to the difficulty of his task. If simpler materials are used (or 'meaningful' ones such as a 'naughty boy' doll hiding from a policeman doll (Donaldson 1978)), children have little difficulty in distinguishing someone else's view from their own (see Flavell (1985) for a review). Beginning in infancy, children come to understand a great deal about what a person can see. They use the other person's direction of gaze to work out what they are looking at from very early indeed; they can use verbal clues to distinguish between different sorts of objects and events (Carpenter *et al.* 1998; Tomasello and Haberl 2003). They know that in order to see an object at least one of the observer's eyes must be open, and aimed in the direction of the object, while no other large opaque object comes between the observed and the observer. They understand about hiding objects (Pratt and Bryant 1990). They also know that what they themselves see is irrelevant to what another person sees. They can use this knowledge to enable an observer to see something, or to prevent this, as well as for their own diagnostic purposes. By four to five they can play hide-and-seek (Peskin and Ardino 2003). They are thus not egocentric in at least some of their assessment and use of other people's vision, though it is not clear whether under-fours are fully aware that lack of vision may mean lack of information (Pillow 1989; Taylor *et al.* 1991; Wimmer *et al.* 1988), and they may think that if two people see the same sight they will interpet it in the same way.

Wimmer *et al.* (1988) questioned children about their own and others' knowledge about a picture in a box. Three-year-olds were able to say whether they knew what the picture in the box was, but couldn't say how they knew (because they had seen it) or why they didn't know (because they hadn't seen it). Seven out of ten four-year-olds could identify the reason for their knowledge or ignorance correctly, showing some understanding of the importance of access to information as a crucial source of knowledge. The researchers argue that even for the youngest children seeing the picture leads to a mental representation of what's in the box, which can be accessed in order to give the correct answer to whether you do or don't know what is in the box. From four years old onwards it also leads to registering the causal connection between having access to information (or not) and having knowledge (or not), for oneself and for other people; that is, understanding access to knowledge develops earlier than understanding what that access causes for one's cognition (Flavell *et al.* 1990; Mitchell and Robinson 1992; Pillow 1989; Pillow and Henrichon 1996; Ruffman and Olson 1989; Taylor *et al.* 1991; Kitchener 2002). This is not surprising, given that young children must see things (in the sense of 'have them come within sight') without 'seeing' them in the epistemic sense of 'see' ('recognise', identify', 'know the significance of') even more than older people do. (The Australian Aborigines encountered by Captain Cook in 1770 took no notice of the 106-foot-long *Endeavour*, too large to be registered as a ship, appearing not to see it until Cook and his sailors disembarked into a smaller rowing boat (Hughes 1987). Children similarly lack experience of artefacts, and indeed of much else.)

One thing that may be problematic here is children's understanding of when they can and cannot be certain about their inferences (Pillow and Henrichon 1996; Pillow 2002; Samuels and McDonald 2002; Kitchener 2002). In a study by Chandler and Helm (1984), children were shown a picture almost entirely obscured by a cardboard cover. A few ambiguous lines could be seen through a hole in the cover, and children, when asked what they were, would typically say they didn't know, or the lines were meaningless scribble. When the cover was removed, the ambiguous lines turned out to be part of the trunk of an elephant. The children were then asked what a naïve observer would see in the lines when the cover was replaced; they said that the lines would be correctly identified as the elephant's trunk. Similar results have been found by Taylor (1988) and Ruffman *et al.* (1991). Children's understanding that the present perceptual experience will yield different information to people whose prior perceptual experience differs shows a major improvement between three and five. What an informed observer knows about an object is assumed to enter the mind of the ignorant observer automatically, an assumption all too often made by adults also!

It has also been suggested that children under school age cannot simultaneously attend to the whole of a picture and to its parts at the same time (e.g. Elkind 1978; Vurpillot 1976). Thus, if shown a 'person' made up of fruits, four- to five-year-olds typically mention the parts rather than the whole, as if the 'person' representation was not available to them. However, Prather and Bacon (1986) found that even two- to three-year-olds could identify both part and whole in a simpler picture (such as a triangle with sides defined by carrots) and 14 per cent spontaneously produced an 'integrated' description; for example, 'It's a triangle made of carrots'. It would seem that both materials and questioning techniques are important, but that multiple representations may be possible even for very young children. It would seem, then, that very young children can distinguish between their own knowledge and another person's when what is in question is inferences about what the other can or cannot see (or hear or know). But they run into difficulties in understanding that the same object may appear different from different positions or on different occasions to different observers. Pillow (1988a) suggests that young children may begin with a passive view of the origin of mental states, believing that the outside world produces an objective and unvarying copy of itself in the mind by being seen (or heard, or whatever), and not understanding that the mind acts on this information to interpret it in ways influenced by each person's idiosyncratic knowledge and subjective states, so that individuals will pick up different information from the same sensory experience and construct different mental representations. A similar account is proposed by Flavell (1988). He brings together a considerable amount of evidence that children under three have learned a great deal about how people (themselves and others) can be 'cognitively connected' to the external world. They have learned, for example, that cognitive connections (such as seeing something) can change over time, are largely independent of other cognitive connections, are independent of other people's cognitive connections, and can entail other, subjective, experiences. However, young children do not understand that these 'connections' are made up of mental representations rather than being objective automatic links; in particular they do not understand that there can be a multiplicity of mental representations and interpretations that are seemingly contradictory.

A similar distinction can be made in the development of the under-standing of 'know'. Children under three may understand 'know' as meaning 'have a true idea about', but it is a later achievement to add to this definition the requirement that the true idea should come from a certain and reliable source or inference, rather than from a guess that luckily turned out to be correct. Distinction between empirical certainties and logical certainties also develops later (e.g. Mitchell and Robinson 1992; Moore *et al.* 1989; Moshman and Franks 1986; Ruffman and Olson 1989; Pillow and Henrichon 1996; Pillow 2002; Samuels and McDonald 2002; Kitchener 2002).

Children may also have particular problems understanding that another person may have a false belief (as opposed to no belief at all as a result of having had no access to information, which, as we have seen, they seem to be able to recognise quite early). Investigation of children's understanding of false belief has been an especially lively and productive area of research. Such understanding is of particular interest to research on children's theory of mind because it elucidates whether the child appreciates that other people may have beliefs that are different from his or her own, and can allow diagnosis of what the child believes are the causes of beliefs. If the child's own beliefs about the situation are true, but the other's would be false, and the child can recognise that the other, acting on false beliefs, would do something different from the child, then we can be sure that the child imputes mental stages of belief to the other person, and predicts the other's behaviour on the basis of the imputed mental stages.

A substantial body of work has now been done using false belief para-digms of various sorts (Flavell 1999; Wellman and Cross 2001; Wellman *et al.* 2001; Kitchener 2002; Saxe *et al.* 2004). In one of the earliest studies (Wimmer and Perner 1983) the child was told a story in which a little boy put some chocolate in place A and then went away. During his absence, the chocolate was moved to place B. The boy then came back, hungry and wanting his chocolate. The child was asked where the little boy would look for his chocolate. Most three-year-olds, and a substantial proportion of four-year-olds, said that the boy would look in place B (where they knew the chocolate now was), not in place A (where the boy last saw it), thus showing that they did not understand where the boy would believe the chocolate to be.

Hogrefe *et al.* (1986) found a developmental lag in children's attribution of ignorance and false belief. Children were told stories where another person was excluded from information that was available to the child, for example that a box labelled 'Smarties' actually contained a pencil. Half of three-year-olds and 80 per cent of four-year-olds could say that the other person would not know what was in the Smarties box, but at this stage the children would not say that the other person would probably have the (false) belief that there were Smarties in the box. They would attribute to the other person their own mental representation of the box's contents; thus, although the other person would not know what was in the box they would be thought to have a mental picture of the box containing a pencil. Just as in the retrospective judgement change in the study by Astington and Gopnik (1988) discussed above, there seems to be a difficulty in admitting alternative mental representations, or perhaps in inhibiting the most obvious representation in favour of a more difficult one. This difficulty may lead to children's repudiation of their own earlier claim of belief. Typically, three-year-olds would say when first seeing the Smarties box 'it has Smarties in'; but after seeing that the contents were in fact pencils, they would say that they had said on first seeing it that it had pencils in, even if reminded of the statement to the opposite effect they had made only a minute or two before (Astington and Gopnik 1988; Gopnik and Slaughter 1991; Schauble 1990; Wimmer and Hart 1991). Three-year-olds seem to have a real conceptual gap here (Astington and Gopnik 1991; Perner 1991a; Wellman 1990; Flavell 1999; Perner et al. 2002): they have a problem in understanding that beliefs involve representations, and how their representations relate to reality. This might be linked to immaturity of brain systems needed for executive control (Saxe et al. 2004; Gathercole et al. 2004; and see pp. 335–338), or to the self-awareness that is deficient in autism (Hobson 2002).

Perner and his colleagues (e.g. Perner 1991b; Hogrefe et al. 1986) believe that there is a similar developmental lag for 'second-order' beliefs ('He thinks that I think that there is a pencil in the box'), success here developing during the early primary school years, but possibly beginning somewhat earlier (Chandler et al. 1989; Hala et al. 1991; Sodian 1991; Wellman et al. 2001). Understanding of this sort makes bluff (and double bluff and all sorts of higher order games of deception) possible. They suggest that there is a repeated cycle of three stages of recognising and using alternative mental representations, first in visual perspective taking, then in knowing about other people's knowledge, then in higher order knowledge attribution ('John kicks Mary because John knows that Mary does not know that the teacher has arrived, and he wants her to know about it so he gives her a kick'). In the first stage the child is totally ignorant of others' beliefs: all other people see what I see or know what I know and so forth. In the second, transitional, stage, the child knows that different views or beliefs exist but has difficulty specifying them for another person and may inappropriately attribute his or her own mental representation to the other. In the third stage the child recognises the need to infer the other's mental representation, can do so and can apply the inference. This sort of achievement is invaluable for the development of interpersonal understanding. Autistic children seem to have particular problems with this (Baron-Cohen *et al.* 2000; Baron-Cohen and Frith 1992; Frith 1990; Frith and Frith 2003; Gillberg 1992; Hermelin 2001; Hill and Frith 2003; Hobson 1991, 2002; Klin *et al.* 1992; Perner *et al.* 1989; Tager-Flusberg 1992; Flavell 1999; Peterson 2002; Saxe *et al.* 2004). The literature offers some interesting accounts of children's understanding of lies and deception (Bussey 1999; Lee and Cameron 2000; Lee *et al.* 2002; Peterson 1995; Polak and Harris 1999; Siegal and Peterson 1996, 1998; Woolley 1995).

This sort of understanding develops rapidly in the preschool years. Accepting multiple representations seems to be easiest in the 'pretend' domain, which flourishes from the second year onwards (e.g. Leslie 1987, 1988a; Lillard 2001, 2002; Taylor 1997, 1999; Taylor *et al.* 2004), or when 'desires' are the focus (Wellman and Woolley 1990; Wellman *et al.* 2001), or when prediction or guessing is explicitly involved, or when the representation is clearly subjective (for example, three-year-olds are said to understand that cats think cat food tastes 'yummy' even though they themselves think it tastes 'yukky'), or when deceit is focused on (Butterworth *et al.* 1991; Chandler *et al.* 1989; Perner 1991a; Peskin 1992). Complete understanding that there may be different mental representations of the same object or event and that these may be equally 'valid' is undoubtedly a very sophisticated achievement indeed (and probably a fragile one, given how often we may fail to appreciate someone else's point of view). It involves a great deal of knowledge about mental events, which means it may make great demands on working memory (Gathercole *et al.* 2004; and pp. 86–87); it includes understanding one's own cognitive processes (and hence it may be metacognitive, see Flavell (1999) and pp. 132–135); it may be related to reasoning, especially about counterfactuals (Guajardo and Turley-Ames 2004; and p. 106) and also embedded in the language and social context of cognition (Wellman 1985a, 1990; Wellman *et al.* 2001; Lohmann and Tomasello 2003); it may be linked to impersonation and having imaginary friends (Taylor *et al.* 2004). It has been said to be an essential component of the skills needed for living with other people (Humphrey 1983), with great importance throughout evolution and hence areas of brain specialised for theory-of-mind processing (Frith and Frith 2003; Saxe *et al.* 2004). Adults' discussion, especially mothers' discussion, of people's beliefs, desires and understanding is associated with individual differences in children's understanding of mental states, which may account for some of the difficulties of deaf and autistic children (Bartsch 2002; Strauss *et al.* 2002; Peterson 2002; Hobson 2002; Meins 1998; Meins and Fernyhough 1999; Meins *et al.* 2002, 2003; Peterson and Slaughter 2003; Hill and Frith 2003; Symons 2004; Baird and Astington 2004). Thus children's understanding of mind is perhaps a central issue in their cognitive and social development, as Wellman (1990), Flavell (1999) and Hobson (2002) argue.

It will already be clear that the tasks used for assessing children's theory of mind differ in which aspect of it they focus on and also in their difficulty. Most studies use tests of only one or two areas of theory of mind and do not treat them psychometrically, but Wellman and Liu (2004) offer a scaled set of tasks, in which children succeed in identifying another person's different desires before they can identify people's different beliefs, and understanding true (but not shared) beliefs precedes understanding false beliefs. Other researchers, including Schult (2002), also show correct identification of desires before intentions, but many other theory-of-mind behaviours need to be integrated into the scale.

Theorists here, as elsewhere in the psychology of cognitive development, differ in their explanations of the causes of the development of children's 'theory of mind'. Birch and Bloom (2004) argue that all that is happening is that the 'curse of knowledge', a tendency to be biased by one's own knowledge when attempting to understand another's perspective, diminishes as the child gets older. A claim for a more radical qualitative change in understanding is commoner in the field. Some theorists have claimed that it is due to an innately specified 'module' devoted to mechanisms for dealing with agents, especially other people (Leslie 1994; Fodor 1983). This 'module' comes into operation as a result of brain maturation, and equips the baby with a distinction between agents, who have an internal source of energy permitting them to operate on their own, and inanimate or inactive entities; then with a first theory of mind, which allows the young child to understand agents as perceiving the world and having goals; and finally with a second, additional, theory of mind which allows the child to see agents as having mental states related to truth, for example pretending, believing, and imagining.

Other researchers (e.g. Perner 1991; Wellman 1985a, 1990; Flavell and Miller 1998; Flavell 1999) also emphasise the coherence, the abstractness, the lawfulness of children's ideas about the domain of minds. They point out that like truly scientific theories, theory of mind allows generalisation, explanation and prediction, and the use of evidence to support ideas, even to the point of denying counter-evidence. They stress the size and pervasiveness, but also the domain-specificity, of the shift in ideas about minds that children go through between the ages of two and five, and suggest that this shift shows that a general structural change and reorganisation is happening, not just the accumulation of new knowledge in essentially unrelated areas. They point out that it is people in the grip of a theory who are most likely to ignore or distort counter-evidence; they compare the children who denied they had a moment ago predicted that there would be Smarties in a Smarties box rather than the pencils they saw there immediately after their prediction (Astington and Gopnik 1988; Hogrefe *et al.* 1986; Wimmer and Hart 1991) with the children who had such difficulty in abandoning their theory about balancing blocks (Karmiloff-Smith 1988;

Karmiloff-Smith and Inhelder 1974/5) and the scientists who may go to even greater lengths to protect their theories (Gosse 1907; Kuhn 1962). It would be the theory-like nature of the understanding that is to a considerable degree responsible for the rapidity of development on so many related concepts over a comparatively short period of time. Like Piagetian schemas, theories have built-in tendencies to self-improvement in the form of increasing coherence, inclusiveness, and flexibility, and the interaction between theory and the evidence available for testing is seen as driving the development of children's understanding, much as it drives the development of knowledge in science. Wellman (1990) summarises this position; Perner (1991a) provides a notably elegant argument of it from basic principles.

Other researchers in the area (e.g. Hobson 1991, 2002) believe that calling children's understanding of minds a 'theory' leads to insufficient recognition of the role of perception and knowledge (as opposed to theory-led inference) in the child's understanding. For example, there are observable regularities in the expression of some mental states, such as surprise or sadness, and these are used by infants, by preschoolers and by adults in not dissimilar ways. The early behaviourist way of understanding minds is certainly added to, but it is not superseded. It is important to these researchers to remind us that general cognitive limitations or strengths may be relevant to children's developing theory of mind; for example, working memory (Gathercole *et al.* 2004), or difficulties in inhibiting initial responses (Flavell and Miller 1998), or language difficulties. The theory that a 'theory of mind' develops between the ages of two and five may introduce too great a discontinuity into our account of development, so that we both underestimate the competence of the very young and overestimate the coherence and abstractness of adults' thinking (Kitchener 2002). Hobson (1991, 2002) prefers to emphasise the role of emotionally charged interactions and relationships with other people. We are biologically programmed to engage in such interactions and relationships, to the extent that we may have direct perceptual experience of other people's emotions just as we do of their physical experience or our own. Experience with other people who model the expressive behaviour of mental states, and who react to and comment on one's own, is the source of awareness of other people's mental states, of reflective self-awareness of one's own, and of one's 'folk-psychology' 'theory' of minds. This experience is something young children seize on with great interest, seeking to discuss other people's actions and motivations with their mothers, for example (Dunn 1988; Dunn *et al.* 1987; Howe and Rinaldi 2004). Disputes with siblings and discussions with mothers predict children's theory of mind development (Hughes and Cutting 1999; Dunn *et al.* 1995, 2001b; Meins 1998; Watson *et al.* 1999; Peterson and Slaughter 2003; Strauss *et al.* 2002; Peterson 2002; Hobson 2002; Symons 2004; Bartsch 2002; Baird and Astington 2004); attachment to the discussing mother is also relevant (Meins *et al.* 2001, 2002, 2003;

Meins and Fernyhough 1999), which reminds us of the social and emotional setting of theory of mind.

Hobson (1991: 47–48) argues:

> Once a child has acquired a grasp of body-anchored and 'outer-directed' subjectively experienced mental states on a largely if not exclusively non-inferential basis, then the child can employ inferences or other intellectual strategies to learn more about its own and others' minds . . . Theorizing is not the primary source of children's knowledge about minds, nor are minds first understood by children as especially private, 'theorizing' minds – they are the minds of people who are perceived and felt to act and feel, as well as turning out to be the minds of people who think and believe . . .

The developmental progression is from an infant's perception and growing understanding of the public, psychologically expressive behaviour and attitudes of persons, to a young child's more sophisticated knowledge of the nature of persons and their potentially but only partially undisclosed minds.

Before we leave children's concepts of mind, a pair of cautions is necessary. The dominant explanations in the field feature the development of a richer understanding of mental life from rudimentary beginnings. Birch and Bloom (2004) have recently argued that what is happening is more like the freeing of a mental state understanding that is rich early on in children's lives from being limited by a bias towards preferring one's own knowledge, and falling back on this preference whenever it is too hard to work out someone else's knowledge, or too much bother. This account might cope better with some of the evidence of children having a sophisticated understanding that other people do not know what you know when it is worth your while to use this understanding to deceive them, and with adults' often shaky use of their knowledge that other people may have different knowledge and opinions and desires from their own. Secondly, there continues to be controversy among professional philosophers and psychologists about what sort of 'philosophy of mind' is correct (or, better, appropriate). Fodor (1990) provides a 'guide' to a number of different positions on this question, and so, more soberly, does Lycan (1989). One central issue is the psychological status of 'beliefs', 'desires', 'intentions', and so forth, in explaining behaviour. Philosophers such as Ryle (1949) and psychologists such as Skinner (1957) have argued, forcefully and influentially, that mental representations and mental states in general do not really exist and so have no role in psychological explanation. They are 'the ghost in the machine', and what is of interest is the machine itself, the behaviour it emits, and the patterning of stimulation and reinforcement in the world that surrounds it. These theorists would see it as at best useless and as at worst misleading to talk of the thinking machine having mental representations such as 'theories of mind'. They restrict their investigations to contingencies between measurable conditions and behaviours and do not attribute 'intentional states' such as beliefs, expectations and desires to the 'thinker'.

A more accepting position acknowledges that our language and our 'commonsense' 'folk' psychology or 'folk epistemology' use concepts of mental states and intentional descriptions. We may, however, use terms such as 'think' or 'believe' or 'intend' as convenient descriptions of how someone's behaviour makes sense to us, without having any idea about whether the description is correct or whether the mental state exists and causes behaviour. The descriptions have developed over the millennia of human social existence because their use facilitates social interaction, not because they were the product of systematic dispassionate study of people's minds. Folk psychology is no more a scientific theory than folk meteorology was (and, as Lillard (1998) points out, it differs between culturally different folks), but it enables good enough 'getting on' with other people, just as 'red sky in the morning, shepherd's warning' gave good enough advice on when to shelter the sheep. There may be dangers of reifying beliefs, desires, etc. in inappropriate ways, and of crediting people with 'theories of mind' that are too coherent and systematic, if there is a flexible *ad hoc* behaviourist reality.

2.14 Coda and caveat

Throughout this review of areas of cognitive development I have mainly been describing studies that describe age differences in children's performance cross-sectionally, using separate samples at different ages. This is the commonest sort of study in many areas of research on cognitive development. Commonly, but not always, the results are presented in terms of young children giving wrong answers and older ones doing better. Often, this is a legitimate interpretation: but not always. Siegal (1991) suggests (as have other researchers, see e.g. Donaldson (1978)) that a great deal of the wrongness of young children's answers to adults' questions about such matters as conservation and theory of mind is caused by the adults' breach of normal conversational rules and children's reaction to an anomalous situation. In a number of experiments he has found, for example, that repetition of questions worsens performance on conservation tasks and on the appearance–reality distinction; that there are order effects on these and on gender constancy tasks; and that children would often explain that a wrong answer was given 'just pretending' or to tease or please the adult questioners. He points out that in the interviews used to test children's cognition the child is dealing with an interrogator who is much larger, more powerful and more knowledgeable, and who is in charge, however much gentleness and friendliness is shown. In such an unequal social interaction, correct answers may be fairly unproblematic, but incorrect answers may be associated with uncertainty about the situation, misinterpretation of what is going on under repeated questioning, attention-seeking or a desire to escape from the interview.

This criticism has to be taken seriously, not least because if it is correct an enormous amount of what is taken as 'fact' in children's cognitive development would turn out to be at best suspect, at worst a set of false negatives. Where researchers have been aware of these problems, and have used complementary methods to get at the child's understanding, I think we can continue to trust their data; but there are uncomfortably many papers in the literature where even the most elementary precautions were not taken, and children were asked silly questions and compared with a non-comparable sample of adults – the local undergraduate population being the normal source of 'adults'. Sometimes it is too easily assumed that what the adults say is 'right' or universal, rather than a culturally specific or historically specific belief that would not stand up to scrutiny. The research on children's ideas of the afterlife or of the effects of brain transplants discussed earlier in this chapter is prominent in my mind here, because the 'findings' particularly offend my own beliefs; though all I am really entitled to do is to ask researchers to consider their own assumptions a little more critically. We need to remember that when people lack information they may confabulate, that is make up an answer; and then stick to it so as not to lose face. We also need to remember that we may often not have adequate language to convey the richness and excellence of our understanding (Pine *et al.* (2004) examine gestures during a problem-solving task, with interesting results). Finally, we need to remember that if you ask a stupid question you are very likely to get a stupid answer. Let readers beware, and researchers think very very carefully about what they are doing!

Chapter 3

Individual differences in cognitive development

Most of the literature on cognitive development focuses on the description of a generalised, universal, normal progress from the cognition of infancy to the cognition of adulthood, with little attention to variation in the rate or detailed patterning of this development, and less to the possibility of different developmental paths. Most of the literature on individual differences in cognition measures them but takes a largely non-developmental view of them, assuming that differences between individuals are stable throughout development, that the more intelligent or creative are so from their earliest years. This bias is there even when researchers on individual differences are looking for the factors that might be affecting the relative quantity and quality of cognition. There is an excuse for this separation, in the pragmatic need to limit researchers' focus and concentrate their efforts, and it has been argued that individual variation and cognitive development in any case have different causes (Anderson 1992). Nevertheless, my own feeling is that there should be some attempt to consider the work on individual differences within cognitive development, as this is likely to improve our understanding of both (see also Richardson (1991), Scarr (1992), Ferrari and Sternberg (1998)). I will consider three of the main 'dimensions' of individual differences in cognition: intelligence, cognitive style and creativity.

3.1 Intelligence

Conceptions of individuals as differing in 'intelligence' are by far the best known and most thoroughly worked-out accounts of 'individual differences'. In general terms, there is some degree of agreement (e.g. Chen *et al.* 1988; Nicholls *et al.* 1986; Sternberg and Detterman 1986; Sternberg and Powell 1983; Ferrari and Sternberg 1998; Sternberg 2004) about what 'intelligent behaviour' is: both laity and psychologist experts believe that intelligent persons will have good vocabularies, read with good comprehension, talk fluently and sensibly, make good decisions, plan well, be able to apply their knowledge to problems, determine how best to achieve goals, be interested in things around them, etc., while less intelligent persons will show fewer of these characteristics. Given a relevant sample of behaviour, most adults within a culture can assess how close an individual is to this sort of prototype, though they may have more difficulty if the individual is from a culture different from their own. I discuss children's conceptions of 'intelligence' with their ideas about people (pp. 184–186).

The list of things 'intelligent' people do in the last paragraph is a fairly general and heterogeneous one. It should also have been very accessible to developmental analysis. Clearly as children get older they develop larger vocabularies, read better, talk more in more elaborate ways, have a larger knowledge base, plan more; whether they change in their interest in things around them, learn better, make better decisions, or reason better is very much more questionable (see Chapter 2). But psychologists theorising intelligence have consistently rejected simple measures of the frequency or complexity of 'intelligent behaviours' (and we would have had to be more specific about what they were and what the relationships were between them) and focused on the entity that they presume underlies them. Basic concepts about the nature of 'intelligence' have influenced this work very profoundly. Francis Galton, pioneering mental testing at the end of the nineteenth century, believed firmly that intelligence was a fixed and inherited capacity underlying all cognitive activity and all educational achievement and social eminence (and largely based on, or measurable via, sensitivity to physical stimuli (Sternberg and Powell 1983; Ferrari and Sternberg 1998)). Those who, like Spearman, Burt and Eysenck, followed this line defined it as 'innate, general cognitive ability', and looked for simple tests that measured general intelligence, 'g', without contamination from different experience, knowledge or education. They developed sophisticated techniques for finding the communality between scores on measures of different sorts of 'intelligent' behaviour, notably factor analysis. They did not develop a sophisticated developmental theory, perhaps because of their focus on innate general intelligence and their emphasis on rather simple measures such as digit span, although some attempts have been made to describe how different pictures of the structure of intelligence emerge from factor analytic studies at different ages. I will discuss this briefly later.

Another strand in attempts to define and measure intelligence has been heavily influenced by educational needs. At the turn of the nineteenth and twentieth centuries, Alfred Binet was asked by the French educational authorities to devise tests that would pick out those children who were not capable of succeeding in the normal school regime, so that they could be given special education rather than be left to fail. He developed a comparatively sophisticated theory of intelligence (Binet and Simon 1916; Sternberg and Powell 1983; Ferrari and Sternberg 1998; Mackintosh 1998), but test items were chosen pragmatically because they represented the typical performance of children at successive ages. Thus individuals could be assessed in terms of where their performance came up to that of children of the same age, and where it was weaker, more like that of younger children. The concept of 'mental age', and later the idea of IQ, which is a comparison between 'mental age' and chronological age, came from this. Most of Binet's items comprised fairly complex tasks similar to those of everyday mental life, involving understanding language and reasoning, with verbal, spatial or numerical materials. Binet saw that the 'normal' children and the 'mentally retarded' children were not two clearly separate groups. 'Intelligence' as measured by his tests varied continuously along a scale, and his mental age score was essentially a measure of average rate of growth of various mental functions from birth to the time of testing, that is, it measured present performance relative to the population norm, as the result of the cumulative performance and achievement to date. Binet's approach did not imply that 'intelligence' was fixed: given favourable opportunities retarded children might make up their deficit, and if things went wrong for the advanced group their rate of development might fall. However, since a test score is the result of the accumulation of earlier growth of mental functions, some degree of constancy in performance is inevitable.

Attempts to devise tests that would make predictions that could be useful to schools more often than not used the tests' agreement with measures of school achievement as a measure of test validity (Luo *et al.* 2003). On the whole, test items that involve using knowledge of the sort required in school show higher correlations with school achievement than do test items with little or no school-relevant content. While this is hardly surprising, it does illustrate how difficult it is to separate experience and potential, how we cannot determine from a measure taken after a particular history of experience what the score would have been after other, different, histories. The problem is obvious when the test used involves knowledge or skills that are clearly acquired to different degrees as a result of different experiences (hence the need to revise vocabulary tests to take out words like 'anti-macassar' or 'haberdashery', which are in much less frequent use than previously), but it remains a problem in less obvious ways even when the test does not have such culturally specific content. Individuals may differ, for example, in how far they have learned to concentrate on psychophysical tasks or to answer questions co-operatively in the unusual social situation of being required to display one's knowledge despite its not being otherwise useable at the moment. Cognitive skills such as these are necessary for good performance in school and in doing intelligence tests; it seems likely, as I discuss in Chapter 5, that they are affected by the practice with which other people, parents and teachers especially, surround the child. This does not preclude the possibility that both test scores and educational achievement are underpinned by some very basic factor such as *g* or 'mental speed', but it does make it hard to investigate this (Luo *et al.* 2003).

Thus there has been a tension between different meanings of 'intelligence' both in the specialised work of psychologists and in the way the term is understood by the general public. Eysenck provided a clear exposition of the three different meanings that have become familiar to psychologists as Intelligence A, Intelligence B and Intelligence C. Intelligence A is:

> the biological fundament of cognitive processing, genetically based (perhaps entirely so), and responsible for individual differences in intellectual competence. Intelligence B, on the other hand, denotes the application of Intelligence A to ordinary life affairs and problems, modified as this inevitably will be by personality differences, socio-economic status, and educational, cultural and other environmental factors . . . Intelligence C refers to the measurement of intelligence (whether A or B) by means of specially constructed tests.
>
> (Eysenck 1986: 1)

Which of these is the most important level of intelligence is something theorists differ about. There is a great deal of very specialised literature on the relationship between different tests of intelligence, which is sometimes purely about Intelligence C, as one intelligence test is used to validate or to criticise another. Eysenck's own work focused very much on Intelligence A, as I will describe later. Many accounts of intelligence deriving from information-processing theory are linked to all three meanings (e.g. Anderson 1992; Carpenter and Just 1986; Sternberg 1985). Whichever meaning is focused on, two issues have arisen: what items of behaviour are both representative of intelligence and measurable, and how possible different components of intelligence fit together. What behaviour is to be chosen and measured often reflects the original Galton–Binet differences as well as whether Intelligence A is preferred to Intelligence B, or vice versa; the organisation of components of intelligence has received different sorts of solutions. The approach in the psychometric literature has been largely centred on techniques such as factor analysis, which have been used in attempts to see how far different test performances can be explained in terms of a general underlying cognitive capacity (g) rather than in terms of more specific abilities not perhaps called on by more than one test. A great many structural models have appeared in the psychometric literature (see e.g. Carroll (1982), Sternberg and Powell (1983), Anderson (1992), Ferrari and Sternberg (1998), Mackintosh (1998)). Many of these result from different applications of factor analytic techniques to a heterogeneous collection of test items. Since, mathematically, there is an infinite number of ways in which factors can be fitted to a set of scores on tests, and since there is no widely accepted mathematical criterion for deciding which factor analysis-derived structure is most acceptable, there are no obvious grounds for claiming one structural model as more 'correct' than others. This approach has involved theory mainly as a way to justify factor structure, rather than using factor structure to test theory. Information-processing approaches to intelligence have more often moved from theory to accounts of the structure of intelligence (see Sternberg 1985) but do not involve much consideration of Intelligence A.

I want also to note that ever since Galton's interest in comparing different individuals and Binet's interest in picking out those who needed special education, measurements of 'intelligence' have involved relative measurements, not absolute ones. Both 'mental age' and IQ are quantified relative to a population norm, not quantities comparable with height or weight or speed of running a marathon. During childhood a considerable year-on-year gain in what the child can actually do is necessary if he or she is to keep up with the population; the five-year-old who scores at the population norm has actually passed a lot more test items than the average child aged four. As children get older, and especially from adolescence onwards, increases in intelligence-related skills change much less, so there is less need to pass more items to remain at the same 'mental age', and IQs are no longer calculated by dividing 'mental age' by chronological age. There are also changes in the standard deviations of how many test items are passed at different ages: this complicates comparisons across ages. Lichten (2004) argues that the focus on relative quantity of intelligence and the absence of thought about 'mental growth' has squeezed development out of intelligence theory, obscured interesting regularities and differences in different areas of 'intelligence', and created some uninterpretable anomalies. He believes that 'mental growth' curves give better clues to all sorts of psychological, educational and social policy puzzles. The IQ community has not yet published refutations of his arguments, and my own skills in psychometrics are not sufficient to settle the question, but it is an interesting example of how assumptions that everyone has been making for more than a century may lead to very puzzling results. Another puzzle, the 'Flynn effect', is discussed below.

The mainstream IQ approach has not given as much attention as one might wish to the development of intelligence, which is our main concern here. The nearest psychometric approximation to a developmental concept is probably R. B. Cattell's distinction (Cattell 1971) between 'fluid' and 'crystallised' intelligence subfactors of g. Fluid intelligence is relatively independent of systematic educational and cultural influences and is best measured by tests that require mental manipulation of given abstract information, for example classification problems using squiggle shapes, inductive reasoning where content is irrelevant to the validity of the argument, figural analogies and series completion like Raven's matrices tasks. Crystallised intelligence represents the person's accumulation of schooling, acculturation and other learning experiences, and is best measured via tests of vocabulary, general knowledge and comprehension, which require more knowledge of the cultural milieu. Both fluid and crystallised intelligence are said to increase through childhood to adolescence, but thereafter fluid intelligence is constant, or, in extreme old age, declines, while crystallised intelligence continues to increase for as long as people continue to accumulate knowledge and experience (Cattell 1971; Horn 1968, 1970).

While these models usefully note the range of influences – from 'brain maturation' to 'educational experience' – that could affect 'intelligence', each of these needs far more specification as to what has an impact, and how, and when, and why, and on what aspect of 'intelligence'. It also leaves open the question of what pattern of cognitive activities constitutes 'intelligence' at different ages, and there is less developmental evidence, and much less developmental theory, on this than one would like. Studies seeking to predict childhood intelligence from testing in infancy (Bornstein and Sigman 1986; Rose et al. 1986; Rose and Feldman 1995, 1997; Slater 1995; Sigman et al. 1991; McCall and Carriger 1993; Dougherty and Haith 1997; Ferrari and Sternberg 1998; Tsao et al. 2004) suggest that infant 'alertness' as shown in habituation and visual attention tasks predicts much of the variation in intelligence test score in early childhood. The evidence base is not completely consistent, but there may be some continuity in fundamental aspects of cognition from infancy to childhood, just as there is some continuity in rankings on more composite intelligence test scores over the years of childhood. (It should be remembered, however, that a substantial proportion of individuals show marked changes in their IQ scores, some merely fluctuating wildly but some moving systematically up or down (Hindley 1965; Hindley and Owen 1978; Petrill et al. 2004; Feinstein and Bynner 2004).)

The interesting findings about alertness in intelligence may usefully be related to recent attempts to identify and study a fundamental substratum of 'intelligence' (Mackintosh 1998). Researchers have sought to find simple measures of brain functioning or basic cognitive processing, which some of them see as the true core of intelligence (e.g. Eysenck 1982, 1986; Jensen 1982; Luo et al. 2003), though not all of them are overtly reductionistic, recognising that the simple measure is part of the complex structure of intelligent behaviour (Anderson 1989a, 1992). It is not as yet clear how far these approaches are coherent and reconcilable. All could be linked to a Galtonian concept, 'mental speed', and the researchers involved do, I think, tend towards the non-developmental model of intelligence as 'innate general cognitive ability'; Luo et al. (2003: 69), for example, suggest that 'mental speed' is 'primarily genetically mediated'. Although early research showed little relationship between 'mental speed' and 'intelligence', some more recent work (e.g. Jensen (1982): for a thorough critical review see Mackintosh (1998)) found quite strong correlations between them. A subject's reaction time (RT) to, for example, a light going on, increases as the number of lights that might possibly go on increases. High IQ subjects have shorter RTs than lower IQ ones, and the difference is greater the more possible lights there are, that is, the rate of increase as well as the actual length of RT is greater for low IQ subjects than for high IQ ones. Other studies measure inspection time (IT). The subject gets very brief exposures to two clearly different stimuli (such as two vertical lines, 3 : 2 in length) and then has an unlimited amount of time to report which is, for example, longer. The individual's IT score is the duration of exposure time at which the subject's judgement is 90–95 per cent correct. There seems to be a moderate negative correlation between IT and non-verbal IQ test scores (Anderson 1992; Mackintosh 1998; Nettelbeck 1998, 2001): lower IQ subjects need to see the stimuli for a longer time in order to be able to compare them correctly. IT is thought to measure how quickly subjects can encode incoming information into short-term memory. However, there has been some variability in the size and significance of the correlations between IT and IQ, with high correlations only being found if the IQ range is large and there are mentally retarded subjects in the group (Vernon 1985). Again, consistency and IQ are positively correlated. IT has been studied developmentally. There is debate about whether it remains the same over age. Anderson (1986, 1988, 1992) argues that it does, though other researchers, notably Nettelbeck and his colleagues, find that IT decreases throughout childhood and adolescence, which suggests an increase in the speed of basic information-processing (Nettelbeck 1986; Nettelbeck and Wilson 1985, 2004; Nettelbeck and Vita 1992; Wilson *et al.* 1992). Inspection time appears to have been stable over the period 1981-2001, unlike measures of *g* (Nettelbeck and Wilson 2004). I discuss the rise in *g* below (pp. 231–235).

Similar replication problems and problematic interpretations of what the test requires seem to be occurring in the somewhat more cognitive tasks reviewed by Cooper and Regan (1982). Hunt *et al.* (1975) looked at correlations between verbal IQ scores and performance on tasks where the subjects had to say 'same' or 'different' in response to pairs of letters that were identical physically (A,A) or in name only (A,a). Their analysis of these tasks suggests that in the name identical (NI) task the subject has the extra job of retrieving the name associated with each visual pattern as compared with the physically identical (PI) task, so the NI–PI time difference represents the amount of time needed to access the names in memory. Subjects with high verbal IQs need less time to do this than subjects with low verbal IQs, so perhaps they have faster access to overlearned verbal material in memory. However, they are also faster on both NI and PI trials, so the results may be picking up a general speed factor rather than differences in how efficiently verbal memory is accessed. We are not yet very close to an account of the relationship between intelligence and other aspects of cognition.

The last approach to be mentioned measures the electrical activity produced by the brain in response to a brief visual or auditory stimulation.

Shortly after stimulation – for example, after the subject has heard a brief tone – there is a peak or 'evoked potential' in central nervous system activity.

The size, latency and frequency of such evoked potentials can be measured, and averaged over a large number of trials to give the 'average evoked potential' or AEP; this measure is then correlated with IQ score. It is suggested that the AEP is a 'picture' of the individual's response to incoming information (A. E. Hendrickson 1982). The Hendrickson model describes how incoming information sets up electrical activity in nerve fibres and biochemical changes in the synapses between successive fibres and cells in the transmission of activity within the brain (for a simple introductory account of brain functioning see Chapter 5). The correct transmission of information is seen as requiring accurate recognition memory at a basic neuronal level, and it is assumed that individuals differ in their accuracy and hence in how long and complex a message they can transmit before an error leads to breakdown. The AEP provides an estimate of this accuracy, in that individuals whose recognition and transmission of information are inaccurate will tend to have varying reactions to the incoming stimulation, sometimes showing a large reaction but tending towards smaller and slower ones that fade quickly. Averaged over a lot of trials, an inaccurate-transmission individual, someone with a lot of erroneous 'noise' in the system, will have a flat, unclear AEP, while a more accurate information processor will have a large, quick, sharp AEP. AEP differences will be paralleled by differences in 'real-life' learning and memory: an individual with a slow and 'crackly' central nervous system will be slow to process information, to create a memory store, to carry out simple and, more notably, complex cognitive processing, and to acquire and organise a knowledge base. Such an individual may thus be expected to do badly on intelligence tests, and on cognitive tasks in general.

The evidence on the association between AEP and IQ has to be said to be inconsistent (Bates and Eysenck 1993; Deary and Caryl 1993; Eysenck 1986; Mackintosh 1998; Vernon 1985). There seem to be reliability problems and replication problems, and Jensen has characterised the area as a thicket of seemingly inconsistent and confusing findings, confounded variables, methodological differences, statistically questionable conclusions, unbridled theoretical speculation, and, not surprisingly, considerable controversy (Jensen 1980: 709). Other reviewers (Eysenck 1986; Vernon 1985) are more positive about AEPs than this; Vernon sees the experimental research as insufficient and suggests that speed of processing, rather than a complex model of accuracy, might account for the results. Schafer (1982) relates evoked potentials to 'neural adaptability', comparing responses to inputs whose timing and nature are known or unpredictable. Unexpected input evokes a larger response than input that is expected, with a bigger difference for intelligent subjects than for mentally retarded ones. This might be seen as higher IQ people being quicker to habituate to completely predictable overlearned stimulation and better at reorienting attention to focus on novel stimulation, thus using limited neural energy and cognitive space more efficiently (this is reminiscent of babies' habituation and later intelligence, see p. 89). There seems to be a high correlation (about 0.8) between neural adaptability, as seen in small AEPs to familiar expected stimulation plus large AEPs to unexpected novel stimulation, and IQ. Vernon (1985) suggests that the Hendricksons' work could be conflated with Schafer's, though the former has the more elaborate biochemical model.

There is a certain plausibility in the idea that the speed and efficiency of the brain are an important component in the speed and efficiency with which a person deals with a cognitive task and hence his or her performance on IQ tests, particularly those where only a limited amount of time is available. I have more to say about this in Chapter 5, where I relate research on the brain to questions of the organisation and development of cognition. However, I see three problems with the accounts of the 'biological determinants of behavioural intelligence' described above. The first is a methodological one. The measurement of 'brain speed' is seriously problematic (Luo et al. 2003). Typically, getting an individual's AEP or reaction time means that he or she must tolerate the placement of electrodes (itself not a simple procedure) and the adjustment of measuring devices, and then must sit and listen to many repetitions of a brief tone or watch for flashes of a light. It cannot be assumed that everyone who undergoes this procedure will be consistent over its duration in motivation, attention or affect, and in so far as these influence cortical activity they may produce variation in AEP or RT. As Mackintosh (1986, 1998) points out, the AEP will show a complex pattern only if the patterns it averages are themselves both complex and constant; if there is variability between trials with peaks of different sizes or at different points in time they will cancel each other out and the average trace will be flatter and shorter than the constituent ones. It does seem to be the case that lower IQ subjects vary more between trials, that is, that their score is less stable and less uniform, and hence their AEP is lower. This could indeed be due to the cognitive difference that Eysenck (1982, 1986) and the Hendricksons are suggesting (A. E. Hendrickson 1982; D. E. Hendrickson 1982); but somewhat less cognitive possibilities, such as ability to maintain a consistent level of attention to a boring task or willingness to co-operate with an experimenter, do suggest themselves. Even the recording of brain activity is to some extent a social activity and we might be unwise to assume that our measures are totally independent of the subject's motivation and ideas about what is going on. This may be particularly important when studying development. Eysenck (1986), without documenting them in detail, reported studies that relate AEP to age, and claimed that with increasing age the evoked potential is larger and arises faster, and the AEP is less variable. This might suggest that children's brains work faster and more efficiently, even on the level of very simple neural responses to simple stimulation, as they get older, a notion that bears an interesting relation to the accounts of information-processing development discussed in Chapter 4, but that may not be congruent with the idea of intelligence as a fixed innate cognitive characteristic. Nor, as I shall describe later, is it a notion that fits in with the account of cognitive development put forward by Mike Anderson. There are also alternative explanations in terms of children's willingness to take part in the procedures of AEP testing.

The second problem is whether evoked potentials are a simple and accurate measure of nervous system information-processing. Even if there are no motivational or attentional problems, the evoked potential is a somewhat indeterminate peak in more general electrical activity, which will be influenced in size and shape by all the other cortical activity going on, and distorted by the indirectness of our measurement. Until we understand how evoked potentials relate to neurone activity on the one hand and to cognitive processes on the other, we can only take them as an indirect measure of the efficiency of information-processing.

The third problem with models like the Hendricksons' is the discrepancy in complexity between the understanding of the brain used in the model, and that emerging from current studies by neuropsychologists (see Chapter 5). 'Neural adaptability', 'neural efficiency' and so forth are crude concepts compared with the delicate analysis of neuroscientists. Brain research on parallel and alternative pathways, multiple spread of information, links between psychologically different systems such as affect and cognition, and so forth, argues against such simplification. Again, these models are comparatively non-developmental. They show a poor fit with the recent evidence on how brain cells and connections continue to change and develop well into adult life, very much under the influence of experience (see Chapter 5). While individual differences in 'neural efficiency' might well lead to individual differences in ability to profit from experience and in what 'experience' is experienced – I find myself not doubting this in the least – individual differences in experience are just as likely to have repercussions for 'neural efficiency', and the models take little account of this possibility. There can be in this a whiff of reductionism, as when Eysenck (e.g. 1986) resolves the debate between Galton's and Binet's approaches so very much in favour of Galton, 'Intelligence A' and the psychophysiological measurement of intelligence, coming near to dismissing the study of Intelligence B as hopelessly unscientific. Mackintosh (1998), after a heroic effort to be fair to these studies, makes a similar point, saying:

> The most obvious explanation of the apparently most reliable effect [of an association between AEP and IQ] is that it is IQ that is responsible for differences in ERP rather than vice versa; the higher your IQ the

fewer resources you need to devote to the task of discriminating two difficult-to-discriminate stimuli.

(1998: 241)

3.1.1 Anderson's model of intelligence and development

Mike Anderson (1989a, 1992, 2001) offers some interesting speculations about the nature of intelligence and its development, which I integrate here with some points from elsewhere. He starts by stating three regularities in the data about intelligence. First, measurements of different cognitive abilities tend to be correlated, for example AEP is correlated with digit span, which is correlated with vocabulary, which is correlated with spatial analogy scores. Second, cognitive abilities increase with age at a similar rate and for a similar portion of the developmental curve. Third, individual differences in test scores are relatively stable over development: the alert baby becomes the bright schoolchild and the competent adult, although adult and child have a great deal of knowledge and many skills that the baby does not. (Feinstein and Bynner (2004), however, find that substantial discontinuities arose in middle childhood for a minority of individuals; these were related to social class, and are discussed later, p. 377.) Theories that centre intelligence on the general speed and efficiency of the individual's neurophysiology explain these regularities in terms of the neural processing that underlies all cognitive activity. These theories look more problematic, however, in dealing with irregularities, with why different abilities are not more strongly correlated, with why some individuals develop much faster in one area than others or have difficulties in one area while doing well in others, with why some individuals develop at a steady rate but others seem to fluctuate in their development. Some theorists have coped with such irregularities by suggesting that there are multiple separate or modular intelligences (e.g. Gardner 1983; Howe 1989a; Fodor 1983; Ferrari and Sternberg 1998), but such theories, emphasising different cognitive processes applied to different areas and acquired relatively independently of each other, have problems in coping with the regularities that we started by noting. Only a theory that deals with intelligence and individual differences within a theory of thinking which specifies how basic neurophysiology relates to different kinds of information-processing can explain both regularities and irregularities.

Anderson, in his model of the 'minimal cognitive architecture' of intelligence, suggests that there is a basic processing mechanism describable at the neurophysiological level. This is used by many different kinds of knowledge system and accounts for the general co-variation of different abilities. Individuals differ in the speed of their basic processing mechanism. People who can process information faster can cram more processing and more information into their limited-capacity working memory before it becomes overloaded. Less information will be lost from working memory unprocessed, more will be usefully processed to solve the current problem or stored conveniently in long-term memory for use in the future. More information can be acquired, and more complex processing can be carried out. People with faster and more efficient basic processing mechanisms will learn more and reason better, getting more out of the same amount of experience, ending up with more and better organised knowledge and more practised processing. The research using RTs and ITs and ERPs described earlier is concerned with this basic processing mechanism.

The basic processing mechanism is not used in the acquisition of all the knowledge and skills we typically develop. Anderson says that some knowledge and skills are developed largely through the operation of processing modules that are common to all, or virtually all, members of the human species, even those who are cognitively abnormal (cf. Fodor 1983; Leslie 1994; Pinker 1994, 1997; Frith and Frith 2003). These modules are the result of millennia of evolutionary usefulness. Anderson uses as example our ability to translate the two-dimensional stimulation on our retinas to a perception of a three-dimensional world. The vast majority of human beings can do this, whatever else is lacking because of immaturity or mental retardation, but such perception is far too complex for any presently existing computer to cope with. Other examples might be drawn from the skills being discovered in very young infants, for example their co-ordination of vocalisation and gesture and their discrimination between people and objects, familiar and unfamiliar people, and television pictures of Mother behaving normally in live conversation with them and of a recording of Mother conversing with them, played back to them with a 30-second delay (Trevarthen 1978, 1980). Other possible modules include the phonological encoding and syntactic analysis of language (Pinker 1994, 1997), and a 'theory of mind', or ability to think of other people as having mental states. Modules like these have evolved to fulfil universal processing functions in our species: brain research (Chapter 5) is discovering a great deal about them. Some are virtually 'wired in', others are 'experience-expectant' in that they utilise the sort of environmental information that has been ubiquitous throughout the evolution of the species and can be relied on to occur in any individual's experience. These depend on experience for their 'fine-tuning', often on experience during a particular 'sensitive period' of development, and if this experience is abnormal or missing the experience-expectant module comes to work abnormally or not at all. The perceptual deficits of kittens without normal visual experience in the first period after their eyes open are an obvious example, paralleled by the acuity problems of human children whose shortsightedness is not corrected early enough.

As well as the experience that can reasonably be expected to occur regularly at a particular point in virtually everybody's life, so that 'experience-expectant' or 'wired-in' processing modules will serve us well, there are many environmental events that are less consistent in their occurrence or timing. The information-processing system has to be able to handle these too, and here another major source of individual differences lies. You can only acquire this somewhat more idiosyncratic knowledge (for example, methods of counting, how to read, the rules of croquet, the skills of microbiology or art history) if it comes within your experience, and you then have to be able to process it appropriately. Anderson suggests that the basic processor is involved here, so that the faster processor will do better at seeing what distinguishes Picasso's paintings from Matisse's, or at counting by fives as well as by units, but that there are also 'specific processors' that may be more efficient in some areas than others; for example, good verbal processing and less good spatial processing. The degree to which people develop cognitive abilities will depend on their general basic processing mechanism and on any relevant specific processor, and individual differences in speed and efficiency will apply to both general and specific mechanisms. 'Ability' will also depend on experience in two ways. If an information-processing module is involved, this must have 'come on-line' normally as a result of maturation within an at least minimally facilitating environment. If the environment has been grossly abnormal, or if the child is too young for the module to be operative, then the module will not operate properly and processing will not be possible. However, most modules need only experience that everyone has, or even no experience of the outside world at all, so there will be little in the way of individual differences in modular functioning. More importantly for individual differences, experience will affect specific processors to a very significant extent: it provides them with the information they process, and without relevant information they will be of little use. They are not 'experience-expectant' but 'experience-dependent'; however, the basic processing mechanism is still important because it limits the efficiency with which use can be made of experience. Anderson believes that the basic processing mechanism is not itself affected by experience: it is this that is 'innate general cognitive ability'.

Intelligence, then, to summarise Anderson's theory, is made up of a basic processing mechanism, processing modules and a number of specific processors. These interact. There is little or nothing in the way of individual differences in modules, which are either there and processing universally available information in a universal way, or are not there and not processing, because the individual is so immature that they have not 'come on-line' or because the environment has been so grossly abnormal that the module has been permanently impaired or because of damage to the central or peripheral nervous systems. The main source of individual differences is variation in the speed of the basic processing mechanism, where faster processors can acquire more information in a given period of time and can do more complex processing without running into the limits of working memory. There is probably no developmental change in the speed of the basic processing mechanism, on the basis of the evidence that inspection time, which is a relatively 'pure' measure of processing speed not much affected by the subject's knowledge and strategies, is only weakly correlated with age (Anderson 1988; Nettelbeck and Wilson 2004). This evidence comes from children old enough to understand the IT task, however, so developmental changes earlier in life remain conceivable: babies may process some information more slowly and less efficiently than older people because of the comparative immaturity of the CNS (see Chapter 5) as well as because of their failure to understand what the task is.

Specific processors, like the basic processing mechanism, vary in their speed from person to person, and one particular person may have faster specific processors of one sort than of another; for example, fast verbal processing and slower spatial processing. The speed of the basic processing mechanism constrains all the specific processors, however, and if it is very slow differences between specific processors may be masked. (This suggestion may seem hard to reconcile with some of the cases of 'idiots savants', who, although severely retarded and presumably the possessors of an impaired basic processing mechanism, may show an outstanding ability to, for example, calculate calendar dates, or do mental arithmetic, or produce elaborate drawings (Hermelin and O'Connor 1990; Howe 1989c; Howe and Smith 1988; O'Connor and Hermelin 1990; Radford 1990; Hermelin 2001; Hobson 2002). One answer to the dilemma might be to attribute these 'islands of excellence' to the functioning of processing modules that focus attention and accumulate information in one particular narrow area. There is still controversy over how 'idiots savants' perform their feats.) A slow basic processing mechanism constrains the complexity of the cognitive processing that can be carried out by a specific processor and also constrains the complexity of knowledge that can be acquired in a specific domain. If basic processing is at a consistent speed throughout development, the baby who processes information slowly and inefficiently in an infant habituation experiment will be the child who is slow to acquire and accumulate knowledge and to use it in later cognitive processing, and so has a low IQ and poor educational achievement compared with children whose faster basic processing mechanisms allow them to get more out of the same experience. Basic processing speed may constrain what can be gained from any particular environment, but of course environments also differ in their usefulness for processing: a slow basic processor with a helpful environment may do very well compared with a fast basic processor whose environment is very unhelpful. Both processors and environments are indispensable for the development of cognition; both contribute to measured individual differences in cognition.

This is an interesting model but it still has problems. First, it does not fully consider motivation, emotion and the social world. Second, it depends on a model of brain processing speed simpler than the structure and function as described by neuroscientists, and on an inconsistent body of experimental evidence. Finally, for most assessment purposes, measurements of the 'intelligence' that incorporates a history of experience and involves using knowledge will be more relevant than purer measures. Just as in diagnosing the causes of reading failure or predicting the course of arithmetical development it has proved more useful to examine the child's use of the component skills of reading or arithmetic than to scrutinise or seek to improve more remote and abstract cognitive skills (see pp. 30–56, 68–84 on reading and arithmetic, Chapter 6 on teaching thinking), in most educational settings variation in intelligent academic behaviour will be better understood by examining the child's performance of school-like tasks microgenetically (Siegler 2005) – perhaps using the zone of proximal development (pp. 308–309) as a diagnostic area – than by looking at inspection time. Sternberg's model of intelligence (Sternberg 1985, 1990; Sternberg *et al.* 1995), less innovative than Anderson's, may be more helpful at this level.

3.1.2 The triarchic theory of intelligence

The 'triarchic' theory of intelligence (Sternberg 1984, 1985, 1990; Sternberg *et al.* 1995; Sternberg and Kaufman 1998) has three subtheories: a subtheory of the components or internal mental mechanisms that underpin an individual's intelligent behaviour; an experiential subtheory of how intelligence is applied differentially to more novel or more familiar situations; and a contextual subtheory of how intelligence serves adaptation to one's environment.

Of these, the componential subtheory is the most elaborately worked out in Sternberg (1985), not surprisingly, given that Sternberg's earlier work was in the field of information-processing. He suggests that there are three basic kinds of components of intelligence: metacomponents, performance components and knowledge-acquisition components. Metacomponents are clearly the constituents of metacognitive activity (p. 132); they are involved in, for example, defining what a task is and how to tackle it, selecting appropriate cognitive processes to accomplish the task and combining them strategically, allocating mental resources, monitoring their operation and evaluating. Performance components are lower-order processes that are called up to execute the plans that the metacomponents put together. They are processes such as inferring relations between stimuli, applying known relations and rules to new stimuli, comparing stimuli, choosing responses, working through chains of logical reasoning, etc. While metacomponents operate on cognitive components, performance components operate on data. Knowledge acquisition components are processes used in gaining new knowledge. The three main ones, necessary for learning and for achieving insights, are selective encoding, selective combination and selective comparison. Relevant information has to be sifted out from what is irrelevant, coded into an integrated plausible useful whole and related to information that has been acquired previously.

Components vary in their specificity: some apply to only one task, some to a larger set, some are required for almost all cognition. They also vary in how closely they are interrelated. In some cases activating one component always activates another, and feedback from one also affects another, but in the present model it is metacomponents that have these sorts of strong links and that also mediate between other components. Sternberg (1985: 110–111) uses the example of solving an anagram to illustrate this. The metacomponents define the task and decide on a certain tentative strategy for unscrambling the letters into another word; immediately the performance component responsible for the first step of the strategy takes over, and successive performance components are called on in turn. This activation produces action that produces feedback as to the operation and success of each performance component. Metacomponents monitor this feedback: if it is unsuccessful, the metacomponent that decides on changes in strategy may take over, and an alternative strategy or alternative solution be tried in the same way. As well as the specific information about the success of this strategy in this case, more general information is being acquired by the metacomponents about how to solve anagrams in general. Knowledge acquisition components sort this out and relate it to previous information stored in long-term memory. Next time the metacomponents define a task as being one of anagram solution, they can call on this accumulation of acquired knowledge about anagrams in general.

Cognitive development occurs in several ways in the subtheory of components. First, the knowledge acquisition components provide the means to a steadily developing store of relevant information. The increasing size of the knowledge base leads to better later acquisition and more subtle and flexible organisation of what is known; there is more to relate new information to, more to guide encoding, combination and comparison, and hence more effective use of knowledge. Second, the metacomponents can monitor, evaluate and modify themselves. Early in development they are largely ineffective but they have an enormous capacity for self-improvement. Self-monitoring by the metacomponents leads to better definition of tasks, better choice of performance components, better allocation of mental resources, and so forth. In principle there is here an unending feedback loop, with the metacomponents transforming themselves from a jalopy to a Rolls-Royce. In practice, as we saw from the developmental literature, we probably settle, unless there is much external pressure for improvement or unusually few limitations of cost, for less perfection, for 'good enough' cognitive motoring.

Sternberg suggests that everyone uses components of these sorts when tackling cognitive tasks, irrespective of their culture and their experience. Experience is, however, the second important dimension of the triarchic theory of intelligence. The components that the componential subtheory describes involve intelligence to the extent that they are applied to relatively novel tasks or situations or become automatic and highly efficient quickly. What is being emphasised in the experiential subtheory is the ability to adapt previous understanding to new demands effectively, as opposed to the routine carrying-out of well-worn strategies and processes in isolation from each other. The ideal test is one that is novel enough to present some challenge, unique enough that routine cognition will not solve it, either because it has a new conceptual structure or because actually doing it requires new processes or a new combination of old processes. It should not, however, be too novel if it is to be useful for diagnostic purposes: if the person has no previously acquired knowledge at all to bring to bear on the task, then it will be impossible for him or her to do anything, intelligent or not, with it. Since the speed with which you give up on a task is affected by many other things than intelligence, a too novel task will provoke little behaviour that is of any use for diagnosing intelligence.

The other important part of the experiential subtheory is its emphasis on automatisation. Sternberg argues (1985: 71) that complex information-processing tasks can only be executed because many of the operations required have become automatic. Arithmetic provides a good example. As I mentioned earlier (pp. 68–82), many arithmetical tasks require considerable knowledge, great accuracy, severe demands on memory and, preferably, an ability to check the plausibility of the answer (for example by estimating before actually calculating a sum). People who are not practised at long division or square roots or whatever do such tasks slowly and painfully (if they know how to at all) and make many mistakes. Computers, completely automated, do the constituent processes fast and accurately; they do so without knowledge, however; hence the gas bills for millions of pounds that are occasionally sent out after a decimal point has somehow been misplaced. Expert or savant human calculators (Smith 1983; Hermelin 2001) appear to have stocked their memories with immense quantities of relevant knowledge, to have devised unusual and ingenious methods for simplifying the calculations and using their results, and to have developed a sense of numbers having idiosyncratic 'personalities' that presumably both distinguish the numbers and motivate the calculator (they sometimes do better when numbers they like rather than ones they dislike appear in the calculations).

It is obvious that experience plays an important part in the development of human intelligence (Ceci and Liker 1986; Ericsson and Charness 1994; Radford 1990; Mackintosh 1998; Ferrari and Sternberg 1998; Sternberg and Grigorenko 2003). The experiential subtheory points out two ways in which both individual differences and developmental changes can be explained. First, individuals with a superior ability to deal with novelty will show more rapid learning and consolidation of smooth, controlled information-processing, so that automatisation will begin earlier in dealing with the task and will proceed faster. Second, the more that processing has become automatic, the fewer cognitive resources it will require, and hence more resources will be available for dealing with the novel aspects of the task. Highly intelligent and more knowledgeable people, and children as their cognitive development progresses, will show better transfer of old learning to new tasks, see better analogies, use their intelligence components more effectively, 'get the hang of' problems and skills more quickly, and have more ways to compensate for their weaknesses.

The final component of the triarchic theory of intelligence is a sub-theory on the context of intelligence. Sternberg is concerned here to link information-processing to the demands of the real world as reflected in definitions of intelligence (by Piaget and others) as 'adaptation'. People are not 'intelligent' in a vacuum, even when taking intelligence tests, and the contextual subtheory outlines different ways in which everyday intelligence is applied. Sternberg (1985) describes three 'basic' processes: 'adaptation', or self-modification to fit one's environment better, to resolve the discrepancy between how one thinks or acts and how one believes one ought to think or act; 'shaping', or modifying the environment, a more risky strategy that often follows the failure of attempts at adaptation and that requires great knowledge of the environment if it is to succeed; and 'selection', or opting out of the unsatisfactory environment and finding a better one. Since the profitability of each of these strategies will depend on the context as well as on the individual, what is 'intelligent' will differ for different individuals in different predicaments and at different times. A Democrat in the USA in 2005, for example, might have found the state of politics unsatisfactory. In accordance with the contextual subtheory, he or she might equally intelligently try a 'shaping' strategy by working for the election of a president with a liberal ideology, or 'selection', by living as completely as possible within a small group of the population that was relatively liberal, or both; or he or she might try to adapt to government policies by shifting to a belief in a nominally mixed but actually capitalist economy in which the poor receive charity at the whim of the well-off rather than having a right to share in the prosperity of the community. A Jewish socialist in Germany in 1933 would have a different range of options. The odds would be overwhelmingly against adapting to National Socialism or shaping it to be more favourable to Jews or left-wingers; 'selection', via emigration or resistance or concealment, would be the only possible long-term choice. Intellectual development in the contextual subtheory occurs through a mixture of these sorts of process, applied to the new environments that children meet as they get older and venture out from the immediate family. The environments of home and school, for example, may make different demands on the child who must therefore act differently in the two settings: it may be easier to shape home to one's predilections than it is to shape school, and easier to select a context within school than it is to select a niche at home.

The contextual subtheory was the least satisfactory part of Sternberg's triarchic model. His more recent work has developed it but, while it does usefully correct the tendency to see real-life intelligence as reducible to scores on IQ tests, it is at risk of becoming a general model of learning styles; I discuss one recent account of it below. It is impossible at present to test much of it, for example to specify the range of ways in which people 'adapt to', 'shape' and 'select' their environments (while their environments are certainly shaping them, and no doubt also 'adapting to' and even 'selecting' them); thus, as with Piaget's assimilation and accommodation model (Chapter 4), it is hard to see how the theory can be falsified. Sternberg and Suben (1986) use Shirley Brice Heath's ethnographic accounts of three communities in the south-eastern United States (Heath 1983) to produce a lively description of how their different environments influence the intelligence that children bring to school, but their account ultimately adds little to Heath's beyond a plea for greater respect for societies whose socialisation processes and view of intelligence are not congruent with the values of schools and of conventional intelligence tests. 'Intelligence is largely the result of a socialisation process, and our understanding and assessment of intelligence must seriously take into account the nature of this process', they conclude (Sternberg and Suben 1986: 233). This is a useful reminder of our responsibilities as citizens: we also need to consider what may happen to people's 'intelligence' if their culture breaks down (Heath 2004). The earlier parts of this chapter dealt with models of intelligence that treated 'intelligence' as independent of culture and capable of being assessed without contamination from cultural effects, and these theorists would still maintain these assertions and reject the criticisms that Sternberg (and I) would make: in Chapter 5 I will return to studies of how environment and experience seem to affect cognition and examine the 'socialisation process'.

3.1.3 Rise in IQ over time: the 'Flynn effect'

One of the most intriguing, debated and unsettling sets of findings on 'intelligence' in recent years has centred on evidence that IQ scores have risen by about thirty points, two standard deviations, in the past fifty years. This rise was first documented by James Flynn (Flynn 1987; see also Flynn (1998, 1999, 2003)), and has become known as the Flynn effect. The rise is found in most of the data sets that have been examined, from both Western and Third World countries (Flynn 1998; Daley *et al.* 2004), and for most major IQ tests such as the Wechsler, Raven's matrices, and the Stanford-Binet, though with uneven gains on different subtests, more on *g*-loaded tests than vocabulary; it does not show up on inspection time measures of intelligence (Nettelbeck and Wilson 2004). After an initial period of worry about whether the samples were adequate, the existence of rise is now accepted by theorists of all ideological stances. One further issue is agreed on by most commentators: the rise cannot be explained by genetic change, as the time period is far too short. Mingroni (2004) does propose a genetic mechanism, 'heterosis', effectively hybrid vigour. The argument is that there has been an increase in geographical mobility over the period of the IQ rise that would have increased the chance that people found partners from outside their immediate neighbourhood and so decreased the amount of inbreeding between close relatives, which is likely to produce offspring with two recessive genes damaging to intelligence. Mingroni argues that this decrease in inbreeding and increase in hybrid vigour could explain the Flynn effect on IQ; and also changes in height, growth rate, myopia, head circumference, head breadth, asthma, autism, and attention deficit disorder. This he calls 'a partial list' of the possible consequences of heterosis. Could he be over-egging the pudding a little bit here? The existence of a beneficial change in the population towards more heterozygosity is an interesting possibility, not least because it is the opposite of the assumption of the early intelligence theorists that eugenics should concentrate on genetic purity rather than cross-breeding. Whatever the viability of this explanation, there is continuing debate with some very unsettling implications.

The first area of perplexity is whether there is evidence of change in people's real-life intelligence as well as their IQ scores. If people two generations ago had average scores two standard deviations lower than the current average, the population norm then would now be considered to be borderline mentally deficient. Looking at it the other way round, what is regarded as an average IQ score now would have been regarded as very highly able then. Do we have evidence of changes in real-life ability on this scale? The evidence is sparse and mixed (Flynn 1999; Mackintosh 1998); there is incontrovertible evidence of small increases, of more people reaching higher educational standards as education becomes universal, prolonged and requires higher final achievements, but it is rare for these to be linked to IQ rises. Meadows et al. (forthcoming) show small rises over a three-year period in maths, literacy and related IQ subtest scores in seven-year-olds, associated with changes in the UK National Curriculum; but not changes in g. Howard (2001) tries to make a case for increased real-life intelligence, citing increases in scientists' productivity and patent applications, decreases in rates of mild mental retardation, and the earlier and earlier achievement of high performance at chess. None of his examples is really convincing, none is large in scale, and the assortment is at best selective. Teachers generally do not feel that they are now facing classrooms of much brighter students, though as they also judge that students' motivation is declining this may get in the way of better performance. Thus we have the paradox of rises in our best measures of the entity that is supposed to underlie both real-life intelligent behaviour and educational achievement, which are much bigger and better documented than improvements in real-life performance.

This paradox is complicated further by the fact that the biggest and securest rises are on tests that are regarded as good measures of *g* or of 'fluid intelligence' rather than on tests that are heavily influenced by education, such as vocabulary (Flynn 1999), where there is little if any rise. As the most conspicuous social change over the past fifty years has been in the amount of education people get and in their educational aspirations, and more people now reach or go beyond basic levels of literacy and numeracy, rises in IQ subtests that use these sorts of skills would be easier to interpret. Intelligence specialists like Jensen (1998) would not be happy to attribute rises in *g* to better education without that better education leaving traces in higher 'crystallised intelligence' too. If *g* has increased, what is stopping its effects showing in tests of crystallised intelligence and the real world? I do not know of any convincing explanation.

As we cannot explain the rise in IQ scores in genetic terms because there has not been enough time for there to have been genetic change in the population, the explanation for the rise has to be environmental, or perhaps an interaction between genes and environment. One possible environmental explanation is that over the time period people simply became more used to taking IQ tests, and so did better on them, but Flynn (1998) dismisses this possibility; it is hard to see why it would apply to Raven's matrices or the WISC similarities test, but not to vocabulary tests. Lynn (1989) argues away the thirty point rise in average IQ over the past fifty years by invoking increase in height and head size over the same period (dubious in Western Europe and North America) and the correlation of 0.21 between head size and IQ scores (such a correlation would account for 5 per cent of the variance). Attempts to explain away the IQ rise as due to fewer forceps deliveries would seem to be equally dubious. It could be argued in direct opposition to this that advances in keeping premature babies alive might have led to more brain-damaged babies surviving, and hence to more individuals with low intelligence test scores.

Explaining IQ rise in terms of better nutrition might work a little better (see Chapter 5 for discussion of links between malnutrition and lower IQ), and this does seem to be a relevant factor in one study in Kenya (Daley *et al.* 2004): but again we have little evidence that there has been a steady rise in nutritional standards in Europe and the USA during the long period of steady IQ rise, or that the improvement was commensurate with the size of the IQ rise, and again it is odd that nutrition-led gains could be visible on IQ tests but not in real-life intelligence (Flynn 1998, 1999). Some of the contributors to Neisser (1998) suggest that the key environmental factor may have been increased exposure to electronic media, initially television, more recently video games and computers. But the rise in IQ began before access to these media, and seeing television and computer games as beneficial to IQ lies uneasily with social concerns about them as 'dumbed down' and more likely to be damaging than helpful.

One possible explanation lies in what has been called the 'multiplier effect' or the 'Matthew effect' (Howe *et al.* 1998; Dickens and Flynn 2001; Ceci *et al.* 2003). This is crucially important to discussions of the contribution of genes and environment to intelligence, so I discuss it later (Chapter 5), but it is relevant to the fifty-year rise in IQ and needs to be noted here too. The argument is that an initially small effect on intelligence may lead to a small change in experience that augments the initial effect, thus leading to a 'virtuous circle' of improvement (or a 'vicious cycle' of deterioration). In the case of the Flynn effect, a small change in the social environment might have a direct effect on children's intelligence; that rise in intelligence in turn might make them select slightly different environments, ones with more books in, for example; this slightly different environment might lead to knowing a little more and picking up information faster, and hence to doing better in school; which could lead to a more intellectually stimulating job, friendship group, partner; which would lead to continued improvement in intelligence, which could lead to better diet and health care in pregnancy and offspring who start life with slightly higher IQs and a more intellectually stimulating environment. Flynn himself gives a more detailed account in a recent paper (Flynn 2003), suggesting that the explanation has to be sociological, centring on the effects of industrialisation and then post-industrialisation. In his account, work roles have shifted towards professional and service sector jobs that require more independent thinking on the job and less rote work (or heavy physical labour). People have become more leisured and family size has decreased, which may have made it possible to engage in more cognitively challenging leisure activities. More parents have been through a longer education system and the benefits are visible in their parenting and their aspirations for their own children's education. Schooling has become universal; however, it is heavily focused on accreditation and teachers believe educational motivation has declined. Hence Flynn suggests a cultural shift away from valuing school achievement and towards problem solving for its own sake, such that *g*-loaded test performance rises but school-related test performance does not. Effectively he is saying that whereas earlier the average was brought down by the low scores of people whose intelligence was stifled by the crippling boredom and exhaustion of their jobs, now more people are living active thinking lives that only the elite enjoyed earlier in history, with benefits for their IQs. It is on the whole an optimistic picture, suggesting that if society prioritises cognitive skills, people's brains can rise to the occasion and ratchet up the average cognitive achievement of the population. I find myself needing rather more substantial evidence that this is a completely accurate picture of how culture has shifted over the time period involved, and it may not fit very well with the fact that the whole of the distribution of *g* has shifted upwards: the IQ elite are also scoring higher, not just the IQ lumpen-proletariat in the low to middling part of the distribution. I look at the effects of psychosocial factors on children's cognitive development later (Chapter 5).

So there is a lot of room for debate about the Flynn effect. Something (or more likely several somethings) has resulted in a rise so big we cannot ignore it, located in the place we would not expect it rather than where we would have thought it would be, and not, so far, amenable to any explanation. Perhaps the origin of the problem is in our belief that we can find and measure an essential intelligence independent of culture; these not yet interpretable rises in IQ remind us that almost certainly we cannot (Sternberg 2004; Sternberg and Kaufman 1998).

3.1.4 Résumé: so what is 'intelligence' anyway?

One scholarly, cool and thorough review of IQ and human intelligence concludes that we have at best tentative answers to what cognitive processes are responsible for differences in performance on IQ tests.

> Factor analysis raised the possibility that, underlying these differences between various kinds of test, there might also be some process or processes common to all. All that can be said is that, to date, experimental analysis has failed to identify any such common process, at least with any degree of rigour or precision, and that it may be safer to assume that IQ tests measure a wide range of different cognitive processes, with only partial overlap between those measured by different types of test.
>
> (Mackintosh 1998: 331)

Despite the progress made by newer models of 'intelligence' such as Anderson's and Sternberg's, it could be argued that we should never have slid (as I deliberately did at the beginning of this chapter) from talking about 'intelligent behaviour' to talking about 'intelligence', that an erroneous and misleading reification has led us astray for nearly a century. This is the position incisively argued by Howe (1989a, 1989b, 1989c). He lists ten criteria that would justify the use of 'intelligence' as an explanatory concept, not just as a descriptive measure, and argues that none of them can be met by our existing research-based knowledge. His central point is that all the claims for the existence in an individual of a stable quantity of a thing called 'intelligence' rest on the positive correlations between measures of performance on cognitive tasks that are presumed to require or involve the use of 'intelligence'. He does not deny that these correlations do exist, but he points out that they are not necessarily due to any particular underlying quality of the individual. Task performance may be related because both tasks require the same knowledge, the same learned skills, the same degree of perseverance or willingness to go 'beyond the information given', not only because they both require 'intelligence'. If the tasks being used for measuring 'intelligence' are of even moderate complexity, they will be highly likely to involve previously learned knowledge, skills and strategies, and it will probably be virtually impossible to specify what these are for any given task, let alone say what their developmental history has been for individuals. Calling the common ground of different tasks 'intelligence' merely provides it with a rather unspecific description.

Howe agrees that this objection applies much less strongly if the tasks used for measuring intelligence are very simple ones, tests of processes not contaminated by prior knowledge. Unfortunately the correlations between such tests have been inconsistent, and in the case of replicable studies have been low (0.3 or less). In any case, even simple measures like IT can be influenced by variables other than 'intelligence'. Thus Howe states that 'intelligence', whether measured by simple psychophysiological tasks, by somewhat more complex tasks involving learning, problem-solving or reasoning, or by traditional 'intelligence tests', remains an unspecified composite of knowledge, skills, strategies, and personality qualities, not necessarily the same from one individual to another or from one test occasion to another, and certainly not an 'innate general cognitive ability'. Anderson's view, of course, would be that Howe is underestimating the importance of basic speed of information-processing, which is seen relatively 'purely' in comparatively simple tests such as inspection time but also contributes in two ways to more complex tasks. First it allows more demanding information-processing to be carried out within the restrictions of working memory while the current task is actually being done, and second it has allowed the accumulation of more and better organised information and the perfecting of more sophisticated cognitive routines earlier in the individual's life (or, in the case of a low processing speed, allowing less to be done in the present with a smaller and less well-processed store of acquired skill and knowledge).

Whether Howe is right or not, it is clearly desirable that our attempts to measure 'intelligence' should be scrutinised so that the reasons why a particular individual functions at a particular level may be more fully understood than a bald IQ figure can indicate. This is of course what responsible users of traditional intelligence tests do, and many would wish also to investigate individuals' performance under other circumstances too, looking at classroom behaviour or at the 'zone of proximal development' (Siegler 2005, and pp. 308–310). Such an approach recognises that, to pick up a rather unpleasing metaphor used by a headmaster of my acquaintance, some people have brains like Minis while others have brains like Porsches, but (to extend the metaphor) the skills of the serviceman and the driver, not to speak of the fuel, the load and the demands of the terrain, are crucial to the way in which the engine runs, and thus to not only the speed at which the car travels but also its safety, the comfort of its occupants and the degree to which it pollutes its environment, to name only three other variables that are at least as important in deciding how 'good' the car's functioning is.

3.1.5 The heritability of intelligence

One major area of the literature on 'intelligence' has not yet been discussed. The definition of intelligence as 'innate general cognitive ability', particularly in those definitions that emphasise intelligence as a consequence of fairly simple differences in the physical working of the brain, implies that intelligence will be heavily influenced by the individual's genes. We know (see Chapter 5) that several genetic abnormalities lead to severe mental retardation, and we are beginning to understand the causal chain between the gene defect or having an abnormal amount of chromosomal material and the behavioural differences of individuals with conditions such as phenylketonuria or Down's syndrome. It is quite clear that the development of the brain is under the control of a complex genetic programme (while also influenced by environmental events) and that, as Scarr and Kidd (1983) elegantly put it, 'the wrong amount of genetic material evidently messes up the program for brain development' (p. 336).

If the 'wrong' genetic material messes up brain development and hence brain performance and hence IQ when it is 'wrong' to a severe degree, might differences in IQ within the normal range have their source in more subtle degrees of genetic wrongness or rightness? It would, paradoxically, be easier to answer this question if there had been fewer attempts to establish a genetic basis for IQ. Investigations of its heritability have occupied much time and energy in the past seventy or eighty years with little profit, much bitter controversy, and some indefensible intervention in the lives of the powerless. Gould (1984) provides a powerful account of some of the atrocities that were a direct result of the belief that intelligence was easily measured, very largely inherited, and not to be improved by education or other environmental interventions; an account that has been very much resented and criticised by believers in IQ testing. Before I review the evidence that this belief is seriously erroneous, there is some conceptual ground to cover.

In the sense in which geneticists use it, 'heritability' means something more precise than 'capable of being inherited', which is the ordinary dictionary definition. Within a population, a trait varies over a certain range. This variance can be partitioned into a component due to relevant genetic differences within the population, a component due to environmental differences, and a component due to the interaction of genetic and environmental differences. Heritability is, at its broadest, the proportion of variation within the population that is due to genetic differences; it is sometimes taken to be that part of the entire genetic component that is due to additive genetic differences between individuals. It may be seen that what proportion of the variation is heritable is affected by how much environmental variation there is: this means that an estimate of heritability of a trait derived from one population with a particular range of environments might not be an appropriate estimate for a population with different environments, or indeed for a genetically different population. Clearly we could not generalise heritability from one population to another: a heritability estimate is always of heritability in the particular population studied, within the particular range of environments it experiences, and at the particular time it is studied. It cannot predict heritability in novel environments; if the new range of environments has more relevant variation, then the proportion of trait variance due to environment will be greater and that due to heredity will be less, and if the new environments vary less, heritability will be greater.

It should be unnecessary to point out that even if a trait is strongly heritable, there can still be environmental influences on how the genetic programme proceeds (Gottesman and Hanson 2005). For example, phenyl-ketonuria is due to a single defective gene that causes a failure to produce the particular enzyme, phenylalanine hydroxylase, required to metabolise phenylalanine, got from protein in most ordinary human diets. This metabolic problem causes an accumulation of phenylalanine that swamps the developing nervous system of the baby, and hence mental retardation develops. Since the genetic defect can be identified at birth and a diet that does not contain phenylalanine can be provided, it is possible to get round the metabolic deficiency, prevent the nervous system from being damaged and reduce the mental retardation to a minimal amount. The gene that causes phenylketonuria remains strongly heritable, but provided people with that gene have an environment free of phenylalanine while their brains are developing (and while, if they are pregnant women, their babies' brains are developing), the gene will not affect the trait of intelligence. Even a high heritability for normal intelligence would not mean that the nature of the environment was irrelevant to its level or its range.

Nor does a heritability estimate tell us how the genes actually affect the trait. In the case of phenylketonuria and some of the other genetic defects that have been studied (but not all those that are known) we have a good idea of what genes are involved and what sort of pathway there is between gene–protein–enzyme activity and physiology and brain functioning, and some (less) idea of how underlying physiology and brain functioning cause differences in intelligence and IQ score. We have this understanding, how-ever, from studies of genes and brains, not from studies of IQ scores and pedigrees. These latter inform us about what sources are relevant to indi-vidual differences in intelligence in a population studied at a particular time under particular conditions; they do not tell us how the relevant sources contribute to the trait, nor which would still be relevant under different conditions, nor even in any very exact way which source is more important. While intuitively we may feel that a heritability of 80 per cent must determine one's score at least four times as much as a heritability of 20 per cent, or that if heritability is 80 per cent and 'environmentality' is 20 per cent the latter is negligible, it is a feeling that has to be resisted. We cannot argue from a population variance estimate to the exact position of an individual, nor ignore the fact that even a relatively strong hereditary influence is still dependent on and influenced by the environment it meets. Without some environment to grow up in, the gene cannot find expression, and even if it has the same effect in every environment in which it is found, somewhere there may be an environment that will change its expression. Plus in any case genes work in conjunction with other genes, not in isolation, and apart from a few catastrophic gene abnormalities, the course of development is due to combinations of genetic and environmental factors.

The traditional way of estimating IQ heritability in a population has been to divide the total variance of that population's IQ scores into a genetic part and an environmental part. This simple model sometimes fits the data well, but it is too simple to be biologically correct. Even the behaviour geneticists (e.g. McHugh and McKusick 1991; Plomin 1986, 1991, 1993, 1994; Scarr and Kidd 1983; Cherny et al. 1994, 1997; Bishop et al. 2003; DeFries et al. 1994; McGue et al. 1993) agree that most human behavioural traits show multifactorial inheritance, that is, their transmission depends on more than one of a number of genetic and environmental factors. The expression of a gene depends on the environment of development: the effect of environmental factors may differ for genetically different individuals, so that there is gene–environment interaction. Environmental factors may be correlated with genotypic ones; a single gene locus (or environmental incident) may be critical for a trait, but its effect may be modified by other gene loci (or environmental factors) that interact with the critical gene (or event); many genes (or many environmental factors) may combine in an additive way to produce a trait. Sophisticated techniques will be necessary to sort out which of these complex patterns of inheritance best describes the relationship between genotype and phenotype for a particular trait. The task is given a further dimension of difficulty by the extensive time that development takes. The individual's genes code for functioning over time, indeed over the whole lifespan to the extremes of old age, including regulation of development, maturing and ageing; 'genetic timing' and 'environmental timing' will fit together in very complicated ways that have profound effects on behaviour, with the influence of genes possibly increasing over time (McCartney et al. 1990; Plomin and Rende 1991). The literature on sensitive periods in perceptual development, for example, shows that the same environmental deficit will have a marked effect at one period in an animal's life and little or no noticeable effect at earlier or later periods (e.g. Aslin et al. 1983; Aslin and Smith 1988; Greenough 1991). In other words, it is inappropriate to say that someone is intelligent or has a good memory or a particularly high degree of artistic ability because he or she has 'the right gene'. Variation within the normal range of cognitive traits may begin with variation in genes, but several genes will be involved and they will have operated in a delicate and intricate pattern of interaction with other genes and environmental factors over a long pathway of development, with the environment and the whole life history contributing to the eventual cognitive ability, just as the genes do.

Much the same needs to be said about the complexity of environment. Many recent behaviour genetic studies divide the environmental part into 'shared environment' (which makes people in the same environment more alike) and 'non-shared environment' (which does not). 'Shared environment' seems, they suggest, to be powerful in early childhood, and has been said to be of trivial importance later. However, a further adjustment to the model is important. Genes may have a direct effect on the brain and behaviour, and may have an indirect effect via interaction with the environment (see Chapter 5). Most heritability estimates count both direct and indirect effects as genetic variation because the heritability theorists argue that the genes determine the environmental experience; but the proximal cause of the indirect effect is actually in the environment, and other theorists would (with just as much correctness) call the result an 'environment' effect (e.g. Ceci 1990). Strictly, both direct and indirect genetic effects depend on both genes and environment, working together in complex ways; like Mackintosh (1998) I doubt whether much is to be gained by using simplified models of 'how much' can be attributed to one or the other.

Having made these warning remarks about heritability estimates, I can turn to the psychological literature. I shall deal with it extremely briefly as there is a great deal of work on the heritability of intelligence and much of it has far too high a ratio of prejudice to considered judgement. Mackintosh (1998) provides a masterly review.

If a trait has a high heritability, that is, if its variation in a population is associated to a high degree with genetic variation, we would expect individuals to be similar on the trait in proportion to the extent to which they shared the same relevant genes (I say 'relevant' since most of our genetic material seems to be virtually identical with our conspecifics, and much is shared with other primates and even mice). Thus genetically identical individuals such as monozygotic twins should be very similar indeed; parents and children, and brothers and sisters, who share an average of half their genes, fairly similar; and differences should increase as degree of relatedness decreases. This argument, of course, underlies the many twin studies and family studies that make up so much of the literature on intelligence. They have indeed found genetic relatedness to be associated with similarity of IQ scores.

Studies of members of the same families, however, have the intrinsic problem that genetically related parents and children and genetically related siblings normally live together, that is, they share each other's environments to a considerable if undefined extent. Further, parents not only pass on genetic material to their children and share their environment, they also do things because of their own genes, including those that they share with the child, which may affect the child; and the child's own genes and behaviour may affect the child's behaviour. Say the father has, and passes on to his daughter, a gene for enjoying reading. (Needless to say, this is an entirely fictitious example. One does not have genes 'for enjoying reading', nor for being intelligent, nor for having a long nose. One has genes that lead to the building of particular proteins at particular times and so, in a long and complex chain of interactions with other genes and with non-genetic influences from the environment, eventually to having a physical or psychological characteristic (Gottesman and Hanson 2005). We are rapidly learning more and more about this chain, and we know for sure that it will never be possible to point to a gene and say 'that's what made the Bachs musical' or 'that's what makes Vanessa Redgrave a great actress'. However, it is worth following the argument as the fictional 'gene for enjoying reading' is a simplification sympathetic to the hereditarian case, which nevertheless fails to stand up even with this advantage. Having this gene, the father will presumably seek opportunities of reading himself and will model 'enjoying reading' to the child, while not modelling those other activities whose time is taken up by the preferred activity of reading. The child, with her genetic predilection for reading, will also be given lots of experience of reading by her father, and will enjoy it; their observation of each other's enjoyment is surely likely to reinforce their activity and their similarity. The child's enthusiasm for books might rekindle an interest in the father that had found little expression while he was too busy with work for many enjoyments; the father's enthusiasm for reading is likely to be expressed in special educational efforts on his daughter's behalf. Even if the daughter does not inherit the 'loving reading' gene, she will still experience her father's enthusiasm for reading, certainly by observing him and probably also by being read to. The father may make special efforts to make reading attractive to this child in a wish to have her share his pleasures and because he knows that there are major educational advantages in liking to read. Parent and child behaviour may be very similar, but the similarity will be due to environmental similarity as well as shared genes. We might expect behavioural similarity to be greatest when there is likely to be parental shaping of young children towards a high level of a trait universally agreed to be desirable (such as reading well or, indeed, being intelligent), and similarity may decrease, particularly when there is less consensus on what level of a trait is best, as children become older and more independent, and leave the environmental pressures of their parents.

There is some evidence for this argument (Luster and Dubow 1992; Scarr and Weinberg 1983; Cherny *et al.* 1994, 1997; DeFries *et al.* 1994; McGue *et al.* 1993; Bishop *et al.* 2003; Spinath *et al.* 2004; Fulker *et al.* 1993; Ferrari and Sternberg 1998).

Gene–environment interactions on these lines may be very common, and they will greatly complicate heritability estimates based on genetically related people who live together. We cannot sort them out at all if our data set only has one child per family, as this does not allow us to distinguish between the effects of the child and the effects of the family environment: if we have a data set with measures on all family members we can use techniques such as multi-level modelling to estimate the effects of individuals, their dyadic relationships, and their family environment. Such work is in progress in my university using the ALSPAC sample, but there are no results yet.

Plomin (1991) and Scarr and McCartney (1983) make similar points about how different types of genotype–environment effects must be considered within developmental theory. First, genetically related people may provide the child with an environment correlated with the child's genotypes, so, for example, through this 'passive' correlation the child who has inherited a genetic tendency to high intelligence may be surrounded by the possessions and activities of highly intelligent parents and siblings. Second, the child's own genetic characteristics may evoke responses from other people that are related to the child's genotype: particular encouragement of the child's interest in books, for example, or alternatively a pressure to 'get your nose out of that book and get some fresh air and exercise'. (Sex-stereotyped provision of toys, or indeed anti-sexist provision of the toys traditionally associated with the opposite sex, would be examples of this 'reactive' correlation between genotype and environment, picking up a comparatively obvious part of the child's genotype.) Third, the child may actively seek or create an environment to the full development of its genetic propensities – 'ecological niche picking' which maximises the impact of congenial aspects of the environment and minimises the less genotypically suitable bits. (These might be compared with Sternberg's ideas about the cultural context of intelligence (Chapter 4).) Scarr and McCartney propose that although 'passive', 'reactive' and 'active' genotype–environment correlations all occur in the course of development, their relative importance changes with age. The influence of passive effects is greatest in infancy, and declines as the child's individuality becomes more recognisable and its opportunities for selecting experiences increase. Reactive effects continue through life, while active effects increase from infancy to adolescence as the child encounters successively wider environments with more variation to select from. This proposal implies that siblings will be more similar as young children, when passive genotype–environment effects dominate and they share the same family environment, than they are as adolescents, when their experience varies more and more and they may even be seeking to be as different from each other as possible (Schachter 1982). There does seem to be some evidence for such a change (see e.g. Bouchard *et al.* (1990), Dumaret and Stewart (1985), Dunn (1991b), Plomin (1986, 1990a, 1990b), Scarr and Weinberg (1983)); for example, the higher correlation between the IQs of adoptive parents and young adopted children than between those of adoptive parents and adopted children grown up to adolescence.

The obvious strategy for getting round this problem is studies of genetically related people reared separately and unrelated people reared together. Earlier work in this area concentrated on studies of twins who had been brought up separately, hence Stephen Jay Gould's remark that the easiest way he knew of to make a living was to be an identical twin whose co-twin had been adopted at birth into another family, and to hire himself out to psychologists trying to estimate the heritability of IQ (and other personality traits). While this early work suggests that identical twins reared separately were still very similar indeed in IQ (i.e. that IQ is highly heritable), there are serious problems with the studies. The numbers of twins are small and they are very possibly not representative of the wider population. Further, the degree to which their environments differed, indeed even the degree to which their environments were separate, is very unclear. Many 'reared apart' twins were adopted by an aunt and brought up near their sibling, which suggests some communality of environment. Where the environment clearly differed, IQ scores tended to differ too (Bouchard *et al.* 1990; Plomin 1994; Ferrari and Sternberg 1998). On the whole, not enough has been done to identify environmental differences that are relevant to intelligence (as we shall see in Chapter 5), and I do rather regret that the resources that went into chasing 'reared apart' twins didn't go into examining environments.

Adoption studies, on the other hand, provide quite useful evidence on the heritability of intelligence. Adopted children are not genetically related to the family that rears them, so genetic differences and environmental differences are not confounded except in so far as the adoption agency tries to provide adoptive parents who resemble the biological ones. When there is more demand for babies to adopt than there are babies given up for adoption, agencies tend to select parents who are above average on such measures of 'suitability' as socio-economic status, educational level, intelligence and character (so far as they can gauge them). Adoptive parents are probably also unusually determined people, since becoming an adoptive parent requires you to convince so many other people of your deservingness and merits; they are probably not altogether representative of the population as a whole. While this does limit the generalisability of the studies somewhat, the fact that adoptive parents tend to provide better than average environments for their children has actually illuminated questions about the variability of IQ, as we shall see.

An ideal adoption study design has information on the IQs of all four parents for each child and compares adopted and biological siblings. While as yet no study provides this, there are two major conclusions from the existing studies (Horn 1983; Scarr and Weinberg 1983; Schiff and Lewontin 1986; Plomin 1994; DeFries *et al.* 1994; Mackintosh 1998; Bishop *et al.* 2003; Haugaard and Hazan 2003). The first is that the correlation between natural parent and child is higher than that between adoptive or rearing parent and child, which supports a stronger role for genes than for environment in intellectual resemblance between parent and child. The correlation between adoptive parents and children, or between adopted siblings, also decreases from early childhood to adolescence, suggesting that their shared environment has some effect while the children are spending all their time in it, but has much less effect once the children have grown old enough to experience (and select) worlds outside the home. The second is that children reared in adoptive families, with their social and economic advantages and with family members of above average intelligence, show a higher level of IQ score than would be expected from their biological parents' scores, if the biological parents come from disadvantaged social classes. This finding supports a strong role for environment in the intellectual level of children. The genes you inherit from your parents may determine the potential you have for intelligence, but the environment in which you are reared determines how nearly you reach that potential.

Two important points arise from the adoption studies of intelligence. The first concerns IQ differences between groups that differ genetically and environmentally. The Minnesota Transracial Adoption Study (Scarr and Weinberg 1983) looked at black, mixed-race and white children adopted into white families. It tested the hypothesis that these children would per-form equally well on IQ tests, that is, that 'racial' differences in IQ are due to cultural factors, not to genetic differences, and its results supported the hypothesis. Both black and mixed-race adopted children scored above the average for Minnesota's white population, considerably above the average for children reared in the black community, though about six IQ points below the natural children of the adoptive parents. This result, similar as it is to Eyferth's study of the illegitimate children of black and white American soldiers who occupied Germany after the Second World War and fathered children on local women (Flynn 1980, 1999), suggest that there is no convincing argument for a genetic cause for the lower average IQ score of American blacks. (Mackintosh (1998) offers a strong refutation of a wide range of studies that have attributed ethnic group differences to genetic inheritance of intelligence.)

The second point I want to make arises from the important French study by Michel Schiff and his colleagues (Duyme 1988, 1990; Schiff and Lewontin 1986; Schiff *et al.* 1982; Duyme *et al.* 1999). This study traced a sample of 32 children adopted within the first month of life into upper-middle-class families. Their biological mothers and the putative fathers were all unskilled workers. The children's IQ scores and school careers were compared with schoolchildren of the general population and of their original social class, and also with biological half-siblings. The children in this comparison group had the same biological mothers as the adopted children, though mostly a different father, and were near them in age. They had not been adopted into upper-middle-class families, however; instead they were being reared in unskilled workers' families, mostly with their biological mother, though some were with grandparents or a foster mother. The results of some of the comparisons made are shown in Table 3.1.

It is quite clear from this that the adopted and non-adopted sibling samples were different from each other (despite sharing the same mother) and closely resembled their social class of rearing. The social class contrast was particularly marked in their school histories: upper-middle-class children were much more likely to make uninterrupted progress through school. We will return to social class differences in educational performance in Chapter 5.

I have talked about heritability of intelligence so far without putting a figure to it. There are several reasons for this. My main reason is that I am personally much more interested in what environments do to the development of the skills of intelligence than in the genetic differences that underpin differences in unanalysed IQ. This is not to diminish the interest and importance of studies of the brain and what makes brains differ in their production of intelligent behaviour; we are fortunate in working at a time when rapid advances are being made in understanding the way the brain works. I look forward to knowing more about it, and I introduce it below (pp. 316–347), but it seems to me unlikely that this knowledge will make environmental effects look unimportant, or establish a definition of intelligence as 'innate general cognitive ability' as being useful for psychological or educational purposes.

My second reason is that experts producing heritability estimates have varied considerably and violently in the figure they settled on. This, plus the lack of explicit and testable models of the genes behind the heritability, makes me disinclined to regard most estimates as scientifically unimpeachable. The 'best guess' of reputable scholars appears to be that the heritability of IQ scores in the white North American and British populations studied is between 40 per cent and 70 per cent (Mackintosh 1998; Ferrari and Sternberg 1998). We know little or nothing about other populations, nor is it entirely clear what range of social classes is included even in the white British and North American samples. These are of course populations with relatively uniform environments and universal education, characteristics that will reduce the environmental variance and thus tend to inflate heritability. As I said earlier, a 'heritability' figure is a property of a

Table 3.1 School careers and IQ scores of French children adopted into middle-class families: comparisons with social class of origin and general population.

Children's social class	Sample	School history			IQ			
					Group IQ Test		WISC IQ	
		No. of failures among 32 children of age of adopted and sibling sample	Failure rate (%) remedial class	Serious failure rate (%) (permanent special education)	Average	% below 85 IQ	Average	% below 85 IQ
Unskilled workers	Half-siblings of adopted children	16.1	66	33	95.1	21	94.2	25
	National surveys	16.5	67	34	95.0	21	–	
Upper middle class	Adopted children	4	17	3	106.8	5	110.6	3
	National surveys	4	17	3	110	3	–	
National norms		11.2	46	18	99.2	16	100	16

Source: Adapted from Schiff and Lewontin 1986: 90.

particular population in a particular environment at a particular time; you cannot generalise the heritability of one sample to another.

The only sensible position to take, it seems to me, is that intelligence is affected by one's genes both directly as they work to produce a more or less adequately functioning brain and indirectly through one's kin's behaviour and the environment one seeks out and elicits oneself; but that it is also malleable, affected by the environments to which one becomes adapted. Environments may be easier to manipulate than genes have been, but they certainly have not been studied in sufficient detail. We will examine both genetic influences and environmental influences on cognitive development in Chapter 5.

3.2 Cognitive style and learning styles

Intelligence is by far the dominant dimension of individual differences in cognition, but there have been other dimensions of cognitive style, some purely psychological, some developed for their educational implications. The first, Field dependence/independence (FDI), originated in Witkin's work (Witkin 1977; Witkin and Goodenough 1981) on basic perceptual processes: it was a bipolar construct such that field-dependent perceivers had difficulty in perceiving the constituent parts of a figure in the visual field as separate from the whole, while field-independent perceivers were skilled at analysing the field into separate parts. It was usually measured using the Embedded Figures Test, in which the task was to pick out a simple figure that made part of the contours of a more complex one, or the Rod and Frame Test in which the rod typically had to be adjusted to a true vertical within a frame that was tilted out of alignment with the vertical. These tasks were seen as good indicators of a much more general cognitive style and personality dimension. Field-independent (FI) people were good at the Embedded Figures Test and other tasks requiring perceptual restructuring because they were autonomous, impersonal, task-oriented people. Field-dependent (FD) people, with a stronger interpersonal orientation and a greater sensitivity to social stimulation, were worse on restructuring tasks because of their reliance on other people and a less task-oriented approach. Early versions of the theory saw FI as clearly superior to FD, but more recently the two have been seen as more equally valid alternatives; for example, FD people might be better at interpersonal and holistic tasks.

Developmentally, FDI could have two sorts of importance. The first concerns what causes it, the second how differences of cognitive style affect other aspects of development. There is weak and inconsistent support for Witkin's hypothesis that field independence is encouraged by parenting that encourages separate autonomous functioning rather than reliance on parental authority (Witkin and Goodenough 1981; Kagan and Kogan 1970; Kogan and Saarni 1989; Kogan 1983) and on biological differences in hemispheric lateralisation (Waber 1977).

As to how being FD or FI would affect other aspects of development, FDI impinges on a wide range of cognitive processes – not just spatial cognition but memory, learning and problem-solving – and has, as I said earlier, social implications also, through its association with different sorts of social competence. It is not clear whether FDI is independent of intelligence: there do seem to be fairly substantial correlations between the Embedded Figures Test and both g and spatial intelligence (Satterly 1976; Vernon 1972), not surprisingly, given the conceptually overlapping test content. Work by Nakamura and his colleagues (Nakamura and Finck 1980; Ruble and Nakamura 1972) suggested that FD children showed more task orientation and FI children more sensitivity to social cues. Children who had a low social orientation and high task effectiveness were all high on field independence; children who had a high social orientation tended to be more FD whether or not they were task-oriented or had a sense of self-effectiveness. However, while FDI remains conceptually unclear and its measurement is fraught with problems, its use as a dimension of cognitive development is uncertain.

It has also been suggested that people differ in their tendency to 'reflection' or 'impulsivity'. These cognitive styles refer to the extent to which a child can delay his or her response when searching for the correct answer to best choice in a context where what response to make is initially uncertain. (This difference in styles cropped up in my discussion of problem-solving, pp. 126–131.) The standard test here was the Matching Familiar Figures Test (MFFT), which requires the subject to find the only picture in a set that is exactly the same as a standard figure. Children who make a choice quickly but also make many errors are called 'impulsive'; those who respond slowly but make few errors are called 'reflective'. It was assumed that impulsivity is a general trait and a disadvantage in most settings, particularly in education; hence the encouragement teachers give children to 'think, don't just guess'.

While there are some doubts about the psychometric adequacy of the MFFT, just as there are about the Rod and Frame and Embedded Figures Tests (Block et al. 1986; Kagan 1987; Kogan 1983; Ferrari and Sternberg 1998), the underlying issue of the relative importance placed on speed and on accuracy is one of great importance for cognitive psychology and for education. Children who are faced with a difficult detailed task may estimate the payoffs of strategies that emphasise speed or accuracy – or economy of effort; they may wish to please the tester or to get out of being tested. There is some evidence that there are indeed complexities in this: teachers rate children who are 'impulsive' as judged by their performance on the MFFT not as behaviourally impulsive but as anxious, cautious, vulnerable and self-doubting (Block *et al.* 1974, 1986; Victor *et al.* 1985; Wapner and Connor 1986). Their MFFT style of fast–inaccurate responding presumably reflects their wish to escape from being tested and failing. It is not a successful strategy but neither is it a sign of general impulsivity. The evidence for reflection–impulsivity as correlated with ability to delay gratification and resist temptation is not strong (Kogan 1976, 1983; Ferrari and Sternberg 1998).

An alternative account of reflection–impulsivity has been put forward by Zelniker and Jeffrey (1976, 1979). They suggest that more reflective children are dealing with the MFFT and other similar tasks in terms of more analysis of detail, while impulsive children do more global holistic processing. The more focused attention of reflective children may be more advantageous in many educational tasks, particularly perhaps if they can adjust the way they distribute their attention to the demands of the task. However, attention deployment and distribution of effort are not likely to be independent: it is certainly possible to increase children's reflectiveness by training them, using a variety of procedures (Kogan 1983: 682). It is not clear, however, how long such improvement lasts, how far it generalises, or whether what changes is the nature of the processing done, the resources devoted to it, or some combination of the two. Nor is it clear what caused individual differences in reflection–impulsivity in the first place.

Baron *et al.* (1986) pick up some of these issues in their discussion of 'cognitive style' as departure from optimally efficient behaviour on cognitive tasks rather than as a halfway house between ability and personality. They centre on 'impulsivity', seeing it as a tendency to stop too soon when trying to discover the solution to a cognitive task. An 'impulsive' child answers with the first possible response that comes to mind, thus risking errors that someone who persisted with thinking about the problem might not make, or gives up too readily when persistence might have produced an answer. This could be seen as underestimating the utility of making further cognitive effort. There will be a number of motivational and metacognitive reasons for such underestimating. A person may not value the payoff of further work, for example preferring the short-term reward of going to a party now to the more distant reward of high achievement, high income and high status that might result from studying but might not from partying (at least at the school pupil stage of the life cycle – things may be different when 'certification' comes from social contacts rather than from academic record). The varying approaches to study that I outline later differ in this sort of way. There may be differences also in the cost of further cognitive effort: cognition that is very painful or effortful may not seem to be worth it. An ideal, non-impulsive, thinker would balance the utility and the cost of thinking, and neither spend too much time polishing a 'good enough' performance nor carelessly throw in an underfinished not quite good enough one. Both over-confidence and under-confidence may be involved in impulsiveness, the former suggesting that further thought is superfluous and the latter that it may not bring about any improvement. A person's characteristic explanations or 'attributions' of success or failure may also lead to giving up too soon or even to not trying at all (Bandura 1995, 1997; Dweck and Elliott 1983; Dweck 1999; Meadows 1986: 149–150, 193–195; Thompson 2004).

The complexity of reasons for impulsive premature answering of a question suggests that it might vary across tasks that differ in the attributions they evoke, the thinking they demand or the payoff they attract. Perhaps 'impulsivity' only applies to some tasks, where the person sees the task as involving intellectual competence, has a standard for what good performance would be on tasks in general and on this task in particular, and has to decide between several possible answers, none of which is immediately known to be right (Kagan *et al.* 1987). Siegler (1986, 1988, 2005) uses an information-processing model of associative strengths of different answers and individual differences in the 'strength' level that is acceptable as an answer; he sees these reflected in the strategy choices of good students, not-so-good students, and perfectionists.

'FDI' and 'reflection–impulsivity' are two examples of how individual differences in cognition have been conceptualised. Schmeck (1988) presents a number of conceptualisations and suggests that they can all be encompassed by 'one broad inclusive dimension of individual difference' of learning style, which he labels 'global versus analytic'. An extreme 'global' style involves field dependence, intuitive and emotional thinking, simultaneous processing of many aspects of experience, a tendency to impulsivity, and the formation of global impressions rather than precisely articulated analyses. Its pathological extreme could be called 'globetrotting' (Entwistle 1988; Pask 1988), an incomplete understanding based on overreadiness to see relationships between ideas or to come to conclusions without examining the evidence. At the other end of the stylistic dimension is an extreme 'analytic' style, involving field independence, sequential organised thinking, dispassionate noting of detailed objective 'facts', critical and logical thinking and a focus on learning step-by-step operations rather than a comprehensive overview. Here the pathological form is 'improvidence', an incomplete understanding based on detailed knowledge of many relevant facts which, however, fail to be integrated with broad principles, a 'can't see the wood for the trees' sort of cognition. Neither extreme is truly functional: an integration of the two, a balance of simultaneous and successive processing, of holism and analysis, varying according to task demands, will be more useful. Schmeck suggests that these cognitive styles develop as a result of the very young child's emotional reaction to failures of parental support and sensitivity. He uses ideas from psychoanalytic theorists such as Winnicott, suggesting that the child's self-awareness leads to pathological cognitive styles if the self-concept is emotionally negative, while self-acceptance is necessary for an integrated flexible cognitive style. There is little evidence on this sequence of causation, and Schmeck does not seem to be aware of the cultural limitations of the model of parent–child relations he uses.

Klein (2003) discusses modality learning styles, especially the contrast between visual and verbal/auditory/aural learning styles which has had some educational influence. The theory here is of opposed types, with individuals being supposed to have a strong preference for a specific modality in their learning style, so that the 'visual' learner needs everything to be presented and processed visually, and the verbal learner would be lost with visual material unless it can be translated into words. This idea is not unlike Gardner's multiple intelligences (Gardner 1983). The research evidence suggests that this polarisation is misleading; most learners prefer a more moderate or even mixed learning opportunity, and vary their preference somewhat according to the demands of the task. In any case, using a range of representations may well be an extremely sensible strategy and a desirable curriculum goal.

Some of the most interesting accounts of cognitive learning styles link them with current motivations. These studies often focus on examination of performance on particular well-defined tasks rather than assuming that 'cognitive style' is consistent over all occasions for learning or problem-solving. The differences they pinpoint cut across the global–analytic dimension: they are associated with different motives for cognitive activity which result in different approaches to it. Three main 'approaches' are suggested (Biggs 1984, 1988; Entwistle 1988; Entwistle *et al.* 1979; Marton 1983, 1988; Riding 1991; Volet and Chalmers 1992), 'surface', 'deep' and 'achieving'. Biggs in particular describes these approaches in students in secondary and tertiary education, but the same motives could no doubt apply earlier in development. 'Surface' students are concerned to obtain success (in terms of getting a qualification or a satisfactory grade) with minimal effort. They wish to avoid failure, and hence worry about tasks taking too long or, alternatively, having been worked on for too short a time for adequate performance. They tend to focus on 'essentials', usually the factual data given in their textbooks and lectures that they judge to be important to their assessors – and work to reproduce them as accurately as possible. They are much less concerned with deeper levels of understanding, and they happily forget what was learned once they succeed in getting the qualification they sought. 'Deep' learners start from an intrinsic interest in the subject-matter and an intention to develop and use a personal understanding of it. Self-actualisation, and enjoyment of learning for its own sake, combine with interest to focus them on the meaning of what they study. They are much less likely than 'surface' students to reproduce facts without amendment or criticism and without reference to underlying principles. 'Achieving' students are primarily interested in doing better than anyone else, getting the highest grades being a concrete demonstration of this. They may use 'deep' or 'surface' strategies, depending on the course requirements and the methods of assessment they face.

Of these three approaches, the theorists see the 'surface' learning style as least worthy of respect. They associate it with weak and anxious students, though acknowledging that curriculum and assessment in a considerable part of the education system may demand rote reproduction, not deep understanding and insight, let alone originality. This point about the inter-action between task demands and student learning styles is an important one. Some theorists assume (as I have pointed out earlier in this chapter) that a single sample of behaviour is sufficient for the diagnosis of cognitive style as this is seen as consistent over different tasks and situations and even developmentally, but fail to provide data that substantiate this view. Even if individuals are consistent in cognitive style, as does seem to be the case in a domain such as academic learning (Pask 1988; Siegler 1988), this consistency may be ascribed in part to institutional constraints such as examination techniques and other 'official' definitions of what is 'proper' learning. Primary school children may be exhorted to 'work it out' or to guess; science students may be expected to learn many highly specific facts and rules rather than go for global comprehension. Pask presents evidence that individuals can adopt the learning style appropriate to a particular task, though this versatility or sensitivity to context is itself differentially evident in different individuals! Siegler (1988) sees it in terms of individual differences in strategy choices, these choices being based on the amount of knowledge and the amount of certainty required for stating an item of knowledge as an answer.

Sternberg (2002) divides learning styles somewhat differently, focusing on the sorts of teaching and learning activities that build up to 'successful intelligence'. He suggests that individual students differ in their preference for memory learning or analytic thinking or creative thinking or practical thinking. He has carried out a series of studies on what happens when the 'match' between student style and teaching style is varied, suggesting that students do best when they have an opportunity to use their preferred style, though it may be advantageous to them to get some practice at working within the other styles. These ideas are relevant to my discussion of 'teaching thinking', Chapter 6.

It seems to me, then, that the accumulated work on 'cognitive style' has not as yet led to any clear conclusion on its place in the study of the development and acquisition of cognition in childhood. The view that 'cognitive style' is a general and stable trait seems to be losing ground to a view that styles are highly susceptible to task and situational influences, a shift that may be paralleled elsewhere in the psychology of cognitive development, where domain-specific models are receiving more attention than very high-level general ones. Similarly there is more recognition now that the demands of a particular task will be a major determinant of whether a cognitive style such as field independence or impulsivity is an advantage or a disadvantage. A more complex developmental progress is implied in this, as to assessment and causal explanations. A great deal needs to be clarified about who does what when, and with what degree of success, and what the antecedents and consequents are. Motivation factors, not much considered by the cognitive style approach, will be at work here; we will need to link it back to metacognitive awareness. As I said apropos of intelligence, it's not just the mental engine that determines performances, it's how you use it and on what.

3.3 Creativity

I shall deal very briefly with work on 'creativity' as an aspect of individual differences in cognition and cognitive development, and shall be critical of much that has been done. Something is said to be 'creative' if it is original and adaptive or appropriate: a 'creative' person is someone who produces original and adaptive ideas, reasoning or compositions. There is a series of problems with this: defining what is 'original' or 'adaptive', attributing it to an individual's 'creativity', recognising it when it occurs, are all complex and difficult. The root of my criticism of the area is the failure of theoreticians to be consistent and exact in their concept of what creativity is and how it works, a very pervasive problem (see Sternberg (1999), Simonton (2003), Runco (2004)). The term is used to refer to the genius of Leonardo da Vinci and to the innovations of young children (or language-trained apes) in coining words to fill a gap in their vocabularies, via the novels of Jane Austen and the school compositions of an eight-year-old, without, I think, sufficient analysis of what these products and behaviours have in common and what differentiates them. Agreeing as I do with Edison's aphorism that 'Genius is one per cent inspiration and ninety-nine per cent perspiration', I want some theoretical differentiation between Leonardo and Washoe. I shall first review the psychometric literature on creativity and then, via a return to earlier work on the intuitions of creative adults, indicate what may be involved in 'real', serious, creativity.

Commonly in the developmental literature, 'creativity' has been measured by and seen as largely synonymous with performance on divergent thinking tests (Guilford 1967; Simonton 1999) and even more narrowly with such tests' measure of 'ideational fluency': that is, for example, how many uses the subject can think of for an object such as a brick. Even if measures with wider implications (but perhaps less objectivity and consensus) such as teacher ratings or excellence of artistic expression are taken, ideational fluency has been seen as the psychometric core of the concept of 'creativity'. The sheer number of responses produced has the considerable merit of being easy to count, hence it is a quick measure reliable between judges, who are less likely to agree on originality and appropriateness. Producing original uses for a brick is usually a consequence of producing many uses; in other words, it does appear that fluency is needed to generate originality (Kogan 1983). Similarly, the evidence that creative people are more likely to think of 'remote associates', not just obvious associates, for example to see that the word 'party' is associated with each of the otherwise heterogeneous set 'line', 'Conservative' and 'stag', is 'unpersuasive' (Perkins 1988).

The identification of ideational fluency with creativity rests on the case that both require a broad deployment of attention, a wider consciousness of possibilities and implications, a freedom and spontaneity of personality that allows ideas to bubble forth. However, Wallach (1971) puts forward a less attractive interpretation: the person who puts on a highly fluent and productive performance on a divergent thinking test may be showing obsessive tendencies, in an unwillingness to give up generating barely different answers, or an anxiety to please the tester, making a large number of responses in order to make a good impression. Here the need to distinguish between quantity and quality is particularly evident (see also Harrington *et al.* (1983)). And if we move out of the developmental literature to consider the 'creativity' of writers like Barbara Cartland (prolific but rather possibly not 'creative') and James Joyce (creative, but not particularly prolific), its importance is reinforced. It appears that it is quality, not quantity, of divergent thinking performance that predicts creativity recognised as such by teachers. Quantity is important, perhaps, if it stems from a willingness to postpone self-censorship, and provides material for further development, not because it is an end in itself (Csikszentmihalyi *et al.* 1993).

The question of how to gauge the 'creativity' of a product is a complex one, and the various indices that might be proposed have all run into two difficulties: first, the lack of unanimity between judges, and second, the lack of correlation between different indices. 'Unusualness' is an obvious criterion, but although it can be assessed on the basis of statistical rarity (brick as building material makes up a higher proportion of 'uses for a brick' than does brick as a source of reddish powder, so the latter is more unusual and thus more 'creative'), some unusual 'uses' might be so bizarre that we might see them as pathological, not as creative (bricks as radio receivers for the messages that little green men on Mars are sending out in an attempt to control my thought waves and make me assassinate William Shakespeare because Martians don't like his plays). 'Appropriateness' has been suggested as a further criterion and as a corrective to this problem, but this is a quality that raters agree on less well: a brick as a pillow seems definitively inappropriate to an American textbook writer (Rebok 1987: 322) but plausible, if dubiously comfortable, to someone who has admired the beautiful ceramic pillows of ancient China. There are historical as well as cultural problems here: some of Mozart's music, Mendel's theory and the mini-skirt all seemed inappropriate when they were first produced – 'too many notes' is supposed to have been one reaction to the first case – but have seemed more or less admirably creative, unusual and appropriate at a later date. Conversely, later thinkers may repudiate earlier 'creativity': the theory that 'ontogeny recapitulates phylogeny', that the development of the individual from conception to maturity recapitulates the evolutionary development of the species, seemed unusual and appropriate to late-nineteenth-century philosophers, biologists and sociologists including Herbert Spencer, G. Stanley Hall and Freud, and also, I suspect, to Piaget (Gould 1977; Meadows 1986). Despite the fact that it displayed two higher level indices of creativity in that it helped to transform what was thought about development and about humanity's place in the universe and gave rise to qualitative shifts and to increases in theorising, and that it provided a simple framework that contained and 'explained' phenomena of a complex diversity, it is now seen as false, hence inappropriate, and not perhaps so very original in the intellectual climate of the nineteenth century. Historians of science and of the arts can often find a precursor theory or product whose existence may be taken to lessen the 'originality', if not the excellence, of what had previously been taken as stunningly creative.

Some writers (e.g. Perkins 1988) are not deterred by these problems, saying that creativity is a 'fuzzy' concept and that we all agree on core instances, so need not be too concerned about disagreement about more marginal ones. I am not sure how much of a 'core' we really do agree on, but unfortunately for developmental psychologists, our definition problem is particularly acute. Children are continually doing things (e.g. early words, early games) that are novel for them and appropriate, but have been done by millions of people before. Or they do things (e.g. invent a name) that are altogether novel and provide an appropriate solution to a problem, but later develop the normal consensual form and give up their earlier 'creative' solution. They are far more engaged in 'pretence' than adults, something that Carruthers (2002) links to creativity, but he does not provide a convincing account of the relation of play, creativity and pretend.

It is not known whether 'creativity', as measured by divergent thinking tests or by teacher ratings, is a stable individual characteristic over the course of development, partly because it is not clear what 'creativity' consists of at different ages (Feldman 1999). It seems that many adult writers wrote also as children, but we do not know how many people write as children or as adults but not both, nor in what ways their writing was 'creative'. Nor is it known what conditions facilitate ideational fluency, let alone 'creativity': the research that suggested that play or 'open' classroom environments fostered such behaviour is seriously flawed (Bennet et al. 1976; Kogan 1983). Torrance (1962, 1988) has had some notable success in identifying creative adolescents and also in training and support activities for students who were under-performing in school, but finer analyses are needed of both input and output.

A considerable amount of research has been done on the relationship between intelligence and creativity (e.g. Freeman et al. 1971; Getzels and

Jackson 1962; Hudson 1970; Wallach and Kogan 1965; Runco 2004). Much of this work is compromised by the two cognitive characteristics being defined in terms of intelligence test scores and creativity test scores, or by the use of ratings of one or the other that are even more approximate (such as school achievement tests as an index of the intelligence of more or less 'creative' professional adults). Not surprisingly, the results are unclear. However, it seems that intelligence and creativity are positively correlated in the general population, so that few persons with low IQ scores are recognised as 'creative' on tests or as professional artists or scientists (but see the research on 'creativity' in so-called idiot savants, e.g. Grigorenko (2003), Hermelin (2001), Howe (1989c), O'Connor and Hermelin (1990), Radford (1990)). IQ does not predict creativity so well at an above-average level: there may be a threshold level of intelligence necessary for creative achievement, but extra IQ points above that level (about 110–120) do not predict extra creativity. There obviously are highly intelligent people who do not produce creative work. Intelligence could therefore be seen as enabling rather than causing creativity. Perkins (1988) floats the idea that highly creative professionals are almost all highly intelligent because they needed high intelligence earlier in their careers in order to get the academic credentials and qualifications necessary for entry to their profession and the opportunity to be creative within it. Their high intelligence might have no further relevance to their present creativity. Whether this argument is persuasive depends on one's view of education and one's definitions of intelligence and creativity. If the criterion for 'creativity' is eminence in a profession such as science or architecture, then undoubtedly educational certification will have been required because people rarely get to work as scientists or architects if they have not completed a formal training extending over many years. 'Creativity' in popular music, on the other hand, might not require educational certification in the creative musician; but what about the marketing apparatus that spots, supports, finances, promotes and shapes the musical talent? Whether the cognitive processes that constitute 'intelligence' enable or promote 'creativity' is perhaps better considered by looking at them in more detail. I will return to the social context of 'creativity' later.

It is quite clear that for many creative people their creativity is very task-specific, and built on a long period of gaining expertise on one particular area (Simonton 2003). The creativity of Chopin and Liszt, for example, was expressed almost entirely in piano music, that of Jane Austen in novels of exquisite social comedy, that of Mendel exclusively in genetics. The cognitive processes involved operate on the basis of very specific content and mastery of form and subject-matter. The psychometric literature on creativity has been very general about processes; 'generate and select' is perhaps the core description (Runco 2004), though tests like the Uses of Objects, even less specifically, require only generation of ideas. It is necessary to find an intermediate level of specificity and precision. A number of relevant activities appear in the reports of creative people about their own cognition (e.g. Getzels and Csikszentmihalyi 1976; Ghiselin 1954; Koestler 1964; Ochse 1990; Sternberg 1999; Simonton 2003). (They also appear in the commentary of psychologists on creative individuals (e.g Gardner 1983, 1993), though many such commentaries are of very poor quality, treating biographical material in an astonishingly arbitrary way.)

Getzels and Csikszentmihalyi (1976), for example, investigated art students who were rated by their teachers as being creative. They spent more time on initial exploratory approaches to their work, were more able to change directions if new ideas or possibilities came up later, did not view their work as fixed and were more independent of precedent and prior thought. All in all they excelled in 'fending off closure', which enabled them to progress beyond the obvious to more novel solutions to problems. Elsewhere, creative people are described as having a preference for looking at problems from contradictory positions, and making particular fertile use of negations. Koestler (1964) emphasised the finding and use of analogies (pp. 110–115): both creativity and humour result, he said, from the intersection of two formerly distinct frames of reference. The problem-solving technique of 'brainstorming' also stresses banning criticism, deferring closure, encouraging fluent production of novel ideas, encouraging add-ons and analogies, and so forth.

To be able to proceed like this requires certain cognitive attitudes, which do indeed turn up in reports on the personalities of creative persons (Nakamura and Csikszentmihalyi 2001; Simonton 2003; Runco 2004). Creativity involves choosing challenges rather than avoiding them, which is linked with autonomy, independence and ambition. It involves valuing appropriateness, which is defined (in perhaps somewhat transcendental terms) as (in the sciences) the consistency, parsimony, generalness and predictive power of theories, or (in the arts) as moral or emotional profundity in the representation of the meaning of life, human nature and so forth. It involves tolerance of risk, the ability to confront uncertainty, to enjoy complexity, to toy with and resolve ambiguity, etc. Such people as creative artists, scientists and architects (Nakamura and Csikszentmihalyi 2001; Ochse 1990) do seem to have these characteristics more than their less creative peers. The creative person also has, however, an exhaustive knowledge of his or her field, a sizeable basic repertoire of strategies and skills and information, acquired through a long and effortful involvement in the area; in short, expertise (Ericsson and Charness 1994; Ericsson 2003). Radford (1990) reviews the literature on exceptional early achievement in a number of different fields: commonly, high achievers are not predictable from early excellence so much as from their investment of time and energy. Whether the creative attitude is applied even outside one's own area of expertise is not clear: some creative persons do seem to have been able to turn their skills to unrelated areas (Rossini was a creative cook as well as a composer), and some of course are expert and even creative in more than one field, Leonardo da Vinci, Freud and Piaget being obvious examples.

The introspections of creative people (Ghiselin 1954; Ochse 1990; Wallas 1926) also provide an interesting summary of the stages of the creative process. The first is the long slog of familiarising oneself with the problem, gathering together and organising what might be the relevant information, acquiring the necessary expertise, investigating each avenue of solution. No solution, no satisfactory action, can be found, despite intensive work trying every possibility that suggests itself. Commonly in those cases where a creative solution is eventually found, the first stage of working hard on a problem is succeeded by a second stage of not working on the problem at all but letting it 'lie fallow': going on holiday (or merely to sleep) or working on something else. This is then followed by a third stage, an 'insight', a 'Eureka' reaction, which suggests the answer. Various dramatic and famous instances of this are reported: Archimedes realising that the volume of an intricate object could be measured by measuring how much water it displaced in a full container, just as his own body displaced water in his overflowing bath, or Kekulé dreaming of how the atoms of carbon and hydrogen fitted together in molecules of benzene in a ring like a snake biting its own tail. The essential fourth stage is the working out and testing of the solution, which obviously resembles the first stage, and may lead to further cycles of hard work and discovery.

Subjectively, this cyclic pattern of the creative act seems plausible, and a recent series of studies finds people who 'slept on a problem' were more likely to develop an insight into its solution (Stickgold and Walker 2004). But of course we do not have systematic data on whether the cycle is indeed significantly associated with creative products, or whether there are many cycles like this that never get past stage 2, or cycles where a solution emerges as a result of stages 1 and 4, without any experience identifiable as 'lying fallow' or 'insight'. Nor do we know what quantity of stage 1 activity or stage 2 inactivity can lead to what profundity of stage 3 insight. Nevertheless, this model of the creative cycle has at least two merits: it reminds us that by no means all cognitive activity is conscious, accessible and controllable, and it is deeply consoling to those of us who find ourselves rather frequently staring into space with an apparently empty mind: 'I'm not daydreaming, I'm letting an insight emerge'. The relevant developmental literature might thus be on play, exploration, 'pretend' and insight rather than on 'creativity' *per se* (Haight and Miller 1992; Harter and Chao 1992; Smith and Simon 1984; Smith *et al.* 1985; Sternberg 1999; Lillard 1994, 2002; Carruthers 2002), but also on motivation, effort, and tutoring (Radford 1990; Ericsson and Charness 1994; Ericsson 2003).

Nakamura and Csikszentmihalyi (2001) make the final and enormously important point that creativity is constituted by forces beyond the innovating individual. Their example is the eminent chemist Linus Pauling, who won the Nobel Prize for chemistry in 1954 for his contributions to the electrochemical theory of valency, nearly discovered the structure of DNA (and was a mentor to Watson and Crick, who first proposed the correct structure), won the Nobel Peace Prize in 1963 for his advocacy of nuclear disarmament, and campaigned for the use of vitamin C for fighting cancer and the common cold. Describing his personal gifts, they say:

> Pauling had the intense curiousity and abiding love of science needed to fuel long, hard work. Moreover he had both a quick, fertile, playful mind suited to theorizing and a prodigious memory that enabled him to amass a vast store of chemical knowledge to draw on in theorizing. He had an exceptional capacity for visualizing, equipping him to analyse three-dimensional structures, and the strong mathematical ability needed for absorbing and applying quantum physics. He had an inclination towards the big picture and was comfortable with approximation and conjecture. [. . .] These personal qualities contributed to Pauling's accomplishments by enabling effective interactions with the domain. Other qualities enabled Pauling to shape, or benefit from, his interactions with the fields. He had infectious enthusiasm; ample self-confidence; and especially importantly [. . .] a legendary ability to clearly, simply and convincingly communicate complex ideas. These qualities helped him persuade the field to accept his ideas. Reciprocally, he showed a responsiveness to stimulation from the field that made varied interactions fruitful. As a student, he readily absorbed lessons, guidance and ideas; throughout his career, he was capable of drawing motivation from competition and scepticism that he encountered rather than being paralysed.
>
> '(Nakamura and Csikszentmihalyi 2001: 338)

But these formidable strengths were not all that determined Pauling's creativity. The field, both the existing body of knowledge, skills, practices, questions, and the people engaged with it, touches the creative process at many points, sometimes positively, sometimes not. It defines what is learned by novices, who internalise a particular version of the field which then informs the work they will do. The version internalised will depend on the version used by the novice's mentors; if they are at the cutting edge so will the novice be, or if they possess innovative skills the novice will learn these, not just the well-tried ones. Well-placed (and well-behaved) novices will also benefit from the social context in which they learn their skills; not just mentors, but collaborators, colleagues and correspondents who generate their own ideas, react with evaluations, and may have complementary skills. The degree to which the field can be receptive to the particular new ideas being generated is also crucial; if they are too different, or not different enough, from the common knowledge of the field, or if they are badly communicated, good ideas may be beaten – for a long time, or even forever – by less good ones; or may not appeal to the patrons who fund the creative person to be creative (neither art patrons nor funding bodies make unproblematic decisions about what activity deserves support, alas).

Thus we have to recognise that when we judge that something is 'creative', our judgement arises from our understanding and experience of the field of knowledge, skills and practices. This field judges the 'creative' persons or products but has also set the agenda for them and provided a lot of what has to be known. The 'creative' person is in turn a member of what the field becomes, and so influences the next generation of creative people. What has been done strongly influences what is done next; the old thing, but better; or the old thing, with variations; or not the old thing, since that would be boring . . .

Chapter 4

Models of cognition in childhood
Metaphors, achievements and problems

I have looked at work describing the knowledge and cognitive skills that develop in childhood, and looked at theories of individual differences. Now to turn to models of the developmental processes behind these changes. In this section I look at theoretical models that seek to explain cognitive development. I begin my discussion of these models by picking out three themes that have run through most of our description of children's thinking and that pervade my discussion of how we explain its development.

The first is the general question of how far children's thinking is different from adults' thinking. Here we can see a wide range of beliefs, from St Paul's eloquent assumption that children's thought is different from and inferior to adults' thought –

> But when that which is perfect is come, then that which is in part shall be done away.
> When I was a child, I spake as a child, I understood as a child, I thought as a child: but when I became a man, I put away childish things.
> For now we see through a glass, darkly; but then face to face: now I know in part; but then shall I know even as also I am known.
> (1 Corinthians 13: 10–12)

– to the contemporary emphasis on the structure and process of children's thought being similar to adults' from the very earliest years of schooling onwards, and the differences being due to children's ignorance of relevant material and their lesser practice at meditating on and describing their own ideas. The second theme is whether we are dealing with 'development', conceived of as a change that is largely generated from inside the individual, and that is largely towards an improved state, or 'learning', conceived to be more from the outside in and by no means necessarily an improvement. There are interesting issues here about the adequacy of such a bipolar distinction between development and learning, and the relationships between the two. The third theme is an equally fundamental one. It is the question of what models are appropriate for cognition. Is it more helpful to think of ourselves as 'in essence limited capacity manipulators of symbols' (Siegler 1983: 129) very similar to slow and inaccurate computers; or as biological organisms with a long evolutionary history that has led to us having a brain that functions in particular ways and leads to particular cognitive activities just as we have evolved lungs, livers and a thumb articulated with fingers so that fine grasping is possible; or as members of social groups taking part in relationships and cultures, and using and developing our cognition within them and inseparable from them? Different models of human nature make different assumptions about the relative importance of the social and the biological, of cognitive processes and physiological structures and problem context. Which metaphors seem appropriate arises from these assumptions and also constrains what questions will be asked and what answers will be seen as possible. I will argue that though we may learn a great deal about cognition by thinking of it as computation, as adaptation or as acculturation, we must be clear and explicit about our basic assumptions and remain aware of how our chosen metaphor may obscure important points that another model would have clarified. The discussion of several models of cognitive development that follows will include some assessment of how adequately the models match up to these demands.

4.1 Piaget's model of cognitive development

We begin with a model that set out its basic assumptions far more elaborately than any other, that took into account a uniquely wide range of biological and philosophical considerations, and that is still the base from which others diverge. Piagetian theory was a tremendous intellectual achievement, and for all its faults, and despite all the idiocies committed on data by people who misunderstood what was important about it, has shaped the field in quite remarkable ways. It gives an abstract account of the cognitive processes that cause development which is still influential and which is in certain respects probably basically correct, needing mainly testing and specification. It gives a more concrete account of cognitive structure that addresses important philosophical issues but is psychologically too rigid, and does not deal adequately with the influence of cognitive material or cognitive context.

It would take several volumes larger than this to describe and evaluate Piagetian theory fully; here I will focus on a few of his most important ideas. Reading Piaget himself is still a rewarding experience – the early work is the most accessible (Piaget 1929, 1930, 1932, 1959, for example), and for the theory issues I am going to discuss Piaget (1983). Among important discussions of his work are Gelman and Baillargeon (1983), Beilin (1992),

Rotman (1977), Vuyk (1981), Smith (1996, 2002), and Shayer (2003). Larivee *et al.* (2000) provide a brief account of post-Piagetian French psychology.

At the core of Piaget's model is the idea that cognition is one form of the adaptation between organism and environment that is seen through all the living world. The child, or indeed the adult, is all its life actively trying to make sense of the world, just as any organism must try to adapt to its environment. I have discussed the implications of evolutionary theory and brain research for cognitive development theory elsewhere (pp. 342, 428–431; see also Young (1987)); Piaget's main work on this, *Biology and Knowledge* (1971b) is still an important book. He said that 'adaptation' in cognition proceeded by means of 'assimilation', which involves relating new information to pre-existing structures of knowledge and understanding, and 'accommodation', which involves developing the old structures into new ones under pressure from new, externally given information or problems or from the pressure of internal contradictions by incompatible structures. These two cognitive processes or twin 'functional invariants' work together throughout the whole of cognitive life (the assimilation of new information must lead to some degree of accommodation in the old system of knowledge, if only to the minor degree of 'ah, here's another *X*: I've seen at least a hundred of those in my time, so now I've seen at least a hundred and one'), and together with the equally innate tendency to organise knowledge into coherent systems and smooth routines they give rise to a series of 'structures' of cognition, that is, ordered rules, categories, procedures and so forth that eventually amount to unified organisations of logical operations.

Piaget believed that all living organisms have this innate and inevitable drive to adapt to their environment, through assimilating new information to the structures of knowledge that have already developed, and accommodating their existing structures of knowledge to the new information that accumulates. His main concern was with human adaptation, with the study of its ontogeny in children a stand-in, to some degree, for its phylogeny in the species – because the fossil record is comparatively uninformative on the thinking of humans over the course of evolution (but see Mithen 1996), the study of the development of thought in children was a substitute for the study of thought in australopithecines or Neanderthals. He recognised that cognitive development had a varied and heterogeneous set of roots. These included physical maturation, especially of the brain; interaction with the physical world; reflection on the logical rules that could be derived from or applied to it; social interaction. Because these were so different, and development was so smooth and universal, he saw equilibration, an unending internal balancing of accommodation and assimilation, as the integrating force behind development: together, assimilation, accommodation and equilibration are the 'functional invariants' of cognitive development. I discuss them in turn below.

4.1.1 Assimilation and accommodation

Assimilation and accommodation are fundamental but abstract concepts that are at one and the same time immensely plausible and immensely hard to tie down to specific behaviour, let alone specific brain activity or specific educational practice. They are almost certainly essential basic components of a good model of cognitive development, though they need considerably more specification (Flavell 1963; Beilin 1992; Gelman and Baillargeon 1983; Beilin and Fireman 2000). Piaget's own main account was given in two books published in English in 1978, where he distinguishes between different sorts of assimilation. He postulated that there is a sort of natural instinct to assimilate in biological systems: 'any scheme of assimilation tends to feed itself, that is, to incorporate outside elements compatible with its nature into itself' (Piaget 1978a), thus driving development on. This happens at three levels. The first is assimilating objects to schemes, as the infant does when grasping a new object, or as scientists had to when a new planet's existence was discovered. The second is assimilation between different schemes, for example eye–hand co-ordination or the sort of alternation between writing and critically reading one's own writing that is achieved by the secondary school pupil (pp. 62–68). The third and highest level is assimilation between subschemes and the totality that integrates them into a coherent whole; the concept of 'gravity', for example, is at the core of physicists' accounts of many quite different localised events, from the motion of the planets round the sun to the falling of Newton's apple. These assimilations are said to involve the scheme 'finding' or 'distinguishing' characteristics that match the scheme or are near neighbours to it, as opposed to others that negate or contradict it, though these too must in the end be co-ordinated into the total scheme. Thus both affirmations and negations are important. A balance between affirmations and negations is necessary for development, just as a balance between assimilation and accommodation is. In play assimilation is dominant over accommodation, while in imitation this imbalance is reversed.

While this account of assimilation and accommodation is of great interest, a number of problems arise. Some cluster around the 'drive to assimilate'. It is not clear to me at what point this drive would be satisfied: the model appears to imply that there could always be further assimilation and accommodation, that the 'natural' state of cognitive development (indeed of existence in general) is progress towards a highly developed, subtle, sophisticated, intricately integrated, perfectly balanced cognitive system. Is this an empirical account of what is really done, or a rational reconstruction of ideal cognition? There is room for real doubt about whether most people really do go in for this sort of thorough thinking-out of everything, and even whether professional scientists do (Kuhn 1962), and there are difficulties over finding analogies and transfer (pp. 110–126);

perhaps here Piaget was using himself as a prototype and forgetting that the rest of us are, probably, sloppier thinkers, content with localised understanding, not pushing its limits outwards, and quite capable of believing contradictory things?

There are problems also over the question of what is or can be assimilated to a scheme, and how this is done. What degree of match, on what dimensions, means that a new object or event affirms a pre-existing scheme? What mismatch negates it? For example, suppose that I initially believed that every word of the Bible was literally true, and that, therefore, we knew the world was created in exactly seven days (in late October of 4004 BC, if I also believed Archbishop Ussher's biblical commentary). What would then be my adaptation to the theory of evolution and the evidence of geology and the fossil record? I could refuse to assimilate this science and stick to creationism; or I could accommodate to the science and reject the literal truth of the Bible; or, like some unhappy nineteenth-century scientists (Thwaite 2002), I could suggest that God during his seven days' work created new rocks and animals containing evidence of an evolutionary history that had never actually happened. Of these three adaptations, the last is inherently unstable, leading for example to a pretty odd sort of God; the first is adaptation by restriction, like the amoeba that successfully protects itself against the drying up of its pond by retreating into a shell-like skin; only the second is likely to lead to further cognitive development and better understanding of the world (and to fit scholarship about the writing of the Bible (Lane-Fox 1991), though creationists of course reject this too). Whether it also leads to better adaptation in a wider sense, such as in Sternberg's triarchic model of intelligence (p. 227), depends on the socio-cultural context; for someone living among fundamentalists it might well lead to blasphemy trials and outright persecution.

This is an extreme example, but a real one. Piaget's examples tend to be *post hoc*, and no one else has yet done better. We may also doubt whether affirmations and negations are equally readily dealt with by the thinker, as negations in logic, and in scientific theory building, seem to be so difficult to manage (see Kuhn (1962), Wason (1977), Siegler (2005)). Further, in many areas it is extremely hard to see whether a new event affirms or negates a scheme; the concept is hard to apply in questions of moral or political judgement, for example, or in the visual arts. Researchers argue that one of the important things we have to learn is, precisely, which kinds of knowledge have to be consistent and which do not (Russell 1978; Bartsch 2002; Danovitch and Keil 2004; Fay and Klahr 1996). Smith (2002) makes a similar point, suggesting that what is important about Piagetian development is the recognition of what knowledge is or isn't necessarily so. Most of the Piagetian literature, however, focuses on areas of knowledge where it is essential to be consistent, systematic and rigorous.

4.1.2 Equilibration

Assimilation, accommodation and organisation, functioning together, were held together by an even more important (and mysterious) process called 'equilibration', Piaget believed. He saw equilibration as central to evolution, to all biological functioning and to cognition in particular. It was a central theoretical concept from the beginning to the end of his career, but it is hard to define it precisely, not least because Piaget's own account of it developed over the years. Essentially, perhaps, it marks his belief that although assimilation, accommodation and organisation are active incessantly to deal with the information and the problems that continually impose themselves on the organism's attention, there was none the less stability in cognition to a considerable degree, not the constant shifting of cognitive structures that constantly change – the maturation of the organism, its second-by-second experience of the environment, the pressures of the social world – might seem to force during development. 'Equilibration' is clearly a force for stability, via a self-regulation that balances external and internal changes. In some cases it works by restoring the previous stable state; in the cases that are more interesting for development, successful adaptation calls for a more radical and pervasive shift if balance is to be regained, an *equilibration majorante* (Piaget 1978a).

It has been regarded as a problematic concept for many years, even by sympathetic commentators (Flavell 1963; Boden 1979; Smith 2002). Why did Piaget believe that cognition was an equilibrated system? He clearly believed that organisms *need* to maintain a stable internal equilibrium within the changes and uncertainties of the outside world, a belief that one can sympathise with. There are a number of biological systems of self-regulation that serve precisely this sort of need: the regulation of body temperature in warm-blooded animals is one example (p. 334). If something goes wrong with either the automatic or the behavioural self-regulation of body temperature, we lose our physiological equilibrium and may become quite seriously, even fatally, damaged, as in cases of heat stroke or hypothermia. 'Durable disequilibria constitute pathological organic or mental states' (Piaget 1968: 102). But recent research (e.g. Dauncey and Bicknell 1999) on the relationship between birth weight, postnatal growth, and disorders such as obesity, heart disease and schizophrenia as an adult suggests there can be early fine-tuning of this regulation into a durable equilibrium that leads to individual differences, and perhaps morbidity, much later. Biological equilibria are not necessarily simple, universal or progressive.

Evolutionary adaptation is another source of Piaget's model of equilibration. Implicit in his views, as in much of biology at the time he was first developing his ideas, is a view of evolution as being adaptation that tends towards improvement; this view is encapsulated by the metaphor of 'the survival of the fittest' in Social Darwinism, and by the common picturing of the evolution of Man (*sic*) as from a shaggy unimpressive character to an upstanding Caucasoid young male, almost complete with briefcase, bowler hat and furled umbrella. Twentieth-century theorising and data gathering have changed this view to a realisation that evolution is not a simple and inevitable progress towards the pinnacle of Western middle-class manhood, but a more contingent and complex history of change, variation and extinction, in which the degree to which the species is 'improved' is judged entirely by its ability to cope with its present environment and adapt to environmental changes (Gould 1977; Oyama *et al.* 2001). Evolutionary equilibration is, if it exists at all, temporary, contingent and not necessarily in every way better and better.

The other root of Piaget's belief in cognitive equilibria must surely be related to the coherence, closure and self-structuring properties of logico-mathematical systems. The number system, for example, or the rules of formal logic, structure reasoning so as to lead on every occasion to true and non-contradictory answers, 'necessary' knowledge. It is always true that '2 + 2 = 4', for example, and always false that '2 + 2 = 5' or '2 + 1 = 4'; if it is true that 'every dog will have his day' then there can be no dog anywhere that has not either already had his day or a legitimate expectation that it will come today or sometime in the future. The main question here, and see pp. 281–283, is whether such perfectly clear and consistent systems of knowledge are representative of knowledge as a whole and whether we use them easily; Piaget seems to have seen them as at least pre-eminently important and desirable. There is some prioritising here of particular sorts of knowledge and cognition, I think; postmodernists might not agree with it.

Equilibration relies extremely heavily on the assumption of invariant regularities and consistencies in thought. It explains *how* cognitive development occurs in terms of 'need' for a coherently organised and consistent way of thinking. The changes and demands of the outside world produce in the thinker small 'perturbations' or 'conflicts' that lead the cognitive system to small automatic adjustments (of assimilation and accommodation) to cope with the conflicts and return either to the original cognitive equilibrium or to a new and better one. It is the momentary non-functioning of a cognitive scheme that both signals the presence of a 'perturbation' and is the sole motivator of efforts to seek a new equilibrium, but the non-functioning does not of itself indicate what the conflict is or how to solve it. Even in his most detailed account (1978a) Piaget did not succeed in specifying what contradictions are noticed or resolved or exactly which lead to cognitive progress. He warned, correctly, that not all contradictions are fruitful, and speculated that structural contradictions are more relevant to cognitive development than are momentary contradictions due to perception or historical accident. A theory of effective spurs to cognitive change would be very useful, but is not available at present. I will outline some of the points that will need to be dealt with. In order to resolve disequilibrium in the direction of cognitive growth, you must be able to recognise (not necessarily consciously, though some theorists (e.g. Smith 2002) think conscious recognition is important) that there is a disequilibrium, and as Rotman (1977) points out this is not unproblematic; you must similarly recognise at least approximately what has caused it, as if you do not your chance of progress must be very small; you must *want* to resolve it, rather than deciding to live with the contradiction (like the White Queen in *Through the Looking Glass* who deliberately practised believing impossible things before breakfast); and you must have some means to improve on the disequilibrated state. There may also be, in many cases, alternative equally plausible or even equally valid resolutions of the contradiction, and in other cases no resolution may be possible, as in various logical and mathematical paradoxes (Hofstadter 1979). Bryant (1982a) argues that confirmation by two schemes leading to the same conclusion may lead to development more effectively than conflict; for example when we check that we got the addition sum right when we added up a column of numbers going from top to bottom by adding them from bottom to top, we learn about the accuracy of our addition programme and develop a new way of doing it. At all stages of developing a cognitive competence we may flip between procedures (Siegler 2005). I discuss the social setting of cognitive confirmation and disagreement elsewhere (pp. 191–194, 406–408).

Piaget did discuss (1978a: 30–8) what makes one state of cognitive equilibrium 'better' than another. Better equilibria can cope with more elements or dimensions; they are both more differentiated and more integrated; they co-ordinate and complete earlier equilibria; they are more flexible; and they provide more possibilities for interacting with a wider environment. This is a plausible description of a better cognitive system but hard to translate into behavioural terms, and there are some problems in founding 'betterness' on increased complexity or width of application. It is obvious that adults do interact in more varied ways with their environment than infants do, and with more different aspects of it, and similarly that human–environment interactions are wider and more differentiated than amoeba–environment interactions. It should not be taken as obvious, however, that this makes humans or adults 'better' or 'better equilibrated' or 'better adapted to their environment' than amoebae or infants are (Midgley 1985; Ruse 1986). Nor does this account explain why 'lower' forms of life (such as amoebae) or of cognition are prevalent and apparently well adapted to the world. Why would we have the traditional tabloid newspapers, for example, if equilibration really pushed cognition ever on?

4.1.3 Stages

Piaget somewhat compounded this problem by his emphasis on the idea that cognitive development formed a single invariant sequence of stages and that any variation found merely reflected differences in rate of development (Larivee *et al.* 2000). He said that the sequence was a result of individual equilibratory construction, not due to an innate teleology of development, though he was clearly sympathetic to the work of biologists such as Waddington who demonstrated how much of embryological development and physical growth was pre-programmed while still under the influence of the organism's experience of the environment. 'Preformationism' has been a non-respectable position in much thinking about cognition (Mischel 1971; Richardson 2000), but in far more subtle, specific and limited forms is now appearing as a basis to theories of cognition. We need to understand a great deal more than we do at present about the nature and mechanisms of genetic programming and central nervous system functioning (and about the nature and mechanisms of the effects of life experiences, which are if anything less well understood and no less complex); but modern biology, as Piaget was perhaps the earliest to see, has a great deal to offer to those concerned with cognition (see e.g. Young 1987). Nevertheless, the claim that the Piagetian sequence of stages is invariant and universal is not unproblematic. Even diagnosis is not clear. Each stage contains 'an aspect of achievement with respect to the stages going before and also an aspect of preparation with respect to the stages coming after' (Piaget 1960b: 13–14). This presumably means that at any given time there may be vestiges of earlier cognition and anticipations of later ones, that is internal inconsistency in stage structure, which is problematic for a simple stage model in that it makes the identification of a clearly differentiated 'stage' difficult, and suggests that the sequence of stages may be logically necessary rather than naturally invariant (Smedslund 1980; Gelman and Baillargeon 1983; Meadows 1975; Klausmeier and Sipple 1982; Smith 2002). Pointing out that achieving a higher stage does not preclude the person sometimes functioning at a lower one (e.g. Smith (2002: 519): 'developmental levels are levels of knowledge, not levels of knowers') does not altogether avoid the difficulty. It raises questions about why the person's thought has lapsed from the better equilibrium of the higher stage; about how much evenness in level should be expected; about whether a given level might be more often found in some domains of knowledge or cognitive task than others; and so forth. These are interesting and important questions (Siegler 2005), but off the agenda of mainstream Piagetian theory.

The cross-cultural evidence suggests that besides these diagnostic problems there are a number of significant variations not just in rate of development, which would have only marginal relevance to the validity of Piaget's theory, but in whether the later stages develop in the sort of form Piaget described. The sort of schooling the culture provides and the sorts of concepts it values seem to be the main determining factors (Dasen 1977; Laboratory of Comparative Human Cognition 1983; Rogoff 1990; Kozulin *et al.* 2003). The evolutionary analogy would itself suggest that a single invariant sequence is less likely than a branching tree-like pattern: certain cognitive adaptations are developed but other possible adaptations remain potential rather than actualised, or are even given up. The time and resources required to develop mathematical or musical ability to the full, for example, might preclude even the normal development of other areas of cognition, let alone developing them too to their full potential. We have no idea how this sort of specialisation would fit with the general universal and relatively content-independent sorts of structures that make up the Piagetian stage sequence.

Piaget's use of 'structures' has been very influential, both at the basic conceptual level, where, as we will see, there are problems, and even more at the level of descriptions of behaviour, where his stage descriptions have caught many psychologists' imaginations. I think that much of this influence is now declining, and Piaget's own interest shifted towards an emphasis on 'procedures' towards the end of his life (Larivee *et al.* 2000). (To some extent, this is a shift in level of description. 'Structures' are the timeless, abstract, universal laws of transformations and relations between objects or concepts, such as the mathematical system of real numbers; 'procedures' are the goal-directed behaviours that, occasion by occasion, we use. For example, commutativity $(8 + 2 + 7 = 7 + 2 + 8 = 2 + 7 + 8$, etc.) is part of the structure that underlies our successful procedures for adding up our bills, top to bottom or bottom to top, pence and pounds together or separately.) Nevertheless, some discussion of 'structures' and 'stages' is appropriate here.

It would be hard to deny that human thought, at least after infancy, is in some senses structured. It has rules, legitimate procedures and hierarchies of concepts. We are not completely bound by these structures, we may not be aware of them, and we do not, on the whole, have adequate descriptions of them, but generally we work within their system. So far, this is commonplace, a very vague description applicable to language, Piaget's formulations, number systems and even the extreme behaviourists' associative networks (Feldman and Toulmin 1976; Goswami 2002; Smith 2002; Wertsch 2005; Halford 2002; Siegler 2005). As we become more detailed, problems start to arise, and I want to discuss the forms some of these take in Piaget's work (see particularly Piaget (1970, 1971b)).

The first problem is that of the ontological nature of 'structures': what sort of existence they have. Are they abstract theoretical descriptions or real cognitive processes located in the child's mind or brain? Piaget's position tended towards reductionism, that thinking is firmly centred in a neurophysiological base, but also that it must have an abstract description, the two levels being isomorphic. His description of the earliest stage of thought was primarily biological, that of the later stages primarily abstract and in terms of formal logic. This general position avoids the dilemma, though what the isomorphisms are remains as yet unknown.

A second problem is that we do not directly observe thinking or other cognitive processes, we infer them from observable behaviour. Inhelder and Piaget (1979), discussing the relationship between procedures and structures, reiterate that the best evidence for the existence of structures in the child's mind is what the child considers possible, impossible, or necessary, and some very interesting and ingenious research has been done in this area. However, unless we are extremely careful, clever and scrupulous, and unless we study behaviour with the right techniques and on the right timescale (Siegler 2005), we may make the wrong inferences, and this is particularly likely when we are studying people different from ourselves or comparing groups different in age, class, or culture. Cole and Means (1981) discuss this question very thoroughly. Their strictures apply to most Piagetian accounts of the inadequacies of young children's thought, which we will come back to. Piaget's formulation, which slides (often almost within a chapter) between structures that are in the theorist's description and identical or virtually identical structures that are in the child, was inadequate. In his early work, Piaget virtually invented the research technique now known as 'microgenesis' (Siegler 2005), and produced immensely fascinating examples of children's cognition as they thought their way through a problem. The performance he describes is often extremely interesting; but in moving to theorising the 'universal' cogniser in terms of competence he lost, I think, some of the richness that he had revealed in cognitive development. It is often problematic to go from performance (which is comparatively observable) to competence (which has to be inferred from a sample of performance and from a theory of what competence is like). Behaviour is an important source of data for theory, but it has to be *interpreted* before its degree of support for theoretical claims can be assessed. This was clearly Piaget's procedure in most of his published 'experiments': a deliberately artificial situation is presented to the child and his thinking about it is probed and then interpreted by the experimenter, this 'thinking' being manifested primarily in the child's talk about the situation and secondarily in his manipulations of the material. The theory arises from the interpretations, not from the overt behaviour; and the behaviour is reported, selectively, as supporting illustration of the theory. Thus it can be for the reader a matter of considerable doubt and difficulty to relate what the child can be observed to do or, very often, say, and the abstract formal mental structures that are said to explain the child's activities, and this I will come back to when I discuss some questions of the empirical validity of Piagetian structures. It was, presumably, not a problem for Piaget, but then he was neither a psychologist nor an empiricist. Elucidating thought by examining language does not seem to have struck him as particularly problematic, even though he believed that language was unable to convey what was not already established in thought, and this would seem to imply that language is, at least slightly, retarded compared with thinking. Unless the lag is very small, this would mean that there would be occasions when the child's language was too underdeveloped to express the greater sophistication of his thinking. Using language to diagnose thought would in these cases give rise to false diagnoses of immature thinking; nor is the interpretation of children's language necessarily unproblematic.

Subtle differences in the test situation or in the language of the adult in the interview in a Piagetian *methode clinique* have been acknowledged as one possible source of inter-individual or intra-individual inconsistencies in reasoning (or 'horizontal decalages'), even by Piaget himself (Piaget 1971a, 1971c; Larivee *et al.* 2000), but he persisted in supposing that horizontal decalages were mainly measurement error, not psychologically meaningful. Some other researchers have seen them as more serious problems for Piagetian theory (Meadows 1975; Donaldson 1978); some as signs that individual differences in development have to be tackled more seriously than Piaget ever did (Larivee *et al.* 2000); some as developmentally important in themselves (Siegler 2005).

There is one further central problem in Piaget's use of structures, which we must deal with before discussing the empirical validity of his work. This is two characteristics of structures that appeared very early in his work on them (Piaget 1952) and that relate to both his biologism and his description of structures in formal and abstract terms. Cognitive structures tend to form structured wholes (*structures-d'ensemble*), and this is what, once they are fully established, the concrete operational stage, the formal operational stage and other logico-mathematical systems consist of. 'Stages' are periods of relative equilibrium in the development of the child's thought, which is said to resemble the development of thought in the human species. There are a number of points here that need a brief comment on a theoretical level; some we will return to, as they raise empirically answerable questions.

The terms '*structure-d'ensemble*' and 'stage' imply the existence of a fairly tight relationship among a set of cognitive structures. On the whole, we would expect the structures that form a *structure-d'ensemble* to develop and appear together, and to react one upon the other. Piaget's theory also suggests that they form at each stage qualitatively different structures, being not just bigger but better (in terms of coherence, complexity and field of application, as we said earlier). Again, at a very general level this would appear really rather likely, but the detail of Piaget's models of *structures-d'ensemble* turns out to be unsatisfactory. Both concrete operations and formal operations are described in terms of logical systems that logicians regard as being of poor quality (see e.g. Boden (1979: 80–86), Ennis (1978)), and that are inferred from behavioural (largely verbal) data in ways that turn out, at least in the case of formal operations, to be quite simply wrong (Bynum *et al.* 1972).

In addition to these difficulties, Piaget's model of stages has changed with development. The earlier model implied a stage sequence where transitions from stage to stage are the disequilibrated periods and are relatively brief, so that there are fairly abrupt changes from stage to stage. It is this model of clearly contrasted stages that dominated most popular accounts of Piagetian theory. In the later model there is a considerably less step-like development, and the preparation, achievement, consolidation and super-seding of, say, concrete operations flow into one another smoothly and cover a period of several years. If this is the better picture (and, as I describe below, the empirical evidence is for this later, more complex model, not for the earlier one), the descriptive value of stage and *structure-d'ensemble* concepts begins to look very slight indeed.

In Piagetian theory the most fundamental structures of thought are applicable to virtually any area of knowledge; they are seen as abstract content-free ways of reasoning. Piaget described them as fitting together into a succession of coherent and qualitatively different stages; the major ones are the sensori-motor, pre-operational, concrete operational and formal operational stages, and there are sequences of substages within the sensori-motor stage and within areas of operational thought, such as conservation of quantity. The structure of each stage is such that thought at any given moment is relatively consistent in its level across different content areas; consistency is especially to be expected at the times when concrete operations and, later, formal operations are fully developed, as both these stages are based on logical models. While logical systems are being con-structed, temporary inconsistencies and fluctuations are to be expected, but the theory retains an emphasis on differences between stages and simi-larities within them. In a child behaving according to the Piagetian model, performance on one test of, say, conservation will predict performance on other conservation tests and on other tests of concrete operations. Further-more, the stage structure limits the possibilities of improving performance by instruction. The child cannot assimilate or accommodate to events that are too incompatible with his or her whole coherent system of under-standing, and instruction can at best produce only a limited and possibly temporary advance, isolated in the area being trained. The Piagetian child is just social enough to learn from disagreement with peers – which can be experienced as like disagreeing with oneself – but Piagetian cognitive development is predominantly endogenous. This is a crucial issue for those concerned with education, and requires some discussion.

The main form of social interaction that Piaget discussed as contributing positively to cognitive development was children's conflict with peers whose reasoning led to a different conclusion. If two children disagree which row of counters 'has more in' in a conservation test, for example, the recog-nition of disagreement was seen as provoking further thought in order to reduce conflict and remove the contradiction. Essentially the children are seeing that they are being disagreed with by someone whom they regard as very much like themselves, and this can amount to a recognition that they might potentially be making a judgement that they disagree with themselves. Disagreement with someone who is felt to be unlike oneself would not spark off an internal conflict, because it would not be recognised as potentially one's own problem. Thus disagreement with an adult, especially correction of one's ideas by an adult, would have little benefit for cognitive development both because adults are viewed as different from children and because the power difference complicates things: the Piagetian child may bow to the adult's authority to the extent of parroting the correction, but will not internalise it.

> In some cases, what is transmitted by instruction is well assimilated by the child because it represents in fact an extension of some spontaneous constructions of his own. In such cases his development is accelerated. But in other cases, the gifts of instruction are presented too soon or too late, or in a manner which precludes assimilation because it does not fit with the child's spontaneous constructions. Then the child's development is impeded, or even deflected into barrenness, as so often happens with the teaching of the exact sciences.
>
> (Piaget 1962: 246)

The impact of other thinkers on the Piagetian child is more subtly considered by Piaget than is apparent from the mainstream accounts of his theory (Smith 2002), but the Piagetian emphasis is certainly on conflict rather than agreement or instruction as the route from others' understanding to an improvement in one's own. There has been a considerable amount of research and discussion (e.g. Almasi 1995; Rogoff 1995; Chinn and Anderson 1998) challenging Piaget's account. It is not clear that conflict is better for cognitive development than co-operation and confirmation, or that symmetrical power relationships give rise to more progress than asymmetrical ones, or intra-individual conflict is 'better' than inter-individual conflict. Undoubtedly, instances of each can make a contribution, and individuals may differ in which they prefer (I saw myself as a Vygotskian parent, but my strongly Piagetian child sometimes seemed to have a mission to refute my years of criticism of Piagetian theory).

Of Piaget's sequence of stages, the sensori-motor stage develops over the first two years or so of the child's life and is therefore not relevant to a book focusing on the school-age child. The school years begin late in the 'pre-operational' period, cover 'concrete operations', and end during 'formal operations'. It is therefore appropriate to provide a very brief account of each stage. The pre-operational stage is described (1) as the period when children begin to use semiotic systems such as language and imagery, and (2) as a time when they lack operational thought, that is, flexible reversible reasoning that allows them to conserve, classify, seriate, co-ordinate perspectives, overcome misleading perceptual impressions, etc. Concrete operational children have these abilities: they can think much more systematically and quantitatively and their thinking is described in terms of formalised logical structures (the 'groupings') relating to classifications and relations in quantity and in space; but their thinking is still tied to the concrete and observable. The final formal operations stage is a more integrated and more abstract development from concrete operations, less tied to concrete content and more capable of dealing with hypothetical material. Formal operations receive a more abstract holistic and rigorous description from Piaget. Logicians as well as psychologists have queried the models given for both the concrete operations and the formal operations stages (Vuyk 1981), and they remain controversial (Smith 2002; Richardson 2000).

With this account of stages, Piagetian theory puts up a challenge that has attracted a good deal of research response. As I have said, direct evidence on the reality of assimilation, accommodation and equilibration has been hard to get: testing the stage model has been somewhat easier, though not altogether unproblematic. Sequences of stages are fairly well confirmed, though there have been some suggestions that their order is logically necessary (e.g. Smedslund 1980) and so of no empirical interest. Rate of progress through the sequence seems to vary somewhat between individuals, but this is far from crucial to Piagetian theory, which is concerned with the idealised 'normal' epistemic subject, not with individual differences (Smith (2002); but see also Larivee et al. (2000)). Rate also varies between cultures, degree of schooling and less formal educational experience being one of the main relevant variables; in some cultures there is little sign of formal operations (Kozulin et al. 2003). This finding is mildly embarrassing for a model that has been taken as claiming that formal operations is a universal high point of human cognition, but in fact Piaget's main account does not explicitly make such a claim (Inhelder and Piaget 1958). The role of social and environmental experience in cognitive development is an important issue that needs more investigation than the main stream of Piagetian thought provided. I discuss it elsewhere in this book (e.g. Chapter 5).

The behaviours typical of different stages appear in a fairly constant order, then, if not at a constant rate. Their appearance can certainly be accelerated by training (Brainerd 1983; Gelman and Baillargeon 1983; Siegler 2005). Contrary to the predictions of the Piagetian account, training does produce improvement in performance that can be considerable, longlasting and pervasive (see also Chapter 5). A variety of training methods have been seen to succeed, and it is not the case that 'neo-Piagetian' models, which conjure up equilibratory mechanisms or provoke discovery, are any more successful than methods involving imitation, didactic interaction, or the following of verbal rules. Initial stage level does not seem to predict the possibility of training or limit how effective it will be. Pre-schoolers have successfully been trained on the concrete operations tasks that they would not be expected to get right for another three or four years, and their performance after training appears as competent as that of untrained eight-year-olds. This has been interpreted as showing that there are minimal differences between the cognitive structures of preschool children and those of primary-school children. It does seem to be clear that Piaget painted far too negative a picture of children's thinking in the preoperational stage, and we might prefer a model of cognitive development that described more preschool competence and (perhaps) a less complete later stage competence, with a gradual consolidatory transition rather than a qualitative shift during the school years (Beilin 1992; Vuyk 1981; Braine and Rumain 1983; Donaldson 1978; Siegler 2005). However, there is some danger of arguing away a developmental change in cognition rather than carefully analysing the extent and nature of the change.

One of the differences between younger and older children is in the degree and type of within-stage consistency they show, or how many *décalages*, that is, slips in level of performance, there are. The question here is how the different areas fit together as structured stages. The usual research design has been the obvious one of seeing how children's performances correlate across a number of tasks that each involve the same logical principles (e.g. conservation) or belong to the same stage (e.g. measure of class inclusion, weight conservation and perspective-taking, which all belong to the concrete operations stage). It is not always altogether clear how large a correlation is required to support the theory of within-stage consistency, and the statistical complexities are considerable. On the whole, research studies have found less consistency between different areas of concrete operations than a simple model of logical structures that are constructed quickly and underlie all tasks would suggest (Brainerd 1978; Gelman and Baillargeon 1983; Klausmeier and Sipple 1982; Larivee *et al*. 2000; Meadows 1975; Siegler 2005). There have also been numerous inconsistencies between different measures of ostensibly the same operation, for example, conservation tests using materials that seem obviously equivalent to the adult but produce obstinately different responses from children (e.g. Beard 1963; Miller 1982; Uzgiris 1964). Some of these *décalages* are due to the 'figurative aspect' of the test situation; for example, if the transformed material in a conservation test looks very different from the original, then children will be less likely to give a conserving response than if the change in appearance is slight. Similarly, various changes in the social situation or in the language used help young children to conserve or manage problems such as class inclusion (e.g. Light *et al*. 1979; Siegel *et al*. 1978). Some *décalages* receive only a last resort explanation: that the objects involved offer more 'resistance' to the thinker. Piaget never dealt with the problem of *décalages* thoroughly. He was less interested in them than in how children managed the general principles underlying operational thought, for example how they had a feeling of certainty despite appearances that suggested otherwise. He thus had little to say about *décalages* except where they were common to all children, hence characteristic of his 'epistemic subject'. Research by Longeot and his colleagues (Longeot 1978; Larivee *et al.* 2000) starts to deal with this omission, and with some of the problems of low correlations within stages, with a model that predicts when consistencies and *décalages* will occur. Longeot points again to the possibility that there may be discrepancies between the logico-mathematical structures of the epistemic subject and the natural thinking of children solving adaptive problems in real life: the distinctions between 'knowing' and 'doing' and between various degrees of 'having a concept' that I mentioned earlier (Siegler 2005).

Recent research carrying on from Piaget's universalistic account of children's thinking describes a plurality of processes in cognitive development and information-processing in a multidimensional model that allows for an account of individual differences (Larivee *et al.* 2000). Individuals develop a mental tool-kit of sets of both propositional processes and analogical processes. Propositional processes involve analytic and sequential processing and follow rules that are independent of the situation, for example logical rules, and they are particularly useful in dealing with logico-mathematical problems of the classic Piagetian type. Analogical processes are more global and more dependent on task content; scripts and prototypical categorisation are key examples. Although some problems or domains are best addressed propositionally rather than analogically, and some the reverse, many can be solved using either sort of process, and individuals may differ in which they can use most easily. It may be advantageous to be able to move between the two flexibly, and development of one set may push on development of the other, presumably through comparison of the strengths and weaknesses of each. Young children may be stronger users of analogical processing than propositional processing, but they are not entirely restricted to perceptual analogies (pp. 113–115). The model also acknowledges the resemblance of the distinction between propositional and analogical processing to the formal and informal reasoning and scientific thinking that Vygotsky discussed (Vygotsky 1978a).

A companion paper by Suizzo (2000) discusses additional sources of individual differences in children's cognitive development. She suggests that the socio-emotional context of cognition is inextricable from problem-solving as emotion involves the appraisal of events in relation to goals (see Chapter 7). This is important for the development of children's understanding of emotion, of themselves and of others, for their motivation to persist with a difficult problem or to take on a new challenge, and their ability to inhibit or plan their actions. She also notes the Vygotskian point that we may want to know not just the level that a child functions at independently but also the level that functioning can reach with the help of another person's support (see pp. 308–309).

The brief discussion in Gelman (2000) links these neo-Piagetian ideas to her own ideas about systematic sources of variability in cognitive development and learning, and what constraints there are for knowledge in different domains (Gelman and Williams 1998). A domain of knowledge is based on a set of interrelated principles that organises its content and the operations that apply within it, and distinguishes it from other domains. Counting principles and arithmetic are Gelman's preferred example (p. 71). Some domains are 'core', and may have an innate basis; others are certainly built up from cultural experience. Experience is mapped on to existing mental structures, and if many examples analogous to the structure are encountered because the environment or the culture is full of them, the domain will develop fast. The organising principles of a core domain may be the same even if the detailed content is different; thus different number names are learned in different cultures but the basic rules of arithmetic are the same though they may operate more smoothly in some cultures than in others (p. 69).

Researchers inspired by Piaget are developing beyond his model. For example, recent work has shown that development is not a smooth progress between qualitatively different stages but involves gradual and inconsistent movement between different cognitive processes (Siegler 2005). There may be alternative paths to the same outcome, and such individual differences need to be accounted for. There is interest also in the possibility that cognitive development is domain-specific rather than, as in Piagetian theory, general across domains. Investigation obviously requires detailed descriptions, with data gathered very carefully; this is very much what Piaget and Inhelder did in the series of studies that are still acknowledged as brilliant investigative observation.

4.2 Information-processing models of cognitive development

I think there are two levels of description of cognition that are quite incontrovertibly important: the neurophysiological workings of brains, and the psychological level of behaviours like recognising faces, understanding language, social cognition and so forth. Information-processing models sit between these two, attempting to provide a theoretical structure for the computational mind-mechanisms behind the behaviour, often but not always guided by what is known about the workings of the brain. Adequate neurophysiological and behavioural descriptions and theories may make computational information-processing ones redundant, but for the moment they have not.

4.2.1 Issues in information-processing

Psychologists using the information-processing approach to the study of cognition and cognitive development (Klahr and MacWhinney 1998; Siegler 2005) describe cognition as largely a matter of handling information in order to solve problems. They are primarily concerned with how information is selected, represented, stored, retrieved, transformed, and so forth. The focus is on what mental processes are used to deal with information, with how they are organised, and with how they change during learning or development. Computation is seen as the basis for human cognition, and sometimes computers are used to test hypothetical accounts of the information-processing that goes into solving a problem. Even if they are not, some attempt is made to specify the hypothetical cognitive processes sufficiently precisely for them to be tenable by experiments with people if not by computer simulation. The cognitive tasks investigated tend to be fairly tightly defined also, and they quite often have a Piagetian or psychometric pedigree. Siegler (1978, 1983, 1984, 1989b, 2005), for example, did extensive analyses of a balance task, and Klahr (Klahr and Wallace 1976; Klahr 1984; Klahr and MacWhinney 1998) of conservation and class inclusion. The basic assumption is that analogies with the ways in which computers process information will be helpful. Just as computers operate by combining a number of microlevel distinct operations in an appropriate sequence, so humans are seen as using a fairly small number of elementary cognitive processes in a structured way over a period of time. Mental processes that mediate in varying ways between stimulus and response are emphasised, and in many aspects human cognition is seen as active and constructive, unlike the passive S-R models of classical behaviourism, and indeed unlike the run-of-the-mill computer.

Like Piagetian models, information-processing approaches to cognitive development seek to describe children's cognitive capabilities and limitations at successive points in their development, and to explain how a later and more advanced understanding emerges from an earlier less adequate one; that is, these models too are concerned with 'what develops' and with 'how this development occurs'. They deal with these questions by trying to specify what cognitive processes the child applies to what information, which processes in which order for how long, and what information, how represented, and when in the processing sequence. They also seek to specify how development occurs, what components of processes and representations are self-modifying, or can be modified by outside influences, or are resistant to change. They seek to describe the 'architecture' of the cognitive system, to deal with both goal-driven and event-driven processes, to explain change processes, and to specify constraints on change (Klahr and MacWhinney 1998). They assume that knowing about adult information-processing (or computer information-processing) can lead to illuminating comparisons with children's information-processing (and vice versa).

The computer analogy suggests a distinction between mind structures (analogous to the computer's hard disc and storage) and cognitive processes (analogous to the computer's software). The 'cognitive processes' of computers are programmed-in and automatic; human ones may be strategic and change with development or learning. Whichever, they operate on the information stored in the mind–computer's storage spaces and may be limited by speed or by the type or quantity of information they can manage. Using an information-processing model, therefore, we are concerned with information representation, storage, retrieval, transformation, re-representation, re-storage, etc., as the person works towards solving a problem. When we consider the development of information processing over childhood we are usually assuming an improvement in such structures and processes as children are supposed to be developing a better knowledge system. Because humans are less precise than computers when applied to the sorts of problems that theorists usually use in this area of research, we will also be concerned with attentional processes and executive control, and, importantly, with reaching answers despite not really having sufficient information.

The core constructs of information-processing models assert that there must be internal representations of information that cognitive processes act upon, generating, manipulating or transforming the initial representation. Representations and processes together make up the knowledge base, and it is assumed that this is large and rich in interconnecting links, so a particular piece of information can be accessed in many different ways from strong association to indirect inference. Although the knowledge base is to all intents and purposes infinitely large, some of its content may be difficult or impossible to reach on occasion, and only a very small subset of knowledge can be acted on at any one time, as only a limited quantity of attentional resources is available to bring knowledge and processes into an active state and maintain them there. Some activation is automatic and requires little or no attention; other processes needing more immediate control make heavy demands on attentional resources. Automatic processing tends to be fast and to make minimal demands on resources, but it is not under voluntary control so it cannot easily be modified. Controlled processing is slower and uses up many more attentional resources, and may be less efficient, but it is easier to modify and fit flexibly to task demands and other varying aspects of each situation.

Traditional information-processing models analyse the mind as a system that represents information as syntactic symbols, operates on these symbols according to logical rules, and stores the resultant symbols in specified localities in a long-term memory store: just like a digital computer that takes in symbolic information into particular locations in its memory, retrieves them to be operated on by a central processing unit, and stores them again in appropriate places in memory. This metaphor for cognition has worked well for tasks that require conscious effort and strategic thought when human beings do them, such as playing chess or doing complex arithmetic to predict whether a beam will balance; it has not succeeded anything like so well with cognitive tasks that human beings perform without conscious or strategic effort, such as building a tower out of blocks or recognising an object in the environment.

4.2.2 Connectionist models

Newer models of information-processing that stay closer to the way we know brain neurones work may provide a better account of this sort of cognition. These are referred to in different ways, as 'parallel distributed processing', 'neural networks', or 'connectionism'. (Richardson (2000) provides an introduction. For fuller discussion of the approach see McClelland *et al.* (1986), Rumelhart and McClelland (1986), Bechtel and Abrahamsen (1991), Clark (1989), Minsky (1988), Elman *et al.* (1997), Klahr and MacWhinney (1998), Siegler (2005), Elman (2005)). What is proposed varies from model to model, but the basic hypothesis is that basic information-processing involves a large number of units working contemporaneously in parallel, with units, like neurones, stimulating or inhibiting each other through networks of connections. These units process very small pieces of information, smaller than a meaningful symbol and so often called 'subsymbols'. Information is not stored in a localisable place but exists as a pattern of excitation and inhibition between units; thus instead of there being a slot in memory in which information about Piaget is stored, the system has information about Piaget only when particular sets of units are active and stimulating or inhibiting each other in particular connection patterns.

Units that are active together have their excitatory connections strengthened and their inhibitory connections weakened; for units that are not active together the reverse happens. This means that over time a network that repeatedly receives the same input will develop a strong set of excitatory connections and inhibitory connections; the units that have repeatedly been active together will come to excite each other more reliably and strongly than ever. Even if only some of the units are activated, the whole configuration will come into play; no single subsymbol of information is crucial and the configuration will be activated even if a few incorrect or irrelevant pieces of information are included in the generally correct package of incoming stimulation. There is no information store, no knowledge of rules, no metacognition, independent of the activated connections. Thus, compared with the older information processing models, there is more emphasis on parallelism in the cognitive system, on distributed knowledge, on the gradual acquisition of knowledge and on gradual decline. Connectionist systems can also reach an answer despite not having sufficient information (a very human characteristic).

Connectionist models appear to have a number of very positive advantages. They seem to be in principle compatible with what we know about the nervous system (Elman (2005); and pp. 316–347), where neurones activate and inhibit each other in complex networks, carrying out basic processing so incredibly rapidly that parallel processing must be involved. The connectionist networks are not strongly deterministic in their functioning, so they can deal with conflicting information and find the best or most probable possible outcome. Thus they can use connections developed over old experiences to deal with new ones, or handle cases that are an exception to the usual rule. When their limits are reached, they do not crash suddenly and completely, but begin to perform less well; just like human brains they show gradually failing performance or 'graceful degradation'. They show 'content addressable memory', where a variety of different cues that are linked to the memory may summon it up: if enough of the units of a particular network are properly activated, the whole circuit comes to function. There is feedback, or 'back propagation', from later stages of processing back to earlier ones. Finally, connectionist networks can learn from experience by changing the weights of connections, the strength of the excitatory or inhibitory links between units; this would be the sort of gradual learning over many trials that is probably what we do when developing our coherent knowledge of language or arithmetic.

These characteristics suggest that connectionist network models may be very useful for some of the most crucial and problematic areas of cognitive development. They might provide a basis for the conceptually and practically difficult distinction between maturation and learning, between the development and the acquisition of cognition. Maturation changes in development might change characteristics of the network such as the maximum number of units that could be involved and the general and threshold activation levels; that is, they would involve the architectural structure of the system. Learning would change the fine-tuned detail of weights of connections between units and of connections between networks. Connectionist models might provide a mathematically based account of the phases of neurological development where there is a rapid proliferation of synapses followed by a period of weeding many of them out (pp. 335–336). They may provide a much more specific account of assimilation and accommodation than Piagetian theory has done. They may clarify whether development is sensibly described as 'stage-like', whether development is from one distinct, well-integrated and general across domains to another separate one, or whether there is continuity across a succession of small and gradual changes. Models of a normally functioning system may be tampered with to model impaired development or the effects of damage, and to suggest how problems might be remedied.

Bechtel and Abrahamsen (1991) and Richardson (1998) argue that the behaviour of connectionist simulations is a result of the interventions of the researcher operating the model, rather than of the model developing itself; thus if the model behaves as the theory predicts this may merely be because of the way it was manipulated, rather than an independent confirmation of the validity of the model. Richardson also points to a gap between different sorts of 'knowledge', quoting Elman *et al.* (1997: 359) as saying 'Knowledge ultimately refers to a specific pattern of synaptic connections in the brain . . . knowledge is the representations that support behaviour'. He argues that a description of 'knowledge' in terms of the connection weights between parts of a connectionist network does not enable us to see whether knowledge improves in development, or how one pattern of connection weights is better or worse than another, or how to remediate a defective one. Finally networks may represent the world but they cannot act on it, nor, I suppose, do they have selective attention or goals or intentions or social contexts.

Klahr and MacWhinney (1998) suggest that connectionist models need to go beyond the limited areas where they have modelled human development quite successfully (there are several examples in models of language acquisition, e.g. Marcus (1993), Karmiloff and Karmiloff-Smith (2001), van Geert (1991), Klahr and MacWhinney (1998), Siegler (2005)) and need to theorise the 'effective environment'; that is, train the connectionist networks in ways that are based on a better understanding of the environmental input that children receive. It seems likely that current enthusiasm for connectionist models may lead to notable advances in our understanding of these and related issues.

4.2.3 Information-processing models of the development of cognition in childhood

To summarise a vast literature ruthlessly, cavalierly even (see Siegler (1983, 1986, 2005), Halford (1993, 2002), Klahr and MacWhinney (1998) for fuller accounts): the rudiments of basic information-handling processes such as recognition, scanning, categorical perception, and various associations between different modalities, events and pieces of information can be observed even in very young children; but each of these shows experience-related and age-related changes in speed, exhaustiveness, flexibility and consistency of use (e.g. Kail 1991a, 1991b; Stigler *et al.* 1988; Klahr and MacWhinney 1998; Siegler 2005). Nevertheless, however much innate specification the human cognitive system starts out with, it does, by and large, change during development.

There are clearly developmental changes in cognitive strategies, one obvious candidate for an important role in cognitive development. Some examples of these are reviewed in my discussion of memory and the skills of reading, writing, arithmetic and general study skills (Chapter 2). In particular, it is clear that young children show less evidence of using deliberate strategic approaches to problems (at least of an academic rather than social or practical sort), and have smaller and less flexible repertoires of strategies than older children. As I discussed earlier (e.g. pp. 31–36, 60–67, 67–83, 90–96), there are considerable improvements in use of cognitive strategies, particularly over the primary school years. Changes in life's task demands, such as the requirements of the school curriculum and the need to co-ordinate home and school worlds, may contribute to this change. Awareness of one's own achievements and activities in remembering seem important also. Such awareness, knowledge about and use of cognition are the concern of the field known as 'metacognition', or cognition whose own subject-matter is cognition. There is some debate over whether metacognition is separate from cognition that is about other aspects of the world, and about the role of conscious awareness; but it seems to be fairly clear that there are changes in children's knowledge about and control of their cognition as they get older.

There is even less doubt that the knowledge base available to children increases as they get older. Theories that concentrated on universal cognitive processes set this sort of developmental change aside as uninteresting, just as studies of learning in adults tried to rule out knowledge as a contaminating variable. Recently there has been more interest in cognitive development within specific domains of knowledge, and these studies have suggested that the amount of knowledge available and the ways in which it is organised may have important effects even on universal cognitive processes, and may be one of the major components of cognitive development (e.g. Chi and Ceci 1987; Keil 1989; Danovitch and Keil 2004). Just as we do not yet understand how metacognition and cognition interact, we do not really understand how content knowledge affects cognitive processes or how knowledge systems should be modelled. I describe some of the relevant work in Chapters 2 and 6. Studies that investigate the sources of knowledge and how it is organised and used will no doubt make more contribution to psychological theory than those that merely describe age difference in content.

As I said earlier, information-processing models seek to describe and explain these changes in knowledge representation and storage, information manipulation, inference, and problem solving. There have been a number of developmental models of general information-processing as well as the specific and detailed accounts of the information-processing that is involved in various levels of success or failure on a particular task, such as predicting the movement of a balance or answering a class inclusion test. The next section offers a very brief summary of the models proposed by Case (1974, 1984, 1985), Kail and Bisanz (1982), Keil (1984), Klahr (1984), Klahr and Wallace (1976), Siegler (1983, 1984, 1986, 1989b) and Sternberg (1984,

1985); Sternberg's model is also discussed in the section in intelligence (Section 3.1).

4.2.4 Examples of information-processing models

Information-processing models of cognitive development could be seen as tending towards the same two separate categories as other accounts of children's cognition, the first category being those that focus on the cognitive system *per se* and describe the very basic structures and processes that underlie all cognitive functioning, a largely syntactic approach, and the second category taking much more account of how the general system is applied to particular tasks. They also differ in how far a real child is visible behind the silicon chips. The first model I will mention gives information-processing a comparatively human face. Case (1974, 1984, 1985) describes the child as:

> an organism that is endowed with certain natural desires, and that encounters certain natural barriers to their realization, but which also has the capability for overcoming these barriers by refining and re-combining the inborn procedures with which it comes equipped.
>
> (Case 1985: 59)

The core model, however, is mechanistic rather than organismic, consisting of figurative, operative and executive *schemes* for handling information that have their roots very early in the child's life, and give rise to four neo-Piagetian *stages* of cognition, with much the same conceptual and evidence problems as Piaget's own model. Though his structural account seems at present less than perfectly justified, Case has some interesting suggestions to make about developmental *processes*. He postulates innate capabilities for setting goals, formulating strategies to meet these goals, and integrating different strategies into more complex and effective ones. Basically (Case 1985: Chapter 12), children have four general regulatory processes that orchestrate their mental activity. These are a tendency to problem-solving, a tendency to exploration, a tendency to imitation, and a capacity for mutual regulation with other people. Problem-solving involves searching for an operation that bridges the gap between the state of affairs that is to be found now and a more desirable goal state. The child, faced with a less than optimum present situation (such as not being able to reach the toy on the floor from his or her seat in the high chair) and able to envisage a more desirable situation (having the toy to hand), searches for a strategy that will transform the former into the latter. The first step in problem-solving is to search for operations that will transform the less pleasant, less desired state of affairs into the more pleasant, more desired one, perhaps by matching the particular features of the problem and the goal ('distant toy', 'I can't move to get it') with features of schemes in the repertoire ('Mummy gets things for me', 'pulling strings moves distant things') and computing some sort of best fit. Next, the proposed sequence of operations ('Get Mummy's attention, point out toy, show I want it back, accept toy') is evaluated for its effectiveness, either after actually being enacted or after an imagined 'dry run'. This can then lead to 'retagging' of the sequence so that it can be more easily accessed if it has succeeded ('when I said "Dolly please" Mummy gave me Dolly *and* a biscuit') or avoided if it has led to a negative outcome ('jumping out of the high chair really hurts'). Finally the schemes used become consolidated, or hierarchically integrated, as essential components run more automatically and inessential ones are dropped, and as separate components come together to form larger invariant units. Our child in the high chair might give up leaning over to stretch out an arm for the toy that is beyond arm's length, but begin to incorporate automatic 'please' and 'thank you' as parents demand an explicit acknowledgement of their services.

Case's second natural developmental process is exploration. Here the child does not have an explicit goal but does have a situation to which several possible schemes could apply. What happens here is a sort of 'suck it and see' procedure: the child tries out various schemes and notes their results. Schemes are chosen because they have features applicable to the starting situation, not because they are relevant to any particular goal, and typically several schemes will be applied in succession. As in problem-solving, the results are evaluated and the schemes retagged, and because several schemes have been tried out freely and in rapid succession they can be consolidated, their components varied, automated, integrated and so forth. Exploration is a 'bottom-up' process, while problem-solving is a 'top-down' one; it is also, in Piagetian terms, heavily assimilatory.

The third natural general developmental process is imitation. Often young children do not know what to do or what results could possibly be obtained, but more experienced people do have this knowledge and may act on it in the child's presence. Children can observe what those around them do and seem to have a strong natural tendency to imitate the actions of others, to get the same result, or for the sake of being like another person, or just for fun. The adult, or more skilled person, models both possible strategies for dealing with the situation and the goals that these strategies can achieve in this case. The child may focus on the action or on the goal; as in the cases of problem-solving and exploration that do not involve modelling themselves on other people, the schemes the child uses are evaluated, retagged and consolidated.

Case's final process is 'mutual regulation', or the adaptation of the child and another person to each other's feelings, cognitions and behaviour. This may be done to serve emotional or social ends, as in attempts to comfort or please, or to achieve dominance through assertion or aggression, or it may be task-oriented as when children and adults co-operate to solve a problem or instruct each other. The same common sub-processes of accessing schemes and experimenting with novel sequences, evaluating the consequences, retagging the schemes and consolidating them, apply. Case's main example here (1985: 270–271) is of what happens during deliberate instruction of a less skilled person by a more skilled one, and he does not elaborate on his brief nomination of affective mutual self-regulation as a means to intellectual development. Nevertheless, it seems to me to be a helpful advance for an information-processing model to make an explicit recognition of social facilitation of development and of cognition's affective roots. Both mutual regulation and imitation are Vygotskian learning processes (pp. 307–312). Both are likely to be adversely affected if the child and its caretaker do not establish a caring relationship and joint activity (pp. 388–393).

All these four general learning processes are seen as arising early in infancy, and as occupying a considerable proportion of young children's time. Both their early emergence and their high frequency suggest that they are quite strong candidates for important developmental processes. Case believes they would give rise to the sort of stage transitions described earlier because they would produce a hierarchical integration of what were previously separate control structures. The sub-processes of activation, evaluation, retagging and consolidation are invariant and resemble Piaget's functional invariants of assimilation, accommodation and equilibration, but in the cases of imitation and mutual regulation are put to use in ways more reminiscent of Bruner and Vygotsky: the child inherits the cultural tools used by adults and, first by mutual regulation, then in more and more internalised ways, can use them as his or her own independent strategies and skills. The cognitive capacities for setting goals, for activating existing schemes in novel sequences in pursuit of these goals, for evaluating the results, and for reworking or 'retagging' sequences that have been evaluated positively so that they can be generated intentionally in future, and for recalling such reworked structures and consolidating them so that they form smoothly functioning executive structures are innate (Case 1984: 27–28). It is not clear how strongly Case means these to be seen as literally invariant over the course of development; as Flavell (1984) points out, it may be misleading rather than helpful to suppose that, for example, the 'goal-setting' of the neonate is very like the 'goal-setting' of the adolescent. Some sort of 'goal-setting' process is indeed likely to be useful both as a means to development and as a means to minute-by-minute survival, but we need more details of what 'goal-setting' is available at different points in development – and in different ecological settings and for individuals with different histories – than Case's reliance on functional invariants provides.

The main maturational constraint that Case discusses is the size of the short-term storage space (STSS) that a child has available for information-processing. Total resources do not change during development, but their distribution between operating and storage does: operating needs fewer resources as operations become more practised, more consolidated and more integrated, so that more space is available for holding their results ready for operation. Operations continue to develop and to become more and more slick for as long as they are practised. Performance on a task will be a function of the strategy sequence used, the demands that that sequence makes on operating space and short-term storage space, the availability of relevant information, and the size of attentional resources. One major cognitive difference between adults and children is the amount of practice they have had on basic cognitive operations, and also on cognitive operations specific to a particular domain. Adults will almost always have had more practice on the general basic operations, but there may be some domains where the child has had more practice than the adult (new topics in the maths curriculum, for example, or childhood crazes such as puns and other word play) and may be the quicker and better thinker.

We know that for many tasks there are developmental changes in strategies and in their demandingness, and in the existence and accessibility of relevant knowledge (Chapter 2). A very precise analysis of tasks, of learner activities, of how tasks and learners change with practice, and of the interdependences between knowledge, strategies and processing is required to determine why there is developmental change; this is not going to be easy to achieve. Meanwhile the 'best guess' seems to be that developmental changes in absolute amount of processing space, if they exist at all, are less important than changes in how they are used. Changes in what information is stored and how it is accessed, and a wider range of more sophisticated processing possibilities that can gather and act on information, seem to be more important. Case does maintain, however, that these changes, which could obviously be very domain-specific, are held together so that cognitive development is homogeneous across domains, the 'homogenising' factor being maturational limits such as the degree of myelinisation of the central nervous system. I will look at what we are beginning to know about how the brain works in cognitive activities in Chapter 5.

Kail and Bisanz (1982) provide another account of the mechanisms of cognitive development, involving increases in the content and integration of the knowledge base, and increase or better use of storage capacity. Knowledge is organised in an associative network whose 'nodes' and linkages are changed by detection of regularities and inconsistencies resulting in streamlining, chunking of knowledge, automatisation of processes and increase in speed. These tend to generate more *sufficient* representations and processes, allowing cognition to apply to a wider range of phenomena without giving rise to too many exceptions and anomalies; modifications following the detection of regularities tend to generate more *efficient* representations and processes as links between elements and processes become smooth and automatic. Altogether there is a fairly steady development towards more complex and more hierarchically integrated cognition. The model places less emphasis on uniform development across domains.

In Sternberg's model (Sternberg 1984, 1985), which is discussed more fully in the section on intelligence (Section 3.1), the main developmental mechanism is strategy construction based on the use of knowledge-acquisition components, performance components (which are processes such as encoding, drawing inferences, mapping relations between similar contents) and metacomponents that select and monitor performance, these last being 'the major basis for the development of intelligence' (Sternberg 1984: 172). Sternberg (1984) includes essays on the mechanisms of cognitive development and further references.

Klahr and Wallace (1976), Klahr (1984) and Klahr and MacWhinney (1998) have 'generalisation' at the core of their developmental model. They focus on regularity detection and redundancy elimination, like Kail and Bisanz. It is thus important that all the relevant information should be accurately encoded, otherwise the self-modifying cognitive system could not work. Siegler's model (Siegler 1983, 1984, 1986) stresses that much of children's knowledge is rule-governed, using 'if . . . then' question–answer patterns. Some aspects of these rules are quite broadly applicable; for example, there may be fall-back rules that are resorted to in several different situations when information-processing demands overwhelm the cognitive system. He sees encoding as central to cognitive development, since if the crucial features are not adequately represented, automatisation, generalisation and strategy construction cannot proceed fruitfully. A comparison of the accounts I have described is set out in Table 4.1. Anderson (1989a, 1992; see also Chapter 3) and Karmiloff-Smith (1991, 1992; pp. 293–294) provide other interesting models.

It is models like these that most nearly come to grips with issues about the relationship of development and learning. Development proceeds by association of new information with old information, either through the two occurring together in a regular way (contingency) or through the two being similar on some dimension; this is of course the assumption that has dominated Learning Theory. The various theorists' proposed processes for change seem to form at least overlapping sets, with a frequent emphasis on self-monitoring and processes for automatisation and the detection of consistencies and inconsistencies. They take different positions on the role of the knowledge base: Case, for example, assumes it is minimally relevant to processing and Keil sees it as the main arena for cognitive change, and there seem to be parallel assertions about whether development is general across all domains and uniform in rate between them, or whether it varies very much from one domain to another. Similarly there is a degree of disagreement about how far development is influenced by the outside world, particularly by interaction with other people: Keil and Case specify instruction as a means to cognitive development; Klahr's model is primarily

Table 4.1 Information-processing accounts of cognitive development: some comparisons between models.

Source	Change in knowledge base?	Change in attentional resources?	Knowledge modification processes	Domain-specific or general cognition?	Other features
Case 1984, 1985	Not emphasised.	In use, not in total capacity; Short Term Storage System increases.	Differentiation and hierarchical integration, executive control structures become more complex. Goal setting, search, evaluation, retagging and consolidation.	Emphasis very much on general parallels across wide range of domains; processes universal, even evolution-based.	Stages: natural processes of problem-solving, exploration, imitation and mutual regulation, including instruction. Affective motives for cognition.
Kail and Bisanz 1982	Number of elements increases; so does amount in chunks. More conceptual links, perceptual less salient.	Increase, possibly in total capacity, possible in effective use related to knowledge.	Addition or deletion of knowledge nodes, strengthening and weakening of links. Inconsistency and regularity detectors. Chunking, automatisation and speed increases.	Model applies across domains but need not be uniform development.	
Keil 1979, 1984	Main source of cognitive change. Structure of knowledge determines processes.	Not emphasised.	Increasing differentiation of knowledge and awareness of links. Higher order relations, coherence and juxtaposition in semantic field. Current knowledge and structural constraints on processing and learning. Processes cannot be independent of structure of knowledge involved.	Specific to domain. Expect experience to affect level.	Emphasis that there is less evidence for complex processing that for complex representation or structure from which processing is derived. Instruction may be important.

Reference					
Klahr 1984, Klahr and Wallace 1976	Knowledge includes time-line record of own cognitive processing.	Better chunking, representation, production.	Self-modifying production systems (equivalent to Piagetian 'reflective abstraction'). Includes conflict resolution rules, selection of better strategies, elimination of redundancies, discrimination, generalisation etc.	Global structural reorganisations from local incremental modifications.	Development mainly internally system-driven, spontaneous not externally taught. Stages, at least in rules.
Siegler 1983, 1984, 1986, 1989b, Klahr and Siegler 1978	Constitutes rules for specific and general problem-solving. Adequate encoding essential.		Encoding, combination processes, monitoring. Synthesis becomes more accurate and efficient. Negative feedback in evaluation and selection of features.	Some processes biologically given, some learned. Experience is important. Analogies with evolution.	This is a process model at an early stage of generalisation from its origins in fine analysis of a limited range of tasks.
Sternberg 1984, 1985	Knowledge acquisition central; selective encoding, and combination comparison. Increase in knowledge and changes in efficiency of its use lead also to more sophisticated later acquisition and easier performance.	Limited capacity, especially metacomponents.	Feedback from performance and acquisition components to metacomponents, which are self-monitoring and deal with feedback. Automatisation, repeated activation leading to detection and use of regularities and inconsistencies. Metacognition important.	Development of local subsystems of knowledge, general global system used in default of good local system.	Includes novice–expert and gifted–retarded descriptions.

internally motivated, system-driven, not taught. Finally, the models centre on a similar range of tasks, problems derived from the cognitive psychology literature, though Case tries to extend his discussion in social and affective areas and Keil's focus is on knowledge systems that seem closer to semantic network studies. Indeed, the same data serve more than one model as evidence: Siegler's documentation of the balance task is used by other theorists for their own purposes.

Flavell (1984), reviewing the models described in Sternberg (1984), finds all of them interesting but none, as yet, convincing. His final comment is that 'there is more variety in *what* gets developed and also more variety in *how* these varied developments get accomplished' (p. 206) than the models, as yet, allow. The comment refers to the possibility that different sorts of learners have different sorts of cognitive processes available to them; for example, that the developmentally early ways of processing information give rise to new mechanisms for processing information so that cognitive development proceeds in new ways. Becoming able to process language for discrepancies and agreements between literal meaning and the message that the speaker intends to convey, or to analyse words into phonemes, to give two examples, changes current understanding of discourse and of spelling respectively *and* gives tools for further developments. Flavell likens this to technological development: things are possible now that we have satellites or laser beams or non-stick cake tins that were impossible or very difficult before. Changes in information-processing mechanisms may be one of the sources of differences between novices and experts, or between the gifted and the ungifted; however, like Keil, I think we should not forget the probability of different knowledge bases here.

It is also important to analyse the demands of the task if we are to understand the performance of people working on it. What they do is constrained by their own cognitive limitations, but it is also directed by what they think the task requires. Individuals may have the crucial knowledge for a particularly effective idiosyncratic strategy, but sometimes a strategy may be used because it is convenient for them on that task, not because it is the best strategy available. On another occasion they may do something different (Siegler 2005). This is important developmentally for a number of reasons. What strategy of processing information is used will depend on what the task is seen to require, hence its familiarity will affect performance. It will also depend on what relevant information is available, and again children may lack information that older problem-solvers would have. The 'costs' of the strategies that could be brought to bear on a task may also be different for children: less easily assessed, in the first place, and less easily leading to a cost–benefit analysis. We may perhaps be, unlike traditional computers, problem-solvers who are willing to settle for a 'good enough' near-solution to a problem if it would be very laborious to give up our not-quite-adequate strategy and replace it with a more efficient but more expensive one. We saw a number of examples of this 'get by by bodging it' in Chapter 2, for example the balancing strategies used by the subjects of the study by Karmiloff-Smith and Inhelder (1974/5), pp. 133–134, and the 'knowledge-telling' strategy in writing (Bereiter and Scardamalia 1987), pp. 60–67. Different forms of representation may be useful for different purposes; different cultures offer different ones (Karmiloff-Smith 1992; Kozulin *et al.* 2003; Valsiner 1997a, 1998a, 2000), though this is not recognised as prominently as it needs to be in information-processing theories that are striving for universal models.

One further point to be made about these models is that they do not use biological evidence. Though several theorists stress that they see their subjects as organisms produced by evolution, the models are mechanistic rather than organismic, even if the machine is an active, constructive and self-modifying one. What is being discussed is also, on the whole, 'cold' cognition rather than 'hot'; the sort of dispassionate, detached, cognition that is brought to bear on formal well-defined 'academic' tasks of not much immediate relevance to the desires of the problem-solver, let alone his or her survival. The cognitive processes described here are not closely linked to affect (except in Case's model, where goals are set by unrealised desires). This may reflect the models' origins in 'cognitive science', where computers and affect are incompatible. In view of the increasing amount of evidence that in the human brain there are strongly structural links between cognition and affect (pp. 435–439), the disassociation of cognition and emotion may be unfortunate.

4.2.5 Cognitive development and representations

Another shift in cognitive development is towards representations of the world that can be used in different ways. The first representations of the infant, or of the novice in a new domain, are likely to be enactive (Bruner 1966). These sorts of representations relate to the procedural ways of knowing discussed earlier (e.g. pp. 76–80, 128, 159, 163). They may be very effective but are implicit and hard to control. An adult will still employ some enactive representations (try working out the tenth letter of the alphabet after 'g') but will also have and use iconic representations and symbolic representations, the latter predominantly language-based.

A newer account of cognitive development (Karmiloff-Smith 1991, 1992) has been developed from Piagetian theory, the information-processing approach, research on certain unusual forms of cognitive disability, and recent findings on brain development. Karmiloff-Smith argues for an epigenetic interaction between innate predispositions and experience that has Piagetian roots but suggests more wired-in constraints and structure than Piaget proposed. She sees knowledge as more domain-specific than Piaget suggested; during the development of a cognitive domain there is a sequence of stages that is similar to the sequence of stages seen in the development of other domains, but there is not necessarily synchrony of stages or stage changes across domains. There are domain-general learning processes but domain-specific structures. The processes described resemble those of classic information-processing models:

> Development and learning, then, seem to take two complementary directions. On the one hand, they involve the gradual process of proceduralization (that is, rendering behavior more automatic and less accessible. On the other hand, they involve a process of 'explicitation' and increasing accessibility (that is, representing explicitly information that is implicit in the procedural representations sustaining the structure of behavior).
>
> (Karmiloff-Smith 1992: 17)

The core of the model is the representation of information. Initially the young child, or the novice in a cognitive domain, may be limited to implicit representations of information. These are essentially procedural or enactive (Bruner, Oliver and Greenfield 1966, pp. 76–80 this volume); the child may solve problems successfully but cannot consciously analyse or vary how the success is achieved. New experience in the domain adds new representations and allows success on new tasks but does little to amend the old representations, until in a process of change that is largely internally generated the child moves into the next phase of development and representations begin to become explicit and accessible to deliberate reflection and modification. The first re-representations can be related to each other, manipulated and contradicted, but it takes further development for them to become accessible for reflection, and more still for them to be expressible verbally; thus they become increasingly flexible, reasoned and deliberate.

> It is from the process of representational redescription, rather than simply from interaction with the external environment, that cognitive flexibility and consciousness ultimately emerge.
>
> (Karmiloff-Smith 1992: 26)

The very general process of representational redescription is common to all domains of knowledge, but it may proceed faster or more securely or further in one domain rather than another. A star dancer may be able to perform a movement beautifully but not describe it verbally; the dance teacher or critic may not be able to move like a dancer but can analyse and describe what the dancer does. Some domains or some representations may come more easily to us than others because of innate predispositions wired in by evolution – as in the modular modules of cognition that she is seeking to go beyond. Some children may have particularly advanced development in a few domains while being considerably impaired in others, as seems to be the case for some children with autism or Williams syndrome. Brains probably quite normally contain multiple neural circuit representations of the same phenomenon (pp. 327–338). Humans, though probably not other animals, can not only build up representations, they can compare and synthesise them, as in analogical reasoning (pp. 110–115); this increases the possibility of metacognition (pp. 132–135). Collectively, humans develop representations into cultural tools, such as language, maps, graphs, caricatures, so that external notations can support (or constrain) cognition. Representations that can be communicated to others enable activities such as teaching and learning from being taught.

> The process of knowledge development is creative, reflexive in the sense that it works itself over, and is always in the context of the task and previous experience continually. Thus, it is inextricably part of the historical, social and cultural context, which both prescribes and prohibits certain tasks and provides possible ways of solving them.
>
> (Meadows 1996: 19)

I quoted Siegler defining people as 'in essence limited capacity manipulators of symbols' (Siegler 1983: 129). This is one possible view, and I will admit to a limited capacity (especially where appreciating this sort of literature is concerned). However, it is potentially a misleadingly narrow view (I would prefer to think that my essence is not symbol-manipulation). It is good to see the richer views presented by Siegler (2005) restore the liveliness of real learners to the picture of cognitive development, and to begin to re-embed it in the social world.

4.3 Vygotsky

Both the Piagetian model and the information-processing approach are based on one key idea: there are psychological structures in people's minds that explain their behaviour, that are invariant across cultures, settings and tasks, and that are essentially independent of the individual's relations to other individuals, to social practices, and to the cultural environment. Psychology is seen as the study of the individual mind's inner workings, which are seen as developing through individual maturation or learning, or individual construction of an internal model of outside reality, or some combination of such factors in the individual mind. At the centre of the theory derived from the work of Vygotsky (and foreshadowed also by Pierre Janet, G. H. Mead, J. M. Baldwin and Hegel: see Broughton and Freeman-Moir (1981), Markova (1982), Kozulin (1986, 1990), Zinchenko (1985), Van der Veer and Valsiner (1988), Valsiner (1998, 2000), Kozulin *et al.* (2003)) is a radical challenge to this key idea: far from being internal and individualistic, cognitive abilities and capacities are formed and built up in part by social phenomena, they are public and intersubjective, created through interaction with the social environment. Any description of cognition that isolates it from the social interaction that constitutes it is seriously incomplete and may provide a distorted and misleading picture. In particular, it is essential to study the development of cognition if its mature forms are to be properly understood. Thus Vygotskian theory rests on quite different philosophical bases from other theories of cognitive development.

For our present purposes, the central idea in Vygotsky's theory of cognitive development is summed up in this frequently cited passage:

> in the process of development, children begin to use the same forms of behaviour in relation to themselves that others initially used in relation to them. Children master the social forms of behaviour and transfer these forms to themselves . . . Logical argumentation first appears among children and only later is united within the individual and internalized. Child logic develops only along with the growth of the child's social speech and whole experience . . . it is through others that we develop into ourselves and . . . this is true not only with regard to the individual but with regard to the history of every function . . . Any higher mental function was external because it was social at some point before becoming an internal, truly mental functioning.
>
> . . . Any function in the child's cultural development appears twice, or on two planes. First it appears on the social plane, and then on the psychological plane. First it appears between people as an interpsychological category, and then within the child as an intrapsychological category.
>
> (Vygotsky 1981, in translation by Wertsch 1981)

Vygotsky's assertion that cognitive development involves the internalisation, transformation and use of routines, ideas and skills that are learned *socially*, from more competent partners, thus forms a unique contrast to the individualistic cognitivist approach. His account also solves, perhaps almost too completely, the 'bootstrapping problem' of explaining how more sophisticated cognitive competences can arise from less sophisticated ones. It is to all intents and purposes impossible to lift yourself up using the straps of the boots you are wearing; similarly it has been hard to see how a child might solve everyday cognitive problems such as realising that a word picks out a particular aspect of an object without previously having a whole complex of concepts about that object and what can be done with it. 'Red' is intended by the knowledgeable speaker to refer to an object's colour, but how are naïve listeners to know that colour is what is meant, not location, size, function, ownership or name, or any combination of these, unless they have a prior notion of colour as a characteristic that can be separated out and commented on? A word can become a name, or a label, for an object only against a background of beliefs about which is being picked out by the word.

Both the origins of these beliefs and their mapping on to language will be problematic for those who assume that cognitive development is by individual construction. One solution is to say that cognitive processes and concepts are, ultimately, innate (e.g. Fodor 1981); a second is to seek precursors of the problematic skills in the hope that a full enough sequence will have small enough steps between successive levels of skill that the transition from one to the next will look easy to explain. Vygotsky's solution makes the innate ideas solution unnecessary, and moves the other to the realm of description, not of explanation. It is that children develop more sophisticated cognitive competences despite having only simpler ones in their own repertoire, because adults (that is, older, more skilled persons available as teachers or models) have the more sophisticated competence and guide the child repeatedly through the relevant behaviour. The child as an individual does not have the resources necessary for the higher level of cognitive functioning, but the teaching adult does. Adult and child interact, the adult providing the structured context within which the child can act as though he or she was competent to solve the problem, and by so acting in such a context, the child can indeed reach the solution successfully. To begin with, the adult has to provide almost all the cognition necessary for the task, but as the child becomes more and more familiar with it the adult can leave more and more for the child to do, until at last the child can undertake the entire task successfully. Repetition of this 'scaffolding' of learning on related tasks extends the child's competence and eventually leaves him or her able to take on new examples with minimal adult support, or alone. The child's independent cognitive behaviour has developed from less sophistication and expertise to more, and the medium of development has been social interaction, apprenticeship to another, more skilled, person. Cognitive development is to be understood largely in terms of the child being led to behave in ways that the culture has developed as cognitively useful. By so behaving, and by practising and reflecting on what is done, the child internalises the cognitive skills of the culture and can develop them and pass them on to the next generation.

Thus, for the Vygotskian, there is no bootstrapping problem; rather the child is helped by the adult in the 'guided reinvention' of the accumulation of knowledge and ways of thinking that preceding generations have constructed. The skills required of the child are of observation and imitation, and of generalisation and decontextualisation, but even these fundamental skills develop under the fostering support of social interaction. Some of the skills learned from adults are what Bruner has called 'cultural amplifiers', cognitive tools that make thinking jobs easier. The Arabic number system that we now use has, I would imagine, made mathematical computation easier than it was for the Romans, with their more cumbersome way of writing numbers, while later inventions such as logarithms and electronic calculating machines have made computation easier still. Other cultural habits of thinking may impede cognitive development, although they are highly serviceable within their particular cultural domain. For example, belief in the literal truth of the Book of Genesis cannot be combined with understanding evolutionary theory, which has proved a most useful cognitive amplifier in its organisation and explanation of biological phenomena, except by separating one's religious and scientific knowledge; and some educational policy-makers have argued that the use of calculators impedes children's understanding of numbers in ways that reliance on traditional computation methods would facilitate. Whether helpful or not, the culture's ways of thinking surround children, are modelled to them by other users and discussed with them, and they may structure their language, their play, their schooling and their social interaction. The developing thinker does not have to create cognition out of an unpeopled vacuum, but may adopt and eventually internalise some of the cognitive content and processes made available by others.

Vygotsky suggested that in the course of development the child's own activities are shaped by the culture, or, more immediately, by the reactions of other people, and thus they move beyond what he agreed was to some extent a biological origin. Pointing, for example, is initially an unsuccessful reach for a too-distant object, which is responded to by the baby's mother as a sign that the baby wants the object. The child's movements are interpreted by the mother as an indicatory gesture. As she comes to the child's aid, the movement that was a gesture 'in-itself' becomes a gesture 'for-others'. The child, with some awareness of the communicative power of the movement, comes to use it as a deliberate gesture: the 'reaching' becomes reduced to movements that signal need but could not themselves achieve the desired object even if it were within reach, and other signals (such as cries, looks at the mother, and eventually words) are added. The child now addresses the gesture to adults who might bring about the desired result of grasping the object, rather than to the object itself, which was the focus of interest in the first place. It also becomes possible to use the gesture for oneself: to point out, or touch, an object as part of directing one's own attention to it, as in counting a set of objects or as in the memory tasks described in Chapter 2. A similar sequence appears in the development of the 'higher mental functions', both processes such as selective attention, logical memory and concept formation, and language, writing, counting, drawing and other 'external' cultural skills (Vygotsky 1978a; Lock 1978; Chapter 2 this volume). The core developmental process is the 'circular reaction', in which the subject reacts to a stimulus not just to adapt to it but also with some anticipation of how the reaction will affect the stimulus field and lead to the next stimulus (Rogoff 1998; Valsiner 2000).

4.3.1 Internalisation

At the heart of this development is one of the most important concepts in Vygotskian theory: 'internalisation'. It has been one of the returning difficulties of philosophy and psychology to understand the relationship between the external and the internal, whether these are contrasted as completely different and unrelated phenomena, or one reduced to the other, or some other relationship between the two postulated, as we see in, for example, the various solutions to the mind–body problem (see Chapter 5). Vygotsky gives an unusually precise answer to how external and internal relate, emphasising above all that it is a developmental relation, a constructive process, where cognitive processes external to an individual are transformed to create a plane of internal processes. Uniquely, he stresses that internalisation is primarily seen in the context of social interactions, and he analyses it in terms of the systems of meaning (semiotic systems) that mediate social functioning, of which language is the most familiar. Internalisation is part of the construction of consciousness through human social interaction: the child takes on self-consciousness and self-concept through social experiences (cf. Lewis and Brooks-Gunn 1979; Mead 1934; pp. 186–194), and cognitive consciousness and competence also arise socially.

> All higher mental functions are internalised social relationships . . . Their composition, genetic structure, and means of action – in a word, their whole nature – is social. Even when we turn to mental processes, their nature remains quasi-social. In their own private sphere, human beings retain the functions of social interaction.
>
> (Vygotsky 1981: 164; see also Wertsch and Stone 1985: 166)

Thus Vygotsky is stressing a close and complex relationship between external social processes and internal psychological ones. The example of memory may help to illuminate this relationship. Cultures have developed their own mnemonic techniques, and these are normally made available to the members of the culture. The very young and the uneducated, who have not yet learned to use the culture's technique, may have ways of remembering that combine a biological basis with the effects of early learning; Vygotsky called these 'mneme' (Kozulin 1990). These ways of remembering may be very effective for the informal and repetitive experiences of the young child; as I described in Chapter 2, we are discovering more and more cognitive effectiveness in young children working on 'ecologically natural' tasks. As the individual is taught the culturally mediated ways of remembering that the culture has developed ('mnemo-techniques'), these may displace the 'natural' processes so that they play a subordinate role in memory, and the memory skills of an acculturated adult represent a complex functional system that will be used more deliberately, more flexibly and with more self-awareness than the child's. To begin with, the child's biologically based memory is the centre of his or her own skill, and the culture's memory skills are an external world; as the cultural skills are learned they become internalised, take over much of the child's memorising and recall, and become integrated with skills of inference, concept use, and story-telling. Non-cultural memory processes remain essential for remembering, as the memory disorders found in patients with various sorts of brain damage show (Mayes 1988), but culturally learned skills may enhance these processes or make up for their deficiencies. The better the cognitive toolbox and the strategies for choosing from it, the better the chance of functioning successfully.

Internalisation changes the complexity of what is done, ultimately for the better but initially, perhaps, for the worse. Culturally provided skills are generally more sophisticated than the skills that they replace, and so the learner cannot usually manage them easily and well. The learner's version of a culturally provided skill will be cruder than the expert's, and it may indeed be cruder than the learner's own pre-existing skills; indeed, Valsiner (2000: 44) describes Vygotsky's idea of development as a succession of periods of steady growth interspersed with periods of crisis periods and regressions as cognition is challenged and reorganised. The small girl trying hard to learn to be 'a ballerina' may move more awkwardly in her ballet lesson than she does normally; the adult writer may resist learning a new word-processing package because text compiles itself more smoothly with the older, simpler one. 'Functional regression' may be part of the internalisation of any complex skill: it may be one of the reasons why cognitive development can seem slow and effortful (cf. Karmiloff-Smith and Inhelder 1974/5; Karmiloff-Smith 1992), and why people switch back and forth between strategies (Siegler 2005).

Internalisation, however, transforms the social process into the psychological, and thereby changes its structure and functions. This inevitably happens because the central process in internalisation is the gradual emergence of control over external processes, including control over external signs and systems of communication. Children perform actions, or use words and signals, without having a full understanding of their significance. They may know from their past successful usage that a particular action is a necessary part of getting the desired result (for example, they may always wash their hands and display their cleanness before meals) without understanding *why* the action is important (because washing hands decreases the possibility of infection from dirt, a goal highly valued by their hygienic mothers). Similarly, a child may know that a word refers to a particular object but not appreciate the full range of meaning it connotes. Social interaction necessarily involves the use of sign forms, including words, that have acquired a rich meaning over the generations of their use. Initial use, which may involve only a fragment of this meaning, progresses through generalisation to include more and more connotations. Vygotsky states that the

> basic distinguishing characteristic of the word is the generalised reflection of reality

and that

> in order to transmit some experience or content of consciousness to another person, there is no other path than to ascribe the content to a known class, to a known group of phenomena, and as we know this necessarily requires generalisation.
>
> Thus it turns out that social interaction necessarily presupposes generalisation and the development of word meaning i.e. generalisation becomes possible with the development of social interaction. Thus higher, uniquely human forms of psychological social interaction are possible only because human thinking reflects reality in a generalized way.

> (Wertsch and Stone 1985: 168)

Generalisation is thus an intrinsic part of human thinking, being a necessary part of learning from your own and other people's experience, and practice in generalising about what other people teach you leads to ever more habitual generalisation. Vygotsky is stressing a complex developmental pattern of relationships between internally arising and externally given generalisation. So far as developmental psychologists' concern with diagnosing children's competence is concerned, two important points arise. The first is that agreement between child and adult as to meaning at one point must not be taken as showing that they have the same full range of generalised meaning. Child and adult may agree on the referent of a word but not on the full meaning, or the child may know that an object is a member of a particular category by virtue of its possessing a particular attribute but not understand whether that attribute is merely characteristic or a defining property (Keil 1981b; Vygotsky 1986; Rogoff 1998; pp. 149–151). Nor will the child initially use word or concept in an adult way. While the child or novice's understanding of words may be based on relatively simple and context-bound relationships between word and object, adults will understand them in terms of a complex system of meaning that involves relationships between words. 'Interested', 'curious', inquisitive', 'nosey', 'enthralled', absorbed', for example, carry subtly varied social and linguistic connotations. Children's difficulties with figurative language provide other examples (pp. 155–164).

The second point is that individuals may differ in their ability to provide generalisations for themselves or for others, and to profit from them. Some individuals may set up for others fertile situations of 'mediated learning' (Feuerstein *et al.* 1980), giving them experiences that an expert has framed, selected, highlighted and scaffolded in such a way that appropriate learning and transfer are facilitated. These may involve elaborated links or emphasis of salient feedback or a host of other comments and actions characteristic of talk between fast language developers and their mothers and lacking in the interchange of slow language developers (Meadows 1996; Rutter *et al.* 2003; Thorpe *et al.* 2003). Some individuals, lacking such cognitive functioning, may fail to generalise even when to do so would prevent them from having to learn to solve each problem from the very beginning. Internalisation itself can presumably be more specific or more general, depending on the characteristics of child, adult, their interaction and the cultural content.

4.3.2 Mediation

As well as an emphasis on the role of interpsychological experience in intrapsychological cognitive development, on the importance of learning with and from other people, Vygotsky's theory has at its core the notion of 'mediation', the use of psychological 'tools' or 'signs', which allows a qualitative change in mental (or socio-historical) life. Language, for example, changes the relations of human beings to each other and to the non-human world from what those relations are in those who cannot use language. Mediation, or the use of communicable systems for representing reality as well as acting on it, is at the foundation of cognitive processes, which therefore cannot be reduced to automatic links between stimulus and response (as the Behaviourist psychology dominant in the West during Vygotsky's lifetime, and important also in Russia, would have argued). Signs, like artefact-type tools, are a product of the history of the culture. (Vygotsky's historical interests are, unfortunately, beyond the scope of this chapter, but see Kozulin (1986, 1990, 2003), Scribner (1985), Van der Veer and Valsiner (1991), Valsiner (2000), Egan and Gadjamaschko (2003).) We have developed and grown up with a collection of symbols and of ways of problem-solving that shape our thinking. If we want to remember something, we can use writing as an *aide-mémoire*, or knots tied in a piece of string such as the Incas used, or rote learning of phrases and rules of rhyme and rhythm that together allow the near-verbatim recall of material such as long traditional stories (Lord 1960) or nursery rhymes. Signs can be used for communication between people or for communication with oneself, in thinking. They are embedded in activity, constructed through the subject's interactions with the world (and particularly, perhaps, with the other people in the world). And the sign systems one has available have a marked effect on the sort of consciousness and degree of cognitive organisation one has. Young children might operate on a practical level of intelligence and on a symbol system level independently, but adults would in most of their experience integrate the enactive and the symbolic levels. Language, the 'psychological tool' *par excellence*, is perhaps the most potent means of integrating practical (or procedural?) and symbolic (or declarative?) knowledge.

> [The child] plans how to solve the problem through speech and then carries out the prepared solution through overt activity. Direct manipulation is replaced by a complex psychological process through which inner motivations and intentions, postponed in time, stimulate their own development and realisation.
>
> (Vygotsky 1978a: 26)

Action is mediated by the use of language for planning (and for monitoring and evaluating and other metacognitive activities), using (because language has social roots) a socially created and socially determined system of symbols and rules. The interweaving of thought and language, and their use within social interactions with more skilled partners who wish the child to learn, allow the child to move from fragmentary use without understanding to a coherent and flexible mastery of representational systems and cognitive skills. There is an increasingly profitable dialectic between the child's actions and the child's representations, and also between the child's understanding and other people's (Vygotsky 1986; Egan and Gadjamaschko 2003).

A microgenetic example of problem-solving from research by Vygotsky's colleague R. Levina illustrates this (Valsiner 2000: 80):

> Anya T., aged 3 yrs 7 months, is faced with solving the problem of retrieving a piece of candy from the top of a cupboard. Among other objects in the room, there is a stick long enough for her to reach the candy and knock it down. Anya first reaches silently. Then she comments 'It is very high' using the cultural tool of language to comment on her action. She then climbs on to a couch and reaches again. Again she uses language, this time to comment on the possibility of getting help – 'I should call Lyuba so she gets it' and to comment again on the problem 'Can't get it, too high'. Then she grasps the stick, leans on it but does not use it; she has begun to bring the second cultural tool in to the problem field. She comments 'No way to get it, very high', holds the stick in one hand and reaches towards the candy with the other. She brings in her background life experience; 'The hand is tired . . . Can't get it. We also have a high cupboard, papa put things on them and I couldn't get them.' Again, she reaches and comments, using language

to describe the problem again and also to describe herself; 'No. I can't reach it. I am still little.' She reaches, stands on the chair, swings the stick, aims at the candy and says 'Pah-pah'. Here at last she unites the cultural tool of the stick with her culturally-derived knowledge of aiming and shooting: the two cultural tools are combined. She laughs, moves the stick forward, looks quickly at the candy, smiling, and gets it with the help of the stick. She comments on her success and on a future use for the stick – 'See, I got it with the stick. I'll hang it up at home, and my cat will be reaching for it.'

4.3.3 Representational systems

Vygotsky places far more emphasis on the origins and characteristics of representational systems than Piagetian or information-processing approaches do, though both of course are very much concerned with how problems are represented. His discussion of these semiotic issues is no more complete than the rest of his work could be, but it includes some points that have emerged as important from our earlier discussion of cognitive skills. Among them are the developmental course of language (and other forms of representation and of thinking) from social roots to a mature form that also incorporates internal communication; the dialectic interaction between the use of procedural knowledge, or 'activity', and declarative knowledge, which become increasingly interdependent as development proceeds; the role of metacognition and symbolic control of behaviour; the interdependence of thinking and language; and the effects on cognition of different cultural tools.

Much of Vygotsky's account of cognitive development focuses on the role of language. He saw it as one of the most important of 'psychological tools', culturally developed ways of behaving towards objects that allow high-level cognitive functioning. Other psychological tools include counting systems, mnemonic techniques, writing, and diagrams and maps. Integrating any of these into a psychological function such as memory or spatial perception transforms the mental functioning, in Vygotsky's view. The psychological tools are not merely facilitators or auxiliaries: their use allows (or even requires) qualitatively different functioning, 'revolutions' in thinking associated with changes in psychological tools. Kozulin (1990: 134–135) uses as an example different ways of measuring the passing of time. Early devices for measuring time used natural processes occurring steadily over time to record the passing of time intervals: for example, the shadow moving across the sundial, sand falling from top to bottom of an egg-timer, or water running to a marked height in a water-clock. Clockwork clocks provide a less immediate representation of passing time: the movements of the cogs, weights, pendulum, springs and so forth are too complex to show us the amount of time that has passed, even if they are visible, and we have to use the 'symbolic time' of the position of the hands on the dial; this means we have to learn to read the clock-face. Electronic digital watches provide a purely symbolic measure of time, and require us to use arithmetical knowledge to judge whether more time has elapsed between one pair of times than between another, as no physical analogue at all remains for the time.

Individuals 'appropriate' psychological tools from their social and cultural milieu. They do not inherit them as instincts or reflexes, they do not normally reinvent them from scratch, they do not discover them in their independent interactions with the natural world. In particular they learn to use tools through face-to-face communication and social interaction with other people who are also using psychological tools. Thus the tools have communication among their functions. Development involves, as we have said, initially interpersonal use of psychological tools, which increasingly become available for intrapersonal use. We hope that in the course of development an individual will appropriate a good range of culturally given tools and also strategies for choosing which one to use in a particular situation.

> Social life creates the necessity of subordinating the individual's behaviour to social demands and in addition creates complex signalisation systems – the means of connection that direct and regulate the formation of conditional connections in the brains of individual humans.
>
> (Vygotsky 1960, translated by Wertsch 1985a)

Language is of course pre-eminent among the 'complex signalisation systems' that Vygotsky considered, and the relationship between was perhaps his central interest (Kozulin 1990, 2003; Vygotsky 1962, 1986). He proposed a distinction between pre-intellectual speech and preverbal thought. Children under two use vocal activity as a means of social contact and emotional expression, and are capable of systematic and goal-directed activity that does not require verbal operations. This first 'primitive' stage is followed by a stage of 'practical intelligence' in which the child's language uses syntactic and logical forms that have parallels in the child's practical problem-solving activity but are not linked to them in any systematic or useful way. In the third stage the child starts to use external symbolic means, such as language or other cultural tools, to help with internal problem-solving. It is at this stage that children can be heard to talk themselves through problems or to count by using their fingers as aids. Finally, such aids are internalised and problem-solving thought uses internal dialogue, while language can be used more to reflect on and develop thought than as a prop to support problem-solving.

Thus Vygotsky saw speech as beginning to have social functions very early in the child's life, developing among the child's 'complex and rich social contacts' into an increasingly powerful tool. Expression of emotions and maintenance of social contacts are followed by the use of language to communicate, to make reference, to represent ideas, to regulate one's own actions, initially within a context of social interaction and shared knowledge but increasingly independently of social partner and of supportive context. The child who talks to himself or herself is regulating and planning mental activities, not, as Piaget suggested, failing to communicate with others because of an overwhelming egocentricity (Vygotsky 1986). Piaget believed that children's immature use of language was due to their lack of understanding of how to communicate with others who did not share their own knowledge, and that it disappeared as they became socialised. Young children do of course have difficulties in telling whether the speaker or the listener is responsible for a communication breakdown (Robinson and Robinson 1977, 1980, 1981). Vygotsky, however, argued that 'egocentric' speech was speech used for overt self-regulation but produced in potentially communicative settings (as in Levina's example above). The child's private monologue is a precursor of the completely 'in the head' talking oneself through a problem which may facilitate solution for adults. Regulation of and by others using language, self-regulation by language; communication with others using language, communication with oneself using language: these merge within the developing individual, as he or she takes part in social interactions within the culture, into mature verbal thought. Language becomes more and more useful as a tool for abstract reflection. It also changes immediate perception and action, which become more and more integrated into a cognitive system which is to a large extent represented through language and expressed in language. The internalisation of perception leads to language mediation, which leads to greater cognitive freedom and flexibility; cultural development fuses with organic development as the culture's higher mental functions are extended to and internalised by individuals. With further development 'egocentric' speech becomes 'inner speech', and the self-regulator's problem-solving dialogue with self is no longer observable. It may only become examinable when the task is difficult, or when an outsider asks for explicit 'talking-through' the problem. Very great task difficulty may force recourse to other regulation; finding another helpful text, or seeking out an expert to answer one's questions or provide further training, for example. The culture's 'psychological tools' have come to determine much of the individual's mental processes (Davydov and Radzikhovskii 1985).

4.3.4 Play and cognitive development

While Piaget saw play as an unequal balance of assimilation and accommodation, Vygotsky explicitly recognised it as an important medium of cognitive development. Valsiner (2000: 43) quotes a passage from a lecture that Vygotsky gave in 1933:

> In play a child is always higher than his average age, higher than his usual everyday behaviour: he is in play as if a head above himself. The play contains, in a condensed way, as if in the focus of a magnifying glass, all tendencies of development; it is as if the child in play tries to accomplish a jump above the level of his ordinary behaviour.
>
> The relationship of play to development should be compared with that of teaching–learning [*obuchenie*] to development. Changes of needs and consciousness of a more general kind lie behind the play. Play is the resource of development and it creates the zone of nearest development. Action in the imaginary field, in the imagined situation, construction of voluntary intention, the formation of the life-plan, will motives – this all emerges in play.

The theme of the importance of play and imagination is also given some discussion in Chapters 3 and 7.

4.3.5 Scaffolding and social interaction

Vygotsky's emphasis on social interaction entails two important consequences that his own interest in education and in mental handicap (defectology) developed (Kozulin 1986; Sutton 1983; Vygotsky 1978a). The first is that more complex cognitive functioning will be possible in a dialogue between two individuals than is possible for those individuals alone, or at least for the less skilled individual, though at a late stage in development an individual may be able to provide his or her own interlocutor. The other consequence is that instruction could be a facilitator of cognitive development, not, as Piaget would have it, at best irrelevant and at worst a distortion (see, especially, Vygotsky (1986), Chapter 6). 'Learning by transaction' is at the heart of cognitive development.

By no means all the evidence that is relevant to these issues comes from Vygotskian research. Other parts of this book offer a general examination of the contribution of social experiences to cognitive development (e.g. pp. 138–139, 159–162, 171–175, 184–186, 374–408). Here I will just mention a few explicitly Vygotskian observational studies in which children have been set to solve a problem with and without an interlocutor. David Wood (Wood 1980, 1988; Wood *et al.* 1978) observed mothers and four-year-olds working together to construct a wooden pyramid. James Wertsch (1978, 1979, 1985a 1985b; Wertsch *et al.* 1980) recorded children working with their mothers on constructing a copy of a 'model' puzzle. Ellice Forman (Forman and Cazden 1985) made a longitudinal study of pairs of children solving problems such as chemistry experiments. On a rather larger scale,

Vygotskian theory underpins the Kamehameha Elementary Education Project (Tharp and Gallimore 1988; Tharp *et al.* 1984). The data from these studies, and from others that are, for example, Piagetian in origin (e.g. Doise and Mugny 1984; Perret-Clermont and Brossard 1985), show that internalisation can be observed in children's use of tutorial interchanges, social interaction may facilitate performance on a task, and the improvement may transfer to similar tasks done alone later. If the limited quantity of focused interaction typically provided in these studies can produce such effects, how much more might day-in, day-out learning from mother? Naturalistic data on cognitively productive social interaction in children's daily lives suggests powerful effects of mother–child interaction on children's language development and development of concepts, as I discussed earlier (pp. 22–32, 186–200). Moerk (1989) argued that the LAD that Chomsky (1976) postulated to explain language development is most probably a LADY, the unfairly undervalued mother whose chatter and listening seems to him (and to other language researchers) to be excellently fitted to producing an expert speaker. Given the Soviet (and indeed Marxist) context of this section, I will not restrain the exhortation 'Mothers of the world unite, you have nothing to lose but your deprecators!'

4.3.6 The 'zone of proximal development'

One important Vygotskian concept that has not yet been discussed is the 'zone of proximal development' (ZPD). He presents it as part of a discussion of the interaction between 'learning' and 'development' (Vygotsky 1978a: 79–91). Here he argues that if we are to provide learning opportunities that will enable the child to develop we must determine at least two developmental levels. The lower of these is the sort of thing that the usual psychological and educational test measures, what the child can do independently; the higher is what the child can do with such assistance as demonstrations, prompts or leading questions.

> The zone of proximal development . . . is the distance between the actual developmental level as determined by independent problem solving and the level of potential development as determined through problem solving under adult guidance or in collaboration with more capable peers.
>
> (Vygotsky 1978a: 86)

Independent unaided problem-solving indicates what cognitive functioning the child has already mastered; problems that the child can only solve with assistance suggest what functions are not yet mature but are in the process of maturation. 'What a child can do with assistance today she will be able to do by herself tomorrow' (Vygotsky 1978a: 87). Diagnosis of the ZPD is necessary both for a full assessment of the child's abilities and for the optimum targeting of instruction. There is little profit from teaching aimed below the bottom of the ZPD because the child's functioning here is already mature, or from teaching aimed above the top of the ZPD, because the difference from the child's actual present functioning may be too great: 'the only "good learning" is that which is [slightly] in advance of development' (Vygotsky 1978a: 89); teaching is good only when it 'awakens and rouses to life those functions which are in a stage of maturing, which lie in the zone of proximal development' (Wertsch and Stone 1985: 165).

How does progress through the ZPD come about? In particular, how can 'good learning' be in advance of development? In one sense, here we are back at the 'bootstrapping problem' that I discussed earlier (pp. 19, 131, 306). As we have seen, Vygotsky saw that play is one of the contexts in which progress is made, but he placed a great deal of emphasis on another: interaction between teacher and pupil, or more expert person and relative novice. Bruner describes the 'teacher lifts the boot-straps' answer. The teacher (adult or more competent peer)

> serves the learner as a vicarious form of consciousness until such a time as the learner is able to master his own action through his own consciousness and control. When the child achieves that conscious control over a new function or conceptual system, it is then that he is able to use it as a tool. Up to that point, the tutor in effect performs the critical function of 'scaffolding' the learning task to make it possible for the child, in Vygotsky's word, to internalise external knowledge and convert it into a tool for conscious control.
>
> (Bruner 1985: 25)

During the earliest periods of learning in the ZPD a child may have a very limited degree of understanding of what the task involves; the teacher offers a model or successive precise and simple directions, and the child merely observes or imitates. Gradually, as the child becomes able to cope with more components of an activity, and has more understanding of how they fit together, an understanding that will include more appreciation of what the goal is and how the means to it work, the adult reduces the assistance given and changes from very directive help to suggestion and encouragement. The adult needs to take less and less responsibility for the successful performance of the activity as the increasingly competent learner takes it on. The developmental task is to move from other-regulation to self-regulation (Brown *et al.* 1983); eventually the child provides his or her own scaffolding.

If there is, as this account implies, a gradual transition from other-regulation to self-regulation as the child moves towards the upper part of the ZPD and becomes able to do independently what previously could only be done with assistance, it follows that there will be changes in the best form for assistance and other-regulation to take. Early in the learning cycle, assistance will be elaborate, explicit and frequent, as when the child is instructed through a close sequence of small steps. Later, assistance will be more abbreviated, less explicit and less frequent, with hints such as 'OK, what else could you look for?' rather than instructions such as 'Get the big yellow one that's over there'. Optimum assistance adapts itself to the learner's successes and failures (Bruner 1983; Tharp and Gallimore 1988; Wertsch 1978, 1979, 1985a; Wood 1980, 1988; Rogoff 1995, 1998, 2003; Chaiklin 2003). The validity, and the educational implications, of this model of fostering cognitive development will be discussed in Chapter 5.

4.3.7 Socio-cultural contexts of development

I must make some reference to the fact that Vygotsky saw his work as a 'socio-cultural' theory of psychological processes. He emphasised that children pick up the socially constructed psychological tools that are available to them, and that these, superimposed on organic development, 'form a single line of socio-biological formation of the child's personality' (in Lee (1985): 74). Thus there will be both cultural and historical patterns in cognition. He used the ethnographic material on cultures that was available to him to investigate these issues, but also used parallels between development in the child and socio-historical development. His colleague A. R. Luria, for example, went in the early 1930s to remote parts of central Asia where the mechanisation and collectivisation of agriculture were transforming the traditional peasant economy and way of life (Luria 1976). His intention was to compare the cognitive processes used by non-literate 'unreformed' peasants and those who were participating in more modern ways of life. He did find some of the differences predicted by Vygotsky, for example illiterate and uneducated peasants sorted objects by their appearance and use (as young children do) while schooled respondents preferred more taxonomic sortings, but considerable controversy arose over the extent of the differences (see e.g. Cole and Griffin (1980)), and even more over their interpretation (it was politically unacceptable to 'denigrate' the peasants by saying their thought was 'childlike'). Part of the problem was the lack of a detailed theory of the cognitive structure and processes provided by and required by the traditional peasant culture. A functional sorting of local artefacts is not self-evidently less useful than a taxonomic one. The sufficiently successful basis for the arrangement of objects in my kitchen cupboards, for example, is largely based on functional attributes such as 'vulnerable to mice', 'delicious but bad for us, keep out of easy reach', 'used here together'; taxonomic classifications (except those isomorphic with the perceptual characteristics of size and weight) are secondary. It seems quite likely that many of the cognitive processes that we take for granted as part of the normal repertoire of skills have become so as a result of us having been schooled in them, and using them in our everyday activities (see e.g. Cole and Means (1981), Rogoff (1998, 2003), for discussion of this).

4.3.8 Activity

The concept of 'activity', which appears in Vygotsky's writings but has been developed since by Soviet psychologists, is of importance here (Davydov and Radzikhovskii 1985; Kozulin 1986; Wertsch 1981; Zinchenko 1985; Kozulin 2003). Socially meaningful activity must be an explanatory principle and a basic unit of analysis in psychology. It is also seen to be a generator of consciousness, and activity mediated by psychological tools and interpersonal communication produces the higher mental functions. The analysis of activities must include consideration of their goals, and their embedding in the social context, for as social structures and processes influence what practical activities are engaged in, and these activities determine cognitive development, ultimately social consciousness and the modes of production (Vygotsky's was an explicitly Marxist theory) determine psychological development. Different cultures (and subcultures) have different activities and different goals; an individual's cognitive activity operates within both cultural constraints and cultural amplifiers, including cultural differences in the way the ZPD operates (see Cole (1985), Rogoff (1990, 1995, 1998, 2003), Stigler, Schweder and Herdt (1990), Valsiner (1988a, 1988b), Winegar (1989)).

As Hundeide (1985), Mellin-Olsen (1987) and other educators have pointed out, the pupil's definition of an activity may differ radically from the teacher's, with resultant difficulties in their learning. As Tharp and Gallimore (1988) argue, the who, where, what, why and when of activity settings need to be considered. It may be more important to examine patterns of differences in cognition than the generalised and abstract models of Piaget and the information-processing theorists have supposed.

Thus Vygotsky's work contrasts with the approaches of Piaget and the 'information-processors' in its insistence on the relevance of the social, cultural and historical milieu to the individual's cognitive development. It also makes a far more incisive analysis of the learning process, and so is of great importance to educators, both in and out of school. There will be some further discussion of what families and schools do to help children learn and develop cognitive skills in Chapter 5, but I will just mention here an apparent paradox. If neo-Vygotskian 'scaffolding' of socially meaningful activity is the best way of helping learning, and schools do rather little of it (not least because it requires a teacher–pupil ratio of approximately one to one; a pretty detailed diagnosis of what skills exist, which are potential, and how to teach each one; and a very sensitively implemented teaching programme over an extended period of time – not the conditions that the ordinary school provides), how is it that schools are at all successful?

One obvious way out of the paradox is to say that schools are in fact *not* at all successful, and certain reviewers of the educational process do indeed take this position, though their proposed remedies range from de-schooling (e.g. the argument associated with Ivan Illich) to a far more authoritarian and didactic use of school time (e.g. various pronouncements by MPs), via an increase in neo-Vygotskian schooling (e.g. Tharp and Gallimore 1988). I have no sympathy with this position: schools seem to me to be remarkably successful under difficult conditions, though they might indeed be more successful if they could be more Vygotskian. Another solution of the paradox is to assert that there are ways of learning that involve less scaffolding by a teacher, and indeed there obviously are, in the various 'conditions of learning' described in so many classic educational textbooks (e.g. Gagné 1985). The 'Piagetian' model used in early childhood education (see Meadows and Cashdan (1988) for a critical discussion) and the traditional rote learning that Tharp and Gallimore (1988) attack so intensely are, in their contrasting ways, methods of learning, and even of facilitating cognitive development. What is interesting here is the relationship between different ways of learning. Might it possibly be the case, for example, that an early history of good scaffolding, so to speak, 'sets up' learners to become their own scaffolders, so that they can both take their own rote learning and mechanical information-processing 'beyond the information given', and act in a Piagetian mode as never-ceasing equilibrators, continually seeking a deeper and broader and more flexible understanding of their worlds?

Chapter 5

Causes of change and variation in cognitive development

This chapter is concerned with *causal* accounts of change and variation in cognitive development. It focuses on biological, environmental and social processes and events that might be thought to produce cognitive development. It is concerned with the basics of the 'how' questions: how is cognition assembled during childhood? What internal and external factors influence the way in which cognitive behaviour develops and how do the developmental processes work? How do an individual's genes and experience interact during cognitive development? It is not a satisfactory answer to such questions, though it may provide a very early sketch map of what sort of terrain will have to be covered. It is not satisfactory for several reasons: in the first place there are my own inadequacies, but beyond that there is the two-strand problem of incomplete description and inadequate theory that characterised even the material on 'what' children's cognition is, which I discussed earlier in this book. 'How' questions, questions of cause, are notoriously harder to answer than descriptive 'what' ones. 'Cause' itself is an elusive and difficult concept; we are going to need to consider such things as what are the events or processes on which cognitive development is conditional, which are *sufficient* causes (all that is required for it to proceed), or *necessary* causes (essential but perhaps not the only thing required) or *contributory* causes (useful, but neither necessary nor sufficient). Distinctions may also have to be made between predisposing factors, precipitating factors, and factors that, once development is on its way, sustain, reverse, limit, amplify, diminish or otherwise modify it. There may be overdetermination, belt and braces and safety pins all, co-operatively or independently, holding up the developmental trousers. We must also recognise that for something as complex as cognition there will perhaps be multiple causation, many factors involved in ways that may vary from person to person and time to time, so that the 'life histories' of cognitive development in different people may be substantially different in what event or process was significant and when. There will be chains of causes: X causes Y, but is itself caused by W which is caused by V which is caused by etc. How far we trace these chains back to the First Cause will depend on many factors: time, persistence, how good the data are, what we consider to be 'real' causes, how many unknown processes we can tolerate between 'cause' and 'effect'; and throughout we will achieve a much more satisfactory account, and have an infinitely better potential for therapeutic or educational intervention, if we consider *how* these causes work.

Understanding development is one key to understanding how biology works, how experience works and the interaction between biological predispositions and environmental information. The general picture is as follows. Human children incorporate (metaphorically) evolved behavioural dispositions just as they incorporate (literally) evolved body structures. Development is a result of genes within environments. Genes exert their effects in fixed programmes that are coded in the DNA of the genotype, and in open programmes that are open to environmental influence and prepared to acquire information from experience. Open programmes may progress using what is experienced only to fine-tune development (experience-expectant) or may be open to more radical influence (experience-dependent). The structure and function of the developing brain are determined by how experiences shape the genetically programmed maturation of the nervous system. The social world, and especially the caregiver, is one crucial source of experiences; these trim or enable genetic potentials by neuronal growth and neurotransmitter production. During critical periods in the early years psychoneuroendocrinological fine-tuning affects the workings of the brain – which may be particularly associated with the current interpersonal experiences of the infant and then with future interpersonal expectations, experience and emotion. What we need to do is to examine how all this happens, co-ordinating our levels of description as far as we can.

Much of the work on cognitive development to be found in the literature is of little use in tackling the 'how' questions. Some of it is concerned only with a 'what' question: what differences are associated with age differences? The 'differences' themselves may be suspect if they come from cross-sectional comparison of samples that are not really equivalent; all too many comparisons of children with 'adults' draw their 'adults' from the population of undergraduate students without considering whether they represent the total population of all adults in the same way as children drawn from ordinary, that is non-selective, schools represent the total population of all children. Age difference data do not in themselves tell us anything much about why there are these differences, let alone how the younger children develop to become like the older ones. At best such data map out what has to be explained; good descriptions of what is the same and what has changed in each successive level provide what has to be explained and thus indicate what the 'how' answer must be. (To take one extreme, if there are *no* age differences, the 'how' will either identify an early completion of development or processes that maintain a stable state, or both.) Age difference data may also serve a useful function by showing that a cognitive process we take for granted in adults is problematic in young children, and thus needs to have its development examined. Piaget's demonstration that young children had difficulty with conservation is an example of this, though his ideas about developmental processes have perhaps stood up better to later work than his age differences description; so many 'age differences' have subsequently been whittled away by demonstrations of very early competence.

Although a case can be made that the causes of 'development' are different from the causes of 'individual differences' (e.g. Anderson 1992; Scarr 1996), I think that part of the problem here is a discussion of development in terms of universally applicable patterns and processes. If there is a cause that applies in the same way at the same point in every individual case, it will be hard to spot precisely because it is so all-pervasive. What we need as well as universals, I think, is an account of *variation* in development, so that we can illuminate how development generally happens by examining development in exceptional cases (as is being done in genetics, where anomalies causing pathological development have proved much easier to identify and understand than the genes associated with more subtle variations that are all within the 'normal' range of behaviour or structure). Cross-sectional age difference data tend to be weak on this sort of examination too; they may set up 'the (normal) five-year-old' and 'the (normal) ten-year old' without much interest in (or even much acknowledgement of) those children who do not fit into the neat age-related patterns. This is understandable, given the difficulty of distinguishing between real individual differences and measurement error, but this sort of 'tidying-up' of data cuts out cases that, by being exceptional, provide good opportunities for investigating the processes that account for deviations from normal development. Radke-Yarrow (1991) makes a powerful argument for a disciplined use of case studies of small samples: such a method would allow investigation of how development proceeds in context and in relation to other aspects of development, and how it is patterned over time.

Correlational data will be helpful in understanding development but do not of themselves answer causal questions. A correlation between A and B does not establish that A causes B, or that B causes A: A and B might be independently related to a third variable, C. For example, in the school age population there will be a positive correlation between height and reading ability; but clearly reading well does not make you grow taller, nor does being tall cause you to read better; rather both height and reading ability are associated with age, the latter via the accumulation of learning and experience for which age stands as an indicator. If A invariably precedes B, that does not establish that A causes B, nor does a lack of A invariably preceding a lack of B establish a causal relation, though this may tell us more than a correlation would. If we have both, plus a finding that supplying the missing A (by training or other intervention) leads to the development of the *B* that would (we suppose) otherwise have been missing, we begin to have a strong case for *A* causing *B*. But we still need an account of *how* the causal chain worked. It will be clear by the end of this chapter that we are not very well provided with either good data or good theory on the 'causes' of cognitive development. Though strong cases have been made in certain areas (for example, the role of phonological awareness in learning to read, of the failure of development of a cognitive coherence mechanism in autism, of mother's use of child-contingent language in language development), it is not yet clear whether these separate islands of causal explanation can be brought together, just as there is uncertainty at the descriptive level over whether there is cognition in general or whether there are more or less autonomous cognitive skills developing separately.

This chapter does not impose a false unity on this heterogeneous literature. It readdresses some of the material used descriptively in the earlier parts of this book to look for *explanations* of how and why cognitive development proceeds as it does. The amount and quality of the relevant material vary enormously. Many different disciplines are potential sources, but there are few interdisciplinary investigations to help bring coherence to a vast, patchy and ambiguous array of evidence. The section necessarily reflects the nature of the literature: it is heterogeneous and uncertain and its efforts at integration are tentative. It begins with an introductory account of work on brains and cognitive development. Although some theorists interested in cognition argue that its 'hardware' level is irrelevant to its 'software' (Anderson 1992; McShane 1991; Marr 1982), like some others interested in cognition (Churchland and Churchland 1990; Churchland 2002; Piaget 1971b), I believe that what *can* be said about cognition is that it is strongly associated with what the physical nature of the brain is, and so the more we seek to understand what current neuroscience implies for cognitive development, the better. Discussion of brain development is followed by a brief look at genetic influences on cognitive development, and at the ways in which factors in the physical environment such as diet and lead pollution can be seen to influence children's cognition. These comparatively physiological sections are followed by a move to the social side of the 'nature–nurture' controversy, with discussion of some aspects of people's social experience. The last major concern of the section is the impact on children's cognitive development of the educational efforts of adults, especially their parents.

5.1 Brains and cognitive development

As neuroscientists continue to make exciting discoveries about how the brain develops and how it works, I think it becomes more and more necessary for psychologists to consider what the impact of discoveries at this level should be on psychological models of cognition and of cognitive development. Some discussion of these issues is the business of this section; I shall leave aside for the moment what ideas should be transmitted in the reverse direction. I feel some hesitation in undertaking this task, given millennia of disagreement about mind–brain relationships, the complexity of the neuroscience evidence and the speed with which it is being refined, revised and elaborated, and our distinctly partial accounts of cognitive behaviour, let alone the problems of linking different areas of research that have extremely different methodologies. However, it does seem essential to try to convey the excitement and importance of understanding brain, cognition and cognitive development together and better. I will not, for reasons of lack of expertise and space, go into much detail on the physiology or anatomy of brains, preferring to refer readers to other sources. Those whose formal education in biology ended early, and indeed anyone who would profit from a thoughtful overview of a vast amount of knowledge, should begin by reading and thinking about J. Z. Young's *Philosophy and the Brain* (1987). Changeux (1987) gives a clear and elegant account of 'neuronal man' and proposes an interesting model of the neuroscience–cognition interface. P. S. Churchland (1986, 2002) writes elegantly on what a 'unified science of the mind–brain' should consider, and P. M. Churchland (1989) also comments on cognitive neurobiology. Greenfield (1996) provides a beautifully illustrated account of nervous systems' structure and biological functioning. Gregory (1988) is of great interest to the general reader, and offers several brief articles on relevant topics, notably a very clear account of 'brain development' by Colwyn Trevarthen. Touwen (1998), Joseph (2000) and Nelson and Bloom (1997) also discuss child development and neuroscience. Spelke (2002), Johnson (1997, 1998) and De Haan and Johnson (2003) write for psychology students, and Goswami (2004), Byrnes and Fox (1998) and Blakemore and Frith (2004) all provide introductory accounts for educationalists. As always, chapters in the *Handbook of Child Psychology* (including Johnson (1998)) are useful reviews.

5.1.1 'Mind' and brain

There has been debate for hundreds of years about the nature of 'mind' and its relation to the brain (for a useful book of readings see Lycan (1989)). The advances made in the physical sciences have led to the success of a model of the world as explainable in terms of physical systems of mindless particles and forces, mechanically interacting and without individual meaning. The workings of our own bodies are rather successfully described in these mechanical and material terms; just as we do not need any longer to explain thunder in terms of the gods' anger or heat in terms of the immaterial spirit 'phlogiston', so we do not need to postulate the existence of an *élan vital* to explain the properties of living organisms, though as we have seen such explanations remain common among children and adults.

However, we experience ourselves (and normally other people and sometimes other animals (Byrne and Whiten 1988; Griffin 1976)) as capable of being conscious, free, morally responsible, rational agents, not just 'meaningless' physically ordered collections of atoms. At the core of the 'mind–body problem' is how to reconcile these two views of the world, to cope with the anomaly of our consciousness, our subjectivity, our capacity to have mental states that refer to something in the world other than themselves, and our sense that 'mind' can cause physical events (as when for example we decide to stop writing and prepare lunch, or to ignore our hunger for a little longer in order to get the mind–body problem out of the way) as well as physical events causing mental ones (seeing, hearing, feeling euphoric because of a drink, and so on), in an otherwise material and mechanical world.

5.1.2 Idealism, dualism and materialism

One solution to this anomaly verges on denying the material nature of the world, viewing it all as a mental construct existing only in one's mind. In this 'idealist' stance, the only thing I can be sure exists is my own collection of mental states, which includes, presumably, an impressive degree of imagination ranging from a sense of having a body that is getting hungry to a recollection of Dr Johnson's comment on Bishop Berkeley's idealism *and* of where to look it up – or imagine I am looking it up, perhaps. (In Boswell's account, he and Johnson talk of this 'ingenious sophistry to prove the non-existence of matter, and that every thing in the universe is merely ideal. I [Boswell] observed, that though we are satisfied his [Berkeley's] doctrine is not true, it is impossible to refute it. I never shall forget the alacrity with which Johnson answered, striking his foot with mighty force against a large stone, till he rebounded from it, "I refute it *thus*"' (Boswell [1791] 1979: 122)). An extreme idealist theory does cope with the mental–physical problem (by denying the independent existence of the physical world), with the world-reference problem (since there is no world outside our imagination) and with subjectivity (since that is all there is). I think it might be hard to give an account in these terms of our different degrees of consciousness, including both its changes and its stability. It also gives rise to some interesting moral problems: could I justifiably feel complacent at the range and detail of my imagination, and what responsibility would I bear for having imagined the genocidal activities of the Nazis and other political persecutions, for example? But ultimately it fails because of its implausibility and, as Dr Johnson points out, the stubborn evidence of our senses that our mental states have to do with material objects. Idealism, in this sense, and science are probably not capable of coexistence.

Thus there are two main alternatives: 'dualism', that there are two distinct kinds of entity in the world, the material and the mental; and a form of 'monism', 'materialism', that mental and physical processes are of the same kind, and that ultimately mental processes are physical. Dualism is not so easily dismissed as idealism, though the problem of how mental and physical, being completely different entities, can interact at all, let alone effectively, is an enormous one. Dualists assert that there is a distinctive *mental* aspect to the mind that is not reducible to physical terms. Some dualists deny that the mind is identical with the brain and think of the mind as a sort of non-physical substance, independent of the body in that it survives it after death, though mind and brain interact causally while the brain is intact (we saw children apparently reasoning like this, pp. 173–174). To dualists, the laws of neuroscience, which describe how the brain works, need have little or nothing to say about how the mind works, because mind and brain are different substances. The very distinguished neurophysiologist, John Eccles, for example, asserted dualistically that there is a self-conscious mind, operating under the higher-order rules of the mental world, monitoring and directing the material and mechanical brain. The non-material mind has the ideas, the emotions and the spirituality, while the brain is a rigidly operating machine doing nothing particularly glorious and certainly explainable in much the same sort of terms as a complex mechanism (Eccles 1989; Popper and Eccles 1977). In effect what he (like those dualists to be found in the general field of artificial intelligence (AI)) is doing is ignoring or trivialising the complexity of the structures and mechanisms that neuroscience is finding in the brain. AI specialists may conceivably be justified in concentrating on cognitive functioning rather than on the physical objects that allow or produce such functioning. However, I feel myself (and see also Churchland and Churchland (1990), Churchland (2002)) that they would be wise to keep an eye on what better accounts of the physical substratum might have to say about limitations or facilitations of particular ways of functioning (why there seem to be quantity and time constraints in short-term memory but not in long-term memory, for example). Neither Eccles nor anyone else gives a good account of the non-material mind and its interactions with the physical.

I don't think we will get very far as scientists (or even as ordinary people) if we separate the cognitive system into a higher-order glorious mind and a crude material brain composed of different substances. Even the subtlest mental events – reasoning, moral feelings, political and aesthetic judgements – can be affected if the brain is affected by drugs or lesions. In addition, it is non-parsimonious to postulate two sorts of entities when one kind might do. For these reasons, and because it is becoming clearer and clearer that the brain, although mechanical in the sense of being describable in terms of physical structures and material processes and subject to scientific investigation, is enormously complex and beautifully organised, 'substance dualism' looks as though it is not viable, and not necessary.

Similar problems arise for another version of dualism, 'property dualism'. Property dualism is more viable, however, or at least is still being more vigorously asserted. The argument is that there are properties of mental functioning that cannot, in principle as well as in current fact, be reduced to physical functioning. Subjective experiences, for example, are produced by the brain and can in turn affect the brain but are not themselves identifiable with any physical properties of the brain: feeling happy, or believing that Napoleon was Emperor of France, are *mental* phenomena that cannot be adequately described and explained in terms of brain states. While this is true of what we can do at present to describe many 'mental states' and 'mental processes', an increasing amount of evidence links specific 'mental' activities to specific physical events in the brain, as I will describe. The debate may perhaps be taken to be about what is the 'best', that is, best documented, most fertile, most intelligible level of description; to do this implies recognising both that changes in our knowledge may lead to changes in which description is 'best', and that there are interesting questions to be asked about the relationships between levels. Neuroscience is showing us, in fact, more and more reasons to assert a monism that goes as far as saying that mentality is not separable from the brain. *All* observed mental activities are associated in time with some corresponding cerebral activity. In comparatively simple cases, for example when the finger is pricked by a pin, we can describe the physical processes that ensue in the nerves of the spinal cord and the brain and the 'mental' feeling of pain (see Wall (1985)). In more complex cases, we cannot yet specify what these physical processes are, but the rapid advances of neuroscience give reason to hope that we may sometime do so. Indeed, Wall's interesting account of 'pain and no pain' provides an argument against dualism by showing that there are variations in the relations between 'input' of stimulation at the periphery of the nervous system and 'output' accounts of what sort and amount of pain is being felt where, which cannot be explained in the dualist terms of a clever interpretative mind monitoring the mechanical proceedings of a simple material brain. The findings of recent neuroscience investigations are showing us more and more about the cerebral events that occur with mental events. For example, when we recognise a face and name its owner there is a fairly constant succession of activation in particular parts of the cortex, first in cells that seem to specialise in face recognition and then in 'naming' cells (see Perrett *et al.* (1985), Young (1987: 125–128), Johnson (1997, 1998)).

It seems sensible to refuse to separate mind (and consciousness) from the brain because consciousness incontrovertibly requires a functioning brain. If the brain is not functioning at all, the individual has no mental events at all; if the brain's functioning is disturbed (for example by damage in particular areas, or by abnormalities in neurotransmitters, or, temporarily, by drugs or alcohol), consciousness and mental functioning are also disturbed. These disturbances tell us, in fact, a lot about both brain functioning and mental events (see below). We do not have any evidence of disembodied minds that, independent of brains, control bodies (or indeed anything else, despite the claims made for 'psychic' or paranormal phenomena). There can be brain functioning without consciousness, if not, perhaps, without any mental events at all. Our brains are ceaselessly active, functioning, for example, while we are asleep, and even when we are awake, they are doing all sorts of things that we are not conscious of at the time, which we may indeed find insuperably hard to become conscious of. For example, we have great difficulty in becoming aware of many of our cognitive processes (see elsewhere in this chapter and in Chapter 2), and much of the information that we know is only called up when required, or only appears when a particular part of the brain is stimulated.

Research on the organisation and functioning of the brain and the nervous system is suggesting a degree of complexity and interrelationship between different parts that rules out very simple models. The sort of reductionism that dualists object to – claims that mental functioning can be entirely explained in terms of a few simple synaptic connections or waves of electrical activity or changes in the amount of a particular brain transmitter or stimulation and response within a single cell – now looks unsatisfactory from the basis of the neurosciences' evidence as well as from the basis of asserting the complexity of mind. Brains just are not simple straight-in/straight-out machines where one thing leads rigidly to another. Rather, they have a number of elaborate 'programs' (Young 1978, 1987) for action that interact and develop over the lifespan, and come into play on the basis of more or less internally modulated rhythms or as demanded by the needs of the moment in ways that assist in keeping the individual alive and, preferably, prospering. All living involves selection and choice, and thus, to be at all efficient, learning, that is, the remembering of experience and its organisation into whatever degree of coherence is possible and useful. Living things that react to a variety of stimuli in various ways may need to have mental activity, and in some cases consciousness or even self-awareness, to be able to use their programs for surviving and reproducing, particularly perhaps if they are social beings (Humphrey 1983). Conscious experience and cognition are closely associated with brain activity; they are not things, even 'mental things', that can exist apart from it. They are characteristic properties of some but not all brain activities, and vary in character according to which parts of the brain are most active; they are not reducible to microlevel processes in a preparation of brain cells. The evidence is more and more of integrating links and interconnections between brain parts that had been thought to function separately. Searle (1984) draws the analogy between mind and brain, on the one hand, and the liquidity of water, the transparency of glass, or the solidity of wood on the other. The surface features of liquidity, solidity and transparency are *caused by* the behaviour of microlevel elements (the interactions between water molecules, the structural relationships of wood or glass molecules); they also *just are* features of those sorts of microlevel elements in those sorts of systems. We can usefully have scientific definitions in terms of the surface features (e.g. liquidity) as well as scientific descriptions of the microlevel elements (e.g. a water molecule). In fact we need both because their descriptive ranges are different; we cannot, for example, reach into a glass of water, pull out one molecule and say 'This one's wet' or 'This one's at 10°C', though such things can be said of the larger system, the water in the glass. The microlevel explanation is neither better nor worse than the macrolevel one. An account at any level of description can be an adequate explanation unless information in terms of other levels of description is needed to clarify the account, to remove ambiguity or prevent misunderstanding (cf. Wittgenstein 1976).

Searle's argument about the 'emergent' quality of mind brings us back to the possible usefulness of our present descriptions of minds. One focus of debate here has been the validity or falsity of 'folk psychology', the common-sense view that most ordinary adults hold about what human cognitive activity is and how it relates us to the world. As folk psychologists, we believe that we each have a mind,

> a unitary, integrated 'control centre' which receives, evaluates, intelligently manipulates, and stores information from the environment, sets goals in the light of the information, designs means for achieving them, and directs the bodily actions by which these means are executed. Our minds, we believe, perform these many different functions, encompassing many different volitional, affective, and cognitive states and processes. An ingredient of this concept is a distinction between an inner subjective realm of sensations, emotions, desires, intentions, plans, beliefs, fantasies, dreams, hypotheses, and other mental states, processes, and events on the one hand, and outer, objective, merely physical existence on the other.
>
> (Forguson 1989: 4)

This characterisation of 'minds' has served us quite well over millennia of social life; but currently debate centres on whether the categories of folk psychology, particularly its emphasis on logical processes and intentional states, are correct characterisations of mental states, and on whether they can be reduced to categories at the neurobiological level of description. One important stream in this complex and often heated debate is 'functionalism'. Much influenced by the computer metaphor for thought, functionalism focuses on cognition as symbol manipulation, and on the syntactic rules that are used to transform one abstract symbol into another. A strong contrast is made between the logical operations on symbols, which are seen as interesting, and the causal relations among the physical states of the computer (machine or brain) which is implementing the logical operations, which are seen as irrelevant, since it is assumed that any mechanism could do the job: human neurone, silicon chips, or old beer cans, if suitably put together, would be functionally equivalent (and equally uninteresting to the functionalists). The core idea of functionalism is that mental states are characterised in terms of the abstract causal relations to environmental input, to other internal states, and to output. Being 'in love', for example, is a mental state that has characteristic causal relations to one's own behaviour, such as giving especial care to one's appearance, writing more poems than usual, rushing to the ringing telephone if there is any possibility that the Beloved is on the other end; to other, internal, states, such as one's beliefs about the Beloved, desire for the Beloved's presence, indifference to others who are normally of some interest, intense emotionality; and to external input, for example a heightened attention to all Beloved-relevant stimulation (and a tendency to see all stimulation of whatever sort as evocative of him or her). How these patterns or characteristic causal relations are realised – in male or female matter, or in nonhuman matter of some sort – is unimportant to the functionalist, whose interest is in the cognitive system in its own right. This stance, of course, is necessary for those who hope to use computers and other machines to model human cognition (pp. 278–295). It is also justified by the true assertion that there may be something important in common if not in the 'being in love' at least in the 'mate seeking' of a human, a chimpanzee, a stickleback and a spider, though there might be different neural events and processes in each species; or indeed that there might be different neural events underlying the 'being in love' of two different humans or of one human on different occasions (King Henry VIII in his successive liaisons and marriages, for example). The argument of multiple realisability, of the same mental relations being instantiated or realised in many differentiable ways, with human central nervous systems being only one sort, reduces the importance of knowing about how human brains work. Neuroscience can only tell us about engineering details – chemical, structural, electrical or molecular – for one particular embodiment of the functional relations that make up brain states, and is therefore seen by the philosophical functionalists as a less useful level of description than cognitive psychology, which focuses directly on the functional organisation of cognition (Pylyshyn 1980).

I feel, for obvious reasons, sympathetic to the view that we continue to need investigations of mental life at the psychological level, that psychology cannot be reduced to neuroscience. However, the functionalist position that neuroscience is *irrelevant* to understanding cognitive functions seems to me to be rash in the extreme. In part, this is because our main alternative access to what functional mental states and processes we have is through folk psychology, the 'common-sense' assumptions listed by Forguson (1989: 4) and vigorously debated by a number of philosophers (e.g. Churchland, P.M. 1989; Churchland, P.S. 1986, 2002; Dennett 1987, 1995, 2003; Fodor 1983; Forguson 1989; Stich 1983; Davis 2004).

The 'homey generalisations' of folk psychology (Churchland 1986), however rich and complicated, are not necessarily so perfect as to need no revision. Cultures differ in their 'folk psychology'; a person's 'folk psychology' changes in the course of his or her development (p. 211); there have also been historical changes in folk psychology, for example a decline in its use of explanations involving possession by demons to account for unacceptable or inexplicable behaviour, and an increase in materialist explanations or metaphors – 'it really gets on my nerves'. Further, folk psychology runs into both philosophical problems and problems of discrepancy with the evidence of scientific psychology. For example, folk psychology assumes that we have more or less direct and correct access to our mental states, that we have 'awareness'. But we have not managed to produce a clear account of what 'awareness' is, let alone what 'consciousness' is (Greenfield 1996), and introspection has many times led people to pronouncements about their mental activities that other external evidence suggests cannot be correct (e.g. Churchland 1989; Nisbett and Wilson 1977). Nor is it impossible that even such complex states as 'awareness' may (in the future) be elucidated by neuroscience, which could help clarify the phenomena that folk psychology is unclear about by reformulating them in more scientific terms. Folk psychology may continue to be what we use in our everyday dealings with other people – it has been used for these purposes for many many more years than scientific psychology or neuroscience has, so its comparatively greater success here is not surprising – but it may be misleading when we are seeking a scientific understanding of mind or brain or cognitive development.

There remains considerable and often heated debate about the nature of 'mind' and its relation to brain. Being neither a philosopher nor a neuroscientist I can do no more than alert readers to this problem, refer them to other discussions (e.g. Blakemore and Greenfield 1987; Bunge 1980; Churchland 1986, 2002) and proceed to questions about how the brain system works in cognition and cognitive development. These are dealt with from a pragmatic view on the mind–brain relation: that ideas, beliefs, memories and so forth are associated with, perhaps attributable to, physical events and structures in the brain.

5.1.3 How the brain works: some important points

J. Z. Young (1985, 1987) emphasises that the brain contains in some form of record all the information that makes possible the actions of our everyday life, including cognition. He points out that all living things have the fundamental purpose of continuing their lives and do this by using what he calls 'programs', instructions for complex sequences of physical changes that deal with information from past and present, from the body and its environment, in order to keep things going or developing. At all sorts of levels in the brain there are programs for functions such as breathing, sleeping and waking, producing coherent language, perceiving particular shapes and orientations (including face recognition), remembering, evaluating, and so on. Brains react to outside sensory stimulation, but their activity is not simply a reflection of this outside stimulation. The brain sometimes seems to have one particular locale that is crucial to running a particular function, for example the reticular formation deep in the core of the brain is crucially involved in sleep–wake cycles, but input from and output to other parts of the brain are also involved in the minute-by-minute running of the program. Increasingly, neuroscience is identifying both the individual parts that are crucially involved in serving a particular brain function *and* the 'democratic' way in which they operate together with other parts. This is a difficult enterprise but one that is progressing rapidly.

The methods of examining activity in normal brains as they work on cognitive tasks include gross electrical recordings, such as electroencephalograms (EEGs) and event-related potentials (ERPs), which involve recording from electrodes placed on the subject's scalp. These have the advantage of being non-invasive (so there are fewer ethical problems about using them on children for research purposes) and of considerable accuracy about the timing of brain activity in relation to stimulation provided by the researcher. (I discussed some research on ERPs and intelligence earlier, pp. 218–223.) On the other hand, the recorded electrical activity is a composite of activity over different areas of the brain, which makes it difficult to clarify localisation of function. Imaging techniques are better on localisation but not so good on timing. Magnetic resonance imaging (especially functional magnetic resonance imaging, fMRI) uses differences in the magnetic properties of substances in the brain to create images of (for example) shifts in blood flow in particular areas, which are believed to be correlated with the level of brain activity in these areas. This technique allows comparison of pictures of brain activity resulting from different combinations of cognitive tasks, with differences in brain activity indicating which tasks activate different brain areas. For example, Posner and Petersen (1988) asked their subjects to look at real words, pseudowords or word-like strings of letters, nonwords, and strings of letter-like forms. All these tasks activated the same area of the occipital lobe, but the real words and the pseudowords activated a further area, and the real words additionally activated regions of the left frontal lobe that are also involved when the task involves defining a word. When the subjects had to process the words phonologically, areas of the left temporal lobe and lower parietal lobe were activated. This technique can show with great precision how different areas of the brain are involved in complex cognitive tasks: the problems have been less precise information about the timing of brain activity, the cost of the equipment, and a more invasive, scary and unpleasant experience for the subject, who has to lie unmoving inside a noisy tube while a giant magnet scans the brain. Obviously, this may be particularly difficult for children. Further, it is not always straightforward to interpret changes in energy use or blood flow in the brain in terms of cognitive activity. Spelke (2002) comments that neuroimaging studies have provided 'rich and useful' descriptions of the neural activity that accompanies psychological functions that are already well understood on the behavioural level, but have been more 'variable and inconclusive' in describing functions that are less well understood psychologically.

However, as cognitive neuroscience advances, an enormous and increasing amount of new information about the brain will show how we should model cognition. We now know for sure that specific elementary cognitive functions are associated with specific regions of the brain, but that beyond the simplest level the picture is of several different areas of brain working together (as in the example of reading in the previous paragraph). Global distinctions, for example between a 'left hemisphere' specialised for 'logical' or 'sequential' processing and a 'right hemisphere' that is holistic and creative, turn out to be myths. We also know that brain functioning is often parallel rather than sequential, that functions may end up as fairly modular and separable having started off as interactive, that there is an enormous amount of interconnectivity within the brain. We know that the brain often does more processing than the minimum required for success on a task, for example the visual system has separate areas for colour, contrast, movement, texture and so forth, which are all used in recognising an object even when some of them are redundant. We know that brain functioning is probabilistic, so that not exactly the same combination of neurones may fire each time a task is done, and not exactly the same areas of brain will be involved for different individuals. There is variation between normal human brains just as there is variation between normal human hands or feet or teeth; the same basic patterns for almost all of us but subtly different details of finger length or tooth spacing that may sometimes be relevant to function but often are not. The length of my fingers or the breadth of my hands, for example, may affect how successful I am as a concert pianist, but not how successful I am as a singer or a drummer or a writer; nor will they be the major contributor to my success as a pianist (see Chapters 2 and 3).

It is clear, then, that the characteristics of brains may be crucial to determining what cognition is and what cognitive development is. The millions of nerve cells in the brain are connected in extraordinarily complex networks not necessarily confined to adjacent areas of the brain. The brain is always active, though individual cells may show no activity at a particular moment, and somehow the *pattern* of activity, of connections between nerve cells and impulses circulating in time between them, signals to our brains which alternative version of a program will keep us functioning optimally at the moment. Brains also develop over time, responding to activation from genes and messages from other parts of the central nervous system, and also to the stimulation that they receive and seek out from the outside world.

This sort of system for dealing with information has some important characteristics worth noticing, some of which differentiate it from at least the present generation of computers. It is ceaselessly active; much of its activity is endogenous; even when it responds to the outside world its response reflects the modulation of ongoing neural circuits as well as the information coming from outside; it selects its input; it has the capacity of keeping itself alive and functioning; it uses parallel processing; it has an enormous ability to learn; its learning and functioning are related to its evaluation of what is best for its genotype. It is also dependent for its actions on receiving signals from both the outside world and endogenous changes in hormonal state. It is the composer of its own music, the conductor, the orchestra, and even much of the audience. There is probably little point in asking *why* brain functioning is like this, as answers can only range from 'it just is' to *post hoc* discussions of, for example, the greater evolutionary usefulness of such a system. But there are all sorts of interesting questions about exactly how the system works and what the system's workings imply for behaviour and development. It is some of these questions that I want to address for psychologists now, by looking a little more closely at some examples of relatively well-documented structure and functioning.

5.1.4 An introductory description of the brain

It is outside the scope of this book to go into detail about the anatomy, physiology and biochemistry of the brain. Greenfield (1996) provides an accessible, well-illustrated picture book, or see Gregory (1988), particularly the section on the nervous system. Byrnes and Fox (1998), Goswami (2004) and Johnson (1997) describe some of the methods for examining brain activity that are revolutionising our understanding. What follows is a very brief and introductory description.

Brains are made up of neurones, which we can think of as doing all the cognition, and glia cells and the vascular system, which are the support system. Glia cells are important for regulation and repair in the brain throughout life. Astroglia cells link the neurones and the microcapillaries of the blood system, providing a constant and precise supply of the glucose and oxygen the brain needs. Brains use a very considerable amount of energy, and with recent developments in technology for observing living brains as they work we are just beginning to see which areas of the brain are metabolising glucose for activity while doing a particular task.

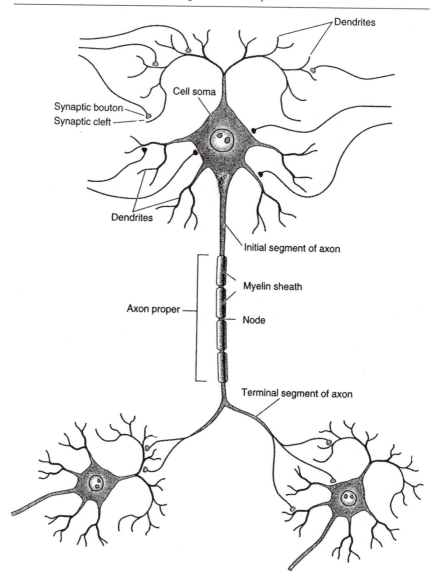

Figure 5.1 The basic structure of nerve cells: schematic drawing of neurone showing axon, dendrites, synapses and glial cells. Adapted from Kingsley (1996).

For our purposes the essential cells for cognition are the nerve cells or neurones. Figure 5.1 shows their basic structure. Neurones are large as body cells go, with a cell body that has many filaments of tissue protruding from it, the dendrites. One protrusion is longer than the others, and this is called the axon; it may be as much as one metre in length. Nerve fibres from one neurone link it to many other neurones, the fibres running between each other in a complex network such that each neurone sends out thousands of fibres that join up with other neurones' central cell bodies and axon and dendrites, and each neurone is covered with thousands of nerve endings from many other neurones. These connections are functional and change as is useful throughout the life of the brain.

The central nervous system integrates signals between nerve cells. Signals consist of impulses that pass from the cell body along the nerve fibres. A neurone becomes active under the influence of many factors, such as the chemical conditions of its local environment, the pattern of excitation and inhibition it is receiving (and has just received), and its characteristic threshold of excitability. Any given neurone, therefore, may be receiving both excitatory and inhibitory messages from thousands of other neurones, and would send signals on to many others. This involves complex patterns of organisation: convergence of nerve endings from many other neurones on to one neurone, and divergence of nerve fibres from one neurone on to many other neurones, and lateral inhibition, emphasising complexity and contrast.

When the electrical impulses of a signal come to the end of a nerve fibre they reach the synapse, a minute gap between the nerve ending and the cell body or dendrites of the next cell. Here a chemical substance is released into the synaptic gap, and these 'neurotransmitters' react with receptor sites on the outgoing side of the synapse, on the post-synaptic neurone, to change the excitability of the neurone and perhaps transmit a further electrical signal to further synapses and further cells in more distant parts of the network. This transmission across the synapse depends on whether the signals from the neurone before the synapse can excite the post-synaptic nerve cell, but transmission can also be prevented by inhibitory signals that weaken or block the signals from the first cell on the incoming side of the synapse.

There are many different neurotransmitters, among them acetylcholine, noradrenaline, dopamine and various hormones and peptides. In some cases a particular neurone activates a particular neurotransmitter, so, for example, cholinergic neurones synthesise and emit acetylcholine, but the various neurones in a chain of nerve fibres may emit and be acted on by different transmitters. Some functions are carried out by parts of the nervous system working together using the same neurotransmitter throughout, for example dopamine is secreted by the neurones concerned with waking the brain from sleep. Other functions are carried out with many neurotransmitters; for example, contraction of the muscles of the alimentary canal involves acetylcholine, noradrenaline and many peptides.

There are connections between the sensory organs (such as eyes, ears, receptor cells in the skin and joints), via the cells of the peripheral nervous system, to the central nervous system (the brain and spinal cord), and outwards from the brain to muscles to allow control of posture and movement. Not all the information that receptors receive is passed on to the central nervous system's highest levels. Activation at the receptors is first processed in them and subsequently at various levels of its progress through the central nervous system. Light signals on the retina, for example, are transformed into electrical signals that pass up the optic nerve and through a succession of 'relay stations' to the visual cortex at the back of the brain. If an unchanging light falls on exactly the same cells of the retina for long enough they eventually cease to be activated by it, and no further signals are sent to the visual cortex until the light changes. Even if information coming from the receptors reaches the brain and results in output signals back to peripheral parts of the body, it may not become conscious; much information about body posture, for example, comes in and is automatically acted on so that we remain upright without having to 'think' about it. To give another example, the brightness of the daylight around us affects our activity levels and emotional states; exposure to bright artificial light stimulation on dull days has become a therapy and a preventative for some cases of depression.

As there are about 10^{12} nerve cells in the brain, as these can be signalling at various levels of intensity from total inactivity to a rapid propagation of large bursts of activity, as they each have very many connections to other nerve cells, as they use a number of different chemical neurotransmitters, and as their firing is organised in time as well as in space, the total pattern of nervous activity in the brain can be seen to be very complicated. The 10^{12} neurones consist of comparatively few different types, and synapses look even more alike; thus it will be hard for anatomical investigations to tell one from another in the branching, interlacing tangles of fibres. Additionally, no two brains will have identical patterns of connections. However, with recent advances in the technology of the neurosciences, enormous progress is being made into discovering how this 'total pattern' is set up and works. Researchers have reached a fairly advanced understanding of how comparatively simple neural circuits work in invertebrate animals such as the sea slug, *Aplysia californica*. They have also made great advances in studying the connection patterns that underlie some of the simpler reflex actions of vertebrates, and in the arrangement of brain cells into maps of the sensory information received from the eyes, the ears and the skin. The functioning of the brain is known to be dependent on its structure; different nerve pathways lead to predictable changes in reflexes, stimulation of particular parts of the brain leads to particular specific sensations or hallucinations, and surgical lesions to the brain or damage to it, for example from accidents or strokes, lead to changes in functioning that vary according to the area damaged. Structure is also dependent on functioning, as my later discussion of brain development in the next section emphasises. There are closely similar and very orderly patterns of neural connections from one

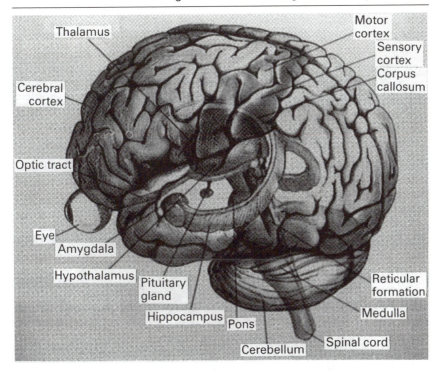

Figure 5.2 The anatomy of the brain (1): schematic drawing showing the left cerebral
hemisphere and the limbic system. From Bloom *et al.* (1985); © by
Educational Broadcasting Corp. Used with permission of W.H. Freeman
and Co.

part of the nervous system to another, so that even if individual neurones
differ a little they are of the same class overall. The details of the circuits
are, as we will see, the result of normal stimulation and functioning of the
growing system during development. Abnormal stimulation will produce
major changes in the connection pattern and consequently in how it functions, and in neurotransmitters.

So far we have talked about neurones and patterns of neurones without
considering the anatomy of the brain. Figures 5.2 and 5.3 show its gross
structure. It is essentially an enlargement of the head end of the spinal
cord. Moving up from the spinal cord we find the hindbrain, the medulla
oblongata and the pons. The cerebellum develops outwards and backwards
from the hindbrain, the midbrain lies immediately above and in front of it,
and the cerebral hemispheres lie around and above all the rest. The left and
right cerebral hemispheres are the familar grey convoluted structures that
we all think of as 'brains'; they are divided into the frontal lobes (which lie
behind the forehead), the temporal lobes (behind the temples), the parietal
lobes (top back of the head), and the occipital lobes (back of the head). The

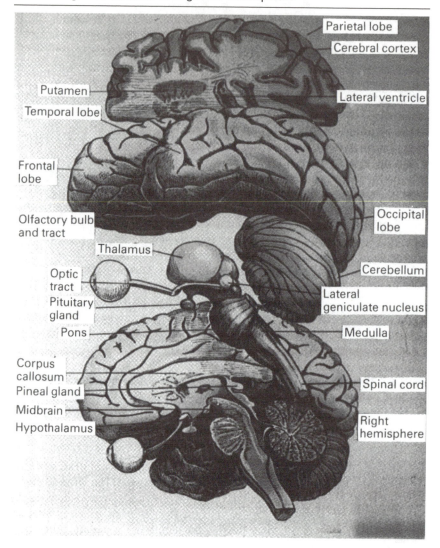

Figure 5.3 The anatomy of the brain (2): schematic drawing showing the internal structures of the brain. From Bloom *et al.* (1985); © by Educational Broadcasting Corp. Used with permission of W.H. Freeman and Co.

nerve cells over much of the cerebral hemispheres are arranged in columns with six layers; vast numbers of nerve fibres run into and out of them and there are millions of connecting 'interneurons'. There are comparatively few types of cells; the cerebral cortex is built up of very many instances of a small number of basic elements. Connections run into the cerebral cortex from the sensory receptors and the lower parts of the brain, and between the two hemispheres, and between different areas of each hemisphere, and to the midbrain, cerebellum and brain stem.

Normally the left cerebral hemisphere is the leading partner in many cognitive activities. It dominates in speech, in language comprehension and in right-hand learned skills such as writing and sewing; it controls the right-hand side of the body. The right hemisphere, associated with the left-hand side of the body, is better at shape perception and hearing non-verbal sounds. However, normally the two hemispheres work together, and neither monopolises any cognitive activity. They are linked by a thick bundle of nerve fibres known as the corpus callosum, and through the brain stem lower in the central nervous system. The two hemispheres can be induced to show evidence of their different 'preferred' capacities in patients where the corpus callosum has been cut (as a treatment for severe and persistent epilepsy), but normally information about the world is constantly reflected to all parts of the brain.

The world provides us with a massive amount of stimulation. The brain selects among this input, emphasising one sort and playing down another. Some of these selective biases are 'wired in' prior to any experience, for example the human infant's selective attention to human voices, faces and smells, but we also learn to attend to or to ignore particular sorts of information. Stimulation of any sort that could become conscious passes to the thalamus, in the midbrain, and from there to the appropriate area of the cortex, where each sense has its own primary sensory area. Each primary sensory area in the cortex is surrounded by its secondary sensory area, and is connected to it by its nerve fibres. Each secondary sensory area is connected with the corresponding secondary sensory area of the other cerebral hemisphere, with all the other secondary sensory areas in its own cerebral hemisphere, and with the association areas, where various kinds of sensory information are elaborated and integrated into a meaningful whole. The different association areas are interconnected and connected to the motor areas, which themselves have connections from the thalamus and from other parts of the cerebral cortex.

Thus there are areas of the cortex specialised for vision (in the occipital lobe), for hearing and for smelling (in the temporal lobe and pyriform cortex), for touch (in the convolution or postcentral gyrus which runs, roughly, from ear to ear), and so forth. In these areas there are orderly 'maps' of incoming stimulation, for example several maps of the retina in the visual cortex. These preserve information about the spatial pattern of visual stimulation. The different maps tend to be concerned with different aspects of the stimulation, for example one may deal with its orientation, another with its colour or movement. Activity in these maps has to be precisely co-ordinated, but organising perception into separate units allows comparatively economical neural networks to function efficiently. Localised processing of a simple characteristic of stimulation such as size or colour is co-ordinated with other processing as required by the task at hand, so that it is widespread cortical activity that makes up complex cognition, even if simple cognition could be said to be localised.

The hypothalamus is a small area in the midbrain under the thalamus. It organises body metabolism and controls body temperature, the states of being awake or asleep and of being aggressive, afraid, and sexually aroused. But the cerebral hemispheres may also be involved in these feelings, assessing their meaning and deciding on a programme of behaviour that may involve modification of stereotyped automatic responses organised in the hypothalamus. Body temperature may be kept constant, for example, by responses such as sweating in which the hypothalamus is the crucial organiser, or by a cerebrally mediated response such as getting up to turn the air conditioner on. Areas of the temporal lobes and a number of other areas including the hypothalamus seem to be involved in emotional states and behaviour, with hormones in the local blood supply being particularly important. The whole of the brain is supplied with blood, which provides it with oxygen, glucose, hormones and other necessary substances. The brain controls the secretion of hormones by the endocrine glands, and is itself subject to the action of these hormones. What we usually think of as 'emotion' and what we usually think of as 'cognition' are not completely separate brain functions.

Although I have been emphasising the interconnectedness of brain structure and of brain functioning, it is probably helpful to an initial understanding of the brain to indicate a few of the relatively localised functions of the brain. The various kinds of cognitive activity discussed in this book are centred in the cerebral hemispheres. Spatial thinking depends on an area in the right hemisphere between the temporal, parietal and occipital lobes; mathematical thinking on approximately the same area in the left hemisphere. Articulating speech and hearing speech depend on areas in and around the left temporal lobe, and language comprehension and verbal memory on the left parietal lobe. The visual cortex is in the occipital lobe at the back of the head. Social behaviour and mood involve the frontal lobes and the regions around the thalamus and hypothalamus. Damage in one of these areas is likely to impair the relevant type of functioning, but so many areas are involved in cognitive tasks of any complexity – doing arithmetic, for example, involves seeing or hearing numbers, memory, reasoning, verbal comprehension, computation, eye movements, either articulation for a verbal answer or the hand, arm, etc. movements of writing, and quite conceivably emotions of anxiety, complacency, triumph or despair – that any brain damage may have some effect on many tasks, and it will take very widespread brain damage to wipe out any function completely. We learn a great deal from studying brain damage, but inferences to normal functioning are not unproblematic (Mayes 1988; Shallice 1989; Byrnes and Fox 1998).

5.1.5 Brain development and cognitive development

Knowledge of how the brain develops has developed at an accelerating pace over the past century (for reviews of more recent research see Gunnar and Nelson (1992), Johnson (1997, 1998, 2000), Spelke (2002), De Haan and Johnson (2003), Gottesman and Hanson (2005), Scerif and Karmiloff-Smith (2005)). Until quite recently it was supposed that the brain had a set of innately wired pathways, which were modified to a relatively small extent by experience, probably by the history of use and disuse of nerve cell connections. Learning, through the establishment of simple conditions reflexes, added all the elaboration of cognition to the preset biology of the brain. This passive associative model fails because it both underestimates the intercoordinations between nerve cells and fails to account for what is now known about their rich and complex developmental history.

The basic processes of brain development are the induction of neurones, proliferation of neurones and glial cells, cell migration, cell death, cell differentiation, formation of synapses and pruning of synapses (de Haan and Johnson 2003a; Luciana 2003; Johnson and Munakata 2005). Beginning soon after conception, the proliferating cells of the embryo differentiate into a three-layered structure, and the nervous system develops from just a few cells on the outermost layer. Neurones divide rapidly from approximately six to eighteen weeks of gestation. They migrate to the position they will occupy in the mature brain, either by being pushed outwards by more recently developing cells, or by active cell migration in which they find their way by clinging to the long glia cells that radiate from the inner to the outer surface of the developing brain. Prenatally, neural induction, neural proliferation, cell migration, and cell differentiation occur in an orderly way, giving rise to the three-dimensional layering of the brain. Once in their final position, neurones differentiate, for example developing a particular pattern of branching of dendrites, longer or shorter axons and more or fewer synapses. This happens at different times in different areas of the brain; in some areas this sort of development continues to puberty or beyond. The pattern of dendritic branches, axons and synapses affects the quantity and quality of the signals that neurones receive and pass on to other neurones. As development proceeds, there are bursts of synaptogenesis in which many more axons, dendrites and synapses are formed, followed by pruning leading to synaptic stabilisation and rearrangement; these are at different times in different brain areas. Cells shrink and die off in the embryo even while proliferation and migration are at their height, and programmed cell death continues throughout foetal development. This probably allows for correction of errors during cell division, could play a role in the elimination of transitory areas whose usefulness is now past, and could allow the number of nerve cell connections to match the size of a target. Synapse formation and pruning also begin prenatally and continue into adulthood, with the usefulness of particular connections being a major force in their survival or deletion. Neurotransmitters probably play a role in signalling to the immature brain which connections should be kept and which pruned out (Whitaker-Azmitia 2001); a failure of neurotransmitters to develop properly may possibly be a contributor to developmental disorders such as autism and Down syndrome. In some cases, the achievement of the maximum density of synaptic connections is associated with a major development in some aspect of cognition (Luciana 2003). However, there is a great deal of cognitive development, and continuing change in links between synapses, at times when there is not rapid change in either brain structure or brain metabolism. After puberty, although new synapses are still formed, synaptic elimination works to stabilise the neural circuits that have been activated by experience and ensure an optimal balance between excitatory and inhibitory neurotransmitters that modulate neuronal activity within cortical networks (Paus 2005).

The idea of 'critical periods' of brain development implies that the brain must have particular experiences within a short time period of development if it is to be able to develop and function normally; that if the experience comes earlier or later it will have no effect. There are some examples of this in the development of the visual cortex, largely documented from studies of visual deprivation of animals (Banks and Salapatek 1983; Johnson 1998). For most cognitive functions, and in humans, it is probably better to think of 'sensitive' periods rather than 'critical' ones, since some learning is still possible even after deprivation in most cases. Findings in cognitive neuroscience also suggest that notions of the brain being 'ready' to learn some specific skill may be problematic; many brain areas appear to be fairly fully developed long before they come to be used for the functions they serve in a mature brain, and some cognitive functions are run by different brain areas in the immature and the mature individual, without being seriously compromised (Spelke 2002). There is debate about whether overall brain size predicts cognitive development once all other factors have been allowed for. A recent study (Gale *et al.* 2004) found that head size (an approximation to overall brain size) at eighteen weeks of gestation and at birth did not predict IQ at age nine years, but head size at ages nine months and nine years, and rate of head growth between these ages, did. Babies who were breastfed, and the babies of more educated mothers, had faster head growth between nine months and nine years and higher IQs. This pattern of findings suggests the complexity of the relationship between brains and the environment, which I return to later (pp. 357–373).

The neurones that integrate nerve impulses from different parts of the nervous system develop patterns of connections and of activity even in the earliest months, before birth. They transmit substances that play a key role in the regulation of nerve cell growth and differentiation throughout the developing brain (and can play something of the same role if implanted into adult brains that have been damaged). By the time the embryo is eight weeks old, and the cells that will develop into the neocortex appear, the lower parts of the brain have already developed an elaborate structure on which further growth is based. The embryo nerve cells interact with each other's genetically controlled messages, with the hormones and growth substances produced by cells, with nerve impulses conducted through the network of nerve connections, and with input from the wider environment provided by the mother's body. Though to begin with nerve cell interactions are generated by activity that is intrinsic to the brain, it is the timing and patterning of external stimulation that plays a major role in determining the precise detail of neural networks, editing, sorting and pruning connections. This creates the basis for detailed perception, elaborated representation and refined cognitive programmes that enable mastery of experience. Development such as this goes on throughout childhood (and perhaps throughout life), with continuity between the early mechanisms of brain growth and the later mechanisms of learning from experience, with brain tissue continuing to be self-organising. Different areas of the brain reach maturity at different ages, so that a particular task may be associated with one area of the brain early in life, and later in development other areas may be implicated in the task. The cerebral cortex is a late developer. Its nerve cells are not distributed in the fully adult pattern until six months after birth, and dendritic connections are not fully mature until adolescence. Many of its features, including a degree of left–right asymmetry and possible lateralisation from this, have developed before birth, but some psychological functions (memory is a possible example) have to be carried out in 'stopgap' ways prior to the maturation of the brain part that serves this function in the adult brain. There are, however, many 'pre-adaptations', where brain structures seem to be in readiness for action before they are needed (Singer 1986; Tees 1986; Goldman-Rakic 1987; Greenough and Black 1992; Johnson 1997, 1998; de Haan and Johnson 2003a; Luciana 2003; Byrnes 2004; Byrnes and Fox 1998; Dong and Greenough 2004).

Another important area of postnatal brain development is the growth of an insulating sheath of myelin around nerve fibres, a process that continues throughout infancy and childhood and into adolescence. Myelinisation leads to faster and more efficient conduction of nerve impulses, and thus of sharing information between various brain areas. This may contribute to more precise and streamlined cognition (Johnson 1997, 1998; Paus 2005), and perhaps may contribute especially significantly to changes in executive control and social cognition (Paus 2005). Although it is not yet well understood, our understanding of the part that myelinisation plays in cognitive development may be advanced by advances in neuroimaging techniques.

I have been focusing on neuroscience, and emphasising that the multiple connections in the brain are laid down during development and elaborated by endogenous changes in the brain and by experience. A brain system does not work in isolation, even before the developing brain has fine-tuned its interconnections by its experience. Brains have social and emotional functions as well as cognitive ones. Some parts of the brain are specialised for social behaviour. Parts of the frontal lobes, again comparatively late in their maturation, are involved in attention to the feelings and emotions of other people. They are linked to areas of the brain concerned with emotion, and are the areas that were lesioned in radical leucotomies and lost in the famous case of Phineas Gage. Both Gage and leucotomised patients were insensible of the effects of their behaviour on other people, as if the effects of social learning had been lost. The crucial point is that the human nervous system develops in a social context and under the influence of a genetic endowment that allows individuals to function as members of a social group. As Trevarthen (1988a: 108) neatly says:

> the state of morphogenetic regulators in an immature organism depends upon the affections and interests of more mature conscious beings, and upon the way the brains of these beings from the preceding generation have been programmed with cultural rituals and beliefs in an earlier childhood. Growing human brains require cultivation by intimate communication with older human brains.

A total understanding of the brain and its cognition must allow for this fact: models using the metaphor of brain-as-computer will be deficient insofar as they do not do so.

5.1.6 The brain's learning and remembering

In Chapters 2 and 4 of this book I discussed some of the psychological models of learning and remembering and their development. These models were, on the whole, descriptions of people's behaviour, not of the 'mechanics' of memory. Here I am concerned with some recent neuroscience studies of what happens in an individual nerve cell or a system of such cells when an organism learns, remembers and forgets.

All animals contain a complex memory record in their DNA, a memory that guides their development within the environments they encounter without, so far as we know, being itself modified by those encounters. This DNA-based memory has the content it does because it has enabled the animal's ancestors to behave in ways that allowed their reproductive survival, ways that are therefore likely to be adequate in future environments not too drastically different from the ancestral ones. (Thus 'evolutionary psychologists' theorising about cognitive development (see e.g. Finlay *et al.* (2001), Suddendorf and Whiten (2001), Fischer and Yan (2002), Carruthers (2002), Reader (2003), Cummins (2004), Keller (2004)) can argue that understanding the 'environment of evolutionary adaptedness' may make useful contributions to understanding modern humans.) Virtually all animals are also capable of at least elementary forms of learning, of a behavioural plasticity that means they can react more effectively to the details of the situation that arise, adapting their remembered programme of action to what is demanded of them on each occasion. This learning probably involves changes in the connections between nerve cells such that useful pathways are selected from the earlier multiplicity of pathways. It is likely that there are short-lived changes in the electrical properties of the neurones that correspond with the changes in behaviour known as the short-term memory system (STM) or working memory. Long-term memory probably involves much more permanent modifications in synapses and nerve cell circuits, including changes in how many synapses there are and in the biochemistry of the neurotransmitters involved in the network. Obviously it is hard to study exactly what is happening in human brains, but similar forms of elementary learning and memory are found across a wide span of the phylogenetic scale. Where plasticity is lacking, or goes wrong, there may be a developmental disorder (Dong and Greenough 2004).

It appears (Bailey and Kandel 1985; Teyler and Fountain 1987; Johnson 1997, 1998; Siegler 2005) that many sorts of learning result from alterations in how excitable nerve cells are and alterations in connections between synapses, particularly through alterations in the strength of already existing connections by modulations in how much chemical neurotransmitter is released. As an organism habituates to a repeated stimulus, there are changes at the presynaptic connection of the sensory neurone on to the motor neurones. Development determines the presence of contacts between sensory and motor neurones, but not the strength of the connections. In habituation, short-term memory involves a transient depression in synaptic efficiency, and long-term memory (lasting for days and weeks, maybe lifetimes) a functional inactivation of previously existing connections, so that habituated animals have fewer active zones with less transmitter released at each. Similarly, sensitised and conditioned animals have enhanced synaptic transmission between sensory neurone and motor neurone, with more zones active, each of which is bigger and emits more neurotransmitter. The chemistry of learning involves a complex sequence of chemicals, resulting in more neurotransmitter flowing in the case of sensitisation and less in the case of habituation. As a long-term change this may possibly include an alteration in how the genetic material can express itself and the subsequent synthesis of chemicals. Similar changes involving selective changes in the efficacy of synaptic connections (long-term potentiation or LTP) seem to occur during the learning processes of animals such as the fruit fly, the octopus, and the rat, and to last for long periods relative to the length of the life of the animal; it seems at least possible that they occur in the much more complex brains of humans and other primates.

The success of neuroscience studies in demonstrating synaptic changes has been considerable. There has not so far been as much progress in the extremely complex task of specifying how changes in different neural pathways become related, as they must do if we can call up the same piece of information to different questions, or if we integrate information from different sources, or if we generalise from one piece of learning to a more universal principle. There is no one particular area in the brain that is the memory store. Although parts of the neocortex are probably involved in the storage of the results of complex learning, and the hippocampus may be involved in memory integration, it seems that memories are stored in the parts of the brain as multiple representations that mediate the perceptions on which these memories are based. There might be multiple memory systems in both working memory and long-term memory, cf. Rumelhart's parallel distributed processing (Rumelhart and McClelland 1986) and connectionist models (pp. 281–283). Such a multiple system might well show the little unevennesses that we may be aware of in ourselves, our good memory for faces and our poor memory for names, for example. Multiple memory representations might help to protect against loss of information. Similarly, declarative memory and procedural memory may operate and be stored somewhat differently. Amnesia (Mayes 1988; Shallice 1989) varies in its effects (as the site of the brain damage causing it also varies), but if the lesions are in the medial temporal region, particularly in the hippocampus, the patients are likely to have a normal short-term memory and to be able to recall a normal amount of information learned long ago, but to have difficulty when required to learn new information or to recall events that occurred at the time just before the amnesia began. Declarative memory is much more affected than procedural memory. Squire (1987) suggests that the crucial areas are necessary for the acquisition and consolidation of declarative memories, in interaction with the cortical association areas where these memory representations are finally stored. Developmentally, declarative memory seems to be a later accomplishment than procedural memory (Bachevalier 1992; Bachevalier and Mishkin 1984; Squire 1987; Schneider 2002; Gathercole 1999; Gathercole *et al.* 2004;   pp. 84–104), which might account for infantile amnesia, the unavailability of memories dating from the first year or two of infancy to the older child or adult.

5.1.7 Learning from experience

There may be interesting analogies to be drawn between learning and the natural selection that occurs during, for example, evolution, and in the working of the body's immune system. If the nervous system does learn and remember by the selection of nerve connections and responses that are useful, and the elimination of those that are not, under the influence of experience, we would expect it to have certain features. Those parts of it concerned in learning should contain a very large number of cells and interconnections, all slightly different; and this is indeed the case. The parts of the human brain most associated with learning, such as the cortex, the hippocampus and the cerebellum, have millions of cells, each of which may receive thousands of synapses; regions such as the hypothalamus, which regulates all sorts of basic physical functions according to innate programmes that work so well normally that they do not need to be modified by learning (though they may be supplemented by a learned system in the cortex, as in the case of body temperature, mentioned elsewhere in this section), have relatively few cells. Cortical cells vary a great deal, too, in what they respond to. In the visual cortex, for example, the young kitten or monkey has cells that innately are most responsive to a particular contour or orientation, but that also respond, to begin with, to other similar stimulation. With visual experience these cells become more sharply tuned and reliable; if the animal's experience is artificially limited, for example by it only being allowed to see an environment of vertical stripes, only those cells that are innately programmed to respond to vertical and near-vertical contours will mature, and those with other orientations will cease to be excitable (Banks and Salapatek 1983; Changeux 1987; Greenough and Black 1992; Johnson 1997, 1998; Dong and Greenough 2004). There seems to be selection by competition, as in this case, and by co-operation, as when simultaneous input from both eyes is necessary for the development of binocular vision cells in the kitten. Young (1987) calls this 'associative synaptogenesis'; it is important because it allows for the development of patterns of cells that record the regular combinations of events that occur in the world, and hence better representations of its regularities, and perhaps its 'affordances' (Gibson 1979).

Greenough et al. (1987) suggest that this learning by selection occurs as an 'experience-expectant' developmental process. The process utilises the sort of environmental information that has been ubiquitous throughout the evolution of the species, and can be relied upon to occur in any individual's experience (unless that individual, like the laboratory kittens mentioned above, has encountered a most unusual seriously distorted environment). Neural mechanisms have evolved that, expecting this normal environmental information, use the input to shape the specifics of neural development. One important mechanism is the innate generation of an enormous number of synaptic connections between neurones, with selection based on experience determining which connections are strengthened and which, so to speak, wither away. The timing of the experience may be crucial. The 'effects' of abnormal experience such as sensory restriction can include impaired behaviour, abnormal neurophysiological development, and less complex morphological development: the degree to which recovery is possible is almost certainly slight at best, though animals such as humans may devise other means of coping with their handicap.

It may seem odd that the evolutionary process has left development dependent on receiving the right sorts of experience at the crucial moment, rather than 'wiring it in'. However, having the genes programme a general outline of what the system should be like, and then taking advantage of expectable experience to get the system finely tuned to environmental details that actually occur, allows for a highly ordered and appropriate pattern to emerge from a much less organised one. Sensory systems seem to start with a strong predisposition to function in a particular way, and if experience is near enough to normal they will do so; while if experience is too far from normal the system will function in an unusual way, usually less effectively, but there may be some compensatory changes in other systems. Myopic children, for example, with less good distance vision, may not find it easy to be expert bird spotters or squash players but are often extremely good at nearsighted or tactile tasks such as reading or needlework (Tees 1986). Goswami (2004) summarises findings of enlarged areas in the hippocampus thought to be specialised for spatial representation in London taxi drivers and enlarged neural representations of the fingers of the left hand in skilled violinists, and functional reorganisation of the sensory areas of the brain in blind people who read Braille. Although the sceptical may argue that people have only succeeded as violinists or taxi drivers because they happened to have brains that could cope with the need to use more than averagely detailed representations in the crucial areas, it does seem possible that brains respond to exercise as other organs of the body do.

Individuals may perhaps differ in various ways, for example the amount of relevant experience they 'expect' or need for adequate functioning, their resistance to adverse experience and their compensation for it, or their ability to produce suitable experience, perhaps through social interaction. 'Neural plasticity' has recently been suggested to be a better basis for differences in g than the 'brain speed' I discussed in Chapter 3 (Garlick 2003; Dong and Greenough 2004). We do not yet have much in the way of neuroscience investigations of individual differences, apart from some very interesting clinical studies; but behavioural studies of, for example, temperament and stress and the child's ecology are suggesting differential vulnerability and strength that may have a biological base (e.g. Garmezy and Rutter 1985; Rutter, 1988, 1992; Cicchetti 2003). Reader (2003) and Reader and Lefebvre (2001), in a study across species, finds that individuals who have a low level of fear of new events, a high level of interest in new events, and a high propensity for social learning are particularly likely to make innovations, show flexible behaviour, use a variety of tools, and have larger association areas in their brains.

As well as the experience that can be reasonably expected to occur regularly at a particular period in virtually everybody's life, so that 'experience-expectant' learning processes can be set to use it in 'fine-tuning' nerve systems, there are many environmental events that are less consistent in their occurrence or timing, perhaps even being unique to only one individual. Brains need to be able to respond to these sorts of experience too. Animals that interact with a miscellany of objects in a complex environment have been shown to do better at a range of cognitive tasks than those reared in the dull, indeed sensorily deprived, cages of the typical laboratory animal (Greenough and Black 1992; Greenough et al. 1987; Dong and Greenough 2004; Reader 2003); comparisons of the brains of rats reared in standard and more complex environments show that the latter probably have more synaptic connections, particularly in the visual cortex but probably also in other cortical and sub-cortical regions. Active interaction with an interesting environment can increase synapse numbers in adult rats (including 'middle-aged' ones) as well as in the developing young, and the experience of being trained on tasks such as maze-running probably also brings about specific morphological changes in the brain. It seems to be possible for experience to give rise to synapse development even at quite late ages, perhaps by synapses being formed quite rapidly as a result of neuronal activity and surviving in so far as they fit the appropriate pattern of connections (Dong and Greenough 2004): a case perhaps of exercise acting on the brain just as it would on the rest of the body. We do not know yet whether these late-formed synapses are the same or are formed in the same way as those that appear early in development. Early development seems to produce a surplus of synapses that are then pruned back by experience to a useful subset. Later in life synapses seem to be generated in response to experience that provides important information, probably in a more localised way but again involving selective preservation of part of a relatively unpatterned growth. While there are spurts in the generation of nerve cells and connections between them in particular areas, Greenough and his colleagues think it improbable that such spurts are synchronous over the brain as a whole (Greenough et al. 1987: 552–553). Understanding how brain growth proceeds is important as a corrective to simplistic models of cognitive growth.

An asynchronous relationship of brain areas, that is, a staggering of the developmental schedule for different functions, would allow one system to act as a foundation for another, for example early visual and motor skills could act as the foundations for later understanding of spatial relations, the activity of the organism in acquiring and organising experience being of the greatest importance. It could also allow for some 'catch-up' growth rectifying earlier disadvantage. This sort of development would involve subtle variations between individuals who had slightly varying experience (Johnson and Munakata 2005; Scerif and Karmiloff-Smith 2005); it is what Gottlieb (1983, 1991) calls 'probabilistic epigenesis' rather than completely predetermined genetic blueprinting.

Psychologists studying people's remembering behaviour have found it useful to distinguish between different sorts of memory, for example 'episodic' and 'semantic' memory, or 'long-term memory' and 'working memory' (pp. 84–104). The hippocampus seems to be crucial for response timing and working memory (Mayes 1988; Shallice 1989). It is also thought to be important in the remembering of temporal and spatial relations between events and objects, needed in building up a 'cognitive map' of the environment (O'Keefe and Nadel 1978; Teyler and Fountain 1987; Young 1987; Goswami 2004; Byrnes and Fox 1998). Young (1987) emphasises how relations in time and space between thousands of individual nerve cells form complex representations of useful information in time and space, organised both in terms of associated facts and in terms of useful programmes for action. Some patients suffering from amnesia have impaired memory for facts ('declarative' information) while their procedural memory for skills using those same facts is, relatively, preserved. Remembering how to act through a sequence of behaviour but not how to describe or reflect on or to vary it significantly has been seen as the sort of capacity for representation young infants have (Bachevalier (1992), cf. Bruner's 'enactive' representation (Bruner 1966)). It may mean that it is possible to operate within a limited familiar world but not to retrieve information voluntarily into consciousness, nor to maintain a consciously accessible personal memory (Goodman and Haith 1987). Exposure to lead pollution seems to have an adverse effect on hippocampal development that might partially account for the impairments of learning and memory found in children with high blood lead levels (see below, section 5.3.1). Exposure to carbon monoxide and to other pollutants (Jacobson *et al.* 1984, 1992; pp. 357–361) may have similar adverse effects.

If we summarise what recent neuroscience studies are suggesting to us about how the brain learns and remembers, it seems to be emerging that such processes depend on the possibility of alterations of the connections between neurones, alterations in their sensitivity, efficacy, number, mapping of interconnections, etc.; and that such alterations, both temporary and permanent, occur throughout life. A number of brain centres operate together as a complex system, so that signals from the outside world and signals from other parts of the body indicate whether (and in what way) an action has been rewarding, and so should be learned and repeated, or not. It has recently been argued (Fiser *et al.* 2004) that sensory input from the outside world is not the dominant driver of neural activity in the higher levels of the visual cortex. Repeated visual stimulation with the same stimulus produces variable responses in the visual cortical neurons rather than direct reflections of the visual stimulation. This may not be random 'noise' in the visual system, but rather spontaneous but patterned activity representing the modulation of ongoing neural circuits. Advantageous programmes are more likely to be repeatedly used and smoothly learned and remembered; less rewarding ones tend to fall out of use. The patterns of connections that are set up by a combination of inheritance of general structures and tendencies and fine-tuning of specifics through environmental experience represent the organism's knowledge of the environment, to some degree as a topographical and time-based map, but more generally as a representation that produces the behaviour appropriate to the environmental situation and the organism's evolutionary goals. Memory and learning can be facilitated or upset by stimulation, lesions, drugs, or toxins; maybe by social experience. Normally brains operate as a united system comprising the knowledge and life patterns of the individual. In these brain workings lies the subjective unity of his or her mind and personality.

5.1.8 Brain areas and cognitive tasks

Recent work in cognitive neuroscience is using the techniques I have described to identify the brain areas that are most active in a range of cognitive tasks, allowing comparison with the models derived from experimental psychology. I will very briefly mention work on attention, memory, reading and mathematics.

Simply attending to something in order to process it involves (*inter alia*) alerting to the information, interrupting other cognitive processes, engaging attention to the task, and inhibiting return of attention to it after it has been done. We have seen that these are not simple tasks and that they develop during childhood (Schul *et al.* 2003). The ascending reticular activating system and the prefrontal cortex seem to be involved in the alerting and interrupting functions, the parietal lobes in disengaging attention, the midbrain in moving attention to a new focus (Byrnes and Fox 1998; Rueda *et al.* 2004). Individuals with impaired functioning in these areas may have attention difficulties.

Remembering information is another requirement for education and cognitive development. Again, research in experimental cognitive psychology suggests a model of memory as multifaceted. Cognitive neuroscience (Byrnes and Fox 1998) confirms this. Human memory is distributed across many different brain regions which work together. Even the simplest stimuli can be encoded in different ways and different brain areas are involved in the different codings: for example, visual coding and response to visual presentation of a word activate areas of the occipital lobe, auditory presentation and encoding activate the primary auditory cortex and language processing areas in the left temporoparietal cortex, areas in the frontal lobe are involved in semantic processing and memory. Frontal cortical regions are involved when subjects are asked to think about their own personal history.

We know from experimental cognitive psychology with adults and children that reading involves co-ordinated processing of orthographic, phonological, syntactic and semantic information. Not surprisingly, cognitive neuroscience studies show that a lot of different areas of the brain are involved (Goswami 2004; Byrnes and Fox 1998). There is activity in the occipital-temporal areas when subjects are processing visual features such as letter shapes. These areas are implicated in processing for the word/nonword distinction too. Areas in the left temporal-parietal junction are involved in phonological processing. Areas in the frontal lobes are activated when real words are presented and have to be defined. Dyslexic children sometimes show reduced activity in these areas, and targeted reading remediation has been shown to increase brain activity in them as well as improving reading performance (e.g. Byrnes and Fox 1998; Goswami 2004; Shaywitz et al. 2004). It appears that learning to read can change the functioning of brains. In a study of literate and illiterate women in Portugal (Castro-Caldas et al. 1998), they were asked to repeat words and nonwords. Different brain areas were activated in the brains of the literate and the illiterate women as they repeated the nonwords. Dyslexic individuals may have brains that were always set up in not quite the optimum way for learning to read, or they may have developed brain differences as a result of their different experience of reading: or both.

Again, neuroscience studies supplement the findings of complex processes in mathematical processing. The evolutionarily old system for processing very small numbers and larger sets for relative number (pp. 69–70) seems to be associated with brain activity bilaterally in the intraparietal areas (Dehaene et al. 2003, 2004; Goswami 2004). Other number knowledge is represented in the brain's language system (Dehaene et al. 2004) along with overlearned verbal sequences and memorised poetry. Counting on the fingers activates an area of the parietal-premotor brain that may also be active during more sophisticated calculation (Goswami 2004); calculation may also involve visuo-spatial areas, as if the subject was using a mental image of the number line. Byrnes and Fox (1998), however, use evidence from brain damage and mathematically disabled children to argue that lower-level maths skills are located in the posterior regions of the left hemisphere and higher-level skills are mediated by the frontal lobes and the right hemisphere. No doubt further neuroscience research will resolve this uncertainty.

Spelke (2002) makes the important point that assessing whether young children have mastered a particular cognitive skill is often complicated by task demands that are in principle separable from the skill of interest. We have seen various examples of this in earlier sections of this book: problems in remembering crucial information in moral judgement tasks, distraction in memory tasks, overload in composition, reporting what you see when your vocabulary is not adequate for putting that into words. Neuroimaging can reveal what is going on by using and comparing tasks with little extraneous demand, for example by measuring and picturing the brain activity of people simply looking at displays rather than requiring them to make a verbal report. It can also allow researchers to give the same task to people at different developmental ages, rather than giving 'age-appropriate' tasks and having to translate between them, which can leave uncertainty about whether 'developmental' changes in performance are due to the development of the child or to changes in the tests. Perhaps even more exciting, a collaboration between neuroscience and education might eventually identify the ways in which educational processes and programmes affect brains, and brains influence people's response to educational processes and programmes (Posner and Rothbart 2005), something that could vastly improve formal education and reduce our vulnerability to suggestions that all children need for their cognitive development is a particular food supplement or activity.

5.2 Genes and cognitive development

My discussion of brain development focused on the complex and inescapable interaction of intrinsic and extrinsic factors in cognitive development, on genetic and environmental effects. We know with certainty that development in general is dependent on both genes and environment; we are beginning to know about how differences in either lead to differences in development. I will present here, briefly, a few comparatively well-studied areas of work on the role of genes in cognitive development. Discussion of the physical environment and the social environment follows this section.

I will begin with two unquestionable facts about genes and cognitive development: genes affect cognitive development, much more than the reverse; and the links between genes and cognitive development form a long and complex causal chain. It is extremely important to emphasise the complexity of this relationship, when we research it, when we consider the findings of research, and when we decide how to lead our lives. In this section I attempt to review what we know about how genes affect cognitive development, and also some of the ways in which they don't.

The basic material of human heredity is deoxyribonucleic acid (DNA), the famous 'double helix', which is made up of four 'bases' arranged in pairs. Every human cell contains a sequence of about 30 billion base pairs. These are arranged in the cell on 46 chromosomes, 23 matched pairs, and within each chromosome the DNA is organised as functioning units called 'genes', which are located in definite positions on the chromosomes and function together to control the development and functioning of the organism. The Human Genome Project has begun the mapping of the genes in the human genotype (International Human Genome Sequencing Consortium 2001, 2004; Venter *et al.* 2001; Stein 2004; Ross *et al.* 2005). There are 20,000 to 25,000 gene units, most of them the same in all humans (about 98 per cent are the same in humans and chimpanzees, about 80 per cent are the same in humans and mice; fruit flies have fewer genes, parsley has more). Genes code for the production in the cell of the specific proteins that have to be made in the right place and right amount and at the right time to keep the body functioning properly. Thus they are essential for the development and functioning of the body and the behaviour it produces, both in producing proteins and in regulating the timing of development; but no single gene is sufficient, genes always work in conjunction with other genes and with the environment that they live in. Genes are turned on and off by other genes as the organism proceeds through its life, in response to environmental stimuli.

> The expression of any one gene is embedded within a biological system influenced by a multitude of other genetic and environmental influences; concepts of gene regulation (expression) and epigenesis are now essential for understanding development.
>
> (Gottesman and Hanson 2005: 10.3)

An individual person has a set of genes, inherited from their parents, which is not quite the same as anyone else's unless they have a twin who came from the same egg and sperm as they did (monozygotic twins), or unless a clone has been made from their own genes. These individuals share the same genotype, and will therefore carry the same genes forward to their own children; but their phenotypes, the body and behaviour they develop, will develop to be very much the same rather than absolutely identical because genes affect development in conjunction with the environment, and even the two twins will not have exactly the same environment. There may in any case be some minor randomness in development and even clones or monozygotic twins will not be exactly identical (Edelman and Gerald 1994).

Early in development, cells can change form or function and then transmit that form or function to future cells in that cell line. For example, an undifferentiated embryo cell may be transformed in development into a brain cell which then through cell division gives rise to other brain cells; had it initially differentiated into a muscle cell, it would have founded a line of muscle cells. As the brain cell does different jobs from the muscle cell, it needs different proteins; the genetic instructions for making proteins that are not needed are turned off during development, are not expressed in that cell. This is an example of the developmental process called 'epigenesis' (Gottesman and Gould 2003; Gottesman and Hanson 2005). Some cases of mental retardation arise when genes are not expressed during development in the normal way; for example, when a methyl group is added to cytosine, one of the bases of DNA, that gene is essentially turned off and neuro-developmental anomalies may result (Shahbazian et al. 2002). The impact of early nutrition on diabetes, obesity and cancer later in life may also be mediated by methylation (Waterland and Jirtle 2004).

It may be helpful here to point out that recent advances in medical genetics are revealing more complex patterns of inheritance than Mendelian genetics allows. Mendel's brilliant work was done on an organism, the garden pea, that behaves genetically as he insightfully described: it has two sets of chromosomes with paired instructions for development (it is 'diploid'), which lead to various 'all-or-none' traits (or 'phenotypes') such as pod shape or pea colour, whichever parent the particular gene comes from, with little or no variability between individuals. Things are not quite so simple as this in human beings. For example, the same gene may lead to different phenotypes in different individuals. The condition known as Von Recklinghausen NF 1 involves an abnormal gene on chromosome 17 (17q11.2) (Pyeritz 1991) and most people affected by it have abnormal pigmentation and benign tumours; some but not all have other tumours, skeletal defects, and mental retardation and learning disabilities. It is not yet clear how these effects are produced and why they vary so much between individuals. In some cases (Hoffman 1991; Pyeritz 1991) genetic information inherited from the mother may be expressed differently from the same information inherited from the father, which violates one of Mendel's laws. This phenomenon is known as 'genetic imprinting'. For example, deletion of part of chromosome 15 (15q11–13) leads on to two different syndromes of mental retardation, Prader-Willi syndrome (which includes being food-obsessed, obese and slow-moving) and Angelman syndrome (which includes hyperactivity). People who inherited the defective chromosome from their mothers show Angelman syndrome; people with Prader-Willi syndrome seem mostly to have inherited the defective chromosome from their fathers. In another sort of genetic imprinting, people who inherit Huntington's disease from their fathers tend to develop it earlier in life than people who inherit it from their mothers. A study of Turner's syndrome by Skuse et al. (1997) suggests that the impact of having only one sex chromosome depends on which parent that chromosome came from. It is not yet clear how genetic imprinting works, though the processes of gene regulation in development seem to be involved. Current research mapping the genome (e.g. Ross et al. 2005; Carrell and Willard 2005) will help clarify this.

Finally, the traditional picture of all or none inheritance and 'dominant' and 'recessive' genes needs to be modified. In Mendel's peas, plants that had a +/– combination were the same as those with a –/– pair at the given locus: the – gene determined a trait identically in the heterozygote +/– and the homozygote –/–. In humans, the same 'dominance' sometimes occurs; but more often careful examination shows that there are intermediate levels of change in phenotype. Sickle cell anaemia appears in people homozygous for the HbS gene; those with one HbS and one HbA gene were thought to be unaffected, indistinguishable from people who had HbA/HbA, so sickle cell anaemia was seen as a 'recessive' trait. More recently, people with HbS/HbA, though not anaemic, have been found to have an abnormal phenotype. Two HbS have different effects from one HbS, which differs in its effects from no HbS. It is now also known that the genetic material in the nucleus of the egg and the nucleus of the sperm is not the only genetic material that affects development. The cytoplasm around the nucleus of each cell contains DNA too (mitochondrial DNA), and this too is inherited by the developing foetus. Most of this material comes from the egg, as the sperm is too small to have much cytoplasm. Thus there is a possibility of 'maternal' or 'cytoplasmic' inheritance. Some rare cases of pathological development of the optic nerves arise in this way.

5.2.1 Genetic anomalies and cognitive development

Once we recognise the complexity of the ways genes work in conjunction with other genes and the environment, we can see that there is complexity too at the level of the outcome. Research trying to establish a genetic basis for phenotypic characteristics such as IQ or schizophrenia may have difficulty finding it if the 'high IQ' phenotypes or 'schizophrenic' phenotypes are not all the same. For example, our prospects of finding a genotype for autism are not good because the phenotype of 'autism' is not the same in all those diagnosed as autistic. We do know that certain genetic anomalies give rise to autistic symptoms, and autistic individuals may have evidence of structural brain abnormalities or altered brain architecture or altered immune systems (Baron-Cohen et al. 2000; Frith and Frith 2003; Hill and Frith 2003; Gottesman and Hanson 2005; Scerif and Karmiloff-Smith 2005); these 'endophenotypes' might be easier to link to genotypes and also more useful for explaining how the child's development has been shifted off the normal path. We know from genetic anomalies that there is a sequence or cascade of effects between gene and phenotype, which environments contribute to as well as genes.

Clearly, genes are important in cognitive development. Some genetic anomalies 'mess up' normal cognitive development in ways we are just beginning to understand. More subtle differences in genes, in partnership with other genes and with the non-genetic environment, undoubtedly make complex contributions to development. Understanding these is going to require good data on people's genes, on their environments, and on their developmental histories, and subtle models and methodologies; it will take a lot of effort (and expense); and it will be of enormous political delicacy (Collins 2004; Karmiloff-Smith and Thomas 2003; Scerif and Karmiloff-Smith 2005).

5.2.1.1 Phenylketonuria

Phenylketonuria (PKU) is a well-known disease associated with an identified abnormal gene on chromosome 12 (Woo 1991). The defective gene leads to the absence of a particular enzyme, phenylalanine hydroxylase, which is needed to convert the phenylalanine from protein in the diet into tyrosine. In the absence of the enzyme, phenylalanine cannot be metabolised and used in the body, and cannot be got rid of. High concentrations of phenylalanine result in an excess of chemicals that are normally present only in minute quantities; in the person with PKU they are present at toxic levels. They interfere with the development and growth of the central nervous system; the brain develops normally to birth, but once the baby starts a diet that contains phenylalanine in protein the developing nerve cells are vulnerable, and the connections between nerve cells begin to be damaged and broken down. Reduced brain development and irreversible mental retardation (with severe emotional and behavioural disturbance) result. Thus the genetic anomaly leads to marked anomalies in cognitive development.

However, it does so only in the normal environment, specifically if the PKU baby receives a normal diet. If a special dietary environment is provided during the period of brain development, if the infant is fed on a diet that does not contain phenylalanine, no such excess of deleterious chemicals is built up and the central nervous system can develop more or less normally. The genetic defect is still there, but it has no effect in the special environment where there is little or no phenylalanine. PKU individuals still cannot produce phenylalanine hydroxylase, but if they do not need it to deal with phenylalanine because their diet contains none, they avoid the most serious consequences of their abnormality. Diets that contain even small amounts of phenylalanine may produce brain damage and some cognitive impairment even in late childhood (Smith *et al.* 1990, 1991).

Once brain development is complete, the individual with PKU is not harmed by a normal diet, as the mature nervous system appears to be resistant to the high levels of toxic chemicals that accumulate. However, if a woman with PKU, whose own retardation has been prevented by a restricted diet during her infancy and childhood, takes an unrestricted diet containing phenylalanine during her pregnancy, the baby may be born with severe mental retardation resulting from excess phenylalanine, even though it has inherited the normal gene for phenylalanine hydroxylase from its father. The build-up of phenylalanine in the pregnant woman does not affect her own brain because her mature nervous system is relatively resistant to it, but it swamps the circulation of the developing foetus and causes abnormal neurological development *in utero*. The child's prenatal environment gives it PKU mental retardation, even though it does not itself have the genetic abnormality that leads to PKU (Konner 1982; Scarr and Kidd 1983; Waisbren 1999).

5.2.1.2 Turner's syndrome

Many other rare genetic defects are associated with mental retardation, through, for example, the errors of metabolism that they cause (Volpe 2000; Dong and Greenough 2004; Johnston *et al.* 2003). Some commoner abnormalities also need to be mentioned here. Some individuals inherit not 46 chromosomes, but a greater or smaller amount of chromosomal material. Most surviving individuals with more or fewer than 46 chromosomes have either anomalous combinations of Xs and Ys, or an extra member for chromosome pair 21. One extra X or Y chromosome does not seem to have a marked consistent effect on cognitive development, and may go unnoticed. The recent mapping of the genes on the X chromosome (Ross *et al.* 2005) shows that many genes on the X chromosome code for proteins known to be important to brain function, which implies that knowing more about the X chromosome may make a major contribution to our understanding of cognition (Check 2005). Having only one sex chromosome, an X (Turner's syndrome), probably does lead to cognitive anomalies (McCauley *et al.* 1987; Rovet and Netley 1982; Skuse *et al.* 1997). Turner's syndrome women tend to do exceptionally poorly on tests of spatial thinking such as mental rotation tasks, and they may also do worse on tests such as the Wechsler items Arithmetic, Digit Span, Picture Completion and Object Assembly. Their verbal intelligence is normal. They appear fairly normal physically during childhood, though of short stature, but they do not produce hormones at the normal levels of adolescence and adulthood and are sterile. There could be a number of possible explanations for their poorer spatial ability. Rovet and Netley, and McCauley *et al.* suggest that their missing X chromosome leads to an acceleration in cell division rates, hence faster brain maturation with less lateralisation and less right hemisphere involvement in nonverbal cognitive abilities. Another possibility is a lack of androgenisation in childhood. S. M. Resnick *et al.* (1986) found that girls who had had elevated levels of androgens prenatally showed enhanced spatial ability when tested in their teens; they also engaged in more activities involving spatial manipulation, though this seemed to be a consequence of their high level of spatial ability, not a cause of it. Hines and Shipley (1984) found evidence of greater cerebral lateralisation in such girls. Skuse *et al.* (1997) present evidence that impairment is related to which parent the X chromosome came from.

5.2.1.3 Fragile X

Another chromosome anomaly that leads to abnormal cognitive development, in this case mental retardation, has attracted a great deal of interest recently because advances in techniques for examining genetic material have led to identifying exactly what part of the chromosome is abnormal, and to a rapidly developing understanding of all the steps between genetic anomaly and behavioural differences (Reiss and Dant 2003; Crnic and Hagerman 2004; or Tager-Flusberg (2003) for a briefer account of the syndrome). Fragile X syndrome is the result of a mutation in a single gene on the X chromosome. Where normal individuals have a comparatively small number of repeats of the CGG triplet at locus Xq27.3 (between 6 and 50), in some individuals the number of repeats is unstable and has increased, probably in successive individuals over several generations. In about 1 in 4000 males and 1 in 8000 females there are more than 200 repeats, and these individuals are categorised as having the 'full mutation' for Fragile X syndrome. It is estimated that about 1 in 500 X chromosomes have between 50 and 200 CGG repeats at locus Xq27.3, and these 'premutation' alleles are unstable and tend to expand when transmitted from parent to child; sometimes a premutation allele transmitted from the mother may undergo a massive expansion at locus Xq27.3 and a full mutation may result. Over the past few years, an extensive body of research has been done using modern techniques of brain imaging as well as classical anatomical techniques, and on animals as well as humans (for a review see Reiss and Dant (2003)). As a result, the complexity of the route from genotype to phenotype is becoming clear. The full mutation leads to a reduced production of a protein (FMRP) essential for normal brain development and function (and essential also to some other physical changes). Animal studies show that during normal brain development FMRP is produced at synapses in response to synaptic activation. While the brain is actively developing new synaptic connections, the levels of FMRP in the brain are increased in response to learning and to enriched environments. In the individual with Fragile X, the reduced levels or abnormalities of FMRP cause abnormalities in the neurones, especially in the dendritic spines, which are not formed and pruned in the normal organised way, so that the neurones resemble the immature and untidy connectivity shown in normal individuals at the very earliest stages of development. There are also abnormalities in neurotransmitters. Certain areas of the brain show highly significant increases in volume, for example the caudate nucleus, where abnormalities are known to produce disturbance in attention and working memory, regulation of mood and social behaviour, and flexibility in response to environmental cues. In other areas there are decreases in volume, for example in the superior temporal gyrus which is important in processing complex language stimuli and implicated in the interpretation of face and gaze, and in the cerebellar vermis, which might produce autistic symptoms. Functional imaging techniques examining brain activity in humans suggest that individuals with Fragile X are generally using appropriate areas of their brains in cognitive tasks but are less able to adapt to increased difficulty than are normal individuals. The nervous system in Fragile X syndrome is, perhaps, poorly modulated, with hyper-arousal and problems of inhibition and habituation forming a basic risk factor for autistic behaviour. It may also be the case that levels of FMRP affect the expression of other genes, and thus that abnormalities in how several genes function may contribute to the problems of individuals with the syndrome. There may also be endocrine abnormalities, with Fragile X individuals having abnormal activation of the hypothalamic–pituitary–adrenal axis and higher levels of cortisol and increased cortisol reactivity.

Given the pervasive nature of the nervous system abnormalities in Fragile X syndrome, it is not surprising that Fragile X individuals show a range of cognitive difficulties. The characteristic set of problems includes age-related decline in IQ, abnormalities in executive function and working memory, disturbance in language and communication, deficits in visuospatial processing, hyperactivity, attentional problems and anxiety, perhaps centring on a deficit in the individual's ability to modulate arousal (Cornish et al. 2004a, 2004b). There is some association with autism, with repetitive behaviours such as hand-flapping and an aversion to eye contact with parents (Cohen et al. 1989; Loehlin et al. 1988; Reiss and Dant 2003; Tager-Flusberg 2003; Turner and Jacobs 1983). These difficulties have a complex developmental course, with considerable variation between individuals, including a gender difference such that the severity of symptoms is commonly greater in boys. Tager-Flusberg (2003) suggests that there is an association between the activation ratio of the normal and Fragile X chromosomes and the degree of severity of the syndrome in females (and in those males who have some normal genes for the production of FMRP). Overall, the rate of Fragile X mental retardation in females is about half the rate in males. Fragile X girls with relatively high IQs may show the other problems despite not being mentally retarded. In general there is increasing developmental delay from infancy onwards, with problems of motor control being noticed early but expressive language problems and cognitive difficulties becoming increasingly serious later, and social withdrawal and poor self-esteem emerging in adolescence. The bases of individual differences are beginning to be researched. Reiss and Dant (2003) summarise studies on a cohort of 120 cases of Fragile X. In this group, lower levels of FMRP are correlated with lower cognitive scores and more social withdrawal and distractibility; cognitive scores and social adaptation are positively correlated, and behaviour problems negatively correlated, with parental IQ and the quality of the home environment. In this research the link with environmental influences was especially strong for boys, with parental IQ, which the researchers interpreted as an index of genetic influences, being rather more important for girls. It may be that further research in the near future will use larger samples to clarify how different factors in the genes and in the environment lead to differences in the nature and the severity of symptoms; but it is already clear that there is an interaction of different genes and environmental variations.

5.2.1.4 Down syndrome

The commonest genetic anomaly leading to mental retardation, indeed one of the commonest causes of moderate to profound mental retardation, is

Down syndrome (DS), which affects about 1 in 1000 births. DS individuals mostly have a third version of chromosome 21 because of an incorrect division of the mother's chromosomes during the formation of the egg. Occasionally the error occurs during the formation of the sperm or during the early development of the embryo. In the latter case, mosaicism, not all the cells may carry the defect, and the impairment of the individual will be dependent on the proportion of cells that have the extra chromosome (Coyle *et al.* 1991; Crnic and Pennington 2000; Capone 2001). Because there are three copies of chromosome 21 instead of two, there are extra genes coding for a range of proteins, with wide-ranging and increasing effects on development. The chromosomal anomaly leads to a number of physical anomalies: the characteristic facial features, heart defects, increased susceptibility to infections, and other physical traits. There is also a high incidence of neurological disorders, for example brains that are smaller and lighter and have abnormal convolutions in several areas, a reduction in the total number and density of neurones, abnormal patterns of dendrites connecting neurones, and variable myelination (Capone 2001). The central nervous system of DS individuals who survive into mid-adulthood invariably develops the pathology characteristic of Alzheimer's disease (Coyle *et al.* 1991; Loehlin *et al.* 1988), and there may be genetic links between the two syndromes (Zaremba 1985).

The cognitive abilities and educational achievements of DS children vary considerably. Carr (1985) ventures the following points as a tentative summary, although there are considerable individual differences: virtually all DS individuals are handicapped to some degree, the majority being severely handicapped. There is progressive decline in IQ scores from near normal in the early months to lower scores in the school years (see also Carr 1988); the DS child seems to have particular difficulty in making progress from sensori-motor intelligence to verbal and conceptual intelligence, with perhaps less consistent test performance than a normal child. There are particular problems in auditory processing, memory, language and metacognition (see also Chapman 1997; Snowling and Gombert 2002; Johnson-Glenberg and Chapman 2004; Laws 2004). The overall pattern of cognitive development proceeds through virtually the same sequence as in cognitively normal children but there is less coherence between achievement in different domains and overall achievement falls further and further behind the normal level, particularly if the child is brought up in an institution. Morss (1985) sees this pattern of 'developmental delay' as reflecting poor learning style. DS children seem to need more exposures to material before they learn spontaneously, and to lack cognitive strategies and transfer.

DS children often show marked language delay. This is associated with hearing difficulties (Davies 1985) and preceded by impairments in vocalisation, referential looking and intersubjective communication between infant and mother in the first year of life (Gunn 1985; Jones 1979). Mothers may have a harder time communicating with the DS child because of the reduced eye contact, less synchronicity of action and less alternation of conversational turns that they achieve; mothers' input becomes correspondingly more directive and restricted. The DS child's lesser linguistic competence provokes less stimulating language from the mother, and may thus contribute to further retardation of language and cognition. Their syntactic production tends to be simpler than normal, though semantic and pragmatic aspects of language may be more nearly normal for their chronological age.

Studies of reading skills in DS children are summarised by Buckley (1985) and Snowling and Gombert (2002). Informal case studies and small surveys show a substantial number of DS children learning to read independently and for pleasure (see also Carr 1988). Three intervention studies produced reading skills in advance of the children's mental ages, in some cases up to their chronological ages. Some children appeared to develop spoken language from reading, rather than the reverse, finding learning to deal with written language easier than dealing with spoken language. This reversal of the usual developmental order may be associated with some of DS children's specific deficits: they commonly have hearing defects that would make hearing speech sounds difficult; they have short-term memory deficits for auditory information; they have articulatory difficulties; and they have difficulties linking auditory and vocal inputs and outputs (Boudreau 2002; Laws and Gunn 2002). These deficits would cumulatively make learning spoken language difficult, in so far as phonological processes are involved; possibly DS children are learning to read outside the phonological route from written word to meaning (see Chapter 2, section 2.2). Buckley's own research (1985) shows them making semantic errors, such as 'closed' for 'shut', 'go to bed' for 'sleep', which would support this interpretation of their learning. However, non-intervention-study measures of reading skills show less impressive achievements (Carr 1988).

I have only been able to give a brief summary of work on cognition in Down syndrome, and so have risked simplifying the picture of their deficits and achievements. I must stress that DS individuals vary just as normal individuals do in their cognitive and personality characteristics: some are profoundly handicapped, some can cope with normal schooling and live comparatively independent lives as adults. However, recent research (O'Connor 1987; Stern 1987; Crnic and Pennington 2000; Capone 2001) has begun to specify precisely the difficulties and deficits that are associated with the syndrome. The chromosomal abnormality causes sensory deficits (and probably central nervous system differences) that affect cognitive processes, but the effects of these on achievement involve interaction with environmental factors. Carr (1988) reports a longitudinal study of DS children from six weeks to twenty-one years. Along with the usual profile of a decline in scores from infancy, she finds some consistent sub-group differences: girls score better than boys on both IQ tests and educational tests; home-raised children do better than those reared away from home on verbal ability, reading-level and arithmetic tests, but not on IQ tests; and non-manual socio-economic status (SES) children do very significantly better than manual SES children on language and arithmetic tests, reading accuracy and reading level scores, and non-significantly better on reading comprehension despite their lack of superiority in IQ. Thus, more advantaged backgrounds were producing more skilled children, skilled in advance of their level of general ability and to a degree that could be a source of real pride and pleasure to the children themselves. The 'resilience and courage' of parents was helping these children to satisfactory lives (Carr 1988: 429). It was also demonstrating again the complex intertwining of genetic and environmental influences in cognitive development: the wonderful devotion of these parents was making an enormous positive contribution to children whose genetic endowment put them at high risk of difficulties.

5.3 The environment and cognitive development

I have provided an introduction to brains and genes in cognitive development, which emphasised the effect of the environment on both development and functioning. It should already be obvious that there are many aspects of 'the environment' that are relevant to cognitive development, and that these could do with more conceptual clarification if they are to be investigated successfully (see pp. 442–444). It will be seen that often different environmental factors are interrelated in mutually reinforcing ways. I will be discussing environmental effects one by one, because this is on the whole how much of the research has been done, but trying to link them where there is evidence and where the answers about the 'how' of cognitive development seem to be suggesting related processes. I begin with environmental aspects that are more 'physical' and move to those that are more 'social'.

5.3.1 Pollution and cognitive development

The functioning and the physical development of the brain are subject to environmental influences as well as genetic ones. High dosages of certain substances, for example mercury and lead, are known to poison the nervous system. Some of the substances are, at a low level, common environmental pollutants. It may be the case that they cause brain damage even at low levels, particularly to the rapidly developing brains of children (Johnston and Goldstein 1998; Johnston *et al.* 2003). Lead is one of the best known of these pollutants, and so there has been public concern about its effects, and steps have been taken to reduce environmental lead levels. It is used less in paints, cosmetics and the canning process than in earlier years, unleaded petrol is now available more freely and used by an increasing number of car drivers, and lead water pipes are no longer installed in domestic water systems, though many remain in older housing. However, lead remains a common potential danger to the developing brain, and children may ingest a considerable amount of lead from the air near roads with heavy traffic, from soft water supplied by lead pipes, from plants grown in contaminated soil, from painted objects that they lick or chew, and from dust licked off dirty fingers, dropped sweets and so forth. (An epidemiological study by Wilson *et al.* (1986) examined children's blood lead levels in the lead smelting town of Port Pirie, South Australia. There was a fairly high degree of pollution throughout the town, but the risk of having a high blood lead level was increased fourfold by having a household member working with lead at the smelter, sixfold by having flaking paint outside the house, threefold by being a nailbiter, fourfold by having dirty hands and fivefold by having dirty clothes, both these last two as rated by the child's teachers. Ambient lead dust ingested orally would seem to be the source here.) Which source is most important will obviously vary; there has been some, somewhat circumstantial, evidence that lead from petrol has been a major contributor (Rutter 1983b).

High levels of lead in the body (measured in the blood or the teeth) are associated with intellectual impairment, behaviour problems such as hyperactivity, and, at the highest levels, gross neuropathology. This is why infants who compulsively pick at and chew painted furnishings or other objects ('pica') are doing themselves no good at all. The severity of these effects is greatest at highest lead levels, and decreases as they decrease. The timing of lead ingestion may influence the behavioural effects, through different stages of neuromaturation perhaps (Shaheen 1984). It used to be thought that lead levels below 40 micrograms (μg) per 100 ml in the blood had no adverse effects. Different studies, and hence different reviews, came to different conclusions: Rutter (1983a) interpreted research to that date as showing a consistent small effect of low levels of lead on psychological functioning; Harvey (1984) preferred a verdict of 'not proven' as did Smith (1985). The inconsistent research results may be due to methodological differences, for example in the measurement of lead levels, in demographic characteristics of samples, in the definition of 'high' and 'low' lead levels used, and in statistical analyses. Moore (2003) discusses the methodological difficulties of the field but implies that the interests of industries that would be affected by legislation against lead pollution may have biased both the research done and some interpretations of research. One important complication is that lead level and social disadvantage are correlated, so the associations between raised lead levels and cognitive deficits in children might be due to confounding social and environmental variables. The latter are hard to control and can only be partialled out in studies of large samples using sophisticated statistical techniques. Small samples and simple analyses could not reveal a small but real effect.

Three studies of school children carried out in the past twenty years have made considerable progress towards clarifying what effects lead at low levels may have on cognition. Silva *et al.* (1988) studied 579 eleven-year-olds in Dunedin, New Zealand, as part of the longitudinal Dunedin Multi-disciplinary Health and Development Study. As well as giving blood samples, the children were assessed for IQ and reading, behaviour problems as seen by teachers and parents, and various background variables such as frequent changes of residence or of school, poor family relations or mental health and some characteristics of the mother. These variables made it possible to take social, environmental and background factors into account. The study showed that raised blood lead level was associated with a very small but statistically significant increase in children's behaviour problems, inattention and hyperactivity; though there was no effect on IQ scores, reading showed a small effect of blood lead level. Fulton *et al.* (1987), Thomson *et al.* (1989) and Raab *et al.* (1990) studied 501 children aged six to nine living in central Edinburgh. Here there was a relationship between blood lead level and ability that was still significant after various social and environmental variables had been controlled for, with even comparatively low levels of blood lead having an effect. Again the Rutter scales were used to assess behaviour disorders in the children, and an interviewer collected data on the home background (these data included an ability test for one of the parents). Blood lead levels were significantly correlated with behaviour and hyperactivity even when confounding variables were taken into account. Again, the size of the correlation was not large; blood lead appeared to be having a small but statistically significant bad effect on ability, achievement and behaviour.

The third study (Fergusson *et al.* 1988a, 1988b, 1988c) measured lead level in teeth and measures of intelligence, cognitive ability and attention/activity level in a birth cohort of New Zealand children. Ninety-five per cent of the children born in the Christchurch region of New Zealand in 1977 gave one of their shed first 'milk' teeth to 'the Christchurch Child Development Study "Tooth Fairy"', who sent them each a thank-you letter and 50 cents and assayed the lead level in each tooth. Dentine lead levels were highest for children from socially disadvantaged families, those who lived in old wooden houses (which might have been painted with paint containing lead), those who had lived for a protracted period on streets with high traffic density, and those who had engaged in pica. Children who were high on more than one of these variables tended to have proportionately higher lead levels. Socially disadvantaged children tended to have higher lead levels even if all these variables were taken into account. The authors speculate that these children may have had greater exposure to industrial lead through living in homes with manual workers, or that there may be systematic differences in diet and exposure to dirt (Fergusson *et al.* (1988a), and the study by Wilson *et al.* (1986) referred to earlier).

The Christchurch researchers then correlated dentine lead levels with cognitive and school achievements made when the children were eight and nine, that is, shortly after they had shed and given up the assessed tooth. It was assumed that both tooth and cognitive scores reflected their accumulated exposure to environmental lead. Measures of parents' education, the family's socio-economic conditions, the child's perinatal and educational history, and of aspects of the home environment (including for how long the child was breastfed, the mother's smoking habits, and measures of mother–child interaction using the HOME Inventory) were correlated with test scores as co-variates for dentine lead levels, thus controlling for variation on these factors. As in other studies, lead level was associated with intelligence test scores but the association was reduced to statistical non-significance if the confounding social disadvantage measures were taken into account. Scores on school achievement tests remained significantly correlated with dentine lead. The lead-test correlations remained stable over the period of a year from age eight to age nine. The researchers suggest that this poorer school performance comes about because even the comparatively low levels of exposures to lead in their sample may cause nervous system damage that leads to deficits in attention, which in turn impair long-term school achievement. Their third paper (Fergusson *et al.* 1988c) shows that dentine lead level is significantly associated with teachers' and mothers' ratings of inattentive and restless behaviour (using items from the Rutter scales). The correlation remained statistically significant when confounding variables were allowed for. It is, however, small. In all three papers, Fergusson *et al.* provide an exemplary tabulation and discussion of the strengths and weaknesses of their evidence; they thus provide conviction for their 'opinion that the weight of the evidence suggests the presence of a very small causal association by which increases in lead values are associated with increases in rates of inattentive/restless behaviour' (Fergusson *et al.* 1988c: 822). However, they point out that their data cannot rule out the possibility that the causation is in the opposite direction: that children who are for other reasons restless and inattentive may act in certain ways which increase the lead in their bodies; they might spend less time in the comparatively clean air of home with a good book and more time out on the streets and scrabbling in the dirt, for example. A study of neonatal blood lead levels (Bellinger 1987) suggests that this reverse causal path, though possible, does not destroy the case for lead causing damage. Samples of blood were taken from the umbilical cords of newborn babies, and lead levels from those samples were correlated with later scores on baby intelligence tests; the correlations were small but significant even when confounding variables were taken into account. The 'overactivity causing lead level' sequence presumably would not apply *in utero*. It has to be noted, however, that some other studies (e.g. Ernhart *et al.* 1986) have found only non-significant results in neonatal assessment, and that other pollutants may have similar effects. For example, Jacobson *et al.* (1984, 1992) found that children who had been exposed prenatally to a high level of poly-chlorinated biphenyls (PCBs) (because their mothers had eaten fish contaminated with PCBs during pregnancy) had worse scores on the Brazelton Neonatal Scales as neonates and more errors in short-term memory at the age of four. Any period of neurological development may be vulnerable.

Thus it seems to be probable that even low-level exposure to lead in the environment (and conceivably to other pollutants) is associated with a tendency to attention deficits, emotional reactivity and hyperactivity and worse performance in school. The effects of lead interact with the effects of other socio-economic variables, probably being more severe for socially disadvantaged children than for middle-class ones (Shaffer 1985). However, the association is not strong: it only shows up in large samples that are carefully measured. Lead does not all by itself cause inattentiveness or educational retardation or delinquency or hyperactivity, but it does contribute to some such problems. Preventing lead poisoning, provided the substitutes for lead have fewer adverse effects, will have small but not insignificant benefits.

5.3.2 Prenatal drug and alcohol use and children's cognitive development

Pregnant women are generally advised that they should give up drink and drugs for the duration of their pregnancies. But some do not, and there are a number of studies suggesting that prenatal exposure to drugs and alcohol may have long-term effects on the baby. The evidence is complex and not completely consistent. Recent research on the association between pregnant women's use of cocaine and their children's cognitive outcomes (Arendt *et al.* 2004; Nelson *et al.* 2004) illustrates the complexities of the field. Both studies used American samples and compared children whose mothers had taken cocaine during their pregnancy and children whose mothers had not. Prenatal cocaine exposure is thought to affect the developing brain, and hence children's language, cognition and behaviour problems. Arendt *et al.* (2004) assessed their sample of 101 exposed and 130 non-exposed children at age seven and found that prenatal drug exposure was associated with lower scores on the Wechsler Intelligence Scale for Children (WISC), but that mothers' vocabulary and HOME scores at age seven were stronger predictors. They conclude that prenatal cocaine exposure may confer some developmental disadvantage, particularly in the visual and motor domains, but that many children whose mothers took cocaine during pregnancy are brought up in inadequate rearing environments; once these were allowed for in a multiple regression analysis there was little sign of effects of prenatal exposure in this sample. Nelson *et al.* (2004) looked at rates of iron deficiency and anaemia and at neurodevelopmental outcomes in two-year-olds and four-year-olds. Cocaine-exposed children were more likely to be anaemic at age four, and anaemia at age two or age four was associated with lower Wechsler Preschool and Primary Scale of Intelligence (WPPSI) scores at four. A history of prenatal exposure to cocaine was associated with higher blood lead levels. Children who had been brought up by foster mothers or adoptive mothers still showed somewhat lower scores, though this finding is complicated by the fact that the mothers whose babies had been separated from them had had higher levels of cocaine use than those who were left to rear their child. This all suggests a complex set of causation between prenatal exposure to cocaine and children's cognition, with pre-natal impairment of delivery of oxygen and nutrients to the foetus, subtle effects on the development of the central nervous system, lower birthweight, anaemia, enhanced gastrointestinal absorption of lead, poorer parenting postnatally, postnatal drug use, and general socio-economic disadvantage all intertwined.

Similarly, children who were heavily exposed to alcohol prenatally may suffer from foetal alcohol syndrome (FAS) and show deficits in intellectual and academic achievements and poor social adaptation, including more disruption of schooling, more getting into trouble with police, and more alcohol or drug problems (Streissguth *et al.* 1991, 2004). We know that prenatal exposure to alcohol leads to abnormal development of the CNS; the main question is whether there is a safe amount. A good environment postnatally may help the children cope with the physical damage that has been done to their developing brains even in the severest cases, if a relatively early diagnosis allows protective measures to be taken.

It seems likely to me that intra-uterine effects will often be complicated by later influences. As well as the effects of the drugs that mothers have taken, we see this in the case of maternal diabetes (Sesma and Georgieff 2003; Luciana 2003), which is associated with preterm delivery but may have its own effects, and in an association between the mother's mental state during pregnancy and the child's outcomes in the early school years, with indications of more difficulties if the mother suffered depression or anxiety on pregnancy (Hammen 2003; Ramchandi *et al.* 2005; Heron *et al.* 2004; Connor *et al.* 2002a, 2002b, 2003). Here the problems of separating the effects of mental state on intra-uterine development and on later development if the mother's depression or anxiety continues after her child is born are obviously very considerable.

5.3.3 Nutrition and cognitive development

It has been clear for at least a century that children who are underfed to a serious degree may grow up (if they survive) to do comparatively poorly in school and on more formal tests of cognitive development. This was obvious to reformers at the turn of the century such as Margaret McMillan, whose pioneering work in nursery education provided for the feeding (and washing) of the children's bodies as well as for the stimulation of their minds (Bradburn 1989). It was obvious to the officials of Boards of Education and Local Education Authorities, such as Sir Cyril Burt (Burt 1955). It is still obvious in the Third World, where half or more of the children in many countries suffer from some degree of malnutrition and around one child in twenty is severely malnourished (World Health Organisation statistics; Lozoff (1989)). What is less obvious is precisely how this poorer performance comes about, and what interventions might reduce the disadvantage. A considerable amount of work has been done on the links between differences in nutrition and differences in cognitive development, but considerable controversy remains (Dobbing 1987; Pollitt 2000; Black 2003a, 2003b; Grantham-McGregor 2002). I will review here some of the research on the effects of severe malnutrition on intellectual performance, and, more briefly, some of the research on dietary effects within a population that is in general well or at least adequately fed. It will be seen that both areas involve complex questions and that many investigations have serious methodological difficulties.

5.3.3.1 Malnutrition and cognitive development

The classic hypothesis was that undernutrition during the vulnerability of a 'critical period' early in life would seriously distort the development of the brain, and, because the brain determines the character and intelligence of the person, would seriously distort his or her cognitive performance (Bedi 1987; Dauncey and Bicknell 1999). The brains of children who die of starvation are lighter in weight and contain fewer cells and less total protein than normal (Smart 1987). The more detailed studies possible on laboratory animals show a wide range of effects of malnutrition, including smaller brain size, decreased numbers of neurones, glial cells, dendrites and synaptic connections, slower peripheral nerve conduction, lower electroencephalograph frequencies in sleep and waking states, delays in myelination, and changes in the pattern of neurotransmitters and other brain chemicals (Bedi 1987; Lozoff 1989; Dauncey and Bicknell 1999). Normal brain development involves the proliferation of brain cells and then a reduction in their number. Undernutrition while cells are being formed leads to a reduced final number; later undernutrition affects the growth and myelinisation of nerve fibres, while the growth and development of the body in general is also retarded. These changes in brain structure should not be interpreted simply, but it is probably not too misleading for the non-expert to think of these malnourished animals as having a deficit in brain development, a reduction in the interconnections of nerve cells and a slowing of the transmission of neural impulses among them. It has been inferred from this that early malnourishment also causes permanent behavioural deficits that cannot be rectified because the underlying brain is damaged.

This pessimistic inference, however, must be resisted. Research has not so far established exactly how the various changes in the brain associated with malnutrition might lead to it functioning less efficiently. Starved animals have smaller brains, for example; but they also have smaller bodies, such as would normally only need smaller brains running them. Structural changes have been found to be particularly marked in the cerebellum; Black (2003a) finds some evidence of an association between zinc deficiency and motor problems in some vulnerable children and Dauncey and Bicknell (1999: 240) report research that found prenatally undernourished rats had delayed motor development, including 'a slightly unsteady gait and non-fluent paw movements', but there are few other reports of deficits in fine motor co-ordination, which the cerebellum controls, in either humans or laboratory animals. Nor is it clear how far deficits in brain development can be compensated for by later development. Environmental enrichment has beneficial effects on brain and behaviour in previously malnourished laboratory animals (see Katz and Davies (1983)), but probably does not completely eliminate the physical effects of malnutrition. In fact it is per-haps as difficult to alter a laboratory animal's nutrition without affecting other aspects of its environment as it is to alter a human child's. A common way of providing infant rats with good or poor nutrition is to alter the size of the litter the mother has to feed; members of a very large litter each get less milk than members of a small one. However, they also have a different sort of social experience: more siblings to interact with, and different mothering, as small, immobile, growth-retarded rat pups elicit more maternal contact than large active pups do (Smart 1987), just as mothers of undernourished human children spend more time in contact with the children, allowing them more time suckling (Galler 1987). This increased maternal contact time has important implications for development, which I will pick up later. For the moment, the point is that even in laboratory studies of animals it is unlikely that nutritional status is the only difference between 'well-nourished' and 'poorly nourished' animals (Winick 1976; Dauncey and Bicknell 1999). Nutritional status has direct effects on brain development, but it also has direct effects on health and mortality, emo-tionality, energy level and exploration, which could bring about further effects on cognitive development as the malnourished, inactive, timid animal fails to explore the stimulation the environment offers. These more or less motivational effects might or might not be reversed when a better diet or different living conditons are introduced, though growth retardation itself will decrease exploratory opportunities, since it leads to mobility developing later and so to restrictions in interaction with the environment. Environments that provide impoverished sensory input are known to affect the development of the brain, decreasing the proliferation of dendrites and synaptic connections: effects that it may be hard to distinguish from the effects of malnutrition. Thus there are several vital gaps in the research data that need filling before it could be validly inferred that malnutrition (aside from the associated deficits in stimulation and experience) causes physical changes in the brain (and that these are permanent and irreversible) which lead (by what pathways?) to deficits in cognitive development (and that these too are permanent and irreversible). There is evidence for changes in the brain; we do not yet know what these imply for the mind.

The realisation of the interaction between nutrition and the environment even in the laboratory is important for studies of human malnutrition, where nutritional and environmental disadvantage coexist inextricably. Most malnourished children live in conditions of poverty, environmental deprivation and social disadvantage, and the effects of malnutrition and the effects of familial and social–environmental disadvantage exacerbate each other (Barrett 1987). World Health Organisation statistics show that a horrifyingly high percentage of children in the developing world (and some even in the United States and Europe) are malnourished, their potential development perhaps thereby impaired, even if not curtailed by early death. A number of research studies 'in the field' have looked for the effects of early nutrition on later achievement (e.g. Grantham-McGregor 1987; Ivanovic *et al.* 2000; Walker *et al.* 2000). Typically, children who have been diagnosed as having marasmus (severe deficiency of protein and calories, particularly in the first year of life) or kwashiorkor (protein deficiency), or children with restricted physical growth, are later compared with adequately fed children. There are enormous difficulties in making a valid comparison, as Rumsey and Rapoport (1983) and Richardson (1984) discuss. Comparison children are often 'matched' on convenient (but fairly gross) socio-economic measures such as being in the same class at school; sometimes siblings who were not malnourished are selected. Neither of these provides a really satisfactory control. Richardson's work in Jamaica examined (by interviews and home observations) a range of environmental variables in hospitalised malnourished boys and in classmates without a history of malnourishment (Richardson 1976, 1984; see also Dobbing (1987: 193–196)). It was found that the malnourished boys were significantly less well off on such variables as caretaker's upbringing, reproductive history and level of capability, housing conditions and crowding, intellectual stimulation at home, amount of schooling and mortality of siblings. These findings cast doubt on any conclusion that the lower IQ and worse school performance of the malnourished boys could be attributed solely to their period of malnutrition rather than to their horribly extensive experience of disadvantage. In a multiple regression analysis, boys from the least disadvantaged settings seemed to suffer less from malnutrition than those from the most disadvantaged settings, being two IQ points behind their comparison classmates, while the most disadvantaged boys showed a nine IQ point deficit. Thus the effects of malnutrition are embedded in a very complex social and biological context, and vary with it. Sibling comparisons reduce the variation to that found within a family, but within-family variation may be especially marked in these studies: if one member of a pair of siblings has been severely malnourished and the other has not, surely they must differ in other aspects of their experience – temperament, parental affection, 'historical' differences such as changes in family income – or why should one sibling have had a more favourable diet than the other? The other siblings may also have been malnourished, but less noticeably.

However difficult the proper control of variables between comparison and malnourished groups may be (Grantham-McGregor 1987; Grantham-McGregor *et al.* 2000; Grantham-McGregor and Ani 2001; Black 2003a, 2003b), many researchers find that undernutrition is associated with long-term and deleterious effects on development. Galler and her colleagues have done a longitudinal study of a sample of 129 children in Barbados who had suffered severe marasmus (protein–energy undernutrition) in infancy, comparing them with 129 children of similar social class who had no history of malnutrition. The children who had suffered a period of undernutrition eventually caught up on physical growth, but continued to have lower cognitive performance and school achievement, with an increase in attention problems and poorer social skills (Galler 1987). Although the environment throughout childhood was somewhat more disadvantaged for the malnourished children than for the controls, Galler concludes that the early period of malnutrition was the major contributor to their impaired development. Richardson, discussing the disparity between Galler's findings in Barbados and his own in Jamaica, suggests that this is too strong a conclusion (Dobbing 1987: 193–197). Both studies indicate that the complexities of how variables in the environment interact in development must be addressed if we are to understand the mechanisms by which a period of undernutrition early in life brings about its effects.

Barrett (1987) criticises the research into malnutrition and cognitive development that used intelligence, conceptualised as 'innate general cognitive ability' and measured with IQ tests, as the main outcome variable. Measuring IQ is justified if the researcher has a theory of a causal relationship between malnutrition and general level of intellectual development, not if IQ is chosen merely because IQ tests are comparatively easily administered. I agree with Barrett that it is regrettable that other variables are not considered: Barrett's own research in Guatemala found that early supplementary feeding of chronically malnourished children did not predict performance on cognitive tests but did have long-term effects on attention, emotional expression, social involvement and persistence (Barrett 1987; Barrett *et al.* 1982). These more fine-grained variables were examined because the researchers hypothesised that malnutrition would disrupt caregiver–child interaction, affecting attention, responsiveness to social stimulation and the ability to elicit responses from others; that the child would learn to withdraw from new situations, would have difficulty in coping with routine stressful situations, would lack persistence, and would be withdrawn and lethargic. Such a pattern of behaviour conserves the energy that is in short supply when calories are lacking, but also tends to isolate the developing child from stimulation and opportunities to learn. Undernourished children demand and receive less stimulating interchange with their caretakers, spend more time in close bodily contact (often suckling for long periods, which maximises the amount of milk taken in, but not the amount of information taken in about the wider outside world), and spend less time in exploring the social and physical environment (Lozoff 1989). If, as may be the case, the child's mother or other caregivers are themselves chronically undernourished, anaemic or depressed, the stimulation offered to the child and the caretakers' responsiveness to the child's initiatives may also be reduced (Cravioto and Arrieta 1979; Salt *et al.* 1988; pp. 382–401). Child and environment, both undernourished and mutually understimulated, form a huddled bundle of helplessness and hopelessness, all their energy needed for bare survival, and the idea of doing well on an IQ test becomes a sick joke. Even sicker and no joke at all is the idea that only the demonstration of long-lasting IQ deficits would justify taking malnutrition seriously and trying to eradicate it.

In contrast to the pervasive chronic malnutrition endemic in the developing world, a few children who are not growing up in poverty suffer periods of starvation early in life because of conditions such as pyloric stenosis (a malformation of the digestive tract that leads to projectile vomiting of food) or cystic fibrosis (a genetically caused condition where food is not digested normally). The period of malnourishment is usually short. Research on the later development of these children, although it cannot separate the effect of the period of undernutrition from other effects of the child's illness such as hospitalisation and stress on the family, does allow some separation of malnutrition and wider social disadvantage. Research findings are inconsistent; there seems to be little effect on IQ scores except when the children are very young, but there may be some deficits in attention and memory (Ellis and Hill 1975; Lloyd-Still *et al.* 1974; Richardson 1984). There are occasional 'natural experiments' when famine strikes a population that is normally well nourished, so that people whose brains were developing fast at the time of the famine can be compared with those undergoing such development at another time, under normal conditions. One such brief atypical famine occurred during the winter of 1944–5 when the occupying forces cut off food supplies to the civilian population of part of Holland and there were severe general nutritional difficulties for about six months. Boys who were foetuses or newborns at the time were tested when they began military service at the age of eighteen, in the early

1960s. No effects of their or their mother's period of acute malnourishment could be found (Stein *et al.* 1975). There are no details of the women's diets in pregnancy, so it is possible that they may have been protected against the general famine in some way, and no details of the boys' condition at birth or through the first year. Nevertheless this was a famine probably comparable with the experimental deprivation that has led to persistently poorer functioning in rats (Dobbing 1987). It did not have effects discernible in testing for army recruitment after nearly twenty years of normal good Dutch feeding. Whether this lack of effect indicates a true absence of deficit due to famine, or initial deficits that were recovered from as these babies grew up, or insufficiently sensitive testing methods obscuring real deficits, it is impossible to tell.

If malnutrition is hypothesised to cause deficits in brain development and consequently in cognition, then preventing malnutrition by providing adequate food should allow more normal brain growth and cognitive development. A research study that provided food supplements for an 'experimental' group drawn from a population at risk from malnutrition and compared them with an unsupplemented matched control group could test the hypothesis. However, as well as the ethical problem of helping only some of those at risk (which implies allowing those not helped to suffer in order to have a cleaner research design) and the wider ethical issues due to the fact that providing food aid changes the ecology of food supplies in the community so that recipients may become dependent on the supplementary feeding and be put at a disadvantage when this form of aid comes to an end (Galbraith 1980), there are problems of comparability between the 'experimental' and 'control' groups and of monitoring the invervention. The nominally 'supplementary' food may replace the child's normal diet, or may be consumed in whole or in part by other members of the family; or if the whole family is fed (to eliminate this latter difficulty), there may be changes in the behaviour of other members of the family that affect their interaction with the child. Supplementing the diet of women during pregnancy and lactation, for example, is likely to enhance their interaction with their babies as well as the babies' brain development. There seems to be some evidence, once these methodological difficulties are taken into account, that supplementation of the food supply of nutritionally deprived populations does have benefits for cognition, particularly if it continues from the child's prenatal life well into early childhood. In several studies children have done better in school readiness tests or made more progress in the first few years of school (Grantham-McGregor 1987; Grantham-McGregor *et al.* 1987; Grantham-McGregor and Ani 2001; Black 2003a; Pollitt 2000), an achievement that might well affect their parents' and teachers' judgement of their potential and thus their later achievement (pp. 401–408). Prevention of malnutrition before it happens is clearly the best course. Intervention that combines nutritional supplementation with rehabilitation through social and educational intervention does seem to be more effective than either alone, and it is worth feeding the mother as well as the child (e.g. Cravioto and Arrieta 1979; Sinisterra 1987; Pollitt 2000).

Even in rich countries, some families report that they sometimes go hungry and do not get enough food to eat. Alaimo *et al.* (2001a and b) examined food insufficiency in a US national sample of more than 5000 children aged between six and sixteen. Their findings agree with those from poorer countries. Children whose families reported that they sometimes or often did not get enough to eat had lower scores on the WISC Block Design and Digit Span and the WRAT reading and arithmetic subtests, and were more likely to have repeated a school grade and to have missed more school days. Teenagers with a family history of food insufficiency were at least twice as likely to have seen a psychologist, to have been suspended from school, and to have social difficulties. Some of this risk of adverse outcomes was removed by adjusting for a range of psychosocial and environmental variables, including gender, poverty status, ethnicity, parental education and employment, lead exposure, crowding and birthweight; but the negative association between food insufficiency and cognitive and psychosocial scores remained. These findings confirm that undernutrition is a problem for children's cognitive development, but it is a problem strongly associated with other problems. General health may be affected – remember that more school days were missed; being hungry may make the child more irritable or distractible in school, impairing learning and the child's ability to cope with stress and relate to peers; parents too may be stressed, may be suffering from undernutrition too if they give what food there is to the child rather than getting an adequate diet themselves; the family very possibly will have some of the other problems associated with poverty, such as poor housing and an unsupportive neighbourhood (Garrett *et al.* 1994; Evans and English 2002; Evans 2004). Food parcels are at best part of the answer; coping with the families' other problems, including help with psychosocial stimulation, may also be necessary (Walker *et al.* 2000).

5.3.3.2 Failure to thrive

Even if the family has the food, getting it into the child is not always easy. 'Failure to thrive' is the term applied to children in industrialised societies who do not grow as expected and whose impaired growth has no identifiable organic cause (Skuse 1984; Chatoor *et al.* 2004). The traditional explanation for these children's difficulties was psychological deprivation, the lack of a warm and responsive relationship with the mother: not being loved enough took away the child's ability to make use of his or her food, not enough psychological nourishment led to not enough physical nourishment. A classic study by Widdowson (1951) documented this happening in orphanage children in the care of two different nurses, one of whom quite incontrovertibly put her charges off their food. But the classic explanation is not now seen as being adequate to explain failure to thrive.

Many children are fussy about their food, and some show food refusal and lack of appetite so extreme it has been called 'infantile anorexia' (Chatoor *et al.* 2004), while showing a normal interest in exploring the world and interacting with other people. Children with this diagnosis are not suffering from maternal neglect, and tend to come from middle-class families. Their cognitive development as toddlers is correlated not with their nutritional status but with psychosocial variables: higher scores were predicted by better reciprocity and lower levels of conflict and noncontingency between mother and child, less maternal intrusiveness during play, higher maternal education and SES, not by what they ate. Children with failure to thrive as indexed by faltering or stunted growth tend to come from disadvantaged low-income families, with problems such as unemployment, overcrowding, marital difficulties, social isolation and adverse environmental conditions. Their mothers report more negative feelings about their own childhoods and more life stresses for themselves and their partners when interviewed during their pregnancy. They have more difficulty feeding their newborn infant; the process of inadequate feeding and nurture seems to start early and to have roots far back in the mother's life and in the wider family environment. Difficulties occur before the infant's growth failure begins, but the growth failure itself and its associated developmental deficits of cognitive delays and behaviour problems (Raynor and Rudolf 1996; Drewett *et al.* 1999, 2001; Boddy *et al.* 2000) are likely to perpetuate the difficulties. Intervention that supports the family as well as feeding the child is necessary (Skuse 1984; Super *et al.* 1990), just as in the case of undernutrition in the non-industrialised world.

5.3.3.3 Minor dietary deficiencies

As well as suffering from undernutrition, children may lack a particular component in the diet, for example having a diet that does not provide them with enough iron, calcium, zinc or vitamins. Some of these specific dietary deficiencies appear to have adverse consequences for cognitive development, though there is considerable (and heated) controversy about this. Lozoff (1988), Pollitt (2000) and Grantham-McGregor and Ani (2001) review research on iron deficiency. Iron deficiency is quite common in infants and children, particularly between six and twenty-four months: iron deficient infants tend to be tired, fearful, irritable, apathetic and distractible. A considerable body of research shows that anaemia is correlated with lower developmental quotients on mental test scores, and with worse motor development, though few studies have controlled for confounding variables. Anaemic infants have been said to improve rapidly when given iron supplements long-term, but controlled research (see Lozoff (1988), Pollitt

(2000, 2001), Grantham-McGregor and Ani (2001) for reviews) suggests that these improvements on tests were probably largely due to practice effects, as anaemic infants treated with placebos and non-anaemic untreated infants also improve. Better controlled studies have failed to find improvement in infants' test scores after two or three months of iron therapy, sufficient to correct their anaemia, though there was some sign of improvement in motor scores. Pollitt's work suggests that iron therapy for anaemic older children might reduce their cognitive impairment, also improving their attention and their energy levels. Anaemia in adults limits work capacity and activity: an anaemic mother might have a hard time providing developmental stimulation for her children. In view of the evidence on the importance of interaction with the mother both for malnourished children (Salt *et al.* 1988; Pollitt 2000; Grantham-McGregor and Ani 2001) and well-fed ones (which I reviewed elsewhere in this section), both parental and child anaemia should be prevented.

Marginal and moderate zinc deficiency seem to be quite common among children with impaired growth and poor cognitive and motor functioning (Black 2003; Salgueiro *et al.* 2002). Zinc is known to be essential for normal foetal growth and development, and of great importance for growth and functioning after birth. Infants with zinc deficiencies may have a range of chronic health problems, including susceptibility to infections, weight loss and stunted growth. Animal studies show effects on brain development (pp. 335–338), but the evidence for this in humans is sparse and inconsistent. There is some evidence of associations between low zinc levels in children and poorer school performance, but there are many issues, such as controlling for confounding variables (such as poverty) and the precise timing of the zinc deficiency, that need to be examined more carefully (Black 2003a, 2003b). Zinc-rich foods tend to be expensive, so poor children are at increased risk of zinc deficiency; but supplementation is unlikely to be enough if it is the only intervention. Again, it is crucial to work on this problem in a joined-up way.

Dietary long-chain polyunsaturated fatty acids are very important for human neurodevelopment, especially for those born prematurely or at a low birth weight (Dauncey and Bicknell 1999). Human breast milk naturally contains such substances, and this may be the reason breast-fed babies tend to do better than formula-fed ones, unless the formula milk is enriched with them. Mothers who eat oily fish during pregnancy and breastfeeding tend to have babies whose development is enhanced (Daniels *et al.* 2004), though too much oily fish could be a bad thing if it comes from contaminated waters (see pp. 357–361).

Benton (1990) and Black (2003b) review research on vitamin and mineral intake and psychological functioning. Many members of the medical profession and nutritionists argue that if the diet supplies sufficient protein and calories all the necessary micronutrients come associated with them, and there are unlikely to be deficiencies. Benton examines the alternative argument that there may be deficiencies, either because some individuals need an especially high intake of particular micronutrients, or because the diet may give rise to a subclinical deficiency even in the average individual. The existing research suggests that this hypothesis needs to be taken seriously. For example, deficiencies in vitamin B_{12} are associated with poorer cognitive functioning in Third World children, in geriatric populations even in wealthy countries, and in children whose mothers who ate a vegan or macrobiotic diet during pregnancy or breastfeeding. As Black (2003b) and Pollitt (2000) point out, the evidence is not conclusive, because there are inconsistencies in findings and not all those studies that support the hypothesis are well designed, using double-blind techniques to rule out positive effects of supplementary diets due to consumer belief, for example. It is also not clear whether supplying micronutrients benefits those who are already taking in the normally recommended quantity as well as those whose diet was clearly very deficient. Finally, we do not know how micronutrients affect cognitive performance and development: whether their effects should be looked for in changes in the chemistry of neurotransmitters in the brain, or in better behaviour such as increased attention to the boring tests used to assess cognition, or in a decrease in ill health; or whether different micronutrient deficiencies compound each other's effects in individuals whose diet is lacking in several nutrients.

5.3.3.4 Too much of a bad thing: Dietary substances and cognitive behaviour

We have discussed the effects on cognitive development of diets that are *deficient*, in calories or vitamins and trace metals. Recently there has been interest in the effects of Western diets of highly processed fatty and sugary food, and suggestions that some food additives and some deficiencies in more 'natural' foods might exert an adverse influence on children's behaviour and hence on their cognition. In part because of the high level of public interest, this has proved to be a difficult area to research: parents' desire to see a positive result from the new diet they are giving their child has led to dramatic improvements in problematic behaviour, which are greatly reduced if the dietary changes are introduced in a properly controlled double-blind fashion. More positive change is seen on parent report of mood and behaviour than on laboratory tests or standard psychometric assessments, a discrepancy that might be due to parental optimism (and an ineffective treatment) or to insensitive formal tests (and a more effective treatment), and is hard to interpret.

Rumsey and Rapoport (1983) assess the behavioural and cognitive effects of certain constituents of diet in children. One substance that children in the United States consume in large quantities is caffeine, which is found in coffee, tea, cocoa, chocolate and cola beverages. Caffeine is known to affect the central nervous system, enhancing arousal and facilitating automatic responding on well-learned tasks. People who normally abstain from caffeine find its side-effects aversive, while high users report positive effects, and withdrawal symptoms if they do not consume caffeine. It has been suggested that caffeine calms down hyperactive children, but placebo effects seem to be involved. It may stimulate anxiety symptoms in some children. Consumption of sugar and refined carbohydrates as a high proportion of the diet may be correlated with more aggressive and destructive behaviour in hyperactive children and with more activity in normally active control children. Food additives have received much publicity as hypothesised causes of hyperactivity in genetically vulnerable or allergic individuals. Here uncontrolled studies have supported the hypothesis but their lack of methodological rigour means that their results are uninterpretable. Properly conducted research shows inconsistencies in results. Rumsey and Rapoport (1983) suggest that possibly some children's behaviour does improve when additives are eliminated from their diet though it is not clear that it worsens again when the additives are secretly reintroduced as a 'challenge'. Very careful research is needed to overcome methodological problems in the selection of cases, the double-blind administration of restrictions and challenges, control for placebo effects and sensitive but objective assessment of behaviour.

A news item in *Nature* (Giles 2004) summarises papers on studies where rodents were fed the equivalent of human junk food. All of them found that rats and mice that had eaten a high-fat, high-cholesterol diet struggled to find their way round mazes, and took longer to recall the solutions to problems they had already solved. The cause of the cognitive damage may be that their diets had a lot of trans-fatty acids (which are routinely added to human food to improve its shelf-life), which probably caused high levels of triglyceride; rats given drugs that reduced triglyceride levels learned their mazes better. If humans are affected by their diets in the same way as these rodents (and the classic work of Widdowson and McCance half a century ago implies this too), a diet of junk food may be damaging to our brains too. Campaigns to improve the quality of school dinners are looking more and more important, not just because of the problems associated with obesity (Wardle 2005) but also because of direct cognitive damage.

Clearly much more work needs to be done on the effects of diet on brains and cognition. Meanwhile, the safest diet for cognition seems to be a healthily mixed, fresh and not over-refined one, just as it is for one's health and one's waistline . . .

5.4 The social world and cognitive development

In an earlier part of this chapter I looked at non-social causes of cognitive development; now I move to the social side of development. A great deal of the literature on the role of other people in children's cognitive development can be placed in three groups. The first points out more or less permanent characteristics of adults, such as their social class or intelligence or family structure, which are associated with different cognitive outcomes for the child. The second looks at activities (and beliefs) of parents that make them, moment by moment, more or less effective supporters or inducers of their children's learning. The third looks at interaction between the child and teachers (or fellow pupils) in a similar way. In discussing this work, I will be seeking elucidation of *how* adults' characteristics or activities or beliefs might affect children's cognition.

We need to remember here the methodological difficulty that complicates discussion of the effects of parent–child interaction just as it bedevils the study of the heritability of intelligence (see pp. 237–247). Parents may be seen to have a significant impact on their children's cognition just as they have been seen to be significantly similar in IQ; but what part of this similarity or this impact is due to their activity, what to the child's actions, what to shared genes and what to shared environment? Genes and environment interact and have their effect in complex ways (e.g. Bishop *et al.* 2003; Cardon *et al.* 1992; Caspi *et al.* 2000; Plomin 1990a, 1993, 1994; Rutter 1988, 1992; Scarr 1992, 1996; pp. 347–350). The association between parent input and child output may come about through one or more of several different routes – sharing genetic material, gene–environment interaction, impact of parents' behaviour, impact of child's behaviour, sharing environments, or combinations of these. The complexity of causes of both the similarities and the differences between parents and children is enormous, and there is extreme difficulty in finding decisive evidence to sort the causes out. It will be necessary to consider whether what seems to be an effect of experiencing a particular type of interaction or other social factor is not in fact largely genetically determined, and whether what seems to be largely genetically determined is not in fact an effect of experiencing a particular type of interaction or other social factor. There clearly is a great deal of genetic programming in development, but we cannot neglect the effect of the environment; as we have seen, the physical environment has significant effects on the brain, and adoption into an advantaged social environment raises IQ. It is also necessary to consider which participant in a social interaction is having the crucial effect on the others; children influence their families and are not passive recipients of family influences.

5.4.1 Family background and children's cognitive development

There has been evidence for at least the past century that cognition or, more specifically, educational achievement is associated with family background. From at least Galton's 'hereditary genius' onwards, children with more middle-class backgrounds or more educated parents do better throughout their educational careers, staying in education longer and having higher achievement at most stages. They also tend to do somewhat better on IQ tests (though not during infancy (Slater 1995)), in particular contributing relatively few cases to the population of marginally subnormal scorers, and to a lesser degree they also tend to do better on Piagetian tests. The socio-economic status (SES) of the family is still a fairly good predictor of children's academic achievement (Blake 1989; Bornstein and Bradley 2003; Bradley and Corwyn 2002; Duncan et al. 1994; Duyme et al. 1999; Hart and Risley 1995; Hoff 2003; Huston et al. 1994; Jencks 1975; McLoyd 1998; Rutter 1985b, 1992; Smith et al. 1997; Schaffer 1992a; White 1982). Social class differences like these have persisted despite the existence of a general rise in achievement and intelligence (pp. 231–235) and of mobility between social classes between generations, and despite the belief in meritocracy and egalitarianism that characterises countries like Britain and the United States.

But social class, or SES, is not of itself a causal variable. It is an index based on the occupation of the head of the family, and thus a guide to the family's income, the parents' education, and, less directly, to a wider set of social circumstances. Research on social class or SES sometimes focuses on comparing people from different categories (with different 'social addresses' (Bronfenbrenner 1979, 1986; Bronfenbrenner et al. 1996, 1998, 2000) rather than on the intervening structures or processes that might explain how the address label comes to be associated with different developmental outcomes. Thus its results are often open to several interpretations. Further, the correlations between SES measures and cognitive outcomes are not enormously high; for example, the extensive and complex analyses of Marjoribanks (1979) found measured 'family environment' correlated 0.45 with achievement in English and mathematics and 0.29 to 0.34 with intelligence. Thus 'family environment' accounted for between 9 per cent and 20 per cent of the variance in cognitive achievement scores. Very importantly, social address studies do not adequately rule out genetic factors: studies that try to control for inherited differences in intelligence by partialling out the mother's IQ or the parents' educational level typically find the correlations between family background and children's performance in school or on IQ tests are reduced (Gottfried 1984; Plomin 1994; Scarr 1996), sometimes to a very insignificant level.

It is not entirely clear how a variable like SES affects children's cognitive achievement, or what sort of explanatory model is appropriate. The correlation between SES and intelligence or educational achievement might reflect class differences in innate 'intelligence' (Eysenck 1971), though the adoption studies I discussed in Chapter 3 (pp. 243–245) suggest it does not. There might be differences in the behaviour that facilitates good performance on IQ tests and in school; there might be different reactions by schools and other tests to children differing in SES. There might be different opportunities available to the different social classes (for example, better-funded schools in wealthier areas), even in a social system that believes it is meritocratic and open to all those who are talented. There might be differences in health. These possibilities are by no means mutually exclusive: indeed, the different disadvantages of poverty tend to co-occur (Evans 2004). Whichever cause may apply, we surely need to look closely at the moment-by-moment way the effect is brought about. Work that looks at more specific variables may be more useful, and it is these variables that I want to discuss more fully. This strategy will make it easier to address the question of why there is variation *within* classes and other overtly similar backgrounds, and to elucidate causal chains. We cannot, however, entirely dismiss class itself as a significant factor in development in so far as it reflects inequalities of health, education and opportunity. Class-based indices may continue to be the most economical predictors of achievement.

The Collaborative Perinatal Project (Broman *et al.* 1987) followed a very large sample in the United States from before birth into the early school years to look for the causes of cognitive deficit. Its findings suggest different causal patterns for mild retardation (IQ between 50 and 69) and severe retardation (IQ less than 50). Severe retardation was likely to be linked to overt central nervous system disorder, mainly Down Syndrome or the after-effects of rubella before birth or meningitis after it. Seventy-two per cent of the severely retarded white children and 14 per cent of the mildly retarded whites had CNS damage. More black children were retarded without definite CNS disorder, but it was again four or five times as common in the severely retarded black children. Children who were later diagnosed as severely retarded were more likely to have had problems in the perinatal period; they were more likely to have poor Agpar scores, that is, to be in poor condition immediately after birth, and to be small in size, have low head circumferences and so forth. That is, the severely retarded children commonly showed symptoms of being at risk of abnormal development at or shortly after birth, and their retardation was caused to a significant degree by problems they were born with, or by later overt physical damage.

Different factors seem to be at work for the mildly retarded children. Mild retardation was linked to SES, being very rare in high SES groups, and commoner in blacks (4.6 per cent) than whites (1.15 per cent). It was associated with lower SES at birth, with lower levels of maternal education, with lower age of the mother at the child's birth, with less maternal care, and with worse housing. There was some association with poor placental functioning, breech deliveries and poorer perinatal condition, factors that predicted severe mental retardation, but these were all less effective than social factors in discriminating between the mildly mentally retarded children and the borderline normal children. White children who were mildly mentally retarded at seven had tended to show poorer early cognitive skills; for example, 42 per cent of them had abnormal expressive language at the age of three. This earlier indication of problems was less clear in black children, where 77 per cent of mildly retarded seven-year-olds had had normal language expression at three. Broman *et al.* (1987) conclude that the causes of mild mental retardation are not primarily medical, but that social and environmental factors predominate. Their data, to their regret, do not clarify such factors.

Feinstein and Bynner (2004), using the 1970-born subjects of the British Cohort Study, examine continuities in cognitive performance over the years of middle childhood, relating change to social class and to economic performance as young adults. The cohort members were assessed on vocabulary and drawing tests at age five and on the British Ability Scale (an IQ measure) and reading at age ten. Just under 12 per cent of children were low scorers (in the bottom quartile) at age five but in the top half at age ten – the 'escapers'; about 12 per cent were in the top quartile at age five but the bottom half at age ten – the 'fallers'. Almost all the 'fallers' came from low SES families. When adult outcomes were examined, individuals who were in the lowest quartile at both five and ten were most likely to suffer outcomes such as low wages, low education, unemployment, criminality, and depression. Escapers were at much less risk of poor outcomes, doing about as well as average children on adult outcomes. Fallers did not do so well as those who were high at both five and ten, suggesting their early high score did not give them protection against later difficulties.

Kim-Cohen *et al.* (2004) looked at how the effects of SES deprivation affected IQ in five-year-old twins. Some children showed resilience in the face of SES adversity, scoring higher on an IQ test and lower on antisocial behaviour than their deprivation would have predicted. There was a genetic component to this resilience, shown by twin similarities, and accounting for a little under half the variance in IQ, but cognitive resilience was also promoted by maternal warmth, stimulating activities, and the child's own sociable temperament. Family cohesiveness, communication and shared meaning may be making important contributions to the children doing better than expected cognitively.

Family background might impinge differently on different individuals within the same family; in effect, they each have their own unique environment despite living together. McCall (1983), Scarr (1985), Harris (1998), Plomin (1989, 1991, 1994) and Plomin and Daniels (1987), for example, claim that there is as much variance within families as between them, that siblings differ as much as unrelated people. As the commentaries on the Plomin and Daniels paper show, this remains a matter of debate (for example, their analysis may not have distinguished adequately between variance within the family and general error variance, and it does not fully deal with gene–environment correlation and interaction). However, it may be as well to look at the contribution of non-shared environment to cognitive development. There is little evidence, indeed little idea of what 'non-shared environment' might be, to show whether it is not impossibly idiosyncratic. However, one way in which children's experience in the family may differ is in their ordinal position in the sequence of siblings. First-born and only children, and singletons, may tend to have earlier and better language development (including higher verbal IQs) and slightly higher scholastic achievement than later born children and twins, especially those in large families with small age gaps between sibs (e.g. Blake 1989; Gottfried and Gottfried 1984; Rutter 1985b; Zajonc 1983). First-born children are known to get more interaction and talk with their parents. They may be more likely to be the leaders than the followers in their play with their younger siblings, particularly having the advantage of more advanced skills to teach their sibs and so consolidate them in themselves, and are more subject to pressure from their parents to achieve developmental milestones and good educational results. Their relatively good performance could therefore be taken as evidence for the effect of parent–child interaction on development. ALSPAC data (Rutter et al. 2003; Thorpe et al. 2003) establish a strong case that the language retardation often shown by twins is associated with the reduced amount of language addressed to each twin compared with a singleton. The ordinal effect cannot easily be explained in non-interactional terms. There is no obvious genetic reason why first-born children should be more intelligent, and though some late-born children may suffer through the association between higher parental age and Down Syndrome, there are reproductive problems also for very young mothers. If the ordinal effect exists (and there is some controversy about it; see e.g. Blake (1989), Galbraith (1982), Plomin (1986)), it is an example of systematic environmental influences on cognitive development that differ for individuals within families.

There are links between family size and achievement. Blake (1989) finds a consistent difference in total educational attainment between the offspring of small and large families in the USA. Those from large families are less likely to complete high school, to get through the earlier stage of grade school without being kept down to repeat a grade, to have high verbal IQ scores, or to have high educational goals. Their achievement is more closely constrained by their social origins, they have less confidence in their abilities than those abilities would justify, and they are more likely to underperform in school relative to their ability scores. These differences between small and large families are found throughout the range of social groups, though they are mitigated by such other social forces as high parental SES, a cultural emphasis on educational attainment or an exceptionally cohesive kin network.

Blake argues that the cause of this difference between sibsize groups in their cognitive attainment is that parents' efforts to support their children's cognition are a crucial factor in its development, and that these parental efforts are 'diluted' if they have to be spread over many children. She cites various pieces of evidence for this explanation: the advantage in verbal IQ but not in non-verbal IQ for children from small families, which suggests parental attention and interaction as a cause; the increased amount of time that such children spend at home engaged in intellectual and cultural pursuits and in playing alone, and the greater frequency of being read to that they report they enjoyed as pre-schoolers; the decrease in sibsize effect in families from social groups that foster educational achievement. Middle children in closely-spaced large families do particularly badly, because they have older siblings who will beat them in the competition for resources, and they will experience a long period while younger siblings are being born and using up parental attention. Blake suggests that these children may have had less interaction with their parents focused on an activity demanding and receiving joint attention, less child-contingent and responsive inter-action, less enthusiasm, more interruption, less success and confidence, and a reduced expectation of what could be achieved. Again, family interaction patterns are seen as crucial, with interaction with parents being assumed to be more supportive for cognitive development and educational attainment than interaction with siblings can be.

Another within-family variation that might be associated with cognitive development is the child's gender. As IQ tests have traditionally been com-posed in such a way as to minimise sex differences, and theorists like Piaget have not shown a strong interest in individual differences, let alone sex-linked ones, the largest body of relevant evidence is on educational achievement. There have been enormous changes in recent decades in the relative performance of boys and girls. Boys used to be more likely to be high achievers, particularly when boys and girls were educated in the same social setting; more recently girls have done better than boys on most measures and even the decline in performance on mathematical subjects that used to affect girls in adolescence has been reduced (Anastasi 1985; Eccles 1985; Walkerdine 1989; Fredricks and Eccles 2002; Jacobs et al. 2002; Fadigan and Hammrich 2004; Van de gaer et al. 2004; Shapka and Keating 2003). The superiority of girls' academic performance could be explained in different ways; explanations in terms of girls' 'faster rate of maturation' are possible (though measuring this 'faster rate of maturation' is not straightforward), but it is fairly clear that small girls seek to co-operate with and talk with their mothers and teachers, and spend less time in rough and tumble play with peers and similar activities of low direct relevance to educational achievement (see Hutt et al. (1989), Meadows and Cashdan (1983), Tizard et al. (1976), Gelman et al. (2004)). A brief report on chim-panzees in the Gombe National Park in Tanzania (Lonsdorf et al. 2004) suggests that this is also the case for young chimpanzees. Females, who tend to spend more time watching their mothers than males do, start to use sticks to fish for termites at younger ages than males, catch more termites per dip, choose sticks of the lengths that their mothers preferred, and use the same fishing techniques as their mothers. Males, who spend their time near the termite mounds 'playing', do learn to fish for termites, but later and with less proficiency. Agostini and Visalberghi (2005), observing capuchin monkeys in Argentina, also find juveniles learning preferentially from adults of the same sex: in this case juvenile males stayed close to adult males and chose the same food targets and places to forage. It seems likely that some of the origins of gender differences in behaviour lie here. Again, boys and girls may have systematically different environments even within the same school or family, more different later in life than earlier.

Siblings have a powerful effect on each other, as we saw early in Judy Dunn's observations (Dunn 1988, 1993; and pp. 191–194). They may have both direct and indirect effects on each other's cognitive development. Older siblings may model or teach new concepts and skills (Maynard 2002) with benefits for their own cognition and self-esteem (Zukrow-Goldring 1995). Parents' and teachers' experience with an older sibling may affect their approach to a younger one (Brody 2004; Brody et al. 2003; Howe and Rinaldi 2004). A sibling's characteristics may affect the whole family and the child's individual experience (Haden 1998; Maynard 2002). Traditionally, families may have structured expectations about the relative achievement and role of children, either successively or by gender: the oldest son goes into the family business; girls are educated only for marriage and family. Siblings' feelings about parents' differential treatment may affect their development (Brody et al. 2003; Haden 1998).

5.4.2 Family language and children's cognition

As much of the way that culture is transmitted both in the home and at school is verbal, we need to refer back here to my discussion of the way in which language in the family affects children's cognitive development (pp. 22–26). Many studies have picked up aspects of language use as potentially relevant to how children acquire language, the style of their ultimate language use, and the ease with which later skills of cognition and literacy are developed (e.g. Hess et al. 1984; Wells 1985; Rice 1989; Snow et al. 1991; Garton 1992; Harris 1992; Crain-Thoreson and Dale 1992; Lieven et al. 1992; Bates et al. 1995; Hart and Risley 1995; Ochs and Schieffelin 1995; Snow 1995; Meadows 1996; Bloom 1998; Huttenlocher 1998; Evans et al. 1999; Hoff and Naigles 2002; Senechal and LeFevre 2002; Williams and Rask 2003; Haney and Hill 2004). For some children, there is a good fit with the language acquisition support system, and language development goes well; for others the fit is more difficult, and they may fall further and further behind (Johnson-Glenberg and Chapman 2004). The causal issues are complex, but much research suggests that children whose parents provide 'child-contingent' language develop language fast and do well cognitively. In this sort of language as used to young children there are various syntactic, semantic and pragmatic modifications that cumulatively provide the young child with a good model to learn from, perhaps such a good model that no Chomskian innate knowledge of language is required. Among the many adjustments of this relatively consistent, organised, simplified and redundant set of utterances are some that become very relevant as the child moves into formal education, where the use of language is similarly high on questions, directions, prompts and modelling of discourse, and is in this way 'foreign' to some young children whose families do not talk like their teachers (Heath 1983).

The meeting of home language and the school is one of the places where home language becomes important outside the home. Teachers and children undoubtedly react to each other's language, affecting the teacher's view of the child's skills and probable achievement and the child's view of whether school is a compatible extension of home. Differences in use of language will also result in differences in cognition about language, and in different shades of expertise in particular uses of language, for example answering display questions, telling stories, realising that what was meant is not literally the same as what was said, that a comment has the function of a command, and so forth (e.g. Heath 1983; King 1978; Robinson 1983). Children whose family experience of language includes school-like language tend to settle into school more easily and to do better there than children whose family language is different from the school's. Some of these children may reject (or be rejected by) the school because of the difference, and their cognitive skills will thus not incorporate those of the school's curriculum; others may become users of two dialects, one for home and one for school. Having two dialects or languages may be experienced as potentially or actually alienating (Heath 1983; Rodriguez 1980), particularly if one of them is subject to negative attitudes and discrimination, and if there is no active support for the bilingual child to learn and use both. In more favourable circumstances being bilingual or bidialectical probably facilitates cognition about language (Diaz 1985, Hyltenstam and Obler 1989; McLaughlin 1984; Paradis and Lebrun 1984; Bishop and Mogford 1993), bringing greater cognitive flexibility and a more advanced conceptualisation of language itself.

Children in school who are using the school's dialect as their own second language, not as native speakers, face a number of disadvantages. Their own language may not have given them so much practice on specialised skills important in the school's language, for example answering display questions, telling or discussing stories, or analysing objects or events; thus they will be less expert in these skills. Their own language may be socially judged as the mark of a stigmatised social group, and stereotypes of that group's behaviour and potential achievement may interfere with recognition of individual children's behaviour and potential. Because teacher and pupil have different languages they may meet communication problems, and at best they may have to translate each other's utterances as well as acting on them. The effort of doing this may divert cognitive resources away from the focus of the interaction, the question the child is to answer or the problem that is to be solved. It may be harder for the teacher to provide help at the appropriate level and for the pupil to internalise the ideas presented in a 'foreign' language. Children from minority groups and from the working class may have to do more work than middle-class children to get the same results. They may be more likely to be labelled as 'stupid' or 'mildly retarded' (cf. Broman *et al.* 1987), just as we would all be less likely to shine on a demanding task if we were simultaneously having to translate it from a less familiar language.

5.4.3 Family 'teaching styles' and children's cognition

Recent studies place family differences in language use in the context of how parents facilitate their children's development and acquisition of cognitive skills. Various researchers have looked at how mothers teach their children, by observing mother and child working together on a task such as drawing a pattern (e.g. Hess and Shipman 1965), assembling a puzzle (e.g. McNaughton and Leyland 1990), constructing a model object (Wertsch 1979; Wertsch *et al.* 1980, 1995; Wood and Middleton 1975; Wood *et al.* 1978), reading a book (Pellegrini *et al.* 1990), number tasks (Saxe *et al.* 1987), discussing people's mental lives (Meins 1997, 1998; Meins and Fernyhough 1999; Meins *et al.* 2002, 2003) or various other games and problems (Freund 1990; Heckhausen 1987; Hodapp *et al.* 1984; Kontos 1983; Petrill and Deater-Deckard 2004). Hubbs-Tait *et al.* (2002) examined mothers' behaviour towards their children in a Head Start programme. Schaffer (1992b) and Rogoff (1998) discuss these 'joint involvement episodes' as context for development. Wood and his colleagues, for example (Wood and Middleton 1975; Wood *et al.* 1978), carefully observed four-year-olds as they assembled a wooden pyramid. The mothers were asked to teach the child how to put the pyramid together and the children were finally assessed on their independent performance. The complexity of the construction was such that a child of four could not complete it alone, but could succeed if given supportive instruction.

Mothers varied in their instruction and children in their success. Wood describes several different ways in which the mother controlled the child's next activity. The least controlling was a general verbal prompt such as 'now you make something'; a more specific verbal instruction, such as 'get four big blocks', would tell the child more about what he or she must do in the next stage of the task. Non-verbal help, such as pointing out the relevant material, preparing material so that the child only has to assemble it, or even doing the work as a demonstration that the child only has to watch, might also be provided. These levels of instruction vary in how much they leave to the child's initiative and how much they take over responsibility for the task.

Wood found that the mother's style of teaching, her use of these different levels, affects how well the child learns to do the task, how far the pyramid is completed when at last the child is asked to assemble it alone. The mothers who teach most effectively seemed to use two 'rules' to guide their choice of levels. The first was that if the child fails to succeed at a given level of help, then the level of help or control should be increased and a little less left to the child's unaided activity. The second rule was that if the child succeeds at a given level, the next instruction may offer a little less help. The child's failure is followed by making things a bit easier, his or her success by allowing them to be a bit more challenging.

This looks like the sort of effective instruction that has been described in language development studies and in Vygotskian theory as 'scaffolding' (pp. 18–26). Bruner encapsulates it thus:

> If the 'teacher' in such a system were to have a motto, it would surely be 'where before there was a spectator, let there now be a participant'. One sets the game, provides a scaffold to assure that the child's ineptitudes can be rescued by appropriate intervention, and then removes the scaffold part by part as the reciprocal structure can stand on its own.
>
> (Bruner 1983: 60)

This scaffolding is seen as an effective language acquisition support system (just as important as the Chomskian language acquisition device, which was internal to the child, p. 18), and an analogous procedure seems to be an effective means of facilitating the cognitive development of young children. (And, to digress for a moment, the social and emotional development; see Eisenberg and Mussen (1989), Heath (1983), Kaye (1984), Meins (1997, 1998), Hubbs-Tait et al. (2002), Howe and Rinaldi (2004)). The learner is inducted into a predictable format of interaction: his or her role in it is orchestrated and supplemented by actions that highlight critical features and information, buffer the learner's attention against distractions, channel the learner's activities so that there is freedom to succeed and not too much freedom to go wrong. Errors are turned into opportunities to learn, procedures are commented on and explained, efforts are praised, and responsibility for doing the task is gradually transferred to the learner, contingent on his or her having demonstrated an ability to succeed.

Wood's pyramid construction studies and other research using the same approach (e.g. Rogoff 1998; Wertsch 1979; Wertsch et al. 1980, 1995) showed an association over the short time period of the study between the mother's teaching style and the child's success in learning a new task. Subsequent work has examined mothers' use of scaffolding styles in their normal play with their children, and has allowed investigation of variables such as the role of the family's social class, the task's difficulty, and the child's ability in determining how scaffolding occurs and works. Pellegrini *et al.* (1990), for example, looked at how the mothers of black children on Head Start preschool programmes interacted with their children over books, and found that mothers' level of teaching was adjusted to their children's competence, thus contradicting suggestions that scaffolding is an exclusively middle-class activity (cf. also Tizard and Hughes (1984)).

Saxe *et al.* (1987) provide interesting documentation of a wide range of aspects of children's early number development. They interviewed and tested 78 children aged two and a half and four and a half, interviewed their mothers about the children's everyday number activities, and recorded mother–child interaction on a set of number-based tasks. The tests given to the child, for example, included reciting counting words to as high a figure as possible, telling a puppet which of two named numbers (e.g. 'three, two' or 'six, eleven') was bigger, reading written numbers, counting items in a set, judging the effect of adding or subtracting one, and counting out items to match the number in a given set. Saxe *et al.* were interested in the mathematical contexts actively negotiated by the child and others, in how the child's own generation of a goal in accord with his or her current conception of numerical activities led to new understandings and in how parental facilitation occurred, via parents' provision of more complex goals, activities or contexts. They were concerned to provide a developmental analysis of the child's understandings, an analysis of the cultural goals the child's activities were directed towards, and an analysis of the way in which the child's goals emerge and shift within an adult-supported activity. They compared working-class and middle-class white Brooklyn children at two and a half to three or four to six years of age. I discussed the children's mathematical cognition earlier (pp. 248–249).

The researchers expected and found a developmental shift over this age range, and social class differences, with a small superiority for middle-class children at two but a large one at four, particularly on tasks involving cardinal number, numerical reproduction and arithmetic that had high-level goals. Children would often use a strategy from a low level of numerical functioning for what was really a higher level task, for example the task of counting a model set and then counting out units to match it was often done by trial-and-error moving of objects without any overt attempts at numerical representation. Children who scored highly tended to have parents who had high aspirations for them, and delivered a high level of stimulation via maternal language and the play materials provided, and via a flexible teaching style coupled with a belief that learning can be influenced.

Mothers and children were observed interacting on two tasks, one where the child had to count a single array and one where the child had to put out as many pennies as there were Cookie Monsters. In both cases there was considerable evidence of successful maternal scaffolding. Mothers matched the type of instruction they gave to how difficult the child was finding each subgoal, giving more specific instructions on harder tasks and more complex instructions to older and more accurate children, and making instructions more specific after the child made an error. Many children succeeded in the tasks when working with the mother but not alone, and were able to adjust their behaviour in correspondence with their mother's instructions, thus achieving more complex goals in interaction. An effective problem-solving environment emerged by negotiation, where the mother adjusted the task's organisation to the child's efforts, and the child's efforts were adapted to the mother's instruction.

Asked about their normal use of numerical activities, more than 70 per cent of mothers said their child showed a marked interest in them and at least three times a week counted something, looked in number books, or used numbers in play. Older children's activities were more complex than younger children's, and middle-class children's than working-class ones', with the range of complexity increasing with age as higher level goals were increasingly added to lower level ones. Mothers reported changing tasks as the same level of numerical reasoning was applied to harder tasks, for example counting more numerous sets of objects, or as the child reached the same goal with less assistance. Usually the mothers had several activities serving similar goals in play at the same time. Children regularly participated in number activities at varying levels of complexity, often activities that were the dyad's own inventions.

The data of Saxe et al. (1987, and see pp. 71, 83, 248–249, 333, 344) on children and mothers involved in everyday mathematics activities suggest there is maternal scaffolding of young children's numerical activities, and that this functions rather effectively. The child's ability to generate numerical goals enables and constrains his or her participation in social number activities; mothers scaffold this participation so that the child achieves more in partnership than alone and so comes to understand goals more advanced than his or her own; this facilitated understanding enables participation in more complex goals and interactions, and so on.

Several American investigators have used instruments such as the Home Observation for Measurement of the Environment (HOME Inventory) to describe features of the family's 'cognitive ecology' (e.g. Bee et al. 1982; Bradley and Caldwell 1980, 1984; Bradley et al. 1989; Gottfried 1984; Luster and Dubow 1992; Rogoff 1995, 1998). The HOME Inventory for newborn to three-year-old children gathers data on mothers' responsivity, avoidance of restriction and punishment, organisation of the environment, play materials, maternal involvement in the child and opportunities for variety in daily stimulation, through a combination of mother's statements and the interviewer's observation, during interview, of her behaviour and the home. Its forty-five items are somewhat heterogeneous and atheoretical, sometimes subjective, and have been criticised as biased towards middle-class values, for example, 'Mother's speech is distinct, clear and audible', 'At least 10 books are present and visible', 'Mother structures child's play periods'. HOME scores do, however, show moderate correlations with cognition and IQ assessments, over quite a number of years, particularly the subscales of maternal involvement and responsivity and play materials (Gregg *et al.* 2004). Correlations using HOME scores from infants are lower than scores from assessments of two-year-olds or older children, a result similar to that of other studies. This might suggest that cognition during infancy may be more heavily genetically programmed, so that environmental variation influences cognitive development less than it may at later ages, though differences in item content and accuracy of assessments may also be relevant.

The dimensions of the inanimate environment that are picked up by HOME and similar instruments as predictors of cognitive development are the availability of age-appropriate play materials, the possibility of free visual and physical exploration of the environment, and lack of over-crowding and unstructured stimulation. MacPhee *et al.* (1984) and Schaffer (1992a) suggest that the core principle of development uniting these is that there should be a reasonable match between the amount of stimulation available and the child's ability to use it. Stimulation that is contingent on the child's need, attractive, predictable and allowing him or her control and independence, that is, stimulation that is like scaffolding, is optimal for development; intrusive or non-contingent stimulation (as from the television being on incessantly) may be unhelpful (Jordan 2004). Other people may be important mediators of the stimulation of the home, as interpreters or simply as providers.

Both quality and quantity of interaction may be important. Sigel and his colleagues describe 'distancing strategies', with which parents encourage children to reflect upon their experience via requiring its representation – 're-presentation' – and so its 'de-contextualisation' (Sigel 1982b; Sigel *et al.* 1991; cf. Donaldson 1978). They believe that differential use of these strategies on the tasks they have set up influences children's behaviour. The pattern of results is complex, with variation between tasks and with differences between the effects of mothers' and fathers' behaviour; but, for example, children were more likely to create 'rational descriptions' in a story task if the mother made 'high-level mental demands'. Distancing strategies were important in association with other factors, including the parents' beliefs about appropriate strategies and the nature of child development (Goodnow 1984; McGillicuddy-DeLisi 1982; Miller 1996b). The context in which the parents' behaviour is measured is important; Sigel's subjects behaved differently on his two tasks while the language used by Wells's subjects, both children and adults, varied significantly according to the activity being engaged in (Wells 1985). A recent British cohort study found amounts of reading to and talking to children, and outings to 'places of interest' were positively correlated with their cognition, and amount of television watching and outings to department stores and funfairs were negatively correlated, independently of other characteristics of family, child and parents (Gregg et al. 2004). Thus different amounts of engaging in particular activities will give differing opportunities for language and interaction that might facilitate cognitive development. For example, reading and 'looking at books' lead to high levels of 'representational speech', particularly, for preschoolers, naming and labelling objects in context, while eating and caretaking lead to relatively high amounts of controlling speech (Davie et al. 1984; Wells 1985).

Parent activities that 'encourage development', in joint play or through providing appropriate and varied materials and experiences, are relevant to cognitive achievement. The core is warm participation in socially and intellectually stimulating interactions, with adults showing reciprocity with children, being responsive to them, and providing emotional support, but also providing some structured, directed experiences with encouragement and praise (Meins 1997, 1998; Hubbs-Tait et al. 2002; Petrill and Deater-Deckard 2004). Possibly the child participant in such interaction derives an enhanced sense of being competent and effective as well as receiving good cognitive opportunities and helpful interpretations and support from the adult; it is worth noting that maternal intrusiveness, being very directive and controlling, is associated with the child doing less well. There are quite consistent positive correlations between the amount of adult–child interaction of this sort and the child's cognitive development, which remain even when maternal IQ and educational level are partialled out in an attempt to control for passive genotype–environment interaction effects (Gottfried 1984; Luster and Dubow 1992) and when other demographic variables are controlled (Gregg et al. 2004). It is not entirely clear which components of the parent's behaviour have direct effects, and which are mediated by other factors, and the best balance of behaviour may vary from task to task and age to age (Hubbs-Tait et al. 2002), but it does seem to be the case that if the parent–child interaction is characterised by positive emotional support, high cognitive stimulation and low parental intrusiveness the child is likely to do well in terms of both cognition and confidence, while the reverse of this pattern is associated with the child doing badly. Thompson (2004) sees parenting and the environment of the home as the basis of individuals' approaches to learning challenges and achievement (see pp. 247–253 on learning styles and Chapter 6 and pp. 184–186 on teaching thinking).

It may be seen that although there is a fair degree of agreement on the general nature of parent–child interaction which correlates with children's cognitive development, interpretative questions, and many questions of detail, remain. The validity of findings is heavily dependent on using the right sort of measurement, in the first place. The HOME Inventory studies, for example, which find a moderate positive correlation between their scales and child outcomes, use a set of items that summarise and may amalgamate behaviour that might usefully be differentiated further. A more microlevel 'ethological' approach might elucidate patterns that are more amenable to theoretical interpretation and more helpful for intervention or training than global 'responsivity' or 'involvement'. Studies such as David Wood's show the advantages of using a finer-grained level of behaviour (and of having a coherent developmental model), but data from ordinary interaction in the home are desirable if an ecologically representative picture is to be drawn. Studies that focus exclusively on one aspect of parent–child interaction, for example language or even more narrowly 'distancing strategies', may elucidate variation in cognitive development associated with this factor but are obliged to consign all other factors, not studied, to the status of sources of error variance. Worse than this, they may not even realise the importance of their focal factor if it is a necessary cause but not powerful except in combination with another, unstudied, factor. A study that compares groups that have and that lack the behaviour pattern of interest over a long period of time is to be desired, as there may be long-term effects of interaction as well as short-term ones, and, as David Wood implies in the 'scaffolding' model, what is facilitative behaviour may well change as the child grows older (or the learner becomes more expert). Finally, we need an explicit theory of *how* interaction affects development so that causal chains can be analysed; it should also be sensitive to the problems of distinguishing between psychosocial and genetic effects, and between parent effects on children and child effects on parents.

5.4.4 Children whose cognition is not 'scaffolded'

I have described a pattern of social interaction between adult and child that may be an important support of good cognitive development. The case for it rests at present on a variety of pieces of evidence that are suggestive rather than conclusive. One component that we have not yet examined is what happens to children who miss out on this sort of social interaction. If it is crucial for normal development, children who have not had it should show abnormalities – specifically, deficits and difficulties – in their cognitive development. If they show no such abnormalities, such support cannot be necessary for development, though it might facilitate it in the normal run of things. I propose to touch on three sorts of case: studies of children who have suffered extreme social deprivation and grossly inadequate (or malevolent) caretaking; studies of social groups that do not normally use 'scaffolding' and 'motherese' as the populations usually studied by psychologists typically do; and studies that make fine-grained analyses of variation in interaction between depressed mothers and their children.

5.4.4.1 Children who have suffered extreme deprivation in early childhood

Some children are subjected to horrible extremes of neglect, abuse and social deprivation; in some cases we have detailed information on what sort of cognitive functioning such children showed after being rescued. There are a few famous cases where it has been claimed that the child may have completely lacked any human contact, living with non-human animals and surviving only because they provided substitute parental care, and these 'feral' children said to resemble 'savages', 'idiots' or 'beasts' (Gesell 1942; Maclean 1979; Zingg 1940; Newton 2002), usually the sort of the animals that it was believed had enabled them to survive – for example, the 'wolf-children' rescued by the Reverend Mr Singh in northern India howled, ran on all fours, and tore at raw meat (Zingg 1940). However, these cases are typically badly documented, and both the description of the state of the children when first found and the treatment they receive in efforts to rehabilitate them may owe more to the rescuers' preconceptions about what is morally correct than to detailed objective observation, systematic assessment or principled pedagogy. The 'feral' child who is an exception to this, being both well-documented and the recipient of a rehabilitation programme inspired by well-thought-out educational principles, is the boy known as 'Victor' (Lane 1976). Victor was captured in the forests of Aveyron in southern France in 1800, when he was aged about thirteen. He had certainly been living wild there for at least three years, and probably his isolation had begun in his early childhood. After his capture he was taken to Paris and put into the care of Jean-Marc Itard and his housekeeper, Madame Guerin. Itard was a remarkable man, a pioneer in the education of the handicapped and the deaf, and he kept a very detailed record of Victor's development. He devised a system of patient and careful training procedures that remarkably anticipate twentieth-century behaviour modification techniques. Victor, when first rescued, functioned at a level of sensori-motor intelligence, sometimes showing remarkable sensory acuity and sometimes no reaction at all; he had no language and no social skills, and little emotional display. Under Madame Guerin's tutelage, and with the supervision and training of Itard, he progressed to some conceptual thought and moral feelings, especially of empathy, but his language development was disappointing, his social skills rudimentary, and his emerging sexuality and emotions disturbing to both the adults responsible for him and the boy himself. Poor Victor showed so little recovery towards a normal developmental course that it has remained a matter of controversy from his own time to ours whether his defective development might not have had physical roots, not just social ones. Here the question that applies to all children neglected to such a degree has to be faced: is it possible that they were so badly treated because those responsible for them believed that they were in some way abnormal, even before they were abandoned? Consideration of Victor's symptoms and achievements has led some psychologists to suggest that he was probably autistic (Bettelheim 1967; Frith 1990), though Lane (1976) maintains that this diagnosis rests on a selective use of the evidence.

Victor's isolation from human contact is unique. It has been more common for children to suffer deprivation of social interaction, perceptual stimulation, sensori-motor experience, emotional support or adequate nutrition while still in the care of adults. Not long after Victor was found in post-Revolutionary France, Kaspar Hauser turned up in post-Napoleonic Bavaria (Frith 1990; Lang n.d.; Phillips 1980; Masson 1996). He was about sixteen; he had a minute vocabulary, much of it used parrot-fashion, but could read and write a little; could barely walk, would eat only bread and water, could not bear strong light but could see in the dark. When he was able to talk about his experience, he said that he had always lived in a dark room with a low ceiling, where he sat on straw on the ground. There he never heard a sound or saw a bright light, was supplied with bread and water by a man who stood behind him to do so, and had only a couple of wooden horses for playthings. He made rapid progress with first a foster family and then a tutor; he was an appealing young man with an air of innocence about him, and rumours developed that he was of noble birth. It was thought that perhaps he was an illegitimate son of Napoleon, or the rightful Crown Prince of Baden, kidnapped from his cradle and cruelly imprisoned by his usurper. He became one of the local celebrities, and indeed he was of interest to a wide circle of aristocrats and politicians including an English nobleman who paid for his keep and education. His cognitive progress slowed down and he was accused of being lazy and inattentive, though whether this was ineradicable deficit or the reaction of a socially petted adolescent to an unsympathetic, even hostile, teacher is unclear. Five years after he first appeared in Nuremberg, he suffered a mysterious knife wound, from which he died. Who he was, where he came from and who killed him cannot be known; people's myths about foundlings and the intrigues of courts obscure the case. But unless he was a uniquely consummate con artist, it does seem that Kaspar Hauser was made to suffer many years of social and physical deprivation, and that he made a notable recovery when returned to normal life in his late teens.

Some modern cases of social deprivation are documented in a fashion that makes inferences about how deprivation affects cognitive development rather easier to draw. Skuse (1984) reviews four well-known cases of extreme deprivation. Three are American. Anna, the illegitimate daughter of a mother whose Stanford-Binet IQ was 50, was kept from infancy until after her fifth birthday wedged into a chair in a storage room, her arms tied above her head. Isabelle, illegitimate daughter of a deaf-mute mother, was kept shut away with her in a dark room until she was nearly seven. Genie was confined to one small bare room by her psychotic father until she was nearly fourteen, beaten and barked at rather than talked to, tied to a potty-chair or confined in a sleeping bag made like a straitjacket in a crib covered with wire mesh (see also Curtiss (1977), Rymer (1993)). Skuse's next case is a pair of monozygotic Czech twins who spent their first year more or less normally in a children's home and the next six months with an aunt, but for the next five and a half years were in the care of a weak-minded father and a stepmother straight out of Grimm's fairy tales, who brought up the two little boys in almost total isolation, beating them, locking them up for long periods in the cellar, and never allowing them out of the house (see also Koluchova 1976). Fujinaga *et al.* (1990) report on two Japanese children similarly brought up, kept in a shed near their parents' house and allowed to crawl in the yard, but beaten, never talked to or played with or treated with affection. For all these children, and for four other children, Mary, Alice, Beth and Louise, who were less cruelly treated and less socially and perceptually deprived (Skuse 1984), fairly detailed information is available on the state they were in when first rescued from their horrible conditions, and on at least some aspects of their later development.

The children are not identical in the deficits they showed initially, nor in how these problems persisted. Some of those who had had very restricted perceptual environments were initially suspected of sensory impairments because their hearing or vision did not fit the usual pattern. For example, Genie, who had been kept in a room where she could not see anything further than ten feet away, was short-sighted to exactly this degree. On the whole there was a very rapid development of normal vision and hearing. All the children initially had severely limited spoken language and gesture and their language comprehension was poor. Once they were rescued, and received normal or enhanced language experience, Isabelle, the Czech twins and three of Skuse's less deprived girls rapidly developed virtually normal language skills, and the Japanese siblings made slower but substantial progress. Anna, Genie and the last of Skuse's cases, Mary, remained severely retarded in their language; Anna and Genie also remained far below age-appropriate levels on non-verbal intelligence tests, though in the other cases non-verbal IQs were superior to verbal IQ scores. All of the children developed good or adequate motor skills; the Japanese boy became a successful marathon runner. The Czech twins, Isabelle, the Japanese siblings, and Skuse's cases Alice, Beth and Louise were able to cope with normal school, and the Czech and Japanese children are known to have held down ordinary jobs.

Skuse suggests that the victims of extreme sensory and social deprivation whom he describes shared a number of characteristic cognitive deficits: 'motor retardation, absent or very rudimentary vocal and symbolic language, grossly retarded perceptuomotor skills' (1984: 563). They also (understandably) lacked emotional and social expression and social skills.

Of these, the language deficit and the social–emotional problems seemed to be most profound, and the rate of improvement in motor and perceptual skills was much faster. Anna, Genie and Mary, who showed some non-verbal abilities but a complete absence of language, had the worst cognitive outcomes; speech therapy and life in a good environment with fostering adults enabled rapid development of language and cognitive abilities in the other children. If anything, cognition recovered rather better than social and emotional skills, though problems with complex language or with attention remained in some cases, and verbal IQ was depressed relative to performance IQ.

More recent, larger scale and more systematic data come from a continuing series of studies of children who suffered grossly deprived institutional rearing followed by adoption into normal families. The children were all Romanian, placed in orphanages in Romania mainly within the first months of their lives. In these institutions they received inadequate food, no individuated care, no social or cognitive stimulation, and were kept in bare and dirty cots in bare and dirty rooms. The English and Romanian Adoptees Study Team (ERA) have published a large number of accounts of these children at successive stages from their entry to the UK through to age eleven (e.g. Castle *et al.* 1999; Chisholm *et al.* 1995; Croft *et al.* 2001; Kaler and Freeman 1994; Kreppner *et al.* 2001; Kreppner *et al.* 1999; O'Connor *et al.* 2000, 2003; Roy, Rutter, and Pickles 2000; Rutter and the English and Romanian Adoptees Study Team 1998; Rutter *et al.* 2001, 2004). At their rescue, these children showed severe retardation of all cognitive and language measures, retarded physical growth, and socio-emotional problems. Most showed a rapid recovery of cognition and language within the first two years in their adoptive families: those who had been rescued from the orphanages before they were six months old were all at age four scoring near or above the norm for British children; those who had been in the institutions for longer varied but showed very considerable catch-up. The improvement continued between ages four and six; increases in weight and IQ were to the normal range, and though head circumference was not so good and there were a lot of residual problems of socio-emotional development, particularly of attachment, most children were functioning well. Kreppner *et al.* (2001) identify problems of inattention and overactivity. Romanian orphan children adopted into Canada and the Netherlands similarly fared surprisingly well (e.g. Benoit *et al.* 1996; Morison *et al.* 1995; Maclean 2003; Zeanah *et al.* 2003).

These distressing cases suggest that growing up under conditions of extreme deprivation will prevent the development of normal cognition and language; but that if there is no overt genetic anomaly (as there was in Mary's case) and no gross malnutrition (as in Anna's and Genie's, and as in the case of some of the Romanian orphans) there may be a rapid improvement in ability, to within the normal range of IQ and cognition, given stimulating loving care in a small group, though there may be longer-lasting problems of attention, overactivity and attachment, and we do not yet know the outcome in adulthood. It is heartening that better conditions produced so much improvement for these children. Although longer privation clearly has a worse effect, there is very little evidence here for a 'critical period' during which the child must have 'scaffolding' and after which it is too late, apart from the failures of Victor and Genie to develop useful language after having none to adolescence. We might use these data, with data on IQ and ageing and on brain development late in life (pp. 343–345), to justify maintaining the working hypothesis that deprivation leads to deficit at any date, but that there can be a good prognosis if stimulation and support are provided after the period of deprivation.

5.4.4.2 Cultural similarities and differences in parent–child interaction

Two assumptions have to be avoided: that all cultures are 'really' the same in the way they handle parent–child interaction, and that cultures that differ from one's own are worse, unnatural, or inefficient. Blatantly wrong though they are, such ethnocentric biases all too easily creep into one's thinking. I therefore approach discussion of how cultures differ and are similar in parental facilitation of children's cognitive development with some caution, and with an instruction to the reader to proceed similarly. My discussion is also very brief.

In general terms, all cultures make arrangements for children's activities and responsibilities that change as the children's competence develops and extends to new situations. Children everywhere participate in cultural activities that socialise them into the skilled roles and behaviour of their culture. Often, perhaps most often, this is done through structuring the child's activities within the family, providing appropriate instruction within joint activities and allowing children to be active participants in their own socialisation. Ethnographic studies of many cultures provide examples: girls learning to weave in Guatemala (Rogoff 1986, 1995, 1998, 2003), becoming a tailor in Liberia (Greenfield and Lave 1982; Lave 1990), learning about 'clean' and 'unclean' behaviours in India (Shweder et al. 1990; Hejmadi et al. 2004). Rogoff (1990, 1998) suggests that the structuring of activities for novices to work in close involvement with others is ubiquitous, though cultures differ in the content that the novice has to learn and in how communication and participation are arranged.

Differences between cultures in the knowledge that the learner has to acquire are easy to acknowledge, harder to identify, harder still to place a value on. Raven (1980) provides a salutary example of the problems that may arise if the skills and knowledge valued by one culture are pushed insensitively on to another: inner-city working-class mothers taught to play with their young children in middle-class ways did so and believed that it would have a good effect on the children's learning behaviour in school, but that it would be at the cost of unfitting the child for the tougher streetwise activities of the neighbourhood. Another example of a cultural difference, this time in the manner of using cognitive skills, comes in the contrast between the individualistic competitive ethos of schooling in much of the West and the self-effacing, co-operative style of non-Western groups such as Native Americans and the Japanese, a stylistic difference that may constitute part of a different sense of self (Markus and Kitayama 1991) and certainly is part of the difficulty such children have in American classrooms (e.g. Tharp and Gallimore 1988; Weinstein 1991). Social groups differ in their attitudes to stories both as consumers and as producers (Cazden 1988; Heath 1983; Weinstein 1991; pp. 36–38), with consequences for the children's cognitive development directly, through the information, skills and attitudes they learn, and indirectly, through other people's evaluations of their storying.

Children grow up with a particular culture and so are presented with (and protected from) problems that differ from culture to culture, and indeed that change in culturally imposed ways as the child gets older. The sorts of children that researchers are most familiar with, Western and middle class, have to become experts in literacy, and so have to learn in early childhood to attend to and use differences in the little two-dimensional squiggles that are letters. Being literate at a high level has its own rewards, but children have to engage with literacy and numeracy because they are among the core skills of the school curriculum, and are national priorities – compulsory parts of the National Curriculum, for example – because they are seen as essential for the economic health and development of the nation. Other groups may have different goals, in which universal literacy is low down the priorities; these goals may be quite as good for the present functioning and the future survival of the group as Western ones are. Understanding development involves studying children's behaviour (and their interaction with other people in particular) in the context of the goals that are locally valued, without imposing our own goals or our assumptions about what goals are worthwhile. It also involves the recognition that all goals have costs attached, that we cannot achieve all possible positive outcomes simultaneously and without any cost, and the recognition that the same ultimate outcome may be achieved in different ways – learning to read is an example of a development that can take several different routes, none of which is clearly 'better' than the others in the long term.

Different cultures prescribe different things to be learned, and also vary how they communicate with children. I have discussed some of the literature on adult–child talk earlier in this section, and will now only make the point that some of the variation in adult–child talk is associated with other differences in adult–child interaction. For example, the other modes of communication available differ if one pair are in skin-to-skin contact and facing the same way and one pair are physically more distant and cannot easily look at the same object (Rogoff 1990, 2003; Trevarthen 1988b). Cultures differ also in the question of whose place it is to initiate talk: in some, adult and child are equals in taking turn in conversation, in others adult initiates and child deferentially responds, in others there is child–older child talk rather than child talk with adults (Ochs 1988, 1990). It must be stressed that parent–child interaction takes place within a context of other people, other potential social partners. Older children or grandparents or other members of the extended family may play with the child more than parents do. These non-parent caregivers may determine children's activities and responsibilities, working with the child in guided participation in the skills of the culture. Being the child's parent in the sense of 'biological parent' is certainly not necessary for such interaction. Western children are, ethnographic studies show, unusually segregated from adult occupational and recreational activities, and learn about the skills of such activities in the separate and specialised context of school much more than non-Western children do. Learning by observation and by eavesdropping will occur less frequently when children are thus excluded from the adult world. Children will have less responsibility for their own learning, and adults will make more formal and explicit attempts to teach them.

5.4.4.3 Cognitive development in the children of depressed mothers

The argument of the earlier parts of this section has been that children need, or at least benefit from, sensitive, child-contingent 'scaffolding' of their attention, thinking and concentration during the early stages of their cognitive development and their education. I move now to work on the development of the children of depressed mothers because it seems possible that depressed mothers are often not able to scaffold their preschoolers' activities, and that this shortage of scaffolding and concomitant emotional difficulties have their effect on the child's cognitive behaviour. (Depression in fathers might also create risk (Cummings et al. 2005), but has been much less researched.)

Depression is alarmingly common among the mothers of young children. Population studies (e.g. Brown and Harris 1978; Richman et al. 1982; Hammen 2003) find noticeable depression in up to 40 per cent of women; low socio-economic status, lack of a confiding relationship, several pre-school children (perhaps especially if they include twins) and no satisfying job increase the risk of depression. It is also becoming apparent that the children of depressed parents are probably at increased risk of psychiatric disorder. The evidence is not yet sufficiently clear to quantify this risk and there are still numerous debates and disagreements: see reviews by Coyne and Downey (1991), Dix (1991), Downey and Coyne (1990), Cummings and Davies

(1994), Hammen (2003). A number of conceptual and methodological problems contribute to this lack of clarity. One is that 'depression' varies from case to case, and there is still controversy about diagnostic criteria (see e.g. Seligman (1975), Rosenhan and Seligman (1995), Barker (1988), Rutter *et al.* (1986)). Samples recruited from people receiving clinical care differ from people recruited from the general population. Sometimes members of a sample are defined as 'depressed' because they are above a conventional cut-off score; those just below and those far below this level are classed together as 'non-depressed', though their mood states may be very different. Depression used to be thought of as involving a single episode that usually resolved without lasting impairment, but it may actually more character-istically involve recurring episodes of severe depression with residual diffi-culties even during more positive periods. Thus the child may be exposed to 'depression' of varying severity for a longer time than any one officially diagnosed episode. Depression is also associated with anxiety and 'per-sonality disorders' such as aggression and undue dependence, and often occurs as a reaction to difficulties in people's lives such as economic adver-sity, poor interpersonal relationships, marital conflict and breakup, lack of social support and housing problems, all of which might be expected to impinge on children directly and independently of their parents' depression. It may be associated with factors that are entirely or largely 'in' the child, such as prematurity, multiple births, serious handicap, difficult 'tempera-ment'; or depression may accompany the stresses and emotional demands of parenting, when one's offspring is simultaneously the best and brightest thing in the universe and the source of one's sleep deprivation, one's anxieties about feeding and health, yet another sticky and indelible stain on the carpet, and some singularly aversive high-pitched noises.

It will not be easy to tease out what psychological difficulty is leading to what, given the variation in mothers' depression, in the degree to which their parenting is supplemented by other people's, and in the age of the child during the period(s) of depression. This last is a particularly important point: what is appropriate parenting changes with age, this being one of the things that good parenting recognises, and the skills needed at one age may be affected by depression more or less than the skills appropriate at another age. Further, children's own reactions to their mother's depression are likely to be age-dependent; children of different ages will probably have had different lengths of time exposed to a mother suffering from episodes of depression or less severe negative feelings. It is hard to compare research samples which are not always completely documented on variables such as these and are often also small enough to show results due to idiosyncrasies of individuals.

Despite these methodological and conceptual problems, some tentative conclusions seem to be emerging (Downey and Coyne 1990; Rutter 1990; Cummings and Davies 1994; Beardslee *et al.* 1998; Brennan *et al.* 2000;

Hammen 2003). School-aged children of depressed parents tend to have more adjustment problems than children of non-depressed parents, including poorer ratings on behaviour and emotion checklists, higher levels of psychiatric treatment, poorer physical health, academic deficits and lack of social competence. In particular, they may be especially liable to becoming depressed themselves.

It is quite possible that parent and child are both distressed and depressed because they share genes or because they share the same unsupportive and stressful environment. However, studies that include detailed observations of parent–child interaction suggest that the link between parental depression and child adjustment, especially the child's cognitive adjustment, may lie centrally in features of the interaction of depressed mothers and their children. I will use as an example a study, the SLUFP project, which I became involved in (Cox et al. 1987; Meadows and Mills 1987; Mills and Funnell 1983; Mills et al. 1985; Pound et al. 1982). The first stage of this study involved detailed observations of depressed and 'control' mothers (the latter demographically very similar but without psychiatric symptoms) at home with their two-year-old children, observations that focused on their joint activity and on episodes of control or distress. The children were observed again in any preschool setting they attended, and during their second term in infant school (at age six), when teacher ratings and scores on a computer vigilance task were added to the intelligence tests taken at two and a half and six. The mothers were extensively interviewed about their lives, marriages and other circumstances at the two-and-a-half-year-old stage, but, regrettably, not at the six-year-old stage. All were white, working-class, British born, inner London, two-parent families with the father in employment at the outset of the study.

It must be said at the outset that some of the depressed mothers were parenting sensitively and sensibly, and their children were problem-free at all ages. But the larger part of the depressed group reported that their children had extensive behaviour problems, and here the mother–child interaction tended to show a less promising pattern, particularly if there was marital discord in the family. These mothers were less likely to respond to their two-year-olds' overtures, to extend their children's behaviour in 'scaffolding' ways, to facilitate social interaction, and to pre-empt conflict by managing the interaction so that problems did not reach overt conflict. They were more likely to be very withdrawn and despairing in mood, or to be intrusive, critical and hostile, reacting to the child's episodes of distress with anger and controllingness. There was less overt positive enjoyment of mother–child interaction, less joint play and less imaginative co-operation, and though there was no decrease in physical warmth and cuddles some of this seemed to be the mother using the child as a comfort object. Some of these children seemed to be carrying the responsibility for looking after their mothers, glancing up from their intelligence test continually to ask

'You all right Mum?', fetching ashtray after ashtray after being asked to get one, in at least one case making the comforting cup of tea.

When the children were seen in school at the age of rising six, it was the children who had had depressed mothers *and* behaviour problems at two who differed from the rest. They were significantly less good at concentrating on school tasks and at developing their activity beyond a very simple repetitive level; they received more poor ratings from teachers on social and academic problem checklists; they had much more difficulty with the formal tests when these involved sustained attention. As I observed them throughout the school day, the metaphor that they built up in my mind was 'anxious puddings': inert, unresponsive, heavily defended children whose first reaction was 'I can't do it' and whose second was to shut themselves off from all occasions when they might have to try. In short, they looked like depressed, under-achieving children who were not engaging themselves with the opportunities that the school offered and were somewhat distressed by its cognitive and social challenges. Given the limited resources of the school system it seemed likely that they might never be enticed out of this into a higher level of engagement, achievement and enjoyment. The continuity of problems from two and a half to six, which was statistically significant at better than the 0.01 level, looked likely to be maintained to later ages.

Other studies have also shown various of the effects we found in our sample; for example: negative self-concept and attributions (Hammen *et al.* 1987, 1990), guilt and anxiety (Radke-Yarrow 1991; Zahn-Waxler and Kochanska 1990), being withdrawn with peers (Zahn-Waxler *et al.* 1984) and with demanding tasks (Kochanska 1991), insecure attachment (Radke-Yarrow and Sherman 1985), attention problems (Cogill *et al.* 1986; Cohler *et al.* 1977; Jacobvitz and Sroufe 1987; Wahler and Dumas 1989), and less parental facilitation of children's activity (Estrada *et al.* 1987; Radke-Yarrow and Kuczynski 1983; Rutter 1990). Attachment between parent and child is an important contributor to children's cognitive development; sensitive responsive parenting protects against risk (Cicchetti 2002).

There may be the beginnings of a case here for some more specific links between parenting and child behaviour than we have seen before. These may act directly on and through cognition and via the participants' emotional states. It seems possible, firstly, that depressed mothers, with sadder, slower and flatter ways of speaking and acting (Bettes 1988; Breznitz and Sherman 1987; Mills *et al.* 1985; Pound *et al.* 1982; Radke-Yarrow *et al.* 1990), with less empathy and involvement in other people's activities (Dix 1991; Slade 1987), and with little or no positive emotion, are much less likely to be able to produce the positive and child-contingent parenting that supports and extends the development of young children's cognition and language. This may be particularly important for young children, who need the scaffolding and emotional support for cognitive effort that they cannot yet sustain for themselves:

> Parenting is a particularly complex form of social interaction. The sustained effortful behaviour that it involves is likely to prove difficult for depressed parents, especially when their children are young and exaggerated affective tone and a high tolerance for aversive behaviour are required.
>
> (Downey and Coyne 1990: 61)

As in the SLUFP sample, this experience of parenting that lacks responsiveness to the child, is non-contingent and non-facilitating, and does not extend the child's activity imaginatively may be associated with slower and more limited development of cognition and language, with a depressed verbal IQ, with less symbolic play and with impaired concentration and engagement in school. Second, parenting that deals with control issues by imposing obedience unilaterally or by abdicating control totally in the face of even minimal child resistance misses the opportunities for teaching children to reason, understand and negotiate that less distressed mothers may provide; its consequences at school age might include difficulties with classroom routine and co-operation with other children, as well as, perhaps, less empathy and understanding. Third, parenting that is sad and helpless seems to be associated with child behaviour that is anxious, guilt-ridden and helpless (Zahn-Waxler and Kochanska 1990); it is one of the clearer and more noteworthy findings emerging from the research literature that the psychiatric problems of the children of depressed parents tend to involve depressive symptoms. The depressed mothers in the SLUFP study often reported that their own mothers had suffered from depression, an apparent stability of symptom over three successive generations. This continuity gets to look nastily inescapable when a further point is added: because depression is unattractive and associated with lack of energy, it may be that the depressed mother suffers from inadequate social support networks outside the family (Brown and Harris 1978; Coyne and Downey 1991), and because depressed mothers tend to have depressed partners and unsupportive marriages (Downey and Coyne 1990), the young child may not have a non-depressed person available either within the family or outside it to provide happier parenting.

I will end this section by stressing three things. First, this is all very much 'work in progress' and this pattern of effects of maternal depression on children's cognitive development is a matter of intelligent speculation rather than of firm fact. Second, it would be wrong, it would be wicked to blame the mothers, who are usually doing as well as anyone could in horribly unhelpful circumstances; rather blame us all for our lack of concern for the support of the psychological health of young children and their caregivers.

Third, to return to the wider subject matter of this book, this area provides important intimations of how the development and acquisition of cognition in childhood are bound up inextricably with emotion, a topic I return to in the final chapter.

5.4.5 Children and poverty

An enormous amount of evidence documents an association between poverty and disadvantage, on the one hand, and risk of poorer developmental outcomes in cognition, emotion and behaviour, on the other (e.g. Ackerman et al. 2004a, 2004b; Bolger et al. 1995; Bornstein and Bradley 2003; Bradley and Corwyn 2002; Bronfenbrenner et al. 1996; Bronfenbrenner and Morris 1998; Duncan et al. 1994; Evans 2004; Felner et al. 1995; Hoff et al. 2002; Huston et al. 1994; Luthar 1999; McLoyd 1998). We are beginning to be able to go beyond the constituents of poverty to see how each might have an effect on children's cognitive development, an essential step in discovering how we can break the cycle of disadvantage. Ackerman et al. (2004a, 2004b), for example, show that contextual risk in the form of family instability and parental maladjustment combined with harsh parenting were associated with children doing worse in adjusting to school, perhaps because they tended to destabilise family functioning. Whether economic adversity persisted was less important for child outcomes than the family functioning variables.

Children living in poverty are likely to be subject to a complex, multifaceted and long-term exposure to multiple risks. For example, study after study, including those cited above, shows that compared with children from richer families they are more at risk of being in a family where relationships are stressed and violent; where marriages break down and parents are absent; where siblings are delinquent and failing school; where the home has worse physical conditions, for example overcrowding, damp, pollution; where family members' physical and mental health is worse; where the family has less support from neighbours, friends and kin; where day-care and schools have less money, less well-trained staff, fewer resources, and a high proportion of pupils with the same social problems; where there are few positive out-of-school activities; where the neighbourhood has more hazards, more traffic, more crime, more pollution, more physical deterioration; and where even opportunities to access a healthy diet are few and expensive. Even if the economic circumstances of a family in poverty improve, this is most often not a big improvement, and the economic respite is often short-lived. As we have seen in this section, exposure to each of these disadvantages may increase the risk of poor cognitive development (and behaviour problems): experience of continued poverty, or of intermittent poverty where the change in income does not take the family far above the official poverty level, can add up to sustained and pervasive disadvantage over a long period.

5.5 The school as a setting for the development and acquisition of cognition

A section on social influences on the development and acquisition of cognition in childhood has to recognise that children are involved in social institutions other than the family, many of which have received little attention. I do not know of much research on children's induction into religious ideas in church settings, for example, nor on the cognitive skills they acquire through youth organisations. The major social institution that is relevant to our present concerns is, however, the school, and the problem here is too much research rather than too little. I shall not seek to summarise the literature on how schools affect children's cognitive development (for American reviews see Brophy (1986), Brophy and Good (1986), Snow *et al.* (1991), Weinstein (1991), and the 1989 volume of the *International Journal of Educational Research*, and for British studies, Mortimore *et al.* (1988, 1989), Rutter (1985b), Rutter *et al.* (1979), Tizard *et al.* (1988), Eccles and Roeser (1998), NICHD Early Child Care Research Network (2004), Rutter and Maughan (2002)). Instead, I will focus on whether effective schooling involves the sort of scaffolding that seems to be associated with effective cognitive functioning in the family.

An enormous quantity of research has been done on why some schools or teachers seem to foster pupils' achievement better than others. This is not a simple problem: it is complicated by differences in the level of skills and knowledge that the pupils start from, by differences in their abilities, by differences in their cognition-related activities outside school, by problems in measuring achievement, by problems in identifying and measuring relevant school or teacher characteristics, and by other complexities. Researchers have not always succeeded in coping with these problems, and 'findings' do not always stand up to further scrutiny. However, a number of points relevant to school 'scaffolding' can be made. Students learn best when they are engaged in academic tasks that are clearly introduced to them and that they can proceed through steadily, making consistent progress with few failures (ideally almost none when they have to work independently, and not many when the teacher is there to provide feedback and guidance); when the teacher has established a classroom orientation towards conscientious academic work, and supervises and instructs actively within the classroom; and when the teacher's behaviour supports students' efforts through behaviour such as question sequences that establish easy facts that have to be combined to answer a harder problem, allowing an appropriate time for a student to produce an answer, providing regular and extensive feedback, praising specifically rather than generally, and acknowledging achievements in a positive but non-intrusive way (Brophy (1986), Fraser (1989), Mortimore *et al.* (1989)). This package of behaviours looks like scaffolding, as it might be manifested under the notably difficult circumstance of having to do it for twenty or thirty learners at once. Class size affects the possibility of relationships where the teachers feel they know their pupils as individuals, and hence the possibility of scaffolding; and hence there are advantages to having small class sizes in terms of benefits for children's achievements (NICHD Network 2004).

'Scaffolding in the classroom' has to be differentiated to fit the characteristics of the learners. Very young pupils need more instruction in the routines and procedures of the classroom and of learning, and, being involved in the development of basic skills, they should have frequent opportunities to practise them and receive feedback on them. Older pupils who have internalised how to be a pupil and are now applying well-learned basic skills may not need to participate in the activity so overtly, and may learn with more impersonal instruction: they can provide a greater degree of scaffolding for themselves. Similarly, low achievers need more structuring of their learning by their teachers: more active instruction, more feedback, higher success rates and smaller steps in cognitive demands, more practice, more support and more encouragement. Thus 'scaffolding' may have to be adjusted to the individual's current competence and permanent or temporary idiosyncrasies; no wonder that teaching is such a demanding and highly skilled activity!

The research on 'effective teaching' focuses on increases in cognitive achievement, often measured as performance on tests or in examinations. Some educationalists (Scheerens and Creemers 1989) would argue that the measures used over-emphasise the acquisition of knowledge that is used only in tests, and that does not become an accessible and applicable part of the learner's knowledge base. This sort of 'knowledge-transforming' learning may require particular sorts of social input; one approach which seems particularly promising is 'co-operative learning' (Brown and Palincsar 1989). This is an alternative to the individualist learning that is required in most classrooms, and that may be inappropriate for many learners (Heath 1983; Tharp and Gallimore 1988).

Brown and Palincsar focus their discussion of co-operative learning on 'reciprocal teaching', which provides a simple introduction to group discussion techniques aimed at understanding and remembering text content. It takes place in a co-operative learning group in which an adult teacher and a group of students take turns leading a discussion on the content of a section of text that they are jointly attempting to understand. Four strategic activities are given guided practice: questioning, clarifying, summarising and predicting. The group member whose turn it is to be leader begins the discussion by asking a question on the main content and ends by summarising it. In between, disagreements are resolved by rereading and discussion of questions and answers; after the summary, the group leader asks for predictions about future content. The adult teacher is the model for these strategic activities initially, and provides feedback and guidance appropriate to the needs of the current discussion leader and the other group members. The group members have joint responsibility for understanding and discussing the text; the leader is responsible for orchestrating the dialogue and the listeners for being supportive critics in the elucidation of content and the resolution.

Why does reciprocal teaching work well? First, it highlights *explanation*. These participants in the discussion have to offer explanations, interpretations, justifications and resolutions to problems. The listeners in the group call on the discussion leaders to back up their arguments with relevant data and so elaborate and extend them, increasing the coherence of the knowledge structure. This involves both support for what is said and arguments that are in conflict with it. The *support* activities of the group include shared responsibility for thinking, which shares out the effort and reduces anxiety because no one contribution need be a complete solution or able to stand independently of others; modelling cognitive processes, because group members share roles such as summariser, recorder, 'yes-butter' and corrector, and can both see how other members perform these roles and use other people's enactments to complement their own performance; and sharing expertise, as individuals' knowledge and skills can be combined and responsibility for covering the ground shared out. The *conflict* activities of the group include insistence on clarification, justification and elaboration, which can result in fundamental cognitive restructuring (Doise and Mugny 1984). Individuals can come to perform these group activities for themselves, as they internalise all the thinking roles, insist on clarifying and justifying themselves and try out their own counterexamples and summaries.

Lave (1990) provides an interesting discussion of the underlying principles of 'understanding-in-practice' and of 'understanding-via-schooling'. He argues that the former is the more powerful source of enculturation:

> knowledge-in-practice, constituted in the settings of practice, based on rich expectations generated over time about its shape, is the site of the most powerful knowledgeability of people in the lived-in world. The encompassing, synthesizing intentions reflected in a theory of understanding-in-practice make it difficult to argue for the separation of cognition and the social world, the form and content of learning, or of learning and its 'applications'. Internalization is a less important vehicle for transmission of the experience the world has to offer, in this view, than activity in relation with the world.
>
> (Lave 1990: 323)

Thus, learning in school may be deeply problematic. School is part of 'real life' – a major part of it for children, fifteen thousand hours or so of it in the West – but it differs from children's non-schooled life in at least two cognitively relevant ways. First, it concentrates to a considerable extent on procedures that are divorced from real-world procedures by being more algorithmic, more closed, and more specific. Second, learning focuses on problems prescribed by the curriculum rather than problems the learners spontaneously want to solve. This may lead to the learners learning procedures and applying them correctly to classroom examples but incorrectly or not at all to analogous problems encountered outside school, as seems to be all too common in everyday mathematics (see section 2.4). The goals of learning have not been clear, the procedure has been overspecified, and the practice has not come to be flexible or to be 'owned', as would have happened in the 'understanding-in-practice' of apprenticeship. At the root of this there may be different metaphors of learning. The dominant one in Western education and psychology makes the subject-matter the environment in which the child moves: the problem-solver moves through the successive steps of the problem as if contained by it. 'Understanding-in-practice' makes the learners constitute the problem for themselves: the child's understanding and goals define the problem, give meaning and value to the subject-matter and the process of learning it, and integrate it into the learner's life and activity.

> Given that the development of an understanding about learning and about what is being learned inevitably accompanies learning, in the more conventional sense, it seems probable that learners whose understanding is deeply circumscribed and diminished through processes of explicit and intense 'knowledge transmission' are likely to arrive at an understanding of themselves as 'not understanding' or as 'bad at what they are doing' even when they are not bad at it (such seems the fate of the vast majority of the alumni of school math classes). On the other hand, learners who understand what they are learning in terms that increasingly approach the breadth and depth of understanding of a master practitioner are likely to understand themselves to be active agents in the appropriation of knowledge, and hence may act as active agents on their own behalf.
>
> (Lave 1990: 325)

I think it may be useful to compare the points that Lave makes here with the literature on the effectiveness of special educational programmes for children from disadvantaged families (e.g. Barnett 1995; Burchinal et al. 1997; Campbell et al. 2001, 2002; Campbell and Ramey 1995; Fan and Chen 2001; Mosteller 1995; Ramey and Ramey 1998; Reynolds 1994; Reynolds et al. 1996, 2004; Reynolds and Temple 1998; Yoshikawa 1995). Because low achievement in educational settings and involvement in delinquency have proved hard to eradicate, and remain associated with poverty and disadvantage, a number of educational interventions have been set up to try to improve achievement and reduce failure. The American Project Head Start and the current British Sure Start are examples of such programmes. Head Start mainly involved enriched experience for children (and sometimes their families) before they went into the ordinary school system. The outcome of this sort of educational 'inoculation' seemed in the early stages to be transitory rises in IQ that reduced to nothing within a couple of years, prompting Jensen (1969) to say that 'compensatory education has been tried and it has failed'. More careful analyses later have shown far more positive effects of Head Start programmes (e.g. Consortium for Longitudinal Studies 1983; Berrueta-Clermont 1984; Garber 1988; Garber and Hodge 1989; V. E. Lee et al. 1988; S. Lee et al. 1988; Reynolds 1994; Sylva 1994; Woodhead 1985, 1988; Zigler and Muenchow 1992; Zigler and Styfco 1993; Zigler and Valentine 1979). Properly conducted intensive preschool intervention for disadvantaged children can lead to short-term gains in IQ that are followed by better school performance and better motivation to work in school, and eventually by less risk of failure in school and anti-social behaviour. The much less intense experience of attendance at preschool groups in the UK is also associated with better educational performance in the primary school for the whole social range of children (Osborn and Milbank 1987; Clark 1988; Jowett and Sylva 1986; Gregg et al. 2004).

Two particularly well-documented projects, the Abecedarian project (Ramey and Ramey 1998) and the Chicago Child-Parent Centers (Reynolds et al. 2004) show what the causal path between intervention and outcome may be. There are three main possibilities: that the intervention improves children's cognitive abilities as measured in standardised tests and these improvements initiate a sequence of improved performance on school tasks and tests that culminate in better school achievement; that the intervention makes families more likely to support the child's cognitive development more effectively; that participation in the programme makes the families seek out better schools for their children and use the schools more effectively. The evidence from these two major studies is that all these things happen. Children's cognition was boosted by their preschool experience and this, plus continuing family support and school support through the later part of their education, led to higher rates of school completion. Programme participation enhanced these little children's cognition and language and their readiness to cope with the demands of formal schooling; this led to higher ratings from teachers, less likelihood of being retained in grade to repeat a year, and more completion of high school. Programme involvement of mothers had a positive effect on both child outcomes and mothers' well-being. School support and family support as they grew older were the major predictors of children avoiding involvement in crime and delinquency. The quality of schooling after the intervention was crucial for the eventual outcome; the early intervention is not so much an 'inoculation' that can prevent failure all by itself as an early advantage that can be built on to lead, eventually, to success.

The message of the literature on cognitive development that I have reviewed in this book is that cognitive development is embedded in emotion and motivation, that it is influenced or even constituted by social interaction, that it can involve play and imagination as well as focused problem-solving and study, that it is not separate from the rest of the child's life.

5.6 Social influences on children's cognitive development: recapitulation and theoretical discussion

In order to make sense of what the existing evidence tells us about social and interactional influences on children's cognition, and to integrate this section with the earlier parts of this book, it may be useful to reconsider, briefly, what the major theories of cognitive development say about social factors in cognitive development. Of the three 'models' of cognitive development discussed in Chapter 4, Vygotsky's says most about social facilitation, Piaget's less, and the information-processing approach least (with the exception of Case's account of the child's innate predilection for observation, imitation and emotionally motivated learning). It is essentially the Vygotskian approach that is most relevant here, though I will first recapitulate and discuss some of Piaget's ideas, and the idea of observation and imitation as the major route to socially based learning.

Piaget (1932, 1983) listed social influences as one of the four major factors behind cognitive development (the others being equilibration, maturation, and the child's individual experience of the physical and logical–mathematical world), but insisted that children must already have the relevant cognitive structures in order to profit from social influences, that social interaction could only complete their development, not create it. Thus social interaction would only affect cognitive development at times when the child's individually constructed cognitive structures are nearing completion, when the child is a 'transitional' conserver, for example, beginning to give up non-conserving answers in favour of conservation. Further, young children were said to be too egocentric to recognise that there might be a discrepancy between their own ideas and someone else's, and therefore would be less able than older children to use such discrepancies and undergo the cognitive conflict that Piaget saw as essential to cognitive development. Finally, Piaget believed that 'symmetrical' interactions between peers would facilitate cognitive development in ways that 'asymmetrical' interactions between adult and child could not, because adult and child are too unlike in cognitive skills and social status for the child to be able to be an active participant in resolving cognitive disagreement. The Piagetian account of social influences on cognitive development therefore limits them quite severely, and focuses centrally on the symmetrical and active negotiation of cognitive conflict between equals.

The long-running debate over whether this Piagetian account is satisfactory continues (pp. 277–278). There is disagreement, for example, about the relative efficiency of intra-individual conflict, inter-individual conflict, and inter-individual co-operation and confirmation and of active and passive engagement, and over whether symmetrical or asymmetrical relationships are more effective facilitators of learning. The role of age in this is also unclear, but if younger children and older children do, as Piaget suggested, differ in their openness to social facilitation of learning, this difference may be contributing to the inconsistency in the findings of different research studies. There are also difficulties about how cognitive changes are assessed: often the criterion is advance to a successful per-formance of a task – to becoming a conserver, for example – and smaller advances, such as a longer period of working on the task even though the right solution is not found, or understanding the solution when someone else gives it, are not looked for, though they might be more likely conse-quences if the amount of exposure to learning opportunities is small.

Thus, although the Piagetian model has given rise to a considerable body of work on the social facilitation of cognitive development, it does not yet provide specific answers about when and how such facilitation occurs, nor about how socially induced learning is incorporated into what remains a mainly individually generated developmental course. Socio-cognitive conflict provokes disequilibrium which the child then equilibrates; thus all the problems with what equilibration is and how it works that I raised in Chapter 4 arise. Finally, the Piagetian model sees other people as a part of the child's total environment not so very different from its other parts, facilitating cognitive development because they hold views of the outside world differing from the child's own, more than because they have social goals and intentions. In view of the increasing evidence of children's ten-dency to treat persons and inanimate objects as different in kind from babyhood onwards (see Kaye (1984), Trevarthen (1982)), we might do well to look at theories that take a more social-centred approach to cognition.

Social learning theory (Bandura 1977b) proposes that children learn by observing and imitating others. It is argued that children naturally imitate (cf. Case 1985), that social reinforcement motivates this, that models to be imitated are usually socially desirable (for example in being more com-petent cognitively than the learner), and that thus children will often learn through observation and imitation of more skilled cognition than their own. In this account of learning, the person who is imitated may not be deliberately modelling behaviour, so the 'social' component of the learning process is in the social reward outcomes of imitation and the social desir-ability of the model, rather than in the process of learning or in social interaction between imitator and imitated. I think it is helpful to be reminded that children do learn by imitation of 'accidental' models, models who are not seeking to teach them, but questions of what 'imitation' is, and how it works, remain. What conditions are necessary for imitation to be possible? How near must the learner's initial skills be to what is imitated? Does behaviour first learned through imitation undergo further change; for example if it is, as Piaget suggested, very much accommodation, is it followed by assimilation, and would that alter the imitated behaviour? Does the way the model presents the behaviour that is imitated affect how easy it is to imitate it, or how durable and well-learned the imitation is? Social learning theory as such has not provided answers to these questions. They are, however, taken seriously in the most influential of current social-centred theories of cognition, that originating in Vygotsky's work.

For Vygotsky (as for G. H. Mead), cognition originates in social inter-action and centres on children's appropriation of cultural tools, goals and activities, which they internalise in their coming to be fully functioning members of their cultures. Interaction with other people, especially more skilled people who take the responsibility for keeping the interaction within the learner's zone of proximal development, and who use language and non-verbal teaching strategies to facilitate the child's learning, is a central part of this. The more competent partner structures the interaction so that the child is able to participate in increasingly complex ways, eventually managing all the actions necessary for a successful completion of the task. There is a transition from other-regulation to self-regulation so that even-tually no support from another person is necessary, though recognition and praise from a skilled other may remain welcome, as the Nobel Prize system shows! Ultimately this 'scaffolding' technique of teaching has been so well internalised by the learners that they can provide it for themselves in new learning situations; the learning child internalises the teacher's actions and reflections, transforming them into his or her own way of solving that particular problem or doing that particular task, but also internalising and developing more general tools – how to observe, how to imitate, how to analyse, how to scaffold one's own cognitive activity or another person's. These powerful 'metacognitive' activities contribute to making the learner into a 'self-running problem-solver' (Meadows and Cashdan 1988). The neo-Vygotskian model of teaching centres on scaffolding: the model of learning involves a wide range of processes ranging from mindless imitation to reflective abstraction of general principles of metacognition. It could thus be seen as the best current candidate for understanding social influences on cognitive development. Whether it is sensible to determine a 'best' model at present is a question in need of further discussion, however.

Chapter 6

Teaching thinking

Formal education has many goals, not all of them universally agreed on, not all of them clear or explicit, not all of them good for the particular individual, not all of them attained. This is not the place to debate, or even to acknowledge, most of them. My concern here is what education might be doing to enhance cognitive development, or facilitate the acquisition of cognitive skills. To do this, I will try to match some of the attributes of successful cognition, of good thinkers, with what we know about possible educational practices. I will also look briefly at some educational programmes intended to teach thinking.

It is clear that people who have developed or acquired a good repertoire of strategies, both high-level general ones and narrower highly specialised ones, and can apply them to a wide range of learning and problem-solving situations, are likely to be highly effective in their cognition. They are likely to be better learners, reasoners, readers, writers, memorisers, scientists, mathematicians, intelligence test takers and so forth than people who have smaller or more rigid repertoires of strategies, will be more likely to be 'Universal Expert' or 'Renaissance Man'. As well as having a good repertoire of strategies, they will know a lot about how, when and why to operate these strategies; that is, they will have a high degree of meta-cognitive knowledge and reflective awareness. This knowledge makes them able to operate strategies effectively on familiar tasks, and to see how they can be applied to new tasks, perhaps in a slightly modified form. They will also need an extensive base of declarative knowledge, the facts on which their cognitive strategies can work, or that can make strategic thought simpler or even unnecessary. Strategy, metacognition and basic knowledge are well co-ordinated in the cognitively competent person: they can operate in the appropriate sequence, often more or less automatically, and flexibly according to how the task's demands are being met. Cognitive experts are also likely to be fast, thus reducing demands on memory and economising on cognitive resources. Finally, good thinkers will have a confident attitude to cognitive tasks; they will be willing to accept cognitive challenges, to extrapolate from the familiar to the unfamiliar, to take risks and to go 'beyond the information given', to make mistakes and learn from them, to succeed and not take their success for granted but be able soberly to identify its sources. In short, they will be people who enjoy thinking.

Human cultures do, on the whole, value such activities, and many invest a great deal of their resources in efforts to equip their young members with cognitive strategies, knowledge and an aptitude for transfer. Cultures differ, of course, in what knowledge and what cognitive skills they emphasise, and in the form the education system takes; but generally a good ability to learn cognitive skills and apply them appropriately to any situation that is met is a universal cultural goal. School systems are commonly held to be responsible for teaching their students to think effectively and are also commonly accused of failing to do so. Evaluating the truth of this accusation is beyond the scope of this book, though a brief overview of some of the research on the differential effectiveness of schools may be found in the preceding chapter. I will here provide a brief account of what psychology suggests are the features of good thinking, and of what might be suggested about how to teach it.

Resnick (1987b: 3) offers a list of 'key features of higher order thinking', which forms one useful starting-point for our discussion.

- Higher order thinking is *nonalgorithmic*. That is, the path of action is not fully specified in advance.
- Higher order thinking tends to be *complex*. The total path is not 'visible' (mentally speaking) from any single vantage point.
- Higher order thinking often yields *multiple solutions*, each with costs and benefits, rather than unique solutions.
- Higher order thinking involves *nuanced judgement* and interpretation.
- Higher order thinking involves the application of *multiple criteria*, which sometimes conflict with one another.
- Higher order thinking often involves *uncertainty*. Not everything that bears on the task at hand is known.
- Higher order thinking involves *self-regulation* of the thinking process. We do not recognise higher order thinking in an individual when someone else 'calls the plays' at every step.
- Higher order thinking involves *imposing meaning*, finding structure in apparent disorder.
- Higher order thinking is *effortful*. There is considerable mental work involved in the kinds of elaborations and judgements required.

The cognitive skills involved here, although called 'higher order', in fact pervade even 'basic skills' such as reading, simple arithmetic, and knowing whether it will soon be tea-time. Research on what happens when people read a passage of text, for example (pp. 50–55), shows that the reader uses a combination of recognising or decoding words, calling on relevant linguistic knowledge, topic knowledge and genre knowledge already stored in memory, and 'high-level' general cognitive processes such as making inferences, noting connections, checking and organising text information and additional external information, deleting irrelevant material and so forth, in order to construct a mental representation not just of the literal extant text itself but of the mental representation the writer hoped to induce in the reader. Knowledge and skills like these are generally agreed to be the main components of what we do when we comprehend text. Successful readers are better at them than unsuccessful readers; to a considerable extent they have become so skilled that text comprehension processes proceed rapidly and automatically (that is, without conscious effort or deliberate attention), and some of them (for example phonological decoding) may even no longer be used unless automatic processing breaks down. Deliberate conscious efforts to comprehend what is read are made when the topic is unfamiliar so that prior knowledge cannot aid interpretation; when the language is unusual or anomalous; when the argument or genre or inferences presented are unusual or complicated – particularly dense, for example – or when the reader intends to study and remember the text rather than just get the gist of it. Skilled readers can both skim and understand text automatically and use deliberate effortful comprehension processes when appropriate. Unskilled readers, including children learning to read, need to be able to apply them too: even beginning reading is not just word recognition or letter-to-sound decoding (Oakhill and Garnham 1988). Worryingly, it seems that children who are having difficulty learning to read may get less opportunity to practise these skills than more successful children because their learning is focused on decoding skills (see Francis (1982), Stanovich (2004)).

Resnick argues that children's difficulties with school mathematics centre on their failure to link their own independently developed mathematical concepts and procedures with the formal rules and algorithms taught in school (cf. pp. 79–83, 299, 301, 304 on mathematical reasoning, and Vygotsky on the development of scientific concepts, pp. 73–77). Again, dealing with a mathematical problem involves recognising the numerical (or algebraic or geometric or whatever) symbols, calling on relevant knowledge that may be entirely mathematical (that is, formal) or may be real-world general knowledge, and producing the appropriate computations. Many mathematical difficulties arise because symbols are manipulated and computations carried out without any reference to their meaning, although consideration of what they mean would allow a check on the accuracy and appropriateness of the manipulations. Conversely, if appropriate algorithms are lacking, even a well-understood practical situation may only be dealt with approximately and by trial and error; only someone who can compute and measure angles accurately will be able to divide a circular cake into seven equal slices; the rest of us have to divide by eight and distribute the extra slice by deservingness or favouritism rather than by the equal shares principle.

As with reading, skilled mathematical problem-solving seems to involve much metacognitive behaviour – checking, monitoring, relating to other instances, evaluating alternative strategies, defining a sequence of sub-goals – and good mathematics learners get more practice at these activities than do poor ones. Much the same is true throughout the rest of the curriculum, as various papers in Dillon and Sternberg (1986) and Sternberg and Grigorenko (2003) argue. Successful thinkers elaborate problems and rearrange them into new forms that are easier to deal with; they evaluate proposed solutions for their consistencies and inconsistencies, and examine their implications; they seek and use analogies with other similar situations. Such processes have long been seen as the defining properties of intelligent behaviour (see Sternberg (1982, 1985), Sternberg and Grigorenko (2003), and pp. 213–214) and have been argued to be among the 'mechanisms of cognitive development' (Siegler 1989b). Recent research in artificial intelligence has found that a number of such basic and general processes are used in many complex tasks. Simulation programmes in several different domains use means–end analysis, sub-goal formation, generate-and-test routines, 'executive' or 'metacognitive' procedures and so forth; for each particular problem these processes are applied to an organised body of domain-specific knowledge.

If we come at cognition a little differently, centring on good reasoning, we come up with a list of cognitive activities that repeats and extends the list so far. Let us take it that good reasoning leads to drawing justified conclusions and being able to evaluate, perhaps to explain them, using evidence that has been interpreted in justifiable ways. Some of the processes of reasoning may be specific to particular domains, but many are universal (Leighton and Sternberg 2004). Good reasoning involves diagnosing situations, searching for, finding and weighing evidence, analysing implications, identifying assumptions, establishing and evaluating beliefs, constructing and evaluating arguments and counterarguments, judging probability and plausibility, and making inferences or drawing conclusions.

Children begin to be good reasoners very early in their lives, find the same things difficult as adults do, and get better and better with practice, increasing knowledge/evidence to reason about, and better metacognition (see pp. 104–115). They become more systematic and coherent in their reasoning, and more accurate about the certainty and probability of their arguments. They need resources of intelligence and of working memory, accessible and helpfully represented domain-specific knowledge, knowledge of the cultural tools of thought that are available, ability to analyse and evaluate arguments and assess the quality of data, sensitivity to missing information, to be able to cope with uncertainty and ambiguity, reflectiveness, curiosity, persistence, ability to take alternative perspectives and handle counterfactuals, metacognitive awareness and skills to manage their reasoning, and a medium to communicate it with, probably but not necessarily language.

There are of course distinctions between different sorts of reasoning. Deductive reasoning involves taking a set of premises and drawing out what is implicit in them as an explicit conclusion, in such a way that the conclusion is safe and final; 'All cats like to sit on laps', 'Mowzer is a cat', therefore 'Mowzer likes to sit on laps'. It is used, in a more probabilistic way, in activities such as medical diagnosis, trouble-shooting equipment malfunctions, and so forth. Inductive reasoning goes beyond the particular information that is contained in the premises to make generalisations that may not be quite so safe. Bertrand Russell's example was the turkey who inferred from the fact that the farmer fed it every morning that he always would; the farmer did, all the way up to the middle of December. Another worthwhile distinction is between reasoning used to come to conclusions, or exploratory reasoning, and the justificatory reasoning used to explain or defend the conclusions reached. The latter may be at best a tidied-up version of the former, with the false starts and waverings edited out. A tidied-up version can be misleading as an educational tool, as in the case of 'experiments' in science curricula that replicate simple versions of historic experiments without the years of work the real original scientists did, and are at best demonstrations. At worst, justificatory 'reasoning' may select and distort the evidence used in order to defend a conclusion that seemed right at the time but is now unpopular; there are all too many political examples. There might be arguments for preferring some of these varieties of reasoning to others; at the very least, a good thinker should be aware of which is in play at a particular time.

A variety of instructional procedures has been applied in the attempt to transmit knowledge and induce understanding. These can be reviewed in terms of how well they serve the goal of producing people with a rich and flexible repertoire of strategies.

One educational approach eschews instruction, advocating that children should discover or invent strategies themselves, either through their own unaided exploration of the world or with an adult as background provider of fertile learning opportunities. This approach, which has been much used in early childhood education, drew much support from Piagetian theory though it has earlier roots, for example in Rousseau's *Émile*. Its guiding principle is encapsulated in Piaget's own summary of his theory:

> Remember also that each time one prematurely teaches a child something he could have discovered for himself, that child is kept from inventing it and consequently from understanding it completely.
>
> (Piaget 1983: 175)

This is a strong position to take, implying as it does that instruction is virtually always a bad thing. Children undoubtedly do invent their own cognitive strategies; for example, in early arithmetic there are many cases of children inventing addition and subtraction strategies (see Hughes (1986), Siegler (1986), and pp. 73–77). However, these strategies often contain mistakes, or 'bugs' (Brown and Burton 1978). Some may in any case be imperfect versions of strategies observed in other people or informally taught by them, not 'inventions *de novo*' (Saxe *et al.* 1987). And the discovery or invention of a complex strategy is likely to depend on prior mastery of simpler ones and of a great deal of knowledge, although it can be taught to someone who has not done this prior learning and then used by them. The number of people who 'spontaneously' discovered logarithms, for example, is considerably smaller than the number of people who have been taught to use them. There are important limits to the potential usefulness of discovery learning (e.g. Brainerd 1978, 1983; Desforges 1989; Meadows and Cashdan 1988; Mayer 2004), though its respect for the child's spontaneous activity is important. Mayer (2004) in particular argues that 'pure' discovery learning, where the learners are left to their own devices, is generally completely unsuccessful, though guided discovery learning may be very effective.

The provision of appropriate models to be observed is another comparatively *laissez-faire* form of education. Clearly we are all able to learn from our observations of other people and our imitations of them: early language learning and early socialisation provide many examples (pp. 22–26), Piaget, Case and Vygotsky all discuss it in their different theories of cognitive development (Chapter 4). No one deliberately taught an under-two-year old, who had better remain anonymous, to protest at adults' unwanted intervention in her affairs by shouting 'Shut up' and 'You're really sick, you're really really sick', but observation of older children (in the first case) and television soap opera (in the second) provided sufficient models. Observing and imitating a model's overt behaviour can be a good way to learn; but in practice, if complex behaviour is involved it requires a comparatively clear model, sufficient time to observe it, and perhaps the prior development of many skills that are components of the model's behaviour. The novice often cannot see what the expert is doing, let alone imitate it, let alone appreciate why it is done. An educationally helpful model will do more than merely model: there will be acts that are demonstrations and instructions and comments on the learner's imitations, not simply parts of the normal execution of the skilled behaviour. Such 'educational modelling' behaviour will be especially necessary for learners who have only an immature repertoire of cognitive and metacognitive skills. It is obviously a component of Vygotskian ways of teaching thinking. Peers and siblings might be especially effective models (Anderson *et al.* 2001; Maynard 2002).

Discovery learning and the observation and imitation of models both presume more activity on the part of the learner than the teacher. Obviously this balance of action and initiative can be reversed. There is a long educational tradition of active teacher intervention in the learning of pupils, so that teachers tell learners things, lead them over and over again through the activity they have to learn, correcting their errors as they take each small step and generally shaping their behaviour. This sort of instruction can be very effective: if the learner goes through the exercises enough times the cognitive processing becomes habitual – practice makes perfect. The danger is that practice may make you set in your ways, prevent you, as Piaget pointed out, from understanding how a strategy works and how it may be modified and applied to new tasks, or from inventing a new strategy that might be better than the taught one. Abstracting such understanding from the use of the strategy will probably require both extensive practice and using it on a gradually widening range of examples (pp. 120–126). Alternatively, instruction can include explanations of how the strategy works, as well as instruction on how to do it. It seems to be most useful to provide the learner with information about how the strategy enhances performance: demonstrating that it is 'cost-effective' is an important component of ensuring the strategy continues to be used. The more that a learner knows about a strategy, the more likely it is to be transferred appropriately to other tasks (Brown *et al.* 1983).

'Instruction' is of course a composite involving modelling, examples, practice and explanation: the teacher presents knowledge (procedural, declarative and metacognitive), samples the learner's understanding of it, and provides further explanation as required, prior to involving the students in practice and discussion of their achievements. Explicit and well-structured instruction can teach children to execute many cognitive strategies; generalising this learning to new tasks requires learning about how, when and where the strategies can be used. Although the main direction of transmission of knowledge is from teacher to learner, the teacher needs to be sensitive to the learner's skills and reactions, particularly perhaps if the learner is very young or very much a novice. The neo-Vygotskian account of cognitive development (pp. 295–312) of course emphasises that thought develops through social interaction. Adults 'scaffold' the child through the task to be carried out, doing the parts the child cannot do and arranging the situation so that the child can take his or her part. They direct attention to currently relevant features of the task; they suggest what might be considered, remembered or done; they model appropriate actions and strategies; they supervise and they provide highlighted feedback on the child's actions. Adult and child take turns to carry out the steps of the task, with responsibility for its execution gradually shifting from adult to child; the strategies needed for the task are modelled, overtly, again and again, and the child practises them again and again; the adult gives the child a little more independence after a successful action, and a little more support if there has been a failure or difficulty. The child is helped to progress through the 'zone of proximal development' (pp. 308–311).

Ann Brown and her colleagues showed that this is a very effective method of instruction (see Brown (1994), Brown and Campione (1986), Brown and Ferrara (1985), Brown and Reeve (1987), Palincsar and Brown (1984)), as well as a direct means for studying cognitive development (Siegler and Crowley (1991), Siegler (2005)), and there are an increasing number of observational studies showing that adults do indeed often engage in this sort of interaction with children (pp. 380–388). It is not yet clear how closely the amount of such interaction a child takes part in is related to the rapidity or quality of cognitive development (but see pp. 388–393) or how the components of 'scaffolded learning and teaching' need to be balanced. One important point about really good scaffolding is that it teaches the learner not just knowledge or strategies but how to be a self-scaffolder, what I have called elsewhere a 'self-running problem-solver' (Meadows and Cashdan 1988). The amount of adult time, sensitivity and commitment required is formidable, so children need to learn to be their own cognitive supports – to be both the trellis and the upward-growing vine, to change the metaphor somewhat. To quote Brown *et al.* (1983: 124):

> Mature thinkers are those who provide conflict trials for themselves, practise through experiments, question their own basic assumptions, provide counter examples to their own rules, and so on. Although a great deal of thinking and learning may remain a social activity, mature reasoners become capable of providing the supportive-other role for themselves through the process of internalisation. Under these systems of tutelage, the child learns not only how to get a particular task done independently but also learns how to set about learning new problems. In other words, the child learns how to learn.

Dweck (1999) provides an interesting argument about the motivating effects of different forms of feedback, and their impact on self-concepts. She identifies a syndrome combining high achievement on familiar tasks and high fear of failure, which prevents the person from taking cognitive risks and from recovering resiliently from any lapses in performance. These individuals are willing to do what they know they can already do, but will not try new challenges and are thoroughly demoralised by difficulties. She suggests that the cause of this is feedback that led the individual to see high achievement as a sign of their ability, and failure as a catastrophic indication that they were not so able as they had thought. When the feedback is in terms such as 'you are clever', 'you are so good at art/science/running/ whatever', then the implication of the occasion when there is a failure is thought to be that 'really you are not so clever/good at it after all'; while if the feedback has been 'you did that really well', 'that was elegantly expressed', 'that is a new way of thinking about it' then the implication of failure can be merely 'you didn't do that so well this time', which implies more possibility of improvement. Willingness to take on reasonable challenges is essential for educational success; people who try may not succeed, but those who refuse to try are guaranteed not to succeed. Dweck therefore recommends that praise should centre on the excellence with which the task was done, rather than on the intrinsic merit of the performer, and cites some evidence that this is more likely to encourage people to take on cognitive challenge. Thompson (2004) makes a similar argument. Bandura's notion of 'self-efficacy' and Seligman's of depression as 'learned helplessness' ally this description to personality and motivation (Bandura 1995, 1997; Rosenhan and Seligman 1995; Seligman 1975). Even the best ways of 'teaching thinking' may founder if the learners' concepts of themselves as learners get in the way (Burnett 1999; Burnett and Proctor 2002; Dart *et al.* 2000; and pp. 184–186).

The desired result of learning to think includes, then, at least four major components: many problem-solving strategies, many metacognitive skills, an enormous knowledge base with which these can operate, and a commitment to thinking well and both independently and socially. The different approaches to teaching that I have outlined can be commented on in terms of how they facilitate each of these components. It does seem that learning to execute complex cognitive strategies is easier if the cognitive processes involved are presented with extensive and explicit detail (Bereiter and Bird 1985; Brown *et al.* 1984; Pressley *et al.* 1987; Mayer 2004; Nickerson 2004). Other less explicit teaching methods can lead to strategy discovery (Bjorklund and Jacobs 1985; Ornstein and Naus 1985; Ornstein *et al.* 1988), but it is not clear how to make discovery highly probable, nor that discovered strategies are better in either cognitive or motivational ways than learned strategies (Mayer 2004). More didactic teaching methods such as guided practice can be useful in increasing the efficiency with which a strategy is used, and, if they include discussion of the importance of the strategy over a range of contexts, may avoid the danger that the strategy will be learned passively and applied by rote only in a very limited range of situations. Knowing when and where to apply a strategy, and knowing which of one's repertoire of strategies will fit a particular task, are related parts of learning to think. The former is probably facilitated by learning about a range of tasks similar to the ones on which the strategy has already been applied, the latter by extensive practice on using the strategy on the task, plus, perhaps, analysis of the structural features of the task (e.g. Chi *et al.* (1980), and pp. 120–126).

'Metacognitive' and skills attitudes, for example that effort is necessary, that it may be more useful to 'get the feel of the problem' generally before attempting to find a solution than to generate a possible solution quickly, that you are a person who can have confidence in your ability to solve problems, probably develop best from teaching that provides a great deal of sensitive individualised interaction between teacher and learner. An attentive teacher can intervene to make sure that the learner's successes are recognised and failures are overcome, can model or instruct helpful strategies that keep motivation at a useful level, and can help the learner to make helpful attributions for success and failure rather than unhelpful ones ('I got that one wrong because I didn't notice X', not 'I got that one wrong because I'm stupid'; 'I got that right because I did Y', not 'I got that right because it was my lucky day'). Discovery learning may have positive effects on motivation because of its encouragement of the learner's autonomy – the 'I did it all myself' boast will come more easily here – but may not encourage metacognitive analysis. Regimented instruction may serve neither motivation nor metacognition well if it bores the learner and omits space for reflection and generalisation. Neither rote learning nor self-centred discovery are immediately compatible with socially co-operative learning, though they could alternate with it.

Finally, many strategies need an extensive and well-organised base of factual knowledge on which to operate. Some are specific to particular domains of knowledge. I have touched on the role of knowledge acquisition in cognitive development elsewhere in this volume (Chapter 2). It may thus be educationally effective to teach strategies and domain-relevant infor-mation at the same time, to seek to link procedural and declarative knowl-edge. It seems likely that having efficient cognitive strategies for use in a particular domain will enhance both the acquisition and the organisation of factual knowledge in that domain (e.g. Chi and Ceci 1987), so that stra-tegies and knowledge basis improve together. Traditional didactic educa-tional methods emphasise the acquisition of knowledge without considering how knowledge structures and cognitive processes interact, and thus risk the production of knowledge that is applied only in a restricted subset of the situations to which it is relevant, and is not easily examined, criticised and revised. Knowledge acquired through dialogue and subjected to metacognitive examination may be both more flexible and more fruitful. If it is, it is not surprising that teaching thinking skills explicitly but within curriculum areas seems to be effective (Leighton and Sternberg 2004).

Among the *bonnes a penser* that could be more prominent as educational goals than they have been, Nickerson (2004) includes an interesting set of points. The first distinction is between reasoning and case building, the latter being intended to support one's own case and undermine the oppo-sition's. The second is between reasoning and rationalising, between using reason to find out what one should do and using reason to put what one believes or has done in the best possible light. The third point is that we may need to resist overly simple causal explanations, to deter ourselves from taking contributing causes as sufficient causes or from thinking that only the first or the most recent cause in a sequence of causes is to be focused on. He argues that we should be aware of the biases that afflict human cognition: our tendency to seek confirmation rather than test our beliefs and conclusions, to discount negative evidence, to be overconfident of our accuracy, to justify or even amend our earlier position using hind-sight ('I told you so!'), to overestimate the degree to which other people share our own knowledge, beliefs, goals and behaviour.

A large number of courses and programmes for improving thinking skills have been composed (for reviews, examples and discussion see Coles and Robinson (1989), Resnick (1987b), Segal *et al.* (1985), Vye *et al.* (1988), Brown (1994), Shymansky *et al.* (1997), McGuinness (1999), Smith *et al.* (2000), Adey *et al.* (2002), Lawson (2003), Venville *et al.* (2003, 2004), Georghiades, (2004b)). Not all these programmes have been formally evaluated, and indeed there should perhaps be some debate about what measure of students' improvement should be taken. One of the commonest measures is students' performance on exercises very similar to those that have been taught, which is an appropriate measure but a limited one in so far as the programmes are supposed to teach skills that can be applied over a wider range of the curriculum. Such transfer is desirable but may be difficult to achieve or maintain (see pp. 120–126). Intelligence test scores or general school achievement measures may also be used, but these are not necessarily sensitive to improvements in specific thinking skills: a standardised reading test score might be a somewhat indirect measure of students' ability to elaborate or summarise text. Conversely, although in normal educational conditions there is a positive correlation between thinking skills and educa-tional achievement, this does not establish a causal relationship between them such that improving thinking skills will also improve educational achievement. Measures of specific thinking skills as applied to problems that vary in their resemblance to those on which the student was trained are needed.

A striking example of positive results on such assessments come from studies by Ann Brown and her colleagues (Brown and Reeve 1987; Brown *et al.* 1984; Ferrara *et al.* 1986; Palincsar and Brown 1984; Brown 1994). They achieved improvement in reading comprehension via a more deliberate and interpretative approach to text, and this transferred to classroom and private reading and was maintained over a period of months. It is not yet clear exactly what was learned; it may have been that the overt self-conscious strategies that were taught continued to be used overtly and self-consciously throughout, or that they became automated to be used consciously only when comprehension broke down; or that practice on these skills activated other aspects of reading, and improvement on these was more important than the taught strategies themselves; or that the programme cured the emotional difficulties associated with the students' earlier history of being poor at reading and so removed obstacles to reading better. Fine-grained microgenetic assessment might tease apart these various possibilities, but it could be argued that there is probably an extensive interaction between cognitive, affective and motivational processes. Another body of work with impressive results within science and maths education comes from Philip Adey and Michael Shayer and their colleagues (Georghiades (2004a, 2004b), Venville *et al.* (2003, 2004), Adey and Shayer (1993), Adey *et al.* (2002), Venville (2004)).

Resnick (1987b) argues that 'prudent educational practice' should teach cognitive skills explicitly but embedded in the traditional school disciplines. A discipline-embedded approach provides a natural knowledge base and environment of instances on which to practise cognitive skills. As she says, 'one cannot reason in the abstract; one must reason about something', even if that 'something' is part of a formal and abstract system such as logic or mathematics. Disciplines also provide traditional criteria for what is good thinking: mathematics has formal proofs, the physical sciences combinations of inductive and deductive thinking and a respect for objective empirical evidence, the arts and humanities somewhat different rules for constructing arguments, weighing alternatives and evaluating evidence. The criteria for 'higher order cognitive skills' listed on p. 410 (Resnick 1987b: 3) enter into disciplines to varying degrees, but practising any discipline using such skills will enhance learning of that discipline and may encourage the use of the skills in others too. Educationally, transfer may be produced most widely if 'higher order' reading, writing, mathematics and reasoning skills, potentially 'enabling disciplines', are focused on (e.g. Lehman *et al.* 1988).

Resnick advocates cultivating a 'disposition' to think in a skilled way. This she sees as facilitated by social interaction, first because it provides models, second because it allows scaffolding, third because social support and social validation may help convince students

> that they have the ability, the permission and even the obligation to engage in a kind of critical analysis that does not always accept problem formulations as presented or that may challenge an accepted position.
>
> (Resnick 1987b: 41)

Here motivational research (Connell and Wellborn 1991; Dweck and Elliot 1983; Dweck 1999; Bandura 1995, 1997; Lepper 1981; Nicholls 1978; and elsewhere in this volume) is clearly relevant.

There are many cognitive skills that can be taught within domains or across them. This is the list provided by Nickerson (2004: 422–432):

- Strive to understand the problem.
- Analyse ends and means.
- Make assumptions explicit.
- Make a representation of the problem.
- Break the problem down into manageable subproblems.
- Work backwards.

- Simplify.
- Consider extreme cases.
- Find an analogous or more familiar problem.
- Analyse and evaluate arguments.
- Judge the plausibility of assertions.
- Estimate what the possible answer might be.
- Be sensitive to missing information.
- Deal effectively with uncertainty.
- Take alternative perspectives.
- Use counterfactual thinking.
- Plan, monitor and assess one's own reasoning.
- Know one's own strengths and weaknesses.
- Be disposed to be reflective, inquisitive, truth-seeking and persistent.

Sternberg (2002: 385) makes the point that individuals may differ in their preferred style of thinking, and teaching thinking may need to recognise this if it is to have positive effects on everyone. His work on 'teaching for successful intelligence' is intended to show how this can be done. He argues that 'people adapt, shape and select by recognising and capitalising on strengths, and by recognising and compensating for or correcting weakness. People do not achieve success in the same way. Each person has to find his or her own "recipe" for success. One of the most useful things a teacher can do is to help a student figure out how to make the most of what he or she does well and to find ways around what he or she does not do so well.' Thus he advocates teaching thinking activities that encourage students to engage in memory learning, analytical learning, creative learning, and practical learning, and suggests that a curriculum that encourages all these gives every student some opportunity to practise their strengths and opportunity to work on their weaker skills. Again, the importance of motivation and metacognition and their interplay with cognition have to be emphasised.

Thompson (2004) argues that one of the major problems leading to under-achievement and thus impeding cognitive development is failure-avoidant behaviour. His picture of how this occurs brings together several of the themes and the strands of research that I have been describing in this book.

At the centre is parent–child interaction that is critical and over-controlling, that emphasises high achievement but does not recognise that it has to be worked for, where feedback is not explicit about why something succeeded or failed and what could be done about it: parental teaching, in short, that lacks the child-contingency, the joint activity towards solution, the calibrating of challenges to an amount that the child is likely to cope with, the gradual transfer of responsibility and the warmth that characterise good Vygotskian scaffolding (pp. 388–393). Parental over-control and parental high demands diminish intrinsic motivation and reduce the scope

Person Variables	Family Environment Variables	Achievement Costs
Personality Variables	**Parenting**	**Effects on Behaviour**
• low self-estimates of ability • uncertain self-worth • sensitivity to evaluative threat • emphasis on ability as a criterion of self-worth • view of ability as trait-like and immutable • ability best indicated when success follows low-effort uncertainty about the causes of achievement outcomes • success viewed as outcome of uncontrollable or external factors	• family conflict • authoritarian parenting style • parental criticism and over-control • socially imposed standards of perfectionism from parents • emphasis on 'perfection with ease' • emphasis on achievement in absence of clear advice as to how it may be achieved • non-contingent evaluative feedback • reinforcement on grounds irrelevant to achievement success	• diminished intrinsic motivation • failure to develop effective study skills • defensive pessimism • propensity to self-handicap in situations of evaluative threat • avoidance of challenge • no persistence if difficulties occur • self-presentational costs of self-handicapping • passivity and helplessness • loss of social support networks

Figure 6.1 Correlates of failure-avoidant behaviour. Adapted from Thompson 2004.

for Piagetian internally led development and finding one's own solution (pp. 277–278). These behaviours have consequences for personality characteristics and motivation, and for metacognition (pp. 132–135): the child lacks confidence in his or her own ability, believes that ability is fixed and cannot be augmented (pp. 184–186), that ability is indicated by each success or failure, that effortless success is what should happen, that metacognitive analyses of the specific causes of each success or failure are less relevant than general ability. With this constellation of beliefs, the child may suffer low intrinsic motivation, defensive pessimism, self-handicapping and self-deprecation, passivity and helplessness, fear of challenge, avoidance behaviours, and depression. The authoritarian, demanding, hothousing sorts of parental behaviour that Thompson describes are thus, perhaps, indicative of ways of teaching that do not improve children's thinking (though evidence from numerous biographies and autobiographies suggests they may sometimes be quite good ways of producing angst and rebellion).

Chapter 7

Questions, problems – and possibilities

The final chapter of the ideal book on the development and acquisition of cognition in childhood might contain one or more of the following components: a recapitulation of the most important points made earlier; an overview of the field that provides a clear and comprehensive synthesis of work to date; an exciting new theory indicating where future research should be done; an inspired and practicable pedagogy and curriculum. This chapter contains none of these components. I would like to be able to provide them, but I cannot. There is little to be gained from summarising earlier chapters when they are themselves all too summary accounts of much more material. The field is too heterogeneous and in parts uncertain to allow a synthesis, though there are more signs of researchers considering issues outside their own immediate interests than there were when I worked on the first edition of this book. I do have theoretical ideas about cognitive development, but not an exciting new theory; indeed, I have learned from examining the theories of cognitive development that I discuss in this book that theoretical progress is more likely to be made at a level where behaviour is carefully specified (as in the analysis of what 'phonological awareness' is and how it relates to reading) than at the level of behaviour so general and all-pervasive that it is abstract and untestable (as, for example, assimilation and accommodation). I have tried to present material on cognitive development that is relevant to the concerns of teachers, but again the research literature suggests that there will never be universally appropriate curriculum and pedagogy (and there remains a substantial discrepancy between the practices that the developmental psychologist who has studied children's cognitive development might suggest and the practices that an under-resourced and over-stressed school system can implement).

So I find I can't end with a solution, or even a set of solutions, that I really believe to be correct. Further, although I believe that what I have said in earlier chapters is, largely, true and may even cohere, and in my life as a parent and teacher I act on it, I do not want it to pass unquestioned. Instead, I am going to highlight some problems and omissions, in the hope that if we can produce some good thinking on these we will make further progress towards understanding the development and acquisition of cognition in childhood.

7.1 Problems of diagnosis

Diagnosing cognitive development involves a troublesome tangle of assessment and conceptualisation problems. It is necessary to know what cognition is involved in a particular task; for example, reading or making a logical inference or conserving number. 'Is involved in' could mean 'what cognition is necessary', 'what cognition is sufficient' and 'what cognition people actually do'; developmentalists necessarily take on this last meaning particularly acutely, as 'people' may well do different things if they differ in age, experience or understanding. Finding out what cognitive processes are necessary or sufficient for a task might be done by armchair analysis or by computer simulation; finding out what people do involves getting out there and assessing them. Any such assessment will have to involve a finely tuned test procedure. False positives may arise if the task allows guessing, hints at the right answer, or could be 'solved' by processes other than the ones thought to be necessary: a child might 'read' a text correctly because it is so familiar it has been memorised, for example. Conversely, there is the problem of false negatives: the child might not understand the task instructions, might not attend to essential information or might forget it part way through, might have misleading ideas about what is being asked for, might not be motivated to address the task properly, might have emotional problems such as anxiety about being tested, might be unable to verbalise an answer even though it has been correctly worked out, might be put off an answer because the experimenter seems to be expecting something else, might be able to succeed on the core of the task but be defeated by something so marginal to it that the researcher has not even contemplated that it could be a problem. All the problems of work with people from a different 'culture' from the tester's (Cole and Means 1981) apply to work with children and may be all the more intractable because we expect them to approach the task with assumptions and expectations very much like our own. The history of work on cognitive development is full of demonstrations that earlier assessments showing children failing on tasks had produced false negatives, and that in other tests of 'the same task' children could succeed (e.g. Hughes and Donaldson (1979) on perspective-taking, Light and Perret-Clermont (1989) on conservation, Golomb (2004) on drawing human figures).

A diagnosis of a child's cognition might be more secure if it rests on the child's response to a range of assessments rather than relying on one test situation. However, this of course raises the problem of inconsistency between test results from different versions of the task. If the different versions have been constructed in a principled way so that the ways in which they differ are clear, then test–test variability may reveal a great deal about the demands of the tasks and what cognition is crucial, what optional. It may also reveal things about the cognition of the individual, because one of the conceptual problems linked to the diagnosis of cognition is what we mean when we say someone 'has' or 'understands' a particular cognitive process or structure, even more perhaps when we say someone 'does not have' it. There may be a good match between 'competence' and 'performance', or disastrous lapses on the one hand and flashes of over-achievement on the other. It may be that even when we have a sufficiently good way to do some cognitive task we may sometimes do it differently. It may be worth thinking how 'understanding' might vary in systematic ways: it might vary in its accessibility, in how well it can be used, in its links to other cognitive contents, in its range of application, in its certainty.

Thinking of cognition as being developed in social contexts, even of it as being constituted by social contexts, will be one crucial dimension of this. Vygotsky's ideas about the zone of proximal development, and Ann Brown's and Robert Siegler's about microgenetic testing (Brown *et al.* 1983; Siegler 2005), suggest that assessment of the child as a collaborator with a more expert person, or of the child during training on the concept, may be a most illuminating part of diagnosing cognitive development. Their analyses suggest that development and learning are both gradual and more wavering than some theorists have supposed. More radically, this view might under-mine the idea that cognition is a matter of internal understanding and that we can attribute competence or the possession of a cognitive rule, process or structure to an individual, in favour of the idea that such rules, processes or structures are only our ways of describing behaviour that was learned in, and cannot ever be independent of, social practices (Gellatly 1989). The behaviour provides instances of cognitive principles: it is not controlled, let alone explained, by them. What we need is good descriptions of behaviour that we link with good models of rules and processes without reifying the latter; and the behaviour will be studied in its social contexts, which must also be well described. Getting such descriptions and models is a goal worth aiming for, but achieving it is not going to be easy.

7.2 Patterns of cognitive development

There are marked changes in cognitive behaviour over the years of child-hood; new concepts, skills and strategies emerge. Do they do so in a con-sistent pattern? How are the various aspects of cognitive development related? Are there consistent sequences or co-occurrences of development? Are changes qualitatitive or quantitative? Are there 'stages'? Are there individual differences between children in their cognitive development? Are any such individual differences quantitative or qualitative, consistent or unpatterned? These are questions that have been controversial for many years; they are also questions whose answers are unclear, even in principle. Among the issues involved are, again, questions of diagnosis and conceptualisation.

When I discussed models of what 'cognitive development' is, in Chapter 4, I outlined Piaget's model (section 4.1), which describes it as largely an organism-generated sequence of universal stages, each characterised by a stable and coherent structure of principles or operations; the information-processing model (section 4.2), which focuses on more local sequences of skills within domains and describes sequences in behaviour that are logically necessary rather than broad general stages; and the Vygotskian model (section 4.3), which sees cognition as socially constituted and again places less emphasis on separate stages (though some of Vygotsky's work, for example the development of concepts, might be a partial exception to this). These models are not competitors but they do differ in their basic conceptual assumptions: Piaget's could be called organismic, information-processing's mechanistic, Vygotsky's social-constructivist. Interest in 'stages' is more common in theories that use an organismic metaphor, and most of the work on cognitive stages centres on the Piagetian model. The degree to which Piagetian stages can be seen in children's cognitive behaviour has been a matter for fierce debate and considerable uncertainty, such that John Flavell, one of the best-informed people in the field, published two incompatible decisions in the same year and called himself 'undecided to the point of public self-contradiction' (Flavell (1985), commenting on Flavell (1982a, 1982b)). It is an intractable problem. Diagnosing a 'stage' is going to involve all the difficulties of assessment and conceptualisation that arise in diagnosing even a single cognitive operation, increasing exponentially as the number of tests and operations increases. If a number of tasks require the same basic cognitive operations and these operations form a coherent stage, then success on these tasks (given tests of equivalent sensitivity or difficulty) should be achieved at much the same time. There is remarkably little evidence of this happening. Rather, a lot of claims of 'stages', including Piaget's and, I suspect, the 'theory of mind' research more recently, relies on the change from A_1 to A_2 occurring over the same age range as the change from B_1 to B_2, C_1 to C_2, and so forth; but the children (and even the researchers) who provided data on A are not the same individuals as those who provided data on B: sometimes the design is completely cross-sectional so that the children who showed behaviour A_1 are a different (younger) sample from those who behaved in an A_2 way. Many years ago, as I began my PhD, I felt that claims of stages would be more firmly grounded if they had evidence on tests of several of the operations that together constituted a stage for all subjects, gathered longitudinally so that the co-occurrence of change could be examined. At that time there were no such studies. Mine (Meadows 1975) found no evidence of 'staginess' in children's performance on nine tests of 'concrete operations', and as these tests were well used in the Piagetian literature, and as the operations that they diagnosed were central to the stage, I emerged from my PhD with little belief in the existence of clear-cut, coherent, rapidly achieved stages. Diehard Piagetians may continue to assert their stage model and point out the faults of the assessments that provide no evidence of stages, but while researchers find rather considerable unevenness and even regression in performance (Flavell 1982b; Gelman and Baillargeon 1983; Klausmeier and Sipple 1982; Meadows 1975; Vuyk 1981; Siegler 2005), the onus is on them to provide a fault-free demonstration of stages. The development of performance is age-related, but being stage-like in the sense of being clearly discontinuous, cohesive, synchronous or even across tasks requires stronger evidence than is available in most areas. Siegler (2005), advocating microgenetic analyses of cognitive development, points out that stage-like data are less likely to emerge from children's behaviour if the intervals between assessments are short, while with long intervals it is easier to find radical, qualitative changes in behaviour.

Stage models of cognitive development tend also to neglect the possibility of individual differences except those related to the individual's position in the stage sequence. Some are not even interested in differences in rate of progress through the stages. One uniform path through the stage sequence is assumed to be normal, natural and inevitable. This may not be a wise assumption; Siegler (2005) shows a lot of fluctuation between different ways to solve a given problem on each occasion it is presented, even when the subjects possessed a completely successful way of doing it. Models of cognitive development that see it as in large part socially constituted and culturally specific, and that link it to motivation and emotion and therefore to personality, would assume that, on the contrary, there would be several different – even many different – pathways from early to mature cognition. Perhaps a biologically based model of cognition, using parallels with evolution, and aware of how brain development proceeds by the proliferation and selective dying-off of nerve cell connections and experience-expectant and experience-dependent development, would similarly propose that there might be marked individual differences in cognitive development. Again, the problems of conceptualisation and diagnosis arise.

In short, there are enormous methodological problems in providing a good account of the 'what' of cognitive development. A number of different approaches are possible; each is, I suspect, necessary but not sufficient. Perhaps the most commonly used is laboratory equipment-type assessment of performance. This can provide data about performance and some of the factors that affect it, but it uses a social situation that is unfamiliar to young children and they may not show optimum performance for the reasons I discussed apropos of 'false negatives' earlier in this section. A *series* of careful experiments, especially if done on a microgenetic timescale, may clarify complex performance and even reveal abilities that have not been apparent in the world outside the laboratory. Laboratory studies can also assess the effects of changes in conditions or compare subjects, and they are very useful for training studies. However the effects shown in the laboratory can only be extrapolated to the outside world with great caution: it will be necessary to examine the 'real world' carefully to see whether the same factors are working in the same way.

Descriptions of what individuals do in the real social world complement laboratory assessments. They can provide evidence on cognitive behaviour and how it is affected by various factors, but real-world conditions are less controlled (and more complex) than the laboratory, and causes and consequences will almost certainly be less clear. Real-life interventions, such as educational programmes, can produce strong evidence for causal effects if they have adequate controls, but it may be difficult to tease out exactly what in the intervention brought about the effect. We have to have dialogue, indeed dialectics, between laboratory and real world studies.

7.3 Problems of explanation

As well as describing the phenomena of cognitive development, we might wish to explain them. As well as the question 'what are children's cognitive behaviours?' there are the questions 'why are they like that?' and 'why and how do they change?' These look like even harder questions than the 'what' ones, and not separate from them. If, for example, we described some aspect of cognition as being unchanged from its earliest measurement to maturity, our 'change' question would concern *lack* of change: 'why is it stable and unmodified for so long?' Uncertainties and errors about 'what' will lead to uncertainties and errors about 'why' and 'how'; uncertainties and errors about 'why' and 'how' will lead to problems about 'what'.

It may be helpful to begin my brief discussion of this problem with the four different sets of causal question that ethologists have found it useful to distinguish. These are the complementary cornerstones of the systematic study of behaviour (Hinde 1982, 1987). What is the proximal cause of behaviour, the immediate stimulus that triggered it? How does the behaviour develop, what is its ontogenetic course from infancy to maturity? What is its function, what is it for? How did this behaviour evolve, how did it change during evolution? These four sorts of 'cause' are distinguishable but also linked, and we are going to have to proceed in a way that allows comparison and cross-classification between attempts to explain behaviour at these different complementary levels.

The 'why' of cognitive development could profitably be looked at, I think, at most of these ethological levels. A complete examination in this way would be an enormous undertaking; here I will just draw together some relevant points, mainly at the evolutionary level. Human beings have, like all other animals, come to be as they are now through a long evolutionary history during which natural selection favoured individuals with particular characteristics, and these characteristics were passed on to succeeding generations. One part of this selection process has worked in such a way that considerable cognitive development after birth is both necessary and possible. What is particularly striking about humans compared with other species is that many infant characteristics – physical ones such as tooth development, psychological ones such as indulgence in play – persist in human beings for much longer than they do in other species (Gould 1977). This 'neoteny', or slowing down of maturation, allows us a much longer period during which we can learn from experience and during which other people can teach us. Human beings produce small numbers of offspring, have minimally sized litters of immature and helpless babies, who therefore need a long period of being taken care of by more adult human beings. Human beings have large brains in large skulls and pelvises too narrow for a large skull to pass through without damage to both mother and baby: the foetus's skull must not get too large before birth and there will therefore be considerable brain growth after it. Human beings amplify their limited sensori-motor powers with tools and therefore need complex cognitive skills for their interaction with the non-human world. Human beings live in social groups and therefore need complex cognitive skills for their interaction with each other. Human beings have spread to almost every physical environment, and created more, so that they face the widest possible range of environmental challenges. Cognitive development in general can be seen as just one inevitable aspect of evolutionary destiny (Wohlwill 1973; Reader 2003; Keller 2004); conversely it has been argued that evolution may have endowed us with certain specialised 'modules' of cognition, or perhaps certain constraints and predilections in our cognitive development (Bjorklund and Pellegrini 2000, 2002).

Development in the cognitive area (and in the affective, the motivational and the social areas) no doubt does have this evolutionary component to it. But two limiting points have to be taken into account. First, the degree to which evolution specifies what cognitive development may be is highly debatable. Given what we know about the openness of the developing brain to learning from experience (Chapter 5), and about the effect of experience on the development of behaviour in our own species and others (Laland and Hoppitt 2003; Reader 2003; Keller 2004), I doubt whether the evolutionary component dictates very much very strongly. Evolutionary change, especially neoteny, offers an increased opportunity for learning and variation at least as much as it prescribes fixed forms of cognitive development. Discussion continues about the possible 'innateness' of various cognitive capacities, for example language, face recognition, distinguishing between the animate and inanimate worlds, notions of causality, notions of number. Part of the problem for developmental psychology (and cognitive science: Samuels 2004) is the complex set of meanings that 'innate' has:

At least six meanings are attached to the term: present at birth; a behavioural difference caused by a genetic difference; adapted over the course of evolution; unchanging throughout development; shared by all members of a species; and not learned.

(Bateson 1991b: 21)

Further than this, something that is innate in even several of these senses may nevertheless be modified subsequently by learning from experience. My ability to vocalise is innate, but my vocal behaviour is substantially modified from its beginnings in infancy by a complex history of learning from experience. I must also point out that many cognitive skills have been invented too recently to be directly subject to evolutionary pressures. Evolution by natural selection takes several generations, and it is unlikely in the extreme that natural selection has provided us with the cognitive skills of computer use, understanding calculus, or even reading. So far as we know, human brains have not changed much in size or complexity over the last few thousand years (Gottlieb 1983; Mithen 1996), although over these years there has been an immense change in the use of cognitive skills, both in their spread across more and more of the population and in the invention of new skills and applications. Whatever evolution-given prerequisite skills we bring to reading, mathematics, science, the arts, or the humanities, we learn to use these skills in ways that go far beyond their evolutionarily specified foundations and are unlikely to be strictly limited by evolution. Cognitive development, like physical maturation, takes place within the normal expectable human environment. Variations in this environment will affect its fine-tuning, and may, if extreme, affect it more radically. Prodigious achievers (Radford 1990) and socially deprived children (Skuse 1984; Meadows 1996; pp. 388–393, 400–401) demonstrate two extremes due very largely to exceptional environments. What sort of environmental experience affects a cognitive skill to a noticeable degree will vary according to what sort of cognitive skill is being considered; cognition such as Piaget's sensori-motor stage, which has presumably been characteristic of most human infancy for thousands and thousands of years, will probably be less affected by experience than recently invented cognitive skills such as computer use or memorising strategies. Enrichment studies, deprivation studies, and, perhaps most of all, training studies, will be useful in examining environmental effects; and, as I discuss in the last section of this chapter, we badly need a good account of the environment in cognitive development.

Both the evolutionary and the functional level of questions about behaviour draw attention to the fact that behaviour requires resources and involves costs and benefits. This is not so often considered in the literature on cognitive development as it might be, and we have no highly developed description of the economics of cognition. I will venture a few preliminary remarks. Cognitive development will depend on the availability of resources within the individual, within other persons, and in the surrounding environment. Resources of working memory (pp. 86–87), of knowledge and skills available from earlier learning (Chapter 2), of motivation and energy (Chapter 5), of a correctly working nervous system (pp. 249–251, 258–259, 417–422) will be necessary inside the individual; external resources will include caregivers' and teachers' structuring of the child's time and space and motivation (pp. 375–406), and the information, sustenance and rewards offered. Deficiencies in one sort of resource may be compensated for by riches in another, as when devoted parents manage to teach a handicapped child to reach average levels of performance in school (pp. 12, 56, 355–357) or a very intelligent child can maintain his or her concentration despite poor parenting that has negatively scaffolded his abilities. Resources may be concentrated on one area of development to the cost of other areas, as in 'hothouse' training of prodigies or the activities of 'idiot savants' (pp. 139, 226, 256). External resources may be controlled initially by the parents, who also use their internal resources to supplement the child's immature capacities, and later more control may be exercised by the child (Chapter 6).

Changing cognitive behaviour may require an input of time and energy higher than is available, so that there is a certain inertia and delay in achieving further growth (e.g. Karmiloff-Smith and Inhelder 1974/5; Siegler 2005). Cognitive processes may be a drain on resources until they are well practised and automatic, when they may contribute positively to further development by providing basic skills or material for analogies or processes that get round difficulties. Environments may require particular sorts of cognition and support particular sorts of cognition; what is 'functional' in the evolutionary long term and the immediate short term will depend on the balance of internal and external needs and resources that the individual is faced with. Genes lead to cognition only indirectly and probabilistically (Scerif and Karmiloff-Smith 2005). Cognition may also be guided, even transformed, by 'cultural amplifiers', devices such as clocks, maps, word processors, political systems and religious rituals, which are provided to the child whose thinking develops to utilise these tools (pp. 304–306). Clearly, no 'explanation' of cognitive development is going to be able to rely on only one factor: a more or less Piagetian list of maturation, social experience, physical experience and assimilation or accommodation looks like the minimum that we must develop.

7.4 Constraints on cognitive development

I mentioned in earlier chapters the problem of how children can ever begin on the task of understanding phenomena that are highly complex and could have an infinite number of structures. One example was the problem of inferring the meaning of a word: how can one work out what a term such as 'red' refers to unless one already has the appropriate concept? Without a concept of 'colour', 'red' might refer to anything to do with the objects it labels: their colour, indeed, but equally that they are pointed out, or that they are heavy, or that they are visible, or that they exist. A number of psychologists suggest that we cannot learn without some *a priori* constraints on our learning, where by constraints is meant 'factors intrinsic to the learner which result in a non-random selection among the logically-possible characteristics of an informational pattern' (Keil 1990: 137). As learners, we have to have something that enables us to choose between the alternative models we could construct of any given occurrrence: a bias towards assuming that a word refers to a whole object, not a part of it, unless that is specifically signalled (Markman 1990; Bloom 1998; pp. 18–22); a bias towards understanding events in causal terms, or needing a causal explanation of events (Brown 1990; Gelman 1990, 2004; Goswami 1998; Hickling and Wellman 2001; pp. 109–110); a bias towards counting in a principled way and basic number comparisons (Gelman 1990; Gelman and Meck 1983, 1986; Dehaene *et al.* 2003, 2004; Sophian 1998; pp. 70, 346), are among the interesting suggestions. Having biases of these sorts would reduce the complexity and the uncertainty of an array to a somewhat more manageable level. To put it in a Piagetian way, we cannot assimilate information unless there is something to assimilate it to; we need a reasonable degree of match between what we already know and what we have to learn.

Constraints on cognition could be of various sorts and have a range of different causes. Some very wide-ranging constraints would arise from the nature of the human nervous system (Chapter 5). Our senses provide us with visual and auditory information that we rely on in our cognition; we make much less use of smell, though it may affect us more than we ordinarily suppose. We seem to learn by building up networks of associations that are constantly being reconstituted and modified. We have a limited attention span and short-term memory and cannot process too many different things at the same time. Characteristics such as these put some constraints on what we learn and how we learn it, and although they are weak constraints, modifiable by experience and training, they operate from birth to death over a wide range of cognitive domains. Some physical characteristics apply over a more limited area: our colour perception and our use of different speech sounds are based on physical sensitivities (pp. 9, 152, 333–334) and have implications for such diverse areas as colour categorisation and learning to read. We may develop skills in these areas that transform them from their constrained beginnings, but a number of biases remain.

As I dicussed earlier (pp. 18–22), Newport (1990), Markman (1990), Woodward and Markman (1998) and Gelman and Williams (1998) argue that there are processing constraints in language learning. Children faced with complex stimuli such as language form a representation of *pieces* of those stimuli only, while adults make a more complex representation of the whole. Children, having only fragmentary representations, are in a better position for analysing them into components and hence learning from them than they would be if they had a complex representation without any idea of how to select an analysis. Computer simulations suggest that it is easier to analyse and learn about fragments than about a very complex whole even if the fragments are random, and there might be biases in what aspects of the stimuli are represented such that the fragments are not random. Newport suggests that it is because they normally function on the basis of analysed scraps rather than on the basis of fully represented wholes that children are able to pick up language to communicate with so quickly, while taking a much longer time to perfect its details and represent it as a whole system to be reflected on; and to do well on component-based learning tasks while being worse than adults on tasks that require the integration of complex stimuli. Markman (1990) suggests further constraints in children's learning of language: they work on the assumption that new words apply to new objects as a whole, not to parts; that different words apply to different objects so that one object should not be referred to by different words; and that names apply taxonomically, not thematically. Thus a child learning a new word, as in 'that's a goose', would constrain its meaning to the newly encountered fowl as an entity, not to its waddle or its feathers; would regard it as inappropriate to an object that already has a known label, such as a chicken; and would apply 'goose' to 'goose-like' objects such as swans and ducks, not to objects thematically linked to geese, such as eggs, ponds, nursery rhymes, feathers, lawnmowers and the night-watchmen of ancient Rome.

Gelman (1990) extends the discussion to cognitive development. She suggests that it is directed by skeletal sets of domain-specific principles, with their rules of application and of which entities they apply to. These constitute the structured outline of the domain. An example is the 'how-to-count' principles (Gelman and Gallistel 1978; Gelman and Meck 1983, 1986; Ginsburg et al. 1998; p. 70), which are related to the wider principles of arithmetical reasoning. These domain-specific principles may constrain learning even if they are not part of the learner's explicitly represented understanding of the domain, as in the counting activities of infants and very young children. Some may be implicit in the general information-processing mechanisms we use (particularly if they apply across domains, as short-term memory's organisation should do), and some might be wired-in to the brain. An example of this might be the way in which we map information across modalities, maintaining a single unitary spatial matrix, so that if we both hear and see an object we do not allocate it two different positions in our mental representation of where things are in space. Wired-in constraints like this may have a critical period during which their functioning becomes integrated and fixed (p. 336). They might also reflect evolutionary internalisation of certain external, physical, constraints on objects (Gottlieb 1983; Keil 1990), perhaps what Gibson called their 'affordances' (Gibson 1979); presumably organisms that generally acted as if a seen object should be heard to be at the seen location and not elsewhere would be more likely to survive and reproduce than those that did not.

Domain-specific principles establish the boundaries of relevant stimulation (for example, the colour of objects is irrelevant to counting them, except when the task is to count objects of a particular colour). They constrain both what information is taken in and how it is responded to. They provide a skeleton that the stimulation can be wrapped around. Thus they help the learner to solve problems of relevance and coherent storage at a time when he or she has not yet learned much: they give a 'leg-up' by providing a kind of mental apparatus that supports learning, structured tools for attending to information and storing it. These are, of course, the sorts of support that the scaffolding adult gives the learner (see Chapters 2, 4 and 5). Perhaps one of the constraints we bring to learning is an attention to other people's selection of information and their structuring of events. Such attention may be behind some of the instances where a 'cultural' innovation (such as washing the sand off your gathered fruit) has spread through the young members of a group of primates (Laland and Hoppitt 2003; Reader 2003; Keller 2004). In some cases this may lead to imitation, in others to the facilitated re-invention of what the first animal did.

Brown (1990) pointed out the importance of understanding the basic causal mechanism for learning about information, for transferring what is learned to other occasions, and for analogical reasoning. She argued that if they do understand causes, children learn relatively easily, are persistent and self-motivated and show goal-directed spontaneous error correction and rehearsal, insightful learning and rapid transfer (p. 120). Children have predispositions to learn about particular kinds of things, showing early sensitivity to critical cues and systematic exploratory learning of the relevant causal knowledge (das Gupta and Bryant 1989). By the age of seven or eight they have fairly efficient general-purpose learning processes, and further learning is a combination of the information they have to acquire and the development of increasingly complex applications of that knowledge.

These domain-specific constraints on development are reminiscent of M. Anderson's suggestion of 'modules' in the development of intelligence (Anderson 1989a, 1992; and see pp. 223–227). We have little hard evidence of their existence, and little that explains why they would exist and how they affect development. A third sort of 'constraint' is perhaps more obvious. What you have learned influences what you learn next, both in the process of learning and in what sort of representation you make of what is learned. Someone who is a novice in an area may learn a new piece of information as an isolated fact, with no close connection to the rest of the domain and no implications for it. The same piece of information will be linked into the domain for the expert, and may confirm, or supplement, or overturn the way the domain is understood. There may be quite strong domain-specific constraints on cognition within that domain, especially in the ways in which prior learning affects new learning. The model we have of a particular topic will affect how we deal with new material on that topic, and, through our use of analogies, may affect our cognition in other domains. Whether this is an advantage or not will depend on the adequacy of the model. Historians writing biographies of Shakespeare are sometimes accused of not appreciating the plays; directors creating a production of a play sometimes introduce interpretations that would not have occurred to the playwright and the original audience.

7.5 Cognition and emotion in development

One of the inadequacies of the earlier chapters of this book has been the omission of anything like an adequate discussion of the interplay of emotion and cognition in cognitive development. This reflects the classic partition of psychology and the refusal to admit any affective streak in cognitive development. Most of the literature on cognitive development pays no attention whatever to emotion. The information-processing model is affect-free as well as asocial, in theoretical principle as well as in practice. Piaget's work touched on emotion in the early stages but, apart from mentioning it as a process that energised cognitive development, said little about it (Suizzo 2000); even Vygotsky's account of cognitive development in culturally based settings and interactions largely neglected the emotional side of people's experience. Studies of intelligence ignore emotion (Sternberg and Dweck being the nearest to considering it), and it remains well below visibility even in work on cognitive style and creativity. Paul Harris's work on children's understanding of emotions fills a gap in the literature on the development of cognitive content (Harris 1989; p. 175), and is one of the examples of how careful experiment and ecologically valid samples can help to clarify important issues; but elsewhere emotion is still a Cinderella of cognitive development.

I won't pretend to be her fairy godmother, but I can begin to bring together some of the recent work that might be put together into the magic coach that will take her to the ball. There begins to be a case for regarding the interface of emotional well-being, cognitive models of the world, and social relationships as a prime area for an integrated understanding of development with applications both to 'normal' development and to developmental psychopathology.

In order to focus my discussion on what seems to me to be most exciting at this point of the book, I am going to deal very briefly indeed with some of the wide range of issues that could be raised. First, although I would have liked to extend my account of the brain and cognitive development with an account of the brain in cognitive-and-emotional development, there are debates here that are not easy to resolve (see e.g. Fisher *et al.* (1990), Gray (1990), Le Doux (1989), Panksepp (1990)). The debate beginning with William James's analysis of emotion in the 1880s continues. While it seems to be agreed that 'emotion' involves perception, appraisal and reaction *vis-à-vis* a disturbing event, there is disagreement over the sequencing and the locality of brain processing involving information about emotion-producing stimulation and their cognitive appraisal. All sorts of complex issues are involved over the conceptual nature of emotion, the identification of the brain areas involved and their interconnections, how affective and cognitive information-processing compare and interact, the specificity or ambiguity of emotional arousal, the accessibility to conscious awareness of affective information-processing, the timing of events in the emotion sequence, how short-term changes in a neural network dealing with an emotional situation are reflected in longer-term ones, and so on. The traditional view was that emotion was a special subjective state, intra-psychic rather than relation-based. They believe that it involves, rather, processes of establishing, maintaining or disrupting relations between a person and the internal or external environment, when such relations are significant to the individual because they are relevant to goals, or involve emotional communication with other individuals, or have purely hedonic qualities of physical pain, discomfort or pleasure. A cognitive appraisal of the individual's relations with the environment establishes their significance and is a necessary component of emotion.

Campos *et al.* (1989) also emphasise that emotions have interpersonal consequences: they function to maintain, elicit or end other people's behaviour and to signal to others. For example, the individual's expressions of joy, of success in progressing towards a goal, function to maintain other people's positive interactions, while expressions of sadness, of relinquishing a relation with the environment, of individual helplessness when adaptive action is impossible, signal to elicit help and comfort from others. The actual reaction of the others is not of course guaranteed: the three-year-old artist's delight at her beautiful felt pen drawing on the kitchen floor may elicit from her mother not joy at its aesthetic qualities but anger at its interference with the maternal goal of clean floors and drawings restricted to proper pieces of paper. However, well-meaning interactants are likely to acknowledge each other's emotions even if they cannot themselves share them: discussion of why emotions are or are not shared or acceptable seems to be an important part of the child's curriculum (Dunn 1988, 1995; Dunn *et al.* 1987, 1995; Brown and Dunn 1996; Cutting and Dunn 1999; Dunn and Hughes 2001b; Meins and Fernyhough 1999; p. 191). It is also possible to argue that human cognition evolved to a highly complex level because individuals living in large permanent social groups had to lead complex social lives, in which an ability to use emotional signals appropriately, and to attend particularly closely to emotion-arousing situations (as small children do), would be especially important (e.g. Byrne and Whiten 1988; Humphrey 1983).

This view of emotion as being concerned with the relationships of events to an individual's needs and goals links it to motivation, to social inter-action and to cognition. It gives equal status to the person's appreciation of the significance of events, the person's feelings that are monitors of events, and the individual's coping strategies, the ways he or she deals with the environment. Such a model necessarily implies developmental change, notably in cognitive appraisal and in coping strategies. I will not attempt a full account of the issues and the data in this area here (Harris (1989), Lazarus (1991), Thompson (1990a) for further discussion), but will merely mention a few points concerning how this development seems to happen. I want to stress the centrality of emotional regulation, of having to com-promise between the perhaps intense and egocentric emotional expression that might come spontaneously (McDowell *et al.* 2000) and the perhaps more demure and restricted emotional expression that the culture's rules of etiquette prescribe. (Etiquette may of course prescribe an amplification and exaggeration of a naturally moderate emotional expression; the most familiar English middle-class example of this is probably making 'thank yous' for gifts that are not especially exciting.) It seems that learning emo-tional regulation fits very well into the apprentice–master model, as it proceeds by a combination of adults doing it for the infant or young child, adults scaffolding the child's attempts, adult and child discussing and reflecting on what is done, and responsibility passing gradually from the more skilled adult to the becoming-skilled child (Thompson 1990b; Cole *et al.* 2004). Similar processes may contribute to the learning of complex social emotions such as guilt (Zahn-Waxler and Kochanska 1990; Ackerman *et al.* 1999a and b) and to recognition of mixed emotions (Harris 1989; Kesten-baum and Gelman 1995). What is perhaps of particular developmental interest is what range of individual differences arise from differences in parental handling of the child's emotions. Thompson (1990a) includes some interesting reviews of the development of children under abnormal parent-ing conditions. More recent work on abused children is suggesting changes in neurotransmitters as a result of their exposure to violence and negative emotion, which may persist and colour their cognition for many years (Cicchetti 2002).

My focus here is on the possibility that people may have 'emotional biases' that influence their cognitive development. Malatesta (1990) argues that individuals become predisposed to a characteristic mood state as a result of biologically based traits such as temperament that are operated on by repetitive social experiences. Certain emotional states are frequent and salient, and become part of feelings about the self, so that they can then influence a wide range of behaviours, such as perception, emotional expression, cognitive processing and social relations. On the whole, there may be considerable stability in this so that something like a strong and pervasive personality trait is built up over time to operate in a self-perpetuating way. La Frenière and Sroufe (1985), for example, found significant stability in measures of aggression, affiliativeness and affect in young children; Kagan (1984) found shyness and behavioural inhibition showing continuity from childhood to early adulthood (see also Kagan *et al.* 1987). Experience of social disadvantage may be associated with learning about emotions and eventual emotional adjustment (Evans and English 2002; Felner *et al.* 1995; Lengua 2002).

There is not a great deal of evidence on how emotional state affects cognition. Experimentally induced moods have been shown to produce short-term cognitive biases in perception, learning, judgement and memory (Anastasi 1985; Bower 1981; Williams *et al.* 1988); children who were habitually aggressive made different appraisals of people's intentions towards them from those of more peaceful children (Dodge *et al.* 1986), and maltreated children and control (non-maltreated) children processed aggressive and non-aggressive stimuli differently (Cicchetti 1990; Rieder and Cicchetti 1989). Mood probably biases attention and ability (and willingness) to concentrate, and may bias what could be considered more purely cognitive processes through its effects on the network of connotations of any stimulus. Particular cognitive activities may come to have emotional connotations themselves (maths anxiety, for example), and cognitive processes may become part of the regulation of emotion (Santostefano 1985).

There are likely to be developmental changes in the perception, appraisal and regulation of emotional states. Infants react to notable changes with emotion, negatively if their goals are interfered with, positively if goals are reached or confirmed. Emotional expressions are detectable from birth, and there seems to be individual stability in the expression of anger and sadness over the first two years. By nine months of age or thereabouts other people's emotional expression may guide the baby's own expression of affect. In babies there is a fairly clear relationship between their emotion, its expression, and the circumstances that caused it: caretakers perceive, interpret, act on and comment on the child's mood, so sensitising the child to emotional cues and the linkages between expression, behaviour and causal stimulation. There are stable individual differences here (Dunn *et al.* 1987) that affect the rate of children's development of emotional discourse and understanding, and of theory of mind (Dunn 2004; Meins 1997; Meins and Fernyhough 1999; Meins *et al.* 2002, 2003; Dunn, J. 2004). Systematic shaping of children's emotional behaviour may be part of the way in which caretakers influence their development; the range and type of comments that caretakers make about emotional states may determine both the child's emotional expression and the sorts of emotional state that can be communicated to others and to oneself (Bretherton 1990; Lewis and Michalson

1983; Miller 1985), perhaps to a psychopathological degree. Interpretations of other people's emotions are also likely to be affected by our own emotional experience. Our 'working model' of people has a strong emotional component.

Perhaps because so much of the work that unites social, emotional and cognitive strands in development stems from a practical interest in developmental psychopathology, which often involved the examination of the mother–child relationship, it focuses on early repeated social interactions with familiar partners as the main source of emotional organisation and cognition. Interaction with caretakers leads to attachment that is secure, or anxious, or ambivalent, or disorganised (Ainsworth *et al.* 1978; Bretherton and Waters 1985; Radke-Yarrow and Sherman 1985), and so to 'working models' of relationships. In secure relationships, these models can become more complex and integrated as the child is confident, communicative, and well in tune with the adult partner. The insecurely attached child, whose signals are consistently ignored or misunderstood, whose efforts are not supported or respected, and who does not get useful feedback from the partner, is at risk of more negative emotional states and of building a cognitive model that is less coherent, less accurate and less modifiable (Bretherton 1990; Rutter 1991; Saarni 1990).

Children who are ill-treated or neglected by their caretakers are one population where the relationship between social, emotional and cognitive development is of particular interest. I have discussed such cases in Chapter 5, and will not extend that discussion here. That research supports the idea that different emotional biases arise, largely through social interactions that elicit, emphasise and allow some emotions more than others. Different 'working models' are built up and cognitive biases contribute to the maintenance of an organisation of cognition and affect and social behaviour through a subjective understanding of the world. This has ramifications for motivation, self-concept, attributional style, metacognition and achievement (e.g. Carr *et al.* 1991; Dweck and Elliot 1983). The fine-tuning of cognitive development has an affective component, and researchers need to recognise this.

7.6 Imagination

The earlier chapters of this book discuss quite a wide range of ways of thinking, but they are primarily problem-solving, skill-based and, to a large extent, literate. Even my discussion of creativity focused on the self-consciously applied skills, attitudes and knowledge that are necessary for significant creative achievement. This bias towards systematic, analytic, evaluative and deliberate cognitive effort reflects the bias of the literature and the preoccupations of educational policy makers, but it neglects 'imagination'. I am unhappy with this, as imaginative play is such a central characteristic of childhood and a source of such delight. I therefore make a few speculative points about 'imagination' here.

There is much philosophical debate about the nature of imagination, which I will not review here (but see Reddiford (1980), Ryle (1949, Chapter 8), Sartre (1972), Warnock (1976), Carruthers (2002)). In psychology and education it carries a contradictory set of associated meanings; on the one hand irrational, merely fanciful, a pale shadow of reality, deceiving, trivial, useless, something that children do but should be educated out of; and on the other hand it is seen as free and poetic, as in the Romantic vision of the child born 'trailing clouds of glory' but all too soon subjected to the shades of the educational prison house. This debate is of course closely related to debate about the nature and worth of 'play', just as play activities are often used as evidence of imagination. However, we clearly must not confuse imagination and play (Meadows 1986: 23–30; Meadows and Cashdan 1988); play involves at various times intelligent exploration, discovery, mastery, problem-solving and imitation, as well as imagination, and imagination can, as I shall discuss, be apparent in situations that are not playful.

The etymological root of 'imagination' is the Latin *imago*, meaning an image or representation, and thus at the core of the concept is the capacity to conceive of what is not actually happening here and now. Such a capacity may have pretty mundane results (as in much of the sex-stereotyped role-play of preschoolers), or it may lead to more unusual results. Like creativity, imagination has to work with knowledge and skills even if it transforms them into the unreal and impossible, and so some domains may not offer many opportunities for imaginative thinking (Barrow 1988). The criteria of 'unusualness' and 'effectiveness' may apply to imagination as well as to creativity, though the same conceptual problems arise (see Chapter 3).

A further set of epithets applied to 'imagination' is made up of terms such as 'fantasy', 'storytelling', 'egocentrism', 'mind-wandering'; varieties of indulgence in the imaginary dissociated from the real. These words are often used pejoratively, to justify the suppression of imagination, and may lie behind the way it has been pushed out of cognition into play. Such a pejorative use may be regrettable, not least because 'reasoning' and 'imagination' are not truly independent (Reddiford 1980; Dias and Harris 1988, 1990). Egan (1988a, 1988b) makes an interesting case for imagination in precisely this sense of fantasy and making stories as a valid component of cognition. He starts from John Dewey's definition of the imaginative as 'a warm and intimate taking-in of the full scope of a situation', a definition that highlights the importance of emotion in cognition. Egan suggests that young children's mental lives are full of imagination, not just because their ignorance makes it difficult for them to distinguish between the improbable but really real (earning a living by wittering on about developmental psychology) and the probable but not really real (Father Christmas, animals that talk, fairies, inter-stellar travel), but also because they are actively engaged in making unified sense of the world, and the freedom and exaggeration of fantasy are an important means to the end they are actively engaged in, making unified sense of the world. The 'mythic' thinking typical of non-literate groups serves the same goal. Fantasy and imagination involve the elaboration of impossibilities, a creative play on the abstractions that lie beneath the fantastic content: abstractions that the child is often emotionally involved in, such as the conflict between good and evil, and the powerlessness of the very young. These sorts of issues are the concern of the myths, fairy stories and folktales that were once a contributor to everyone's way of understanding the world and are now part of the province of childhood. Egan suggests that mythic understanding dominates the thinking of young children (and that their curriculum should therefore be centred on it) and remains a constituent of mature understanding. I think his account has a lot of faults – not a great deal of behavioural evidence, some unclear definitions, some value-laden judgements – but it does make the useful point that there are a variety of *bonnes à penser* (Egan 1988b: 63), of 'good things to think with', and imaginative thinking is one collection of these, which has been comparatively neglected.

The various cultural activities that children engage with might be expected to affect their imagination. Heath (1983) shows this for casual story-telling and later school composition; the contribution of favourite books is well known (p. 56). The impact of newer media on children's imagination is still very much debated.

Marjorie Taylor (Taylor 1997, 1999; Taylor and Carlson 1997; Taylor *et al.* 2004) has provided a number of interesting accounts of children's imaginary friends. A substantial minority of young children have imaginary companions, sometimes playing an important role in the emotional life of the child; some of these survive, covertly, for years. Some children impersonate a favourite character, such as a superhero. Taylor and her colleagues see these imagination-based activities as positive for the child, suggesting for example that children who do not imagine other characters are low on emotion understanding and theory of mind. With further research, we may find out both why some children do not fantasise and whether it does indeed have positive effects on development.

7.7 Final section

In this book I have examined our understanding of the child as thinker, dealing with material describing children's thinking, examining dimensions of individual differences, looking at theoretical models and causal influences. The work has been heterogeneous. I have had to piece together evidence from varying approaches in a number of different fields, a process that inevitably means some poorly fitting assemblies and yawning gaps, because the research methods of many studies, while adequate for the work's immediate purposes, are not adequate for the big developmental questions.

> Behavioural research on children, for the most part, is not geared to investigating transactions, encompassing a multiplicity of influences, measuring environment in non-static and developmental terms, addressing developmental questions developmentally, or accounting for individual differences in development . . . [The] discrepancy between conceptual sophistication, on the one hand, and paradigmatic and methodological insufficiencies, on the other, brings an unsettling disequilibrium to developmental research.
>
> (Radke-Yarrow 1991: 391–392)

However, as Piaget claimed that being in 'an unsettling disequilibrium' was a major spur to cognitive development, I want to take this potentially depressing summary as a challenge, not as a criticism. So, in this final section, I want to begin to suggest some shifts in research paradigm that may help us tackle the not yet answered questions of the field. The choice of 'questions' reflects my own priorities (on the psychology–education–parenting interface) and my own research experience (a shift from assessment within the Piagetian paradigm to direct and extended observation of behaviour in 'real-world' contexts). This is a summary restatement of themes that will have emerged from the earlier chapters of this book, and I hope that people reading this section will refer back to relevant material elsewhere.

Children's development occurs in, and has to be examined in, environments. This is so obvious as to be taken for granted, but we do not have anything like a good or thorough analysis and understanding of environments. They are too often ignored, or simplified, or dismissed as too variable and arbitrary to be studied scientifically. Or they are dealt with in terms of single variables such as structural features that are assumed to affect all individuals equally and so need no direct measurement. Examples such as studies of the effect of preschool attendance that do not look at the variation in quality within each preschool setting, or of the effects of 'social address' variables such as being part of a one-parent family, come to mind. These studies tell us something about differences between group averages but leave the causal variables underexposed. Further research looking at variables within groups, or using variables that are good candidates for bringing about causal change directly, will be necessary.

We have to take the study of environments seriously. They may be studied experimentally. Here it has to be assumed that behaviour in a laboratory simulation of the 'real world' bears a reasonably close resemblance to behaviour in the real world itself. At the extreme, it is assumed that children answering a stranger's questions in a strange laboratory (or in an unfrequented and presumably less strange corner of their school) will answer in a way representative of their ordinary thinking and talking. The problem here is whether this situation produces behaviour that does indeed occur elsewhere, or whether it leads on the contrary to a serious mis-representation of the child. Even if the latter is not the case, it will be necessary to compare the artificial and the real environments carefully at some point. The same problem of representativeness applies of course to 'real-life' environments: have they been sampled in a way that represents all the ways in which the environment is, day by day, or at least those parts of life in the environment thought to be important in principle? A sample of parental behaviour would show less child-contingent language for children between six and ten than for babies if it was restricted to the small hours of the morning, for example. This would not necessarily show that babies got more child-contingent language than older children *in toto*!

Environments may be assessed by asking the people who live in them to describe or rate them, a procedure that can also produce interesting data but that is, necessarily, an indirect and possibly subjectively-biased meas-ure. It may be the only possible method for large-scale studies (which also often use gross structural variables such as SES or family size), but it is no substitute for fine-grained, systematic and extended observation of interaction in the environment.

Such observation needs to be based on a sensible conceptualisation of the environment, and, because it is likely to be time-consuming, expensive, and demanding so far as the environments studied are concerned, it would be wise to embark on it informed by the relevant theoretical literature and by the insights as to variables worth study gained from the less conclusive methodologies that I have just criticised. Because of the 'economic' problems of systematic observation, samples are likely to be small, and the work may verge on case study. Intensive studies of a small number of cases have been rare in recent work on cognitive development, though they made significant contributions earlier in the history of psychology, have made up a large part of research in language development and developmental psychopathology, and contribute much of the evidence on the effects of brain damage (see Shallice (1989) on this methodology in this last area, and Scerif and Karmiloff-Smith (2005) on genes and cognitive development). They will be especially useful for answering questions about children who are unusual; for example, children whose early level of achievement is extraordinarily high, or who suffer appalling conditions as they grow up, or who do not respond as usual to training or testing. They may include investigation of several different aspects of behaviour, or several different conditions or life events, that have different effects in combination from their influences singly. Longitudinal case studies can pick up irregularities in the pace of development, which are averaged out of view in large samples but may provide important clues to the processes of developmental change (and checks on the validity of a developmental model, as in my study of Piagetian stages). In an ideal world, the subjects of case studies would be in a known position relative to the population as a whole, for example being the intensively studied part of a population study. An account by Doria Pilling (1990) provides an example of the usefulness of such linkage between case studies and a population studied with questionnaires. She writes about members of the 1958 National Child Development Study cohort, who, despite suffering severe social disadvantage in early childhood, were relatively successful as young adults, with relatively good educational achievement or well above average economic status in their twenties. These individuals' histories add to what we know about the importance of parental support for their children's cognitive development. Similarly, studies such as Quinton and Rutter (1988), ALSPAC and current work on depression, mothering, and outcomes for the children (see Chapter 5) clarify what other research methods suggest, and document the complex histories that lead development down different pathways from childhood to adult life.

I think longitudinal studies are going to be another essential part of coming to understand cognitive development. Again, they are more expensive (and much slower) than cross-sectional studies, though they do not always need to extend over very long periods. They require a particularly clear conceptualisation of what are 'continuities' and what are 'changes' in behaviour, various precautions to separate the effects of increases in competence with development from increases in familiarity with and confidence in the test situation, and, inconveniently, a scrupulous and sophisticated understanding of the appropriate statistical techniques. The comparatively intense contact between researcher and subject also brings the ethics of research to the foreground as an issue: a one-off session of testing with a child in school may not require much more than the agreement of all interested parties and careful handling of the child's sensitivities by the tester, but getting data about ecologically real behaviour over a long period of time has to be recognised to be a big demand on subjects for, perhaps, little return. Researchers have to be concerned to minimise the costs and maximise the benefits to their subjects. They also have to recognise that their relationship with their subjects will not be a neutral one, and ethical problems may arise for them as researcher and as morally responsible person. What do you do if the child's answers to your questions suggest experience of sexual abuse from a family member, or if the parents ask for advice on the education of their child? Can you withhold advice that would lead to a change in the child's experience that you would rather exclude from your research design?

I am now almost at the end of this discussion of the child as thinker, or rather at the place where my discussion stops for the moment, as further discussion is not only possible but essential. I will end by recapitulating points made in various earlier sections.

1   Children do their thinking, as we all do, in a world that presents a particular set of physical, social and conceptual problems in a particular range of settings and experiences. What makes for successful thinking depends on the problem and its context. It is appropriate to read this book with some care and a lot of critical thought, but not with the warm unreasoning engagement you might bring to a favourite light novelist, nor with the sort of attention to the sound of what is said that you might bring to poetry. 'Good' and 'poor' performance are, to a considerable extent, situation-specific.

2   The point that there are different sorts of good performance makes untenable the idea of 'development' as a uni-dimensional progress from less advanced to more advanced functioning; for example, more 'complex' cognition. Evolutionary theory makes a similar point. In general evolution has led to more complexity only if more complexity leads to a higher degree of reproductive success. Very simple organisms may persist without any change towards complexity for millions of years if they are successful in reproducing in their environments and there is no relevant environmental change to reduce this success. Even in human beings, the correlation between greater cognitive complexity and greater reproductive success is not self-evidently high and positive (the eugenicists at the turn of the century, and a sprinkling of mainly right-wing theorists to this day, advocated control of people's reproduction precisely because they believed the correlation was high and negative and that the stupid would out-breed the intelligent). Development may tend towards better success, but what 'success' is will depend on the environmental challenges that the organism meets.

3   As well as there being different sorts of good performance reached by different paths, different paths or different means may lead to the same end, more or less effectively or efficiently or happily. Almost all Western children learn to read, but they do so in a number of different ways. Their repertoire of reading processes is somewhat related to the path to reading that they have taken, but there seems to be little long-term developmental significance in what path you take except through the disadvantage suffered by children who are slow to read. Those children have extra problems with school subjects for which normal reading level is assumed, may suffer from being less skilled than their peers, may have comorbid psychiatric disorders (Carroll *et al.* 2005) and may miss out on the enjoyment and information that can be gained from reading.

4   Given this co-variation of context, performance and development, what may be important about cognitive 'complexity' is the availability of a range of alternative strategies and the ability to select between them as appropriate to the particular situation. People whose repertoire of strategies is very limited or inflexible may do very well if they encounter

only familiar problems, but much less well if a problem demands a new or modified strategy. This implies that cognitive processes have to become somewhat independent from the contexts in which they were first developed, to become at least potentially autonomous tools. Moving from being scaffolded by a more expert person to being able to support one's own cognition is an example of this. The process will never be complete, and cognition is always, I repeat, embedded in a context.

5   We badly need to understand 'contexts' better. Since my discussion of what this involves is only a few pages back, I will leave this assertion without further elaboration.

6   However, we have good reason to believe that the social and inter-personal context is particularly important in the development of complex cognitive skills. It has been argued that human language and cognition evolved to serve social purposes: primates that live in large permanent groups engage in long-term relationships, multi-party inter-actions and co-operative alliances, which require cognitive complexity and sophisticated social cognition. We have incontrovertible evidence that much of cognitive development in childhood involves the acqui-sition of culturally specific cognitive skills through culturally specified social interaction: being observer and apprentice to the work skills of your parent, or being taught to read or do calculus in formal schooling. Some cognition is less social than this, in that the individual child addresses the physical world directly in some area where the adult has no vested interest. Many of the topics Piaget himself addressed were of this sort, and parental interest in teaching conservation to their pre-school children is largely post-Piagetian. There may even be parental implying of non-conservation in suggestions that there is less of a disliked foodstuff on the plate if it is cut up into bits. But even in areas independent of adults there will be social components to the cognition as both the 'non-social' task and the 'individual' thinker are related to a wide range of social tasks and understandings. *Descriptions* of tasks and of thinking can, perhaps, leave aside this social dimension, but its omission from models will leave them incomplete as *explanations* of development.

7   The socialness of cognition implies a number of interesting possibilities. Conceivably, socially based cognition will be more advanced than cognition that is more separate from the social world. For example, we may be able to achieve more in co-operation with another person than we can alone; when we are having difficulties with a cognitive task we may talk ourselves through it in a sort of internal dialogue; we may understand a point or carry through a process better in a task with social content than in one with non-social content (provided the social content fits our social experience); we may have a more complex and

effective understanding of the social world than we have of the non-social world, being better folk psychologists than folk physicists.

8   Further, the socialness of cognition implies, as does the connectedness of the 'cognitive' and 'emotional' areas of the brain, that there will be an intimate interplay between cognition and emotion in both the short term and the long term. The person's self-concept and understanding of other people will have to be considered here. So will his or her motivation to engage with a cognitive problem or with learning a cognitive skill.

Thus, having begun this book by widening conventional definitions of cognitive development somewhat to include culturally based cognitive skills such as reading and writing, using the traditional dividing-up of psychology into cognitive, affective, conative and social areas, I have ended it by arguing that these areas should not be separated in any strong sense, that much that is of interest in developmental psychology lies in the areas of overlap between the four. This makes things more complex, but also more exciting. I hope I have conveyed some of the excitement as well as some of the problems, and that this book will help further development of work on 'the child as thinker'.

References

Aber, J. L. and Allen, J. P. (1987) The effects of maltreatment on young children's socio-emotional development: an attachment theory perspective. *Developmental Psychology* 23, 406–444.

Achenbach, T. M. and Edelbrock, C. S. (1981) Behavioral problems and competencies reported by parents of normal and disturbed children aged four through sixteen. *Monographs of the Society for Research in Child Development* 46(1).

Ackerman, B. P. (1986) Children's sensitivity to comprehension failure in interpreting a nonliteral use of an utterance. *Child Development* 57, 485–497.

Ackerman, B. P. (1997) The role of setting information in children's memory retrieval. *Journal of Experimental Child Psychology* 65, 238–260.

Ackerman, B. P., Brown, E. D. and Izard, C. E. (2004a) The relations between contextual risk, earned income and the school adjustment of children from economically disadvantaged families. *Developmental Psychology* 40(2), 204–216.

Ackerman, B. P., Brown, E. D. and Izard, C. E. (2004b) The relations between persistent poverty and contextual risk and children's behavior in elementary schools. *Developmental Psychology* 40(2), 367–377.

Ackerman, B. P., Izard, C. E., Schoff, K., Youngstrom, E. and Kogos, J. (1999) Contextual risk, caregiver emotionality and the problem behaviors of six- and seven-year-old children from economically disadvantaged families. *Child Development* 70, 1415–1427.

Ackerman, B. P., Kogos, J., Youngstrom, E., Schoff, K. and Izard, C. E. (1999) Family instability and the problem behaviors of children from economically disadvantaged families. *Developmental Psychology* 35, 258–268.

Ackerman, P. L., Sternberg, R. J. and Glaser, R. (1989) *Learning and Individual Differences: Advances in Theory and Research*. New York: Freeman.

Acredolo, C. and Horobin, K. (1987) Development of relational reasoning and avoidance of premature closure. *Developmental Psychology* 23, 13–21.

Acredolo, C., O'Connor, J., Banks, L. and Horobin, K. (1989) Children's ability to make probability estimates. *Child Development* 60, 933–945.

Acredolo, L. and Goodwyn, S. (1988) Symbolic gesturing in normal infants. *Child Development* 59, 450–466.

Adams, J. and Hitch, G. J. (1998) Children's mental arithmetic and working memory. In Donlan, C. (ed.), *The Development of Mathematical Skills*. Hove, UK: Psychology Press.

Adams, M. J. (2004) Modelling the connections between word recognition and reading. In R. B. Ruddell and N. J. Unrau (eds), *Theoretical Models and Processes of Reading*. Newark, DE: International Reading Association.

Adams, M. J., Treiman, R. and Pressley, M. (1998) Reading, writing and literacy. *Handbook of Child Psychology*, vol. 4. New York: Wiley.

Adey, P., Robertson, A. and Venville, G. (2002) Effects of a cognitive acceleration programme on Year 1 pupils. *British Journal of Educational Psychology* 72, 1–25.

Adey, P. and Shayer, M. (1993) An exploration of long-term transfer effects following an extended intervention program in the high school science curriculum. *Cognition and Instruction* 11(1), 1–29.

Adi-Japha, E. and Freeman, N. H. (2001) Development of differentiation between writing and drawing systems. *Developmental Psychology* 37, 101–114.

Agostini, I. and Visalberghi, E. (2005) Social influences on the acquisition of sex-typical foraging patterns by juveniles in a group of wild tufted Capuchin monkeys (Cebus nigritus). *American Journal of Primatology* 65(4), 335–351.

Ainsworth, M., Blehar, M. C., Waters, E. and Wall, S. (1978) *Patterns of Attachment: a Psychological Study of the Strange Situation*. Hillsdale, NJ: Lawrence Erlbaum Associates, Inc.

Akhtar, N., Jipson, J. and Callanan, M. A. (2001) Learning words through over-hearing. *Child Development* 72, 416–430.

Akhtar, N. and Montague, L. (1999) Early lexical acquisition: the role of cross-situational learning. *First Language* 19, 347–358.

Alaimo, K., Olson, C. M. and Frongillo, E. A. (2001a) Food insufficiency and American school-aged children's cognitive, academic and psychosocial development. *Pediatrics* 108, 44–53.

Alaimo, K., Olson, C. M. and Frongillo, E. A. (2001b) Food insufficiency, family income and health in U.S. preschool and school-aged children. *American Journal of Public Health* 91, 781–786.

Aldhous, P. (1992) The promise and pitfalls of molecular genetics. *Science* 257, 164–165.

Alexander, J. M., Carr, M. and Schwanenflugel, P. J. (1995) Development of metacognition in gifted children; directions for future research. *Developmental Review* 15, 1–37.

Alexander, K. L., Entwistle, D. R. and Dauber, S. L. (1993) First-grade classroom behavior: its short- and long-term consequences for school performance. *Child Development* 64, 801–814.

Alexander, T. M. and Enns, J. T. (1988) Age changes in the boundaries of fuzzy categories. *Child Development* 59, 1372–1386.

Alibali, M. W. (1999) How children change their minds: strategy change can be gradual or abrupt. *Developmental Psychology* 35, 127–145.

Allen, G. L., Kirasic, K. C., Siegel, A. W. and Herman, J. F. (1979) Developmental issues in cognitive mapping: the selection and utilisation of environmental landmarks. *Child Development* 50, 1062–1070.

Allen, G. L. and Ondracek, P. J. (1995) Age-sensitive cognitive abilities related to children's acquisition of spatial knowledge. *Developmental Psychology* 31, 934–945.

Allen, J. P., Philliber, S., Herrling, S. and Kuperminc, G. P. (1997) Preventing teen pregnancy and academic failure: experimental evaluation of a developmentally based approach. *Child Development* 64, 729–742.

Allhusen, V., Belsky, J., Booth, C. L. *et al.* (2004a) Affect dysregulation in the mother–child relationship in the toddler years: antecedents and consequences. *Development and Psychopathology* 16(1), 43–68.

Allhusen, V., Belsky, J., Booth-LaForce, C. *et al.* (2004b) Fathers' and mothers' parenting behavior and beliefs as predictors of children's social adjustment in the transition to school. *Journal of Family Psychology* 18(4), 628–638.

Allhusen, V., Belsky, J., Kersey, H. B. *et al.* (2005) Predicting individual differences in attention, memory, and planning in first graders from experiences at home, child care, and school. *Developmental Psychology* 41(1), 99–114.

Alloway, T. P., Gathercole, S. E., Willis, C. and Adams, A.-M. (2004) A structural analysis of working memory and related cognitive skills in young children. *Journal of Experimental Child Psychology* 87(2), 85–106.

Allport, D. A. (1980) Patterns and actions. In G. Claxton (ed.), *Cognitive Psychology: New Directions*. London: Routledge.

Almasi, J. (1995) The nature of fourth-graders' sociocognitive conflicts in peer-led and teacher-led discussions of literature. *Reading Research Quarterly* 30, 314–351. *American Educational Research Journal* 40(4), 929–960.

Ames, G. J. and Murray, F. B. (1982) When two wrongs make a right: promoting cognitive change by social conflict. *Developmental Psychology* 18, 894–897.

Anastasi, A. (1985) Reciprocal relations between cognitive and affective development – with implications for sex differences. *Nebraska Symposium on Motivation*, vol. 32. Lincoln: University of Nebraska Press.

Anderson, J. R. (1983) *The Architecture of Cognition*. Cambridge, MA: Harvard University Press.

Anderson, J. R. (1987) Skill acquisition: compilation of weak-method problem solution. *Psychological Review* 94, 192–210.

Anderson, J. R. and Thompson, R. (1989) Use of analogy in a production system architecture. In S. Vosniadou and A. Ortony (eds), *Similarity and Analogical Reasoning*. Cambridge, UK: Cambridge University Press.

Anderson, M. (1986) Inspection time and IQ in young children. *Personality and Individual Differences* 5, 677–686.

Anderson, M. (1988) Inspection time, information processing and the development of intelligence. *British Journal of Experimental Psychology* 6, 43–57.

Anderson, M. (1989a) New ideas in intelligence. *The Psychologist* 2(3), 92–94.

Anderson, M. (1989b) Letter. *The Psychologist* 2(8), 331.

Anderson, M. (1992) *Intelligence and Cognitive Development*. Oxford, UK: Blackwell.

Anderson, M. (2001) Annotation: conceptions of intelligence. *Journal of Child Psychology and Psychiatry* 42, 287–298.

Anderson, R. C. (2004) Role of the reader's schema in comprehension, learning and memory. In R. B. Ruddell and N. J. Unrau (eds), *Theoretical Models and Processes of Reading*. Newark, DE: International Reading Association.

Anderson, R. C., Nguyen-Jahiel, K., McNurlen, B., Archodidou, A., Kim, S.-Y., Reznitskaya, A., Tillmanns, M. and Gilbert, L. (2001) The snowball phenomenon: spread of ways of talking and ways of thinking across groups of children. *Cognition and Instruction* 19(1), 1–46.

Andersson, B. E. (1992) Effects of day-care on cognitive and socio-emotional competence of thirteen-year-old Swedish schoolchildren. *Child Development* 63, 20–36.

Angoff, W. H. (1988) The nature–nurture debate, aptitudes, and group differences. *American Psychologist* 43, 713–720.

Anooshian, L. J. and Young, D. (1981) Developmental changes in cognitive maps of a familiar neighbourhood. *Child Development* 52, 341–348.

Antell, S. E. and Keating, D. P. (1983) Perception of numerical invariance in neonates. *Child Development* 54, 695–701.

Anthony, J. L. and Lonigan, C. J. (2004) The nature of phonological awareness: converging evidence from four studies of preschool and early grade school children. *Journal of Educational Psychology* 96(1), 43–55.

Applebee, A. (1978) *The Child's Conception of Story*. Chicago: University of Chicago Press.

Arendt, R. E., Short, E. J., Singer, L. T., Minnes, S., Hewitt, J., Flynn, S., Carlson, L. M., Min, M., Klein, N. and Flannery, D. (2004) Children prenatally exposed to cocaine: developmental outcomes and environmental risks at seven years of age. *Journal of Developmental and Behavioral Pediatrics* 25(2), 83–90.

Arnheim, R. (1956) *Art and Visual Perception: A Psychology of the Creative Eye*. London: Faber.

Arsenio, W. F. (1988, 1992) Children's conceptions of the situational affective consequences of sociomoral events. *Child Development* 59(6), 1611–1622.

Arsenio, W. F. and Kramer, R. (1992) Victimizers and their victims – children's conceptions of the mixed emotional consequences of moral transgressions. *Child Development* 63(4), 915–927.

Arterberry, M. E. and Bornstein, M. H. (2001) Three-month-old infants' categorisation of animals and vehicles based on static and dynamic attributes. *Journal of Experimental Child Psychology* 80, 333–346.

Ashcraft, M. H. and Fierman, B. A. (1982) Mental addition in third, fourth and sixth graders. *Journal of Experimental Child Psychology* 33, 216–234.

Aslin, R. N., Jusczyk, P. W. and Pisoni, D. B. (1998) Speech and auditory processing during infancy: constraints on and precursors to language. *Handbook of Child Psychology*, vol. 2. New York: Wiley.

Aslin, R. N., Pisoni, D. B. and Jusczyk, P. W. (1983) Auditory development and speech perception in infancy. In M. M. Haith and J. J. Campos (eds), *Handbook of Child Psychology*, vol. 2. New York: Wiley.

Aslin, R. N. and Smith, L. B. (1988) Perceptual development. *Annual Review of Psychology* 39, 435–471.

Astington, J. W. (1995) *The Child's Discovery of Mind*. Cambridge, MA: Harvard University Press.

Astington, J. W. (2001) The future of theory-of-mind research: Understanding motivational states, the role of language, and real-world consequences *Child Development* 72(3), 685–687.

Astington, J. W. and Gopnik, A. (1988) Knowing you've changed your mind: children's understanding of representational change. In J. W. Astington, P. L. Harris and D. R. Olson (eds), *Developing Theories of Mind*. Cambridge, UK: Cambridge University Press.

Astington, J. W. and Gopnik, A. (1991) Theoretical explanations of children's understanding of the mind. *British Journal of Developmental Psychology* 9, 7–31.

Astington, J. W., Harris, P. L. and Olson, D. R. (eds) (1988) *Developing Theories of Mind.* Cambridge, UK: Cambridge University Press.

Astuti, M., Solomon, G. and Carey, S. (2004) Constraints on conceptual development. *Monographs of the Society for Research in Child Development* 69(3), serial no. 277.

Atkinson, R. C. and Shiffrin, R. M. (1968) Human memory: a proposed system and its control processes. In K. W. Spence and J. T. Spence (eds), *Advances in the Psychology of Learning and Motivation,* vol. 2. New York: Academic Press.

Attili, G. (1989) The case of ambivalence: the interface between emotional and cognitive development. In A. de Ribaupierre (ed.), *Transition Mechanisms in Child Development.* Cambridge, UK: Cambridge University Press.

Au, T. K., Sidle, A. L. and Rollins, K. B. (1993) Developing intuitive understanding of conservation and contamination: invisible particles of a plausible mechanism. *Developmental Psychology* 29, 286–289.

Avis, J. and Harris, P. L. (1991) Belief–desire reasoning among Baka children: evidence for a universal conception of mind. *Child Development* 62, 460–467.

Azmitia, M. (1988) Peer interaction and problem-solving: when are two heads better than one? *Child Development* 59, 87–96.

Azmitia, M. and Perlmutter, M. (1989) Social influences on young children's cognition: state of the art and future directions. In H. W. Reese (ed.), *Advances in Child Development and Behavior,* vol. 21. New York: Academic Press.

Bachevalier, J. (1992) Cortical versus limbic immaturity: relation to infantile amnesia. In M. Gunnar and C. A. Nelson (eds), *Developmental Behavioral Neuroscience.* Minnesota Symposium on Child Psychology, vol. 24. Hillsdale, NJ: Lawrence Erlbaum Associates, Inc.

Bachevalier, J. and Mishkin, M. (1984) An early and a late developing system for learning and retention in infant monkeys. *Behavioral Neurosciences* 98, 770–778.

Baddeley, A. (1986) *Working Memory.* Oxford, UK: Oxford University Press.

Baddeley, A. (1996) Exploring the central executive. *Quarterly Journal of Experimental Psychology* A49, 5–28.

Baddeley, A. (1999) *Essentials of Human Memory.* Hove, UK: Psychology Press.

Baddeley, A. (2000) The episodic buffer: a new component of working memory? *Trends in Cognitive Science* 4, 417–423.

Baddeley, A., Gathercole, S. and Papagno, C. (1998) The phonological loop as a language learning device. *Psychological Review* 105, 158–173.

Baddeley, A. and Hitch, G. (1974) Working memory. In G. A. Bower (ed.), *Recent Advances in Learning and Motivation,* vol. 8. New York: Academic Press.

Baddeley, A. D. (1976) *The Psychology of Memory.* New York: Harper & Row.

Baddeley, A. D. (1990) *Human Memory.* London: Lawrence Erlbaum Associates Ltd.

Baddeley, A. D. and Lewis, V. J. (1981) Interactive processes in reading: the inner voice, the inner ear and the inner eye. In A. M. Lesgold and C. A. Perfetti (eds), *Interactive Processes in Reading.* Hillsdale, NJ: Lawrence Erlbaum Associates, Inc.

Bahrick, H. P., Bahrick, P. O. and Wittinlinger, R. P. (1975) Fifty years of memory for names and places: a cross-sectional approach. *Journal of Experimental Psychology: General* 104, 54–75.

Bailey, C. and Kandel, E. R. (1985) Molecular approaches to the study of short-term and long-term memory. In C. W. Coen (ed.), *Functions of the Brain*. Oxford, UK: Clarendon Press.

Baird, J. A. and Astington, J. W. (2004) The role of mental state understanding in the development of moral cognition and moral action. *New Directions for Child and Adolescent Development* 103, 37–49.

Bakeman, R. and Brown, J. V. (1980) Early interaction: consequences for social and mental development at three years. *Child Development* 51, 437–447.

Baker, L. (1984) Spontaneous versus instructed use of multiple standards for evaluating comprehension: effects of age, reading proficiency and type of standard. *Journal of Experimental Child Psychology* 38, 289–311.

Baker, L. and Brown, A. L. (1984) Metacognitive skills of reading. In D. Pearson (ed.), *Handbook of Reading Research*. New York: Longmans, Green.

Baldwin, J. M. (1895) *Mental Development in the Child and Race*. New York: Macmillan.

Bandura, A. (1977a) Self-efficacy: toward a unifying theory of behavioral change. *Psychological Review* 84, 191–215.

Bandura, A. (1977b) *Social Learning Theory*. Englewood Cliffs, NJ: Prentice Hall.

Bandura, A. (1981) Self referent thought: a developmental analysis of self-efficacy. In J. H. Flavell and L. Ross (eds), *Social Cognitive Development*. Cambridge, UK: Cambridge University Press.

Bandura, A. (1997) *Self-efficacy: The Exercise of Control*. New York: Freeman.

Bandura, A. (ed.) (1995) *Self-efficacy in Changing Societies*. Cambridge, UK: Cambridge University Press.

Banks, M. S. and Salapatek, P. (1983) Infant visual perception. In M. M. Haith and J. J. Campos (eds), *Handbook of Child Psychology*, vol. 2, series ed. P. H. Mussen. New York: Wiley.

Baranes, R., Perry, M. and Stigler, J. W. (1989) Activation of real-world knowledge in the solution of word problems. *Cognition and Instruction* 6, 287–318.

Baringa, M. (1996) Learning defect identified in the brain. *Science* 273, 867–868.

Barker, P. (1988) *Basic Child Psychiatry* Oxford, UK: Blackwell Scientific.

Barnes, D. M. (1989) 'Fragile X' syndrome and its puzzling genetics. *Science* 243, 171–172.

Barnes, S., Gutfreund, M., Satterly, D. J. and Wells, C. G. (1983) Characteristics of adult speech which predict children's language development. *Journal of Child Language* 10, 65–84.

Barnett, W. (1995) Long-term effects of early childhood programs on cognitive and school outcomes. *The Future of Children* 5(3), 25–50.

Baron, J. (1978) Intelligence and general strategies. In G. Underwood (ed.), *Strategies in Information Processing*. New York: Academic Press.

Baron, J. (1985) *Rationality and Intelligence*. Cambridge, UK: Cambridge University Press.

Baron, J. (1988) *Thinking and Deciding*. Cambridge, UK: Cambridge University Press.

Baron, J., Badgio, P. C. and Gaskins, I. W. (1986) Cognitive style and its improvement: a normative approach. In R. J. Sternberg (ed.), *Advances in the Psychology of Human Intelligence*. Hillsdale, NJ: Lawrence Erlbaum Associates, Inc.

Baron, J. and Sternberg, R. (eds) (1987) *Teaching Thinking Skills*. New York: Freeman.

Baron-Cohen, S. (1992) Out of sight or out of mind? Another look at deception in autism. *Journal of Child Psychology and Psychiatry* 33, 1141–1156.

Baron-Cohen, S. (1995) *Mind-Blindness: An Essay on Autism and Theory of Mind*. Cambridge, MA: MIT Press.

Baron-Cohen, S., Baldwin, D. A. and Crowson, M. (1997) Do children with autism use the speaker's-direction-of-gaze strategy to crack the code of language? *Child Development* 68, 48–57.

Baron-Cohen, S. and Frith, U. (1992) Autism and misrepresentation. *The Psychologist* 5, 163.

Baron-Cohen, S., Leslie, A. M. and Frith, U. (1985) Does the autistic child have a 'theory of mind'? *Cognition* 21, 37–46.

Baron-Cohen, S., Tager-Flusberg, H. and Cohen, D. J. (2000) *Understanding Other Minds: Perspectives from Developmental Cognitive Neuroscience*. Oxford, UK: Oxford University Press.

Barrett, D. E. (1987) Undernutrition and child behaviour: what behaviours should we measure and how should we measure them? In J. Dobbing (ed.), *Early Nutrition and Later Achievement*. London: Academic Press.

Barrett, D. E., Radke-Yarrow, M. and Klein, R. E. (1982) Chronic malnutrition and child behavior: effects of early caloric supplementation on social–emotional functioning at school age. *Development Psychology* 18, 541–566.

Barrett, M. (1995) Early lexical development. In P. Fletcher and B. MacWhinney (eds), *The Handbook of Child Language*. Oxford, UK: Blackwell.

Barrett, M. D. and Light, P. H. (1976) Symbolism and intellectual realism in children's drawings. *British Journal of Educational Psychology* 46, 198–202.

Barrow, R. (1988) Some observations on the concept of imagination. In K. Egan and D. Nadaner (eds), *Imagination and Education*. Milton Keynes, UK: Open University Press.

Barsalou, L. (1987) The instability of graded structure: implications for the nature of concepts. In U. Neisser (ed.), *Concepts and Conceptual Development: Ecological and Intellectual Factors in Categorisation*. Cambridge, UK: Cambridge University Press.

Barsalou, L. (1989) Intra-concept similarity and its implications for inter-concept similarity. In S. Vosniadou and A. Ortony (eds), *Similarity and Analogy*. Cambridge, UK: Cambridge University Press.

Bartlett, F. C. (1932) *Remembering*. Cambridge, UK: Cambridge University Press.

Bartsch, K. (2002) The role of experience in children's developing folk epistemology: review and analysis from the theory-theory perspective. *New Ideas in Psychology* 20, 145–161.

Bartsch, K. and Wellman, H. M. (1988) Young children's conceptions of distance. *Developmental Psychology* 24(4), 532–541.

Barwick, J., Valentine, E., West, R. and Wilding, J. (1989) Relations between reading and musical abilities. *British Journal of Educational Psychology* 59, 253–257.

Bates, E. (1997) Origins of language disorders: a comparative approach. *Developmental Neuropsychology* 13, 447–476.

Bates, E., Bretherton, I. and Snyder, L. (1988) *From First Words to Grammar: Individual Differences and Dissociable Mechanisms.* Cambridge, UK: Cambridge University Press.

Bates, E., Bretherton, I., Beeghly-Smith, M. and McNew, S. (1982) Social bases of language development: a reassessment. In H. W. Reese and L. P. Lipsitt (eds), *Advances in Child Development and Behavior*, vol. 16. New York: Academic Press.

Bates, E., Dale, P. S. and Thal, D. (1995) Individual differences and their implications for theories of language development. In P. Fletcher and B. MacWhinney (eds), *The Handbook of Child Language.* Oxford, UK: Blackwell.

Bates, E. and MacWhinney, B. (1979) A functionalist approach to the acquisition of grammar. In E. Ochs and B. Schieffelin (eds), *Developmental Pragmatics.* New York: Academic Press.

Bates, E. and MacWhinney, B. (1989) Functionalism and the competition model. In B. MacWhinney and E. Bates (eds), *The Crosslinguistic Study of Sentence Processing.* Cambridge, UK: Cambridge University Press.

Bates, T. C. and Eysenck, H. J. (1993) Intelligence, inspection time and decision time. *Intelligence* 17(4), 523–532.

Bateson, P. (ed.) (1991a) *The Development and Integration of Behaviour: Essays in Honour of Robert Hinde.* Cambridge, UK: Cambridge University Press.

Bateson, P. (1991b) Levels and processes. In P. Bateson (ed.), *The Development and Integration of Behaviour: Essays in Honour of Robert Hinde.* Cambridge, UK: Cambridge Univesity Press.

Bauer, P., Wenner, J. A., Dropik, P. L. and Wewerka, S. S. (2000) Parameters of remembering and forgetting in the transition from infancy to early childhood. *Monographs of the Society for Research in Child Development* 65(4), serial no. 263.

Bauer, P. J. (1997) The development of memory in early childhood. In N. Cowan (ed.), *The Development of Memory in Children.* Hove, UK: Psychology Press.

Bauer, P. J., Burch, M. M. and Kleinknecht, E. E. (2002) Developments in early recall memory: Normative trends and individual differences. *Advances in Child Development and Behaviour* 30, 103–152.

Baumwell, L., Tamis-LeMonda, C. S. and Bornstein, M. H. (1997) Maternal verbal sensitivity and child language comprehension. *Infant Behaviour and Development* 20, 247–258.

Beal, C. R. (1987) Repairing the message: children's monitoring and revision skills. *Child Development* 58, 401–408.

Beard, R. (1963) The order of concept development: studies in two fields. *Educational Review* 15, 105–117, 228–237.

Beardslee, W. R., Versage, E. M. and Gladstone, T. R. (1998) Children of affectively ill parents: a review of the past ten years. *Journal of the American Academy of Child and Adolescent Psychiatry* 37, 1134–1141.

Bearison, D. J., Magzamen, S. and Filardo, E. K. (1986) Socio-cognitive conflict and cognitive growth in young children. *Merrill-Palmer Quarterly* 32, 51–72.

Bechtel, W. and Abrahamsen, A. (1991) *Connectionism and the Mind: An Introduction to Parallel Processing in Networks.* Oxford, UK: Blackwell.

Becker, H. J. (2000) Who's wired and who's not: children's access to and use of computer technology. *The Future of Children* 10, 44–75.

Bedi, K. S. (1987) Lasting neuroanatomical changes following under-nutrition during early life. In J. Dobbing (ed.), *Early Nutrition and Later Achievement.* London: Academic Press.

Bee, H. L., Barnard, K. E., Eyres, S. J., Gray, C. A., Hammond, M. A., Spietz, L. A., Snyder, C. and Clark, B. (1982) Prediction of IQ and language skills from perinatal status, child performance, family characteristics and mother–infant interaction. *Child Development* 53, 1334–1356.

Beech, J. and Colley, A. (eds) (1987) *Cognitive Approaches to Reading.* Chichester, UK: Wiley.

Beilin, H. and Fireman, G. (2000) The foundation of Piaget's theories: mental and physical action. *Advances in Child Development and Behavior* 27, 221–246.

Beilin, H. (1980) Piaget's theory: refinement, revisionism or rejection? In R. G. Kluwe and H. Spada (eds), *Developmental Models of Thinking.* New York: Academic Press.

Beilin, H. (1992) Piaget's enduring contribution to developmental psychology. *Developmental Psychology* 28, 191–204.

Bellinger, D. (1987) Longitudinal analyses of prenatal and postnatal lead exposure and early cognitive development. *New England Journal of Medicine* 316, 1037–1043.

Belloc, H. (1940) *Cautionary Verses.* London: Duckworth.

Bellugi, U., Bihrle, A., Neville, H., Doherty, S. and Jernigan, T. (1992) Language, cognition and brain organisation in a neurodevelopmental disorder. In M. Gunnar and C. A. Nelson (eds), *Developmental Behavioral Neuroscience.* Minnesota Symposium on Child Psychology, vol. 24. Hillsdale, NJ: Lawrence Erlbaum Associates, Inc.

Belsky, J. (1981) Early human experience: a family perspective. *Developmental Psychology* 17, 3–23.

Belsky, J., Booth, C. L., Bradley, R. *et al.* (2004) Multiple pathways to early academic achievement. *Harvard Educational Review* 74(1), 1–29.

Belsky, J., Booth-LaForce, C. L., Bradley, R., Brownell, C. A., Campbell, S. B., *et al.* (2004) Does class size in first grade relate to children's academic and social performance or observed classroom processes? *Developmental Psychology* 40(5), 651–664.

Belsky, J., Booth-LaForce, C. L., Bradley, R. *et al.* (2005) Pathways to reading: the role of oral language in the transition to reading. *Developmental Psychology* 41(2), 428–442.

Belsky, J., Booth-LaForce, C. L., Bradley, R. *et al.* (2005) A day in third grade: a large-scale study of classroom quality and teacher and student behavior. *Elementary School Journal* 105(3), 305–323.

Belsky, J., Rovine, M. and Taylor, D. G. (1984) The Pennsylvania Infant and Family Development Project, III: the origins of individual differences in infant–mother attachment: maternal and infant contributions. *Child Development* 55, 718–728.

Bennett, N. with Jordan, J., Long, G. and Wade, B. (1976) *Teaching Styles and Pupil Progress.* London: Open Books.

Bennett, W. J. (1987) The role of the family in the nurture and protection of the young. *American Psychologist* 42, 246–250.

Benoit, T. C., Jocelyn, L. J., Moddemann, D. M. and Embree, J. E. (1996)

Romanian adoption: the Manitoba experience. *Archives of Pediatric and Adolescent Medicine* 150, 1278–1282.

Benton, D. (1990) Vitamin/mineral supplementation and intelligence. *The Lancet* 336, 175–176.

Benton, D. (1992) The Benton and Roberts study. *The Psychologist* 5, 403–406.

Benton, D. and Cook, R. (1991) Vitamin and mineral supplements improve the intelligence scores and concentration of 6-year-old children. *Personality and Individual Differences* 12, 1151–1158.

Benton, D. and Roberts, G. (1988) Effects of vitamin and mineral supplementation on intelligence of a sample of schoolchildren. *The Lancet* i, 140–143.

Bereiter, C. and Bird, M. (1985) Use of thinking aloud in identification and teaching of reading comprehension strategies. *Cognition and Instruction* 2, 91–130.

Bereiter, C. and Scardamalia, M. (1982) From conversation to composition: the role of instruction in a developmental process. In R. Glaser (ed.), *Advances in Instructional Psychology*, vol. 2. Hillsdale, NJ: Lawrence Erlbaum Associates, Inc.

Bereiter, C. and Scardamalia, M. (1987) *The Psychology of Written Composition*. Hillsdale, NJ: Lawrence Erlbaum Associates, Inc.

Bereiter, C. and Scardamalia, M. (1989) Intentional learning as a goal of instruction. In L. B. Resnick (ed.), *Knowing, Learning and Instruction*. Hillsdale, NJ: Lawrence Erlbaum Associates, Inc.

Berg, C. A. and Sternberg, R. J. (1985) Response to novelty: continuity versus discontinuity in the developmental course of intelligence. In H. Reese (ed.), *Advances in Child Development and Behavior*, vol. 19. New York: Academic Press.

Bergeman, C. S. and Plomin, R. (1988) Parental mediators of the genetic relationship between home environment and infant mental development. *British Journal of Developmental Psychology* 6, 11–19.

Bergeson, T. R. and Trehub, S. E. (1999) Mothers' singing to infants and preschool children. *Infant Behavior and Development* 22(1), 51–64.

Bering, J. and Bjorklund, D. F. (2004) The natural emergence of reasoning about the afterlife as a developmental regularity. *Developmental Psychology* 40(2), 217–233.

Berlin, B. and Kay, P. (1969) *Basic Color Terms: Their Universality and Evolution*. Berkeley: University of California Press.

Berndt, T. J. and Heller, K. A. (1985) Measuring children's personality attributions. In S. R. Yussen (ed.), *The Growth of Reflection in Children*. New York: Academic Press.

Berrueta-Clermont, J. R. (1984) *Changed Lives: The Effects of the Perry Preschool Project*. Ypsilanti, MI: High/Scope Press.

Berry, J. W., Irvine, S. H. and Hunt, E. B. (1988) *Indigenous Cognition: Functioning in Cultural Context*. Dordrecht, The Netherlands: Martinus Nijhoff.

Bertenthal, B. I. and Fischer, K. W. (1978) Development of self-recognition in the infant. *Developmental Psychology* 14, 44–50.

Berthoud-Papandropolou, I. (1978) An experimental study of children's ideas about language. In A. Sinclair, R. J. Jarvella and W. J. M. Levelt (eds), *The Child's Conception of Language*. New York: Springer-Verlag.

Berti, A. E. (1991) Capitalism and socialism: how 7th graders understand and misunderstand the information presented in their geography textbooks. *European Journal of Psychology of Education* 6, 411–421.

Berti, A. E. and Bombi, A. S. (1988) *The Child's Construction of Economics.* Cambridge, UK: Cambridge University Press.

Bettelheim, B. (1967) *The Empty Fortress: Infantile Autism and the Birth of the Self.* New York: Free Press.

Bettes, B. (1988) Maternal depression and motherese: temporal and intonational features. *Child Development* 59, 1089–1096.

Beveridge, M. (ed.) (1982) *Children Thinking through Language.* London: Edward Arnold.

Beveridge, M. and Brierly, C. (1982) Classroom constructs: an interpretive approach to young children's language. In M. Beveridge (ed.), *Children Thinking through Language.* London: Edward Arnold.

Bialystock, E. (1986) Factors in the growth of linguistic awareness. *Child Development* 57, 498–510.

Bialystok, E. (1997) Effects of bilingualism and biliteracy on children's emerging concepts of print. *Developmental Psychology* 33, 429–440.

Bialystok, E., Luk, G. and Kwan, E. (2005) Bilingualism, biliteracy, and learning to read: interactions among languages and writing systems. *Scientific Studies of Reading* 9(1), 43–61.

Bibace, R. and Walsh, M. E. (eds) (1981) Children's conceptions of illness. *New Directions for Child Development*, vol. 14. San Francisco: Jossey-Bass.

Biggs, J. B. (1984) *The role of metalearning in study processes.* Paper given at British Psychological Society Education Section Conference, Cambridge, September 1984.

Biggs, J. B. (1988) Approaches to essay writing. In R. R. Schmeck (ed.), *Learning Strategies and Learning Styles.* New York: Plenum Press.

Bigler, R. S., Averhart, C. J. and Liben, L. S. (2003) Race and the workforce: occupational status, aspirations and stereotyping among African American children. *Developmental Psychology* 39(3), 572–580.

Bijou, S. W. (1989) Psychological linguistics: implications for a theory of initial development and method of research. In H. W. Reese (ed.), *Advances in Child Development and Behavior*, vol. 21. New York: Academic Press.

Bijstra, J., van Geert, P. and Jackson, S. (1989) Conversation and the appearance–reality distinction: what do children really know and what do they answer? *British Journal of Developmental Psychology* 7, 43–53.

Billow, R. M. (1975) A cognitive developmental study of metaphor comprehension. *Developmental Psychology* 11, 415–423.

Billow, R. M. (1981) Observing spontaneous metaphor in children. *Journal of Experimental Child Psychology* 31, 430–445.

Binet, A. and Simon, T. (1916) *The Development of Intelligence in Children.* Baltimore: William & Wilkins.

Birch, S. A. J. and Bloom, P. (2004) Understanding children's and adults' limitations in mental state reasoning. *Trends in Cognitive Sciences* 8(6), 255–260.

Bishop, D. V. M. (1997) *Uncommon Understanding: Development and Disorders of Language Comprehension in Children.* Hove, UK: Psychology Press.

Bishop, D. V. M. (2000) How does the brain learn language? Insights from the study of children with and without language impairment. *Developmental Medicine and Child Neurology* 42, 133–142.

Bishop, D. V. M. and Mogford, K. (eds) (1993) *Language Development in Exceptional Circumstances.* Hove, UK: Lawrence Erlbaum Associates Ltd.

Bishop, D. V. M. and Snowling, M. J. (2004) Developmental dyslexia and specific language impairment: Same or different? *Psychological Bulletin* 130(6), 858–886.

Bishop, E. G., Cherny, S. S., Corley, R., Plomin, R., DeFries, J. C. and Hewitt, J. K. (2003) Development genetic analysis of general cognitive ability from 1 to 12 years in a sample of adoptees, biological siblings, and twins. *Intelligence* 31, 31–49.

Bjorklund, D. F. (1997) The role of immaturity in human development. *Psychological Bulletin* 122, 153–169.

Bjorklund, D. F. and Jacobs, J. W. III (1985) Associative and categorical processes in children's memory: the role of automaticity in the development of organisation in free recall. *Journal of Experimental Child Psychology* 39, 599–617.

Bjorklund, D. F. and Zeman, B. R. (1982) Children's organisation and metamemory awareness in their recall of familiar information. *Child Development* 53, 799–810.

Bjorklund, D. E. and Pellegrini, A. D. (2000) Child development and evolutionary psychology. *Child Development* 71(6), 1687–1708.

Bjorklund, D. F., Pellegrini, A. D. and Bjorkland, D. F. (2002) *The origins of human nature: evolutionary developmental psychology.* Washington, DC: American Psychological Association.

Black, J. E. and Greenough, W. T. (1991) Developmental approaches to the memory process. In J. L. Martinez and R. P. Kesner (eds), *Learning and Memory: A Biological View.* New York: Academic Press.

Black, J. E., Jones, T. A., Nelson, C. A. and Greenough, W. T. (1998) Neuronal plasticity and the developing brain. In N. E. Alessi, J. T. Coyle, S. I. Harrison and E. Eth (eds), *Handbook of Child and Adolescent Psychiatry*, vol. 6, pp. 31–53. New York: Wiley.

Black, M. M. (2003a) The evidence linking zinc deficiency with children's cognitive and motor functioning. *Journal of Nutrition* 133, 1473S–1476S.

Black, M. M. (2003b) Micronutrient deficiencies and cognitive functioning. *Journal of Nutrition* 133, 3927S–3931S.

Blake, J. (1989) *Family Size and Achievement.* Berkeley: University of California Press.

Blakemore, C. and Greenfield, S. (1987) *Mindwaves: Thoughts on Intelligence, Identity and Consciousness.* Oxford, UK: Blackwell.

Blakemore, S.-J. and Frith, U. (2004) *How the Brain Learns: Towards a New Learning Science.* Oxford, UK: Blackwell.

Blakemore, S.-J., Winston, J. and Frith, U. (2004) Social cognitive neuroscience: where are we heading? *Trends in Cognitive Sciences* 8(5), 216–222.

Blasi, A. (1999) Emotions and moral motivation. *Journal for the Theory of Social Behaviour* 29(1), 1–19.

Blasi, A. (2004) Moral functioning: moral understanding and personality. In D. Lapsley and D. Narvaez (eds), *Moral Development, Self, and Identity.* Mahwah, NJ: Lawrence Erlbaum Associates, Inc.

Bleeker, M. A. and Jacobs, J. E. (2004) Achievement in math and science: do mothers' beliefs matter 12 years later? *Journal of Educational Psychology* 96(1), 97–109.

Blinkhorn, S. and Hendrickson, D. E. (1982) Averaged evoked responses and psychometric intelligence. *Nature* 295, 596–597.

Block, J., Block, J. H. and Harrington, D. M. (1974) Some misgivings about the Matching Familiar Figures Test as a measure of reflection–impulsivity. *Developmental Psychology* 10, 611–632.

Block, J., Gjerde, P. F. and Block, J. H. (1986) More misgivings about the Matching Familiar Figures Test as a measure of reflection–impulsivity: absence of construct validity in preadolescence. *Developmental Psychology* 22, 820–831.

Block, N. (ed.) (1981) *Imagery*. Cambridge, MA: Bradford Books/MIT Press.

Block, N. (1983) Mental pictures and cognitive science. *Philosophical Review* 92, 499–541.

Bloom, D. (2004) Children think before they speak. *Nature* 430, 410–411.

Bloom, F. E., Lazerson, A. and Hofstadter, L. (1985) *Brain, Mind and Behavior*. New York: W. H. Freeman.

Bloom, L. (1998) Language acquisition. In D. Kuhn and R. S. Siegler (eds), *Handbook of Child Psychology, vol. 2, Cognition, Perception and Language*. New York: Wiley.

Bloom, L., Margulis, C., Tinker, E. and Fujita, N. (1996) Early conversations and word learning: contributions from child and adult. *Child Development* 67, 3154–3175.

Bloom, P. (2000) *How Children Learn the Meaning of Words*. Cambridge, MA: MIT Press.

Boal-Palheiros, G. M. and Hargreaves, D. J. (2001) Listening to music at home and at school. *British Journal of Music Education* 18(2), 103–118.

Bobrow, D. and Collins, A. M. (eds) (1975) *Representation and Understanding*. New York: Academic Press.

Boddy, J., Skuse, D. and Andrews, B. (2000) The developmental sequelae of non-organic failure to thrive. *Journal of Child Psychology and Psychiatry* 41, 1003–1014.

Boden, M. (1979) *Piaget*. London: Fontana.

Boden, M. (1982) Is equilibration important? A view from artificial intelligence. *British Journal of Psychology* 73, 165–173.

Boden, M. (1987) *Artificial Intelligence and Natural Man*. Brighton, UK: Harvester.

Boden, M. (1988) *Computer Models of Mind*. Cambridge, UK: Cambridge University Press.

Boden, M. (1989) *Artificial Intelligence in Psychology*. Boston: MIT Press.

Boden, M. (1990) *The Creative Mind*. London: Weidenfeld & Nicolson.

Bolger, K. E., Patterson, D. J., Thompson, W. and Kupersmidt, J. B. (1995) Psychosocial adjustment amongst children suffering persistent and intermittent family economic hardship. *Child Development* 66, 1107–1129.

Bolter, J. F. and Long, C. J. (1985) Methodological issues in research in developmental neuropsychology. In L. C. Hartlage and C. F. Telzrow (eds), *The Neuropsychology of Individual Differences*. New York: Plenum Press.

Bonino, S. and Cattelino, E. (1999) The relationship between cognitive abilities and social abilities in childhood. *International Journal of Behavioral Development* 23, 19–36.

Booth, J. R., Perfetti, C. A. and MacWhinney, B. (1999) Quick, automatic, and general activation of orthographic and phonological representations in young readers. *Developmental Psychology* 35, 3–19.

Borkowski, J. G. (1985) Signs of intelligence: strategy generalisation and metacognition. In S. R. Yussen (ed.), *The Growth of Reflection in Childhood*. New York: Academic Press.

Bornstein, M. and Bradley, R. H. (eds) (2003) *Socioeconomic Status, Parenting and Child Development*. Mahwah, NJ: Lawrence Erlbaum Associates, Inc.

Bornstein, M., Cote, L., Maital, S., Painter, K., Park, S.-Y., Pascual, L., Pecheux, M.-G., Ruel, J., Venuti, P. and Vyt, A. (2004) Cross-linguistic analysis of vocabulary in young children: Spanish, Dutch, French, Hebrew, Italian, Korean and American English. *Child Development* 75(4), 1115–1139.

Bornstein, M., Haynes, M. O. and Painter, K. M. (1998) Sources of child vocabulary competence: a multivariate model. *Journal of Child Language* 25, 367–393.

Bornstein, M. and Lamb, M. (eds) (1999) *Developmental Psychology: An Advanced Textbook*, 4th edn. Mahwah, NJ: Lawrence Erlbaum Associates, Inc.

Bornstein, M. H. and Sigman, M. D. (1986) Continuity in mental development from infancy. *Child Development* 57, 251–274.

Borthwick, S. J. and Davidson, J. W. (2002) Developing a child's identity as a musician: a family 'script' perspective. In R. A. R. MacDonald, D. J. Hargreaves and D. E. Miell (eds), *Musical Identities*. Oxford, UK: Oxford University Press.

Boswell, J. [1791] (1979) *The Life of Johnson*. Harmondsworth, UK: Penguin Books.

Bouchard, T. J., Jr, Lykken, D. T., McGue, M., Segal, N. and Tellegen, A. (1990) Sources of human psychological differences: the Minnesota study of twins reared apart. *Science* 250, 223–228.

Boudreau, D. (2002) Literacy skills in children and adolescents with Down syndrome. *Reading and Writing* 15(5–6), 497–525.

Bower, G. H. (1981) Mood and memory. *American Psychologist* 36, 129–148.

Bower, G. H., Gilligan, S. G. and Monteiro, K. P. (1981) Selectivity of learning caused by affective states. *Journal of Experimental Psychology: General* 110(4), 451–473.

Bowerman, M. (1989) Learning a semantic system: what role do cognitive predispositions play? In M. L. Rice and R. L. Schiefelbusch (eds), *The Teachability of Language*. Baltimore: Brookes.

Bradburn, E. (1989) *Margaret McMillan: Portrait of a Pioneer*. London: Routledge.

Bradley, L. and Bryant, P. E. (1983) Categorising sounds and learning to read: a causal connection. *Nature* 301, 419–421.

Bradley, R. H., Belsky, J., Booth, C. *et al.* (2003) Child care and common communicable illnesses in children aged 37 to 54 months. *Archives of Pediatrics & Adolescent Medicine* 157(2), 196–200.

Bradley, R. H. and Caldwell, B. M. (1980) The relation of the home environment, cognitive competence, and IQ among males and females. *Child Development* 51, 1140–1148.

Bradley, R. H. and Caldwell, B. M. (1984) 174 children: a study of the relationship between home environment and cognitive development during the first five years. In A. W. Gottfried (ed.), *Home Environment and Early Cognitive Development*. New York: Academic Press.

Bradley, R. H., Caldwell, B. M. and Corwyn, R. F. (2003) The child care HOME inventories: assessing the quality of family child care homes. *Early Child Research Quarterly* 18(3), 294–309.

Bradley, R. H., Caldwell, B. M. and Rock, S. L. (1988) Home environment and school performance: a ten-year follow-up and examination of three models of environmental action. *Child Development* 59, 852–867.

Bradley, R. H., Caldwell, B. M., Rock, S. L., Ramey, C. T., Barnard, K. E., Gray, C., Hammond, M. A., Mitchell, S., Gottfried, A. W., Siegel, L. and Johnson, D. L. (1989) Home environment and cognitive development in the first 3 years of life: a collaborative study involving six sites and three ethnic groups in North America. *Developmental Psychology* 25, 217–235.

Bradley, R. H. and Corwyn, R. F. (2002) Socioeconomic status and child development. *Annual Review of Psychology* 53, 371–399.

Bradley, R. H. and Corwyn, R. F. (2005) Productive activity and the prevention of behavior problems. *Developmental Psychology* 41(1), 89–98.

Braine, M. D. S. and Rumain, B. (1983) Logical reasoning. In J. H. Flavell and E. M. Markman (eds), *Handbook of Child Psychology*, vol. 3, series ed. P. H. Mussen. New York: Wiley.

Brainerd, C. J. (1978) *Piaget's Theory of Intelligence*. Englewood Cliffs, NJ: Prentice Hall.

Brainerd, C. J. (1979) *The Origins of the Number Concept*. New York: Praeger.

Brainerd, C. J. (ed.) (1982) *Progress in Cognitive Development, vol. 1, Children's Logical and Mathematical Cognition*. New York: Springer-Verlag.

Brainerd, C. J. (1983) Modifiability of cognitive development. In S. Meadows (ed.), *Developing Thinking*. London: Methuen.

Brainerd, C. J., Kingma, J. and Howe, M. L. (1985) On the development of forgetting. *Child Development* 56, 1103–1119.

Brand, C. and Deary, I. Z. (1982) Intelligence and 'inspection time'. In H. J. Eysenck (ed.), *A Model for Intelligence*. Berlin: Springer-Verlag.

Bransford, J. D. (1979) *Human Cognition*. Belmont, CA: Wadsworth.

Bransford, J. D., Goldman, S. R. and Vye, N. J. (1991) Making a difference in people's ability to think. In L. Okagaki and R. J. Sternberg (eds), *Directors of Development: Influences on the Development of Children's Thinking*. Hillsdale, NJ: Lawrence Erlbaum Associates, Inc.

Breitmayer, B. J. and Ramey, C. T. (1986) Biological nonoptimality and quality of postnatal environment as codeterminants of intellectual development. *Child Development* 57, 1151–1165.

Bremner, J. G. (1980) The infant's understanding of space. In M. V. Cox (ed.), *Are Young Children Egocentric?* London: Batsford.

Brennan, P., Hammen, C., Andersen, M., Bor, W., Najman, J. and Williams, G. (2000) Chronicity, severity, and timing of maternal depressive symptoms: relationships with child outcomes at age 5. *Developmental Psychology* 36, 759–766.

Brenneman, K., Massey, C., Machad, S. F. and Gelman, R. (1996) Young children's plans differ for writing and drawing. *Cognitive Development* 11, 397–419.

Breslow, L. (1981) Reevaluation of the literature on the development of transitive influences. *Psychological Bulletin* 89(2), 325–351.

Bretherton, I. (1985) Attachment theory. In I. Bretherton and E. Waters (eds), *Growing Points of Attachment Theory and Research*. Monographs of the Society for Research in Child Development, vol. 50, pp. 3–35.

Bretherton, I. (1990) Open communication and internal working models: their role in the development of attachment relationships. In R. A. Thompson (ed.), *Socioemotional Development*. Nebraska Symposium on Motivation, 1988, vol. 36. Lincoln: University of Nebraska Press.

Bretherton, I. and Beeghly, M. (1982) Talking about internal states: the acquisition of an explicit theory of mind. *Developmental Psychology* 18, 906–921.

Bretherton, I., Fritz, J., Zahn-Waxler, C. and Ridgeway, D. (1986) Learning to talk about emotions: a functionalist approach. *Child Development* 57, 529–548.

Bretherton, I., McNew, S. and Beeghly-Smith, M. (1981) Early person knowledge as expressed in gestural and verbal communication: when do infants acquire a 'theory of mind'? In M. E. Lamb and L. R. Sherrod (eds), *Infant Social Cognition*. Hillsdale, NJ: Lawrence Erlbaum Associates, Inc.

Bretherton, I. and Waters, E. (eds) (1985) *Growing Points of Attachment Theory and Research*. Monographs of the Society for Research in Child Development, vol. 50, pp. 1–320.

Brewin, C. (1985) Depression and causal attributions: what is their relation? *Psychological Bulletin* 9, 297–309.

Brewster, A. B. (1982) Chronically ill hospitalised children's concepts of their illness. *Pediatrics* 69, 355–362.

Breznitz, Z. and Sherman, T. (1987) Speech patterning of natural discourse of well and depressed mothers and their young children. *Child Development* 58, 395–400.

Briars, D. J. and Siegler, R. S. (1984) A featural analysis of preschoolers' counting knowledge. *Developmental Psychology* 20, 607–618.

Brissenden, T. (1988) *Talking about Mathematics*. Oxford, UK: Blackwell.

Broberg, A. G., Hwang, C. P., Lamb, M. E. and Bookstein, F. L. (1990) Factors related to verbal abilities in Swedish preschoolers. *British Journal of Developmental Psychology* 8, 335–349.

Brody, G. H. (2004) Siblings' direct and indirect contributions to child development. *Current Directions in Psychological Science* 13(2), 124–126.

Brody, G. H., Kim, S., Murry, V. M. and Brown, A. C. (2003) Longitudinal direct and indirect pathways linking older sibling competence to the development of younger sibling competence. *Developmental Psychology* 39, 618–620.

Brody, G. H., Pellegrini, A. D. and Sigel, I. E. (1986) Marital quality and mother–child and father–child interactions with school-aged children. *Developmental Psychology* 22, 291–296.

Brodzinsky, D. M. (1982) Relationship between cognitive style and cognitive development: a 2-year longitudinal study. *Developmental Psychology* 18, 617–626.

Broman, S., Nichols, P. L., Shaughnessy, P. and Kennedy, W. (1987) *Retardation in Young Children: A Developmental Study of Cognitive Deficit*. Hillsdale, NJ: Lawrence Erlbaum Associates, Inc.

Bromley, D. B. (1978) Natural language and the development of the self. *Nebraska Symposium on Motivation*, 1977. Lincoln: University of Nebraska Press.

Bronfenbrenner, U. (1979) *The Ecology of Human Development*. Cambridge, MA: Harvard University Press.

Bronfenbrenner, U. (1986) Ecology of the family as a context for human development. *Developmental Psychology* 22, 723–742.

Bronfenbrenner, U. and Evans, G. W. (2000) Developmental science in the 21st century: emerging theoretical models, research designs, and empirical findings. *Social Development* 9, 115–125.

Bronfenbrenner, U., McClelland, P., Wethington, E., Moen, P. and Ceci, S. (1996) *The State of Americans: This Generation and the Next*. New York: Free Press.

Bronfenbrenner, U. and Morris, P. (1998) The ecology of developmental process. In W. Damon (ed.), *Handbook of Child Psychology*, vol. 1. New York: Wiley.

Brooks, P. J., Tomasello, M., Dodson, K. and Lewis, L. B. (1999) Young children's overgeneralizations with fixed transitivity verbs. *Child Development Today and Tomorrow*. San Francisco: Jossey-Bass.

Brophy, J. (1986) Teacher influences on student achievement. *American Psychologist* 41, 1069–1077.

Brophy, J. and Good, T. (1986) Teacher behaviour and student achievement. In M. Wittrock (ed.), *Third Handbook of Research on Teaching*. New York: Macmillan.

Broughton, J. M. B. (1978) Development of concepts of self, mind, reality and knowledge. In W. Damon (ed.), *New Directions for Child Development*, vol. 1. San Francisco: Jossey-Bass.

Broughton, J. M. B. (1982) Genetic logic and the developmental psychology of philosophical concepts. In J. M. B. Broughton and D. J. Freeman-Moir (eds), *The Cognitive–Developmental Psychology of James Mark Baldwin*. Norwood, NJ: Ablex.

Broughton, J. M. B. and Freeman-Moir, D. J. (1981) *The Cognitive–Developmental Psychology of James Mark Baldwin: Current Theory and Research in Genetic Epistemology*. Norwood, NJ: Ablex.

Brown, A. L. (1975) The development of memory: knowing, knowing about knowing, and knowing how to know. In H. W. Reese (ed.), *Advances in Child Development and Behavior*, vol. 10. New York: Academic Press.

Brown, A. L. (1988) Motivation to learn and understand: on taking charge of one's own learning. *Cognition and Instruction* 5, 311–321.

Brown, A. L. (1989) Analogical learning and transfer: what develops? In S. Vosniadou and A. Ortony (eds), *Similarity and Analogical Reasoning*. Cambridge, UK: Cambridge University Press.

Brown, A. L. (1990) Domain-specific principles affect learning and transfer in children. *Cognitive Science* 14, 107–133.

Brown, A. L. (1994) The advancement of learning. *Educational Researcher* 23(8), 4–12.

Brown, A. L. (1997) Transforming schools into communities of thinking and learning about serious matters. *American Psychologist* 52, 399–413.

Brown, A. L. and Barclay, C. R. (1976) The effects of training specific mnemonics on the metamnemonic efficiency of retarded children. *Child Development* 47, 71–80.

Brown, A. L., Bransford, J. D., Ferrara, R. A. and Campione, J. C. (1983) Learning, remembering and understanding. In J. H. Flavell and E. M. Markman (eds), *Handbook of Child Psychology, vol. 3, Cognitive Development*, series ed. P. H. Mussen. New York: Wiley.

Brown, A. L. and Campione, J. C. (1972) Recognition memory for perceptually similar pictures in preschool children. *Journal of Experimental Child Psychology* 95, 55–62.

Brown, A. L. and Campione, J. C. (1986) Psychological theory and the study of learning disabilities. *American Psychologist* 41, 1059–1068.

Brown, A. L. and Campione, J. C. (1988) Communities of learning and thinking: or a context by any other name. *Contributions to Human Development* 21, 108–126.

Brown, A. L. and Day, J. D. (1983) Macrorules for summarising texts: the development of expertise. *Journal of Verbal Learning and Verbal Behaviour* 22, 1–14.

Brown, A. L. and De Loache, J. S. (1978) Skills, plans and self-regulation. In R. S. Siegler (ed.), *Children's Thinking: What Develops?* Hillsdale, NJ: Lawrence Erlbaum Associates, Inc.

Brown, A. L. and Ferrara, R. (1985) Diagnosing zones of proximal development. In J. V. Wertsch (ed.), *Culture, Communication and Cognition*. Cambridge, UK: Cambridge University Press.

Brown, A. L. and Kane, M. J. (1988) Preschool children can learn to transfer: learning to learn and learning from example. *Cognitive Psychology* 20, 493–523.

Brown, A. L. and Palincsar, A. S. (1989) Guided, cooperative learning and individual knowledge acquisition. In L. B. Resnick (ed.), *Knowing, Learning and Instruction*. Hillsdale, NJ: Lawrence Erlbaum Associates, Inc.

Brown, A. L., Palincsar, A. S. and Armbruster, B. B. (1984) Instructing comprehension: fostering activities in interactive learning situations. In H. Mandl, N. Stein and T. Trabasso (eds), *Learning and Comprehension of Texts*. Hillsdale, NJ: Lawrence Erlbaum Associates, Inc.

Brown, A. L. and Reeve, R. A. (1987) Bandwidths of competence: the role of supportive contexts in learning and development. In L. S. Liben (ed.), *Development and Learning: Conflict or Congruence?* Hillsdale, NJ: Lawrence Erlbaum Associates, Inc.

Brown, A. L. and Scott, M. S. (1971) Recognition memory for pictures in preschool children. *Journal of Experimental Child Psychology* 11, 401–412.

Brown, G. and Harris, T. (1978) *Social Origins of Depression*. London: Tavistock.

Brown, J. R. and Dunn, J. (1996) Continuities in emotion understanding from three to six years. *Child Development* 67, 789–802.

Brown, J. S. and Burton, R. B. (1978) Diagnostic models for procedural bugs in basic mathematical skills. *Cognitive Science* 2, 155–192.

Brown, R. (1958) How shall a thing be called? *Psychological Review* 65, 14–21.

Brozek, J. (1978) Nutrition, malnutrition and behavior. *Annual Review of Psychology* 29, 157–177.

Bruce, D., Dolan, A. and Phillips-Grant, K. (2000) On the transition from childhood amnesia to the recall of personal memories. *Psychological Science* 11, 360–364.

Bruck, M. and Genesee, F. (1995) Phonological awareness in young second language learners. *Journal of Child Language* 22, 307–324.

Bruner, J. S. (1957) Going beyond the information given. In H. Gruber (ed.), *Contemporary Approaches to Cognition*. Cambridge, MA: Harvard University Press.

Bruner, J. S. (1966) On cognitive growth. In J. S. Bruner, R. R. Olver and P. M. Greenfield (eds), *Studies in Cognitive Growth*. New York: Wiley.

Bruner, J. S. (1968) *Toward a Theory of Instruction*. New York: Norton.

Bruner, J. S. (1973) Organisation of early skilled action. *Child Development* 44, 1–11.

Bruner, J. S. (1976) From communication to language – a psychological perspective. *Cognition* 3, 255–287.

Bruner, J. S. (1983) *Child's Talk*. New York: Norton.

Bruner, J. S. (1985) Vygotsky: a historical and conceptual perspective. In J. V. Wertsch (ed.), *Culture Communication and Cognition*. Cambridge, UK: Cambridge University Press.

Bruner, J. S., Goodnow, J. J. and Austin, G. A. (1956) *A Study of Thinking*. New York: Wiley.

Bruner, J. S., Olver, R. and Greenfield, P. M. (eds) (1966) *Studies in Cognitive Growth*. New York: Wiley.

Bryant, P. and Nunes, T. (2002) Children's understanding of mathematics. In U. Goswami (ed.), *Blackwell Handbook of Cognitive Development*. Oxford, UK: Blackwell.

Bryant, P. E. (1974) *Perception and Understanding in Young Children*. London: Methuen.

Bryant, P. E. (1982a) The role of conflict and of agreement between intellectual strategies in children's ideas about measurement. *British Journal of Psychology* 73, 243–252.

Bryant, P. E. (ed.) (1982b) Piaget: issues and experiments. *British Journal of Psychology* 73(2), 157–313.

Bryant, P. E. (1985) Parents, children and cognitive development. In R. A. Hinde, A.-N. Perret-Clermont and J. Stevenson-Hinde (eds), *Social Relationships and Cognitive Development*. Oxford, UK: Clarendon Press.

Bryant, P. E. and Alegria, J. (1990) The transition from spoken to written language. In A. de Ribaupierre (ed.), *Transition Mechanisms in Child Development*. Cambridge, UK: Cambridge University Press.

Bryant, P. E. and Bradley, L. (1980) Why children sometimes write words which they do not read. In U. Frith (ed.), *Cognitive Processes in Spelling*. London: Academic Press.

Bryant, P. E. and Bradley, L. (1983) Psychological strategies and the development of reading and writing. In M. Matthew (ed.), *The Psychology of Written Language*. Chichester, UK: Wiley.

Bryant, P. E. and Bradley, L. (1985) *Children's Reading Problems*. Oxford, UK: Blackwell.

Bryant, P. E., Bradley, L., Maclean, M. and Crossland, J. (1989) Nursery rhymes, phonological skills and reading. *Journal of Child Language* 16, 407–428.

Bryant, P. E., Devine, M., Ledward, A. and Nunes, T. (1997) Spelling with apostrophes and understanding possession. *British Journal of Educational Psychology* 67, 91–110.

Bryant, P. E. and Goswami, U. (1987) Phonological awareness and learning to read. In J. Beech and A. Colley (eds), *Cognitive Approaches to Reading*. Chichester, UK: Wiley.

Bryant, P. E. and Impey, L. (1986) The similarities between normal children and dyslexic adults and children. *Cognition* 24, 121–137.

Bryant, P. E., Jones, P., Claxton, V. and Perkins, J. (1972) Recognition of shapes across modalities by infants. *Nature* 240, 303–304.

Bryant, P. E., Maclean, M., Bradley, L. L. and Crossland, J. (1990) Rhyme and alliteration, phoneme detection, and learning to read. *Developmental Psychology* 26, 429–438.

Bryant, P. E., Nunes, T. and Aidinis, A. (1999) Different morphemes, same spelling problems: cross-linguisitc developmental studies. In M. Harris and G. Hatano (eds), *Learning to Read and Write: A Cross-linguistic Perspective*. Cambridge, UK: Cambridge University Press.

Bryant, P. E. and Trabasso, T. (1971) Transitive inferences and memory in young children. *Nature* 232, 456–458.

Bucci, W. (1978) The interpretation of universal affirmative propositions. *Cognition* 6, 55–77.

Buckley, S. (1985) Attaining basic educational skills: reading, writing and number. In D. Lane and B. Stratford (eds), *Current Approaches to Down's Syndrome*. London: Holt, Rinehart & Winston.

Buijzen, M. and Valkenburg, P. M. (2003) The effects of television advertising on materialism, parent–child conflict, and unhappiness: a review of research. *Applied Developmental Psychology* 24, 437–456.

Bull, R. and Espy, K. (2005) Working memory, executive functioning and children's mathematics. In S. Pickering (ed.), *Working Memory and Education*. New York: Academic Press.

Bull, R. and Johnston, R. S. (1997) Children's arithmetic difficulties: contributions from processing speed, item identification and short-term memory. *Journal of Experimental Child Psychology* 65, 1–24.

Bull, R., Johnston, R. S. and Roy, J. A. (1999) Exploring the roles of the visuo-spatial sketch pad and central executive in children's arithmetical skills: views from cognition and developmental neuropsychology. *Developmental Neuropsychology* 15, 421–442.

Bull, R. and Scerif, G. (2001) Executive functioning as a predictor of children's mathematical ability: inhibition, switching and working memory. *Developmental Neuropsychology* 19, 273–293.

Bullinger, A. and Chatillon, J.-F. (1983) Recent theory and research of the Genevan School. In J. H. Flavell and E. M. Markman (eds), *Handbook of Child Psychology*, vol. 3. New York: Wiley.

Bullock, M. (1985) Animism in childhood thinking: a new look at an old question. *Developmental Psychology* 21, 217–255.

Bunge, M. (1980) *The Mind–Body Problem*. Oxford, UK: Pergamon.

Burchinal, M. R., Campbell, F. A., Bryant, D. M., Wasik, B. H. and Ramney, C. T. (1997) Early intervention and mediating processes in cognitive performance of children of low-income African American families. *Child Development* 68, 935–954.

Burden, R. L. (1987) Feuerstein's Instrumental Enrichment Programme: important issues in research and evaluation. *European Journal of Psychology of Education* 2(1), 3–16.

Burgess, S. R., Hecht, S. A. and Lonigan, C. J. (2002) Relations of home literacy environment (HLE) in the development of reading-related abilities: a one-year longitudinal study. *Reading Research Quarterly* 37, 408–426.

Burnett, P. (1999) Children's self-talk and academic self-concepts. *Educational Psychology in Practice* 15(3), 195–200.

Burnett, P. and Proctor, R. (2002) Elementary school students' learner self-concepts, academic self-concepts and approaches to teaching. *Educational Psychology in Practice* 18(40), 325–333.

Burns, E. A., House, J. D. and Ankenbauer, M. R. (1986) Sibling grief reaction to sudden infant death syndrome. *Pediatrics* 78, 458–487.

Burt, C. (1937) *The backward child.* London: University of London Press.

Burt, C. (1955) *The Subnormal Mind.* Oxford, UK: Oxford University Press.

Bus, A. G. and vanIJzendoorn, M. H. (1988) Mother–child interactions, attachment and emergent literacy: a cross-sectional study. *Child Development* 59, 1262–1272.

Bus, A. and vanIJzendoorn, M. (1995) Mothers reading to their 3-year-olds: the role of mother–child attachment security in becoming literate. *Reading Research Quarterly* 30, 998–1015.

Bussey, K. (1999) Lying and truthfulness: children's definitions, standards and evaluative reactions. *Child Development* 63, 129–137.

Butterworth, B. (1999) *The Mathematical Brain.* London: Macmillan.

Butterworth, G. (1975) Object identity in infancy: the interaction of spatial location codes in determining search errors. *Child Development* 46, 866–870.

Butterworth, G. (1977) Object disappearance and error in Piaget's Stage IV task. *Journal of Experimental Child Psychology* 23, 391–401.

Butterworth, G. (1978) Thought and things: Piaget's theory. In A. Burton and J. Radford (eds), *Perspectives on Thinking.* London: Methuen.

Butterworth, G., Harris, P., Leslie, A. and Wellman, H. (1991) *Perspectives on the Child's Theory of Mind.* Oxford, UK: Oxford University Press.

Butterworth, G. and Hicks, L. (1977) Visual proprioception and postural stability in infancy. *Perception* 6, 255–262.

Butterworth, G. and Light, P. (eds) (1982) *Social Cognition: Studies of the Development of Understanding.* Brighton, UK: Harvester.

Bynum, T. W., Thomas, J. A. and Weitz, L. J. (1972) Truth-functional logic in formal operational thinking. *Developmental Psychology* 7, 129–132.

Byrne, R. W. and Whiten, A. (1988) *Machiavellian Intelligence: Social Expertise and the Evolution of Intellect in Monkeys, Apes and Humans.* Oxford, UK: Clarendon Press.

Byrnes, J. (1988) Formal operations: a systematic reformulation. *Developmental Review* 8, 66–87.

Byrnes, J. and Fox, N. A. (1998) The educational relevance of research in cognitive neuroscience. *Educational Psychology Review* 10(3), 297–342.

Byrnes, J. P. (2004) The neurological basis of learning, development, and discovery: Implications for science and mathematics instruction. *Science Education* 88(6), 984–986.

Cain, K., Oakhill, J. and Bryant, P. (2004) Children's reading comprehension ability: concurrent prediction by working memory, verbal ability, and component skills. *Journal of Educational Psychology* 96(1), 31–42.

Cain, K. M. and Dweck, C. (1995) The relation between motivational patterns and achievement cognitions throughout the elementary school years. *Merrill-Palmer Quarterly* 41, 25–52.

Calkins, L. (1983) *Lessons from a Child: On the Teaching and Learning of Writing.* Exeter, NH: Heinemann.

Callaghan, T. C. and Rankin, M. P. (2002) Emergence of graphic symbol functioning and the question of domain specificity: a longitudinal training study. *Child Development* 73, 359–373.

Callanan, M. A. (1985) How parents label objects for young children: the role of input in the acquisition of category hierarchies. *Child Development* 56, 508–523.

Camaioni, L. (1990) The role of social interaction in the transition from communication to language. In A. de Ribaupierre (ed.), *Transition Mechanisms in Child Development*. Cambridge, UK: Cambridge University Press.

Cameron-Faulkner, T., Lieven, E. and Tomasello, M. (2003) A construction based analysis of child directed speech. *Cognitive Science* 27(6), 843–873.

Campbell, F. A. and Ramey, C. T. (1995) Cognitive and school outcomes for African-American students at middle adolescence: positive effects of early intervention. *American Educational Research Journal* 32, 743–772.

Campbell, F. A., Pungello, E. P., Miller-Johnson, S., Burchinal, M. and Ramey, C. T. (2001) The development of cognitive and academic abilities; growth curves from an early childhood educational experiment. *Developmental Psychology* 37, 231–242.

Campbell, F. A., Ramey, C. T., Pungello, E. P., Sparling, J. and Miller-Johnson, S. (2002) Early childhood education: young adult outcomes from the Abecedarian Project. *Applied Developmental Science* 6, 42–57.

Campbell, J. and Xue, Q. (2001) Cognitive arithmetic across cultures. *Journal of Experimental Psychology General* 130(2), 299–315.

Campbell, R. and Butterworth, B. (1985) Phonological dyslexia and dysgraphia in a highly literate subject: a developmental case and associated deficits of phonemic awareness. *Quarterly Journal of Experimental Psychology* 37A, 435–475.

Campbell, R. and Sais, E. (1995) Accelerated metalinguistic (phonological) awareness in bilingual children. *British Journal of Developmental Psychology* 13, 61–68.

Campione, J. C., Brown, A. L. and Ferrara, R. A. (1982) Mental retardation and intelligence. In R. J. Sternberg (ed.), *Handbook of Human Intelligence*. Cambridge, UK: Cambridge University Press.

Campione, J. C., Brown, A. L., Ferrara, R. A. and Bryant, N. R. (1984) The zone of proximal development: implications for individual differences and learning. In B. Rogoff and J. Wertsch (eds), *New Directions for Cognitive Development: The Zone of Proximal Development*. San Francisco: Jossey-Bass.

Campos, J. J., Campos, R. G. and Barrett, K. C. (1983) Emergent themes in the study of emotional development and emotional regulation. *Developmental Psychology* 25, 394–402.

Cantor, J. H. and Spiker, C. (1989) Children's learning revisited: the contemporary scope of the Modified Spence Discrimination Theory. In H. W. Reese (ed.), *Advances in Child Development and Behavior*, vol. 21. New York: Academic Press.

Caplan, M. Z. and Hale, D. F. (1989) Preschoolers' responses to peers' distress and beliefs about bystander intervention. *Journal of Child Psychology and Psychiatry* 30(2), 231–242.

Capone, G. T. (2001) Down syndrome: advances in molecular biology and the neurosciences. *Developmental and Behavioral Pediatrics* 22(1), 40–59.

Capron, C. and Duyme, M. (1989) Assessment of effects of socio-economic status on IQ in a full cross-fostering study. *Nature* 340, 552–554.

Caramazza, A., McCloskey, M. and Green, B. (1981) Naive beliefs in 'sophisticated' subjects: misconceptions about trajectories of objects. *Cognitia* 9, 117–123.

Cardon, L. R., Fulker, D. W., De Fries, J. C. and Plomin, R. (1992) Continuity and change in general cognitive ability from 1–7 years of age. *Developmental Psychology* 28, 64–73.

Carey, S. (1985) *Conceptual Change in Childhood.* Cambridge, MA: MIT Press.

Carey, S. (1986a) Cognitive science and science education. *American Psychologist* 41(10), 1123–1130.

Carey, S. (1986b) Constraints on semantic development. In W. Demopoulos and A. Marras (eds), *Language Learning and Concept Acquisition.* Norwood, NJ: Ablex.

Carey, S. (1987) Theory change in childhood. In B. Inhelder, D. de Caprona and A. Cornu-Wells (eds), *Piaget Today.* Hillsdale, NJ: Lawrence Erlbaum Associates, Inc.

Carey, S. (1988) Conceptual differences between children and adults. *Mind and Language* 3(3), 167–181.

Carey, S. (1991) Knowledge acquisition: enrichment or conceptual change. In S. Carey and R. Gelman (eds), *The Epigenesis of Mind.* Hove, UK: Lawrence Erlbaum Associates Ltd.

Carey, S. and Gelman, R. (eds) (1991) *The Epigenesis of Mind.* Hove, UK: Lawrence Erlbaum Associates Ltd.

Carlson, S. M., Moses, L. J. and Hix, H. R. (1998) The role of inhibitory processes in young children's difficulties with deception and false belief. *Child Development* 69(3), 672–691.

Carlson, S. M., Wong, A., Lemke, M. and Cosser, C. (2005) Gesture as a window on children's beginning understanding of false belief. *Child Development* 76(1), 73–86.

Carpenter, M., Akhtar, N. and Tomasello, M. (1998) Fourteen- through 18-month-old infants differentially imitate intentional and accidental actions. *Infant Behavior and Development* 21, 315–330.

Carpenter, P. A. and Just, M. A. (1986) Spatial ability: an information-processing approach to psychometrics. In R. J. Sternberg (ed.), *Advances in the Psychology of Human Intelligence.* Hillsdale, NJ: Lawrence Erlbaum Associates, Inc.

Carpenter, T. P. (1986) Conceptual knowledge as a foundation for procedural knowledge. In J. Hiebert (ed.), *Conceptual and Procedural Knowledge: The Case of Mathematics.* Hillsdale, NJ: Lawrence Erlbaum Associates, Inc.

Carpenter, T. P. and Moser, J. M. (1983) The acquisition of addition and subtraction concepts. In R. Lesh and M. Landau (eds), *Acquisition of Mathematics Concepts and Processes.* New York: Academic Press.

Carpenter, T. P., Moser, J. M. and Romberg, T. A. (eds) (1982) *Addition and Subtraction: A Cognitive Perspective.* Hillsdale, NJ: Lawrence Erlbaum Associates, Inc.

Carr, J. (1985) The development of intelligence. In D. Lane and B. Stratford (eds), *Current Approaches to Down's Syndrome.* London: Holt, Rinehart & Winston.

Carr, J. (1988) Six weeks to twenty-one years old: a longitudinal study of children with Down's syndrome and their families. *Journal of Child Psychology* 29, 407–431.

Carr, M., Borkowski, J. G. and Maxwell, S. E. (1991) Motivational components of underachievement. *Developmental Psychology* 27, 108–118.

Carr, M., Kurtz, B. E., Schneider, W., Turner, L. A. and Borkowski, J. G. (1989) Strategy acquisition and transfer among American and German children:

environmental influences on metacognitive development. *Developmental Psychology* 25(5), 765–771.

Carraher, T. N., Carraher, D. W. and Schiemann, A. D. (1985) Mathematics in the streets and in schools. *British Journal of Developmental Psychology* 3, 21–29.

Carrasquillo, A. (1987) Bilingualism, early language and cognitive development. In B. Fillion, C. N. Hedley and E. C. Di Martino (eds), *Home and School: Early Language and Reading*. Norwood, NJ: Ablex.

Carrell, L. and Willard, H. F. (2005) X-inactivation profile reveals extensive variability in X-linked gene expression in females. *Nature* 434, 400–404.

Carroll, J. B. (1982) The measurement of intelligence. In R. J. Sternberg (ed.), *Handbook of Human Intelligence*. Cambridge, UK: Cambridge University Press.

Carroll, J. B. (1993) Human cognitive abilities: a survey of factor analytic studies. Cambridge, UK: Cambridge University Press.

Carroll, J. M., Maughan, B., Goodman, R. and Meltzer, H. (2005) Literacy difficulties and psychiatric disorders: evidence for comorbidity. *Journal of Child Psychology and Psychiatry* 46(5), 524–532.

Carroll, J. M. and Snowling, M. (2004) Language and phonological skills in children at high risk of reading difficulties. *Journal of Child Psychology and Psychiatry and Allied Disciplines* 45, 631–640.

Carruthers, P. (1992) *Human Knowledge and Human Nature*. Oxford, UK: Oxford University Press.

Carruthers, P. (2002) Human creativity: its cognitive basis, its evolution, and its connections with childhood pretence. *British Journal of Philosophy of Science* 53, 225–249.

Carter, P., Pazak, B. and Kail, R. (1983) Algorithms for processing spatial information. *Journal of Experimental Child Psychology* 36, 284–304.

Case, R. (1974) Structures and strictures, some functional limitations on the course of cognitive growth. *Cognitive Psychology* 6, 544–573.

Case, R. (1984) The process of stage-transition: a neo-Piagetian view. In R. J. Sternberg (ed.), *Mechanisms of Cognitive Development*. New York: Freeman.

Case, R. (1985) *Intellectual Development: Birth to Adulthood*. New York: Academic Press.

Case, R. (1996) Modelling the dynamic interplay between general and specific change in children's conceptual understanding. In R. Case and Y. Okamoto (eds), *The Role of Central Conceptual Structures in the Development of Children's Thought*. Monographs of the Society for Research in Child Development, vol. 61.

Case, R. (1998) The development of conceptual structures. In D. Kuhn and R. S. Siegler (eds), *Handbook of Child Psychology, vol. 2, Cognition, Perception and Language*. New York: Wiley.

Case, R., Hayward, S., Lewis, M. and Hurst, P. (1988) Towards a neo-Piagetian theory of cognitive and emotional development. *Developmental Review* 8, 1–51.

Case, R., Marini, Z., McKeough, A., Denis, S. and Goldberg, J. (1986) Horizontal structure in middle childhood: cross-domain parallels in the course of cognitive growth. In I. Levin (ed.), *Stage and Structure: Reopening the Debate*. Norwood, NJ: Ablex.

Caspi, A., Elder, G. H. and Bem, D. J. (1987) Moving against the world: life-course patterns of explosive children. *Developmental Psychology* 23, 208–313.

Caspi, A., Taylor, A., Moffitt, T. and Plomin, R. (2000) Neighbourhood risk affects children's mental health: environmental risks identified in a genetic design. *Psychological Science* 11, 338–342.

Cassidy, J. (1988) Child–mother attachment and the self in six-year-olds. *Child Development* 59, 121–134.

Cassidy, K. W., Fineberg, D. S., Brown, K. and Perkins, A. (2005) Theory of mind may be contagious, but you don't catch it from your twin. *Child Development* 76(1), 97–106.

Castle, J., Groothues, C., Bredenkamp, D., Beckett, C., O'Connor, T. G., Rutter, M. and the English and Romanian Adoptees Study Team (1999) Effects of quality of early institutional care on cognitive attainment. *American Journal of Orthopsychiatry* 69, 424–437.

Castro-Caldas, A., Petersson, K. M., Reis, A., Stone-Elander, S. and Ingvar, M. (1998) The illiterate brain: learning to read and write during childhood influences the functional organisation of the adult brain. *Brain* 121, 1053–1063.

Cataldo, S. and Ellis, N. (1988) Interactions in the development of spelling, reading and phonological skills. *Journal of Research in Reading* 11(2), 86–109.

Cattell, R. B. (1971) *Abilities: Their Structure, Growth and Action*. Boston: Houghton-Mifflin.

Cavanaugh, J. C. and Perlmutter, M. (1982) Metamemory: a critical examination. *Child Development* 53, 11–28.

Cazden, C. (1988) *Classroom Discourse: The Language of Teaching and Learning*. Portsmouth, NH: Heinemann.

Ceci, S. (1990) *On Intelligence . . . More or Less: a Bio-Ecological Theory of Intellectual Development*. New York: Prentice Hall.

Ceci, S. J. (1991) How much does schooling influence general intelligence and its cognitive components? A reassessment of the evidence. *Developmental Psychology* 27, 703–722.

Ceci, S., Barnett, S. M. and Kanaya, T. (2003) Developing childhood proclivities into adult competencies. In R. L. Sternberg and E. L. Grigorenko (eds), *The Psychology of Abilities, Competencies and Expertise*. Cambridge, UK: Cambridge University Press.

Ceci, S. J. and Bronfenbrenner, U. (1985) Don't forget to take the cup cakes out of the oven: prospective memory, strategic time monitoring, and context. *Child Development* 56, 152–164.

Ceci, S. J. and Liker, J. (1986) A day at the races: the study of IQ, expertise and cognitive complexity. *Journal of Experimental Psychology: General* 115, 225–226.

Ceci, S. J. and Williams, W. M. (1997) Schooling, intelligence, and income. *American Psychologist* 52(10), 1051–1058.

Cellérier, G. (1987) Structures and functions. In B. Inhelder, D. de Caprona and A. Cornu-Wells (eds), *Piaget Today*. Hillsdale, NJ: Lawrence Erlbaum Associates, Inc.

Chaiklin, S. (2003) The zone of proximal development in Vygotsky's analysis of learning and instruction. In A. Kozulin, B. Gindis, V. Ageyev and S. Miller (eds), *Vygotsky's Educational Theory in Cultural Context*. Cambridge, UK: Cambridge University Press.

Chall, S. J. (1967) *Learning to Read: the Great Debate*. New York: McGraw-Hill.

Chall, S. J. (1983) *Stages of Reading Development*. New York, McGraw-Hill.

Chall, S. J., Jacobs, V. and Baldwin, L. (1990) *The Reading Crisis: Why Poor Children Fall Behind*. Cambridge, MA: Harvard University Press.

Chan, C. K. and Siegel, L. S. (2001) Phonological processing in reading Chinese among normally achieving and poor readers. *Journal of Experimental Child Psychology* 80, 23–43.

Chan, L. and Nunes, T. (1998) Children's understanding of the formal and functional characteristics of written Chinese. *Applied Psycholinguistics* 19, 115–131.

Chandler, M. (1988) Doubt and developing theories of mind. In J. W. Astington, P. L. Harris and D. R. Olsen (eds), *Developing Theories of Mind*. Cambridge, UK: Cambridge University Press.

Chandler, M., Fritz, A. S. and Hala, S. M. (1989) Small-scale deceit: deception as a marker of 2, 3 and 4 year olds' theory of mind. *Child Development* 60, 1263–1277.

Chandler, M. and Helm, D. (1984) Developmental changes in the contributions of shared experience to social role-taking competence. *International Journal of Behavioural Development* 7, 145–156.

Chandler, M. J. and Lalonde, C. E. (1994) Surprising, magical and miraculous turns of events: children's reactions to violations of their early theories of mind and matter. *British Journal of Developmental Psychology* 12, 83–96.

Chang, F. and Burns, B. M. (2005) Attention in preschoolers: associations with effortful control and motivation. *Child Development* 76(1), 247–263.

Changeux, J. P. (1987) *Neuronal Man*. Oxford, UK: Oxford University Press.

Chapman, D. A. and Scott, K. G. (2001) The impact of maternal intergenerational risk factors on adverse developmental outcomes. *Developmental Review* 21, 305–325.

Chapman, M. and Lindenberger, U. (1988) Functions, operations and decalage in the development of transitivity. *Developmental Psychology* 24, 542–551.

Chapman, M. and McBride, M. L. (1992) Beyond competence and performance: children's class inclusion strategies, superordinate class cues, and verbal justifications. *Developmental Psychology* 28, 319–327.

Chapman, R. (1997) Language development in children and adolescents with Down syndrome. *Mental Retardation and Developmental Disabilities Research Reviews* 3, 307–312.

Chapman, R. (2000) Children's language learning: an interactionist perspective. *Journal of Child Psychology and Psychiatry* 41, 33–54.

Charity, A. H., Scarborough, H. S. and Griffin, D. M. (2004) Familiarity with school English in African American children and its relation to early reading achievement. *Child Development* 75(5), 1340–1356.

Chase, W. G. and Simon, H. (1973) Perception in chess. *Cognitive Psychology* 4, 55–58.

Chatoor, I., Surles, J., Ganiban, J., Beker, L., Paez, L. M. and Kerzner, B. (2004) Failure to thrive and cognitive development in toddlers with infantile anorexia. *Pediatrics* 113(5), 440–447.

Check, E. (2005) The X factor. *Nature* 434, 266–267.

Chen, C. and Stevenson, H. W. (1995) Motivation and mathematics achievement: a comparative study of Asian-American, Caucasian American and East Asian high school students. *Child Development* 66, 1215–1234.

Chen, M. J., Holman, J., Francis-Jones, N. and Burmeister, L. (1988) Concepts of intelligence of primary school, high school and college students. *British Journal of Experimental Psychology* 6, 71–82.

Cheng, P. and Holyoak, K. (1985) Pragmatic reasoning schemas. *Cognitive Psychology* 17, 391–416.

Cherlin, A. J., Furstenberg, F. F., Chase-Lansdale, P. L., Kiernan, K. E., Robins, P. K., Morrison, D. R. and Teitler, J. O. (1991) Longitudinal studies of effects of divorce on children in Great Britain and the United States. *Science* 252, 1386–1389.

Cherny, S. S., Fulker, D. W. and Hewitt, J. K. (1997) Cognitive development from infancy to middle childhood. In R. L. Sternberg and E. Grigorenko (eds), *Intelligence: Heredity and Environment*. New York: Cambridge University Press.

Cherny, S. S., Fulker, D. W., Emde, R. N., Robinson, J., Corley, R. P., Reznick, S. J. and DeFries, J. C. (1994) A developmental-genetic analysis of continuity and change in the Bayley Mental development index from 14 to 24 months of age: the MacArthur Twin Study. *Psychological Science* 5, 354–360.

Chi, M. T. H. (1978) Knowledge structures and memory development. In R. S. Siegler (ed.), *Children's Thinking: What Develops?* Hillsdale, NJ: Lawrence Erlbaum Associates, Inc.

Chi, M. T. H. (ed.) (1983) *Trends in Memory Development Research*. Basle, Switzerland: Karger.

Chi, M. T. H. and Ceci, S. (1987) Content knowledge: its role, representation and restructuring in memory development. In *Advances in Child Development and Behavior*, vol. 20. New York: Academic Press.

Chi, M. T. H., Feltovich, P. and Glaser, R. (1980) Categorisation and representation of physics problems by experts and novices. *Cognitive Science* 5, 121–152.

Chi, M. T. H., Hutchinson, J. E. and Robin, A. F. (1989) How inferences about novel domain-related concepts can be constrained by structured knowledge. *Merrill-Palmer Quarterly* 35(1), 27–62.

Chi, M. T. H. and Koeske, R. D. (1983) Network representation of a child's dinosaur knowledge. *Developmental Psychology* 19(1), 29–39.

Cicchetti, D. (2003) Editorial: Experiments of nature: Contributions to developmental theory. *Development and Psychopathology* 15(4), 833–835.

Chinn, C. A. and Anderson, R. C. (1998) The structure of discussions that promote reasoning. *Teachers' College Record* 100, 315–368.

Chisholm, K., Carter, M. C., Ames, E. W. and Morison, S. J. (1995) Attachment security and indiscriminately friendly behaviour in children adopted from Romanian orphanages. *Development and Psychopathology* 7, 283–294.

Chliounaki, K. and Bryant, P. E. (2002) Construction and learning to spell. *Cognitive Development* 17, 1489–1499.

Chomsky, N. (1968) *Language and Mind*. New York: Harcourt Brace Jovanovich.

Chomsky, N. (1986) *Knowledge of Language: Its Nature, Origin and Use*. New York: Praeger.

Chukovsky, K. (1976) The sense of nonsense verse. In J. S. Bruner, A. Jolly and K. Sylva (eds), *Play: Its Role in Development and Evolution*. Harmondsworth, UK: Penguin Books.

Churchland, P. M. (1989) *A Neurocomputational Perspective: The Nature of Mind and the Structure of Science*. Cambridge, MA: Bradford & MIT Press.

Churchland, P. M. and Churchland, P. S. (1990) Could a machine think? *Scientific American*, January, 26–31.

Churchland, P. S. (1986) *Neurophilosophy: Toward a Unified Understanding of the Mind/Brain*. Cambridge, MA: MIT Press.

Churchland, P. S. (2002) *Brain-wise: Studies in Neurophilosophy*. Cambridge, MA: MIT Press.

Cicchetti, D. (1990) The organisation and coherence of socioemotional, cognitive, and representational development: illustrations through a developmental psychopathology perspective on Down's syndrome and child maltreatment. In R. A. Thompson (ed.), Socioemotional development. *Nebraska Symposium on Motivation*, 1988, vol. 36. Lincoln: University of Nebraska Press.

Cicchetti, D. (2002) The impact of social experience on neurobiological systems: illustration from a constructivist view of child maltreatment. *Cognitive Development* 17, 1407–1428.

Clark, A. (1989) *Microcognition: Philosophy, Cognitive Science, and Parallel Distributed Processing*. Cambridge, MA: MIT Press.

Clark, E. V. (1973) Non-linguistic strategies and the acquisiton of word meanings. *Cognition* 2, 161–182.

Clark, E. V. (1983) Meaning and concepts. In H. H. Flavell and E. M. Markman (eds), *Handbook of Child Psychology*, vol. 3. New York: Wiley.

Clark, H. and Clark, E. (1977) *Psychology and Language*. New York: Harcourt Brace.

Clark, M. (1988) *Children under Five: Educational Research and Evidence*. London: Gordon and Breach.

Clark, M. M. (1976) *Young Fluent Readers*. London: Heinemann.

Clay, M. (1979) *Reading: The Patterning of Complex Behaviour*. London: Heinemann.

Clay, M. (1983) Getting a theory of writing. In B. Kroll and G. Wells (eds), *Explorations in the Development of Writing*. Chichester, UK: Wiley.

Cochran-Smith, M. (1984) *The Making of a Reader*. Norwood, NJ: Ablex.

Coe, R. N. (1984) *When the Grass was Taller: Autobiography and the Experience of Childhood*. New Haven, CT: Yale University Press.

Coen, C. W. (ed.) (1985) *Functions of the Brain*. Oxford, UK: Clarendon Press.

Cogill, S. R., Caplan, H. L., Alexandra, H., Robson, K. M. and Kumar, R. (1986) Impact of maternal depression on cognitive development of young children. *British Medical Journal* 292, 1165–1167.

Cohen, D. and Mackeith, S. A. (1991) *The Development of Imagination*. London: Routledge.

Cohen, G. (1983) *The Psychology of Cognition*. London: Academic Press.

Cohen, I. L., Vietze, P. M., Sudhalter, V., Jenkins, E. C. and Brown, W. T. (1989) Parent–child dyadic gaze patterns in fragile X males and in non-fragile X males with autistic disorder. *Journal of Child Psychology and Psychiatry* 30(6), 857–864.

Cohler, B. J., Grunebaum, H. U., Weiss, J. L., Gamer, E. and Gallant, D. H. (1977) Disturbance of attention among schizophrenic, depressed and well mothers and their young children. *Journal of Child Psychology and Psychiatry* 18, 115–135.

Cole, M. (1985) The zone of proximal development: where culture and cognition create each other. In J. V. Wertsch (ed.), *Culture, Communication and Cognition*. Cambridge, UK: Cambridge University Press.

Cole, M. (1990) Cognitive development and formal schooling: the evidence from cross-cultural research. In L. C. Moll (ed.), *Vygotsky and Education*. New York: Cambridge University Press.

Cole, M. (2002) Culture and development. In H. Keller, Y. H. Poortinga and A. Scholmerich (eds), *Between Biology and Culture: Perspectives on Ontogenetic Development*. Cambridge, UK: Cambridge University Press.

Cole, M. and Griffin, P. (1980) Cultural amplifiers reconsidered. In D. R. Olson (ed.), *The Social Foundations of Language and Thought*. New York and London: Norton.

Cole, M. and Means, B. (1981) *Comparative Studies of How People Think: An Introduction*. Cambridge, MA: Harvard University Press.

Cole, P. M. (1986) Children's spontaneous control of facial expression. *Child Development* 57, 1309–1321.

Cole, P. M., Martin, S. E. and Dennis, T. A. (2004) Emotion regulation as a scientific construct: methodological challenges and directions for child development research. *Child Development* 75(2), 317–333.

Coleman, A. (1985) *Utopia on Trial: Vision and Reality in Planned Housing*. London: Hilary Shipman.

Coleman, M. (1982) *Take one, leave one: young children's concepts of subtraction*. Unpublished M.Ed. thesis, University of Bristol.

Coles, M. J. and Robinson, W. D. (1989) *Teaching Thinking: A Survey of Programmes in Education*. Bristol: The Bristol Press.

Collerson, J. (1983) One child and one genre: developments in letter writing. In B. Kroll and G. Wells (eds), *Explorations in the Development of Writing*. Chichester, UK: Wiley.

Colley, A. M. (1987) Text comprehension. In J. R. Beech and A. M. Colley (eds), *Cognitive Approaches to Reading*. Chichester, UK: Wiley.

Collins, A. and Smith, E. E. (1982) Teaching the process of reading comprehension. In D. K. Detterman and R. J. Sternberg (eds), *How and How Much Can Intelligence Be Increased?* Norwood, NJ: Ablex.

Collins, F. S. (2004) The case for a US prospective cohort study of genes and environment. *Nature* 429, 475–477.

Collins, W. A. and Gunnar, M. R. (1990) Social and personality development. *Annual Review of Psychology* 42, 387–416.

Comeau, L., Cormier, P., Grandmaison, E. and Lacroix, D. (1999) A longitudinal study of phonological processing skills in children learning to read in a second language. *Journal of Educational Psychology* 91, 29–43.

Connell, J. P. and Wellborn, J. G. (1991) Competence, autonomy and relatedness: a motivational analysis of self-system processes. In *Minnesota Symposium on Child Psychology*, vol. 23. Hillsdale, NJ: Lawrence Erlbaum Associates, Inc.

Conroy, J. S. (1984) *Towards a framework for language functioning in learning mathematics*. Paper given at the Fifth International Congress on Mathematics Education, Adelaide, Australia, August 1984.

Consortium for Longitudinal Studies (1983) *As the Twig is Bent*. London: Lawrence Erlbaum Associates Ltd.

Conway, M. and Rubin, D. C. (1993) The structure of autobiographical memory. In A. F. Collins, S. E. Gathercole, M. A. Conway and P. E. Morris (eds), *Theories of Memory*. Hillsdale, NJ: Lawrence Erlbaum Associates, Inc.

Cook, M. (1984) *Levels of Personality*, London: Holt, Rinehart & Winston.

Coon, H., Fulker, D. W., De Fries, J. C. and Plomin, R. (1990) Home environment and cognitive ability of seven-year-old children in the Colorado Adoption Project: genetic and environmental etiologies. *Developmental Psychology* 26, 459–468.

Cooper, H., Lindsay, J. J., Nye, B. and Greathouse, S. (1998) Relationships among attitudes about homework, amount of homework assigned and completed, and student achievement. *Journal of Educational Psychology* 90, 70–83.

Cooper, H., Valentine, J. C., Nye, B. and Lindsay, J. J. (1999) Relationships between five after school activities and academic achievement. *Journal of Educational Psychology* 91(2), 369–378.

Cooper, L. A. and Regan, D. T. (1982) Attention, perception and intelligence. In R. J. Sternberg (ed.), *Handbook of Human Intelligence*. Cambridge, UK: Cambridge University Press.

Cooper, L. A. and Shepard, R. N. (1984) Turning something over in the mind. *Scientific American* 251(6), 106–114.

Cormier, S. M. and Hagman, J. D. (1987), *Transfer of Learning: Contemporary Research and Applications*. San Diego, CA: Academic Press.

Cornell, E. H., Heth, C. D. and Broda, L. S. (1989) Children's wayfinding: response to instructions to use environmental landmarks. *Developmental Psychology* 25(5), 755–764.

Cornish, K., Sudhalter, V. and Turk, J. (2004a) Attention and language in Fragile X. *Mental Retardation and Developmental Disabilities Research Reviews* 10(1), 11–16.

Cornish, K., Turk, J., Wilding, J., Sudhalter, V., Munir, F., Kooy, F. and Hagerman, R. (2004b) Deconstructing the attention deficit in fragile X syndrome: a developmental neuropsychological approach. *Journal of Child Psychology and Psychiatry* 45(6), 1042–1053.

Correa, J., Nunes, T. and Bryant, P. (1998) Young children's understanding of division: the relationship between division terms in a non-computational task. *Journal of Educational Psychology* 90(2), 321–329.

Cosmides, L. and Tooby, J. (1994) Origins of domain specificity: evolution of functional organisation. In L. A. Hirschfeld and S. A. Gelman (eds), *Mapping the Mind: Domain Specificity in Cognition and Culture*. Cambridge, UK: Cambridge University Press.

Cote, N. and Goldman, S. R. (2004) Building representations of informational text: evidence from children's think-aloud protocols. In R. B. Ruddell and N. J. Unrau (eds), *Theoretical Models and Processes of Reading*. Newark, DE: International Reading Association.

Courage, M. L. and Howe, M. L. (2004) Advances in early memory development research: insights about the dark side of the moon. *Developmental Review* 24(1), 6–32.

Cousins, J. H., Siegel, A. W. and Maxwell, S. E. (1983) Wayfinding and cognitive mapping in large-scale environments: a test of a developmental model. *Journal of Experimental Child Psychology* 35, 1–20.

Covington, M. V. (1987) Instruction in problem-solving planning. In S. L. Friedman, E. K. Scholnick and R. R. Cocking (eds), *Blueprints for Thinking: The*

Role of Planning in Cognitive Development. New York: Cambridge University Press.

Cowan, N. (ed.) (1997) *The Development of Memory in Children*. Hove, UK: Psychology Press.

Cowan, P. (1982) The relationship between emotions and cognitive development. In W. Damon (ed.), *New Directions for Child Development*, vol. 16. San Francisco: Jossey-Bass.

Cowie, H. (ed.) (1984) *The Development of Children's Imaginative Writing*. London: Croom Helm.

Cox, A. D., Puckering, C., Pound, A. and Mills, M. (1987) The impact of maternal depression in young children. *Journal of Child Psychology and Psychiatry* 28, 917–928.

Cox, M. V. (1986) *The Child's Point of View: The Development of Cognition and Language*. Brighton, UK: Harvester.

Cox, M. V. (ed.) (1980) *Are Young Children Egocentric?* London: Batsford.

Cox, M. V. (1993) *Children's drawings of the human figure*. Hove, UK: Lawrence Erlbaum Associates Ltd.

Coyle, J. T., Oster-Granite, M. L., Reeves, R., Hohmann, C., Corsi, P. and Gearhart, J. (1991) Down's syndrome and the Trisomy 16 Mouse: impact of gene imbalance on brain development and aging. In P. R. McHugh and V. A. McKusick (eds), *Genes, Brain and Behaviour*. New York: Raven Press.

Coyne, J. C. and Downey, G. (1991) Social factors and psychopathology: stress, social support, and coping processes. *Annual Review of Psychology* 42, 401–425.

Crain-Thoreson, C. and Dale, P. S. (1992) Do early talkers become early readers? Linguistic precocity, preschool language, and emergent literacy. *Developmental Psychology* 28, 421–429.

Cravioto, J. and Arrieta, R. (1979) Stimulation and mental development of malnourished infants. *The Lancet* 2, 899.

Crisafi, M. A. and Brown, A. L. (1986) Analogical transfer in very young children: combining two separately learned solutions to reach a goal. *Child Development* 57, 953–968.

Crnic, L. and Hagerman, R. (eds) (2004) Fragile X syndrome: frontiers of understanding gene–brain–behavior relationships. *Mental Retardation and Developmental Disabilities Research Reviews* 10, 1–2.

Crnic, L. S. and Pennington, B. F. (eds) (1987) Developmental psychology and the neurosciences. *Child Development* 58, 533–538.

Crnic, L. and Pennington, B. (2000) Down syndrome: neuropsychology and animal models. In C. Rovee-Collier, L. P. Lipsitt and H. Hayne (eds), *Progress in Infancy Research*, vol. 1. Mahwah, NJ: Lawrence Erlbaum Associates, Inc.

Croft, C., O'Connor, T. G., Keaveney, L., Groothues, C., Rutter, M. and the English and Romanian Adoptees Study Team (2001) Longitudinal change in parenting associated with developmental delay and catch-up. *Journal of Child Psychology and Psychiatry* 42, 649–659.

Cromer, R. (1987) Language acquisition, language disorder and cognitive development. In W. Yule and M. Rutter (eds), *Language Development and Disorders*. London: MacKeith Press and Oxford, UK: Blackwell Scientific Publications.

Cromer, R. (1991) *Language and Thought in Normal and Handicapped Children*. Oxford, UK: Blackwell.

Crook, C. H. (1984) Factors influencing the use of transparency in children's drawing. *British Journal of Developmental Psychology* 2, 213–221.

Crook, C. H. (1985) Knowledge and appearance. In N. H. Freeman and M. V. Cox (eds), *Visual Order*. Cambridge, UK: Cambridge University Press.

Crook, T., Raskin, A. and Eliot, J. (1981) Parent–child relationships and adult depression. *Child Development* 52, 950–957.

Crowder, R. G. (1982) *The Psychology of Reading: An Introduction*. Oxford, UK: Oxford University Press.

Csikszentmihalyi, M., Rathunde, K. and Whalen, S. (1993) *Talented Teenagers: The Roots of Success and Failure*. New York: Cambridge University Press.

Cuddy-Casey, M. and Orvaschel, H. (1997) Children's understanding of death in relation to child suicidality and homicidality. *Clinical Psychology Review* 17(1), 33–45.

Cummings, E. M. and Davies, P. T. (1994) Maternal depression and child development. *Journal of Child Psychology and Psychiatry* 35, 73–112.

Cummings, E. M., Keller, P. S. and Davies, P. T. (2005) Towards a family process model of maternal and paternal depressive symptoms: exploring multiple relations with child and family functioning. *Journal of Child Psychology and Psychiatry* 46(5), 479–489.

Cummins, D. D. (2004) The evolution of reasoning. In J. P. Leighton and R. J. Sternberg (eds), *The Nature of Reasoning*. Cambridge, UK: Cambridge University Press.

Cunningham, C. C., Glenn, S. M., Wilkinson, P. and Sloper, P. (1985) Mental ability, symbolic play and receptive and expressive language of young children with Down's syndrome. *Journal of Child Psychology and Psychiatry* 26, 255–265.

Cunningham, J. G. and Weaver, S. L. (1989) Young children's knowledge of their memory span: effects of task and experience. *Journal of Experimental Child Psychology* 48, 32–44.

Curtiss, S. (1977) *Genie: A Psycholinguistic Study of a Modern-day 'Wild Child'*. New York: Academic Press.

Cutting, A. L. and Dunn, J. (1999) Theory of mind, emotion understanding, language, and family background: individual differences and interrelations. *Child Development* 70, 853–865.

Czerniewska, P. (1992) *Learning about Writing*. Oxford, UK: Blackwell.

Daley, T. C., Whaley, S. E., Sigman, M. D., Espinosa, M. P. and Neumann, C. (2003) IQ on the rise: the Flynn effect in rural Kenyan children. *Psychological Science* 14(3), 215–219.

Damon, W. and Hart, D. (1982) The development of self-understanding from infancy through adolescence. *Child Development* 53, 841–864.

Damon, W. and Hart, D. (1988) *Self-understanding in Childhood and Adolescence*. Cambridge, UK: Cambridge University Press.

Daniels, D. and Plomin, R. (1985) Differential experiences of siblings in the same family. *Developmental Psychology* 21, 747–760.

Daniels, J. L., Longnecker, M. P., Rowland, A. S., Golding, J. and the ALSPAC Study Team. (2004) Fish intake during pregnancy and early cognitive development of offspring. *Epidemiology* 15, 394–402.

Danovitch, J. H. and Keil, F. C. (2004) Should you ask a fisherman or a biologist?

Developmental shifts in ways of clustering knowledge. *Child Development* 75(3), 918–931.

Darlington, R. B. (1991) The long-term effects of model preschool programs. In L. Okagaki and R. J. Sternberg (eds), *Directors of Development: Influences on the Development of Children's Thinking*. Hillsdale, NJ: Lawrence Erlbaum Associates, Inc.

Dart, B., Burnett, P., Purdie, N., Boulton-Lewis, G., Campbell, J. and Smith, D. (2000) Students' conceptions of learning, the classroom environment, and approaches to learning. *Journal of Educational Research* 93(4), 262–270.

Darwin, C. (1872) *The Expression of the Emotions in Man and Animals*. London: Murray.

Dasen, P. (1977) Are cognitive processes universal? A contribution to cross-cultural Piagetian psychology. In N. Warren (ed.), *Studies in Cross-cultural Psychology*. London: Academic Press.

das Gupta, P. and Bryant, P. E. (1989) Young children's causal inferences. *Child Development* 60, 1138–1146.

Dauncey, M. J. and Bicknell, R. J. (1999) Nutrition and neurodevelopment: mechanisms of developmental dysfunction and disease in later life. *Nutrition Research Reviews* 12, 231–253.

Davidson, P. M. (1987) Early function concepts: their development and relation to certain mathematical and logical abilities. *Child Development* 58, 1542–1555.

Davie, C. E., Hurt, S. J., Vincent, E. and Mason, M. (1984) *The Young Child at Home*. Windsor, UK: NFER-Nelson.

Davidson, J. W., Howe, M. J. A., Moore, D. G. *et al.* The role of parental influences in the development of musical performance. *British Journal of Developmental Psychology* 14, 399–412.

Davies, B. (1985) Hearing problems. In D. Lane and B. Stratford (eds), *Current Approaches to Down's Syndrome*. London: Holt, Rinehart & Winston.

Davis, A. (2004) The credentials of brain-based learning. *Journal of Philosophy of Education* 38(1), 21–35.

Davis, J. A. and Dobbing, J. (eds) *Scientific Foundations of Pediatrics*. London: Heinemann Medical.

Davis, P. J. (1987) Repression and the inaccessibility of affective memories. *Journal of Personality and Social Psychology* 53, 585–593.

Davis, R. B. (1986) Conceptual and procedural knowledge in mathematics: a summary analysis. In J. Hiebert (ed.), *Conceptual and Procedural Knowledge: The Case of Mathematics*. Hillsdale, NJ: Lawrence Erlbaum Associates, Inc.

Davydov, V. V. and Radzikhovskii, L. A. (1985) Vygotsky's theory and the activity-oriented approach in psychology. In J. V. Wertsch (ed.), *Culture, Communication and Cognition*. Cambridge, UK: Cambridge University Press.

Day, J., French, L. A. and Hall, M. (1985) Social influences on cognitive development. In D. L. Forrest-Pressley, G. E. MacKinnon and G. T. Waller (eds), *Metacognition, Cognition and Human Performance*. Orlando, FL: Academic Press.

Dean, A., Malik, M., Richards, W. and Stringer, S. (1986) Effects of parental maltreatment on children's conceptions of interpersonal relationships. *Developmental Psychology* 22, 617–626.

Dean, R. S. (1985) Foundation and rationale for neuropsychological bases of individual differences. In L. C. Hartlage and C. F. Telzrow (eds), *The Neuro-psychology of Individual Differences*. New York: Plenum Press.

Deary, I. J. and Caryl, P. G. (1993) Intelligence, EEG and evoked potentials. In P. A. Vernon (ed.), *Biological Approaches to the Study of Human Intelligence*. Norwood, NJ: Ablex.

DeFries, J. C., Plomin, R. and Fulker, D. W. (1994) *Nature and Nurture during Middle Childhood*. Cambridge, MA: Blackwell.

De Fries, J. C., Plomin, R. and La Buda, M. C. (1987) Genetic stability of cognitive development from childhood to adulthood. *Developmental Psychology* 23, 4–12.

De Haan, M. and Johnson, M. (2003) Mechanisms and theories of brain development. In M. De Haan and M. Johnson (eds), *The Cognitive Neuroscience of Development*. Hove, UK: Psychology Press.

De Haan, M. and Johnson, M. (eds) (2003) *The Cognitive Neuroscience of Development*. Hove, UK: Psychology Press.

Dehaene, S., Molko, N., Cohen, L. and Wilson, A. J. (2004) Arithmetic and the brain. *Current Opinion in Neurobiology* 14, 216–224.

Dehaene, S., Piazza, M., Pinel, P. and Cohen, L. (2003) Three parietal circuits for number processing. *Cognitive Neuropsychology* 20, 467–506.

De Jong, G. (1989) The role of explanation in analogy: or, the curse of an alluring name. In S. Vosniadou and A. Ortony (eds), *Similarity and Analogical Reasoning*. Cambridge, UK: Cambridge University Press.

de Jong, P. F. and van der Leij, A. (1999) Specific contributions of phonological abilities to early reading acquisition: Results from a Dutch latent variable longitudinal study. *Journal of Educational Psychology* 91(3), 450–476.

De Koning, E., Hamers, J., Sijtsma, K. and Vermeer, A. (2002) Teaching inductive reasoning in primary education. *Developmental Review* 22, 211–241.

DeLoache, J. S. (1987) Rapid change in the symbolic functioning of young children. *Science* 238, 1556–1557.

DeLoache, J. S. (1989) The development of representation in young children. In W. H. Reese (ed.), *Advances in Child Development and Behavior*, vol. 22. New York: Academic Press.

DeLoache, J. S. (1991) Symbolic functioning in very young children: understanding of pictures and models. *Child Development* 62, 736–752.

DeLoache, J. S. (2000) Dual representation and young children's use of scale models. *Child Development* 71, 329–338.

DeLoache, J. S. (2002) Symbolic development. In U. Goswami (ed.), *Blackwell Handbook of Cognitive Development*. Oxford, UK: Blackwell.

DeLoache, J. S. (2004) Becoming symbol-minded. *Trends in Cognitive Sciences* 8(2), 66–70.

DeLoache, J. S. and Burns, N. M. (1994) Early understanding of the representational function of pictures. *Cognition* 52, 83–110.

DeLoache, J. S., Kolstad, V. and Anderson, K. N. (1991) Physical similarity and young children's understanding of scale models. *Child Development* 62, 111–126.

DeLoache, J. S., Miller, K. F. and Pierroutsakos, S. L. (1998a) Reasoning and problem solving. In D. Kuhn and R. S. Siegler (eds), *Handbook of Child Psychology, vol. 2, Cognition, Perception and Language*. New York: Wiley.

DeLoache, J. S., Miller, K. F. and Rosengren, K. S. (1997) The credible shrinking room: very young children's performance with symbolic and non-symbolic relations. *Psychological Science* 8, 308–313.

DeLoache, J. S., Pierroutsakos, S. L., Uttal, D. H., Rosengren, K. S. and Gottlieb, A. (1998b) Grasping the nature of pictures. *Psychological Science* 9, 205–210.

DeLoache, J. S., Simcock, G. and Marzolf, D. P. (2004) Transfer by very young children in the symbolic retrieval task. *Child Development* 75(6), 1708–1718.

DeLoache, J. S., Uttal, D. H. and Rosengren, K. S. (2004) Scale errors offer evidence for a perception–action dissociation early in life. *Science* 304, 1027–1029.

Dempster, F. N. (1981) Memory span: sources of individual and developmental differences. *Psychological Bulletin* 89, 63–100.

Denham, S. A., Renwick, S. M. and Holt, R. W. (1991) Working and playing together: prediction of preschool social–emotional competence from mother–child interaction. *Child Development* 62, 242–249.

Dennett, D. (1979) *Brainstorms*. Hassocks, UK: Harvester.

Dennett, D. (1987) *The Intentional Stance*. Cambridge, MA: MIT Press.

Dennett, D. (1995) *Darwin's Dangerous Idea: Evolution and the Meanings of Life*. London: Allen Lane.

Dennett, D. (2003) *Freedom Evolves*. London: Allen Lane.

Derbaix, C. and Pecheux, C. (2003) A new scale to assess children's attitude toward TV advertising. *Journal of Advertising Research* 43(4), 390–399.

de Ribaupierre, A. (1990) *Transition Mechanisms in Child Development*. Cambridge, UK: Cambridge University Press.

DES (1990) *English in the National Curriculum*, No. 2. London: HMSO.

Desforges, C. (ed.) (1989) *Early Childhood Education*. Edinburgh, UK: Scottish Academic Press for the *British Journal of Educational Psychology*.

Desforges, C. and Cockburn, A. (1987) *Understanding the Mathematics Teacher*. Basingstoke, UK: Falmer Press.

Deutsch, D. (1982) *The Psychology of Music*. New York: Academic Press.

DHSS (1980) *Inequalities in Health*. Report of a working group on inequalities in health; Chairman, Sir Douglas Black. London: Department of Health and Social Security.

Dias, M. G. and Harris, P. L. (1988) The effect of make-believe play on deductive reasoning. *British Journal of Developmental Psychology* 6, 207–221.

Dias, M. G. and Harris, P. L. (1990) The influence of the imagination on reasoning by young children. *British Journal of Developmental Psychology* 8, 305–318.

Diaz, R. M. (1985) Bilingual cognitive development: addressing three gaps in current research. *Child Development* 56, 1376–1388.

Dickens, W. T. and Flynn, J. R. (2001) Heritability estimates versus large environmental effects: the IQ paradox resolved. *Psychological Review* 108(2), 346–369.

Dickinson, D. K. and Sprague, K. E. (2002) The nature and impact of early childhood care environments on the language and early literacy development of children from low income families. In S. B. Neuman and D. K. Dickinson (eds), *Handbook of Early Literacy Research*. New York: Guilford.

Dickinson, J. (1990) Adolescent representations of socio-economic status. *British Journal of Developmental Psychology* 8, 351–371.

Dietrich, K. N., Berger, O. G., Succop, P. A., Hammond, P. B. and Bornschein, R. L. (1993) The developmental consequences of low to moderate prenatal and postnatal lead exposure: intellectual attainment in the Cincinnati Lead Study cohort following school entry. *Neurotoxicology and Teratology* 13, 37–44.

Dillon, R. F. and Sternberg, R. J. (1986) *Cognition and Instruction*. New York: Academic Press.

Di Martino, E. C. (1987) The language of social regulation in young children. In B. Fillion, C. N. Hedley and E. C. Di Martino (eds), *Home and School: Early Language and Reading*. Norwood, NJ: Ablex.

di Sessa, A. (1982) Unlearning Aristotelian physics: a study of knowledge-based learning. *Cognitive Science* 6, 37–76.

di Sessa, A. (1983) Phenomenology and the evolution of intuition. In D. Gentner and A. L. Stevens (eds), *Mental Models*. Hillsdale, NJ: Lawrence Erlbaum Associates, Inc.

Dix, T. (1991) The affective organisation of parenting: adaptive and maladaptive processes. *Psychological Bulletin* 110, 3–25.

Dixon, J. A. and Moore, C. F. (1996) The developmental role of intuitive principles in choosing mathematical strategies. *Developmental Psychology* 32, 241–253.

Dobbing, J. (1987) The later development of the brain and its vulnerability. In J. Dobbing (ed.), *Early Nutrition and Later Achievement*. London: Academic Press.

Dodge, K. A., Pettit, G. and Bates, J. (1994) Socialization mediators of the relationship between socio-economic status and child conduct problems. *Child Development* 65, 649–665.

Dodge, K. A., Pettit, G. S., McClaskey, C. L. and Brown, M. M. (1986) Social competence in children. *Monographs of the Society for Research in Child Development* 51, 1–80.

Doise, W. (1985) Social regulations in cognitive development. In R. A. Hinde, A.-N. Perret-Clermont and J. Stevenson-Hinde (eds), *Social Relationships and Cognitive Development*. Oxford, UK: Clarendon Press.

Doise, W. and Mugny, G. (1984) *The Social Development of the Intellect*. Oxford, UK: Pergamon.

Donaldson, M. (1978) *Children's Minds*. London: Fontana.

Donaldson, M. (1982) Conservation: what is the question? *British Journal of Psychology* 73(2), 199–208.

Donaldson, M. and Balfour, G. (1981) Less is more: a study of language comprehension. *British Journal of Psychology* 59, 461–471.

Donaldson, M., Grieve, R. and Pratt, C. (eds) (1983) *Early Childhood Development and Education*. Oxford, UK: Blackwell.

Dong, W. and Greenough, W. T. (2004) Plasticity of nonneuronal brain tissue roles in developmental disorders. *Mental Retardation and Developmental Disabilities Reviews* 10, 85–90.

Donlan, C. (ed.) (1998) *The Development of Mathematical Skills*. Hove, UK: Psychology Press.

Dorval, B. and Eckerman, C. O. (1984) Developmental trends in the quality of conversation achieved by small groups of acquainted peers. *Monographs of the Society for Research in Child Development* 49(2), 1–91.

Dougherty, T. M. and Haith, M. M. (1997) Infant expectations and reaction time as predictors of childhood speed of processing and IQ. *Developmental Psychology* 33, 146–155.

Dowker, A. (1989) Rhymes and alliteration in poems elicited from young children. *Journal of Child Language* 16, 181–202.

Downey, G. and Coyne, J. C. (1990) Children of depressed parents: an integrative review. *Psychological Bulletin* 108, 50–76.

Downing, J. (1979) *Reading and Reasoning*. New York: Springer-Verlag.

Drewett, R. F., Corbett, S. S. and Wright, C. M. (1999) Cognitive and educational attainments at school age of children who failed to thrive in infancy: a population-based study. *Journal of Child Psychology and Psychiatry* 40, 551–561.

Drewett, R. F., Wolke, D., Asefa, M., Kaha, M. and Tessema, F. (2001) Malnutrition and failure to thrive: is there a sensitive period? A nested case–control study. *Journal of Child Psychology and Psychiatry* 42, 181–187.

Droege, K. L. and Stipek, D. J. (1993) Children's use of dispositions to predict classmates' behaviour. *Developmental Psychology* 29, 646–654.

Dumaret, A. and Stewart, J. (1985) IQ, scholastic performance and behaviour of sibs raised in contrasting environments. *Journal of Child Psychiatry and Psychology* 26, 553–580.

Duncan, G. J., Allhusen, V., Belsky, J. *et al.* (2003) Modeling the impacts of child care quality on children's preschool cognitive development. *Child Development* 74(5), 1454–1475.

Duncan, G. J., Brooks-Gunn, J. and Klebanov, P. (1994) Economic deprivation and early childhood development. *Child Development* 65, 296–318.

Dunn, J. (1987) Understanding feelings: the early stages. In J. Bruner and H. Haste (eds), *Making Sense: The Child's Construction of the World*. London: Methuen.

Dunn, J. (1988) *The Beginnings of Social Understanding*. Oxford, UK: Blackwell.

Dunn, J. (1991a) Relationships and behaviour: the significance of Robert Hinde's work for developmental psychology. In P. Bateson (ed.), *The Development and Integration of Behaviour*. Cambridge, UK: Cambridge University Press.

Dunn, J. (1991b) The developmental importance of differences in siblings' experiences within the family. In K. Pillemer and K. McCartney (eds), *Parent–Child Relations Throughout Life*. Hillsdale, NJ: Lawrence Erlbaum Associates, Inc.

Dunn, J. (1992) Lessons from the study of children's conversations. *Merrill-Palmer Quarterly* 38, 139–149.

Dunn, J. (1993) *Young Children's Close Relationships*. London: Sage.

Dunn, J. (ed.) (1995) Connections between emotion and understanding in development. *Cognition and Emotion* 9(2/3), special issue.

Dunn, J. (2004) *Children's friendships*. Oxford, UK: Blackwell.

Dunn, J., Bretherton, I. and Munn, P. (1987) Conversations about feeling states between mothers and their young children. *Developmental Psychology* 23, 132–139.

Dunn, J., Brown, J. R. and Maguire, M. (1995) The development of children's moral sensibility: individual differences and emotional understanding. *Developmental Psychology* 31, 649–659.

Dunn, J. and Hughes, C. (2001a) 'I got some swords and you're dead!': violent fantasy, antisocial behavior, and moral sensitivity in young children. *Child Development* 72, 491–505.

Dunn, J. and Hughes, C. (2001b) Young children's understanding of emotions within close relationships. *Cognition and Emotion* 12, 171–190.

Dunn, J. and Kendrick, C. (1982) *Siblings: Love, Envy and Understanding.* London: Grant McIntyre.

Dunn, J., Plomin, R. and Nettles, M. (1985) Consistency of mothers' behavior towards infant siblings. *Developmental Psychology* 21, 1188–1195.

Duyme, M. (1988) School success and social class: an adoption study. *Developmental Psychology* 24, 203–209.

Duyme, M. (1990) Antisocial behaviour and post-natal environment: a French adoption study. *Journal of Child Psychology and Psychiatry* 31(5), 699–710.

Duyme, M., Dumaret, A. and Tomkiewicz, S. (1999) How much can we boost IQs of dull children?: A late adoption study. *Proceedings of the National Academy of Sciences* 96, 8790–8794.

Dweck, C. (1999) *Self-theories: Their Role in Motivation, Personality and Development.* Philadelphia: Psychology Press.

Dweck, G. S. and Elliott, E. S. (1983) Achievement motivation. In E. M. Hetherington (ed.), *Handbook of Child Psychology.* New York: Wiley.

Eccles, J. (1985) Sex differences in achievement patterns. In *Nebraska Symposium on Motivation,* vol. 32. Lincoln: University of Nebraska Press.

Eccles, J. (1989) *Evolution of the Brain: Creation of the Self.* London: Routledge.

Eccles, J. and Roeser, R. (1998) School and community influences on human development. In M. Bornstein and M. Lamb (eds), *Developmental Psychology: An Advanced Textbook.* Mahwah, NJ: Lawrence Erlbaum Associates, Inc.

Eckler, J. A. and Weininger, O. (1989) Structural parallels between pretend play and narratives. *Developmental Psychology* 25(5), 736–743.

Eckstein, S. G. and Shemesh, M. (1992) Mathematical models of cognitive development. *British Journal of Mathematical and Statistical Psychology* 45, 1–18.

Edelman, Gerald M. (1994) *Bright air, brilliant fire: on the matter of the mind.* London: Penguin.

Eden, G. F. and Zeffiro, T. A. (1998) Neural systems affected in developmental dyslexia revealed by functional neuroimaging. *Neuron* 21, 279–282.

Edwards, B. (1979) *Drawing on the Right Side of the Brain.* Los Angeles, CA: J. P. Tarcher.

Edwards, C. P. and Lewis, M. (1979) Young children's concepts of social relations: social functions and social objects. In M. Lewis and L. A. Rosenblum (eds), *The Child and its Family: Genesis of Behaviour,* vol. 2. New York: Plenum Press.

Edwards, J. (1986) Language and educational disadvantage: the persistence of linguistic 'deficit' theory. In K. Durkin (ed.), *Language Development in the School Years.* London: Croom Helm.

Egan, K. (1988a) The origins of imagination and the curriculum. In K. Egan and D. Nadaner (eds), *Imagination and Education.* Milton Keynes: Open University Press.

Egan, K. (1988b) *Primary Understanding: Education in Early Childhood.* New York: Routledge.

Egan, K. and Gadjamaschko, N. (2003) Some cognitive tools of literacy. In A. Kozulin, B. Gindis, V. Ageyev and S. Miller (eds), *Vygotsky's Educational Theory in Cultural Context.* Cambridge, UK: Cambridge University Press.

Egan, K. and Nadaner, D. (eds) (1988) *Imagination and Education.* Milton Keynes: Open University Press.

Egeland, B., Jacobvitz, D. and Sroufe, L. A. (1988) Breaking the cycle of abuse. *Child Development* 59, 1080–1088.

Ehri L. (1999) Phases of development in learning to read words. In J. Oakhill and R. Beard (eds), *Reading Development and the Teaching of Reading: A Psychological Perspective*. Oxford, UK: Blackwell.

Ehri, L. C., Wilce, L. S. and Taylor, B. B. (1987) Children's categorisation of short vowels in words and the influence of spellings. *Merrill-Palmer Quarterly* 33(3), 393–421.

Eimas, P. D., Siqueland, E. R., Jusczyk, P. W. and Vigorito, J. (1971) Speech perception in infants. *Science* 171, 304–306.

Eisbach, A. O'D. (2004) Children's developing awareness of diversity in people's trains of thought. *Child Development* 75(6), 1694–1707.

Eisenberg, A. R. (1985) Learning to describe past experiences in conversation. *Discourse Processes* 8, 177–204.

Eisenberg, N. and Mussen, P. H. (1989) *The Roots of Prosocial Behaviour in Children*. Cambridge, UK: Cambridge University Press.

Eisenberg, N. and Sayer, J. (1988) *Empathy and its Development*. Cambridge, UK: Cambridge University Press.

Eiser, C. (1985) *The Psychology of Childhood Illness*. New York: Springer-Verlag.

Eiser, C. and Eiser, J. R. (1987) Explaining illness to children. *Communication and Cognition* 20(2/3), 277–290.

Eiser, C., Eiser, J. R. and Lang, J. (1989) Scripts in children's reports of medical events. *European Journal of Psychology of Education* 4(3), 377–384.

Eiser, C. and Patterson, D. (1983) 'Slugs and snails and puppy-dogs' tails': children's ideas about the insides of their bodies. *Child: Care, Health and Development* 9, 233–240.

Eiser, C., Patterson, D. and Eiser, J. R. (1983) Children's knowledge of health and illness: implications for health education. *Child: Care, Health and Development* 9, 285–292.

Eiser, C., Town, C. and Tripp, J. H. (1988) Illness experience and related knowledge amongst children with asthma. *Child: Care, Health and Development* 14, 11–24.

Elkind, D. (1978) *The Child's Reality: Three Developmental Themes*. Hillsdale, NJ: Lawrence Erlbaum Associates, Inc.

Elley, W. B. (1989) Vocabulary acquisition from listening to stories. *Reading Research Quarterly* 24, 174–187.

Ellis, A. W. (1984) *Reading, Writing and Dyslexia in Cognitive Analysis*. London: Lawrence Erlbaum Associates Ltd.

Ellis, C. E. and Hill, D. E. (1975) Growth, intelligence and school performance in children with cystic fibrosis who have had an episode of malnutrition during infancy. *Journal of Pediatrics* 87, 565–568.

Ellis, H. D. (1990) Developmental trends in face recognition. *The Psychologist* 3, 114–119.

Ellis, N. (1988) The development of literacy and short-term memory. In M. M. Gruneberg, P. E. Morris and R. N. Sykes (eds), *Practical Aspects of Memory: II*. Chichester, UK: Wiley.

Ellis, N. and Large, B. (1987) The development of reading: as you seek so shall you find. *British Journal of Psychology* 78, 1–28.

Ellis, N. and Large, B. (1988) The early stages of reading: a longitudinal study. *Applied Cognitive Psychology* 2, 47–76.

Ellis, S. and Rogoff, B. (1982) The strategies and efficacy of child versus adult teachers. *Child Development* 53, 730–735.

Elman, J. (2005) Connectionist models of cognitive development: where next? *Trends in Cognitive Science* 9(3), 111–117.

Elman, J., Bates, E., Karmiloff-Smith, A., Johnson, M., Parisi, D. and Plunkett, K. (eds) (1997) *Rethinking Innateness: A Connectionist Perspective on Development.* Cambridge, MA: MIT Press.

Emery, R. E. and Laumann-Billings, L. (1998) An overview of the nature, causes and consequences of abusive family relationships. *American Psychologist* 53, 121–135.

Emler, N. (1998) Sociomoral understanding. In A. Campbell and S. Muncer (eds), *The Social Child.* Hove, UK: Psychology Press.

Emler, N. and Dickinson, J. (1985) Children's representations of social inequalities: the effects of social class. *British Journal of Developmental Psychology* 3, 191–198.

Emler, N. and Valiant, G. (1982) Social interaction and cognitive conflict in the development of spatial co-ordination skills. *British Journal of Psychology* 73, 295–304.

English, L. (1992) Children's use of domain-specific knowledge and domain-general strategies in novel problem solving. *British Journal of Educational Psychology* 62, 203–216.

Ennis, R. H. (1978) Conceptualization of children's logical competence: Piaget's propositional logic and an alternative proposal. In L. S. Siegel and C. J. Brainerd (eds), *Alternatives to Piaget.* New York: Academic Press.

Entwistle, D. R. and Stevenson, H. W. (1987) Schools and development. *Child Development* 58, 1149–1150.

Entwistle, N. (1988) Motivational factors in approaches to learning. In R. R. Schmeck (ed.), *Learning Strategies and Learning Styles.* New York: Plenum Press.

Entwistle, N., Hanley, M. and Ratcliffe, G. (1979) Approaches to learning and levels of understanding. *British Educational Research Journal* 5, 99–114.

Epstein, H. T. (1974a) Phrenoblysis: special brain and mind growth periods: I. Human brain and skull development. *Developmental Psychobiology* 7, 207–216.

Epstein, H. T. (1974b) Phrenoblysis: special brain and mind growth periods: II. Human mental development. *Developmental Psychobiology* 7, 217–224.

Epstein, H. T. (1990) Stages in human mental growth. *Journal of Educational Psychology* 82, 876–880.

Ericsson, K. A. (2003) The search for general abilities and basic capacities; theoretical implications from the modifiability and complexity of mechanisms mediating expert performance. In R. L. Sternberg and E. L. Grigorenko (eds), *The Psychology of Abilities, Competencies and Expertise.* Cambridge, UK: Cambridge University Press.

Ericsson, K. A. and Charness, N. (1994) Expert performance: its structure and acquisition. *American Psychologist* 49, 725–747.

Ericsson, K. A., Chase, W. G. and Faloon, S. (1980) Acquisition of a memory skill. *Science* 208, 1181–1182.

Ernhart, C. B., Wolf, A. W., Kennard, M. J., Erhard, P., Filipovich, H. F. and

Sokol, R. J. (1986) Intrauterine exposure to low levels of lead: the status of the neonate. *Archives of Environmental Medicine* 41(5), 287–291.

Ervin-Tripp, S. and Strage, A. (1985) Parent–child discourse. In T. A. Van Dijk (ed.), *Handbook of Discourse Analysis, vol. 3, Discourse and Dialogue*. London: Academic Press.

Estes, D., Wellman, H. and Woolley, J. D. (1989) Children's understanding of mental phenomena. In H. W. Reese (ed.), *Advances in Child Development and Behavior*, vol. 22. New York: Academic Press.

Estrada, P., Arsenio, W. F., Hess, R. D. and Holloway, S. (1987) Affective quality of the mother–child relationship: longitudinal consequences for children's school-relevant cognitive functioning. *Developmental Psychology* 23, 210–215.

Evans, G. W. (2004) The environment of childhood poverty. *American Psychologist* 59(20), 77–92.

Evans, G. W. and English, K. (2002) The environment of poverty: multiple stressor exposure, psychophysiological stress, and socioemotional adjustment. *Child Development* 73, 1238–1248.

Evans, G. W., Maxwell, L. E. and Hart, B. (1999) Parental language and verbal responsiveness to children in crowded homes. *Developmental Psychology* 35(4), 1020–1023.

Evans, J. St B. T. (2002) Logic and human reasoning: An assessment of the deduction paradigm. *Psychological Bulletin* 128, 978–990.

Evans, J. St B. T. and Feeney, A. (2004) The role of prior belief in reasoning. In J. P. Leighton and R. J. Sternberg (eds), *The Nature of Reasoning*. Cambridge, UK: Cambridge University Press.

Eysenck, H. J. (1971) *Race, Intelligence and Education*. London: Temple Smith.

Eysenck, H. J. (ed.) (1982) *A Model for Intelligence*. Berlin, Germany: Springer-Verlag.

Eysenck, H. J. (1986) The theory of intelligence and the psychophysiology of cognition. In R. J. Sternberg (ed.), *Advances in the Psychology of Human Intelligence*, vol. 3. Hillsdale, NJ: Lawrence Erlbaum Associates, Inc.

Eysenck, M. W. (1988) Anxiety and attention. *Anxiety Research* 1, 9–16.

Eysenck, M. W. and Keane, M. T. (1990) *Cognitive Psychology: A Student's Handbook*. London: Lawrence Erlbaum Associates Ltd.

Fabricius, W. V., Sophian, C. and Wellman, H. M. (1987) Young children's sensitivity to logical necessity in their inferential search behavior. *Child Development* 58, 409–423.

Fadigan, K. A. and Hammrich, P. L. (2004) A longitudinal study of the educational and career trajectories of female participants of an urban informal science education program. *Journal of Research in Science Teaching* 41(8), 835–860.

Fagan, J. F. (1973) Infants' delayed recognition memory and forgetting. *Journal of Experimental Child Psychology* 16, 424–450.

Fagan, J. F. (1976) Infants' recognition of invariant features of faces. *Child Development* 45, 351–356.

Fagan, J. F. and Singer, L. T. (1983) Infant recognition memory as a measure of intelligence. In L. P. Lipsitt (ed.), *Advances in Infancy Research*, vol. 2. Norwood, NJ: Ablex.

Falk, R. and Wilkening, F. (1998) Children's construction of fair chances: adjusting probabilities. *Developmental Psychology* 34(6), 1340–1357.

Fan, X. T. and Chen, M. (2001) Parental involvement and students' academic achievement: a meta-analysis. *Educational Psychology Review* 13, 1–22.

Farr, M. (1985) *Advances in Writing Research, vol. 1, Children's Early Writing Development*. Norwood, NJ: Ablex.

Farrar, M. J. (1990) Discourse and the acquisition of grammatical morphemes. *Journal of Child Language* 17, 607–624.

Farrar, M. J. and Goodman, G. S. (1992) Developmental changes in event memory. *Child Development* 63, 173–187.

Farrar, M. J., Raney, G. E. and Boyer, M. E. (1992) Knowledge, concepts and inferences in childhood. *Child Development* 63, 673–691.

Fay, A. L. and Klahr, D. (1996) Knowing about guessing and guessing about knowing: preschoolers' understanding of indeterminacy. *Child Development* 67, 689–716.

Fehr, L. A. (1978) Methodological inconsistencies in the measurement of spatial perspective taking ability: a cause for concern. *Human Development* 21, 302–315.

Feigenson, L., Dehaene, S. and Spelke, E. (2004) Core systems of number. *Trends in Cognitive Sciences* 8(7), 307–314.

Feinstein, L. and Bynner, J. (2004) The importance of cognitive development in middle childhood for adult socio-economic status, mental health, and problem behavior. *Child Development* 75(5), 1329–1339.

Feldman, C. F. (1988) Early forms of thought about thoughts: some simple linguistic expressions of mental state. In J. W. Astington, P. L. Harris and D. R. Olson (eds), *Developing Theories of Mind*. Cambridge, UK: Cambridge University Press.

Feldman, C. F. and Toulmin, S. (1976) Logic and the theory of mind. In *Nebraska Symposium on Motivation*. Lincoln: University of Nebraska Press.

Feldman, D. (1999) The development of creativity. In R. J. Sternberg (ed.), *The Handbook of Creativity*. Cambridge, UK: Cambridge University Press.

Felner, R. D., Brand, S., DuBois, D. L., Adan, A., Mulhall, P. and Evans, E. (1995) Socioemotional disadvantage, proximal environmental experiences, and socio-emotional and academic adjustment in early adolescence: investigation of a mediated effects model. *Child Development* 66, 774–792.

Fenson, L. (1985) The transition from construction to sketching in children's drawings. In N. H. Freeman and M. V. Cox (eds), *Visual Order*. Cambridge, UK: Cambridge University Press.

Fenson, L., Dale, P. S., Reznick, J. S., Bates, E., Thal, D. and Pethick, S. J. (1994) Variability in early communicative development. *Monographs of the Society for Research in Child Development* 59, serial no. 242.

Ferguson, C. A. and Slobin, D. A. (eds) (1973) *Studies of Child Language Development*. New York: Holt, Rinehart & Winston.

Fergusson, D. M., Fergusson, J. E., Horwood, L. J. and Kinzett, N. G. (1988a) A longitudinal study of dentine lead levels, intelligence, school performance and behaviour: Part 1, Dentine lead levels and exposure to environmental risk factors. *Journal of Child Psychology and Psychiatry* 29, 781–792.

Fergusson, D. M., Fergusson, J. E., Horwood, L. J. and Kinzett, N. G. (1988b) Part 2, Dentine lead and cognitive ability. *Journal of Child Psychology and Psychiatry* 29, 793–810.

Fergusson, D. M., Fergusson, J. E., Horwood, L. J. and Kinzett, N. G. (1988c) Part

3, Dentine lead levels and attention/activity. *Journal of Child Psychology and Psychiatry* 29, 811–824.

Ferrara, R. A., Brown, A. L. and Campione, J. C. (1986) Children's learning and transfer of inductive reasoning rules: studies of proximal development. *Child Development* 57, 1087–1099.

Ferrari, M. and Sternberg, R. J. (1998) The development of mental abilities and styles. In D. Kuhn and R. S. Siegler (eds), *Handbook of Child Psychology, vol. 2, Cognition, Perception and Language*. New York: Wiley.

Ferreiro, E. (1999) Oral and written words: are they the same units? In T. Nunes (ed.), *Learning to Read: An Integrated View from Research and Practice*. Dordrecht, The Netherlands: Kluwer.

Feuerstein, R., Rand, Y., Hoffman, M. and Miller, R. (1980) *Instrumental Enrichment*. Baltimore: University Park Press.

Field, T., Sandberg, D., Garcia, R., Vega-Lahr, N., Goldstein, S. and Guy, L. (1985) Pregnancy problems, post-partum depression and early mother–infant interactions. *Developmental Psychology* 21, 1152–1156.

Finlay, B. L., Darlington, R. B. and Nicastro, N. (2001) Developmental structure in brain evolution. *Brain and Behavior Science* 24, 263–308.

Fischer, K. W. (1987) Relations between brain and cognitive development. *Child Development* 58, 623–632.

Fischer, K. W. and Bidell, T. (1991) Constraining nativist inferences about cognitive capacities. In S. Carey and R. Gelman (eds), *The Epigenesis of Mind*. Hove, UK: Lawrence Erlbaum Associates Ltd.

Fischer, K. W., Shaver, P. R. and Carnochan, P. (1990) How emotions develop and how they organise development. *Cognition and Emotion* 4, 81–127.

Fischer, K. W. and Bidell, T. R. (1998) Dynamic development of psychological structures in action and thought. In W. Damon and R. Lerner (eds), *Handbook of Child Psychology, vol. 1, Theoretical models of human development*. New York: Wiley.

Fischer, K. W. and Yan, Z. (2002) Darwin's construction of the theory of evolution: microdevelopment of explanations of variation and change in species. In N. Granott and J. Parziale (eds), *Microdevelopment: Transition Processes in Development and Learning*. Cambridge, UK: Cambridge University Press.

Fiser, J., Chiu, C. and Weliky, M. (2004) Small modulation of ongoing cortical dynamics by sensory input during natural vision. *Nature* 431, 573–578.

Fisher, R. (1990) *Teaching Children to Think*. Oxford, UK: Blackwell.

Fisher, R. (1998) *Teaching Thinking*. London: Cassell.

Fisher, S. E. and DeFries, J. C. (2002) Developmental dyslexia: genetic dissection of a complex cognitive trait. *Neuroscience* 3, 767–780.

Fivush, R. (1984) Learning about school: the development of kindergarteners' school scripts. *Child Development* 55, 1697–1709.

Fivush, R. (1987) Scripts and categories: interrelationships in development. In U. Neisser (ed.), *Concepts and Conceptual Development*. Cambridge, UK: Cambridge University Press.

Fivush, R., Gray, J. T. and Fromhoff, F. A. (1987) Two-year-olds talk about the past. *Cognitive Development* 2, 393–409.

Fivush, R., Haden, C. and Adam, S. (1995) Structure and coherence of preschoolers' personal narratives over time: implications for childhood amnesia. *Journal of Experimental Psychology* 60, 32–56.

Fivush, R. and Hamond, N. R. (1989) Time and again: effects of repetition and retention interval on 2 year olds' event recall. *Journal of Experimental Child Psychology* 47, 259–273.

Fivush, R., Kuebli, J. and Clubb, P. A. (1992) The structure of events and event representations: a developmental analysis. *Child Development* 63, 188–201.

Fivush, R. and Nelson, K. (2004) Culture and language in the emergence of autobiographical memory. *Psychological Science* 15(9), 573–577.

Flavell, J. H. (1963) *The Developmental Psychology of Jean Piaget*. Princeton, NJ: Van Nostrand.

Flavell, J. H. (1971) First discussant's comments: what is memory development the development of? *Human Development* 14, 272–278.

Flavell, J. H. (1977) *Cognitive Development*. Englewood Cliffs, NJ: Prentice Hall.

Flavell, J. H. (1978a) The development of knowledge about visual perception. In *Nebraska Symposium on Motivation*, 1977. Lincoln: University of Nebraska Press.

Flavell, J. H. (1978b) Comments on Brown and De Loache's paper. In R. S. Siegler (ed.), *Children's Thinking: What Develops?* Hillsdale, NJ: Lawrence Erlbaum Associates, Inc.

Flavell, J. H. (1982a) On cognitive development. *Child Development* 53, 1–10.

Flavell, J. H. (1982b) Structures, stages and sequences in cognitive development. In *Minnesota Symposium on Child Psychology* vol. 15. Hillsdale, NJ: Lawrence Erlbaum Associates, Inc.

Flavell, J. H. (1984) Discussion. In R. J. Sternberg (ed.), *Mechanisms of Cognitive Development*. New York: W. H. Freeman.

Flavell, J. H. (1985) *Cognitive Development*, 2nd edn. Englewood Cliffs, NJ: Prentice Hall.

Flavell, J. H. (1986) The development of children's knowledge about the appearance–reality distinction. *American Psychologist* 41, 418–425.

Flavell, J. H. (1988) The development of children's knowledge about the mind: from cognitive connections to mental representations. In J. W. Astington, P. L. Harris and D. R. Olson (eds), *Developing Theories of Mind*. Cambridge, UK: Cambridge University Press.

Flavell, J. H. (1999) Cognitive development: children's knowledge about the mind. *Annual Review of Psychology* 50, 21–45.

Flavell, J. H. (2001) Development of children's knowledge about the mental world. *International Journal of Behavioural Development* 24, 15–23.

Flavell, J. H., Beach, D. R. and Chinsky, J. M. (1966) Spontaneous verbal rehearsal in a memory task as a function of age. *Child Development* 37, 283–299.

Flavell, J. H., Flavell, E. R., Green, F. L. and Moses, L. J. (1990) Young children's understanding of fact beliefs versus value beliefs. *Child Development* 61, 915–928.

Flavell, J. H., Green, F. L. and Flavell, E. R. (1986) Development of knowledge about the appearance–reality distinction. *Monographs of the Society for Research in Child Development* 51(1), serial no. 212.

Flavell, J. H., Green, F. L. and Flavell, E. R. (1989) Young children's ability to differentiate appearance–reality and level 2 perspectives in the tactile modality. *Child Development* 60, 201–213.

Flavell, J. H., Green, F. L. and Flavell, E. R. (1995) Young children's knowledge about thinking. *Monographs of the Society for Research in Child Development* 60(1), serial no. 243.

Flavell, J. H., Green, F. L., Flavell, E. R. and Grossman, J. B. (1997) The development of children's knowledge about inner speech. *Child Development* 68, 39–47.

Flavell, J. H., Green, F. L., Flavell, E. R. and Lin, N. T. (1999) Development of children's knowledge about unconsciousness. *Child Development* 70, 396–412.

Flavell, J. H. and Markman, E. M. (eds) (1983) *Handbook of Child Psychology, vol. 3, Cognitive Development*. New York: Wiley.

Flavell, J. H. and Miller, R. H. (1998) Social cognition. In D. Kuhn and R. S. Siegler (eds), *Handbook of Child Psychology, vol. 2, Cognition, Perception and Language*. New York: Wiley.

Flavell, J. H. and Ross, L. (eds) (1981) *Social Cognitive Development: Frontiers and Possible Futures*. Cambridge, UK: Cambridge University Press.

Flavell, J. H. and Wellman, H. M. (1977) Metamemory. In R. V. Kail and J. W. Hagen (eds), *Perspectives on the Development of Memory and Cognition*. Hillsdale, NJ: Lawrence Erlbaum Associates, Inc.

Fletcher, P. and MacWhinney, B. (eds) (1995) *The Handbook of Child Language*. Oxford, UK: Blackwell.

Flynn, E., O'Malley, C. and Wood, D. (2004) A longitudinal microgenetic study of the emergence of false belief understanding and inhibition skills. *Developmental Science* 7(1), 103–115.

Flynn, J. R. (1980) *Race, IQ and Jensen*. London: Routledge & Kegan Paul.

Flynn, J. R. (1987) Massive IQ gains in 14 nations: what IQ tests really measure. *Psychological Bulletin* 101, 171–191.

Flynn, J. R. (1998) IQ gains over time: toward finding the causes. In U. Neisser (ed.), *The Rising Curve: Long-term Gains in IQ and Related Measures*. Washington, DC: American Psychological Association.

Flynn, J. R. (1999) Searching for justice: the discovery of IQ gains over time. *American Psychologist* 54(1), 5–20.

Flynn, J. R. (2003) Movies about intelligence: the limitations of *g*. *Current Directions in Psychological Science* 12(3), 95–99.

Fodor, J. A. (1976) *The Language of Thought*. Hassocks, UK: Harvester.

Fodor, J. A. (1981) *Representations: Philosophical Essays on the Foundations of Cognitive Science*. Brighton, UK: Harvester.

Fodor, J. A. (1983) *The Modularity of Mind*. Cambridge, MA: MIT Press.

Fodor, J. A. (1990) Fodor's guide to mental representation: the intelligent Auntie's vade-mecum. *A Theory of Content and Other Essays*. Cambridge, MA: MIT Press.

Foorman, B. and Siegel, A. W. (1986) *Acquisition of Reading Skills: Cultural Constraints and Cognitive Universals*. Hillsdale, NJ: Lawrence Erlbaum Associates, Inc.

Forbes, D. D. S. (1988) A two-year-old's memory observed. *The Psychologist* 1, 27–31.

Ford, M. E. (1979) The construct validity of egocentrism. *Psychological Bulletin* 86, 1169–1188.

Forgas, J. (ed.) (1981) *Social Cognition*. New York: Academic Press.

Forguson, L. (1989) *Common Sense*. London: Routledge.

Forguson, L. and Gopnik, A. (1988) The ontogeny of commonsense. In J. W. Astington, P. L. Harris and D. R. Olson (eds), *Developing Theories of Mind*. Cambridge, UK: Cambridge University Press.

Forman, E. A. and Cazden, C. B. (1985) Exploring Vygotskian perspectives in education: the cognitive value of peer interaction. In J. V. Wertsch (ed.), *Culture, Communication and Cognition*. Cambridge, UK: Cambridge University Press.

Forrest-Pressley, D., MacKinnon, G. and Waller, T. (1985) *Metacognition, Cognition and Human Performance*, vols 1 and 2. Orlando, FL: Academic Press.

Fowler, W. (ed.) (1986) *Early Experience and the Development of Competence*. San Francisco: Jossey-Bass.

Francis, H. (1992) Patterns of reading development in the first school. *British Journal of Educational Psychology* 62, 225–232.

Francis, J. (1982) *Learning to Read: Literate Behaviour and Orthographic Knowledge*. London: George Allen & Unwin.

Fraser, B. J. (1989) Research syntheses on school and instructional effectiveness. *International Journal of Educational Research* 13(7), 707–719.

Frederiksen, C. H. and Dominic, J. F. (1981) *Writing: The Nature, Development and Teaching of Written Communication, vol. 2, Writing: Process, Development and Communication*. Hillsdale, NJ: Lawrence Erlbaum Associates, Inc.

Fredricks J. A. and Eccles, J. S. (2002) Children's competence and value beliefs from childhood through adolescence: growth trajectories in two male-sex-typed domains. *Developmental Psychology* 38(4), 519–533.

Freeman, J., Butcher, H. J. and Christie, T. (1971) *Creativity: A Selective Review of Research*. London: Society for Research into Higher Education.

Freeman N. and Cox, M. V. (eds) (1985) *Visual Order: The Nature and Development of Pictorial Representation*. Cambridge, UK: Cambridge University Press.

Freeman, N. (1975) Do children draw men with arms coming out of their head? *Nature* 254, 416–417.

Freeman, N. (1980) *Strategies of Representation in Young Children: Analysis of Spatial Skills and Drawing Processes*. London: Academic Press.

Freeman, N. (1987) Current problems in the development of representational picture-production. *Archives de Psychologie* 55, 127–152.

Freeman, N. (1988) Children's drawings of humans. In R. L. Gregory (ed.), *The Oxford Companion to the Mind*. Oxford, UK: Oxford University Press.

Freeman, N., Lloyd, S. and Sinha, C. G. (1980) Infant search tasks reveal early concepts of containment and canonical usage of objects. *Cognition* 8, 243–262.

Freeman, N. H. (1995) The emergence of a framework theory of pictorial reasoning. In C. Lange-Kuettner and G. V. Thomas (eds), *Drawing and Looking*. London: Harvester.

Freud, S. (1973) *Introductory Lectures on Psychoanalysis*, vol. 2 of the Pelican Freud Library. Harmondsworth, UK: Penguin Books.

Freud, S. (1977) *Three Essays on the Theory of Sexuality*, vol. 7 of the Pelican Freud Library. Harmondsworth, UK: Penguin Books.

Freund, L. S. (1990) Maternal regulation of children's problem-solving behaviour and its impact on children's performance. *Child Development* 61, 113–126.

Freund, L. S., Baker, L. and Sonnenschein, S. (1990) Developmental changes in strategic approaches to classification. *Journal of Experimental Child Psychology* 49, 343–362.

Friedman, S. L., Scholnick, E. K. and Cocking, R. R. (eds) (1987) *Blueprints for Thinking: The Role of Planning in Cognitive Development.* New York: Cambridge University Press.

Frith, U. (1980a) Reading and spelling skills. In M. Rutter (ed.), *Scientific Foundations of Developmental Psychiatry.* London: Heinemann.

Frith, U. (ed.) (1980b) *Cognitive Processes in Spelling.* London: Academic Press.

Frith, U. (1990) *Autism.* Oxford, UK: Blackwell.

Frith, U. and Frith, C. D. (2003) Development and neurophysiology of mentalizing. *Philosophical Transactions of the Royal Society of London* B358, 459–473.

Frydman, O. and Bryant, P. (1988) Sharing and the understanding of number equivalence by young children. *Cognitive Development* 3, 323–339.

Frye, D. and Moore, C. (eds) (1991) *Children's Theories of Mind: Mental States and Social Understanding.* Hove, UK: Lawrence Erlbaum Associates Ltd.

Fujinaga, T., Kasuga, T., Uchida, N. and Saiga, H. (1990) Long-term follow-up study of children developmentally retarded by early environmental deprivation. *Genetic, Social and General Psychology Monographs* 116, 1.

Fulker, D. W., Cherny, S. S. and Cardon, L. R. (1993) Continuity and change in cognitive development. In R. Plomin and G. E. McClearn (eds), *Nature, Nurture and Psychology.* Washington, DC: American Psychological Association.

Fulton, M., Raab, G. M., Thomson, G. O. B., Laxen, D. P. H., Hunter, R. and Hepburn, W. (1987) Influence of blood lead on the ability and attainment of children in Edinburgh. *The Lancet* i, 1221–1226.

Furnham, A. (1992) Lay understanding of science: young people and adults' ideas of scientific concepts. *Studies in Science Education* 20, 29–64.

Furnham, A., (1999) Economic socialization: a study of adults' perceptions and uses of allowances (pocket money) to educate children. *British Journal of Developmental Psychology* 17, 585–604.

Furnham, A. and Kirkcaldy, B. (2000) Economic socialization: German parents' perceptions and implementation of allowances to educate children. *European Psychologist* 5(3), 200–215.

Furstenberg, F., Brooks-Gunn, J. and Morgan, S. P. (1969) *Adolescent Mothers in Later Life.* Cambridge, UK: Cambridge University Press.

Furth, H. (1980) *The World of Grownups.* New York: Elsevier North Holland.

Fuson, K. C. (1990) Conceptual structures for multiunit numbers: implications for learning and teaching multidigit addition, subtraction and place value. *Cognition and Instruction* 7, 343–403.

Fuson, K. C. and Briars, D. (1990) Using a base-ten blocks learning–teaching approach for first and second grade place value and multidigit addition and subtraction. *Journal for Research in Mathematics Education* 21, 180–206.

Fuson, K. C. and Hall, J. W. (1983) The acquisition of early number word meanings: a conceptual analysis and review. In H. P. Ginsburg (ed.), *The Development of Mathematical Thinking.* New York: Academic Press.

Fuson, K. C. and Kwon, Y. (1992) Korean children's understanding of multidigit addition and subtraction. *Child Development* 63, 491–506.

Fuson, K. C., Pergament, G. G., Lyons, B. G. and Hall, J. W. (1985) Children's conformity to the cardinality rule as a function of set size and counting accuracy. *Child Development* 56, 1429–1436.

Fuson, K. C., Richards, J. and Briars, D. J. (1982) The acquisition and elaboration of the number word sequence. In C. J. Brainerd (ed.), *Progress in Cognitive Development, vol. 1, Children's Logical and Mathematical Cognition*. New York: Springer-Verlag.

Gagné, R. M. (1985) *The Conditions of Learning and Theory of Instruction*. New York: Holt, Rinehart & Winston.

Galbraith, J. K. (1980) *The Nature of Mass Poverty*. Harmondsworth, UK: Penguin Books.

Galbraith, R. C. (1982) Sibling spacing and intellectual development: a closer look at the confluence models. *Developmental Psychology* 18, 151–173.

Gale, C. R., O'Callaghan, F. J., Godfrey, K. M., Law, C. M. and Martyn, C. N. (2004) Critical periods of brain growth and cognitive function in children. *Brain* 127, 321–329.

Gallaway, C. and Richards, B. (eds) (1994) *Input and Interaction in Language Acquisition*. Cambridge, UK: Cambridge University Press.

Galler, J. R. (1987) The interaction of nutrition and environment in behavioural development. In J. Dobbing (ed.), *Early Nutrition and Later Achievement*. London: Academic Press.

Galotti, K. M. (1989) Approaches to studying formal and everyday reasoning. *Psychological Bulletin* 105(3), 331–351.

Galotti, K. M., Komatsu, L. K. and Voelz, S. (1997) Children's differential performance on deductive and inductive syllogisms. *Developmental Psychology* 33, 70–78.

Ganger, J. and Brent, M. R. (2004) Reexamining the vocabulary spurt. *Developmental Psychology* 40, 621–632.

Garber, R. (1988) The Milwaukee Project: Preventing mental retardation in children at risk. Washington, DC: American Association on Mental Retardation.

Garber, R. and Hodge, D. (1989) Risk for deceleration in the rate of mental development. *Developmental Review* 9, 259–300.

Gardner, H. (1973) *The Arts and Human Development*. New York: Wiley.

Gardner, H. (1974) Metaphors and modalities: how children project polar adjectives onto diverse domains. *Child Development* 45, 84–91.

Gardner, H. (1980) *Artful Scribblers*. New York: Basic Books.

Gardner, H. (1983) *Frames of Mind: The Theory of Multiple Intelligences*. London: Heinemann.

Gardner, H. (1998) Extraordinary cognitive achievements (ECA): a symbol systems approach. In R. M. Lerner (ed.), *Handbook of Child Psychology, vol. 1, Theoretical Models of Human Development*, pp. 415–466. New York: Wiley.

Gardner, W. and Rogoff, B. (1990) Children's deliberateness of planning according to task circumstances. *Developmental Psychology* 26, 480–487.

Garlick, D. (2003) Integrating brain science research with intelligence research. *Current Directions in Psychological Science* 12(5), 185–189.

Garmezy, N. and Rutter, M. (1985) Acute reactions to stress. In M. Rutter and L. Hersov (eds), *Child and Adolescent Psychiatry: Modern Approaches*. Oxford, UK: Blackwell.

Garner, R. (1987) *Metacognition and Reading Comprehension*. Norwood, NJ: Ablex.

Garnham, A. (1983) What's wrong with story grammars. *Cognition* 15, 145–154.

Garnham, A. (1985) *Psycholinguistics: Central Topics*. London: Methuen.

Garrett, P., Ng'andu, N. and Ferron, J. (1994) Poverty experiences of young children and the quality of their home environment. *Child Development* 65, 331–345.

Gartley, W. and Bernasconi, M. (1967) The concept of death in children. *Journal of Genetic Psychology* 110, 71–85.

Garton, A. (1992) *Social interaction and the development of language and cognition.* Hove, UK: Lawrence Erlbaum Associates Ltd.

Garton, A. (2004) *Exploring Cognitive Development: The Child as Problem-solver.* Oxford, UK: Blackwell.

Gathercole, S. E. (1998) The development of memory. *Journal of Child Psychology and Psychiatry* 39(1), 3–27.

Gathercole, S. E. (1999) Cognitive approaches to the development of short-term memory. *Trends in Cognitive Science* 3(11), 410–419.

Gathercole, S. and Pickering, S. (2000a) Working memory deficits in children with low achievements in the national curriculum at 7 years of age. *British Journal of Educational Psychology* 70, 177–194.

Gathercole, S. and Pickering, S. (2000b) Assessment of working memory in six- and seven-year-old children. *Journal of Educational Psychology* 92, 377–390.

Gathercole, S. E. and Baddeley, A. D. (1989a) The role of phonological memory in normal and disordered language development. In C. Von Euler, I. Lundberg and G. Lennerstrand (eds), *Brain and Reading.* London: Macmillan.

Gathercole, S. E. and Baddeley, A. D. (1989b) Development of vocabulary in children and short-term phonological memory. *Journal of Memory and Language* 28, 200–213.

Gathercole, S. E., Pickering, S. J., Ambridge, B. and Wearing, H. (2004) The structure of working memory from 4 to 15 years of age. *Developmental Psychology* 40(2), 177–190.

Gauvain, M. (1993) The development of spatial thinking in everyday activity. *Developmental Review* 13, 92–121.

Gauvain, M. (2001) *The Social Context of Cognitive Development.* New York: Guilford Press.

Gauvain, M. and Rogoff, B. (1986) The influence of the goal on children's expectations and memory of large-scale space. *Developmental Psychology* 22, 72–77.

Gauvain, M. and Rogoff, B. (1989) Collaborative problem-solving and children's planning skills. *Developmental Psychology* 25, 139–151.

Geary, D. C., Bow-Thomas, C. C., Liu, F. and Siegler, R. S. (1996) Development of arithmetical competencies in Chinese and American children: influence of age, language, and schooling. *Child Development* 67, 2022–2044.

Geary, D. C., Hoard, M. K., Byrd-Craven, J. and De Soto, M. C. (2004) Strategy choices in simple and complex arithmetic: contributions of working memory and counting knowledge for children with mathematical disability. *Journal of Experimental Child Psychology* 88(2), 121–151.

Gelb, I. J. (1963) *A Study of Writing.* Chicago: University of Chicago Press.

Gellatly, A. (1989) The myth of cognitive diagnostics. In A. Gellatly, D. Rogers and J. A. Sloboda (eds), *Cognition and Social Worlds.* Oxford, UK: Clarendon Press.

Gelman, R. (1990) First principles organise attention to and learning about relevant data: number and the animate–inanimate distinction as examples. *Cognitive Science* 14, 79–106.

Gelman, R. (1991) Epigenetic foundations of knowledge structures: initial and transcendent constructions. In S. Carey and R. Gelman (eds), *The Epigenesis of Mind*. Hove, UK: Lawrence Erlbaum Associates Ltd.

Gelman, R. (2000) Domain specificity and variability in cognitive development. *Child Development* 71(4), 854–856.

Gelman, R. and Baillargeon, R. (1983) A review of some Piagetian concepts. In J. H. Flavell and E. Markman (eds), *Handbook of Child Psychology, vol. 3, Cognitive Development*. New York: Wiley.

Gelman, R. and Gallistel, C. R. (1978) *The Child's Understanding of Number*. Cambridge, MA: Harvard University Press.

Gelman, R. and Meck, E. (1983) Preschoolers' counting: principle before skill. *Cognition* 13, 343–359.

Gelman, R. and Meck, E. (1986) The notion of principle: the case of counting. In J. Hiebert (ed.), *Conceptual and Procedural Knowledge: The Case of Mathematics*. Hillsdale, NJ: Lawrence Erlbaum Associates, Inc.

Gelman, R. and Spelke, E. (1981) The development of thoughts about animate and inanimate objects: implications for research on social cognition. In J. H. Flavell and L. Ross (eds), *Social Cognitive Development*. Cambridge, UK: Cambridge University Press.

Gelman, R. and Williams, E. M. (1998) Enabling constraints for cognitive development and language. In D. Kuhn and R. S. Siegler (eds), *Handbook of Child Psychology, vol. 2, Cognition, Perception and Language*. New York: Wiley.

Gelman, S. A. (2003) *The Essential Child: Origins of Essentialism in Everyday Thought*. Oxford, UK: Oxford University Press.

Gelman, S. A. (2004) Psychological essentialism in children. *Trends in Cognitive Sciences* 8(9), 404–409.

Gelman, S. A. and Kremer, K. E. (1991) Understanding natural cause: children's explanations of how objects and their properties originate. *Child Development* 62, 396–414.

Gelman, S. A. and Opfer, J. (2002) Development of the animate–inanimate distinction. In U. Goswami (ed.), *Blackwell Handbook of Cognitive Development*. Oxford, UK: Blackwell.

Gelman, S. A. and O'Reilly, A. W. (1988) Children's inductive inferences within superordinate categories: the role of language and category structure. *Child Development* 59, 876–887.

Gelman, S. A., Taylor, M. G. and Nguyen, S. P. (2004) *Mother–Child Conversations about Gender. Monographs of the Society for Research in Child Development* 69(1), serial no. 275.

Gelman, S. A. and Wellman, H. M. (1991) Insides and essences: early understandings of the non-obvious. *Cognition* 38, 213–244.

Genesee, F. (1989) Early bilingual development: one language or two? *Journal of Child Language* 16(1), 161–179.

Gentner, D. (1977) Children's performance on a spatial analogies task. *Child Development* 48, 1034–1039.

Gentner, D. (1988) Metaphor as structure-mapping: the relational shift. *Child Development* 59, 47–59.

Gentner, D. (1989) The mechanisms of analogical learning. In S. Vosniadou and A. Ortony (eds), *Similarity and Analogical Reasoning*. Cambridge, UK: Cambridge University Press.

Gentner, D. and Gentner, D. R. (1983) Flowing waters or teeming crowds: mental models of electricity. In D. Gentner and A. L. Stevens (eds), *Mental Models*. Hillsdale, NJ: Lawrence Erlbaum Associates, Inc.

Gentner, D. and Stevens, A. L. (eds) (1983) *Mental Models*. Hillsdale, NJ: Lawrence Erlbaum Associates, Inc.

Gentner, D. and Holyoak, J. (1997) Reasoning and learning by analogy: introduction. *American Psychologist* 52, 32–34.

Gentner, D. and Markman, A. B. (1997) Structure mapping in analogy and similarity. *American Psychologist* 52, 45–56.

Gentner, D. and Toupin, C. (1986) Systematicity and surface similarity in the development of analogy. *Cognitive Science* 10, 277–300.

Georghiades, P. (2004a) Making children's conceptions of electricity more durable by means of situated metacognition. *International Journal of Science Education* 26(1), 85–99.

Georghiades, P. (2004b) From the general to the situated: three decades of metacognition. *International Journal of Science Education* 26(3), 365–383.

Gesell, A. (1942) *Wolf Child and Human Child*. London: The Scientific Book Club.

Getzels, J. W. and Csikszentmihalyi, M. (1976) *The Creative Vision: A Longitudinal Study of Problem Finding*. New York: Wiley.

Getzels, J. W. and Jackson, P. W. (1962) *Creativity and Intelligence*. New York: Wiley.

Ghent-Braine, L., Schauble, L., Kugelmass, S. and Winter, A. (1993) Representation of depth by children: spatial strategies and lateral biases. *Developmental Psychology* 29(3), 466–479.

Ghiselin, B. (ed.) (1954) *The Creative Process*. Berkeley: University of California Press.

Gholson, B. and Beilin, H. (1979) A developmental model of human learning. In H. W. Reese and L. P. Lipsitt (eds), *Advances in Child Development and Behavior*, vol. 13. New York: Academic Press.

Gibson, E. J. (1969) *Principles of Perceptual Learning and Development*. New York: Appleton-Century-Crofts.

Gibson, E. J. (1988) Exploratory behaviour in the development of perceiving, acting and the acquiring of knowledge. *Annual Review of Psychology* 39, 1–42.

Gibson, J. J. (1979) *The Ecological Approach to Visual Perception*. Boston: Houghton-Mifflin.

Gick, M. L. and Holyoak, K. J. (1987) The cognitive basis of knowledge transfer. In S. Cormier and J. D. Hagman (eds), *Transfer of Learning: Contemporary Research and Applications*. San Diego, CA: Academic Press.

Giles, H. and St Clair, R. N. (eds) (1985) *Recent Advances in Language, Communication and Social Psychology*. London: Lawrence Erlbaum Associates Ltd.

Giles, J. (2004) High-fat diet is bad for the brain. *Nature News* 26 October 2004. http://www.nature.com/news/2004/041025/pf/041025-11_pf. html

Giles, J. W. and Heyman, G. D. (2005) Young children's beliefs about the relationship between gender and aggressive behavior. *Child Development* 76(1), 107–121.

Gilhooly, K. J. (2004) Working memory and reasoning. In J. P. Leighton and R. J. Sternberg (eds), *The Nature of Reasoning*. Cambridge, UK: Cambridge University Press.

Gilligan, C. (1982) In a different voice: psychological theory and women's development. Cambridge, MA: Harvard University Press.

Gillberg, C. L. (1992) Autism and autistic-like conditions: subclasses among disorders of empathy. *Journal of Child Psychology and Psychiatry* 33, 813–842.

Gilstrap, L. L. and Ceci, S. J. (2005) Reconceptualizing children's suggestibility: bidirectional and temporal properties. *Child Development* 76(1), 40–53.

Ginsburg, H. P. (1977) *Children's Arithmetic: The Learning Process.* New York: Van Nostrand.

Ginsburg, H. P. (ed.) (1983) *The Development of Mathematical Thinking.* New York: Academic Press.

Ginsburg, H. P., Klein, A. and Starkey, P. (1998) The development of children's mathematical thinking: connecting research with practice. In I. E. Siegel and K. A. Renninger (eds), *Handbook of Child Psychology, vol. 4, Child Psychology in Practice.* New York: Wiley.

Girotto, V. (2004) Task understanding. In J. P. Leighton and R. J. Sternberg (eds), *The Nature of Reasoning.* Cambridge, UK: Cambridge University Press.

Girotto, V., Light, P. and Colborn, C. (1988) Pragmatic schemas and conditional reasoning in children. *Quarterly Journal of Experimental Psychology* 40A(3), 469–482.

Glaser, R. (1984) Education and thinking: the role of knowledge. *American Psychologist* 39, 93–104.

Gleason, J. B., Hay, D. and Cain, L. (1989) Social and affective determinants of language acquisition. In M. L. Rice and R. L. Schiefelbusch (eds), *The Teachability of Language.* Baltimore: Brooks.

Glucksberg, S. and Keysar, B. (1990) Understanding metaphorical comparisons: beyond similarity. *Psychological Review* 97(1), 3–18.

Gnepp, J. and Hess, D. L. R. (1986) Children's understanding of verbal and facial display rulers. *Development Psychology* 22, 103–108.

Gnepp, J. and Klayman, J. (1992) Recognition of uncertainty in emotional inferences: reasoning about emotionally equivocal situations. *Developmental Psychology* 28, 145–158.

Gnepp, J., McKee, E. and Domanic, J. A. (1987) Children's use of situational information to infer emotion: understanding emotionally equivocal situations. *Developmental Psychology* 23, 114–123.

Goldberg, S. (2000) *Attachment and development.* London: Arnold.

Goldberg, W. A. and Easterbrooks, M. A. (1984) Role of marital quality in toddler development. *Developmental Psychology* 20, 504–514.

Goldberg, W. A., Greenberger, E. and Nagel, S. K. (1996) Employment and achievement: mother's work involvement in relation to children's achievement behaviours and mother's parenting behaviours. *Child Development* 67, 1512–1527.

Goldin-Meadow, S. and Mylander, C. (1998) Spontaneous sign systems created by deaf children in two cultures. *Nature* 391, 279–281.

Goldman, A. I. (1986) *Epistemology and Cognition.* Cambridge, MA: Harvard University Press.

Goldman, R. and Goldman, J. (1982) *Children's Sexual Thinking.* London: Routledge & Kegan Paul.

Goldman-Rakic, P. S. (1987) Development of cortical circuitry and cognitive function. *Child Development* 58, 601–622.

Golinkoff, R. M., Mervis, C. B. and Hirsh-Pasek, K. (1994) Early object labels –the case for a developmental lexical principles framework. *Journal of Child Language* 21(1), 125–155.

Golomb, C. (2004) *The Child's Creation of a Pictorial World.* Mahwah, NJ: Lawrence Erlbaum Associates, Inc.

Golomb, C. and Galasso, L. (1995) Make believe and reality: explorations of the imaginary realm. *Developmental Psychology* 31, 800–810.

Golomb, C. and Kuersten, R. (1996) On the transition from pretence play to reality: what are the rules of the game? *British Journal of Developmental Psychology* 12, 203–217.

Goodman, G. S. and Goodman, Y. M. (1979) Learning to read is natural. In L. B. Resnick and P. A. Weaver (eds), *Theory and Practice of Early Reading*, vol. 1. Hillsdale, NJ: Lawrence Erlbaum Associates, Inc.

Goodman, G. S. and Haith, M. M. (1987) Memory development and neurophysiology: accomplishments and limitations. *Child Development* 58, 713–717.

Goodnow, J. J. (1973) Compensation arguments on conservation tasks. *Developmental Psychology* 8(1), 140.

Goodnow, J. J. (1977) *Children's Drawing.* London: Fontana.

Goodnow, J. J. (1984) On being judged 'intelligent'. *International Journal of Psychology* 19, 391–406.

Goodnow, J. J. (1990) The socialization of cognition. In J. W. Stigler, R. A. Shweder and G. H. Herdt (eds), *Cultural Psychology: Essays on Comparative Human Development.* Cambridge, UK: Cambridge University Press.

Goody, J. (1977) *The Domestication of the Savage Mind.* Cambridge, UK: Cambridge University Press.

Goody, J. and Watt, I. (1968) The consequences of literacy. In J. Goody (ed.), *Literacy in Traditional Societies.* Cambridge, UK: Cambridge University Press.

Goodyer, I. M. (1990) *Life Experiences, Development and Childhood Psychopathology.* Chichester, UK: Wiley.

Gopnik, A. (1988) Concepts and semantic development as theory change. *Mind and Language* 3(3), 197–216.

Gopnik, A. and Graf, P. (1988) Knowing how you know: young children's ability to identify and remember the sources of their beliefs. *Child Development* 59, 1366–1371.

Gopnik, A. and Slaughter, V. (1991) Young children's understanding of changes in their mental states. *Child Development* 62, 98–110.

Gopnik, A. and Schulz, L. (2004) Mechanisms of theory formation in young children. *Trends in Cognitive Sciences* 8(8), 371–377.

Gordon, E. W. and Armour-Thomas, E. (1991) Culture and cognitive development. In L. Okagaki and R. J. Sternberg (eds), *Directors of Development: Influences on the Development of Children's Thinking.* Hillsdale, NJ: Lawrence Erlbaum Associates, Inc.

Gorman, K. S. and Pollitt, E. (1996) Does schooling buffer the effects of early risk? *Child Development* 67, 314–326.

Gosse, E. (1907) *Father and Son.* London: Heinemann.

Goswami, U. (1986) Children's use of analogy in learning to read: a developmental study. *Journal of Experimental Child Psychology* 42, 73–83.

Goswami, U. (1988a) Orthographic analogies and reading development. *Quarterly Journal of Experimental Psychology* 40A, 239–268.

Goswami, U. (1988b) Children's use of analogy in learning to spell. *British Journal of Developmental Psychology* 6, 21–33.

Goswami, U. (1989) Relational complexity and the development of analogical reasoning. *Cognitive Development* 4, 251–268.

Goswami, U. (1990a) A special link between rhyming skill and the use of orthographic analogies by beginning readers. *Journal of Child Psychology and Psychiatry* 31(2), 301–311.

Goswami, U. (1990b) Phonological priming and orthographic analogies in reading. *Journal of Experimental Child Psychology* 49, 323–340.

Goswami, U. (1991a) Analogical reasoning: what develops? A review of research and theory. *Child Development* 62, 1–22.

Goswami, U. (1991b) Learning about spelling sequences: the role of onsets and rimes in analogies in reading. *Child Development* 62, 1110–1123.

Goswami, U. (1992) *Analogical Reasoning in Children*. Hove, UK: Lawrence Erlbaum Associates Ltd.

Goswami, U. (1995) Transitive relational mappings in 3- and 4-year-olds: the analogy of Goldilocks and the Three Bears. *Child Development* 66, 877–892.

Goswami, U. (1996) Analogical reasoning and cognitive development. *Advances in Child Development and Behaviour* 26, 91–138.

Goswami, U. (1998) *Cognition in Children*. Hove, UK: Psychology Press.

Goswami, U. (2002) Inductive and deductive reasoning. In U. Goswami (ed.), *Blackwell Handbook of Cognitive Development*. Oxford, UK: Blackwell.

Goswami, U. (2004) Neuroscience and education. *British Journal of Educational Psychology* 74, 1–14.

Goswami, U. and Brown, A. L. (1990a) Higher-order structure and relational reasoning: contrasting analogical and thematic relations. *Cognition* 36, 207–226.

Goswami, U. and Brown, A. L. (1990b) Melting chocolate and melting snowmen: analogical reasoning and causal relations. *Cognition* 35, 69–96.

Goswami, U. and Bryant, P. (1990) *Phonological Skills and Learning to Read*. Hove, UK: Lawrence Erlbaum Associates Ltd.

Gottesman, I. I. and Gould, T. D. (2003) The endophenotype concept in psychiatry: etymology and strategic intentions. *American Journal of Psychiatry* 160(4), 636–645.

Gottesman, I. L. and Hanson, D. R. (2005) Human development: biological and genetic processes. *Annual Review of Psychology* 56, 10: 1–10:24.

Gottfried, A. E., Fleming, J. S. and Gottfried, A. W. (1998) Role of cognitively developed stimulating home environment in children's academic intrinsic motivation: a longitudinal study. *Child Development* 69, 1448–1460.

Gottfried, A. W. (ed.) (1984) *Home Environment and Early Cognitive Development: Longitudinal Research*. New York: Academic Press.

Gottfried, A. W. and Gottfried, A. E. (1984) Home environment and cognitive development of young children of middle-socioeconomic-status families. In A. W. Gottfried (ed.), *Home Environment and Early Cognitive Development: Longitudinal Research*. New York: Academic Press.

Gottfried, G. M., Gelman, S. and Schultz, J. (1999) Children's understanding of the brain: from early essentialism to biological theory. *Cognitive Development* 14, 147–174.

Gottlieb, G. (1983) The psychobiological approach to developmental issues. In M. M. Haith and J. J. Campos (eds), *Handbook of Child Psychology*, vol. 2. New York: Wiley.

Gottlieb, G. (1991) Experimental canalization of behavioural development: theory. *Developmental Psychology* 27, 4–13.

Gottlieb, G., Wahlsten, D. and Lickliter, R. (1998) The significance of biology for human development. In W. Damon (ed.), *Handbook of Child Psychology*, vol 1, pp. 233–273. New York: Wiley.

Gould, E., Reeves, A. J., Graziano, M. S. and Gross, C. G. (1999) Neurogenesis in the neocortex of adult primates. *Science* 286, 548–555.

Gould, S. J. (1977) *Ontogeny and Phylogeny*. Cambridge, MA: Harvard University Press.

Gould, S. J. (1984) *The Mismeasure of Man*. Harmondsworth, UK: Penguin Books.

Gould, S. J. (1987) *Time's Arrow, Time's Cycle: Myth and Metaphor in the Discovery of Geological Time*. Cambridge, MA: Harvard University Press.

Granott, N. (2002) How microdevelopment creates macrodevelopment: reiterated sequences, backward transitions, and the zone of current development. In N. Granott and J. Parziale (eds), *Microdevelopment: Transition Processes in Development and Learning*. Cambridge, UK: Cambridge University Press.

Granott, N. and Parziale, J. (eds) (2002) *Microdevelopment: Transition Processes in Development and Learning*. Cambridge, UK: Cambridge University Press.

Grant, K. E., Compos, B. E., Stuhlmacher, A., Thurm, A., McMahon, S. and Halpert, J. (2003) Stressors and child and adolescent psychopathology: moving from markers to mediators of risk. *Psychological Bulletin* 129, 447–466.

Grantham-McGregor, S. (1987) Field studies in early nutrition and later achievement. In J. Dobbing (ed.), *Early Nutrition and Later Achievement*. London: Academic Press.

Grantham-McGregor, S. (2002) Linear growth retardation and cognition. *The Lancet* 359, 542.

Grantham-McGregor, S. and Ani, C. (2001) A review of studies on the effect of iron deficiency on cognitive development in children. *Journal of Nutrition* 131, 649S–668S.

Grantham-McGregor, S., Powell, C., Walker, S. and Chang, S. (1994) The long-term follow-up of severely malnourished children who participated in an intervention program. *Child Development* 63, 428–439.

Grantham-McGregor, S., Schofield, W. and Powell, C. (1987) The development of severely malnourished children who received psychosocial stimulation: six year follow-up. *Pediatrics* 79, 247–254.

Grantham-McGregor, S. M. and Walker, S. P., Chang, S. (2000) Nutritional deficiencies and later behavioural development. *Proceedings of the Nutrition Society* 59(1), 47–54.

Gratch, G., Appel, K. J., Evans, W. F., Le Compte, G. K. and Wright, N. A. (1974) Piaget's Stage IV object concept error: evidence of forgetting or object conception? *Child Development* 45, 71–77.

Graves, D. (1983) *Writing: Teachers and Children at Work*. Exeter, NH: Heinemann.

Gray, E. M. (1991) Analysis of diverging approaches to simple arithmetic. *Educational Studies in Mathematics* 22, 551–574.

Gray, J. A. (1987) The mind–brain identity as a scientific hypothesis: a second look. In C. Blakemore and S. Greenfield (eds), *Mindwaves*. Oxford, UK: Blackwell.

Gray, J. A. (1990) Brain systems that mediate both emotion and cognition. *Cognition and Emotion* 4, 269–288.

Greenfield, P. M. and Lave, J. (1982) Cognitive aspects of formal education. In D. Wagner and H. Stevenson (eds), *Cultural Perspectives on Child Development*. San Francisco: Freeman.

Greenfield, P. M. and Suzuki, L. K. (1998) Culture and human development: implications for parenting, education, pediatrics and mental health. In I. Sigel (ed.), *Handbook of Child Psychology*, vol. 4. New York: Wiley.

Greenfield, S. (1996) *The Human Mind Explained*. London: Cassell.

Greenough, W. T. (1984) Structural correlates of information storage in the mammalian brain: a review and hypothesis. *Trends in Neurosciences* 7, 229–233.

Greenough, W. T. (1986) What's special about development? Thoughts on the bases of experience-sensitive synaptic plasticity. In W. T. Greenough and J. M. Juraska (eds), *Developmental Neuropsychology*. New York: Academic Press.

Greenough, W. T. (1991) Experience as a component of normal development: evolutionary considerations. *Developmental Psychology* 27, 14–17.

Greenough, W. T. and Black, J. E. (1992) Induction of brain structure by experience: substrates for cognitive development. In M. Gunnar and C. A. Nelson (eds), *Developmental Behavioural Neuroscience*. Minnesota Symposium on Child Psychology, vol. 24. Hillsdale, NJ: Lawrence Erlbaum Associates, Inc.

Greenough, W. T., Black, J. E. and Wallace, C. S. (1987) Experience and brain development. *Child Development* 58, 539–559.

Greenough, W. T. and Juraska, J. M. (eds) (1986) *Developmental Neuropsychology*. New York: Academic Press.

Gregg, P., Washbrook, E., Propper, C., Burgess, S. and Meadows, S. *Up To 5. Draft Report to DfES. Preliminary results under project: Understanding the Impact of Poverty on Children of the 90s*. Prepared by CMPO Research Team, University of Bristol.

Gregory, R. L. (1987) In defence of artificial intelligence – reply to John Searle. In C. Blakemore and S. Greenfield (eds), *Mindwaves*. Oxford, UK: Blackwell.

Gregory, R. L. (ed.) (1988) *The Oxford Companion to the Mind*. Oxford, UK: Oxford University Press.

Grice, H. P. (1975) Logic and conversation. In P. Cole and J. L. Morgan (eds), *Syntax and Semantics, vol. 3, Speech Acts*. New York: Academic Press.

Griffin, D. R. (1976) *The Question of Animal Awareness*. New York: Rockefeller University Press.

Griffiths, M. and Wells, G. (1983) Who writes what, and why. In B. Kroll and G. Wells (eds), *Explorations in the Development of Writing*. Chichester, UK: Wiley.

Grigorenko, E. L. (2001) Developmental dyslexia: an update on genes, brains and the environment. *Journal of Child Psychology and Psychiatry and Allied Disciplines* 42, 91–125.

Grigorenko, E. L. (2003) Expertise and mental disabilities: bridging the unbridge-able? In R. L. Sternberg and E. L. Grigorenko (eds), *The Psychology of Abilities, Competencies and Expertise*. Cambridge, UK: Cambridge University Press.

Grigson, J. (1980) *Jane Grigson's Vegetable Book*. Harmondsworth, UK: Penguin Books.

Grize, J.-B. (1987) Operatory logic. In B. Inhelder, D. de Caprona and A. Cornu-Wells (eds), *Piaget Today*. Hillsdale, NJ: Lawrence Erlbaum Associates, Inc.

Groen, G. J. and Parkman, J. M. (1972) A chronometric analysis of simple addition. *Psychological Review* 97, 329–343.

Grotevant, H. and Carlson, C. (1987) Family interaction coding systems: a descriptive review. *Family Process* 26, 49–74.

Gruneberg, M. M., Morris, P. E. and Sykes, R. N. (eds) *Practical Aspects of Memory*, vol. 2. Chichester, UK: Wiley.

Guajardo, N. R. and Turley-Ames, K. J. (2004) Preschoolers' generation of different types of counterfactual statements and theory of mind understanding. *Cognitive Development* 19, 53–80.

Guilford, J. P. (1967) *The Nature of Human Intelligence*. New York: McGraw-Hill.

Gunn, P. (1985) Speech and language. In D. Lane and B. Stratford (eds), *Current Approaches to Down's Syndrome*. London: Holt, Rinehart & Winston.

Gunnar, M. (1998) Quality of early care and buffering of neuroendocrine stress reactions: potential effects on the developing human brain. *Preventive Medicine* 27, 208–231.

Gunnar, M. and Maratsos, M. (eds) (1992) *Modularity and Constraints in Language and Cognition*. Minnesota Symposium on Child Psychology, vol. 25. Hillsdale, NJ: Lawrence Erlbaum Associates, Inc.

Gunnar, M. and Nelson, C. A. (eds) (1992) *Behavioral Developmental Neuroscience*. Minnesota Symposium on Child Psychology, vol. 24. Hillsdale, NJ: Lawrence Erlbaum Associates, Inc.

Gutfreund, M. (1989) *Bristol Language Development Scales*. Windsor, UK: NFER-Nelson.

Haddon, M. (2003) *The Curious Incident of the Dog in the Night-time*. London: Jonathan Cape.

Haden, C. (1998) Reminiscing with different children: relating maternal style consistency and sibling similarity in talk about the past. *Developmental Psychology* 34, 99–114.

Haden, C. A., Haine, R. A. and Fivush, R. (1997) Developing narrative structure in parent-child reminiscing across the preschool years. *Developmental Psychology* 33(2), 295–307.

Haden, C., Ornstein, P. A., Eckerman, C. O. and Didow, S. M. (2001) Mother–child conversational interactions as events unfold: linkages to subsequent remembering. *Child Development* 72, 1016–1031.

Hagen, J. W. and Hale, G. H. (1973) The development of attention in children. *Nebraska Symposium on Motivation*, 1973. Lincoln: University of Nebraska Press.

Hagen, J. W., Hargrove, S. and Ross, W. (1973) Prompting and rehearsal in short-term memory. *Child Development* 44, 201–204.

Hagerman, R. J. (1992) Fragile X syndrome: advances and controversy. *Journal of Child Psychology and Psychiatry* 33, 1127–1140.

Haight, W. and Miller, P. J. (1992) The development of everyday pretend play:

a longitudinal study of mothers' participation. *Merrill-Palmer Quarterly* 38, 331–349.

Haith, M. M. and Campos, J. (eds) (1983) *Handbook of Child Psychology, vol. 2, Infancy and Development Psychobiology.* New York: Wiley.

Hala, S. and Chandler, M. (1996) The role of strategic planning in accessing false-belief understanding. *Child Development* 67, 2948–2966.

Hala, S., Chandler, M. and Fritz, A. S. (1991) Fledgling theories of mind: deception as a marker of three-year-olds' understanding of false beliefs. *Child Development* 62, 83–97.

Halford, G. S. (1993) Children's understanding: the development of mental models. Hillsdale, NJ: Lawrence Erlbaum Associates, Inc.

Halford, G. S. (2002) Information-processing models of cognitive development. In U. Goswami (ed.), *Blackwell Handbook of Cognitive Development.* Oxford, UK: Blackwell.

Hall, N. (1987) *The Emergence of Literacy.* London: Hodder & Stoughton.

Hall, W. S. (1989) Reading comprehension. *American Psychologist* 44, 157–161.

Halliday, M. A. K. (1975) *Learning How to Mean.* London: Edward Arnold.

Halverson, C. F. and Waldrop, M. F. (1976) Relations between preschool activity and aspects of intellectual and social behaviour at age 7½. *Developmental Psychology* 12, 107–112.

Hamlyn, D. W. (1978) *Experience and the Growth of Understanding.* London: Routledge & Kegan Paul.

Hamlyn, D. W. (1990) *In and Out of the Box: On the Philosophy of Cognition.* Oxford, UK: Blackwell.

Hammen, C. (2003) Risk and protective factors for children of depressed parents. In S. S. Luthar (ed.), *Resilience and Vulnerability: Adaptation in the Context of Childhood Adversities.* Cambridge, UK: Cambridge University Press.

Hammen, C., Burge, D. and Stansbury, K. (1990) Relationship of mother and child variables to child outcomes in a high-risk sample: a causal modeling analysis. *Developmental Psychology* 26, 24–30.

Hammen, C., Gordon, D., Burge, D., Adrian, C., Jaenicke, C. and Hiroto, D. (1987) Maternal affective disorders, illness and stress: risk for children's psycho-pathology. *American Journal of Psychiatry* 144, 736–741.

Hampson, S. E. (1982) *The Construction of Personality.* London: Routledge & Kegan Paul.

Hampton, J. A. (1990) *Concepts.* London: Lawrence Erlbaum Associates Ltd.

Han, J. J., Leichtman, M. D. and Wang, Q. (1998) Autobiographical memory in Korean, Chinese and American children. *Developmental Psychology* 34, 701–713.

Han, W.-J. (2005) Maternal nonstandard work schedules and child cognitive outcomes. *Child Development* 76(1), 137–154.

Haney, M. and Hill, J. (2004) Relationships between parent-teaching activities and emergent literacy in preschool children. *Early Child Development and Care* 174(3), 215–228.

Hannon, P. (1989) How should parental involvement in the teaching of reading be evaluated? *British Educational Research Journal* 15, 33–40.

Hansen, J. and Bowey, J. A. (1992) Orthographic rimes as functional units of reading in fourth grade children. *Australian Journal of Psychology* 44, 37–44.

Harbeck, C. and Peterson, L. (1992) Elephants dancing in my head: a developmental approach to children's concepts of specific pains. *Child Development* 63, 138–149.

Hargreaves, D. J. (1986) *The Developmental Psychology of Music.* Cambridge, UK: Cambridge University Press.

Harper, L. V. and Huie, K. S. (1987) Relations among preschool children's adult and peer contacts and later academic achievement. *Child Development* 58, 1051–1065.

Harrington, D. M., Block, J. H. and Block, J. (1983) Predicting creativity in preadolescence from divergent thinking in early childhood. *Journal of Personality and Social Psychology* 45, 609–623.

Harris, J. R. (1998) *The Nurture Assumption.* London: Bloomsbury.

Harris, M. and Hatano, G. (eds) (1999) *Learning to Read and Write: A Cross-linguistic Perspective.* Cambridge, UK: Cambridge University Press.

Harris, P. L. (1983a) Infant cognition. In M. M. Haith and J. J. Campos (eds), *Handbook of Child Psychology,* vol. 2. New York: Wiley.

Harris, P. L. (1983b) The child as psychologist. In M. Donaldson, R. Grieve and C. Pratt (eds), *Early Childhood Development and Education.* Oxford, UK: Blackwell.

Harris, P. L. (1983c) Children's understanding of the link between situation and emotion. *Journal of Experimental Child Psychology* 36, 490–509.

Harris, P. L. (1989) *Child and Emotion: The Development of Psychological Understanding.* Oxford, UK: Blackwell.

Harris, P. L. (1990) Children's understanding of mixed emotions. In A. de Ribaupierre (ed.), *Transition Mechanisms in Child Development: the Longitudinal Perspective.* Cambridge, UK: Cambridge University Press.

Harris, P. L. (1994) Unexpected, impossible and magical events: children's reactions to causal violations. *British Journal of Developmental Psychology* 12, 1–8.

Harris, P. L., Brown, E., Marriott, C., Whittall, S. and Harmer, S. (1991) Monsters, Ghosts and Witches – Testing the limits of the fantasy–reality distinction in young children. *British Journal of Developmental Psychology* 9, 105–123 Part 1.

Harris, P. L., Donnelly, K., Guz, G. R. and Pitt-Watson, R. (1986) Children's understanding of the distinction between real and apparent emotion. *Child Development* 57, 895–909.

Harris, P. L. and Gross, D. (1988) Children's understanding of real and apparent emotions. In J. W. Astington, P. L. Harris and D. R. Olson (eds), *Developing Theories of Mind.* Cambridge, UK: Cambridge University Press.

Harris, P. L. and Lipian, M. S. (1989) Understanding emotion and experiencing emotion. In C. Saarni and P. L. Harris (eds), *Children's Understanding of Emotion.* Cambridge, UK: Cambridge University Press.

Harris, P. L. and Nunez, M. (1996) Understanding of permission rules by preschool children. *Child Development* 67, 1572–1591.

Hart, B. and Risley, T. R. (1995) *Meaningful Differences in the Everyday Experience of Young American Children.* Baltimore: Brookes.

Hart, B. and Risley, T. R. (1999) *The Social World of Children Learning to Talk.* Baltimore: Paul Brookes.

Hart, R. A. (1979) *Children's Experience of Place: A Developmental Study.* New York: Irvington Press.

Harter, S. (1998) The development of self-representations. In N. Eisenberg (ed.),

Handbook of Child Psychology, vol. 3, Social, Emotional and Personality Development. New York: Wiley.

Harter, S. (1999) *The Construction of the Self: A Developmental Perspective.* London: Guilford Press.

Harter, S. and Buddin, B. J. (1987) Children's understanding of the simultaneity of two emotions: a five-stage developmental acquisition sequence. *Developmental Psychology* 23, 388–399.

Harter, S. and Chao, C. (1992) The role of competence in children's creation of imaginary friends. *Merrill-Palmer Quarterly* 38, 350–363.

Hartlage, L. C. and Telzrow, C. F. (eds) (1985) *The Neuropsychology of Individual Differences.* New York: Plenum Press.

Hartlage, P. L. (1985) A survey of developmental neurologic conditions: implications for individual neuropsychological differences. In L. C. Hartlage and C. F. Telzrow (eds), *The Neuropsychology of Individual Differences.* New York: Plenum Press.

Hartley, D. (1985) *Understanding the Primary School.* London: Croom Helm.

Harvey, P. G. (1984) Lead and children's health: recent research and future questions. *Journal of Child Psychology and Psychiatry* 25, 517–522.

Hasselhorn, M. (1992) Task dependency and the role of category typicality and metamemory in the development of an organisational strategy. *Child Development* 63, 202–214.

Hatano, G., Siegler, R. S., Richards, D. D., Inagaki, K., Stavy, R. and Wax, N. (1993) The development of biological knowledge: a multi-national study. *Cognitive Development* 8, 47–62.

Hatcher, P. J., Hulme, C. and Snowling, M. (2004) Explicit phonological training combined with reading instruction helps young children at risk of reading failure. *Journal of Child Psychology and Psychiatry and Allied Disciplines* 45, 338–358.

Haugaard, J. J. and Hazan, C. (2003) Adoption as a natural experiment. *Development and Psychopathology* 15(4), 909–926.

Haugeland, J. (1985) *Artificial Intelligence: The Very Idea.* Cambridge, MA: MIT Press.

Hawkins, T., Pea, R. D., Glick, J. and Scribner, S. (1984) 'Merds that laugh don't like mushrooms': evidence for deductive reasoning by preschoolers. *Developmental Psychology* 20, 584–594.

Hayes, B. K. and Younger, K. (2004) Category-use effects in children. *Child Development* 75(6), 1719–1732.

Hayes, J. R. (2004) A new framework for understanding cognition and affect in writing. In R. B. Ruddell and N. J. Unrau (eds), *Theoretical Models and Processes of Reading.* Newark, DE: International Reading Association.

Hayne, H. (2004) Infant memory development: implications for childhood amnesia. *Developmental Review* 24(1), 33–73.

Hayward, C. (1982) *Literary theme development in the nursery classroom.* Unpublished M.Ed. thesis, University of Bristol.

Heath, S. B. (1982) What no bedtime story means. *Language in Society* 11, 49–76.

Heath, S. B. (1983) *Ways with Words.* Cambridge, UK: Cambridge University Press.

Heath, S. B. (1986) What no bedtime story means: narrative skills at home and at school. In B. Schieffelin and E. Ochs (eds), *Language-Socialisation across*

Cultures. Cambridge, UK: Cambridge University Press (originally published 1982 in *Language in Society* 11, 49–76).

Heath, S. B. (1989) The learner as cultural member. In M. L. Rice and R. L. Schiefelbusch (eds), *Teachability of Language*. Baltimore: Brookes.

Heath, S. B. (2000) Linguistics in the study of language in education. *Harvard Educational Review* 70(1), 49–59.

Heath, S. B. (2004) The children of Trackton's children: spoken and written language in social change. In R. B. Ruddell and N. Unrau (eds), *Theoretical Models and Processes of Reading*. Newark, DE: International Reading Association.

Heckhausen, J. (1987) Balancing for weaknesses and challenging developmental potential: a longitudinal study of mother–infant dyads in apprenticeship interactions. *Developmental Psychology* 23, 762–770.

Hejmadi, A., Rozin, P. and Siegal, M. (2004) Once in contact, always in contact: conceptions of essence and purification in Hindu Indian and American children. *Developmental Psychology* 40(4), 467–476.

Henderson, L. (1982) *Orthography and Word Recognition in Reading*. London: Academic Press.

Hendrickson, A. E. (1982) The biological basis of intelligence: theory. In H. J. Eysenck (ed.), *A Model for Intelligence*, Berlin, Germany: Springer-Verlag.

Hendrickson, D. E. (1982) The biological basis of intelligence: measurement. In H. J. Eysenck (ed.), *A Model for Intelligence*. Berlin, Germany: Springer-Verlag.

Hendrickson, D. E. and Hendrickson, A. E. (1980) The biological basis of individual differences in intelligence. *Personality and Individual Differences* 1, 3–33.

Henn, H. (1987) The National Writing Project in Manchester. *Greater Manchester Primary Contact* 4(3).

Hermelin, B. (2001) *Bright Splinters of the Mind*. London: Jessica Kingsley.

Hermelin, B. and O'Connor, N. (1990) Art and accuracy: the drawing ability of idiot-savants. *Journal of Child Psychology and Psychiatry* 31(2), 217–228.

Heron, J., O'Connor, T. G., Evans, J., Golding, J., Glover, V. and ALSPAC Study Team (2004) The course of anxiety and depression through pregnancy and the postpartum in a community sample. *Journal of Affective Disorders* 80, 65–73.

Hespos, S. J. and Spelke, E. S. (2004) Precursors to spatial language. *Nature* 430, 453–456.

Hess, R. D., Holloway, S. D., Dickson, W. P. and Price, G. G. (1984) Maternal variables as predictors of children's school readiness and later achievement in vocabulary and mathematics in sixth grade. *Child Development* 55, 1902–1912.

Hess, R. D. and Shipman, V. C. (1965) Early experience and the socialisation of cognitive modes in children. *Child Development* 36, 869–886.

Hewstone, M. (1989) *Causal Attribution: From Cognitive Processes to Collective Beliefs*. Oxford, UK: Blackwell.

Heyman, G. D. and Dweck, C. S. (1998) Children's thinking about traits: implications for judgements of self and others. *Child Development* 64, 391–403.

Heyman, G. D. and Gelman, S. A. (2000) Beliefs about the origin of human psychological traits. *Developmental Psychology* 36, 663–678.

Heyman, G. D. and Legare, C. H. (2004) Children's beliefs about gender differences in the academic and social domains. *Sex Roles* 50(3–4), 227–239.

Hickling, A. K. and Wellman, H. (2001) The emergence of children's causal explanations and theories: evidence from everyday conversation. *Developmental Psychology* 37, 668–683.

Hiebert, J. (ed.) (1986) *Conceptual and Procedural Knowledge: the Case of Mathematics.* Hillsdale, NJ: Lawrence Erlbaum Associates, Inc.

Hiebert, J. (1988) A theory of developing competence with written mathematical symbols. *Educational Studies in Mathematics* 19(3), 333–355.

Hiebert, J. and Lefevre, P. (1986) Conceptual and procedural knowledge in mathematics: an introductory analysis. In J. Hiebert (ed.), *Conceptual and Procedural Knowledge: The Case of Mathematics.* Hillsdale, NJ: Lawrence Erlbaum Associates, Inc.

Hiebert, J. and Wearne, D. (1992) Links between teaching and learning place value with understanding in the first grade. *Journal for Research in Mathematics Education* 23, 68–122.

Hiebert, J. and Wearne, D. (1996) Instruction, understanding and skill in multidigit addition and subtraction. *Cognition and Instruction* 14, 251–283.

Hill, E. L. and Frith, U. (2003) Understanding autism: insights from mind and brain. *Philosophical Transactions of the Royal Society of London* B358, 281–289.

Hill, N. E. and Taylor, L. C. (2004) Parental school involvement and children's academic achievement. *Current Directions in Psychological Science* 13(2), 161–164.

Hinde, R. A. (1982) *Ethology.* London: Fontana.

Hinde, R. A. (1987) *Individuals, Relationship and Culture: Links between Ethology and the Social Sciences.* Cambridge, UK: Cambridge University Press.

Hinde, R. A., Perret-Clermont, A.-N. and Stevenson-Hinde, J. (eds) (1985) *Social Relationships and Cognitive Development.* Oxford, UK: Clarendon Press.

Hindley, C. B. (1965) Stability and change in abilities up to five years: group trends. *Journal of Child Psychology and Psychiatry* 6, 85–100.

Hindley, C. B. and Owen, C. F. (1978) The extent of individual change in IQ for ages between 6 months to 17 years, in a British longitudinal sample. *Journal of Child Psychology and Psychiatry* 19, 329–350.

Hines, M. and Shipley, C. (1984) Prenatal exposure to diethyl-stilbestrol (DES) and the development of sexually dimorphic cognitive abilities and cerebral lateralisation. *Developmental Psychology* 20, 81–94.

Hirsh-Pasek, K. and Golinkoff, R. (1996) *The Origins of Grammar.* Cambridge, MA: MIT Press.

Ho, C. S.-H. and Bryant, P. E. (1997a) Phonological skills are important in learning to read Chinese. *Developmental Psychology* 33, 946–951.

Ho, C. S.-H. and Bryant, P. E. (1997b) Learning to read Chinese beyond the logographic phase. *Reading Research Quarterly* 32, 276–289.

Ho, C. S.-H., Chan, D. W. O., Tsang, S. M. and Lee, S. H. (2002) The cognitive profile and multiple deficit hypothesis in Chinese developmental dyslexia. *Developmental Psychology* 38, 543–553.

Ho, C. S.-H. and Fuson, K. C. (1998) Children's knowledge of teen quantities as tens and ones: comparison of Chinese, British, and American kindergarteners. *Journal of Educational Psychology* 90, 536–544.

Hobson, P. (2002) *The Cradle of Thought.* London: Macmillan.

Hobson, R. P. (1990) On acquiring knowledge about people and the capacity to pretend: response to Leslie (1987). *Psychological Review* 91(1), 114–121.

Hobson, R. P. (1991) Against the theory of 'theory of mind'. *British Journal of Developmental Psychology* 9, 33–51.

Hodapp, R. M., Goldfield, E. G. and Boyatzis, C. J. (1984) The use and effectiveness of maternal scaffolding in mother–infant games. *Child Development* 55, 772–781.

Hodges, R. M. and French, L. A. (1988) The effect of class and collection labels on cardinality, class-inclusion and number conservation tasks. *Child Development* 59, 1387–1396.

Hofer, M. A. (1987) Early social relationships: a psychobiologist's view. *Child Development* 58, 633–647.

Hoff, E. (2003) The specificity of environmental influence: socio-economic status affects early vocabulary development via maternal speech. *Child Development* 74, 1368–1378.

Hoff, E., Laursen, B. and Tardiff, T. (2002) Socioeconomic status and parenting. In M. H. Bornstein (ed.), *Handbook of Parenting*. Mahwah, NJ: Lawrence Erlbaum Associates, Inc.

Hoff, E. and Naigles, L. (2002) How children use input to acquire a lexicon. *Child Development* 73(2), 418–433.

Hoff-Ginsburg, E. (1986) Function and structure in maternal speech: their relation to the child's development of syntax. *Developmental Psychology* 22, 155–163.

Hoffman, M. (1991) Unraveling the genetics of Fragile X syndrome. *Science* 252, 1070.

Hofstadter, D. R. (1979) *Godel, Escher, Bach: An Eternal Golden Braid*. Harmondsworth, UK: Penguin Books.

Hogrefe, G.-J., Wimmer, H. and Perner, J. (1986) Ignorance vs. false belief: a developmental lag in attribution of epistemic states. *Child Development* 57, 567–582.

Holland, J., Holyoak, K. J., Nisbett, R. E. and Thagard, P. R. (1986) *Induction: Processes of Inference, Learning and Discovery*. Cambridge, MA: MIT Press.

Hollich, G., Hirsh-Pasek, K., Golinkoff, R. M., Brand, R. J., Brown, E., Chung, H., Hennon, E. A. and Rocori, C. (2000) Breaking the language barrier: an emergentist coalition model for the origins of word learning. *Monographs of the Society for Research on Child Development* 65, serial no. 262.

Holyoak, K. J. and Nisbett, R. E. (1988) Induction. In R. J. Sternberg and E. E. Smith (eds), *The Psychology of Human Thought*. Cambridge, UK: Cambridge University Press.

Honderich, T. (1987) Mind, brain and self-conscious mind. In C. Blakemore and S. Greenfield (eds), *Mindwaves*. Oxford, UK: Blackwell.

Horn, J. L. (1968) Organisation of abilities and the development of intelligence. *Psychological Review* 75, 242–259.

Horn, J. L. (1970) Organisation of data on life-span development of human abilities. In L. R. Goulet and P. B. Baltes (eds), *Life-span Developmental Psychology: Research and Theory*. New York: Academic Press.

Horn, J. M. (1983) The Texas Adoption Project: adopted children and their intellectual resemblance to biological and adoptive parents. *Child Development* 54, 268–277.

Horn, W. F. and Packard, T. (1985) Early identification of learning problems: a meta-analysis. *Journal of Educational Psychology* 77, 597–607.

Hotopf, W. H. N. (1977) An examination of Piaget's theory of perception. In B. A. Geber (ed.), *Piaget and Knowing: Studies in Genetic Epistemology.* London: Routledge & Kegan Paul.

House, B. J. (1989) Some current issues on children's selective attention. In H. W. Reese (ed.), *Advances in Child Development and Behavior*, vol. 21. New York: Academic Press.

Hoving, K. L., Spencer, T., Robb, K. Y. and Schulte, D. (1978) Developmental changes in visual information processing. In P. A. Ornstein (ed.), *Memory Development in Children.* Hillsdale, NJ: Lawrence Erlbaum Associates, Inc.

Howard, R. W. (2001) Searching the real world for signs of rising population intelligence. *Personality and Individual Differences* 30, 1039–1058.

Howe, C., Tolmie, A. and Rodgers, C. (1992) The acquisition of conceptual knowledge in science by primary schoolchildren: group interaction and the understanding of motion down an incline. *British Journal of Developmental Psychology* 10, 113–130.

Howe, M. J. A. (1984) *A Teacher's Guide to the Psychology of Learning.* Oxford, UK: Blackwell.

Howe, M. J. A. (1989a) Separate skills or general intelligence: the autonomy of human abilities. *British Journal of Educational Psychology* 59, 351–360.

Howe, M. J. A. (1989b) Letter. *The Psychologist* 2(6), 244.

Howe, M. J. A. (1989c) *Fragments of Genius: Idiots Savants and the Psychological Investigation of Remarkable Feats by Mentally Retarded Individuals.* London: Routledge.

Howe, M. J. A., Davidson, J. W. and Sloboda, J. A. (1998) Innate talents: reality or myth? *Behavioral and Brain Sciences* 21(3), 399–442.

Howe, M. J. A. and Smith, J. (1988) Calendar calculating in 'idiots savants': how do they do it? *British Journal of Psychology* 79, 371–386.

Howe, M. L., Brainerd, C. J. and Kingma, J. (1985) Storage–retrieval processes of normal and learning-disabled children: a stages-of-learning analysis of picture–word effects. *Child Development* 56, 1120–1133.

Howe, M. L. and Courage, M. L. (1997) The emergence and early development of autobiographical memory. *Psychological Review* 104, 499–523.

Howe, M. L. and Courage, M. L. (1993) On resolving the enigma of infantile amnesia. *Psychological Bulletin* 113(2), 305–326.

Howe, M. L. and Courage, M. L. (eds) (2004) The nature and consequences of very early memory development. *Developmental Review* 24(1), 1–158.

Howe, M. L., Cicchetti, D., Toth, S. L. and Cerrito, B. M. (2004) True and false memories in maltreated children. *Child Development* 75(5), 1402–1417.

Howe, M. L., O'Sullivan, J. T., Brainerd, C. J. and Kingma, J. (1989) Localizing the development of ability differences in organised memory. *Contemporary Educational Psychology* 14, 336–356.

Howe, N. and Rinaldi, C. M. (2004) You be the big sister': Maternal–preschooler discourse, perspective-taking, and sibling caretaking. *Infant and Child Development* 13, 217–234.

Howley, M. and Howe, C. (2004) Social interaction and cognitive growth: an examination through the role-taking skills of deaf and hearing children. *British Journal of Developmental Psychology* 22, 219–243.

Huang, H. S. and Hanley, J. R. (1995) Phonological awareness and visual skills in learning to read Chinese and English. *Cognition* 54, 73–98.

Hubbs-Tait, L., Culp, A. M., Culp, R. E. and Miller, C. E. (2002) Relation of maternal cognitive stimulation, emotional support, and intrusive behavior during Head Start to children's kindergarten cognitive abilities. *Child Development* 73(2), 110–131.

Huber, S., Krist, H. and Wilkening, F. (2003) Judgment and action in speed adjustment tasks: experiments in a virtual environment. *Developmental Science* 6(2), 197–210.

Hudson, L. (1970) The question of creativity. In P. E. Vernon (ed.), *Creativity*. Harmondsworth, UK: Penguin Books.

Hudspeth, W. J. and Pribram, K. H. (1990) Stages of brain and cognitive maturation. *Journal of Educational Psychology* 82, 881–884.

Huffman, M. A. and Hirata, S. (2004) An experimental study of leaf swallowing in captive chimpanzees: insights into the origin of a self-medicative behaviour and the role of social learning. *Primates* 45, 113–118.

Hughes, C. and Cutting, A. L. (1999) Nature, nurture, and individual differences in early understanding of mind. *Psychological Science* 10, 429–432.

Hughes, M. (1983) What is difficult about learning arithmetic? In M. Donaldson, R. Grieve and C. Pratt (eds), *Early Childhood Development and Education*. Oxford, UK: Blackwell.

Hughes, M. (1986) *Children and Number: Difficulties in Learning Mathematics*. Oxford, UK: Blackwell.

Hughes, M. and Donaldson, M. (1979) The use of hiding games for studying the coordination of viewpoints. *Educational Review* 31, 133–140.

Hughes, R. (1987) *The Fatal Shore*. London: Collins Harvill.

Hulme, C. (1987) Reading retardation. In J. R. Beech and A. M. Colley (eds), *Cognitive Approaches to Reading*. Chichester, UK: Wiley.

Hulme, C., Thomson, N., Muir, C. and Lawrence, A. (1984) Speech rate and the development of short-term memory span. *Journal of Experimental Child Psychology* 38, 241–253.

Humphrey, N. (1976) The social function of intellect. In P. Bateson and R. Hinde (eds), *Growing Points in Ethology*. Cambridge, UK: Cambridge University Press.

Humphrey, N. (1983) *Consciousness Regained: Chapters in the Development of the Mind*. Oxford, UK: Oxford University Press.

Hundeide, K. (1985) The tacit background of children's judgements. In J. V. Wertsch (ed.), *Culture, Communication and Cognition*. Cambridge, UK: Cambridge University Press.

Hunt, E. B. (1978) Mechanisms of verbal ability. *Psychological Review* 85, 109–130.

Hunt, E. B. (1983) On the nature of intelligence. *Science* 219, 141–146.

Hunt, E. B., Lunneborg, C. and Lewis, J. (1975) What does it mean to be high verbal? *Cognitive Psychology* 7, 194–227.

Huston, A. C. and Wright, J. C. (1998a) Mass media and children's development. In I. E. Siegel and K. A. Renniger (eds), *Handbook of Child Psychology, vol. 4, Child Psychology in Practice*. New York: Wiley.

Huston, A. C., McLoyd, V. C. and Garcia Coll, C. (eds) (1994) Children in poverty. *Child Development* 65(2), special issue.

Hutt, J., Tyler, S., Hutt, C. and Christopherson, H. (1989) *Play, Exploration and Learning: A Natural History of the Preschool.* London: Routledge.

Huttenlocher, J. (1998) Language input and language growth. *Preventive Medicine* 27, 195–199.

Huttenlocher, J. and Burke, D. (1976) Why does memory span increase with age? *Cognitive Psychology* 8, 1–31.

Huttenlocher, J., Levine, S. and Vevea, J. (1998) Environmental input and cognitive growth: a study using time period comparisons. *Child Development* 69, 1012–1029.

Huttenlocher, J., Newcombe, N. and Vasukyeva, M. (1999) Spatial scaling in young children. *Psychological Science* 10, 393–398.

Hyltenstam, K. and Obler, L. K. (1989) *Bilingualism across the Lifespan.* Cambridge, UK: Cambridge University Press.

Inagaki, K. and Hatano, G. (2004) Vitalistic causality in young children's naïve biology. *Trends in Cognitive Sciences* 8(9), 356–362.

Ingram, N. and Butterworth, G. (1989) The young child's representation of depth in drawing: process and product. *Journal of Experimental Child Psychology* 47, 356–369.

Inhelder, B. and Piaget, J. (1958) *The Growth of Logical Thinking from Childhood to Adolescence.* New York: Basic Books.

Inhelder, B. and Piaget, J. (1964) *The Early Growth of Logic in the Child.* London: Routledge.

Inhelder, B. and Piaget, J. (1973) *Memory and Intelligence.* London: Routledge & Kegan Paul.

Inhelder, B. and Piaget, J. (1979) Procédures et structures. *Archives de Psychologie* 47, 165–176.

International Human Genome Sequencing Consortium (2001) Initial sequencing and analysis of the human genome. *Nature* 409, 860–921.

International Human Genome Sequencing Consortium (2004) Finishing the euchromatic sequence of the human genome. *Nature* 431, 931–945.

Isbell, B. J. and McKee, L. (1980) Society's cradle: an anthropological perspective on the socialisation of cognition. In J. Sants (ed.), *Developmental Psychology and Society.* London: Macmillan.

Istomina, Z. M. (1975) The development of voluntary memory in preschool-age children. *Soviet Psychology* 13, 5–64.

Ivanovic, D. M., Leiva, B. P., Perez, H. T., Inzunza, N. B., Almagia, A. F., Toro, T. D., Urrutia, M. S., Cervilla, J. O. and Bosch, E. D. (2000) Long-term effects of severe undernutrition during the first year of life on brain development and learning in Chilean high-school graduates. *Nutrition* 16, 1056–1063.

Jacobs, J. E., Lanza, S., Osgood, D. W., Eccles, J. S. and Wigfield, A. (2002) Changes in children's self-competence and values: gender and domain differences across grades one through twelve. *Child Development* 73(2), 509–527.

Jacobsen, T. and Hofmann, V. (1997) Children's attachment representations: longitudinal relations to school behavior and academic competency in middle childhood and adolescence. *Developmental Psychology* 33, 703–710.

Jacobson, J. L., Jacobson, S. W., Padgett, R. J., Brumitt, G. A. and Billings, R. L. (1992) Effects of prenatal PCB exposure on cognitive processing efficiency and sustained attention. *Developmental Psychology* 28, 297–307.

Jacobson, J. L., Jacobson, S. W., Schwartz, P. M., Fein, G. G. and Dowler, J. K. (1984) Prenatal exposure to an environmental toxin: a test of the multiple effects model. *Developmental Psychology* 20, 523–532.

Jacobson, J. L. and Wille, D. E. (1986) The influence of attachment pattern on developmental changes in peer interaction from the toddler to the preschool period. *Child Development* 57, 338–347.

Jacobvitz, D. and Sroufe, L. A. (1987) The early caregiver–child relationship and attention-deficit disorder with hyperactivity in kindergarten: a prospective study. *Child Development* 58, 1496–1504.

Jaffee, S. and Hyde, J. S. (2000) Gender differences in moral orientation: a meta-analysis. *Psychological Bulletin* 126(5), 703–726.

Jager, S. and Wilkening, F. (2001) Development of cognitive averaging: when light and light makes dark. *Journal of Experimental Child Psychology* 79(4), 323–345.

Jahoda, G. (1979) The construction of economic reality by some Glaswegian children. *European Journal of Social Psychology* 9, 115–127.

Jahoda, G. (1984) The development of thinking about socio-economic systems. In H. Tajfel (ed.), *The Social Dimension*, vol. 1. Cambridge, UK: Cambridge University Press.

James, W. (1890) *The Principles of Psychology*. New York: Dover.

Jarman, C. (1979) *The Development of Handwriting Skills*. London: Basil Blackwell.

Jaswal, V. K. (2004) Don't believe everything you hear: preschoolers' sensitivity to speaker intent in category induction. *Child Development* 75(6), 1871–1885.

Jencks, C. (1975) *Inequality: A Reassessment of the Effect of Family and Schooling in America*. Harmondsworth, UK: Penguin Books.

Jennings, K. D., Harmon, R. J., Morgan, G. A., Gaiter, J. L. and Yarrow, L. J. (1979) Exploratory play as an index of mastery motivation: relationships to persistence, cognitive functioning and environment measures. *Developmental Psychology* 215, 386–394.

Jensen, A. R. (1969) How much can we boost IQ and scholastic achievement? *Harvard Educational Review* 39, 1–123.

Jensen, A. R. (1980) *Bias in Mental Testing*. New York: Free Press.

Jensen, A. R. (1982) Reaction time and psychometric *g*. In H. J. Eysenck (ed.), *A Model for Intelligence*. Berlin, Germany: Springer-Verlag.

Jensen, A. R. (1989) Review: Raising IQ without increasing 'g'? *Developmental Review* 9, 234–258.

Jensen, A. R. (1998) *The g Factor: The Science of Mental Ability*. Westport, CT: Praeger.

Jimerson, S., Egeland, B. and Teo, A. (1999) A longitudinal study of achievement trajectories associated with change. *Journal of Educational Psychology* 91(1), 116–126.

Johnson, C. N. (1988) Theory of mind and the structure of conscious experience. In J. W. Astington, P. L. Harris and D. R. Olson (eds), *Developing Theories of Mind*. Cambridge, UK: Cambridge University Press.

Johnson, C. N. and Wellman, H. M. (1982) Children's developing conceptions of the mind and brain. *Child Development* 53, 222–234.

Johnson, D. (1991) *The effectiveness of a genre-based approach to the academic literacy of teacher-trainers and teacher-trainees in Zimbabwe*. Unpublished PhD thesis, University of Bristol.

Johnson, J. and Pascual-Leone, J. (1989) Developmental levels of processing in metaphor interpretation. *Journal of Experimental Child Psychology* 48, 1–31.

Johnson, K. E., Mervis, C. B. and Boster, J. S. (1992) Developmental changes in the structure of the mammal domain. *Developmental Psychology* 28, 74–83.

Johnson, K. E., Scott, P. and Mervis, C. B. (2004) What are theories for? Concept use throughout the continuum of dinosaur experience. *Journal of Experimental Child Psychology* 87, 171–200.

Johnson, M. H. (1998) The neural basis of cognitive development. In D. Kuhn and R. S. Siegler (eds), *Handbook of Child Psychology, vol. 2. Cognition, Perception, and Language*, 5th edn, pp. 1–49. New York: Wiley.

Johnson, M. and Munakata, Y. (2005) Processes of change in brain and cognitive development. *Trends in Cognitive Science* 9(3), 152–156.

Johnson, M. H. (1997) *Developmental Cognitive Neuroscience*. Oxford, UK: Blackwell.

Johnson, M. H. (2000) Functional brain development in infants: effects of an interactive specialization network. *Child Development* 71, 75–81.

Johnson-Glenberg, M. C. and Chapman, R. S. (2004) Predictors of parent–child language during novel task play: a comparison between typically developing children and individuals with Down syndrome. *Journal of Intellectual Disability Research* 48(3), 225–238.

Johnson-Laird, P. (1983) *Mental Models*. Cambridge, UK: Cambridge University Press.

Johnson-Laird, P. N. (1988) *The Computer and the Mind: An Introduction to Cognitive Science*. Cambridge, MA: Harvard University Press.

Johnson-Laird, P. N. (1989) Analogy and the exercise of creativity. In S. Vosniadou and A. Ortony (eds), *Similarity and Analogical Reasoning*. Cambridge, UK: Cambridge University Press.

Johnson-Laird, P. N. (2004) Mental models and reasoning. In J. P. Leighton and R. J. Sternberg (eds), *The Nature of Reasoning*. Cambridge, UK: Cambridge University Press.

Johnson-Laird, P. N., Oakhill, J. and Bull, D. (1986) Children's syllogistic reasoning. *Quarterly Journal of Experimental Psychology* 38A, 35–38.

Johnson-Laird, P. N. and Wason, P. C. (eds) (1977) *Thinking*. Cambridge, UK: Cambridge University Press.

Johnston, M. and Goldstein, G. (1998) Selective vulnerability of the developing brain to lead. *Current Opinion in Neurology* 11, 689–693.

Johnston, M. V., Alemi, L. and Harum, K. H. (2003) Learning, memory and transcription factors. *Pediatric Research* 53(3), 369–374.

Jones, L. and Pellegrini, A. D. (1996) The effects of social relationships, writing media, and microgenetic development on first grade students' written narratives. *American Educational Research Journal* 33, 691–718.

Jones, O. H. M. (1979) A comparative study of mother–child communication with Down's syndrome and normal infants. In D. Shaffer and J. Dunn (eds), *The First Year of Life*. Chichester, UK: Wiley.

Jordan, A. (2004) The role of media in children's development: an ecological perspective. *Journal of Developmental and Behavioral Pediatrics* 25(3), 196–206.

Jorm, A. F. (1983) Specific reading retardation and working memory: a review. *British Journal of Psychology* 74, 311–342.

Joseph, R. (2000) Fetal brain behaviour and cognitive development. *Developmental Review* 20(1), 81–98.

Jowett, S. and Sylva, K. (1986) Does kind of preschool matter? *Educational Research* 28, 21–31.

Joyce, J. [1916] (1960) *A Portrait of the Artist as a Young Man.* Harmondsworth, UK: Penguin Books.

Juel, C. and Minden-Cupp, C. (2000) Learning to read words: linguistic strategies and instructional units. *Reading Research Quarterly* 35, 458–492.

Juel, C. and Minden-Cupp, C. (2004) Learning to read words: linguistic units and instructional strategies. In R. B. Ruddell and N. J. Unrau (eds), *Theoretical Models and Processes of Reading.* Newark, DE: International Reading Association.

Jusczyk, P. W., Friederici, A. D., Wessels, J. M. I., Svenjerud, V. Y. and Jusczyk, A. M. (1993) Infants' sensitivity to the sound patterns of native language words. *Journal of Memory and Language* 32, 402–420.

Jusczyk, P. W., Houston, D. M. and Newsome, M. (1999) The beginnings of word segmentation in English-learning infants. *Cognitive Psychology* 39, 159–207.

Jussim, L. (1986) Self-fulfilling prophecies: a theoretical and integrative review. *Psychological Review* 93(4), 429–445.

Just, M. A. and Carpenter, P. A. (1987) *The Psychology of Reading and Language Comprehension.* Boston: Allyn & Bacon.

Kagan, J. (1964) Information processing in the child: the significance of analytic and reflective attitudes. *Psychological Monographs* 78, 578.

Kagan, J. (1984) *The Nature of the Child.* New York: Basic Books.

Kagan, J. (1987a) Misgivings about the Matching Familiar Figures Test: a brief reply. *Developmental Psychology* 23, 739–740.

Kagan, J. (ed.) (1987b) *The Emergence of Moral Concepts in Young Children.* Chicago: University of Chicago Press.

Kagan J., Kearsley, R. B. and Zelazo, P. R. (1978) *Infancy: Its Place in Human Development.* Cambridge, MA: Harvard University Press.

Kagan, J. and Kogan, N. (1970) Individual variation in cognitive processes. In P. H. Mussen (ed.), *Carmichael's Manual of Child Psychology*, vol. 1, 3rd edn. New York: Wiley.

Kagan, J., Lapidus, D. R. and Moore, M. (1978) Infant antecedents of cognitive functioning: a longitudinal study. *Child Development* 49, 1005–1023.

Kagan, J., Reznick, S. J. and Snidman, N. (1987) The physiology and psychology of behavioural inhibition in children. *Child Development* 55, 2212–2225.

Kahneman, D., Slovic, P. and Tversky, A. (1982) *Judgment under Uncertainty: Heuristics and Biases.* New York: Cambridge University Press.

Kail, R. (1986) Sources of age differences in speed of processing. *Child Development* 57, 969–987.

Kail, R. (1988) Reply to Stigler, Nusbaum and Chalip. *Child Development* 59, 1154–1157.

Kail, R. (1990) *The Development of Memory in Children*, 3rd edn (1st edn 1979, 2nd edn 1984). San Francisco: Freeman.

Kail, R. (1991a) Processing time declines exponentially during childhood and adolescence. *Developmental Psychology* 27, 259–266.

Kail, R. (1991b) Developmental change in speed of processing during childhood and adolescence. *Psychological Bulletin* 109, 490–501.

Kail, R. and Bisanz, J. (1982) Information processing and cognitive development. *Advances in Child Development and Behaviour*. New York: Academic Press.

Kail, R. V. and Hagen, J. W. (eds) (1977) *Perspectives on the Development of Memory and Cognition*. Hillsdale, NJ: Lawrence Erlbaum Associates, Inc.

Kaler, S. R. and Freeman, B. J. (1994) Analysis of environmental deprivation: cognitive and social development in Romanian orphans. *Journal of Child Psychology and Psychiatry* 35, 769–781.

Kalil, A. and Ziol-Guest, K. M. (2005) Single mothers' employment dynamics and adolescent well-being. *Child Development* 76(1), 196–211.

Kamin, L. J. (1974) *The Science and Politics of I.Q.* Potomac, MD: Lawrence Erlbaum Associates, Inc.

Kamler, B. and Kilarr, G. (1983) Looking at what children can do. In B. Kroll and G. Wells (eds), *Explorations in the Development of Writing*. Chichester, UK: Wiley.

Karmiloff, K. and Karmiloff-Smith, A. (2001) *Pathways to Language: From Fetus to Adolescent*. Cambridge, MA: Harvard University Press.

Karmiloff-Smith, A., (1979) *A Functional Approach to Child Language: A Study of Determiners and Reference*. Cambridge, UK: Cambridge University Press.

Karmiloff-Smith, A. (1981) Getting developmental differences or studying child development? *Cognition* 10, 151–158.

Karmiloff-Smith, A. (1984) Children's problem solving. In M. Lamb, A. Brown and B. Rogoff (eds), *Advances in Developmental Psychology*, vol. 3. Hillsdale, NJ: Lawrence Erlbaum Associates, Inc.

Karmiloff-Smith, A. (1986) From meta-processes to conscious access: evidence from children's metalinguistic and repair data. *Cognition* 23, 95–147.

Karmiloff-Smith, A. (1988) The child is a theoretician, not an inductivist. *Mind and Language* 3(3), 183–195.

Karmiloff-Smith, A. (1991) Beyond modularity: innate constraints and developmental change. In S. Carey and R. Gelman (eds), *The Epigenesis of Mind*. Hove, UK: Lawrence Erlbaum Associates Ltd.

Karmiloff-Smith, A. (1992) *Beyond Modularity: A Developmental Perspective on Cognitive Science*. Cambridge, MA: Bradford.

Karmiloff-Smith, A., Grant, J., Jones, M.-C., Sims, K. and Cuckle, P. (1996) Rethinking metalinguistic awareness: representing and accessing what counts as a word. *Cognition* 58, 197–219.

Karmiloff-Smith, A. and Inhelder, B. (1974/5) If you want to get ahead, get a theory. *Cognition* 3, 195–212.

Karmiloff-Smith, A. and Thomas, M. (2003) What can developmental disorders tell us about the neurocomputational constraints that shape development? The case of Williams syndrome. *Development and Psychopathology* 15(4), 969–990.

Karpov, Y. V. and Haywood, H. C. (1998) Two ways to elaborate Vygotsky's concept of mediation: implications for instruction. *American Psychologist* 53, 27–36.

Katz, H. B. and Davies, C. A. (1983) The separate and combined effects of early undernutrition and environmental complexity at different ages on cerebral measures in rats. *Developmental Psychobiology* 16, 47–58.

Kaye, K. (1984) *The Mental and Social Life of Babies.* London: Methuen.

Keasey, B. (ed.) (1977) Social cognitive development. *Nebraska Symposium on Motivation*, vol. 25. Lincoln: University of Nebraska Press.

Kee, D. W. (1994) Developmental differences in associative memory: strategy use, mental effort, and knowledge access interaction. *Advances in Child Development and Behavior* 25, 7–32.

Keegan, R. T. (1996) Creativity from childhood to adulthood: a difference of degree and not of kind. In M. A. Runco (ed.), *New Directions for Child Development* 72, 57–66.

Keeney, T. J., Cannizzo, S. R. and Flavell, J. H. (1967) Spontaneous and induced verbal rehearsal in a recall task. *Child Development* 38, 953–966.

Keil, F. (1991) The emergence of theoretical beliefs as constraints on concepts. In S. Carey and R. Gelman (eds), *The Epigenesis of Mind*. Hove, UK: Lawrence Erlbaum Associates Ltd.

Keil, F. C. (1979) *Semantic and Conceptual Development.* Cambridge, MA: Harvard University Press.

Keil, F. C. (1981a) Children's thinking: what never develops? *Cognition* 10, 159–166.

Keil, F. C. (1981b) Constraints on knowledge and cognitive development. *Psychological Review* 88, 197–227.

Keil, F. C. (1984) Mechanisms in cognitive development and the structure of knowledge. In R. J. Sternberg (ed.), *Mechanisms of Cognitive Development*. New York: Freeman.

Keil, F. C. (1986) The acquisition of natural kind and artifact terms. In W. Demopoulos and A. Marras (eds), *Language Learning and Concept Acquisition*. Norwood, NJ: Ablex.

Keil, F. C. (1987) Conceptual development and category structure. In U. Neisser (ed.), *Concepts and Conceptual Development*. Cambridge, UK: Cambridge University Press.

Keil, F. C. (1989) *Concepts, Kinds and Cognitive Development.* Boston: MIT Press.

Keil, F. C. (1990) Constraints on constraints: surveying the epigenetic landscape. *Cognitive Science* 14, 135–168.

Keil, F. C. (1992) The origins of an autonomous biology. In M. Gunnar and M. Maratsos (eds), *Modularity and Constraints in Language and Cognition*. Minnesota Symposium on Child Psychology, vol. 25. Hillsdale, NJ: Lawrence Erlbaum Associates, Inc.

Keil, F. C. and Batterman, N. (1984) A characteristic-to-defining shift in the development of word meaning. *Journal of Verbal Learning and Verbal Behaviour* 23, 221–236.

Keil, F. C. and Kelly, M. H. (1986) Theories of constraints and constraints on theories. In W. Demopoulos and A. Marras (eds), *Language Learning and Concept Acquisition*. Norwood, NJ: Ablex.

Keller, H. (2002) Development as the interface between biology and culture: a conceptualisation of early ontogenetic differences. In H. Keller, Y. H. Poortinga and A. Scholmerich (eds), *Between Biology and Culture: Perspectives on Ontogenetic Development*. Cambridge, UK: Cambridge University Press.

Keller, M. (2004) Self in relationship. In D. Lapsley and D. Narvaez (eds), *Moral Development, Self, and Identity*. Mahwah, NJ: Lawrence Erlbaum Associates, Inc.

Kemler-Nelson, D. G., Hirsh-Pasek, K., Jusczyk, P. W. and Cassidy, K. W. (1989)

How the prosodic cues in motherese might assist language learning. *Journal of Child Language* 16, 53–68.

Kemp, N. and Bryant, P. E. (2003) Do beez buzz? Rule-based and frequency-based knowledge in learning to spell plural –s. *Child Development* 74(1), 63–74.

Kendler, T. S. (1967) Experimental analysis of inferential behavior in children. *Advances in Child Development and Behaviour* 3, 157–191.

Kendler, T. S. and Kendler, H. H. (1974) Effect of training and stimulus variables on reversal-shift ontogeny. *Journal of Experimental Child Psychology* 17(1), 87–106.

Kestenbaum, R. and Gelman, S. A. (1995) Preschool children's identification and understanding of mixed emotions. *Cognitive Development* 10, 443–458.

Khalidi, M. A. (2002) Nature and nurture in cognition. *British Journal of Philosophy of Science* 53, 251–272.

Kihlstrom, J. F. and Harackiewicz, J. M. (1982) The earliest recollection: a new survey. *Journal of Personality* 50, 134–147.

Kim-Cohen, J., Moffitt, T., Caspi, A. and Taylor, A. (2004) Genetic and environmental processes in young children's resilience and vulnerability to socioeconomic deprivation. *Child Development* 75(3), 651–668.

Kimura, Y. and Bryant, P. E. (1983) Reading and writing in English and Japanese: a cross-cultural study of young children. *British Journal of Psychology* 1, 143–153.

King, R. (1978) *All Things Bright and Beautiful?* London: Wiley.

Kinlaw, C. R. and Kurtz-Costes, B. (2003) The development of children's beliefs about intelligence. *Developmental Review* 23, 125–161.

Kinsbourne, M. (1980) Brain-based limitations on mind. In R. W. Rieber (ed.), *Mind and Body.* New York: Academic Press.

Kinsbourne, M. and Hiscock, M. (1983) The normal and deviant development of functional lateralisation of the brain. In M. M. Haith and J. J. Campos (eds), *Handbook of Child Psychology, vol. 2, Infancy and Developmental Psychobiology.* New York: Wiley.

Kirtley, C., Bryant, P., Maclean, M. and Bradley, L. (1989) Rhyme, rime and the onset of reading. *Journal of Experimental Child Psychology* 48, 224–245.

Kisilevsky, B. S., Hains, S. M. J., Jacquet, A.-Y., Granier-Deferre, C. and Lecanuet, J. P. (2004) Maturation of fetal responses to music. *Developmental Science* 7(5), 550–559.

Kister, M. C. and Patterson, C. J. (1980) Children's conceptions of the causes of illness: understanding of contagion and use of immanent justice. *Child Development* 51, 839–846.

Kitchener, R. (2002) Folk epistemology: an introduction. *New Ideas in Psychology* 20, 89–105.

Kitchener, R. F. (1986) *Piaget's Theory of Knowledge: Genetic Epistemology or Scientific Reason.* New Haven, CT: Yale University Press.

Kitcher, P. (1988) The child as parent of the scientist. *Mind and Language* 3(3), 217–228.

Klaczynski, P. A., Schuneman, M. J. and Daniel, D. B. (2004) Theories of conditional reasoning: a developmental examination of competing hypotheses. *Developmental Psychology* 4, 359–371.

Klahr, D. (1984) Transition processes in quantitative development. In R. J. Sternberg (ed.), *Mechanisms of Cognitive Development*. New York: Freeman.

Klahr, D. and Dunbar, K. (1988) Dual search space during scientific reasoning. *Cognitive Science* 12, 1–48.

Klahr, D. and MacWhinney, B. (1998) Information processing. In D. Kuhn and R. S. Siegler (eds,) *Handbook of Child Psychology, vol. 2, Cognition, Perception and Language*. New York: Wiley.

Klahr, D. and Siegler, R. S. (1978) The representation of children's knowledge. In H. W. Reese and L. P. Lipsitt (eds), *Advances in Child Development*. New York: Academic Press.

Klahr, D. and Wallace, G. (1976) *Cognitive Development: An Information-processing View*. New York: Lawrence Erlbaum Associates, Inc.

Klaue, K. (1992) The development of depth representation in children's drawings: effects of graphic surface and visibility of the model. *British Journal of Developmental Psychology* 10, 71–83.

Klausmeier, H. J. and Sipple, T. S. (1982) Factor structure of the Piagetian stage of concrete operations. *Contemporary Educational Psychology* 7, 161–180.

Klein, J. (2004) Who is most responsible for gender differences in scholastic achievements: pupils or teachers? *Educational Research* 46(2), 183–193.

Klein, P. D. (2003) Rethinking the multiplicity of cognitive resources and curricular representations: alternatives to 'learning styles' and 'multiple intelligences'. *Journal of Curriculum Studies* 35(1), 45–81.

Klein, P. S., Forbes, G. B. and Nadar, P. R. (1975) Effects of starvation in infancy (pyloric stenosis) on subsequent learning abilities. *Journal of Pediatrics* 87, 8–15.

Klin, A., Volkmar, F. R. and Sparrow, S. S. (1992) Autistic social dysfunction: some limitations of the theory of mind hypothesis. *Journal of Child Psychology and Psychiatry* 33, 861–876.

Kobasigawa, A. (1977) Retrieval factors in the development of memory. In R. V. Kail and J. W. Hagen (eds), *Perspectives on the Development of Memory and Cognition*. Hillsdale, NJ: Lawrence Erlbaum Associates, Inc.

Kochanska, G. (1991) Patterns of inhibition to the unfamiliar in children of normal and affectively ill mothers. *Child Development* 62, 250–263.

Koestler, A. (1964) *The Act of Creation*. London: Hutchinson.

Kogan, N. (1976) *Cognitive Styles in Infancy and Early Childhood*. Hillsdale, NJ: Lawrence Erlbaum Associates, Inc.

Kogan, N. (1983) Stylistic variation in childhood and adolescence: creativity, metaphor and cognitive styles. In J. H. Flavell and E. M. Markman (eds), *Handbook of Child Psychology*, vol. 3. New York: Wiley.

Kogan, N. and Saarni, C. (1989) Cognitive styles in children: some evolving trends. *Early Child Development and Care* 43, 101–128.

Kohlberg, L. (1984) *Essays on Moral Development: vol. 2. The Psychology of Moral Development*. San Francisco: Harper and Row.

Kohlmann, C.-W., Schumacher, A. and Streit, R. (1988) Trait anxiety and parental child-rearing behavior: support as a moderator variable? *Anxiety Research* 1, 53–64.

Kohn, M. (1977) *Social Competence, Symptoms and Underachievement in Childhood: A Longitudinal Perspective*. New York: Wiley.

Koluchova, J. (1976) Severe deprivation in twins: a case study. In A. M. Clarke and A. D. B. Clarke (eds), *Early Experience: Myth and Reality*. London: Open Books.

Komatsu, L. K. and Galotti, K. M. (1986) Children's reasoning about social, physical and logical regularities: a look at two worlds. *Child Development* 57, 413–420.

Konner, M. (1982) *The Tangled Wing: Biological Constraints on the Human Spirit*. London: Heinemann.

Kontos, S. (1983) Adult–child interaction and the development of metacognition. *Journal of Educational Research* 77, 43–64.

Koslowski, B. and Maqueda, M. (1993) What is confirmation bias and when do people have it? *Merrill-Palmer Quarterly* 39, 104–130.

Kozulin, A. (1986) Vygotsky in context. In A. Kozulin (ed.), *L. S. Vygotsky, Thought and Language*. Cambridge, MA: MIT Press.

Kozulin, A. (1990) *Vygotsky's Psychology*. Brighton, UK: Harvester.

Kozulin, A. (2003) Psychological tools and mediated learning. In A. Kozulin, B. Gindis, V. Ageyev and S. Miller (eds), *Vygotsky's Educational Theory in Cultural Context*. Cambridge, UK: Cambridge University Press.

Kozulin, A., Gindis, B., Ageyev, V. and Miller, S. (eds) (2003) *Vygotsky's Educational Theory in Cultural Context*. Cambridge, UK: Cambridge University Press.

Krasner, S. M. and Beinart, H. (1989) 'The Monday Group': a brief intervention with the siblings of infants who died from Sudden Infant Death Syndrome (SIDS). *Newsletter of the Association for Child Psychology and Psychiatry* 11(4), 11–17.

Kreppner, J. M., O'Connor, T. G., Dunn, J., Anderson-Wood, L. and the English and Romanian Adoptees Study Team (1999) The pretend and social role play of children exposed to severe early deprivation. *British Journal of Development Psychology* 17, 319–332.

Kreppner, J. M., O'Connor, T. G., Rutter, M. and the English and Romanian Adoptees Study Team (2001) Can inattention/overactivity be an institutional deprivation syndrome? *Journal of Abnormal Child Psychology* 29(6), 513–528.

Kreutzer, M., Leonard, C. and Flavell, J. (1975) An interview study of children's knowledge about memory. *Monographs of the Society for Research in Child Development* 40(1), serial no. 159.

Kristeva, J. (1986) *The Kristeva Reader*. Oxford, UK: Blackwell.

Kroll, B. and Wells, G. (eds) (1983) *Explorations in the Development of Writing*. Chichester, UK: Wiley.

Kuhl, P., Andruski, J., Chistovich, I., Chistovich, L., Kozhenikova, E., Ryskina, V. et al. (1997) Cross-language analysis of phonetic units in language addressed to infants. *Science* 277, 684–686.

Kuhn, D. (1989) Children and adults as intuitive scientists. *Psychological Review* 96(4), 674–689.

Kuhn, D. (1992) Thinking as argument. *Harvard Educational Review* 62, 155–174.

Kuhn, D. (1993) Connecting scientific and informal reasoning. *Merrill-Palmer Quarterly* 39, 74–103.

Kuhn, D. (2002a) A multi-component system that constructs knowledge: insights from microgenetic study. In N. Granott and J. Parziale (eds), *Microdevelopment: Transition Processes in Development and Learning*. Cambridge, UK: Cambridge University Press.

Kuhn, D. (2002b) What is scientific reasoning and how does it develop? In U. Goswami (ed.), *Blackwell Handbook of Cognitive Development*. Oxford, UK: Blackwell.

Kuhn, D. (2003) Metacognitive development. In L. Balter and C. S. LeMonda (eds), *Child Psychology: A Handbook of Contemporary Issues*. Hove, UK: Psychology Press.

Kuhn, D., Amsel, E. and O'Loughlin, M. (1988) *The Development of Scientific Thinking Skills*. San Diego, CA: Academic Press.

Kuhn, D., Garcia-Mila, M., Zohar, A. and Andersen, C. (1995) Strategies of knowledge acquisition. *Monographs of the Society for Research in Child Development* 60(4), serial no. 245.

Kuhn, T. S. (1962) *The Structure of Scientific Revolutions*. Chicago: Chicago University Press.

Kulhavy, R. W., Lee, J. B. and Caterino, L. C. (1985) Conjoint retention of maps and related discourse. *Contemporary Educational Psychology* 10, 28–37.

Kurtz, B. E. and Weinert, F. E. (1989) Metamemory, memory performance and causal attributions in gifted and average children. *Journal of Experimental Child Psychology* 48, 45–61.

Kuzmak, S. D. and Gelman, R. (1986) Young children's understanding of random phenomena. *Child Development* 57, 559–566.

Laboratory of Comparative Human Cognition (1982) Culture and intelligence. In R. J. Sternberg (ed.), *Handbook of Human Intelligence*. Cambridge, UK: Cambridge University Press.

Laboratory of Comparative Human Cognition (1983) Culture and cognitive development. In W. Kessen (ed.), *Handbook of Child Psychology, vol. 1, History Theory and Method*. New York: Wiley.

La Buda, M. C., De Fries, J. C., Plomin, R. and Fulker, D. W. (1986) Longitudinal stability of cognitive ability from infancy to early childhood: genetic and environmental etiologies. *Child Development* 57, 1142–1150.

La Frenière, P. J. and Sroufe, A. (1985) Profiles of peer competence in the preschool: interrelations between measures, influences of social ecology, and relation to attachment history. *Developmental Psychology* 21, 46–69.

Lakoff, G. (1987) *Women, Fire and Dangerous Things: What Categories Reveal About the Mind*. Chicago: Chicago University Press.

Laland, K. N., Hoppitt, W. (2003) Do animals have culture? *Evolutionary Anthropology* 12(3), 150–159.

Lamont, A. (2002) Musical identities and the school environment. In Raymond A. R. MacDonald, David J. Hargreaves and Dorothy Miell (eds), *Musical Identities*. Oxford, UK: Oxford University Press.

Lamont, A. (2003) Toddlers' musical preferences – Musical preference and musical memory in the early years. *Annals of the New York Academy of Sciences* 999, 518–519.

Landau, B. and Gleitman, L. (1985) *Language and Experience: Evidence from the Blind Child*. Cambridge, MA: Harvard University Press.

Landau, B., Smith, L. B. and Jones, S. S. (1988) The importance of shape in early lexical learning. *Cognitive Development* 3, 299–321.

Lane, D. and Stratford, B. (1985) *Current Approaches to Down's Syndrome*. London: Holt, Rinehart & Winston.

Lane, H. (1976) *The Wild Boy of Aveyron*. London: George Allen & Unwin.

Lane, J. (1990) The culture of acquisition and the practice of understanding. In J. W. Stigler, R. A. Shweder and G. H. Herdt (eds), *Cultural Psychology: Essays on Comparative Human Development*. Cambridge, UK: Cambridge University Press.

Lane, S. R. and Lane, S. A. (1986) Rationality, self-esteem and autonomy through collaborative enquiry. *Oxford Review of Education* 12(3), 263–273.

Lane-Fox, R. (1991) The unauthorized version: truth and fiction in the Bible. London: Viking.

Lang, A. (ed.) (n.d.) *The True Story Book*. London: Longmans.

Lange, G., Mackinnon, C. E. and Nida, R. E. (1989) Knowledge, strategy and motivational contributions to preschool children's object recall. *Developmental Psychology* 25(5), 772–779.

Lange, G. and Pierce, S. H. (1992) Memory-strategy learning and maintenance in preschool children. *Developmental Psychology* 28, 453–462.

Lansdown, R. and Benjamin, G. (1985) The development of the concept of death in children aged 5–9 years. *Child Care, Health and Development* 11, 13–20.

Lapsley, D. and Narvaez, D. (2004a) A social-cognitive approach to the moral personality. In D. Lapsley and D. Narvaez (eds), *Moral Development, Self, and Identity*. Mahwah, NJ: Lawrence Erlbaum Associates, Inc.

Lapsley, D. and Narvaez, D. (eds) (2004b) *Moral Development, Self, and Identity*. Mahwah, NJ: Lawrence Erlbaum Associates, Inc.

Larivee, S., Normandeau, S. and Parent, S. (2000) The French Connection: some contributions of French-language research in the Post-Piagetian era. *Child Development* 71(4), 823–839.

Larkin, J. (1983) The role of problem representation in physics. In D. Gentner and A. L. Stevens (eds), *Mental Models*. Hillsdale, NJ: Lawrence Erlbaum Associates, Inc.

Larkin, J., McDermott, J., Simon, D. P. and Simon, H. A. (1980) Expert and novice performance in solving physics problems. *Science* 208, 1335–1342.

Larson, R. W. and Verma, S. (1999) How children and adolescents spend time around the world: work, play and developmental opportunities. *Psychological Bulletin* 125, 701–736.

Lash, J. P. (1980) *Helen and Teacher*. London: Allen Lane.

Laszlo, J. L. and Bairstow, P. J. (1985) *Perceptual–Motor Development: Developmental Assessment and Therapy*. London: Holt, Rinehart & Winston.

Laurendeau, M. and Pinard, A. (1970) *The Development of the Concept of Space in the Child*. New York: International Universities Press.

Lave, J. (1990) The culture of acquisition and the practice of understanding. In J. W. Stigler, R. A. Shweder and G. H. Herdt (eds), *Cultural Psychology: Essays on Comparative Human Development*. Cambridge, UK: Cambridge University Press.

Lawler, R. W. (1981) The progressive construction of mind. *Cognitive Science* 5, 1–30.

Laws, G. (2004) Contributions of phonological memory, language comprehension and hearing to expressive language of adolescents and young adults with Down syndrome. *Journal of Child Psychology and Psychiatry* 45(6), 1085–1095.

Laws, G. and Gunn, D. (2002) Relationships between reading, phonological skills and language development in individuals with Down syndrome. *Reading and Writing* 15(5–6), 527–548.

Lawson, A. E. (1985) A review of research on formal reasoning and science teaching. *Journal of Research in Science Teaching* 22, 569–617.

Lawson, A. E. (2003) The nature and development of hypothetico-predictive argumentation with implications for science teaching. *International Journal of Science Education* 25(11), 1387–1408.

Lazar, A. and Torney-Purta, J. (1991) The development of the subconcepts of death in young children: a short-term longitudinal study. *Child Development* 62, 1321–1333.

Lazarus, R. S. (1991) Progress on a cognitive motivational relational theory of emotion. *American Psychologist* 46, 819–834.

Lea, S. E. G., Tarpy, R. M. and Webley, P. (1987) *The Individual in the Economy.* Cambridge, UK: Cambridge University Press.

Leach, P. (1979) *Who Cares? A New Deal for Mothers and Their Small Children.* Harmondsworth, UK: Penguin Books.

Leahy, R. L. (1981) Development of the conception of economic inequality, I: descriptions and comparisons of rich and poor people. *Child Development* 52, 523–532.

Leahy, R. L. (1983) Development of the conception of economic inequality, II: explanations, justifications and concepts of social mobility and change. *Developmental Psychology* 19, 111–125.

Le Doux, J. (1989) Cognitive–emotional interactions in the brain. *Cognition and Emotion* 3, 267–289.

Lee, B. (1985) Intellectual origins of Vygotsky's semiotic analysis. In J. V. Wertsch (ed.), *Culture, Communication and Cognition.* Cambridge, UK: Cambridge University Press.

Lee, K. and Cameron, C. A. (2000) Extracting truth information from lies: the emergence of representation–expression distinction in preschool children. *Merrill-Palmer Quarterly* 40, 1–20.

Lee, K. and Karmiloff-Smith, A. (2002) Macro- and micro-developmental research: assumptions, research strategies, constraints and utilities. In N. Granott and J. Parziale (eds), *Microdevelopment: Transition Processes in Development and Learning.* Cambridge, UK: Cambridge University Press.

Lee, K., Cameron, C. A., Doucette, J. and Talwar, V. (2002) Phantoms and fabrications: young children's detection of implausible lies. *Child Development* 73(6), 1688–1702.

Lee, S.-Y., Stigler, J. W. and Stevenson, H. W. (1986) Beginning reading in Chinese and English. In B. Foorman and A. Siegel (eds), *Acquisition of Reading Skills.* Hillsdale, NJ: Lawrence Erlbaum Associates, Inc.

Lee, V. E., Stigler, J. W. and Schnur, E. (1988) Does Head Start work? A 1-year follow-up comparison of disadvantaged children attending Head Start, no preschool and other preschool programs. *Developmental Psychology* 24, 210–222.

Lee, V. W. and Croninger, R. (1994) The relative importance of home and school in the development of literacy skills for middle-grade students. *American Journal of Education* 102, 286–329.

Leeson, R. (1993) *Smart Girls.* London: Walker Books.

Lehman, D., Lempert, R. O. and Nisbett, R. E. (1988) The effects of graduate training on reasoning. *American Psychologist* 43, 431–442.

Leighton, J. (2004) Defining and describing reason. In J. P. Leighton and R. J. Sternberg (eds), *The Nature of Reasoning*. Cambridge, UK: Cambridge University Press.

Leighton, J. P. and Sternberg, R. J. (eds) (2004) *The Nature of Reasoning*. Cambridge, UK: Cambridge University Press.

Leinbach, M. D., Hort, B. E. and Fagot, B. I. (1997) Bears are for boys: metaphorical associations in children's gender stereotypes. *Cognitive Development* 12, 107–130.

Lemaire, P. and Siegler, R. S. (1995) Four aspects of strategic change: contributions to children's learning of multiplication. *Journal of Experimental Psychology: General* 124, 83–97.

Lenat, D. B. and Brown, J. S. (1984) Why AM and Eurisko appear to work. *Artificial Intelligence* 23, 269–294.

Lengua, L. J. (2002) The contribution of emotionality and self-regulation to the understanding of children's response to multiple risk. *Child Development* 73, 144–161.

Leonard, C. M. (2003) Neural substrate of speech and language development. In M. De Haan and M. Johnson (eds), *The Cognitive Neuroscience of Development*. Hove, UK: Psychology Press.

Leonard, L. B. (1998) *Children with Specific Language Impairment*. Cambridge, MA: MIT Press.

Lepper, M. R. (1981) Intrinsic and extrinsic motivation in children: detrimental effects of superfluous social controls. *Minnesota Symposium on Child Psychology*, vol. 14. Hillsdale, NJ: Lawrence Erlbaum Associates, Inc.

Lerner, R. M. (1998) Theories of human development: contemporary perspectives. *Handbook of Child Psychology*, vol. 1. New York: Wiley.

Lesh, R. and Landau, M. (eds) (1983) *Acquisition of Mathematics Concepts and Processes*. New York: Academic Press.

Leslie, A. M. (1987) Pretense and representation: the origins of 'Theory of Mind'. *Psychological Review* 94, 412–426.

Leslie, A. M. (1988a) Some implications of pretense for mechanisms underlying the child's theory of mind. In J. W. Astington, P. L. Harris and D. R. Olson (eds), *Developing Theories of Mind*. Cambridge, UK: Cambridge University Press.

Leslie, A. M. (1988b) The child's understanding of the mental world. In R. L. Gregory (ed.), *The Oxford Companion to the Mind*. Oxford, UK: Oxford University Press.

Leslie, A. M. (1990) Pretence, autism and the basis of 'Theory of Mind'. *The Psychologist* 3, 120–123.

Leslie, A. M. (1994) ToMM, ToBY, and agency: core architecture and domain specificity. In L. A. Hirschfeld and S. A. Gelman (eds), *Mapping the Mind: Domain Specificity in Cognition and Culture*. Cambridge, UK: Cambridge University Press.

Leslie, A. M. and Frith, U. (1990) Prospects for a cognitive neuro-psychology of autism: Hobson's choice. *Psychological Review* 97(1), 122–131.

Levin, I. (1982) The nature and development of time concepts in children: the effects of interfering cues. In W. J. Friedman (ed.), *The Developmental Psychology of Time*. New York: Academic Press.

Levin, I. (ed.) (1986) *Stage and Structure: Reopening the Debate*. Norwood, NJ: Ablex.

Levine, S. C., Jordan, N. C. and Huttenlocher, J. (1992) Development of calculation abilities in young children. *Journal of Experimental Child Psychology* 53, 72–103.

Levinson, P. J. and Carpenter, R. L. (1974) An analysis of analogical reasoning in children. *Child Development* 45, 857–861.

Lewis, M. and Brooks-Gunn, J. (1979) *Social Cognition and the Acquisition of Self*. New York: Plenum Press.

Lewis, M. and Michalson, L. (1983) *Children's Emotions and Moods: Developmental Theory and Measurement*. New York: Plenum Press.

Lewis, M. and Ramsay, D. (2004) Development of self-recognition, personal pronoun use, and pretend play during the 2nd year. *Child Development* 75(6), 1821–1831.

Lewis, V. (1987) *Development and Handicap*. Oxford, UK: Blackwell.

Li, J. (2003) U.S. and Chinese cultural beliefs about learning. *Journal of Educational Psychology* 95, 258–267.

Li, J. (2004) Learning as a task or a virtue: U.S. and Chinese preschoolers explain learning. *Developmental Psychology* 40(4), 595–605.

Liaw, F. and Brooks-Gunn, J. (1994) Cumulative familial risks and low-birth-weight children's cognitive and behavioural development. *Journal of Clinical Child Psychology* 23, 360–372.

Liben, L. S. (1981) Spatial representation and behavior: multiple perspectives. In L. S. Liben and N. Newcombe (eds), *Spatial Representation and Behavior across the Life Span*. New York: Academic Press.

Liben, L. S. (1999) Developing an understanding of external spatial representations. In I. E. Sigel (ed.), *Development of mental representation: theories and applications*, pp. 297–321. Mahwah, NJ: Lawrence Erlbaum Associates, Inc.

Liben, L. S. (2003) Beyond point and shoot: children's developing understanding of photographs as spatial and expressive representations. In R. V. Kail (ed.), *Advances in Child Development and Behaviour*, vol. 31, pp. 1–42.

Liben, L. S., Bigler, R. S. and Korgh, H. R. (2001) Pink and blue collar jobs: children's judgements of job status and job aspirations in relation to sex of worker. *Journal of Experimental Child Psychology* 79, 346–363.

Liben, L. S., Kastens, K. A. and Stevenson, L. M. (2002) Real-world knowledge through real-world maps: a developmental guide for navigating the educational terrain. *Developmental Review* 22, 267–322.

Liberman, I. Y. and Shankweiler, D. (1991) Phonology and beginning reading. In L. Rieben and C. A. Perfetti (eds), *Learning to Read*. Hove, UK: Lawrence Erlbaum Associates Ltd.

Liberman, I. Y., Shankweiler, D., Liberman, A. and Fowler, C. (1977) Phonetic segmentation and reading in the beginning reader. In A. S. Reber and D. L. Scarborough (eds), *Toward a Psychology of Reading*. New York: Wiley.

Lichten, W. (2004) On the law of intelligence. *Developmental Review* 24, 252–288.

Lidz, J. and Gleitman, L. R. (2004) Argument structure and the child's contribution to language learning. *Trends in Cognitive Sciences* 8(4), 157–161.

Lieven, E., Behrens, H., Speares, J. and Tomasello, M. (2003) Early syntactic creativity: a usage-based approach. *Journal of Child Language* 30, 333–370.

Lieven, E. V. M. (1978) Conversations between mothers and young children: individual differences and their possible implication for the study of language learning. In N. Waterson and C. Snow (eds), *The Development of Communication*. Chichester, UK: Wiley.

Lieven, E. V. M. (1982) Context process and progress in young children's speech. In M. Beveridge (ed.), *Children Thinking through Language*. London: Edward Arnold.

Lieven, E. V. M., Pine, J. M. and Dresner Barnes, H. (1992) Individual differences in early vocabulary development: redefining the referential–expressive distinction. *Journal of Child Language* 19, 287–301.

Light, P. H. (1979) *The Development of Social Sensitivity*. Cambridge, UK: Cambridge University Press.

Light, P. H. (1983) Social interaction and cognitive development: a review of post-Piagetian research. In S. Meadows (ed.), *Developing Thinking*. London: Methuen.

Light, P. H. (1986) Context, conservation and conversation. In M. Richards and P. H. Light (eds), *Child of Social Worlds*. Cambridge: Polity Press.

Light, P. H., Buckingham, N. and Robbins, A. H. (1979) The conservation task as an interactional setting. *British Journal of Educational Psychology* 49, 304–310.

Light, P. H. and Humphreys, J. (1981) Internal relationships in young children's drawings. *Journal of Experimental Child Psychology* 31, 521–530.

Light, P. H. and Perret-Clermont, A.-N. (1989) Social context effects in learning and testing. In A. Gellatly, D. Rogers and J. A. Sloboda (eds), *Cognition and Social Worlds*. Oxford, UK: Clarendon Press.

Lillard, A. (1994) Making sense of pretense. In C. Lewis and P. Mitchell (eds), *Children's Early Understanding of Mind*. Hillsdale, NJ: Lawrence Erlbaum Associates, Inc.

Lillard, A. (1996) Body or mind: children's categorization of pretense. *Child Development* 67, 1717–1734.

Lillard, A. (1998) Ethnopsychologies: cultural variations in theory of mind. *Psychological Bulletin* 123, 3–33.

Lillard, A. (2001) Pretend play as Twin Earth: a social-cognitive analysis. *Developmental Review* 21, 495–531.

Lillard, A. (2002) Pretend play and cognitive development. In U. Goswami (ed.), *Blackwell Handbook of Cognitive Development*. Oxford, UK: Blackwell.

Linn, M. C. (1986) Science. In R. F. Dillon and R. J. Sternberg (eds), *Cognition and Instruction*. New York: Academic Press.

Linn, M. C. and Peterson, A. C. (1985) Emergence and characterization of sex differences in spatial ability: a meta-analysis. *Child Development* 56, 1479–1498.

Lipman, M., Sharp, A. M. and Oscanyan, F. S. (1980) *Philosophy in the Classroom* Philadelphia: Temple University Press.

Little, T. D. and Widaman, K. F. (1995) A production task evaluation of individual differences in mental addition skill development. *Journal of Experimental Child Psychology* 60, 361–392.

Livesley, W. J. and Bromley, D. B. (1973) *Person Perception in Childhood and Adolescence*. London: Wiley.

Lloyd-Still, J. D., Hurwitz, I. and Shwachman, H. (1974) Intellectual development after severe malnutrition in infancy. *Pediatrics* 43, 306–311.

Lock, A. (ed.) (1978) *Action, Gesture and Symbol: The Emergence of Language.* London: Academic Press.

Lock, A., Service, V., Brito, A., Young, A. and Chandler, P. (1989) The social structuring of infant cognition. In A. Slater and G. Bremner (eds), *Infant Development*. London: Lawrence Erlbaum Associates Ltd.

Locurto, C. (1988) On the malleability of IQ. *The Psychologist* 11, 431–435.

Loeb, S., Fuller, B., Kagan, S. L. and Carroll, B. (2004) Child care in poor communities: early learning effects of type, quality and stability. *Child Development* 75, 47–65.

Loehlin, J. C., Horn, J. M. and Willerman, L. (1989) Modelling IQ change: evidence from the Texas Adoption Project. *Child Development* 60, 993–1004.

Loehlin, J. C., Willerman, L. and Horn, J. M. (1988) Human behaviour genetics. *Annual Review of Psychology* 38, 101–133.

Loftus, E. F. (1979) *Eyewitness Testimony*. Cambridge, MA: Harvard University Press.

Lohman, D. F. (1989) Human intelligence: an introduction to advances in theory and research. *Review of Educational Research* 59, 333–373.

Lohmann, H. and Tomasello, M. (2003) The role of language in the development of false belief understanding: a training study. *Child Development* 74(4), 1130–1144.

Longeot, F. (1978) *Les Stades operatoires de Piaget et les facteurs de l'intelligence.* Grenoble, France: Presses Universitaires de Grenoble.

Longstreth, L. E., David, B., Carter, L., Flint, D., Owen, J., Rickert, M. and Taylor, E. (1981) Separation of home intellectual environment and material IQ as determinants of child IQ. *Developmental Psychology* 7, 532–541.

Longuet-Higgins, H. C. (1987) *Mental Processes: Studies in Cognitive Science.* Cambridge, MA: MIT Press.

Lonigan, C., Burgess, S. and Anthony, J. (2000) Development of emergent literacy and early reading skills in preschool children: evidence from a latent-variable longitudinal study. *Developmental Psychology* 36, 596–613.

Lonsdorf, E. V., Eberly, L. E. and Pusey, A. E. (2004) Sex differences in learning in chimpanzees. *Nature* 428, 715–716.

Lorch, E. P., Bellack, D. R. and Augsbach, L. H. (1987) Young children's memory for televised stories: effects of importance. *Child Development* 58, 453–463.

Lord, A. B. (1960) *The Singer of Tales*. Cambridge, MA: Harvard University Press.

Lourenco, O. and Machado, A. (1996) In defence of Piaget's theory: a reply to 10 common criticisms. *Psychological Review* 103, 143–164.

Lovett, M. W. (1987) A developmental approach to reading disability: accuracy and speed criteria of normal and deficient reading skill. *Child Development* 58, 234–260.

Lovett, S. B. and Pillow, B. H. (1995) Development of the ability to distinguish between comprehension and memory: evidence from strategy selection tasks. *Journal of Educational Psychology* 87(4), 523–536.

Lovett, S. B. and Pillow, B. H. (1996) Development of the ability to distinguish between comprehension and memory: evidence from goal-state evaluation tasks. *Journal of Educational Psychology* 88(3), 546–562.

Lozoff, B. (1988) Behavioral alterations in iron deficiency. *Advances in Pediatrics* 35, 331–360.

Lozoff, B. (1989) Nutrition and behavior. *American Psychologist* 44, 231–236.

Luciana, M. (2003) Cognitive development in children born preterm: implications for theories of brain plasticity following early injury. *Development and Psychopathology* 15(4), 1017–1047.

Luo, D., Thompson, L. A. and Detterman, D. K. (2003) The causal factor underlying the correlation between psychometric g and scholastic performance. *Intelligence* 31, 67–83.

Luria, A. R. (1969) *The Mind of a Mnemonist.* London: Cape.

Luria, A. R. (1976) *Cognitive Development: Its Cultural and Social Foundations.* Cambridge, MA: Harvard University Press.

Luster, T. and Dubow, E. (1992) Home environment and maternal intelligence as predictors of verbal intelligence: a comparison of preschool and school-age children. *Merrill-Palmer Quarterly* 38, 151–175.

Luthar, S. (1999) *Poverty and Children's Adjustment.* Los Angeles: Sage.

Lycan, W. G. (1989) *Mind and Cognition.* Oxford, UK: Blackwell.

Lynn, R. (1989) A nutrition theory of the secular increases in intelligence: positive correlations between height, head size and IQ. *British Journal of Educational Psychology* 59, 372–377.

Lynn, R. (1993) Nutrition and intelligence. In P. A. Vernon (ed.), *Biological Approaches to the Study of Human Intelligence.* Norwood, NJ: Ablex.

Lytton, H. and Romney, D. M. (1991) Parents' differential socialization of boys and girls: a meta-analysis. *Psychological Bulletin* 109, 267–296.

Mabbott, D. J. and Bisanz, J. (2003) Developmental change and individual differences in children's multiplication. *Child Development* 74(4), 1091–1107.

McBride-Chang, C. (1996) Models of speech perception and phonological processing in reading. *Child Development* 67, 1836–1856.

McBride-Chang, C. (1999) The ABCs of the ABCs: the development of letter-name and letter-sound knowledge. *Merrill-Palmer Quarterly* 45, 285–308.

McBride-Chang, C., Bialystok, E., Chong, K. K. Y. and Li, Y. (2004) Levels of phonological awareness in three cultures. *Journal of Experimental Child Psychology* 89(2), 93–111.

McBride-Chang, C. and Ho, C. S.-H. (2000) Developmental issues in Chinese children's character acquisition. *Journal of Educational Psychology* 92, 50–55.

McBride-Chang, C. and Kail, R. V. (2002) Cross-cultural similarities in the predictors of reading acquisition. *Child Development* 73(5), 1392–1407.

McCabe, A. (1989) Differential language learning styles in young children: the importance of context. *Developmental Review* 9, 1–20.

McCall, R. B. (1983) Environmental effects on intelligence: the forgotten realm of discontinuous nonshared within-family factors. *Child Development* 54, 408–415.

McCall, R. B. (1990) The neuroscience of education: more research is needed before application. *Journal of Educational Psychology* 82, 885–888.

McCall, R. B., Meyers, E. D., Hartman, J. and Roche, A. F. (1983) Developmental changes in head-circumference and mental-performance growth rates: a test of Epstein's phrenoblysis hypothesis. *Developmental Psychobiology* 16, 457–468.

McCall, R. B. and Carriger, M. S. (1993) A meta-analysis of infant habituation and recognition memory performance as predictors of later IQ. *Child Development* 64, 57–79.

McCartney, K. (1984) The effect of quality of daycare environment on children's language development. *Developmental Psychology* 20, 244–260.

McCartney, K., Harris, M. J. and Bernieri, F. (1990) Growing up and growing apart: a developmental meta-analysis of twin studies. *Psychological Bulletin* 107, 226–237.

McCartney, K., Wagner Robeson, W., Jordan, E. and Mouradian, V. (1991) Mothers' language with first- and second-born children: a within-family study. In K. Pillemer and K. McCartney (eds), *Parent–Child Relations throughout Life*. Hillsdale, NJ: Lawrence Erlbaum Associates, Inc.

McCauley, E., Kay, T., Ho, J. and Treder, R. (1987) The Turner syndrome: cognitive deficits, affective discrimination and behaviour problems. *Child Development* 58, 464–473.

McClelland, J. L., Rumelhart, D. E. and the PDP Research Group (1986) *Parallel Distributed Processing: Explorations in the Micro-structure of Cognition, vol. 2, Psychological and Biological Models*. Cambridge, MA: MIT Press.

McCloskey, M., Caramazza, A. and Green, B. (1980) Curvilinear motion in the absence of external forces: naive beliefs about the motion of objects. *Science* 210, 1139–1141.

Maccoby, E. and Jacklin, C. (1974) *The Psychology of Sex Differences*. Stanford, CA: Stanford University Press.

McDevitt, T. M., Hess, R. D., Kashiwagi, K., Dickson, W. P., Miyake, N. and Azuma, H. (1987) Referential communication accuracy of mother–child pairs and children's later scholastic achievement: a follow-up study. *Merrill-Palmer Quarterly* 33, 171–185.

MacDonald, R. A. R., Hargreaves, D. J. and Miell, J. D. (eds) (2002) *Musical Identities*. Oxford, UK: Oxford University Press.

McDowell, D. J., O'Neil, R. and Parke, R. D. (2000) Display rule activation in a disappointing situation and children's emotional reactivity: relations with social competence. *Merrill-Palmer Quarterly* 46, 306–324.

McGillicuddy-DeLisi, A. V. (1982) The relationship between parents' beliefs about development and family constellation, socioeconomic status, and parents' teaching strategies. In L. M. Laosa and I. E. Sigel (eds), *Families as Learning Environments for Children*. New York: Plenum Press.

McGilly, K. and Siegler, R. S. (1989) How children choose among serial recall strategies. *Child Development* 60, 172–182.

McGlaughlin, A., Empson, J., Morrissey, M. and Sever, J. (1980) Early child development and the home environment: consistencies at and between four pre-school stages. *International Journal of Behavioural Development* 3, 299–309.

McGue, M. (1989) Nature–nurture and intelligence. *Nature* 340, 507–508.

McGue, M., Bouchard, T. J., Iacona, W. G. and Lykken, D. T. (1993) Behavioral genetics and cognitive ability: a life-span approach. In R. Plomin and G. E. McClearn (eds), *Nature, Nurture and Psychology*. Washington, DC: American Psychological Association.

McGuinness, C. (1999) *From Thinking Skills to Thinking Classrooms*. London: Department for Education and Employment.

McHugh, P. R. and McKusick, V. A. (eds) (1991) *Genes, Brain and Behaviour*. New York: Raven Press.

Mackay, D., Thompson, B. and Schaub, P. (1970) *Breakthrough to Literacy*. London: Longman.

Mackintosh, N. J. (1986) The biology of intelligence. *British Journal of Psychology* 77, 1–18.

Mackintosh, N. J. (1998) *IQ and Human Intelligence*. Cambridge, UK: Cambridge University Press.

McKusick, V. A. (1991) Advances in medical genetics in the past 30 years. In P. R. McHugh and V. A. McKusick (eds), *Genes, Brain and Behaviour*. New York: Raven Press.

McLaughlin, B. (1984) *Second Language Acquisition in Childhood, vol. 1, Preschool Children*. Hillsdale, NJ: Lawrence Erlbaum Associates, Inc.

Maclean, C. (1979) *The Wolf Children*. Harmondsworth, UK: Penguin Books.

McLean, J. F. and Hitch, G. J. (1999) Working memory impairments in children with specific arithmetical learning difficulties. *Journal of Experimental Child Psychology* 74, 240–260.

Maclean, K. (2003) The impact of institutionalisation on child development. *Development and Psychopathology* 15(4), 853–884.

Maclean, M., Bryant, P. and Bradley, L. (1987) Rhymes, nursery rhymes, and reading in early childhood. *Merrill-Palmer Quarterly* 33(3), 255–281.

McLoyd, V. C. (1998) Socio-economic disadvantage and child development. *American Psychologist* 53, 185–204.

McNally, S., Eisenberg, N. and Harris, J. D. (1991) Consistency and change in maternal child-rearing practices and values: a longitudinal study. *Child Development* 62, 190–198.

McNamara, T. P. (1986) Mental representations of spatial relations. *Cognitive Psychology* 18, 87–121.

McNaughton, S. (1987) *Being Skilled: The Socializations of Learning to Read*. London: Methuen.

McNaughton, S. and Leyland, J. (1990) The shifting focus of maternal tutoring across different difficulty levels on a problem-solving task. *British Journal of Developmental Psychology* 8, 147–155.

McNeill, D. (1966) Developmental psycholinguistics. In F. Smith and G. A. Miller (eds), *The Genesis of Language: A Psycholinguistic Approach*. Cambridge, MA: MIT Press.

McNiece, R., Bidgood, P. and Soan, P. (2004) An investigation into using national longitudinal studies to examine trends in educational attainment and development. *Educational Research* 46, 119–136.

MacPhee, D., Ramey, C. T. and Yeates, K. O. (1984) Home environment and early cognitive development: implications for intervention. In A. W. Gottfried (ed.), *Home Environment and Early Cognitive Development: Longitudinal Research*. Orlando, FL: Academic Press.

McShane, J. (1980) *Learning to talk*. Cambridge, UK: Cambridge University Press.

McShane, J. (1991) *Cognitive Development: An Information-processing Approach*. Oxford, UK: Blackwell.

Magnusson, D. and Stattan, H. (1998) Person–context interaction theories. *Handbook of Child Psychology*, vol. 1. New York: Wiley.

Main, M. and George, C. (1985) Responses of abused and disadvantaged toddlers to distress in agemates: a study in the day care setting. *Developmental Psychology* 21, 407–412.

Majid, A., Bowerman, M., Kita, S., Haun, D. B. M. and Levinson, S. C. (2004) Can language restructure cognition? The case for space. *Trends in Cognitive Sciences* 8(3), 108–114.

Malatesta, C. Z. (1990) The role of emotions in the development and organisation of personality. In R. A. Thompson (ed.), Socioemotional development. *Nebraska Symposium on Motivation*, 1988, vol. 36. Lincoln: University of Nebraska Press.

Mandell, F., McAnulty, E. H. and Carlson, A. (1983) Unexpected death of an infant sibling. *Pediatrics* 72(5), 652–657.

Mandler, J. M. (1983) Representation. In P. H. Mussen (ed.), *Handbook of Child Psychology*, vol. 3. New York: Wiley.

Mandler, J. M. (1998) Representation. In D. Kuhn and R. S. Siegler (eds), *Handbook of Child Psychology, vol. 2, Cognition, Perception and Language*. New York: Wiley.

Mandler, J. M. (2004a) *The Foundations of Mind: Origins of Conceptual Thought*. New York: Oxford University Press.

Mandler, J. M. (2004b) *A Synopsis of The Foundations of Mind: Origins of Conceptual Thought*. New York: Oxford University Press. Target article with commentaries and response. *Developmental Science* 7(5), 499–505.

Mandler, J. M. and Johnson, N. S. (1977) Remembrance of things parsed: story structure and recall. *Cognitive Psychology* 9, 111–151.

Mann, V. A., Tobin, P. and Wilson, R. (1987) Measuring phonological awareness through the invented spellings of kindergarten children. *Merrill-Palmer Quarterly* 33(3), 365–391.

Mant, C. M. and Perner, J. (1988) The child's understanding of commitment. *Developmental Psychology* 24(3), 343–351.

Many, J. E., Fyfe, R., Lewis, G. and Mitchel, E. (2004) Traversing the topical landscape: exploring students' self-directed reading–writing–research processes. In R. B. Ruddell and N. J. Unrau (eds), *Theoretical Models and Processes of Reading*. Newark, DE: International Reading Association.

Maratsos, M. (1983) Some current issues in the study of the acquisition of grammar. In P. H. Mussen (ed.), *Handbook of Child Psychology*, vol. 3. New York: Wiley.

Maratsos, M. (1989) Innateness and plasticity in language acquisition. In M. L. Rice and R. L. Schiefelbusch (eds), *The Teachability of Language*. Baltimore: Brookes.

Maratsos, M. (1998) The acquisition of grammar. In D. Kuhn and R. S. Siegler (eds), *Handbook of Child Psychology, vol. 2, Cognition, Perception and Language*. New York: Wiley.

Marchman, V. and Bates, E. (1994) Continuity in lexical and morphological development: a test of the critical mass hypothesis. *Journal of Child Language* 21, 339–366.

Marcus, G. E. (1993) Negative evidence in language acquisition. *Cognition* 46, 53–85.

Marean, G. C., Werner, L. A. and Kuhl, P. K. (1992) Vowel categorisation by very young infants. *Developmental Psychology* 28, 396–405.

Marjoribanks, K. (1979) *Families and their Learning Environments: an Empirical Analysis*. London: Routledge.

Markman, E., Cox, B. and Machida, S. (1981) The standard sorting task as a measure of conceptual organisation. *Developmental Psychology* 17, 115–117.

Markman, E. M. (1973) The facilitation of part–whole comparisons by use of the collective noun 'family'. *Child Development* 44, 837–840.

Markman, E. M. (1977) Realising that you don't understand: a preliminary investigation. *Child Development* 48, 986–992.

Markman, E. M. (1979) Realising that you don't understand: elementary school children's awareness of inconsistencies. *Child Development* 50, 643–655.

Markman, E. M. (1981) Comprehension monitoring. In W. P. Dickson (ed.), *Children's Oral Communication Skills.* New York: Academic Press.

Markman, E. M. (1987) How children constrain the possible meanings of words. In U. Neisser (ed.), *Concepts and Conceptual Development.* Cambridge, UK: Cambridge University Press.

Markman, E. M. (1989) *Categorization and Naming in Children: The Problem of Induction.* Boston: MIT Press.

Markman, E. M. (1990) Constraints children place on word meaning. *Cognitive Science* 14, 57–77.

Markman, E. M. and Callahan, M. A. (1983) An analysis of hierarchical classification. In R. J. Sternberg (ed.), *Advances in the Psychology of Human Intelligence*, vol. 2. Hillsdale, NJ: Lawrence Erlbaum Associates, Inc.

Markova, I. (1982) *Paradigms, Thought and Language.* New York: Wiley.

Markova, I. (1987) *Human Awareness: Its Social Development.* London: Hutchinson.

Markovits, H. (2004) The development of deductive reasoning. In J. P. Leighton and R. J. Sternberg (eds), *The Nature of Reasoning.* Cambridge, UK: Cambridge University Press.

Markovits, H. and Barrouillet, P. (2002) The development of conditional reasoning: A mental model account. *Developmental Review* 22(1), 5–36.

Marks, L. E., Hammeal, R. J. and Bornstein, M. H. (1987) Perceiving similarity and comprehending metaphor. *Monographs of the Society for Research in Child Development* 52(1), serial no. 215.

Markus, H. R. and Kitayama, S. (1991) Culture and the self: implications for cognition, emotion and motivation. *Psychological Review* 98, 224–253.

Marler, P. and Terrace, H. (1984) *The Biology of Learning.* Berlin, Germany: Springer-Verlag.

Marmurek, H. H. C. and Rinaldo, R. (1992) The development of letter and syllable effects in categorisation, reading aloud and naming. *Journal of Experimental Child Psychology* 53, 277–299.

Marr, D. (1982) *Vision: A Computational Investigation into the Human Representation and Processing of Visual Information.* San Francisco: Freeman.

Marsh, R. W. (1985) Phrenoblysis: real or chimera? *Child Development* 56, 1059–1061.

Marshall, J. C. (1987a) Routes and representations in the processing of written language. In E. Keller and M. Gopnik (eds), *Motor and Sensory Processes in Language.* Hillsdale, NJ: Lawrence Erlbaum Associates, Inc.

Marshall, J. C. (1987b) The cultural and biological context of written language. In J. Beech and A. Colley (eds), *Cognitive Approaches to Reading.* Chichester, UK: Wiley.

Marshall, N. (2004) The quality of early child care and children's development. *Current Directions in Psychological Science* 13(4), 165–168.

Martin, C. L. and Ruble, D. (2004) Children's search for gender cues. *Current Directions in Psychological Science* 13(2), 67–70.

Martlew, M. (1983) *The Psychology of Written Language: Development and Educational Perspectives.* Chichester, UK: Wiley.

Marton, F. (1983) Beyond individual differences. *Educational Psychology* 3, 289–304.

Marton, F. (1988) Describing and improving learning. In R. R. Schmeck (ed.), *Learning Strategies and Learning Styles.* New York: Plenum Press.

Marton, F., Asplund Carlsson, M. and Halasz, L. (1992) Differences in understanding and the use of reflective variation in reading. *British Journal of Educational Psychology* 62, 1–16.

Marzolf, D. P. and DeLoache, J. S. (1994) Transfer in young children's understanding of spatial representations. *Child Development* 65, 1–15.

Mason, L. (2003) High school students' beliefs about math, mathematical problem-solving, and their achievement in math: a cross-sectional study. *Educational Psychology* 23, 73–85.

Mason, L. and Scrivani, L. (2004) Enhancing students' mathematical beliefs: an intervention study. *Learning and Instruction* 14, 153–176.

Massey, C. M. and Gelman, R. (1988) Preschoolers' ability to decide whether a photographed unfamiliar object can move itself. *Developmental Psychology* 24(3), 307–317.

Masson, J. M. (1996) *The Lost Prince: The Unsolved Mystery of Kaspar Hauser.* New York: Simon and Schuster.

Masterson, J., Laxon, V. and Stuart, M. (1992) Beginning reading with phonology. *British Journal of Psychology* 83, 1–12.

Matthews, G. (1980) *Philosophy and the Young Child.* Cambridge, MA: Harvard University Press.

Matthews, M. H. (1984) Cognitive mapping abilities of young boys and girls. *Geography* 69, 327–336.

Matthews, M. H. (1987) The influence of gender on the environmental cognition of young boys and girls. *Journal of Genetic Psychology* 147, 295–302.

Matthews, M. H. (1992) *Making Sense of Place: Children's Understanding of Large-scale Environments.* Hemel Hempstead, UK: Harvester.

Mayer, R. (1982a) Different problem solving strategies for algebra word and equation problems. *Journal of Experimental Psychology: Learning, Memory and Cognition* 8, 448–462.

Mayer, R. (1982b) Memory for algebra story problems. *Journal of Educational Psychology* 74, 119–216.

Mayer, R. (1985) Mathematical ability. In R. J. Sternberg (ed.), *Human Abilities: An Information-processing Approach.* New York: Freeman.

Mayer, R. (2004) Should there be a three-strikes rule against pure discovery learning? *American Psychologist* 59(1), 14–19.

Mayes, A. R. (1988) *Human Organic Memory Disorders.* Cambridge, UK: Cambridge University Press.

Maynard, A. E. (2002) Cultural teaching: the development of teaching skills in Maya sibling interactions. *Child Development* 73, 969–982.

Mead, G. H. (1934) *Mind, Self and Society*. Chicago: University of Chicago Press.

Meadows, S. (1975) *The development of concrete operations: a short-term longitudinal study*. PhD thesis, University of London.

Meadows, S. (1977) An experimental investigation of Piaget's analysis of class inclusion. *British Journal of Psychology* 68(2), 229–237.

Meadows, S. (ed.) (1983) *Developing Thinking: Approaches to Children's Cognitive Development*. London: Methuen.

Meadows, S. (1986) *Understanding Child Development*, London: Hutchinson.

Meadows, S. (1996) *Parenting Behaviour and Children's Cognitive Development*. Hove, UK: Psychology Press.

Meadows, S. and Cashdan, A. (1983) *Teaching Styles in Nursery Education: Final Report to SSRC*. Sheffield, UK: Sheffield City Polytechnic.

Meadows, S. and Cashdan, A. (1988) *Helping Children Learn: Contributions to a Cognitive Curriculum*. London: David Fulton.

Meadows, S., Herrick, D. and Feiler, A. (forthcoming) Improvement in SATs Reading scores at KS1; grade inflation or better achievement? *British Educational Research Journal*.

Meadows, S. and Mills, M. (1987) End of grant report to ESRC on project C00232101: Preschool parenting style and children's cognition: follow-up on starting school.

Medin, D. L. and Wattenmaker, W. D. (1987) Category cohesiveness, theories and cognitive archeology. In U. Neisser (ed.), *Concepts and Conceptual Development*. Cambridge, UK: Cambridge University Press.

Mehler, J., Bertoncini, J., Barrier, J. and Jassik-Gerschenfeld, D. (1978) Infant recognition of mother's voice. *Perception* 7, 491–497.

Meichenbaum, D., Burland, S., Gruson, L. and Cameron, R. (1985) Metacognitive assessment. In S. R. Yussen (ed.), *The Growth of Reflection in Children*. New York: Academic Press.

Meins, E. (1997) Security of attachment and maternal tutoring strategies: interaction within the zone of proximal development. *British Journal of Developmental Psychology* 15, 129–144.

Meins, E. (1998) The effects of security of attachment and maternal attribution of meaning on children's linguistic acquisitional style. *Infant Behaviour and Development* 21(2), 237–252.

Meins, E. and Fernyhough, C. (1999) Linguistic acquisitional style and mentalising development: the role of maternal mind-mindedness. *Cognitive Development* 14(3), 363–380.

Meins, E., Fernyhough, C., Fradley, E. and Tuckey, M. (2001) Rethinking maternal sensitivity: Mothers' comments on infants' mental processes predict security of attachment at 12 months. *Journal of Child Psychology and Psychiatry* 42(5), 637–648.

Meins, E., Fernyhough, C., Wainwright, R., Das Gupta, M., Fradley, E. and Tuckey, M. (2002) Maternal mind-mindedness and attachment security as predictors of theory of mind understanding. *Child Development* 73(6), 1715–1726.

Meins, E., Fernyhough, C., Wainwright, R., Clark-Carter, D., Das Gupta, M., Fradley, E. and Tuckey, M. (2003) Pathways to understanding mind: construct validity and predictive validity of maternal mind-mindedness. *Child Development* 74(4), 1194–1211.

Mellin-Olsen, S. (1987) *The Politics of Mathematics Education*. Dordrecht, The Netherlands: Reidel.

Meltzoff, A. N. (1995) What infantile memory tells us about infantile amnesia: long-term and deferred imitation. *Journal of Experimental Child Psychology* 59, 497–515.

Meltzoff, A. N. and Decety, J. (2003) What imitation tells us about social cognition: a rapprochement between developmental psychology and cognitive neuroscience. *Philosophical Transactions of the Royal Society of London* B358, 491–500.

Merriman, W. E., Evey-Burkey, J. A., Marazita, J. M. and Jarvis, L. H. (1996) Young two-year-olds' tendency to map novel verbs on to novel actions. *Journal of Experimental Child Psychology* 63, 466–498.

Mervis, C. B. (1987) Child-basic object categories and early lexical development. In U. Neisser (ed.), *Concepts and Conceptual Development*. Cambridge, UK: Cambridge University Press.

Messer, D. J. (1994) *The Development of Communication: From Social Interaction to Language*. New York: Wiley.

Meyers, M. and Paris, S. (1978) Children's metacognitive knowledge about reading. *Journal of Educational Psychology* 70, 680–690.

Midgley, M. (1985) *Evolution as a Religion: Strange Hopes and Stranger Fears*. London: Methuen.

Miller, A. (1985) *Thou Shalt Not Be Aware: Society's Betrayal of the Child*. London: Pluto Press.

Miller, A. (1987) *For Your Own Good: Hidden Cruelty in Child-rearing and the Roots of Violence*. London: Virago.

Miller, A. (1990) *The Untouched Key: Tracing Childhood Trauma in Creativity and Destructiveness*. London: Virago.

Miller, J. and Davis, D. (1997) Poverty history, marital history and quality of children's home environments. *Journal of Marriage and Family* 59, 996–1007.

Miller, J. E. and Korenman, S. (1994) Poverty and children's nutritional status in the United States. *American Journal of Epidemiology* 140, 233–243.

Miller, K. E., Smith, C. M., Zhu, J. and Zhang, H. (1995) Preschool origins of cross-national differences in mathematical competence: the role of number-naming systems. *Psychological Science* 6, 56–60.

Miller, K. F. and Paredes, D. R. (1990) Starting to add worse: effects of learning to multiply on children's addition. *Cognition* 37, 213–242.

Miller, P. and Sperry, L. L. (1987) The socialization of anger and aggression. *Merrill-Palmer Quarterly* 33(1), 1–31.

Miller, P. H. and De Marie-Dreblow, D. (1990) Social-cognitive correlates of children's understanding of displaced aggression. *Journal of Experimental Child Psychology* 49, 488–504.

Miller, P. H. and Seier, W. L. (1994) Strategy utilization deficiencies in children: when, where, and why. *Advances in Child Development and Behaviour* 25, 107–156.

Miller, P. H. and Zalenski, R. (1982) Preschoolers' knowledge about attention. *Developmental Psychology* 18(6), 871–875.

Miller, P. J., Mintz, J., Hoogstra, L., Fung, H. and Potts, R. (1992) The narrated self: young children's construction of self in relation to others in conversational stories of personal experience. *Merrill-Palmer Quarterly* 38, 45–68.

Miller, P. J., Wiley, A. R., Fung, H. and Liang, C.-H. (1997) Personal story-telling as a medium of socialization in Chinese and American families. *Child Development* 68, 557–568.

Miller, S. A. (1982) On the generalizability of conservation: a comparison of different kinds of transformation. *British Journal of Psychology* 73(2), 221–230.

Miller, S. A. (1986a) Certainty and necessity in the understanding of Piagetian concepts. *Developmental Psychology* 22(1), 3–18.

Miller, S. A. (1986b) Parents' beliefs about their children's cognitive abilities. *Developmental Psychology* 22, 276–284.

Mills, C. M. and Keil, F. C. (2004) Knowing the limits of one's understanding. *Journal of Experimental Child Psychology* 87, 1–32.

Mills, M. and Funnell, E. (1983) Experience and cognitive processing. In S. Meadows (ed.), *Developing Thinking*. London: Methuen.

Mills, M., Puckering, C., Pound, A. and Cox, A. (1985) What is it about depressed mothers that influences their children's functioning? In J. Stevenson (ed.), *Recent Advances in Developmental Psychopathology*. Oxford, UK: Pergamon.

Milne, A. A. (1926) *Winnie-the-Pooh*. London: Methuen.

Mingroni, M. A. (2004) The secular rise in IQ: giving heterosis a closer look. *Intelligence* 32, 65–83.

Minsky, M. (1988) *The Society of Mind*. New York: Simon & Schuster.

Mischel, T. (ed.) (1971) *Cognitive Development and Epistemology*. New York: Academic Press.

Mitchell, P. and Robinson, E. J. (1992) Children's understanding of the evidential connotations of 'know' in relation to overestimation of their own knowledge. *Journal of Child Language* 19, 167–182.

Mithen, S. (1996) *The Prehistory of the Mind*. London: Thames and Hudson.

Mix, K. S., Levine, S. C. and Huttenlocher, J. (1999) Early fraction calculation ability. *Developmental Psychology* 35, 164–174.

Moely, B. E. (1977) Organisational factors in the development of memory. In R. V. Kail and J. W. Hagen (eds), *Perspectives on the Development of Memory and Cognition*. Hillsdale, NJ: Lawrence Erlbaum Associates, Inc.

Moerk, E. L. (1989) The LAD was a lady and the tasks were ill-defined. *Developmental Review* 9(1), 21–57.

Moffitt, T. E., Caspi, A., Harkness, A. R. and Silva, P. A. (1993) The natural history of change in intellectual performance: Who changes? How much? Is it meaningful? *Journal of Child Psychology and Psychiatry and Allied Disciplines* 34, 455–506.

Molfese, D. and Segalowitz, S. J. (eds) (1988) *Brain Lateralisation in Children: Developmental Implications*. New York: Guilford Press.

Moll, L. C. (ed.) (1990) *Vygotsky and Education: Instructional Implications and Applications of Socio-historical Psychology*. Cambridge, UK: Cambridge University Press.

Moog, H. [1968] (English translation 1976) *The Musical Experience of the Pre-school Child*. London: Schott Music.

Moore, C., Bryant, D. and Furrow, D. (1989) Mental terms and the development of certainty. *Child Development* 60, 167–171.

Moore, C., Pure, K. and Furrow, D. (1990) Children's understanding of the modal experience of speaker certainty and uncertainty and its relation to the development of a representational theory of mind. *Child Development* 61, 722–730.

Moore, C. F. (2003) *Silent Scourge: Children, Pollution, and Why Scientists Disagree.* Oxford, UK: Oxford University Press.

Moore, E. G. J. (1986) Family socialization and the IQ test performance of traditionally and transracially adopted black children. *Developmental Psychology* 22, 317–326.

Moore, R. (1986) *Childhood's Domain.* London: Croom Helm.

Moravcsik, J. M. (1990) *Thought and Language.* London: Routledge.

Morgan, F. (1989) Writing in perspective. *Education* 174(14), 303.

Morgan, J. L. and Demuth, K. (eds) (1996) Signal to syntax: bootstrapping from speech to grammar in early acquisition. Hillsdale, NJ: Lawrence Erlbaum Associates, Inc.

Morison, S., Ames, E. W. and Chisholm, K. (1995) The development of children adopted from Romanian orphanages. *Merrill-Palmer Quarterly* 41, 411–430.

Morrison, F. J., Holmes, D. L. and Haith, M. M. (1974) A developmental study of the effects of familiarity on short-term visual memory. *Journal of Experimental Child Psychology* 18, 412–425.

Morss, J. R. (1985) Early cognitive development: difference or delay? In D. Lane and B. Stratford (eds), *Current Approaches to Down's Syndrome.* London: Holt, Rinehart & Winston.

Mortimore, P. and Mortimore, J. (1986) Education and social class. In R. Rogers (ed.), *Education and Social Class.* Lewes, UK: Falmer Press.

Mortimore, P., Sammons, P., Stoll, L., Lewis, D. and Ecob, R. (1989) A study of effective junior schools. *International Journal of Educational Research* 13(7), 753–768.

Mortimore, P., Simmons, P., Stoll, L., Lewis, D. and Ecob, R. (1998) *School Matters: The Junior Years.* Wells, UK: Open Books.

Morton, J. (1980) The logogen model and orthographic structure. In U. Frith (ed.), *Cognitive Processes in Spelling.* London: Academic Press.

Morton, J. (1990) The development of event memory. *The Psychologist* 1, 3–10.

Morton, J., Hammersley, R. H. and Bekerian, D. A. (1992) Headed records: a model for memory and its failures. *Cognition* 20, 1–23.

Morton, J. and Patterson, K. (1980) A new attempt at an interpretation, or an attempt at a new interpretation. In M. Coltheart, K. Patterson and J. Marshall (eds), *Deep Dyslexia.* London: Routledge.

Moses L. J. and Flavell, J. (1990) Inferring false beliefs from actions and reactions. *Child Development* 61, 929–945.

Moshman, D. (1998) Cognitive development beyond childhood. *Handbook of Child Psychology*, vol. 2.

Moshman, D. and Franks, B. A. (1986) Development of the concept of inferential validity. *Child Development* 57, 153–165.

Moshman, D. and Timmons, M. (1982) The construction of logical necessity. *Human Development* 25, 309–323.

Mosteller, F. (1995) The Tennessee study of class size in the early school grades. *Future of Children* 5(2), 113–127.

Movshon, J. A. and Van Sluyters, R. C. (1981) Visual neuronal development. *Annual Review of Psychology* 32, 477–522.

Mumford, M. D. and Gustafson, S. B. (1988) Creativity syndrome: integration, application and innovation. *Psychological Bulletin* 103, 27–43.

Munakata, Y. (2004) Computational cognitive neuroscience of early memory development. *Developmental Review* 24(1), 132–153.

Munn, P. (1998) Symbolic function in preschoolers. In C. Donlan (ed.), *The Development of Mathematical Skills*. Hove, UK: Psychology Press.

Murachver, T., Pipe, M., Gordon, R., Owens, J. L. and Fivush, R. (1996) Do, show, and tell: Children's event memories acquired through direct experience, observation, and stories. *Child Development* 67, 3029–3044.

Murphy, G. L. and Medin, D. L. (1985) The role of theories in conceptual coherence. *Psychological Review* 92, 289–316.

Murphy, K., McKone, E. and Slee, J. (2003) Dissociations between implicit and explicit memory in children: the role of strategic processing and the knowledge base. *Journal of Experimental Child Psychology* 84, 125–165.

Muter, V., Hulme, C., Snowling, M. and Stevenson, J. (2004) Phonemes, rimes, vocabulary and grammatical skills as foundations of early reading development. *Developmental Psychology* 40(5), 665–681.

Myers, N. A. and Perlmutter, M. (1978) Memory in the years from two to five. In P. A. Ornstein (ed.), *Memory Development in Children*. Hillsdale, NJ: Lawrence Erlbaum Associates, Inc.

Myles-Worsley, M., Cromer, C. C. and Dodd, D. H. (1986) Children's preschool script reconstruction: reliance on general knowledge as memory fades. *Developmental Psychology* 22(2), 22–30.

Nagy, W. E. and Scott, J. A. (2004) Vocabulary processes. In R. B. Ruddell and N. J. Unrau (eds), *Theoretical Models and Processes of Reading*. Newark, DE: International Reading Association.

Naigles, L. and Hoff-Ginsburg, E. (1998) Why are some verbs learned before other verbs? Effect of input frequency and structure in children's early verb use. *Journal of Child Language* 25, 95–120.

Nakamura, C. Y. and Finck, D. N. (1980) Relative effectiveness of socially-oriented and task-oriented children and predictability of their behaviours. *Monographs of the Society for Research in Child Development* 45(3–4), serial no. 185.

Nakamura, J. and Csikszentmihalyi, M. (2001) Catalytic creativity: the case of Linus Pauling. *American Psychologist* 56(4), 337–341.

Napolitano, A. C. and Sloutsky, V. M. (2004) Is a picture worth a thousand words? The flexible nature of modality dominance in young children. *Child Development* 75(6), 1850–1870.

Naslund, J. C. and Schneider, W. (1991) Longitudinal effects of verbal ability, memory capacity and phonological awareness on reading performance. *European Journal of Psychology of Education* 6, 375–392.

Nation, K., Adams, J. W., Bowyer-Crane, C. A. and Snowling, M. J. (1999) Working memory deficits in poor comprehenders reflect underlying language impairments. *Journal of Experimental Child Psychology* 73(2), 139–158.

Naus, M. J., Ornstein, P. A. and Aivano, S. (1977) Developmental changes in memory: the effects of processing time and rehearsal instructions. *Journal of Experimental Psychology* 23, 237–251.

Nazzi, T., Bertoncini, J. and Mehler, J. (1998) Language discrimination by newborns: towards an understanding of the role of rhythm. *Journal of Experimental Psychology: Human Perception and Performance* 24, 756–766.

Nazzi, T. and Gopnik, A. (2001) Linguistic and cognitive abilities in infancy: when does language become a tool for categorisation? *Cognition* 80, 30–37.

Needleman, H. L., Gunnoe, C., Leviton, A., Reed, M., Peresie, H., Maher, C. and Barrett, P. (1979) Deficits in psychologic and classroom performance of children with elevated dentine lead levels. *New England Journal of Medicine* 300, 689–695.

Neisser, U. (ed.) (1987) *Concepts and Conceptual Development: Ecological and Intellectual Factors in Categorisation.* Cambridge, UK: Cambridge University Press.

Neisser, U. (ed.) (1998) *The Rising Curve: Long-term Gains in IQ and Related Measures.* Washington, DC: American Psychological Association.

Neisser, U., Boodoo, G., Bouchard, T. J., Jr, Boykin, A. W., Brody, N., Ceci, S. J., Halpern, D. F., Loehlin, J. C., Perloff, R., Sternberg, R. J. and Urbina, S. (1996) Intelligence: knowns and unknowns. *American Psychologist* 51(2), 77–101.

Nelson, C. A. and Bloom, F. E. (1997) Child development and neuroscience. *Child Development* 68(5), 970–989.

Nelson, C. A. and Webb, S. J. (2003) A cognitive neuroscience perspective on early memory development. In M. De Haan and M. Johnson (eds), *The Cognitive Neuroscience of Development.* Hove, UK: Psychology Press.

Nelson, K. (ed.) (1989a) *Narratives from the Crib.* Cambridge, MA: Harvard University Press.

Nelson, K. (1996) *Language in Cognitive Development.* New York: Cambridge University Press.

Nelson, K. and Fivush, R. (2004) The emergence of autobiographical memory: a social cultural developmental theory. *Psychological Review* 111(2), 486–511.

Nelson, K. E. (1971) Memory development in children: evidence from non-verbal tasks. *Psychonomic Science* 25, 346–348.

Nelson, K. E. (1973) Structure and strategy in learning to talk. *Monographs of the Society for Research in Child Development* 38(1–2), serial no. 149.

Nelson, K. E. (1978) How young children represent knowledge of their world in and out of language. In R. S. Siegler (ed.), *Children's Thinking: What Develops?* Hillsdale, NJ: Lawrence Erlbaum Associates, Inc.

Nelson, K. E. (1981) Social cognition in a script framework. In J. H. Flavell and L. Ross (eds), *Social Cognitive Development: Frontiers and Possible Futures.* Cambridge, UK: Cambridge University Press.

Nelson, K. E. (1985) *Making Sense: The Acquisition of Shared Meaning.* London: Academic Press.

Nelson, K. E. (1986) *Event Knowledge: Structure and Function in Development.* Hillsdale, NJ: Lawrence Erlbaum Associates, Inc.

Nelson, K. E. (1989b) Strategies for first language teaching. In M. L. Rice and R. L. Schiefelbusch (eds), *The Teachability of Language.* Baltimore: Brookes.

Nelson, K. E. and Gruendel, J. (1979) At morning it's lunchtime: a scriptal view of children's dialogues. *Discourse Processes* 2, 73–94.

Nelson, K. E. and Gruendel, J. (1981) Generalised event representations, basic building blocks of cognitive development. *Advances in Developmental Psychology,* vol. 1. Hillsdale, NJ: Lawrence Erlbaum Associates, Inc.

Nelson, K. E. and Kosslyn, S. M. (1976) Recognition of previously labelled or unlabelled pictures by 5 year olds and adults. *Journal of Experimental Child Psychology* 21, 40–45.

Nelson, S., Lerner, E., Needlman, R., Salvator, A. M. S. and Singer, L. T. (2004) Cocaine, anemia, and neurodevelopmental outcomes in children: a longitudinal study. *Journal of Developmental and Behavioral Pediatrics* 25(1), 1–9.

Nesselroade, J. R. and Baltes, P. B. (1979) *Longitudinal Research in the Study of Behaviour and Development*. London: Academic Press.

Nettelbeck, T. (1986) Inspection time and intelligence. In P. A. Vernon (ed.), *Speed of Information Processing and Intelligence*. New York: Ablex.

Nettelbeck, T, (2001) Correlation between inspection time and psychometric abilities – A personal interpretation. *Intelligence* 29(6), 459–474.

Nettelbeck, T. and Vita, P. (1992) Inspection time in two childhood age cohorts: a constraint or a developmental function? *British Journal of Developmental Psychology* 10, 180–197.

Nettelbeck, T. and Wilson, J. (1985) A cross-sequential analysis of developmental differences in speed of visual information processing. *Journal of Experimental Child Psychology* 40, 1–22.

Nettelbeck, T. and Wilson, C. (2004) The Flynn effect: smarter not faster. *Intelligence* 32, 85–93.

Nettelbeck, T. and Young, R. (1989) Inspection time and intelligence in 6 year old children. *Personality and Individual Differences* 10, 605–614.

Newcombe, N. and Dubas, J. S. (1992) A longitudinal study of predictors of spatial ability in adolescent females. *Child Development* 63, 37–46.

Newcombe, N. E., Rogoff, B. and Kagan, J. (1977) Developmental changes in recognitive memory for pictures of objects and scenes. *Developmental Psychology* 13, 337–341.

Newell, A. and Simon, H. A. (1972) *Human Problem-solving*. Englewood Cliffs, NJ: Prentice Hall.

Newman, D., Griffin, P. and Cole, M. (1989) *The Construction Zone*. Cambridge, UK: Cambridge University Press.

Newport, E. L. (1990) Maturational constraints on language learning. *Cognitive Science* 14, 11–28.

Newton, M. (2002) *Savage Girls and Wild Boys: A History of Feral Children*. London: Faber.

NICHD Early Child Care Research Network (Spring 2004) Multiple pathways to early academic achievement. *Harvard Educational Review*, 1–29.

Nicholls, A. L. and Kennedy, J. M. (1992) Drawing development: from similarity of features to depiction. *Child Development* 63, 227–241.

Nicholls, J. G. (1978) The development of the concepts of effort and ability, perception of academic attainment, and the understanding that difficult tasks require more ability. *Child Development* 49, 800–814.

Nicholls, J. G., Patashnick, M. and Mettetal, G. (1986) Children's conceptions of ability and intelligence. *Child Development* 57, 636–645.

Nickerson, R. (2004) Teaching thinking. In J. P. Leighton and R. J. Sternberg (eds), *The Nature of Reasoning*. Cambridge, UK: Cambridge University Press.

Nicolson, R. and Fawcett, A. (1990) Automaticity: a new framework for dyslexia research? *Cognition* 35, 159–182.

Nielsen, R. (2002) Disclosure of variation. *Nature* 434, 288–289.

Ninio, A. and Bruner, J. S. (1978) The achievement and antecedents of labelling. *Journal of Child Language* 5, 1–15.

Nisan, M. (2004) Judgment and choice in moral functioning. In D. Lapsley and D. Narvaez (eds), *Moral Development, Self, and Identity*. Mahwah, NJ: Lawrence Erlbaum Associates, Inc.

Nisbett, R. and Ross, L. (1980) *Human Inference: Strategies and Shortcomings of Social Judgement*. Englewood Cliffs, NJ: Prentice Hall.

Nisbett, R. and Wilson, T. (1977) Telling more than we know: verbal reports on mental processes. *Psychological Review* 84, 231–259.

Nold, E. W. (1981) Revising. In C. H. Fredericksen and J. F. Dominic (eds), *Writing: The Nature, Development and Teaching of Written Communication*, vol. 2. Hillsdale, NJ: Lawrence Erlbaum Associates, Inc.

Novak, J. D. (1988) Learning science and the science of learning. *Studies in Science Education* 15, 77–101.

Nucci, L. (2002a) Because it is the right thing to do. *Human Development* 45(2), 125–129.

Nucci, L. (2002b) Exploring borders: Understanding culture and psychology. *Contemporary Psychology* 47(6), 705–707.

Nucci, L. (2002c) The development of moral reasoning. In U. Goswami (ed.), *Blackwell Handbook of Cognitive Development*. Oxford, UK: Blackwell.

Nucci, L. (2004) Reflections on the moral self construct. In D. Lapsley and D. Narvaez (eds), *Moral Development, Self, and Identity*. Mahwah, NJ: Lawrence Erlbaum Associates, Inc.

Nunes, T. and Bryant, P. (1995) Do problem situations influence children's understanding of the commutativity of multiplication? *Mathematical Cognition* 1, 245–260.

Nunes, T., Bryant, P. E. and Bindman, M. (1997) Morphological spelling strategies: developmental stages and processes. *Developmental Psychology* 33(4), 637–649.

Nunner-Winkler, G. (2004) Sociohistoric changes in the structure of moral motivation. In D. Lapsley and D. Narvaez (eds), *Moral Development, Self, and Identity*. Mahwah, NJ: Lawrence Erlbaum Associates, Inc.

Nunner-Winkler, G. and Sodian, B. (1988) Children's understanding of moral emotions. *Child Development* 59, 1323–1338.

Nuttall, D. L., Goldstein, H., Prosser, R. and Rasbash, J. (1989) Differential school effectiveness. *International Journal of Educational Research* 13(7), 769–776.

Oakhill, J. and Garnham, A. (1988) *Becoming a Skilled Reader*. Oxford, UK: Blackwell.

O'Brien, D. (1987) The development of conditional reasoning: an iffy proposition. In H. W. Reese (ed.), *Advances in Child Development and Behavior*, vol. 20. New York: Academic Press.

Ochs, E. (1988) *Culture and Language Development: Language Acquisition and Language Socialisation in a Samoan Village*. Cambridge, UK: Cambridge University Press.

Ochs, E. (1990) Indexicality and socialization. In J. W. Stiger, R. A. Shweder and G. H. Herdt (eds), *Cultural Psychology*. Cambridge, UK: Cambridge University Press.

Ochs, E. and Schieffelin, B. (eds) (1979) *Developmental Pragmatics*. New York: Academic Press.

Ochs, E. and Schieffelin, B. (1983) *Acquiring a Conversational Competence*. London: Routledge & Kegan Paul.

Ochs, E. and Schieffelin, B. (1995) The impact of language socialisation on grammatical development. In P. Fletcher and B. MacWhinney (eds), *The Handbook of Child Language*. Oxford, UK: Blackwell.

Ochse, R. (1990) *Before the Gates of Excellence: the Determinants of Creative Genius*. Cambridge, UK: Cambridge University Press.

O'Connor, N. (1987) Cognitive psychology and mental handicap. *Journal of Mental Deficiency Research* 31, 329–336.

O'Connor, N. and Hermelin, B. (1984) Idiot savant calendrical calculators: maths or memory? *Psychological Medicine* 14, 801–806.

O'Connor, N. and Hermelin, B. (1990) The recognition failure and graphic success of idiot-savant artists. *Journal of Child Psychology and Psychiatry* 31(2), 203–215.

O'Connor, T. (2003) Natural experiments to study the effects of early experience: progress and limitations. *Development and Psychopathology* 15(4), 837–852.

O'Connor, T. G., Heron, J., Golding, J., Glover, V. and ALSPAC Study Team (2003) Maternal antenatal anxiety and behavioural/emotional problems in children: a test of a programming hypothesis. *Journal of Child Psychology and Psychiatry* 44(7), 1025–1036.

O'Connor, T. G., Heron, J., Glover, V. and ALSPAC Study Team (2002a) Antenatal anxiety predicts child behavioral/emotional problems independently of postnatal depression. *Journal of the American Academy of Child and Adolescent Psychiatry* 41, 1470–1477.

O'Connor, T. G., Heron, J., Golding, J., Beveridge, M. and Glover, V. (2002b) Maternal antenatal anxiety and children's behavioural/emotional problems at 4 years. *Report from the Avon Longitudinal Study of Parents and Children, British Journal of Psychiatry* 180, 502–508.

O'Connor, T. G., Marvin, R. S., Rutter, M., Olrick, J., Britner, P. A. and the English and Romanian Adoptees Study Team (2003) Child–parent attachment following severe early institutional deprivation. *Development and Psychopathology* 15, 19–38.

O'Connor, T. G., Rutter, M., Beckett, C., Keaveney, L., Kreppner, J. and the English and Romanian Adoptees Study Team (2000) The effects of global severe privation on cognitive competence: extension and longitudinal follow-up. *Child Development* 71(2), 376–390.

Okagaki, L. and Sternberg, R. J. (eds) (1991) *Directors of Development: Influences on the Development of Children's Thinking*. Hillsdale, NJ: Lawrence Erlbaum Associates, Inc.

O'Keefe, J. and Nadel, L. (1978) *The Hippocampus as a Cognitive Map*. Oxford, UK: Clarendon Press.

Olson, D. R. (1977) From utterance to text: the bias of language in speech and writing. *Harvard Educational Review* 47, 257–281.

Olson, D. R. (ed.) (1980a) *The Social Foundations of Language and Thought: Essays in Honor of Jerome S. Bruner*. New York: Norton.

Olson, D. R. (1980b) Some social aspects of learning in oral and written language. In D. R. Olson (ed.), *The Social Foundations of Language and Thought: Essays in Honor of Jerome S. Bruner*. New York: Norton.

Olson, D. R. (1988) On the origins of beliefs and other intentional states in children.

In J. W. Astington, P. L. Harris and D. R. Olson (eds), *Developing Theories of Mind*. Cambridge, UK: Cambridge University Press.

Olson, D. R. and Astington, J. W. (1986) Children's acquisition of metalinguistic and metacognitive verbs. In W. Demopoulos and A. Marras (eds), *Language Learning and Concept Acquisition*. Norwood, NJ: Ablex.

Olson, D. R. and Torrance, N. (eds) (1991) *Literacy and Orality*. Cambridge, UK: Cambridge University Press.

Olson, D. R. and Torrance, N. G. (1983) Literacy and cognitive development. In S. Meadows (ed.), *Developing Thinking*. London: Methuen.

Olson, S. L., Bates, J. E. and Bayles, K. (1985) Mother–infant interaction and the development of individual differences in children's cognitive competence. *Developmental Psychology* 20, 166–179.

Olson, S. L., Bates, J. E. and Kaskie, B. (1992) Caregiver–infant interaction antecedents of children's school-age cognitive ability. *Merrill-Palmer Quarterly* 38, 309–330.

O'Neill, S. A. (2002) The self-identity of young musicians. In R. A. R. Macdonald, D. J. Hargreaves and D. E. Miell (eds), *Musical Identities*. Oxford, UK: Oxford University Press.

Opie, I. and Opie, P. (1967) *The Lore and Language of Schoolchildren*. London: Oxford University Press.

Opie, I. and Opie, P. (1969) *Children's Games in Street and Playground*. Oxford, UK: Clarendon Press.

Opie, I. and Opie, P. (1985) *The Singing Game*. Oxford, UK: Oxford University Press.

Orbach, I., Gross, Y., Glaubman, H. and Berman, D. (1985) Children's perception of death in humans and animals as a function of age, anxiety and cognitive ability. *Journal of Child Psychology and Psychiatry* 26, 453–463.

Ordonez, C. L., Carlo, M. S., Snow, C. E. and McLaughlin, B. (2002) Depth and breadth of vocabulary in two languages: which vocabulary skills transfer? *Journal of Educational Psychology* 94(4), 719–728.

Ornstein, P. A., Baker-Ward, L. and Naus, M. J. (1988) The development of children's mnemonic skills. In F. Weinert and M. Perlmutter (eds), *Memory Development: Universal Changes and Individual Development*. Hillsdale, NJ: Lawrence Erlbaum Associates, Inc.

Ornstein, P. A. and Naus, M. J. (1985) Effects of the knowledge base on children's memory knowledge. In H. W. Reese (ed.), *Advances in Child Development and Behavior*, vol. 19. New York: Academic Press.

Orton, A. (1987) *Learning Mathematics: Issues, Theory and Classroom Practice*. London: Cassell.

Ortony, A. (1988) Metaphor. In R. L. Gregory (ed.), *The Oxford Companion to the Mind*. Oxford, UK: Oxford University Press.

Osborn, A. F. and Milbank, J. (1987) *The Effects of Early Education*. Oxford, UK: Clarendon Press.

Osofsky, J. (1995) The effects of exposure to violence on young children. *American Psychologist* 50, 782–788.

O'Sullivan, J. T. (1996) Children's metamemory about the influence of conceptual relations on recall. *Journal of Experimental Child Psychology* 62, 1–29.

O'Sullivan, J. T., Howe, M. L. and Marche, T. A. (1996) Children's beliefs about long term retention. *Child Development* 67, 2989–3009.

Overton, W. F. (1998) Developmental psychology: philosophy, concepts and methodology. *Handbook of Child Psychology*, vol. 1. New York: Wiley.

Oyama, S., Griffiths, P. E. and Gray, R. D. (2001) *Cycles of Contingency: Developmental Systems and Evolution*. Cambridge, MA: MIT Press.

Paik, J. H. and Mix, K. S. (2003) U.S. and Korean children's comprehension of fraction names: a re-examination of cross-national differences. *Child Development* 74(1), 144–154.

Palermo, D. S. (1989) Knowledge and the child's developing theory of the world. *Advances in Child Development and Behaviour* 21, 269–297.

Palincsar, A. and Brown, A. L. (1984) Reciprocal teaching of comprehension-fostering and monitoring activities. *Cognition and Instruction* 1, 117–175.

Palisin, H. (1986) Preschool temperament and performance on achievement tests. *Developmental Psychology* 22, 766–770.

Panksepp, J. (1990) Gray zones at the emotion/cognition interface: a commentary. *Cognition and Emotion* 4, 289–302.

Papousek, H. (1967) Experimental studies of appetitional behaviour in human newborns and infants. In H. W. Stevenson, E. H. Hess and H. L. Rheingold (eds), *Early Behaviour*. New York: Wiley.

Pappas, S., Ginsburg, H. P. and Jiang, M. (2003) SES differences in young children's metacognition in the context of mathematical problem solving. *Cognitive Development* 18, 431–450.

Paradis, M. and Lebrun, Y. (1984) *Early Bilingualism and Child Development*. Lisse, The Netherlands: Swets & Zeitlinger.

Paris, S. G. (1978) The development of inference and transformation as memory operations. In P. A. Ornstein (ed.), *Memory Development in Children*. Hillsdale, NJ: Lawrence Erlbaum Associates, Inc.

Paris, S. G. and Jacobs, J. E. (1984) The benefits of informed instruction for children's reading awareness and comprehension skills. *Child Development* 55, 2083–2093.

Paris, S. G. and Lindauer, B. K. (1978) Constructive aspects of children's comprehension and memory. In R. V. Kail and J. W. Hagen (eds), *Perspectives on the Development of Memory and Cognition*. Hillsdale NJ: Lawrence Erlbaum Associates, Inc.

Parke, R. (1989) Social development in infancy: a 25-year perspective. In H. W. Reese (ed.), *Advances in Child Development and Behavior*, vol. 21. New York: Academic Press.

Parkes, C. M. (1972) *Bereavement: Studies in Grief in Adult Life*. London: Tavistock.

Parkins, E. J. (1988) Equilibration and cognition: a review and elaboration of Piaget's genetic epistemology. *Genetic, Social and General Psychology Monographs* 114(1), 77–96.

Pascual-Leone, J. (1970) A mathematical model for the transition rule in Piaget's developmental stages. *Acta Psychologica* 32, 301–345.

Pask, G. (1988) Learning strategies, teaching strategies and conceptual or learning style. In R. R. Schmeck (ed.), *Learning Strategies and Learning Styles*. New York: Plenum Press.

Patel, A. (2003) Language, music and the brain. *Nature Neuroscience* 6(7), 674–681.

Patterson, C. J., Kupersmidt, J. B. and Vaden, N. A. (1990) Income level, gender, ethnicity and household composition as predictors of children's school-based competence. *Child Development* 61, 485–494.

Patterson, K. E. and Morton J. (1985) From orthography to phonology: an attempt at an old interpretation. In K. E. Patterson, J. C. Marshall and M. Coltheart (eds), *Surface Dyslexia: Neuropsychological and Cognitive Studies of Phonological Reading.* Hillsdale, NJ: Lawrence Erlbaum Associates, Inc.

Pauen, S. and Wilkening, F. (1997) Children's analogical reasoning about natural phenomena. *Journal of Experimental Child Psychology* 67(1), 90–113.

Paus, T. (2005) Mapping brain maturation and cognitive development in adolescence. *Trends in Cognitive Science* 9(2), 60–68.

Peery, J. C., Peery, I. W. and Draper, T. W. (1987) *Music and Child Development.* New York: Springer-Verlag.

Pellegrini, A. D., Galda, L. and Flor, D. (1997a) Relationships, individual differences and children's use of literate language. *British Journal of Educational Psychology* 67, 139–152.

Pellegrini, A. D., Galda, L., Flor, D., Bartini, M. and Charak, D. (1997b) Close relationships, individual differences and early literacy learning. *Journal of Experimental Child Psychology* 67, 409–422.

Pellegrini, A. D., Galda, L., Stahl, S. and Shockley, B. (1995) The nexus of social and literacy experiences at home and school: implications for primary school oral language and literacy. *British Journal of Educational Psychology* 65, 273–285.

Pellegrini, A. D., Perlmutter, J. C., Galda, L. and Brody, G. H. (1990) Joint reading between black Head Start children and their mothers. *Child Development* 61, 443–453.

Pellegrini, D. S., Masten, A. S., Garmezy, N. and Ferrarese, M. J. (1987) Correlates of social and academic competence in middle childhood. *Journal of Child Psychology and Psychiatry* 28, 699–714.

Pennington, B. F. (1990) The genetics of dyslexia. *Journal of Child Psychology and Psychiatry* 31(2), 193–201.

Perera, K. (1984) *Children's Writing and Reading: Analysing Classroom Language.* Oxford, UK: Blackwell.

Perfetti, C. A., Beck, I., Bell, L. C. and Hughes, C. (1987) Phonemic knowledge and learning to read are reciprocal: a longitudinal study of first-grade children. *Merrill-Palmer Quarterly* 33(3), 283–319.

Perkins, D. N. (1981) *The Mind's Best Work.* Cambridge, MA: Harvard University Press.

Perkins, D. N. (1988) Creativity. In R. J. Sternberg and E. E. Smith (eds), *The Psychology of Human Thought.* Cambridge, UK: Cambridge University Press.

Perlmutter, M. (ed.) (1980) *New Directions for Child Development, vol. 10, Children's Memory.* San Francisco: Jossey-Bass.

Perlmutter, M. (ed.) (1985) Intellectual development. *Minnesota Symposium on Child Psychology,* vol. 19. Hillsdale, NJ: Lawrence Erlbaum Associates, Inc.

Perner, J. (1988a) Developing semantics for theories of mind: from propositional attitudes to mental representation. In J. W. Astington, P. L. Harris and D. R. Olson (eds), *Developing Theories of Mind.* Cambridge, UK: Cambridge University Press.

Perner, J. (1988b) Higher-order beliefs and intentions in children's understanding of social interaction. In J. W. Astington, P. L. Harris and D. R. Olson (eds), *Developing Theories of Mind*. Cambridge, UK: Cambridge University Press.

Perner, J. (1991a) *Understanding the Representational Mind*. Cambridge, MA: MIT Press.

Perner, J. (1991b) On representing that: the asymmetry between belief and desire in children's theory of mind. In D. Frye and C. Moore (eds), *Children's Theories of Mind: Mental States and Social Understanding*. Hove, UK: Lawrence Erlbaum Associates Ltd.

Perner, J. and Davies, G. (1991) Understanding the mind as an active information processor: do young children have a 'copy theory of mind'? *Cognition* 39, 51–69.

Perner, J., Frith, U., Leslie, A. M. and Leekam, S. R. (1989) Exploration of the autistic child's theory of mind: knowledge, belief and communication. *Child Development* 60, 689–700.

Perner, J., Lang, B. and Kloo, D. (2002) Theory of mind and self-control. *Child Development* 73(3), 752–767.

Perner, J., Leekam, S. and Wimmer, H. (1987) Three-year olds' difficulty with false belief: the case for a conceptual deficit. *British Journal of Developmental Psychology* 5, 125–137.

Perner, J. and Ogden, J. E. (1988) Knowledge for hunger: children's problem with representation in imputing mental states. *Cognition* 29, 47–61.

Perret-Clermont, A.-N. (1980) *Social Interaction and Cognitive Development*. London: Academic Press.

Perret-Clermont, A.-N. and Brossard, A. (1985) On the interdigitation of social and cognitive processes. In R. A. Hinde, A.-N. Perret-Clermont and J. Stevenson-Hinde (eds), *Social Relationships and Cognitive Development*. Oxford, UK: Clarendon Press.

Perret-Clermont, A.-N. and Schubauer-Leoni, M. L. (1981) Conflict and cooperation as opportunities for learning. In W. P. Robinson (ed.), *Communication in Development*. London: Academic Press.

Perrett, D. I. *et al.* (1985) Visual analysis of body movements by neurones in the temporal cortex in the macaque monkey: a preliminary report. *Behavioural Brain Research* 16, 153–170.

Peskin, J. (1992) Ruse and representations: on children's ability to conceal information. *Developmental Psychology* 28, 84–89.

Peskin, J. and Ardino, V. (2003) Representing the mental world in children's social behavior: playing hide-and-seek and keeping a secret. *Social Development* 12(4), 496–512.

Peters, A. M. (1983) *The Units of Language Acquisition*. Cambridge, UK: Cambridge University Press.

Peters, M. (1991) Sex differences in human brain size and the general meaning of differences in brain size. *Canadian Journal of Psychology* 45, 507–522.

Peterson, C. (1995) The role of perceived intention to deceive in children's and adults' concepts of lying. *British Journal of Developmental Psychology* 13, 237–260.

Peterson, C. (2002) Drawing insight from pictures: the development of concepts of false drawing and false beliefs in children with deafness, normal hearing and autism. *Child Development* 73(5), 1442–1459.

Peterson, C. and Slaughter, V. (2003) Opening windows into the mind: mothers' preference for mental state explanations and children's theory of mind. *Cognitive Development* 18, 399–429.

Peterson, S. E., Fox, P., Posner, M. I., Mintun, M. and Raichle, M. (1988) Positron emission tomographic studies of the cortical anatomy of single word processing. *Nature* 331, 585–589.

Petrill, S. A., Lipton, P. A., Hewitt, J. K. Plomin, R., Cherny, S. S., Corley, R. and DeFries, J. C. (2004) Genetic and environmental contributions to general cognitive ability through the first 16 years of life. *Developmental Psychology* 40(5), 805–812.

Petrill, S. A. and Deater-Deckard, K. (2004) Task orientation, parental warmth and SES account for a significant proportion of the shared environmental variance in general cognitive ability in early childhood: evidence from a twin study. *Developmental Science* 7(1), 25–32.

Pettit, G. S., Dodge, K. A. and Brown, M. M. (1988) Early family experience, social problem solving patterns, and children's social competence. *Child Development* 59, 107–120.

Philips, D., Voran, M., Kisker, E., Howes, C. and Whitbook, M. (1994) Childcare for children in poverty: opportunity or inequity? *Child Development* 65, 472–492.

Phillips, J. (1980) Kaspar Hauser. *The Times*, 16 August, 7.

Piaget, J. (1929) *The Child's Conception of the World*. London: Routledge & Kegan Paul.

Piaget, J. (1930) *The Child's Conception of Physical Causality*. London: Routledge & Kegan Paul.

Piaget, J. (1932) *The Moral Judgment of the Child*. Harmondsworth, UK: Penguin Books.

Piaget, J. (1952) *The Child's Conception of Number*. New York: Basic Books.

Piaget, J. (1954) *The Construction of Reality in the Child*. New York: Basic Books.

Piaget, J. (1959) *The Language and Thought of the Child*. London: Routledge & Kegan Paul.

Piaget, J. (1960a) The general problems of the psychobiological development of the child. In J. Tanner and B. Inhelder (eds), *Discussions on Child Development*, vol. 4. London: Tavistock.

Piaget, J. (1960b) The general problems of the psychobiological development of the child. In J. Tanner and B. Inhelder (eds), *Discussions on Child Development*, vol. 4, p. 307. London: Tavistock.

Piaget, J. (1962) *Play, Dreams and Imitation in Childhood*. New York: Norton.

Piaget, J. (1968) *Six Psychological Studies*. London: University of London Press.

Piaget, J. (1969) *The Child's Conception of Time*. London: Routledge & Kegan Paul.

Piaget, J. (1970) *Genetic Epistemology*. New York: Columbia University Press.

Piaget, J. (1971a) The theory of stages in cognitive development. In D. R. Green, M. P. Ford and G. B. Flanner (eds), *Measurement and Piaget*. New York: McGraw-Hill.

Piaget, J. (1971b) *Biology and Knowledge*. Edinburgh, UK: Edinburgh University Press.

Piaget, J. (1971c) *Structuralism*. London: Routledge & Kegan Paul.

Piaget, J. (1977) *The Grasp of Consciousness: Action and Concept in the Young Child*. London: Routledge & Kegan Paul.

Piaget, J. (1978a) *The Development of Thought: Equilibration of Cognitive Structures.* Oxford, UK: Blackwell.

Piaget, J. (1978b) *Success and Understanding.* London: Routledge & Kegan Paul.

Piaget, J. (1983) Piaget's theory. In W. Kessen (ed.), *Handbook of Child Psychology, vol. 1, History, Theory and Method.* New York: Wiley (previously published 1970 in P. H. Mussen (ed.), *Carmichael's Manual of Child Psychology,* 3rd edn, vol. 1, New York: Wiley).

Piaget, J. and Inhelder, B. (1956) *The Child's Conception of Space.* London: Routledge & Kegan Paul.

Piaget, J. and Inhelder, B. (1969) *The Psychology of the Child.* London: Routledge & Kegan Paul.

Piaget, J. and Inhelder, B. (1975) *The Origin of the Idea of Chance in Children.* New York: Norton.

Piaget, J., Inhelder, B. and Szeminska, A. (1960) *The Child's Conception of Geometry.* London: Routledge & Kegan Paul.

Piatelli-Palmarini, M. (1989) Evolution, selection and cognition: from 'learning' to parameter setting in biology and in the study of language. *Cognition* 31, 1–44.

Pick, H. L. and Lockman, J. J. (1981) From frames of reference to spatial representations. In L. S. Liben, A. H. Patterson and N. Newcombe (eds), *Spatial Representation and Behaviour across the Life Span.* New York: Academic Press.

Pillemer, D. B., Goldsmith, L. R., Panter, A. T. and White, S. H. (1988) Very long-term memories of the first year in college. *Journal of Experimental Psychology: Learning, Memory and Cognition* 14, 709–715.

Pillemer, D. B. and White, S. H. (1989) Childhood events recalled by children and adults. In H. W. Reese (ed.), *Advances in Child Development and Behavior,* vol. 21. New York: Academic Press.

Pillemer, K. and McCartney, K. (eds) (1991) *Parent–Child Relations Throughout Life.* Hillsdale, NJ: Lawrence Erlbaum Associates, Inc.

Pilling, D. (1990) *Escape from Disadvantage.* London: Falmer Press.

Pilling, D. (1992) Escaping from a bad start. In B. Tizard and V. Varma (eds), *Vulnerability and Resilience in Human Development.* London: Jessica Kingsley.

Pillow, B. (2002) Children's and adults' evaluation of the certainty of deductive inferences, inductive inferences, and guesses. *Child Development* 73(3), 779–792.

Pillow, B. and Henrichon, A. J. (1996) There's more to the picture than meets the eye: young children's difficulty understanding biased interpretations. *Child Development* 67, 803–819.

Pillow, B. H. (1988a) The development of children's beliefs about the mental world. *Merrill-Palmer Quarterly* 34(1), 1–32.

Pillow, B. H. (1988b) Young children's understanding of attentional limits. *Child Development* 59, 38–46.

Pillow, B. H. (1989) Early understanding of perception as a source of knowledge. *Journal of Experimental Child Psychology* 47, 116–129.

Pine, J. M. (1992) How referential are 'referential' children? Relationships between maternal-report and obervational measures of vocabulary composition and usage. *Journal of Child Language* 19, 75–86.

Pine, K. J. and Nash, A. (2003) Barbie or Betty? Children's preference for branded products and evidence for gender-linked differences. *Developmental and Behavioral Pediatrics* 24(4), 219–224.

Pine, K. J., Lufkin, N. and Messer, D. (2004) More gestures than answers: children learning about balance. *Developmental Psychology* 40(6), 1059–1067.

Pinker, S. (1994) *The Language Instinct: The New Science of Language and Mind*. London: Allen Lane.

Pinker, S. (1997) *How the Mind Works*. London: Allen Lane.

Plomin, R. (1986) *Development, Genetics and Psychology*. Hillsdale, NJ: Lawrence Erlbaum Associates, Inc.

Plomin, R. (1989) Environment and genes: determinants of behavior. *American Psychologist* 44, 105–111.

Plomin, R. (1990a) *Nature and Nurture*. Pacific Grove, CA: Brooks/Cole.

Plomin, R. (1990b) The role of inheritance in behaviour. *Science* 248, 183–188.

Plomin, R. (1991) Behavioural genetics. In P. R. McHugh and V. A. McKusick (eds), *Genes, Brain and Behavior*. New York: Raven Press.

Plomin, R. (1993) Genetic change and continuity from fourteen to twenty-four months. *Child Development* 64(5), 1354–1376.

Plomin, R. (1994) *Genetics and Experience: The Interplay Between Nature and Nurture*. London: Sage.

Plomin, R. and Daniels, D. (1987) Why are children in the same family so different from one another? *Behavioral and Brain Sciences* 10, 1–60.

Plomin, R. and Rende, R. (1991) Human behavioral genetics. *Annual Review of Psychology* 42, 161–190.

Polak, A. and Harris, P. (1999) Deception by young children following noncompliance. *Developmental Psychology* 35, 561–568.

Pollitt, E. (2000) Developmental sequel from early nutritional deficiencies: conclusive and probability judgments. *Journal of Nutrition* 130, 350S–353S.

Pollitt, E. (2001) The developmental and probabilistic nature of the functional consequences of iron-deficiency anaemia in children. *Journal of Nutrition* 131(2), 669S–675S.

Pomerantz, E. and Ruble, D. N. (1997) Distinguishing multiple dimensions of conceptions of ability: implication for self-evaluation. *Child Development* 68, 1165–1180.

Pomerantz, E. and Saxon, J. L. (2001) Conceptions of ability as stable and self-evaluative processes: a longitudinal examination. *Child Development* 72, 152–173.

Pool, D. L., Shweder, R. A. and Much, N. C. (1983) Culture as a cognitive system: differentiated rule understandings in children and other savages. In E. T. Higgins, D. N. Ruble and W. W. Hartrup (eds), *Social Cognition and Social Development: A Socio-Cultural Perspective*. Cambridge, UK: Cambridge University Press.

Poortinga, Y. P. and van de Vijver, F. J. R. (1988) Culturally invariant parameters of cognitive functioning. In J. W. Berry, S. H. Irvine and E. B. Hunt (eds), *Indigenous Cognition: Functioning in Cultural Contexts*. Dordrecht, The Netherlands: Martinus Nijhoff.

Popper, K. R. (1967) *Objective Knowledge*. Oxford, UK: Clarendon Press.

Popper, K. R. and Eccles, J. C. (1977) *The Self and its Brain*. Berlin, Germany: Springer-Verlag.

Posner, J. K. and Vandell, D. L. (1999) After-school activities and the development of low-income urban children: a longitudinal study. *Developmental Psychology* 35(3), 868–879.

Posner, M. and Rothbart, M. (2005) Influencing brain networks: implications for education. *Trends in Cognitive Science* 9(3), 99–110.

Posner, M. I. and Peterson, S. E. (1990) The attention system of the human brain. *Annual Review of Neuroscience* 13, 25–42.

Poulsen, D., Kintsch, E., Kintsch, W. and Premack, D. (1979) Children's comprehension and memory for stories. *Journal of Experimental Child Psychology* 28, 379–403.

Pound, A., Mills, M., Puckering, C. and Cox, A. (1982) Maternal depression and family functioning. In C. M. Parkes and J. Stevenson-Hinde (eds), *The Place of Attachment in Human Behaviour*. London: Tavistock.

Powell, M. B. and Thomson, D. M. (1996) Children's memory of an occurrence of a repeated event: effects of age, repetition, and retention interval across three question types. *Child Development* 67, 1988–2004.

Power, F. C. (2004) The moral self in community. In D. Lapsley and D. Narvaez (eds), *Moral Development, Self, and Identity*. Mahwah, NJ: Lawrence Erlbaum Associates, Inc.

Prather, P. A. and Bacon, J. (1986) Developmental differences in part–whole identification. *Child Development* 57, 549–558.

Pratt, C. and Bryant, P. E. (1990) Young children understand that looking leads to knowing (so long as they are looking into a single barrel). *Child Development* 61, 973–982.

Pressley, M., Borkowski, J. G. and O'Sullivan, J. (1985a) Children's metamemory and the teaching of memory strategies. In D. L. Forrest-Pressley, G. E. Mackinnon and T. G. Waller (eds), *Metacognition, Cognition and Human Performance*, vol. 1. Orlando, FL: Academic Press.

Pressley, M., Forrest-Pressley, D. L., Elliott-Faust, D. and Miller, G. E. (1985b) Children's use of cognitive strategies, how to teach strategies, and what to do if they can't be taught. In M. Pressley and C. J. Brainerd (eds), *Cognitive Learning and Memory in Children*. New York: Springer-Verlag.

Pressley, M. and Levin, J. R. (1980) The development of mental imagery retrieval. *Child Development* 51, 558–560.

Pressley, M., Snyder, B. L. and Cariglia-Bull, T. (1987) How can good strategy use be taught to children? Evaluation of six alternative approaches. In S. M. Cormier and D. J. Hagman (eds), *Transfer of Learning: Contemporary Research and Applications*. San Diego, CA: Academic Press.

Presson, C. C. (1982) The development of map reading skills. *Child Development* 53, 196–199.

Presson, C. C. (1987) The development of spatial cognition: secondary uses of spatial information. In N. Eisenberg (ed.), *Contemporary Topics in Developmental Psychology*. New York: Wiley.

Puckering, C. and Rutter, M. (1987) Environmental influences on language development. In W. Yule and M. Rutter (eds), *Language Development and Disorders*. London: MacKeith Press and Oxford, UK: Blackwell Scientific Publications.

Pumphrey, P. and Elliot, C. (eds) (1990) *Children's Difficulties in Reading, Spelling and Writing*. London: Falmer Press.

Pyeritz, R. E. (1991) Formal genetics in humans: Mendelian and non-Mendelian inheritance. In P. R. McHugh and V. A. McKusick (eds), *Genes, Brain and Behaviour*. New York: Raven Press.

Pylyshyn, Z. W. (1978) When is attribution of beliefs justified? *Behavioral and Brain Sciences* 1, 592–593.

Pylyshyn, Z. W. (1980) Computation and cognition: issues in the foundation of cognitive science. *Behavioral and Brain Sciences* 3, 111–134.

Pylyshyn, Z. W. (1981) The imagery debate: analogue media versus tacit knowledge. *Psychological Review* 88, 16–45.

Quinton, D. and Rutter M. (1988) *Parenting Breakdown: The Making and Breaking of Inter-generational Links.* Aldershot, UK: Avebury.

Raab, G. M., Thomson, G. O. B., Boyd, L., Fulton, M. and Laxen, D. P. H. (1990) Blood lead levels, reaction time, inspection time and ability in Edinburgh children. *British Journal of Developmental Psychology* 8, 101–118.

Rabbitt, P. M. A. (1988) Human intelligence. *Quarterly Journal of Experimental Psychology* 40A, 167–185.

Rachlin, H. (1989) *Judgment, Decision and Choice.* San Francisco: Freeman.

Radford, J. (1990) *Child Prodigies and Exceptional Early Achievers.* Lewes, UK: Harvester.

Radke-Yarrow, M. (1991) The individual and the environment in human behavioural development. In P. Bateson (ed.), *The Development and Integration of Behaviour.* Cambridge, UK: Cambridge University Press.

Radke-Yarrow, M., Belmont, B., Nottelmann, E. and Bottomly, L. (1990) Young children's self-conceptions: origins in the natural discourse of depressed and normal mothers and their children. In D. Cichetti and M. Beeghly (eds), *The Self in Transition.* Chicago: University of Chicago Press.

Radke-Yarrow, M. and Kuczynski, L. (1983) Perspectives and strategies in child-rearing: studies of rearing by normal and depressed mothers. In D. Magnusson and V. Allen (eds), *Human Development: An Interactional Perspective.* New York: Academic Press.

Radke-Yarrow, M. and Sherman, T. (1985) Interaction of cognition and emotions in development. In R. A. Hinde, A.-N. Perret-Clermont and J. Stevenson-Hinde (eds), *Social Relationships and Cognitive Development.* Oxford, UK: Clarendon Press.

Rakoczy, H., Tomasello, M. and Striano, T. (2004) Young children know that trying is not pretending: A test of the 'behaving-as-if' construal of children's early concept of pretense. *Developmental Psychology* 40(3), 388–399.

Ramchandani P., Stein A., Evans J., O'Connor, T. G. and ALSPAC Study Team (2005) Paternal depression in the postnatal period and child development: a prospective population study. *Lancet* 365, 2201–2205.

Ramey, C. T. and Ramey, S. L. (1998) Early intervention and early experience. *American Psychologist* 53, 109–120.

RAND Reading Study Group (2004) A research agenda for improving reading comprehension. In R. B. Ruddell and N. J. Unrau (eds), *Theoretical Models and Processes of Reading.* Newark, DE: International Reading Association.

Raven, J. (1980) *Parents, Teachers and Children: A Study of an Educational Home Visiting Scheme.* London: Hodder & Stoughton, for the Scottish Council for Research in Education.

Raymond, C. L. and Benbow, C. P. (1986) Gender differences in mathematics: a function of parental support and student sex typing? *Developmental Psychology* 22, 808–819.

Raynor, P. and Rudolf, M. (1996) What do we know about children who fail to thrive? *Child: Care, Health and Development* 22, 241–250.

Reader, S. (2003) Innovation and social learning: individual variation and brain evolution. *Animal Biology* 53(2), 147–158.

Reader, S. M. (2003) Innovation and social learning: individual variation and brain evolution. *Animal Biology* 53(2), 147–158.

Reader, S. M. and Lefebvre, L. (2001) Social learning and sociality. *Behavioural Brain Sciences* 24(2), 353–355.

Rebok, G. W. (1987) *Lifespan Cognitive Development*. New York: Holt, Rinehart & Winston.

Reddiford, G. (1980) Imagination, rationality and teaching. *Journal of Philosophy of Education* 14, 205–213.

Reese, E. (2002) Social factors in the development of autobiographical memory: the state of the art. *Social Development* 11, 124–142.

Reese, H. W. (1989) Discrimination set learning in children. In H. W. Reese (ed.), *Advances in Child Development and Behavior*, vol. 21. New York: Academic Press.

Reiss, A. L., Abrams, M. T., Singer, H. S., Ross, J. L. and Denckla, M. B. (1996) Brain development, gender and IQ in children: a volumetric imaging study. *Brain* 119, 1763–1774.

Reiss, A. L. and Dant, C. C. (2003) The behavioural neurogenetics of fragile X syndrome: analysing gene–brain–behavior relationships in child developmental psychopathology. *Development and Psychopathology* 15(4), 927–968.

Repetti, R., Taylor, S. E. and Seeman, T. E. (2002) Risky families: family social environments and the mental and physical health of offspring. *Psychological Bulletin* 128, 330–366.

Resnick, L. B. (1983) A developmental theory of number understanding. In H. P. Ginsburg (ed.), *The Development of Mathematical Thinking*. New York: Academic Press.

Resnick, L. B. (1987a) Constructing knowledge in school. In L. S. Liben (ed.), *Development and Learning*. Hillsdale, NJ: Lawrence Erlbaum Associates, Inc.

Resnick, L. B. (1987b) *Education and Learning to Think*. Washington, DC: National Academy Press.

Resnick, L. B. (1987c) The development of mathematical intuition. In M. Perlmutter (ed.), *Minnesota Symposium on Child Psychology*, vol. 19. Hillsdale, NJ: Lawrence Erlbaum Associates, Inc.

Resnick, L. B. (1989a) Developing mathematical knowledge. *American Psychologist* 44, 162–169.

Resnick, L. B. (1989b) *Knowing, Learning and Instruction: Essays in Honor of Robert Glaser*. Hillsdale, NJ: Lawrence Erlbaum Associates, Inc.

Resnick, L. B., Berenbaum, S. A., Gottesman, I. I. and Bouchard, T. J. (1986) Early hormonal influence on cognitive functioning in congenital adrenal hyperplasia. *Developmental Psychology* 22, 191–198.

Resnick, L. B. and Weaver, P. A. (1979) *Theory and Practice of Early Reading*, vols 1 and 2. Hillsdale, NJ: Lawrence Erlbaum Associates, Inc.

Resnick, S. M., Gottesman, I. I., Berenbaum, S. A. and Bouchard, T. J. (1986) Early hormonal influences on cognitive functioning in congenital adrenal-hyperplasia. *Developmental Psychology* 22(2), 191–198.

Reynolds, A. J. (1994) Effects of a preschool plus follow-on intervention for children at risk. *Developmental Psychology* 30, 787–804.

Reynolds, A. J., Mavrogenes, N. A., Bezruczko, N. and Hagemann, M. (1996) Cognitive and family support mediators of preschool effectiveness: a confirmatory analysis. *Child Development* 67, 1119–1140.

Reynolds, A. J., Ou, S.-R. and Topitzes, J. W. (2004) Paths of effects of early childhood intervention on educational attainment and delinquency: a confirmatory analysis of the Chicago Child-Parent Centers. *Child Development* 75(5), 1299–1328.

Reynolds, A. J. and Temple, J. A. (1998) Extended early childhood intervention and school achievement: age 13 findings from the Chicago Longitudinal Study. *Child Development* 69, 231–246.

Ricciuti, H. N. (1991) Malnutrition and cognitive development: research–policy linkages and current research directions. In L. Okagaki and R. J. Sternberg (eds), *Directors of Development: Influences on the Development of Children's Thinking*. Hillsdale, NJ: Lawrence Erlbaum Associates, Inc.

Rice, C., Koinis, D., Sullivan, K., Tager-Flusberg, H. and Winner, E. (1997) When 3-year-olds pass the appearance–reality test. *Developmental Psychology* 33, 54–61.

Rice, M. L. (1989) Children's language acquisition. *American Psychologist* 44, 149–156.

Rice, M. L. and Woodsmall, L. (1988) Lessons from television: children's word learning when viewing. *Child Development* 59, 420–429.

Richardson, K. (1991) *Understanding Intelligence*. Milton Keynes, UK: Open University Press.

Richardson, K. (2000) *Models of Cognitive Development*. Hove, UK: Psychology Press.

Richardson, S. A. (1976) The relation of severe malnutrition in infancy to the intelligence of school children with differing life histories. *Pediatric Research* 10, 57–61.

Richardson, S. A. (1984) The consequences of malnutrition for intellectual development. In J. Dobbing (ed.), *Scientific Studies in Mental Retardation*. London: Royal Society of Medicine, and Macmillan.

Richman, N., Stevenson, J. and Graham, P. (1982) *Pre-school to School: A Behavioural Study*. London: Academic Press.

Riding, R. and Mathias, D. (1991) Cognitive styles and preferred learning mode, reading attainment and cognitive ability in 11 year old children. *Educational Psychology* 11, 383–393.

Riding, R. J. (ed.) (1991) Learning styles, double issue of *Educational Psychology* 11(3 and 4), 193–393.

Rieben, L. and Perfetti, C. A. (1991) *Learning to Read*. Hove, UK: Lawrence Erlbaum Associates Ltd.

Rieder, C. and Cicchetti, D. (1989) An organisational perspective on cognitive control functioning and cognitive–affective balance in maltreated children. *Developmental Psychology* 25, 482–493.

Riley, M. S., Greeno, J. G. and Heller, J. I. (1983) The development of children's problem-solving ability in arithmetic. In H. P. Ginsburg (ed.), *The Development of Mathematical Thinking*. New York: Academic Press.

Rittle-Johnson, B. and Siegler, R. S. (1998) The relationship between conceptual and procedural knowledge in learning mathematics: a review. In C. Donlan (ed.), *The Development of Mathematical Skills*. Hove, UK: Psychology Press.

Rizzo, T. A. and Corsaro, W. A. (1988) Toward a better understanding of Vygotsky's process of internalisation: its role in the development of the concept of friendship. *Developmental Review* 8, 219–237.

Roberts, G. C., Block, J. H. and Block, J. (1984) Continuity and change in parents' child-rearing practices. *Child Development* 55, 586–597.

Robins, L. and Rutter M. (1991) *Straight and Devious Pathways from Childhood to Adulthood*. Cambridge, UK: Cambridge University Press.

Robinson, E. J. (1983) Metacognitive development. In S. Meadows (ed.), *Developing Thinking*. London: Methuen.

Robinson, E. J. and Mitchell, P. (1992) Children's interpretation of messages from a speaker with a false belief. *Child Development* 63, 639–652.

Robinson, E. J., Nye, R., Thomas, G. V. (1994) Children's conception of the relationship between pictures and their referents. *Cognitive Development* 9, 165–191.

Robinson, E. J. and Robinson, W. P. (1977) Development in the understanding of the cause of success and failure in verbal communication. *Cognition* 5, 363–378.

Robinson, E. J. and Robinson, W. P. (1978) Development of understanding about communication: message inadequacy and its role in causing communication failure. *Genetic Psychology Monographs* 98, 233–279.

Robinson, E. J. and Robinson, W. P. (1980) Egocentrism in verbal referential communication. In M. V. Cox (ed.), *Are Young Children Egocentric?* London: Batsford.

Robinson, E. J. and Robinson, W. P. (1981) Ways of reacting to communication failure in relation to the development of children's understanding about verbal communication. *European Journal of Social Psychology* 11, 189–208.

Robinson, E. J. and Robinson, W. P. (1982) The achievement of children's verbal referential communication skills: the role of metacognitive guidance. *International Journal of Behavioural Development* 5, 329–355.

Robinson, E. J. and Robinson, W. P. (1983) Communication and metacommunication: quality of children's instructions in relation to judgments about the adequacy of instructions and the locus of responsibility for communication failure. *Journal of Experimental Child Psychology* 36, 305–320.

Robinson, F. P. (1946) *Effective Study*. New York: Harper & Row.

Rodgers, B. (1983) The identification and prevalence of specific reading retardation. *British Journal of Educational Psychology* 53, 369–373.

Rodgers, J. L. (1998) A critique of the Flynn effect: massive IQ gains, methodological artefacts, or both? *Intelligence* 26(4), 337–356.

Rodriguez, R. (1980) An education in language. In L. Michaels and C. Ricks (eds), *The State of the Language*. Berkeley: University of California Press.

Roe, A. (1979) A psychologist examines sixty-four eminent scientists. In P. E. Vernon (ed.), *Creativity: Selected Readings*. Harmondsworth, UK: Penguin Books.

Roedder-John, D. (1999) Consumer socialization of children: a retrospective look at twenty-five years of research. *Journal of Consumer Research* 26(3), 183–213.

Rogers, C. (1978) The child's perception of other people. In H. McGurk (ed.), *Issues in Childhood Social Development*. London: Methuen.

Rogoff, B. (1982) Integrating context or cognitive development. In M. E. Lamb and A. L. Brown (eds), *Advances in Developmental Psychology*, vol. 2. Hillsdale, NJ: Lawrence Erlbaum Associates, Inc.

Rogoff, B. (1986) Adult assistance of children's learning. In T. E. Raphael (ed.), *The Contexts of School Based Literacy*. New York: Random House.

Rogoff, B. (1990) *Apprenticeship in Thinking*. Oxford, UK: Oxford University Press.

Rogoff, B. (1995) Observing sociocultural activity on three planes: participatory appropriation, guided particpation, and apprenticeship. In J. V. Wertsch, P. del Rio and A. Alvarez (eds), *Sociocultural Studies of Mind*. Cambridge, UK: Cambridge University Press.

Rogoff, B. (1998) Cognition as a collaborative process. In D. Kuhn and R. S. Siegler (eds), *Handbook of Child Psychology, vol. 2, Cognition, Perception, and Language*, 5th edn, pp. 679–744. New York: Wiley.

Rogoff, B. (2003) *The Cultural Nature of Human Development*. Oxford, UK: Oxford University Press.

Rogoff, B. and Gardner, W. (1984) Adult guidance of cognitive development. In B. Rogoff and J. Lave (eds), *Everyday Cognition: Its Development in Social Context*. Cambridge, MA: Harvard University Press.

Rogoff, B., Goodman-Turkanis, C. and Bartlett, L. (2002) *Learning Together: Children and Adults in a School Community*. Oxford, UK: Oxford University Press.

Rondal, J. (1987) Language development and mental retardation. In W. Yule and M. Rutter (eds), *Language Development and Disorders*. London: MacKeith Press and Oxford, UK: Blackwell Scientific Publications.

Rosa, A., Ochaita, E., Moreno, E., Fernandez, E., Carretero, M. and Pozo, J. (1984) Cognitive development in blind children: a challenge to Piagetian theory. *Quarterly Newsletter of the Laboratory of Comparative Human Cognition* 6, 75–81.

Rosch, E. H. (1978) Principles of categorization. In E. H. Rosch and B. B. Lloyd (eds), *Cognition and Categorization*. Hillsdale, NJ: Lawrence Erlbaum Associates, Inc.

Rosch, E. H. (1981) Prototype classification and logical classification: the two systems. In E. Scholnick (ed.), *New Trends in Cognitive Representation: Challenges to Piaget's Theory*. Hillsdale, NJ: Lawrence Erlbaum Associates, Inc.

Rosch, E. H. and Lloyd, B. B. (eds) (1978) *Cognition and Categorization*. Hillsdale, NJ: Lawrence Erlbaum Associates, Inc.

Rosch, E. H., Mervis, C. B., Gray, W. D., Johnson, D. M. and Boyes-Braem, P. (1976) Basic objects in natural categories. *Cognitive Psychology* 8, 382–439.

Rose, D. H., Slater, A. S. and Perry, J. (1986) Prediction of childhood intelligence from habituation in early infancy. *Intelligence* 10, 251–263.

Rose, K. (1983) *King George V*, London: Weidenfeld.

Rose, S. (1998) *Lifelines*. London: Penguin.

Rose, S. A. and Blank, M. (1974) The potency of context in children's cognition: an illustration through conservation. *Child Development* 45, 499–502.

Rose, S. A. and Feldman, J. F. (1995) Prediction of IQ and specific cognitive abilities at 11 years from infancy measures. *Developmental Psychology* 31, 685–696.

Rose, S. A. and Feldman, J. F. (1997) Memory and speed: their role in the relation of infant information processing to later IQ. *Child Development* 68, 630–641.

Rose, S. A., Feldman, J. F. and Jankowski, J. J. (2004) Infant visual recognition memory. *Developmental Review* 24(1), 74–100.

Rose, S. A., Feldman, J. F. and Wallace, I. F. (1988) Individual differences in infants' information processing: reliability, stability and prediction. *Child Development* 59, 1177–1197.

Rose, S. P. R. (1981) What should a biochemistry of learning and memory be about? *Neuroscience* 6, 811–821.

Rose, S. P. R. (1988) Memory: biological bases. In R. L. Gregory (ed.), *The Oxford Companion to the Mind*. Oxford, UK: Oxford University Press.

Rosengren, K. S., Gelman, S. A., Kalish, C. W. and McCormick, K. (1991) As time goes by: children's early understanding of growth in animals. *Child Development* 62, 1302–1320.

Rosengren, K. S., Kalish, C. W., Hickling, A. K. and Gelman, S. A. (1994) Exploring the relation between preschool children's magical beliefs and causal thinking. *British Journal of Developmental Psychology* 12, 69–82.

Rosenhan, D. L. and Seligman, M. E. P. (1995) *Abnormal Psychology*. New York: Norton.

Rosenshine, B. (1987) Direct instruction. In M. J. Durkin (ed.), *The International Encyclopedia of Teaching and Teacher Education*, pp. 257–263. Oxford, UK: Pergamon.

Ross, L. (1981) The 'intuitive scientist' formulation and its developmental implications. In J. H. Flavell and L. Ross (eds), *Social Cognitive Development*. Cambridge, UK: Cambridge University Press.

Ross, M. *et al.* (2005) The DNA sequence of the human X chromosome. *Nature* 434, 325–337.

Rotman, B. (1977) *Jean Piaget: Psychologist of the Real*. Hassocks, UK: Harvester Press.

Roulstone, S., Loader, S., Northstone, K., Beveridge, M. and ALSPAC Team (2002) The speech and language of children aged 25 months: descriptive data from the Avon Longitudinal Study of Parents and Children. *Early Child Development and Care* 172, 259–268.

Rovee-Collier, C. (1997) Disassociations in infant memory: rethinking the development of implicit and explicit memory. *Psychological Review* 104, 467–498.

Rovee-Collier, C. and Hayne, H. (1987) Reactivation of infant memory: implications for cognitive development. In H. W. Reese (ed.), *Advances in Child Development and Behavior*. New York: Academic Press.

Rovet, J. and Netley, C. (1982) Processing deficits in Turner's syndrome. *Developmental Psychology* 18(1), 77–94.

Rowe, S. and Wertsch, J. (2002) Vygotsky's model of cognitive development. In U. Goswami (ed.), *Blackwell Handbook of Cognitive Development*. Oxford, UK: Blackwell.

Rowe, S. M. and Wertsch, J. V. (1999) The educated mind: how cognitive tools shape our understanding. *Teachers College Record* 101(2), 267–269

Roy, P., Rutter, M. and Pickles, A. (2000) Institutional care: risk from family background or pattern of rearing? *Journal of Child Psychology and Psychiatry* 41, 139–141.

Ruble, D. N. and Nakamura, C. Y. (1972) Task orientation versus social orientation in young children and their attention to relevant social cues. *Child Development* 43, 471–480.

Ruddell, R. B. and Unrau, N. J. (2004a) Reading as a meaning-constructing process: The reader, the text and the teacher. In R. B. Ruddell and N. J. Unrau (eds), *Theoretical Models and Processes of Reading*. Newark, DE: International Reading Association.

Ruddell, R. B. and Unrau, N. J. (eds) (2004b) *Theoretical Models and Processes of Reading*. Newark, DE: International Reading Association.

Rueda, M. R., Fan, J., McCandliss, B. D., Halparin, J. D., Gruber, D. B., Lercari, L. P. and Posner, M. I. (2004) Development of attentional networks during childhood. *Neuropsychologia* 42, 1029–1040.

Ruffman, T. (1999) Children's understanding of logical inconsistency. *Child Development* 70, 872–886.

Ruffman, T., Olson, D. R. and Astington, J. W. (1991) Children's understanding of visual ambiguity. In G. Butterworth, P. L. Harris, A. M. Leslie and H. M. Wellman (eds), *Perspectives on the Child's Theory of Mind*. Oxford, UK: Oxford University Press.

Ruffman, T., Perner, J., Olson, D. R. and Doherty, M. (1993) Reflecting on scientific thinking: children's understanding of the hypothesis–evidence relation. *Child Development* 64, 1617–1636.

Ruffman, T. K. and Olson, D. R. (1989) Children's ascription of knowledge to others. *Developmental Psychology* 25, 601–606.

Rumelhart, D. E. (1977) Toward an interactive model of reading. In S. Dornic (ed.), *Attention and Performance*, vol. 6. Hillsdale, NJ: Lawrence Erlbaum Associates, Inc.

Rumelhart, D. E. (1989) Toward a microstructural account of human reasoning. In S. Vosniadou and A. Ortony (eds), *Similarity and Analogical Reasoning*. Cambridge, UK: Cambridge University Press.

Rumelhart, D. E. and McClelland, J. L. (eds) (1986) *Parallel Distributed Processing: Explorations in the Microstructure of Cognition*. Cambridge, MA: MIT Press.

Rumsey, J. M. and Rapoport, J. L. (1983) Assessing behavioral and cognitive effects of diet in pediatric populations. In R. J. Wurtman and J. J. Wurtman (eds), *Nutrition and the Brain, vol. 6, Physiological and Behavioral Effects of Food Constituents*. New York: Raven Press.

Runco, M. A. (2004) Creativity. *Annual Review of Psychology* 55, 657–687.

Ruse, M. (1986) *Taking Darwin Seriously: A Naturalistic Approach to Philosophy*. Oxford, UK: Blackwell.

Russell, J. (1978) *The Acquisition of Knowledge*. London: Macmillan.

Russell, J. (1981a) Dyadic interaction in a logical reasoning problem requiring inclusion ability. *Child Development* 51, 1322–1325.

Russell, J. (1981b) Why 'socio-cognitive conflict' may be impossible: the status of egocentric errors in the dyadic performance of a spatial task. *Educational Psychology* 1, 159–169.

Russell, J. (1982) Propositional attitudes. In M. Beveridge (ed.), *Children Thinking through Language*. London: Edward Arnold.

Russell, J. (1984) *Explaining Mental Life: Some Philosophical Issues in Psychology.* London: Macmillan.

Russell, J. (1988) Making judgments about thoughts and things. In J. W. Astington, P. L. Harris and D. R. Olson (eds), *Developing Theories of Mind.* Cambridge, UK: Cambridge University Press.

Russell, J., Mills, I. and Reiff-Musgrove, P. (1990) The role of symmetrical and asymmetrical social conflict in cognitive change. *Journal of Experimental Child Psychology* 49, 58–78.

Rutter, M. (1978) Early sources of security and competence. In J. S. Bruner and A. Garton (eds), *Human Growth and Development.* Oxford, UK: Oxford University Press.

Rutter, M. (1981) *Maternal Deprivation Reassessed.* Harmondsworth, UK: Penguin Books.

Rutter, M. (1983a) Cognitive deficits in the pathogenesis of autism. *Journal of Child Psychology and Psychiatry* 24, 513–531.

Rutter, M. (1983b) Low level lead exposure: sources, effects and implications. In M. Rutter and R. R. Jones (eds), *Lead versus Health.* Chichester, UK: Wiley.

Rutter, M. (1985a) Family and school influences on behavioural development. *Journal of Child Psychology and Psychiatry* 26, 349–368.

Rutter, M. (1985b) Family and school influences on cognitive development. *Journal of Child Psychology and Psychiatry* 26(5), 683–704.

Rutter, M. (ed.) (1988) *Studies of Psychosocial Risk: The Power of Longitudinal Data.* Cambridge, UK: Cambridge University Press.

Rutter, M. (1990) Commentary: some focus and process considerations regarding effects of parental depression on children. *Developmental Psychology* 26, 60–67.

Rutter, M. (1991) A fresh look at 'maternal deprivation'. In P. Bateson (ed.), *The Development and Integration of Behaviour.* Cambridge, UK: Cambridge University Press.

Rutter, M. (1992) Nature, nurture and psychopathology: a new look at an old topic. In B. Tizard and V. Varma (eds), *Vulnerability and Resilience in Human Development.* London: Jessica Kingsley.

Rutter, M. and the English and Romanian Adoptees (ERA) Study Team (1998) Developmental catch-up, and deficit, following adoption after severe global early privation. *Journal of Child Psychology and Psychiatry* 39, 465–476.

Rutter, M. and Giller, H. (1983) *Juvenile Delinquency.* Harmondsworth, UK: Penguin Books.

Rutter, M., Izard, C. E. and Read, P. B. (1986) *Depression in Young People: Developmental and Clinical Perspectives.* New York: Guilford Press.

Rutter, M. and Jones, R. R. (eds) (1983) *Lead versus Health: Sources and Effects of Low Level Lead Exposure.* Chichester, UK: Wiley.

Rutter, M., Kreppner, J., O'Connor, T. G. and the English and Romanian Adoptees Study Team (2001) Specificity and heterogeneity in children's response to profound privation. *British Journal of Psychiatry* 179, 97–103.

Rutter, M. and Madge, N. (1976) *Cycles of Disadvantage.* London: Heinemann.

Rutter, M. and Maughan, B. (2002) School effectiveness findings: 1979–2002. *Journal of School Psychology* 40, 451–475.

Rutter, M., Maughan, B., Mortimore, P. and Ouston, J., with Smith, A. (1979)

Fifteen Thousand Hours: Secondary Schools and their Effects on Children. London: Open Books.

Rutter, M., O'Connor, T. G. and the English and Romanian Adoptees Study Team (2004) Are there biological programming effects for psychological development? Findings from a study of Romanian adoptees. *Developmental Psychology* 40(1), 81–94.

Rutter, M. and Schopler, E. (eds) (1978) *Autism: A Reappraisal of Concepts and Treatment.* New York: Plenum Press.

Rutter, M., Thorpe, K., Greenwood, R., Northstone, K. and Golding, J. (2003) Twins as a natural experiment to study the causes of mild language delay: I: Design; twin–singleton differences in language, and obstetric risks. *Journal of Child Psychology and Psychiatry* 44, 326–341.

Rutter, M., Tizard, J., Yule, W., Graham, P. and Whitmore, K. (1976) Research report: Isle of Wight studies 1964–1974. *Psychological Medicine* 6, 313–332.

Rutter, M. and Yule, W. (1976) Reading difficulties. In M. Rutter and L. Hersov (eds), *Child Psychiatry: Modern Approaches.* Oxford, UK: Blackwell.

Ryan, E. B., Ledger, G. W. and Weed, K. A. (1987) Acquisition and transfer of an integrative imagery strategy by young children. *Child Development* 58, 443–452.

Ryle, G. (1949) *The Concept of Mind.* London: Hutchinson.

Rymer, R. (1993) *Genie: Escape from a Silent Childhood.* London: Michael Joseph.

Saarni, C. (1990) Emotional competence: how emotions and relationships become integrated. In R. A. Thompson (ed.), Socioemotional development, *Nebraska Symposium on Motivation*, 1988, vol. 36. Lincoln: University of Nebraska Press.

Sabbagh, M. and Taylor, M. (2000) Neural correlates of theory-of-mind reasoning: an event-related potential study. *Psychological Science* 11, 46–50.

Sacks, O. (1985) *The Man Who Mistook His Wife for a Hat.* London: Duckworth.

Saffran, J., Aslin, R. and Newport, E. (1996) Statistical learning by 8-month-old infants. *Science* 274, 1926–1928.

Sales, J. M. and Fivush, R. (2005) Social and emotional functions of mother-child reminiscing about stressful events. *Social Cognition* 23(1), 70–90.

Salgueiro, M. J., Zubillaga, M. B., Lysionek, A. E., Caro, R. A., Weill, R. and Boccio, J. R. (2002) The role of zinc in the growth and development of children. *Nutrition* 18, 510–519.

Salt, P., Galler, J. R. and Ramsey, F. C. (1988) The influence of early malnutrition on subsequent behavioral development: VII, The effects of maternal depressive symptoms. *Developmental and Behavioral Pediatrics* 9, 1–5.

Samuels, A. and Taylor, M. (1994) Children's ability to distinguish fantasy events from real-life events. *British Journal of Developmental Psychology* 12, 417–427.

Samuels, M. C. and McDonald, J. (2002) Elementary school-age children's capacity to choose positive diagnostic and negative diagnostic test. *Child Development* 73(3), 857–866.

Samuels, R. (2004) Innateness in cognitive science. *Trends in Cognitive Science* 8(3), 136–141.

Santostefano, S. (1985) *Cognitive Control Therapy with Children and Adolescents.* Elmsford, NY: Pergamon Press.

Sapp, F., Lee, K. and Muir, D. (2000) Three-year-olds' difficulties with the appearance–reality distinction: is it real or apparent? *Developmental Psychology* 36, 547–560.

Saracho, O. (1985) Young children's play behaviours and cognitive ages. *Early Child Development and Care* 22, 1–18.

Sartre, J.-P. (1972) *The Psychology of Imagination*. London: Methuen.

Satterly, D. J. (1976) Cognitive styles, spatial ability and school achievement. *Journal of Educational Psychology* 68, 36–42.

Saunders, G. (1988) *Bilingual Children*. Clevedon, PA: Multilingual Matters.

Saxe, G. B. (1988) The mathematics of child street vendors. *Child Development* 59, 1415–1425.

Saxe, G. B., Guberman, S. R. and Gearhart, M. (1987) Social processes in early number development. *Monographs of the Society for Research in Child Development* 52(2), serial no. 216.

Saxe, R., Carey, S. and Kanwisher, N. (2004) Understanding other minds: linking developmental psychology and functional neuroimaging. *Annual Review of Psychology* 55, 87–124.

Scarborough, H. S. and Dobrich, W. (1994) On the efficacy of reading to preschoolers. *Developmental Review* 14, 245–302.

Scardamalia, M. (1977) Information processing capacity and the problem of horizontal décalage: a demonstration using combinatorial reasoning tasks. *Child Development* 48, 28–37.

Scardamalia, M. (1981) How children cope with the cognitive demands of writing. In C. H. Fredericksen and J. F. Dominic (eds), *Writing: The Nature, Development and Teaching of Written Communication*, vol. 2. Hillsdale, NJ: Lawrence Erlbaum Associates, Inc.

Scardamalia, M. and Bereiter, C. (1983) The development of evaluative, diagnostic and remedial capabilities in children's composing. In M. Martlew (ed.), *The Psychology of Written Language: Development and Educational Perspectives*. Chichester, UK: Wiley.

Scardamalia, M. and Bereiter, C. (1986) Writing. In R. F. Dillon and R. J. Sternberg (eds), *Cognition and Instruction*. New York: Academic Press.

Scarr, S. (1985) Constructing psychology: making facts and fables for our times. *American Psychologist* 40, 499–512.

Scarr, S. (1992) Developmental theories for the 90s: development and individual differences. *Child Development* 63, 1–19.

Scarr, S. (1996) How people make their own environments: implications for parents and policy makers. *Psychology, Public Policy and Law* 2(2), 204–228.

Scarr, S. (1997a) Behaviour-genetics and socialization theories of intelligence: truce and reconciliation. In R. J. Sternberg and E. Grigorenko (eds), *Intelligence, Heredity and Environment*, pp. 3–41. Cambridge, UK: Cambridge University Press.

Scarr, S. and Carter-Saltzman, L. (1982) Genetics and intelligence. In R. Sternberg (ed.), *Handbook of Human Intelligence*. Cambridge, UK: Cambridge University Press.

Scarr, S. and Kidd, K. K. (1983) Developmental behaviour genetics. In P. H. Mussen (ed.), *Handbook of Child Psychology*, vol. 2. New York: Wiley.

Scarr, S. and McCartney, K. (1983) How people make their own environments: a theory of genotype > environment effects. *Child Development* 54, 424–435.

Scarr, S. and Weinberg, R. A. (1983) The Minnesota adoption studies: genetic differences and malleability. *Child Development* 54, 260–267.

Scerif, G. and Karmiloff-Smith, A. (2005) The dawn of cognitive genetics? Crucial developmental caveats. *Trends in Cognitive Science* 9(3), 126–136.

Schachter, F. F. (1982) Sibling deidentification and split-parent identification: a family trend. In M. Lamb and B. Sutton-Smith (eds), *Sibling Relationships*. Hillsdale, NJ: Lawrence Erlbaum Associates, Inc.

Schafer, E. W. (1982) Neural adaptability: a biological determinant of behavioural intelligence. *International Journal of Neuroscience* 17, 183–191.

Schafer, G. (2005) Infants can learn decontextualized words before their first birthday. *Child Development* 76(1), 87–96.

Schaffer, H. R. (1992a) Early experience and the parent–child relationship: genetic and environmental interactions as developmental determinants. In B. Tizard and V. Varma (eds), *Vulnerability and Resilience in Human Development*. London: Jessica Kingsley.

Schaffer, H. R. (1992b) Joint involvement episodes as context for development. In H. McGurk (ed.), *Childhood Social Development*. Hove, UK: Lawrence Erlbaum Associates Ltd.

Schaffer, H. R. and Crook, C. K. (1980) Child compliance and maternal control techniques. *Developmental Psychology* 16, 54–61.

Schank, R. C. (1980) Language and memory. *Cognitive Science* 4, 243–284.

Schank, R. C. and Abelson, R. (1977) *Scripts, Plans, Goals and Understanding*. Hillsdale, NJ: Lawrence Erlbaum Associates, Inc.

Schatschneider, C., Fletcher, J. M., Francis, D. J., Carlson, C. D. and Foorman, B. R. (2004) Kindergarten prediction of reading skills: a longitudinal comparative analysis. *Journal of Educational Psychology* 96(2), 265–282.

Schauble, L. (1990) Belief and revision in children: the role of prior knowledge and strategies for generating evidence. *Journal of Experimental Child Psychology* 49, 31–57.

Scheerens, J. and Creemers, B. P. M. (1989) Conceptualizing school effectiveness. *International Journal of Educational Research* 13(7), 691–706.

Schieffelin, B. B. and Cochran-Smith, M. (1984) Learning to read culturally: literacy before schooling. In H. Goelman, A. Oberg and F. Smith (eds), *Awakening to Literacy*. London: Heinemann.

Schiff, M., Duyme, M., Dumaret, A. and Tomkiewicz, S. (1982) How much could we boost scholastic achievement and I.Q. scores: a direct answer from a French adoption study. *Cognition* 12, 165–196.

Schiff, M. and Lewontin, R. (1986) *Education and Class: the Irrelevance of IQ Genetic Studies*. Oxford, UK: Clarendon Press.

Schliemann, A. D. and Carraher, D. W. (2002) The evolution of mathematical reasoning: everyday versus idealised understandings. *Developmental Review* 22, 242–266.

Schmeck, R. R. (1988) *Learning Strategies and Learning Styles*. New York: Plenum Press.

Schneider, W. (1985) Developmental trends in the metamemory–memory behavior relationship. In D. L. Forrest-Pressley, G. E. MacKinnon and T. G. Waller (eds), *Metacognition, Cognition and Human Performance*, vol. 1. Orlando, FL: Academic Press.

Schneider, W. (2002) Memory development in childhood. In U. Goswami (ed.), *Blackwell Handbook of Cognitive Development*. Oxford, UK: Blackwell.

Schneider, W. and Bjorklund, D. F. (1998) Memory. In D. Kuhn and R. S. Siegler (eds), *Handbook of Child Psychology, vol. 2, Cognition, Perception and Language.* New York: Wiley.

Schneider, W. and Körkel, J. (1989) The knowledge base and text recall: evidence from a short-term longitudinal study. *Contemporary Educational Psychology* 14, 382–393.

Schneider, W., Kron, V., Hunnerkopf, M. and Krajewski, K. (2004) The development of young children's memory strategies: first findings from the Wurzburg Longitudinal Memory Study. *Journal of Experimental Child Psychology* 88, 193–209.

Schneider, W. and Pressley, M. (1989) *Memory Development between 2 and 20.* Berlin, Germany: Springer-Verlag.

Schneider, W. and Weinert, P. E. (1990) Universal trends and individual differences in memory development. In A. de Ribaupierre (ed.), *Transition Mechanisms in Child Development.* Cambridge, UK: Cambridge University Press.

Schoenfeld, A. H. (1989) Explorations of students' mathematical beliefs and behaviour. *Journal for Research in Mathematics Education* 20, 338–355.

Scholl, B. J. and Leslie, A. M. (2001) Minds, modules and meta-analysis. *Child Development* 72, 696–701.

Scholnick, E. K. and Wing, C. S. (1992) Speaking deductively: using conversation to trace the origins of conditional thought in children. *Merrill-Palmer Quarterly* 38, 1–20.

Schul, R., Townsend, J. and Stiles, J. (2003) The development of attentional orienting during the school-age years. *Developmental Science* 6(3), 262–272.

Schult, C. A. (2002) Children's understanding of the distinction between intentions and desires. *Child Development* 73(6), 1727–1747.

Schutte, A. R., Spencer, J. P. and Schoner, G. (2003) Testing the dynamic field theory: working memory for locations becomes more spatially precise over development. *Child Development* 74(5), 1393–1417.

Schwartzman, H. (1978) *Transformations: The Anthropology of Children's Play.* New York: Plenum Press.

Scribner, S. (1985) Vygotsky's uses of history. In J. V. Wertsch (ed.), *Culture, Communication and Cognition.* Cambridge, UK: Cambridge University Press.

Scribner, S. and Cole, M. (1981) *The Psychology of Literacy.* Cambridge, MA: Harvard University Press.

Searle, J. R. (1984) *Minds, Brains and Science.* Harmondsworth, UK: Penguin Books.

Searle, J. R. (1990) Is the brain's mind a computer program? *Scientific American,* January, 20–25.

Segal, J. W., Chipman, S. F. and Glaser, R. (eds) (1985) *Thinking and Learning Skills,* 2 vols. Hillsdale, NJ: Lawrence Erlbaum Associates, Inc.

Seidenberg, M. (1997) Language acquisition and use: learning and applying probabilistic constraints. *Science* 275, 1559–1603.

Seitz, V., Rosenbaum, L. K. and Apfel, N. H. (1985) Effects of family support intervention: a ten-year follow-up. *Child Development* 56, 376–391.

Selfe, L. (1977) *Nadia: A case of extraordinary drawing ability in an autistic child.* London: Academic Press.

Selfe, L. (1983) *Normal and Anomalous Representational Drawing Ability in Children*. London: Academic Press.

Seligman, M. E. P. (1975) *Helplessness: On Depression, Development and Death*. New York: Freeman.

Selman, R. L. (1980) *The Growth of Interpersonal Understanding*. New York: Academic Press.

Selman, R. L. (1981) The child as a friendship philosopher. In S. R. Asher and J. M. Gottman (eds), *The Development of Children's Friendships*. Cambridge, UK: Cambridge University Press.

Senechal, M. and LeFevre, J. (2002) Parental involvement in the development of children's reading skills: a five-year longitudinal study. *Child Development* 73(2), 445–460.

Senner, W. (ed.) (1989) *The Origins of Writing*. Lincoln: University of Nebraska Press.

Serafine, M. L. (1988) *Music as Cognition: The Development of Thought in Sound*. New York: Columbia University Press.

Sesma, H. W. and Georgieff, M. (2003) The effect of adverse intrauterine and newborn environments on cognitive development: the experiences of premature delivery and diabetes during pregnancy. *Development and Psychopathology* 15(4), 991–1015.

Shaffer, D. (1985) Brain damage. In M. Rutter and L. Hersov (eds), *Child and Adolescent Psychiatry: Modern Approaches*. Oxford, UK: Blackwell.

Shaheen, S. J. (1984) Neuromaturation and behaviour development: the case of childhood lead poisoning. *Developmental Psychology* 20, 542–550.

Shallice, T. (1989) *From Neuropsychology to Mental Structures*. Cambridge, UK: Cambridge University Press.

Shantz, C. U. (1983) Social cognition. In J. H. Flavell and E. M. Markman (eds), *Handbook of Child Psychology*, vol. 3. New York: Wiley.

Shantz, C. U. (ed.) (1989) Children's cognitive and social-cognitive development: domain specificity and generality. *Merrill-Palmer Quarterly* (invitational issue), 35(1), 1–142.

Shapka, J. D. and Keating, D. P. (2003) Effects of a girls-only curriculum during adolescence: performance, persistence, and engagement in mathematics and science.

Sharon, T. and DeLoache, J. S. (2003) The role of perseveration in children's symbolic understanding and skill. *Developmental Science* 6(3), 289–296.

Shatz, M. (1978) The relationship between cognitive processes and the development of communication skills. *Nebraska Symposium on Motivation*, 1977. Lincoln: University of Nebraska Press.

Shatz, M. and Gelman, R. (1973) The development of communication skills. *Monographs of the Society for Research in Child Development* 38(5), serial no. 152.

Shatz, M. and Gelman, R. (1977) Beyond syntax: the influence of conversational constraints on speech modifications. In C. E. Snow and C. A. Ferguson (eds), *Talking to Children*. Cambridge, UK: Cambridge University Press.

Shayer, M. (2003) Not just Piaget: not just Vygotsky, and certainly not Vygotsky as alternative to Piaget. *Learning and Instruction* 13, 465–484.

Shaywitz, B. A., Shaywitz, S. E., Blackman, B. *et al.* (2004) Development of left occipitotemporal systems for skilled reading in children after a phonologically-based intervention. *Biological Psychiatry* 55, 926–933.

Shahbazian, M. D., Sun, Y. L. and Zoghbi, H. Y. (2002) Balanced X chromosome inactivation patterns in the Rett syndrome brain. *American Journal of Medical Genetics* 111(2), 164–168.

Shepard, R. N. (1967) Recognition memory for words, sentences and pictures. *Journal of Verbal Learning and Verbal Behaviour* 6, 156–163.

Shields, M. M. and Duveen, G. (1982) *The young child's image of the personal and social world: some aspects of the child's representation of persons*. Paper presented at the International Sociological Association Conference, Mexico City, August 1982.

Shonk, S. M. and Cicchetti, D. (2001) Maltreatment, competency deficits, and risk for academic and behavioural maladjustment. *Developmental Psychology* 37, 3–17.

Shrager, J. and Siegler, R. S. (1998) SCADS: A model of children's strategy choices and strategy discoveries. *Psychological Science* 9(5), 405–410.

Shu, H. (2003) Chinese writing system and learning to read. *International Journal of Psychology* 38(5), 274–285.

Shu, H. and Anderson, R. C. (1997) Role of radical awareness in the character and word acquisition of Chinese children. *Reading Research Quarterly* 32, 78–89.

Shu, H., Anderson, R. C. and Wu, N. (2000) Phonetic awareness: knowledge of orthography–phonology relationships in the character acquisition of Chinese children. *Journal of Educational Psychology* 92, 56–62.

Shu, H., Chen, X., Anderson, R. C., Wu, N. and Xuan, Y. (2003) Properties of school Chinese: implications for learning to read. *Child Development* 74(1), 27–47.

Shultz, T. R. and Cloghesy, K. (1981) Development of recursive awareness of intention. *Developmental Psychology* 17, 465–471.

Shuter-Dyson, R. and Gabriel, C. [1968] (2nd edn, 1981) *The Psychology of Musical Ability*. London: Methuen.

Shweder, R. A., Mahapatra, M. and Miller, J. G. (1990) Culture and moral development. In J. W. Stigler, R. A. Shweder and G. H. Herdt (eds), *Cultural Psychology: Essays on Comparative Human Development*. Cambridge, UK: Cambridge University Press.

Shymansky, J. A., Yore, L. D. and Treagust, D. F., Thiele, R. B., Harrison, A., Waldrip, L. D., Stocklmayer, S. M. and Venville, G. (1997) Examining the construction process: a study of changes in level 10 students' understanding of classical mechanics. *Journal of Research on Science Teaching* 34(6), 571–593.

Siegal, M. (1988) Children's knowledge of contagion and contamination as causes of illness. *Child Development* 59, 1353–1359.

Siegal, M. (1991) *Knowing Children: Experiments in Conversation and Cognition*. Hove, UK: Lawrence Erlbaum Associates Ltd.

Siegal, M. and Beattie, K. (1991) Where to look first for children's knowledge of false beliefs. *Cognition* 38, 1–12.

Siegal, M., Butterworth, G. and Newcombe, P. A. (2004) Culture and children's cosmology. *Developmental Science* 7(4), 308–324.

Siegal, M. and Peterson, C. (1996) Breaking the mould: a fresh look at children's understanding of questions about lies and mistakes. *Developmental Psychology* 32, 322–334.

Siegal, M. and Peterson, C. C. (1998) Preschoolers' understanding of lies and innocent and negligent mistakes. *Developmental Psychology* 34(2), 332–341.

Siegal, M. and Robinson, J. (1987) Order effects in children's gender constancy responses. *Developmental Psychology* 23, 283–286.

Siegal, M. and Share, D. L. (1990) Contamination sensitivity in young children. *Developmental Psychology* 26, 455–458.

Siegal, M., Waters, L. J. and Dinwiddy, L. S. (1988) Misleading children: causal attributions for inconsistency under repeated questioning. *Journal of Experimental Child Psychology* 45, 438–456.

Siegel, J. (1988) *Educating Reason: Rationality, Critical Thinking and Education.* London: Routledge.

Siegel, L. S. (1972) Development of the concept of seriation. *Developmental Psychology* 6, 135–137.

Siegel, L. S. (1978) The relationship of language and thought in the preoperational child: a reconsideration of nonverbal alternatives to Piagetian tasks. In L. S. Siegel and C. J. Brainerd (eds), *Alternatives to Piaget.* New York: Academic Press.

Siegel, L. S. and Ryan, E. B. (1988) Development of grammatical-sensitivity, phonological, and short-term memory skills in normally achieving and learning disabled children. *Developmental Psychology* 24(1), 28–37.

Siegel, L. S., McCabe, A. E., Brand, J. and Matthews, L. (1978) Evidence for the understanding of class inclusion in preschool children: linguistic factors and training effects. *Child Development* 49, 688–693.

Siegler, R. S. (1976) Three aspects of cognitive development. *Cognitive Psychology* 8, 481–520.

Siegler, R. S. (1981) Developmental sequences within and between concepts. *Monographs of the Society for Research in Child Development* 46, 1–74.

Siegler, R. S. (1983) Information processing approaches to development. In W. Kessen (ed.), *Handbook of Child Psychology*, vol. 1. New York: Wiley.

Siegler, R. S. (1984) Mechanisms of cognitive growth: variation and selection. In R. J. Sternberg (ed.), *Mechanisms of Cognitive Development.* New York: Freeman.

Siegler, R. S. (1986) *Children's Thinking.* Englewood Cliffs, NJ: Prentice Hall.

Siegler, R. S. (1987) The perils of averaging data over strategies: an example from children's addition. *Journal of Experimental Psychology: General* 116, 250–264.

Siegler, R. S. (1988) Individual differences in strategy choices. *Child Development* 59, 833–851.

Siegler, R. S. (1989a) How domain-general and domain-specific knowledge interact to produce strategy choices. *Merrill-Palmer Quarterly* 35(1), 1–26.

Siegler, R. S. (1989b) Mechanisms of cognitive development. *Annual Review of Psychology* 40, 353–379.

Siegler, R. S. (1995) How does change occur: a micro genetic study of number conversation. *Cognitive Psychology* 28, 225–273.

Siegler, R. S. (1996) *Emerging Minds: The Process of Change in Children's Thinking.* New York: Oxford University Press.

Siegler, R. S. (2005) Microgenetic Analyses of Learning. Unpublished paper prepared for D. Kuhn and R. S. Siegler (eds.), *Handbook of Child Psychology*, 6th edn.

Siegler, R. S. (ed.) (1978) *Children's Thinking: What Develops?* Hillsdale, NJ: Lawrence Erlbaum Associates, Inc.

Siegler, R. S. (2002) Microgenetic studies of self-explanation. In N. Granott and J. Parziale (eds), *Microdevelopment: Transition Processes in Development and Learning*. Cambridge, UK: Cambridge University Press.

Siegler, R. S. (2004) Turning memory development inside out. *Developmental Review* 24(4), 469–475.

Siegler, R. S. and Crowley, K. (1991) The microgenetic method: a direct means for studying cognitive development. *American Psychologist* 46, 606–620.

Siegler, R. S. and Richards, D. D. (1982) The development of intelligence. In R. J. Sternberg (ed.), *Handbook of Human Intelligence*. Cambridge, UK: Cambridge University Press.

Siegler, R. S. and Robinson, M. (1982) The development of numerical under-standings. In H. W. Reese and L. P. Lipsitt (eds), *Advances in Child Development and Behaviour*, vol. 16. New York: Academic Press.

Siegler, R. S. and Shipley, C. (1987) The role of learning in children's strategy choices. In L. S. Liben (ed.), *Development and Learning*. Hillsdale, NJ: Lawrence Erlbaum Associates, Inc.

Sigel, I. (1982a) Reproductive, perinatal and environmental factors as predictors of the cognitive and language development of preterm and fullterm infants. *Child Development* 53, 963–973.

Sigel, I. (1982b) The relationship between parental distancing strategies and the child's cognitive behavior. In L. M. Laosa and I. E. Sigel (eds), *Families as Learning Environments for Children*. New York: Plenum Press.

Sigel, I., Stinson, E. T. and Flaugher, J. (1991) Socialisation of representational competence in the family: the distancing paradigm. In L. Okagaki and R. J. Sternberg (eds), *Directors of Development: Influences on the Development of Children's Thinking*. Hillsdale, NJ: Lawrence Erlbaum Associates, Inc.

Sigman, M., Cohen, S. E., Beckwith, L., Asarnow, R. and Parmelee, A. H. (1991) Continuity in cognitive-abilities from infancy to 12 years of age. *Cognitive Development* 6(1), 47–57.

Sigman, M. and Whaley, S. E. (1998) The role of nutrition in the development of intelligence. In V. Neisser (ed.), *The Rising Curve: Long Term Gains in IQ and Related Measures*, pp. 155–182. Washington, DC: American Psychological Association.

Silk, A. M. J. and Thomas G. V. (1986) Development and differentiation in chil-dren's figure drawings. *British Journal of Psychology* 77, 399–410.

Silk, A. M. J. and Thomas, G. V. (1988) The development of size scaling in children's figure drawings. *British Journal of Developmental Psychology* 6, 285–299.

Silva, P. A., Hughes, P., Williams, S. and Faed, J. M. (1988) Blood lead, intelli-gence, reading attainment and behaviour in eleven-year-old children in Dunedin, New Zealand. *Journal of Child Psychology and Psychiatry* 29, 43–52.

Silven, M., Poskiparta, E. and Niemi, P. (2004) The odds of becoming a precocious reader of Finnish. *Journal of Educational Psychology* 96(1), 152–164.

Simon, H. (1981) *The Sciences of the Artificial*. Cambridge, MA: MIT Press.

Simonton, D. K. (1999) Talent and its development: an emergenic and epigenetic model. *Psychological Review* 106, 435–457.

Simonton, D. K. (2003) Expertise, competence and creative ability: the perplexing complexities. In R. L. Sternberg and E. L. Grigorenko (eds), *The Psychology of Abilities, Competencies and Expertise*. Cambridge, UK: Cambridge University Press.

Sinclair, A., Jarvella, R. J. and Levelt, W. J. M. (1978) *The Child's Conception of Language*. Berlin, Germany: Springer-Verlag.

Sinclair, H. (1987) Conflict and congruence in development and learning. In L. S. Liben (ed.), *Development and Learning*. Hillsdale, NJ: Lawrence Erlbaum Associates, Inc.

Sinclair, H. and Sinclair, A. (1986) Children's mastery of written numerals and the construction of basic number concepts. In J. Hiebert (ed.), *Conceptual and Procedural Knowledge: The Case of Mathematics*. Hillsdale, NJ: Lawrence Erlbaum Associates, Inc.

Singer, D. G. and Singer, J. L. (1990) *The House of Make-Believe: Play and the Developing Imagination*. Cambridge, MA: Harvard University Press.

Singer, J. L. (ed.) (1973) *The Child's World of Make-believe*. New York: Academic Press.

Singer, J. L. (1975) *Daydreaming and Fantasy*. London: Allen & Unwin.

Singer, W. (1986) Neuronal activity as a shaping factor in postnatal development of visual cortex. In W. T. Greenough and J. M. Juraska (eds), *Developmental Neuropsychology*. New York: Academic Press.

Singer-Freeman, K. and Goswami, U. (2001) Does half a pizza equal half a box of chocolates? Proportional matching in an analogy task. *Cognitive Development* 16, 811–829.

Singley, M. K. and Anderson, J. R. (1989) *The Transfer of Cognitive Skills*. Cambridge, MA: Harvard University Press.

Sinisterra, L. (1987) Studies on poverty, human growth and development: the Cali experience. In J. Dobbing (ed.), *Early Nutrition and Later Achievement*. London: Academic Press.

Skinner, B. F. (1957) *Verbal Behaviour*. New York: Appleton Century Crofts.

Skuse, D. (1984) Extreme deprivation in early childhood, I: diverse outcomes for three children in an extraordinary family; II: theoretical issues and a comparative review. *Journal of Child Psychology and Psychiatry* 25, 523–542, 543–572.

Skuse, D. H., James, R. S., Bishop, D. V. M., Coppin, B., Dalton, P., Aamodt-Leeper, G., Bacarase-Hamilton, M., Creswell, C., McGurk, R. and Jacobs, P. A. (1997) Evidence from Turner's syndrome of an imprinted X-linked locus affecting cognitive function. *Nature* 387, 705–708.

Slade, A. (1987) A longitudinal study of maternal involvement and symbolic play during the toddler period. *Child Development* 58, 367–375.

Slater, A. (1995) Individual differences in infancy and later IQ. *Journal of Child Psychology and Psychiatry* 36, 69–112.

Slaughter, V. and Heron, M. (2004) Origins and early development of human body knowledge. *Monographs of the Society for Research in Child Development* 69(2), serial no. 276.

Slaughter, V. and Lyons, M. (2003) Learning about life and death in early childhood. *Cognitive Psychology* 46, 1–30.

Slobin, D. (1985) *The Cross-linguistic Study of Language Acquisition*, vols 1 and 2. Hillsdale, NJ: Lawrence Erlbaum Associates, Inc.

Slobin, D., Gerhardt, J., Kyratis, A. and Guo-Jiangsheng, I. (eds) (1996) *Social Interaction, Social Context and Language: Essays in Honour of Susan Ervin-Tripp*. Hillsdale, NJ: Lawrence Erlbaum Associates, Inc.

Sloboda, J. A. (1985) *The Musical Mind: The Cognitive Psychology of Music*. Oxford, UK: Oxford University Press.

Sloboda, J. A. and Rogers, D. (1987) *Cognitive Processes in Mathematics*. Oxford, UK: Oxford University Press.

Smart, J. L. (1987) The need for and the relevance of animal studies of early undernutrition. In J. Dobbing (ed.), *Early Nutrition and Later Achievement*. London: Academic Press.

Smedslund, J. (1980) Analyzing the primary code: from empricism to apriorism. In D. R. Olson (ed.), *The Social Foundations of Language and Thought*. New York: Norton.

Smetana, J. G., Kelly, M. and Twentyman, C. T. (1984) Abused, neglected and nonmaltreated children's conceptions of moral and socio-conventional transgressions. *Child Development* 55, 277–287.

Smith, B. S., Ratner, H. H. and Hobart, C. J. (1987) The role of cuing and organisation in children's memory for events. *Journal of Experimental Child Psychology* 44, 1–24.

Smith, C. L., Maclin, D., Houghton, C. and Hennessey, M. G. (2000) Sixth-grade students' epistemologies of science; the impact of school science experiences on epistemological development. *Cognition and Instruction* 18(3), 349–422.

Smith, E. E., Langston, C. and Nisbett, R. (1992) The case for rules in reasoning. *Cognitive Science* 16, 1–40.

Smith, F. (1973) *Psycholinguistics and Reading*. New York: Holt, Rinehart & Winston.

Smith, F. (1978) *Reading*. Cambridge, UK: Cambridge University Press.

Smith, F. (1982) *Writing and the Writer*. London: Heinemann.

Smith, I., Beasley, M. G. and Ades, A. E. (1990) Intelligence and quality of dietary treatment in phenylketonuria. *Archives of Disease in Childhood* 65, 472–478.

Smith, I., Beasley, M. G. and Ades, A. E. (1991) Effect on intelligence of relaxing the low phenylalanine diet in PKU. *Archives of Disease in Childhood* 66, 311–316.

Smith, J. D. and Caplan, J. (1988) Cultural differences in cognitive style development. *Developmental Psychology* 24, 46–52.

Smith, J. R., Brooks-Gunn, J. and Klebanov, P. (1997) Consequences of living in poverty for young children's cognitive and verbal ability and early school achievement. In G. Duncan and J. Brooks-Gunn (eds), *Consequences of Growing Up Poor*. New York: Russell Sage Foundation.

Smith, L. (2002) Piaget's model. In U. Goswami (ed.), *Blackwell Handbook of Cognitive Development*. Oxford, UK: Blackwell.

Smith, L. (ed.) (1996) *Critical Readings on Piaget*. London: Routledge.

Smith, L. B. (1989a) From global similarities to kinds of similarities: the construction of dimensions in development. In S. Vosniadou and A. Ortony (eds), *Similarity and Analogical Reasoning*. Cambridge, UK: Cambridge University Press.

Smith, L. B. (1989b) A model of perceptual classification in children and adults. *Psychological Review* 96, 125–144.

Smith, L. B. and Sera, M. D. (1992) A developmental analysis of the polar structure of dimensions. *Cognitive Psychology* 24, 99–142.

Smith, M. (1985) Recent work on low-level lead exposure and its impact on behaviour, intelligence and learning. *Journal of the American Academy of Child Psychiatry* 24, 24–32.

Smith, P. K. and Simon, T. (1984) Object play, problem-solving and creativity in children. In P. K. Smith (ed.), *Play in Animals and Humans*. Oxford, UK: Blackwell.

Smith, P. K., Simon, T. and Emberton, R. (1985) Play, problem-solving and experimenter effects. *British Journal of Developmental Psychology* 3, 105–107.

Smith, S. B. (1983) *The Great Mental Calculators*. New York: Columbia University Press.

Snow, C. E. (1995) Issues in the study of input: finetuning, universality, individual and developmental differences, and necessary causes. In P. Fletcher and B. MacWhinney (eds), *The Handbook of Child Language*. Oxford, UK: Blackwell.

Snow, C. E., Barnes, W. S., Chandler, J., Goodman, I. F. and Hemphill, L. (1991) *Unfulfilled Expectations: Home and School Influences on Literacy*. Cambridge, MA: Harvard University Press.

Snowling, M. (2002) Reading development and dyslexia. In U. Goswami (ed.), *Blackwell Handbook of Cognitive Development*. Oxford, UK: Blackwell.

Snowling, M. (2004) Language skills and learning to read. *The Psychologist* 17(8), 438–441.

Snowling, M. and Gombert, J.-E. (eds) (2002) Language and reading skills of persons with neuro-developmental disorders. *Reading and Writing* 15, special issue.

Snowling, M. J. (1987) *Dyslexia: A Cognitive Developmental Perspective*. Oxford, UK: Blackwell.

Snowling, M. J. (1991) Developmental reading disorders. *Journal of Child Psychology and Psychiatry* 32, 49–77.

Sodian, B. (1991) The development of deception in young children. *British Journal of Developmental Psychology* 9, 173–188.

Sodian, B., Taylor, C., Harris, P. L. and Perner, J. (1991) Early deception and the child's theory of mind: false trails and genuine markers. *Child Development* 62, 468–483.

Sodian, B. and Wimmer, H. (1987) Children's understanding of inference as a source of knowledge. *Child Development* 58, 424–433.

Solomon, Y. (1989) *The Practice of Mathematics*. London: Routledge.

Somerville, S. C. and Bryant, P. E. (1985) Young children's use of spatial coordinates. *Child Development* 56, 604–613.

Song, M.-J. and Ginsburg, H. P. (1987) The development of informal and formal mathematical thinking in Korean and U.S. children. *Child Development* 58, 1286–1296.

Sophian, C. (1988) Early developments in children's understanding of number: inferences about numerosity and one-to-one correspondence. *Child Development* 59, 1397–1414.

Sophian, C. (1998) A developmental perspective on children's counting. In

C. Donlan (ed.), *The Development of Mathematical Skills*. Hove, UK: Psychology Press.

Sophian, C., Garyantes, D. and Chang, C. (1997) When three is less than two: early developments in children's understanding of fractional quantities. *Developmental Psychology* 89, 309–317.

Sophian, C. and Wood, A. (1997) Proportional reasoning in young children: the parts and the whole of it. *Journal of Educational Psychology* 89, 309–317.

Sophian, C., Wood, A. and Vong, K. I. (1995) Making numbers count: the early development of numerical inferences. *Developmental Psychology* 31, 263–273.

Spear-Swerling, L. (2004) A road map for understanding reading disability and other reading problems: origins, prevention, and intervention. In R. B. Ruddell and N. J. Unrau (eds), *Theoretical Models and Processes of Reading*. Newark, DE: International Reading Association.

Speece, M. W. and Brent, S. B. (1984) Children's understanding of death. *Child Development* 55, 1671–1686.

Spelke, E. S. (2002) Developmental neuroimaging: a developmental psychologist looks ahead. *Developmental Science* 5(3), 392–396.

Spencer, C., Blades, M. and Morsley, K. (1989) *The Child in the Physical Environment: the Development of Spatial Knowledge and Cognition*. Chichester, UK: Wiley.

Spiker, C. C. (1989) Cognitive psychology: mentalistic or behavioristic? In H. W. Reese (ed.), *Advances in Child Development and Behavior*, vol. 21. New York: Academic Press.

Spilich, G. J., Vesonder, G. T., Chiesi, H. L. and Voss, J. F. (1979) Text processing of domain-related information for individuals with high and low domain knowledge. *Journal of Verbal Learning and Verbal Behaviour* 18, 275–290.

Spinath, F. M., Price, T. S., Dale, P. S. and Plomin, R. (2004) The genetic and environmental origins of language disability and ability. *Child Development* 75(2), 445–454.

Spinillo, A. G. and Bryant, P. (1991) Children's proportional judgments – The importance of half. *Child Development* 62(3), 427–440.

Spiro, R. J. (2004) Principled pluralism for adaptive flexibility in teaching and learning to read. In R. B. Ruddell and N. J. Unrau (eds), *Theoretical Models and Processes of Reading*. Newark, DE: International Reading Association.

Squire, L. R. (1987) *Memory and Brain*. Oxford, UK: Oxford University Press.

Squire, S. and Bryant, P. (2003) Children's understanding and misunderstanding of the inverse relation in division. *British Journal of Developmental Psychology* 21, 507–526.

Sroufe, L. A. (1979) Socioemotional development. In J. D. Osofsky (ed.), *Handbook of Infant Development*. New York: Wiley.

Sroufe, L. A. (1983) Infant–caregiver attachment and patterns of adaptation in preschool: the roots of maladaptation and competence. *Minnesota Symposium on Child Development*, vol. 16. Hillsdale, NJ: Lawrence Erlbaum Associates, Inc.

Sroufe, L. A. and Fleeson, J. (1986) Attachment and the construction of relationships. In W. Hartup and Z. Rubin (eds), *Relationships and Development*. Hillsdale, NJ: Lawrence Erlbaum Associates, Inc.

Stage, S. A. and Wagner, R. K. (1992) Development of young children's phonological and orthographic knowledge as revealed by their spellings. *Developmental Psychology* 28, 287–296.

Stambrook, M. and Parker, K. C. H. (1987) The development of the concept of death in childhood. *Merrill-Palmer Quarterly* 33(2), 133–157.

Standing, L. (1973) Learning 10,000 pictures. *Quarterly Journal of Experimental Psychology* 25, 207–222.

Stanovich, K. E. (2004) Matthew effects in reading: some consequences of individual differences in the acquisition of literacy. In R. B. Ruddell and N. J. Unrau (eds), *Theoretical Models and Processes of Reading*. Newark, DE: International Reading Association.

Starkey, P. (1992) The early development of numerical reasoning. *Cognition* 43, 93–126.

Starkey, P. and Cooper, R. S. (1980) Perception of number by human infants. *Science* 100, 1033–1035.

Starkey, P. and Gelman, R. (1982) The development of addition and subtraction abilities prior to formal schooling. In T. P. Carpenter, J. M. Moser and T. A. Romberg (eds), *Addition and Subtraction: A Developmental Perspective*. Hillsdale, NJ: Lawrence Erlbaum Associates, Inc.

Starkey, P., Spelke, E. S. and Gelman, R. (1990) Numerical abstraction by human infants. *Cognition* 36, 97–127.

Steedman, C. (1982) *The Tidy House*. London: Virago.

Steel, S. and Funnell, E. (2001) Learning multiplication facts: a study of children taught by discovery methods in England. *Journal of Experimental Child Psychology* 79(1), 37–55.

Steele J. (2003) Children's gender stereotypes about math: The role of stereotype stratification. *Journal of Applied Social Psychology* 33(12). 2587–2606.

Stein, L. D. (2004) Human genome: end of the beginning. *Nature* 431, 915–916.

Stein, Z., Susser, M., Saenger, G. and Marolla, F. (1975) *Famine and Human Development*. Oxford, UK: Oxford University Press.

Stern, J. (1987) The biochemical approach to mental handicap. *Journal of Mental Deficiency Research* 31, 357–364.

Sternberg, R. and Suben, O. (1986) The socialization of intelligence. In M. Perlmutter (ed.), Perspectives on intellectual development. *Minnesota Symposium on Child Development*, vol. 19. Hillsdale NJ: Lawrence Erlbaum Associates, Inc.

Sternberg, R. J. (ed.) (1982) *Handbook of Human Intelligence*. Cambridge, UK: Cambridge University Press.

Sternberg, R. J. (ed.) (1984) *Mechanisms of Cognitive Development*. New York: Freeman.

Sternberg, R. J. (1985) *Beyond IQ: A Triarchic Theory of Human Intelligence*. New York: Cambridge University Press.

Sternberg, R. J. (1988a) Explaining away intelligence: a reply to Howe. *British Journal of Psychology* 79, 527–533.

Sternberg, R. J. (1988b) *The Nature of Creativity: Contemporary Psychological Perspectives*. Cambridge, UK: Cambridge University Press.

Sternberg, R. J. (1990) *Metaphors of Mind: Conceptions of the Nature of Intelligence*. New York: Cambridge University Press.

Sternberg, R. J. (ed.) (1999) *The Handbook of Creativity*. Cambridge, UK: Cambridge University Press.

Sternberg, R. J. (2002) Raising the achievement of all students: teaching for successful intelligence. *Educational Psychology Review* 14(4), 383–393.

Sternberg, R. J. (2004) Culture and intelligence. *American Psychologist* 59(5), 325–338.

Sternberg, R. J. and Davidson, J. E. (eds) (1986) *Conceptions of Giftedness*. New York: Cambridge University Press.

Sternberg, R. J. and Detterman, D. K. (1986) *What is Intelligence?* Norwood, NJ: Ablex.

Sternberg, R. J. and Gardner, M. K. (1982) A componential interpretation of the general factor in human intelligence. In H. J. Eysenck (ed.), *A Model for Intelligence*. Berlin, Germany: Springer-Verlag.

Sternberg, R. J. and Grigorenko, E. L. (eds) (2003) *The Psychology of Abilities, Competencies and Expertise*. Cambridge, UK: Cambridge University Press.

Sternberg, R. J. and Kaufman, J. C. (1998) Human abilities. *Annual Review of Psychology* 49, 479–502.

Sternberg, R. J. and Powell, J. (1983) The development of intelligence. In J. H. Flavell and E. M. Markman (eds), *Handbook of Child Psychology*, vol. 3. New York: Wiley.

Sternberg, R. J. and Smith E. E. (1988) *The Psychology of Human Thought*. Cambridge, UK: Cambridge University Press.

Sternberg, R. J., Wagner, R. K., Williams, W. M. and Horvath, J. A. (1995) Testing common sense. *American Psychologist* 50, 912–926.

Stevens, J. H. and Bakeman, R. (1985) A factor analytic study of the HOME scale for infants. *Developmental Psychology* 21, 1196–1203.

Stevenson, D. L. and Baker, D. P. (1987) The family–school relation and the child's school performance. *Child Development* 58, 1348–1357.

Stevenson, H. W., Chen, C., Lee, S.-Y. and Fuligni, A. J. (1991) Schooling, culture and cognitive development. In L. Okagaki and R. J. Sternberg (eds), *Directors of Development: Influences on the Development of Children's Thinking*. Hillsdale, NJ: Lawrence Erlbaum Associates, Inc.

Stevenson, H. W., Lee, S.-Y. and Stigler, J. W. (1986) Mathematics achievement of Chinese, Japanese and American children. *Science* 231, 693–699.

Stevenson, H. W., Parker, T., Wilkinson, A., Hegion, A. and Fish, E. (1976) Longitudinal study of individual differences in cognitive development and scholastic achievement. *Journal of Educational Psychology* 68, 377–400.

Stewart, A. J. and Healy, J. M. (1989) Linking individual development and social change. *Psychological Bulletin* 44, 30–42.

Stich, S. P. (1983) *From Folk Psychology to Cognitive Science: The Case Against Belief*. Cambridge, MA: MIT Press.

Stickgold, R. and Walker, M. (2004) To sleep, perchance to gain creative insight? *Trends in Cognitive Sciences* 8(5), 191–192.

Stigler, J. W., Lee, S.-Y. and Stevenson, H. W. (1987) Mathematics classrooms in Japan, Taiwan and the United States. *Child Development* 58, 1272–1285.

Stigler, J. W., Nusbaum, H. C. and Chalip, L. (1988) Developmental changes in speed of processing: central limiting mechanism or skill transfer? *Child Development* 59, 1144–1153.

Stigler, J. W., Schweder, R. A. and Herdt, G. (1990) *Cultural Psychology: Essays on Comparative Human Development*. Cambridge, UK: Cambridge University Press.

Stipek, D., Feiler, R., Daniels, D. and Milburn, S. (1995) Effects of different instructional approaches on young children's achievement and motivation. *Child Development* 66(1), 209–223.

Stipek, D. J. (1988) Declining perceptions of competence: a consequence of changes in the child or in the educational environment? *Journal of Educational Psychology* 80, 352–356.

Stipek, D. J. and Daniels, D. H. (1988) Declining perceptions of competence – A consequence of changes in the child or in the educational environment. *Journal of Educational Psychology* 80(3), 352–356.

Stipek, D. J. and Gralinski, J. H. (1996) Children's beliefs about intelligence and school performance. *Journal of Educational Psychology* 88, 397–407.

Stipek, D. J. and Tannart, L. M. (1984) Children's judgements of their own and their peers' academic competence. *Journal of Educational Psychology* 76, 75–84.

Strauss, M. S. and Curtis, L. E. (1981) Infant perception of numerosity. *Child Development* 52, 1146–1152.

Strauss, S., Ziv, M. and Stein, A. (2002) Teaching as a natural cognition and its relations to preschoolers' developing theory of mind. *Cognitive Development* 17, 1473–1487.

Strayer, F. F., Moss, E. and Blicharski, T. (1989) Biosocial bases of representational activity during early childhood. In L. T. Winegar (ed.), *Social Interaction and the Development of Children's Understanding*. Norwood, NJ: Ablex.

Streeter, L. A. (1976) Language perception of 2-month-old infants shows effects of both innate mechanisms and experience. *Nature* 259, 39–41.

Streissguth, A. P., Aase, J. M., Clarren, S. K., Randels, S. P., LaDue, R. A. and Smith, D. F. (1991) Fetal alcohol syndrome in adolescents and adults. *Journal of the American Medical Association* 265, 1961–1967.

Streissguth, A. P., Barr, H. M., Bookstein, F. L., Sampson, P. D. and Olson, H. C. (1999) The long-term neurocognitive consequences of prenatal alcohol exposure: a 14-year study. *Psychological Science* 10, 186–190.

Streissguth, A. P., Bookstein, F. L., Barr, H. M., Sampson, P. L., O'Malley, K. and Young, J. K. (2004) Risk factors for adverse life outcomes in fetal alcohol syndrome and fetal alcohol effects. *Journal of Developmental and Behavioral Pediatrics* 25(4), 228–238.

Streissguth, A. P., Bookstein, F. L., Sampson, P. D. and Barr, H. M. (1995) Attention: prenatal alcohol and continuities of vigilance and attentional problems from 4 through 14 years. *Development and Psychopathology* 1, 419–446.

Stuart, M. (1990) Factors influencing word recognition in pre-reading children. *British Journal of Psychology* 81, 135–146.

Stuart, M. and Coltheart, M. (1988) Does reading develop in a series of stages? *Cognition* 30, 139–181.

Stubbs, M. (1980) *Language and Literacy: The Sociolinguistics of Reading and Writing*. London: Routledge & Kegan Paul.

Styles, M. (1989) *Collaboration and Writing*. Milton Keynes, UK: Open University Press.

Subbotsky, E. (1994) Early rationality and magical thinking in preschoolers: space and time. *British Journal of Developmental Psychology* 12, 97–108.

Suddendorf, T. (2003) Early representational insight: twenty-four month-olds can use a photo to find an object in the world. *Child Development* 74(3), 896–870.

Suddendorf, T. and Whiten, A. (2001) Mental evolution and development: evidence for secondary representation in children, great apes and other animals. *Psychological Bulletin* 127, 629–650.

Sugarman, S. (1981) The cognitive basis of classification in very young children: an analysis of object ordering trends. *Child Development* 52, 1172–1178.

Sugarman, S. (1983) *Children's Early Thought: Developments in Classification.* Cambridge, UK: Cambridge University Press.

Suizzo, A.-M. (2000) The social–emotional and cultural contexts of cognitive development: neo-Piagetian perspectives. *Child Development* 71(4), 846–849.

Super, C. M., Clement, J., Vuori, L., Christiansen, N., Mora, J. O. and Herrera, M. G. (1981) Infant and caretaker behaviour as mediators of nutritional and social intervention in the barrios of Bogota. In T. M. Field, A. M. Sostek, P. Vietze and P. H. Liederman (eds), *Culture and Early Interactions.* Hillsdale, NJ: Lawrence Erlbaum Associates, Inc.

Super, C. M., Herrera, M. G. and Mora, J. O. (1990) Long-term effects of food supplementation and psychosocial intervention on the physical growth of Colombian infants at risk of malnutrition. *Child Development* 61, 29–49.

Sutherland, R., Pipe, M.-E., Schick, K., Murray, J. and Gobbo, C. (2003) Knowing in advance: the impact of prior event information on memory and event knowledge. *Journal of Experimental Child Psychology* 84, 244–263.

Sutton, A. (1983) An introduction to Soviet developmental psychology. In S. Meadows (ed.), *Developing Thinking.* London: Methuen.

Swanson, H. L. (2003) Age-related differences in learning disabled and skilled readers' working memory. *Journal of Experimental Child Psychology* 85, 1–31.

Swanwick, K. (1988) *Music, Mind and Education.* London: Routledge.

Swift, J. [1726] (1985) *Gulliver's Travels.* Harmondsworth, UK: Penguin Books.

Sylva, K. (1994) School influences on children's development. *Journal of Child Psychology and Psychiatry* 35, 135–170.

Sylvester-Bradley, B. (1985) Failure to distinguish between people and things in early infancy. *British Journal of Developmental Psychology* 3, 281–292.

Symons, D. K. (2004) Mental state discourse, theory of mind, and the internalisation of self–other understanding. *Developmental Review* 24, 159–188.

Szechter, L. E. and Liben, L. S. (2004) Parental guidance in preschoolers' understanding of spatial–graphic representations. *Child Development* 75(3), 869–885.

Tager-Flusberg, H. (1992) Autistic children's talk about psychological states: deficits in the acquisition of a theory of mind. *Child Development* 63, 161–172.

Tager-Flusberg, H. (2003) Developmental disordes of genetic origin. In M. De Haan and M. Johnson (eds), *The Cognitive Neuroscience of Development.* Hove, UK: Psychology Press.

Tamis-LeMonda, C. S., Shannon, J. D., Cabrera, N. J. and Lamb, M. E. (2004) Fathers and mothers at play with their 2- and 3-year-olds: contributions to language and cognitive development. *Child Development* 75(6), 1806–1820.

Tardif, T. (1996) Nouns are not always learned before verbs: evidence from Mandarin speakers' early vocabularies. *Developmental Psychology* 32, 492–504.

Taylor, E. (1980) The development of attention. In M. Rutter (ed.), *Scientific Foundations of Developmental Psychiatry.* London: Heinemann.

Taylor, E. (1984) Diet and behaviour. *Archives of Disease in Childhood* 59, 97–98.

Taylor, E. (1985) Syndromes of overactivity and attention deficit. In M. Rutter and

L. Hersov (eds), *Child and Adolescent Psychiatry: Modern Approaches*. Oxford, UK: Blackwell.

Taylor, M. (1988) The development of children's understanding of the seeing–knowing distinction. In J. W. Astington, P. L. Harris and D. R. Olson (eds), *Developing Theories of Mind*. Cambridge, UK: Cambridge University Press.

Taylor, M. (1997) The role of creative control and culture in children's fantasy/reality judgements. *Child Development* 68, 1015–1017.

Taylor, M. (1999) *Imaginary Companions and the Children Who Create Them*. New York: Oxford University Press.

Taylor, M. and Carlson, S. M. (1997) The relation between individual differences in fantasy and theory of mind. *Child Development* 68, 436–455.

Taylor, M., Carlson, S. M., Maring, B. L., Gerow, L. and Charley, C. M. (2004) The characteristics and correlates of fantasy in school-age children: imaginary companions, impersonation, and social understanding. *Developmental Psychology* 40(6), 1173–1187.

Taylor, M., Cartwright, B. S. and Bowden, T. (1991) Perspective taking and theory of mind: do children predict interpretive diversity as a function of differences in observers' knowledge? *Child Development* 62, 1334–1351.

Taylor, M. G. (1996) The development of children's beliefs about social and biological aspects of gender differences. *Child Development* 67, 1555–1571.

Teale, W. H. (1984) Reading to young children: its significance for literacy development. In H. Goelman, A. Oberg and F. Smith (eds), *Awakening to Literacy*. London: Heinemann.

Teasdale, T. W., Fuchs, J. and Goldschmidt, E. (1988) Degree of myopia in relation to intelligence and educational level. *The Lancet* 8264, 1351–1353.

Tees, R. C. (1986) Experience and visual development: behavioral evidence. In W. T. Greenough and J. M. Juraska (eds), *Developmental Neuropsychology*. New York: Academic Press.

Tenenbaum, H. and Leaper, C. (2003) Parent–child conversations about science: the socialisation of gender inequities? *Developmental Psychology* 39, 34–47.

Teyler, T. J. and Fountain, S. B. (1987) Neuronal plasticity in the mammalian brain: relevance to behavioural learning and memory. *Child Development* 58, 698–712.

Tharp, R. G. and Gallimore, R. (1988) *Rousing Minds to Life: Teaching, Learning and Schooling in Social Context*. Cambridge, UK: Cambridge University Press.

Tharp, R. G., Jordan, C., Speidel, G. E. Au, K., Klein, T., Calkins, R., Scoat, K. and Gallimore, R. (1984) Product and process in applied developmental research: education and the children of a minority. In M. E. Lamb, A. L. Brown and B. Rogoff (eds), *Advances in Developmental Psychology*, vol. 3. Hillsdale, NJ: Lawrence Erlbaum Associates, Inc.

Thatcher, R. W., Walker, R. A. and Guidice, S. (1987) Human cerebral hemispheres develop at different rates and ages. *Science* 236, 1110–1113.

Theakston, A. L., Lieven, E., Pine, J. and Rowland, C. (2004) Semantic generality, input frequency and the acquisition of syntax. *Journal of Child Language* 31, 61–99.

Thomas, G. V. and Silk, A. M. J. (1990) *An Introduction to the Psychology of Children's Drawings*. Brighton, UK: Harvester.

Thomas, G. V. and Tsalimi, A. (1988) Effects of order of drawing head and trunk on their relative sizes in children's human figure drawings. *British Journal of Developmental Psychology* 6, 191–203.

Thomas, G. V., Nye, R. and Robinson, E. J. (1994) How children view pictures: children's responses to pictures as things in themselves and as representations of something else. *Cognitive Development* 9, 141–164.

Thomas, K. M. and Casey, B. J. (2003) Methods for imaging the developing brain. In M. De Haan and M. Johnson (eds), *The Cognitive Neuroscience of Development*. Hove, UK: Psychology Press.

Thomassen, J. W. M. and Teulings, H.-L. H. M. (1983) The development of handwriting. In M. Martlew (ed.), *The Psychology of Written Language*. Chichester, UK: Wiley.

Thompson, L. A., Fagen, J. F. and Fulker, D. W. (1991) Longitudinal prediction of specific cognitive abilities from infant novelty preference. *Child Development* 62, 530–538.

Thompson, L. A. and Massaro, D. W. (1989) Before you see it, you see its parts: evidence for feature encoding and integration in preschool children and adults. *Cognitive Psychology* 21, 334–362.

Thompson, R. A. (ed.) (1990a) Socioemotional development. *Nebraska Symposium on Motivation*, 1988, vol. 36. Lincoln: University of Nebraska Press.

Thompson, R. A. (1990b) Emotion and self-regulation. In R. A. Thompson (ed.), Socioemotional development. *Nebraska Symposium on Motivation*, 1988, vol. 36. Lincoln: University of Nebraska Press.

Thompson, T. (2004) Failure-avoidance: parenting, the achievement environment of the home and strategies for reduction. *Learning and Instruction* 14, 3–26.

Thomson, G. O. B., Raab, G. M., Hepburn, W. S., Hunter, R., Fulton, M. and Laxen, D. P. H. (1989) Blood-lead levels and children's behaviour: results from the Edinburgh Lead Study. *Journal of Child Psychology and Psychiatry* 30, 515–528.

Thorpe, K., Greenwood, R., Eivers, A. and Rutter, M. (2001) Prevalence and developmental course of 'secret language'. *International Journal of Language and Communication Disorders* 36, 43–62.

Thorpe, K. J. (1988) *Metacognition and attribution for learning outcome amongst children in the primary school.* Unpublished PhD thesis, University of Bristol.

Thorpe, K., Rutter, M. and Greenwood, R. (2003) Twins as a natural experiment to study the causes of mild language delay: II: Family interaction risk factors. *Journal of Child Psychology and Psychiatry* 44, 342–355.

Thorstad, G. (1991) The effect of orthography on the acquisition of literacy skills. *British Journal of Psychology* 82, 527–537.

Thurber, J. (1953) The secret life of James Thurber. *The Thurber Carnival*. Harmondsworth, UK: Penguin Books.

Thwaite, A. (2002) *Glimpses of the Wonderful: The Life of Philip Henry Gosse.* London: Faber and Faber.

Tierney, R. J., Soter, A., O'Flanahan, J. F. and McGinley, W. (1989) The effects of reading and writing upon thinking critically. *Reading Research Quarterly* 24, 134–173.

Tizard, B. (1986) The impact of the nuclear threat on children's development. In M. P. M. Richards and P. H. Light (eds), *Children of Social Worlds*. Cambridge: Polity Press.

Tizard, B., Blatchford, P., Burke, J., Farquhar, C. and Plewis, I. (1988) *Young Children at School in the Inner City*. Hove, UK: Lawrence Erlbaum Associates Ltd.

Tizard, B. and Hughes, M. (1984) *Young Children Learning*. London: Fontana.

Tizard, B., Hughes, M., Pinkerton, G. and Carmichael, H. (1982) Adults' cognitive demands at home and at nursery school. *Journal of Child Psychology and Psychiatry* 23(2), 108–117.

Tizard, B., Philps, J. and Plewis, I. (1976) Play in preschool centres. *Journal of Child Psychology and Psychiatry* 17, 251–274.

Tizard, B., Schofield, W. and Hewison, J. (1981) Collaboration between teachers and parents in assisting children's reading. *British Journal of Educational Psychology* 52, 1–5.

Tomasello, M. (1992) *First Verbs: A Case Study of Early Grammatical Development*. Cambridge, UK: Cambridge University Press.

Tomasello, M. (1997) Language in cognitive development: emergence of the mediated mind. *Contemporary Psychology* 42(12), 1080–1083.

Tomasello, M. (1998) *The new psychology of language: cognitive and functional approaches*. Cambridge, UK: Cambridge University Press.

Tomasello, M. (2000) Do young children have adult syntactic competence? *Cognition* 74, 209–253.

Tomasello, M. and Haberl, K. (2003) Understanding attention: 12- and 18-month-olds know what is new for other persons. *Developmental Psychology* 39(5), 906–912.

Tomasello, M. and Rakoczy, H. (2003) What makes human cognition unique? From individual to shared to collective intentionality. *Mind and Language* 18(2), 121–147.

Tong, S., Baghurst, P. A., Sawyer, M. G., Burns, J. and McMichael, A. J. (1998) Declining blood lead levels and changes in cognitive function during childhood: the Pont Pirie Cohort study. *Journal of the American Medical Association* 280, 1915–1919.

Torrance, E. P. (1962) *Guiding Creative Talent*. Englewood Cliffs, NJ: Prentice Hall.

Torrance, E. P. (1988) The nature of creativity as manifest in testing. In R. J. Sternberg (ed.), *The Nature of Creativity: Contemporary Psychological Perspectives*. Cambridge, UK: Cambridge University Press.

Torrey, J. W. (1979) Reading that comes naturally: the early reader. In T. G. Waller and G. Mackinnon (eds), *Reading Research: Advances in Theory and Practice*, vol. 1. New York: Academic Press.

Totereau, C., Barrouillet, P. and Fayol, M. (1998) Overgeneralisation of number inflections in the learning of written French: the case of noun and verb. *British Journal of Developmental Psychology* 16, 447–464.

Touwen, B. (1998) The brain and development of function. *Developmental Review* 18, 503–526.

Towse, J. N. and Saxton, M. (1997) Linguistic influences on children's number concepts: Methodological and theoretical considerations. *Journal of Experimental Child Psychology* 66(3), 362–375.

Trabasso, T. (1975) Representation, memory and reasoning: how do we make transitive inferences? In A. D. Pick (ed.), *Minnesota Symposium on Child Psychology*, vol. 9. Hillsdale, NJ: Lawrence Erlbaum Associates, Inc.

Trabasso, T. and Nicholas, D. W. (1980) Memory and inferences in the comprehension of narratives. In F. Wilkening, J. Becker and T. Trabasso (eds), *Information Integration by Children*. Hillsdale, NJ: Lawrence Erlbaum Associates, Inc.

Trainor, L. J. (1996) Infant preference for infant-directed versus noninfant-directed playsongs and lullabies. *Infant Behavior and Development* 19, 83–92.

Trainor, L. J., Wu, L. and Tsang, C. D. (2004) Long-term memory for music: infants remember tempo and timbre. *Science* 7(3), 289–296.

Tramontana, M. G., Hooper, S. R. and Selzer, S. C. (1988) Research on the preschool prediction of later academic achievement: a review. *Developmental Review* 8, 89–146.

Trehub, S. E. (2003) The developmental origins of musicality. *Nature Neuroscience* 6(7), 669–673.

Trevarthen, C. (1978) Communication and cooperation in early infancy. In M. Bullowa (ed.), *Before Speech*. Cambridge, UK: Cambridge University Press.

Trevarthen, C. (1980) The foundations of intersubjectivity: development of interpersonal and cooperative understanding in infants. In D. R. Olson (ed.), *The Social Foundations of Language and Thought*. New York and London: Norton.

Trevarthen, C. (1982) The primary motives for cooperative understanding. In G. Butterworth and P. Light (eds), *Social Cognition: Studies of the Development of Understanding*. Brighton, UK: Harvester.

Trevarthen, C. (1988a) Brain development. In R. L. Gregory (ed.), *The Oxford Companion to the Mind*. Oxford, UK: Oxford University Press.

Trevarthen, C. (1988b) Universal cooperative motives: how infants begin to know language and skills of culture. In G. Jahoda and I. Lewis (eds), *Ethnographic Perspectives on Cognitive Development*. Beckenham, UK: Croom Helm.

Trevarthen, C. (2002) Origins of musical identity: evidence from infancy for musical social awareness. In R. A. R. Macdonald, D. J. Hargreaves and D. E. Miell (eds), *Musical Identities*. Oxford, UK: Oxford University Press.

Trevarthen, C. and Hubley, P. (1978) Secondary intersubjectivity: confidence, confiding and acts of meaning in the first year. In A. Lock (ed.), *Action, Gesture and Symbol: The Emergence of Language*. London: Academic Press.

Trevarthen, C. and Logotheti, K. (1989) Child and culture: genesis of cooperative knowing. In A. Gellatly, D. Rogers and J. A. Sloboda (eds), *Cognition and Social Worlds*. Oxford, UK: Clarendon Press.

Troseth, G. L. and DeLoache, J. S. (1998) The medium can obscure the message: young children's understanding of video. *Child Development* 69, 950–965.

Truss, L. (2003) *Eats, Shoots and Leaves*. London: Profile Books.

Tsao, F.-M., Liu, H.-M. and Kuhl, P. K. (2004) Speech perception in infancy predicts language development on the second year of life; a longitudinal study. *Child Development* 74(4), 1067–1084.

Tucker, D. M. (1992) Developing emotions and cortical networks. In M. Gunnar and C. A. Nelson (eds), Developmental Behavioral Neuroscience. *Minnesota Symposium on Child Psychology*, vol. 24. Hillsdale, NJ: Lawrence Erlbaum Associates, Inc.

Tucker, N. (1981) *The Child and the Book*. Cambridge, UK: Cambridge University Press.

Tulving, E. (1972) Episodic and semantic memory. In E. Tulving and W. Donaldson (eds), *Organisation of Memory*. New York: Academic Press.

Tulving, E. (2002) Episodic memory: from mind to brain. *Annual Review of Psychology* 53, 1–25.

Tunmer, W. E., Herriman, M. L. and Nesdale, A. R. (1988) Metalinguistic abilities and beginning reading. *Reading Research Quarterly* 23(2), 134–158.

Turiel, E. (1983) *The Development of Social Knowledge*. New York: Cambridge University Press.

Turiel, E. (1998) The development of morality. In W. Damon and R. Lerner (eds), *Handbook of Child Psychology, vol. 2, Social, Emotional and Personality Development*. New York: Wiley.

Turner, G. and Jacobs, P. (1983) Marker (X)-linked mental retardation. *Advances in Human Genetics* 13, 83–112.

Uttal, D. H. and Wellman, H. M. (1989) Young children's representation of spatial information acquired from maps. *Developmental Psychology* 25, 128–138.

Uzgiris, I. (1964) Situational generality of conservation. *Child Development* 35, 831–841.

Valentine, E. R. (1982) *Conceptual Issues in Psychology*. London: George Allen & Unwin.

Valkenburg, P. M. and Cantor, J. (2001) The development of the child into a consumer. *Applied Developmental Psychology* 22, 61–72.

Valsiner, J. (1984) Construction of the zone of proximal development: the socialisation of meals. *New Directions for Child Development* 23, 65–76.

Valsiner, J. (1989) Collective coordination of progressive empowerment. In L. Winegar (ed.), *Social Interaction and the Development of Children's Understanding*. Norwood, NJ: Ablex.

Valsiner, J. (ed.) (1988a) *Child Development within Culturally Structured Environments, vol. 1, Parental Cognition and Adult–Child Interaction*. Norwood, NJ: Ablex.

Valsiner, J. (ed.) (1988b) *Child Development within Culturally Structured Environments, vol. 2, Social Co-construction and Environmental Guidance in Development*. Norwood, NJ: Ablex.

Valsiner, J. (1997) *Culture and the Development of Children's Action*. Chichester, UK: Wiley.

Valsiner, J. (1998a) *The Guided Mind*. Cambridge, MA: Harvard University Press.

Valsiner, J. (1998b) The development of the concept of development: historical and epidemiological perspectives. In W. Damon and R. Lerner (eds), *Handbook of Child Psychology, vol. 1, Theoretical Models of Human Development*. New York: Wiley.

Valsiner, J. (2000) *Culture and Human Development*. London: Sage.

Van de gaer, E., Pustjens, H., Van Damme, J. and De Munter, A. (2004) Effects of single-sex versus co-educational classes and schools on gender differences in progress in language and mathematics achievement. *British Journal of the Sociology of Education* 25(3), 307–322.

Vandenberg, B. (1990) Play and problem solving: an elusive connection. *Merrill-Palmer Quarterly* 36, 261–272.

Van den Broek, P., Young, M., Tzeng, Y. and Linderholm, T. (2004) The landscape model of reading: inferences and the online construction of a memory representation. In R. B. Ruddell and N. J. Unrau (eds), *Theoretical Models and Processes of Reading*. Newark, DE: International Reading Association.

Van der Veer, R. and Valsiner, J. (1988) Lev Vygotsky and P. Janet: on the origin of the concept of sociogenesis. *Developmental Review* 8, 52–65.

Van der Veer, R. and Valsiner, J. (1991) *Understanding Vygotsky: a Quest for Synthesis*. Oxford, UK: Blackwell.

Van Geert, P. (1991) A dynamic systems model of cognitive and language growth. *Psychological Review* 98, 3–53.

Van Houtte M. (2004) Why boys achieve less at school than girls: the difference between boys' and girls' academic culture. *Educational Studies* 30(2), 159–173.

Vasilyeva, M. and Huttenlocher, J. (2004) Early development of scaling ability. *Developmental Psychology* 40(5), 682–690.

Vaughan, H. G. and Kurtzberg, D. (1992) Electrophysiologic indices of human brain maturation and cognitive development. In M. Gunnar and C. A. Nelson (eds), Developmental behavioral neuroscience: *Minnesota Symposium on Child Psychology*, vol. 24. Hillsdale, NJ: Lawrence Erlbaum Associates, Inc.

Veenman, M. V. J., Wilhelm, P. and Beishuizen, J. J. (2004) The relation between intellectual and metacognitive skills from a developmental perspective. *Learning and Instruction* 14, 89–109.

Vellutino, F. R. and Scanlon, D. M. (1987) Phonological coding, phonological awareness and reading ability: evidence from a longitudinal and experimental study. *Merrill-Palmer Quarterly* 33(3), 321–363.

Vellutino, F. R., Fletcher, J. M., Snowling, M. J. and Scanlon, D. M. (2004) Specific reading disability (dyslexia): what have we learned in the past four decades? *Journal of Child Psychology and Psychiatry and Allied Disciplines* 45, 12–40.

Venter, J. C., Adams, M. D., Myers, E. W. *et al.* (2001) The sequence of the human genome. *Science* 291, 1304–1351.

Venville, G. (2004) Young children learning about living things: a case study of conceptual change from ontological and social perspectives. *Journal of Research on Science Teaching* 41(5), 449–480.

Venville, G., Adey, P. and Larkin, S. (2003) Fostering thinking through science in the early years of schooling. *International Journal of Science Education* 25(11), 1313–1331.

Venville, G., Rennie, L. and Wallace, J. (2004) Decision making and sources of knowledge: how students tackle integrated tasks in science, technology and mathematics. *Research in Science Education* 34(2), 115–135.

Vernon, P. A. (1985) Individual differences in general cognitive ability. In L. C. Hartlage and C. F. Telzrow (eds), *The Neuropsychology of Individual Differences*. New York: Plenum Press.

Vernon, P. E. (1972) The distinctiveness of field independence. *Journal of Personality* 40, 366–391.

Victor, J. B., Halverson, C. F. and Montague, R. B. (1985) Relations between reflection–impulsivity and behavioral impulsivity in preschool children. *Developmental Psychology* 21, 141–148.

Viding, E., Spinath, F. M., Price, T. S., Bishop D. V. M., Dale P. S. and Plomin R. (2004) Genetic and environmental influence on language impairment in 4-year-old same-sex and opposite-sex twins. *Journal of Child Psychology and Psychiatry* 45(2), 315–325.

Volet, S. E. and Chalmers, D. (1992) Investigation of qualitative differences in university students' learning goals, based on an unfolding model of stage development. *British Journal of Educational Psychology* 62, 17–34.

Volpe, J. (ed.) (2000) Special issue on normal and abnormal development of the CNS. *Mental Retardation and Developmental Disabilities Research Reviews* 6(1).

Vosniadou, S. (1987) Children and metaphors. *Child Development* 58, 870–885.

Vosniadou, S. and Ortony, A. (1983) The emergence of the literal–metaphorical–anomalous distinction in young children. *Child Development* 54, 154–161.

Vosniadou, S. and Ortony, A. (eds) (1989) *Similarity and Analogical Reasoning.* Cambridge, UK: Cambridge University Press.

Vosniadou, S., Ortony, A., Reynolds, R. E. and Wilson, P. T. (1984) Sources of difficulty in children's understanding of metaphorical language. *Child Development* 55, 1588–1606.

Voss, J. (1989) Problem solving and the educational process. In A. Lesgold and R. Glaser (eds), *Foundations for a Psychology of Education.* Hillsdale, NJ: Lawrence Erlbaum Associates, Inc.

Votruba-Drzal, E., Coley, R. L. and Chase-Lansdale, P. L. (2004) Child care and low-income children's development: direct and moderated effects. *Child Development* 75(1), 296–312.

Vuchinich, S., Vuchinich, R. and Coughlin, C. (1992) Family talk and parent–child relationships: towards integrating deductive and inductive paradigms. *Merrill-Palmer Quarterly* 38, 69–94.

Vurpillot, E. (1976) *The Visual World of the Child.* New York: International Universities Press.

Vuyk, R. (1981) *Overview and Critique of Piaget's Genetic Epistemology, 1965–1980,* vols 1 and 2. London: Academic Press.

Vye, N. J., Delcols, V. R., Burns, M. S. and Bransford, J. D. (1988) Teaching thinking and problem solving: illustrations and issues. In R. J. Sternberg and E. E. Smith (eds), *The Psychology of Human Thought.* Cambridge, UK: Cambridge University Press.

Vygotsky, L. S. (1960) The development of higher mental functions. Quoted in J. V. Wertsch (1985a) *Vygotsky and the Social Formation of Mind.* Cambridge, MA: Harvard University Press.

Vygotsky, L. S. (1962) *Thought and Language.* Cambridge, MA: MIT Press.

Vygotsky, L. S. (1971) *The Psychology of Art.* Cambridge, MA: MIT Press.

Vygotsky, L. S. (1976) Play and its role in the mental development of the child. In J. S. Bruner, A. Jolly and K. Sylvia (eds), *Play, its Role in Development and Evolution.* Harmondsworth, UK: Penguin Books.

Vygotsky, L. S. (1978a) *Mind in Society: The Development of Higher Psychological Processes,* eds M. Cole, V. John-Steiner, S. Scribner and E. Souberman. Cambridge, MA: Harvard University Press.

Vygotsky, L. S. (1978b) The prehistory of written language. In M. Cole, V. John-Steiner, S. Scribner and E. Souberman (eds), *Mind in Society: The Development of Higher Psychological Processes.* Cambridge, MA: Harvard University Press.

Vygotsky, L. S. (1981) The genesis of higher mental functions. In J. V. Wertsch (ed.), *The Concept of Activity in Soviet Psychology.* Armonk, NY: M. E. Sharpe.

Vygotsky, L. S. (1986) *Thought and Language,* new edn, ed. A. Kozulin. Cambridge, MA: MIT Press.

Waber, D. P. (1977) Biological substrates of field dependence: implications of the sex difference. *Psychological Bulletin* 84, 1076–1087.

Wachs, T. D. (1987) Specificity of environmental action as manifest in environmental correlates of infants' mastery motivation. *Developmental Psychology* 23, 782–790.

Waggoner, J. E. and Palermo, D. S. (1989) Betty is a bouncing bubble: children's comprehension of emotion-descriptive metaphors. *Developmental Psychology* 25(1), 152–163.

Wagner, D. A. (1982) Ontogeny in the study of culture and cognition. In D. A. Wagner and H. W. Stevenson (eds), *Cultural Perspectives on Child Development*. San Francisco: Freeman.

Wagner, D. A. and Spratt, J. E. (1987) Cognitive consequences of contrasting pedagogies: the effects of Quranic preschooling in Morocco. *Child Development* 58, 1207–1219.

Wagner, R. K. and Torgeson, J. K. (1987) The nature of phonological processing and its causal role in the acquisition of reading skills. *Psychological Bulletin* 101, 192–212.

Wagner, R. K., Torgesen, J. K. and Rashotte, C. A. (1994) Development of reading-related phonological processing abilities: new evidence of bi-directional causality from a latent variable longitudinal study. *Developmental Psychology* 30, 73–87.

Wagner, R. K., Torgesen, J. K., Rashotte, C. A., Hecht, S. A., Barker, T. A., Burgess, S. R., Donahue, J. and Garon, T. (1997) Changing relations between phonological processing abilities and word-level reading as children develop from beginning to skilled readers: a 5 year longitudinal study. *Developmental Psychology* 33, 468–479.

Wahler, R. G. and Dumas, J. E. (1989) Attentional problems in dysfunctional mother–child interactions: an interbehavioral model. *Psychological Bulletin* 105, 116–130.

Waisbren, S. E. (1999) Developmental and neuropsychological outcomes in children born to mothers with phenylketonuria. *Mental Retardation and Developmental Disabilities Research Reviews* 5(2), 125–131.

Wakeley, A., Rivera, S. and Langer, J. (2000a) Can young infants add and subtract? *Child Development* 71, 1525–1534.

Wakeley, A., Rivera, S. and Langer, J. (2000b) Not proved: reply to Wynn. *Child Development* 71, 1537–1539.

Walker, D., Greenwood, C., Hart, B. and Carta, J. (1994) Prediction of school outcomes based on early language production and socioeconomic-factors. *Child Development* 65(2), 606–621.

Walker, S. P., Grantham-McGregor, S., Powell, C. A. and Chang, S. M. (2000) Effects of growth restriction in early childhood on growth, IQ, and cognition at 11 to 12 years and the benefits of nutritional supplementation and psychosocial stimulation. *Journal of Pediatrics* 137, 36–41.

Walkerdine, V. (1988) *The Mastery of Reason*. London: Routledge.

Walkerdine, V. (1989) *Counting Girls Out*. London: Virago.

Walkerdine, V. and Lucey, H. (1989) *Democracy in the Kitchen*. London: Virago.

Wall, P. D. (1985) Pain and no pain. In C. W. Coen (ed.), *Functions of the Brain*. Oxford, UK: Clarendon Press.

Wallach, M. A. (1971) Creativity. In P. H. Mussen (ed.), *Carmichael's Manual of Child Psychology*, 3rd edn, vol. 1. New York: Wiley.

Wallach, M. A. and Kogan, N. (1965) *Modes of Thinking in Young Children: A Study of the Creativity–Intelligence Distinction*. New York: Holt, Rinehart & Winston.

Wallas, G. (1926) *The Art of Thought*. London: Cape.

Wang, Q. (2004) The emergence of cultural self-constructs: autobiographical memory and self-description in European American and Chinese children. *Developmental Psychology* 40(1), 3–15.

Wapner, J. G. and Connor, K. (1986) The role of defensiveness in cognitive impulsivity. *Child Development* 57, 1370–1374.

Ward, S., Wackman, D. B. and Wartella, E. (1977) *How Children Learn to Buy: The Development of Consumer Information-processing Skills*. Beverly Hills, CA: Sage.

Wardle, J. (ed.) (1992) Nutrition and I.Q., special issue of *The Psychologist* 5, 399–413.

Wardle, J. (2005) The triple whammy. *The Psychologist* 18(4), 216–219.

Warnock, M. (1976) *Imagination*. London: Faber.

Wason, P. C. (1977) On the failure to eliminate hypotheses. In P. N. Johnson-Laird and P. C. Wason (eds), *Thinking*. Cambridge, UK: Cambridge University Press.

Wason, P. C. and Johnson-Laird, P. N. (1972) *The Psychology of Reasoning*. London: Batsford.

Waterland, R. A. and Jirtle, R. L. (2004) Early nutrition, epigenetic changes at transposons and imprinted genes, and enhanced susceptibility to adult chronic diseases. *Nutrition* 20(1), 63–68.

Watson, A. C., Nixon, C. L., Wilson, A. and Capage, L. (1999) Social interaction skills and theory of mind in young children. *Developmental Psychology* 35(2), 386–391.

Watson, J. K., Gelman, S. A. and Wellman, H. M. (1998) Young children's understanding of the non-physical nature of thoughts and the physical nature of the brain. *British Journal of Developmental Psychology* 16, 321–335.

Watson, M. W. (1984) Development of social role understanding. *Developmental Review* 4, 192–213.

Waxman, S. R. and Hatch, T. (1992) Beyond basics: preschool children label objects flexibly at multiple hierarchical levels. *Journal of Child Language* 19, 153–166.

Weatherford, D. L. (1982) Spatial cognition as a function of size and scale of the environment. In R. Cohen (ed.), *New Directions for Child Development: Children's Conceptions of Spatial Relationships*. San Francisco: Jossey-Bass.

Weikart, D. (1978) *An Economic Analysis of the Ypsilanti Perry Preschool Project*. Ypsilanti, MI: High/Scope Educational Research Foundation.

Weinstein, C. S. (1991) The classroom as a social context for learning. *Annual Review of Psychology* 42, 493–525.

Weissberg, J. A. and Paris, S. G. (1986) Young children's remembering in different contexts: a reinterpretation of Istomina's study. *Child Development* 57, 1123–1129.

Weisz, J. R., Yeates, K. O., Robertson, D. and Beckham, J. C. (1982) Perceived contingency of skill and chance events: a developmental analysis. *Developmental Psychology* 18, 898–905.

Weizman, Z. O. and Snow, C. E. (2001) Lexical output as it relates to children's vocabulary acquisition: Effects of sophisticated exposure as a support for meaning. *Developmental Psychology* 37, 265–279.

Wellman, H. (2002) Understanding the psychological world: developing a theory of mind. In U. Goswami (ed.), *Blackwell Handbook of Cognitive Development.* Oxford, UK: Blackwell.

Wellman, H., Cross, D. and Watson, J. (2001) Meta-analysis of theory-of-mind development: the truth about false belief. *Child Development* 72, 655–684.

Wellman, H. M. (1983) Metamemory revisited. In M. T. H. Chi (ed.), *Trends in Memory Development Research.* New York: Karger.

Wellman, H. M. (1985a) The child's theory of mind: the development of conceptions of cognition. In S. R. Yussen (ed.), *The Growth of Reflection in Children.* New York: Academic Press.

Wellman, H. M. (1985b) The origins of metacognition. In D. L. Forrest-Pressley, G. E. MacKinnon and T. G. Waller (eds), *Metacognition, Cognition and Human Performance.* Orlando, FL: Academic Press.

Wellman, H. M. (1988) First steps in the child's theorizing about the mind. In J. W. Astington, P. L. Harris and D. R. Olson (eds), *Developing Theories of Mind.* Cambridge, UK: Cambridge University Press.

Wellman, H. M. (1990) *The Child's Theory of Mind.* Cambridge, MA: MIT Press.

Wellman, H. M. and Cross, D. (2001) Theory of mind and conceptual change. *Child Development* 72, 702–707.

Wellman, H. M. and Estes, D. (1986) Early understanding of mental entities: a reexamination of childhood realism. *Child Development* 57, 910–923.

Wellman, H. M. and Hickling, A. K. (1994) The mind's 'I': children's conception of the mind as an active agent. *Child Development* 65, 1564–1580.

Wellman, H. M. and Liu, D. (2004) Scaling of theory-of-mind tasks. *Child Development* 75(2), 523–541.

Wellman, H. M., Phillips, A. T., Dunphy-Lelii, S. and LaLonde, N. (2004) Infant social attention predicts preschool social cognition. *Developmental Science* 283–288.

Wellman, H. M. and Woolley, J. D. (1990) From simple desires to ordinary beliefs: the early development of everyday psychology. *Cognition* 35, 245–275.

Wells, C. G. (1981a) Pre-school literacy related activities and success in school. In D. R. Olson (ed.), *The Nature and Consequences of Literacy.* Cambridge, UK: Cambridge University Press.

Wells, C. G. (1981b) Some antecedents of early educational attainment. *British Journal of Sociology of Education* 2, 181–200.

Wells, C. G. (1982a) Influences of the home on language development. In A. Davies (ed.), *Language and Learning in School and Home.* London: SSRC, Heinemann.

Wells, C. G. (1982b) *Language, Learning and Education.* Bristol: Centre for the Study of Language and Communication.

Wells, C. G. (1985) Preschool literacy-related activities and success in school. In D. R. Olson, N. Torrance and A. Hildyard (eds), *Literacy, Language and Learning: The Nature and Consequences of Reading and Writing.* Cambridge, UK: Cambridge University Press.

Wells, C. G. (1986) Variation in child language. In P. Fletcher and M. Garman (eds), *Language Acquisition.* Cambridge, UK: Cambridge University Press.

Wells, G. and Gutfreund, M. (1987) The conversational requirements for language learning. In W. Yule and M. Rutter (eds), *Language Development and Disorders*. London: MacKeith Press and Oxford, UK: Blackwell Scientific Publications.

Werner, H. (1948) *The Comparative Psychology of Mental Development*. Chicago: Follett.

Wertsch, J. V. (1978) Adult–child interaction and the roots of metacognition. *Quarterly Newsletter of the Laboratory of Comparative Human Cognition* 2(1), 15–18.

Wertsch, J. V. (1979) From social interaction to higher psychological process: a clarification and application of Vygotsky's theory. *Human Development* 22, 1–22.

Wertsch, J. V. (ed.) (1981) *The Concept of Activity in Soviet Psychology*. Armonk, NY: M. E. Sharpe.

Wertsch, J. V. (1985a) *Vygotsky and the Social Formation of Mind*. Cambridge, MA: Harvard University Press.

Wertsch, J. V. (ed.) (1985b) *Culture, Communication and Cognition*. Cambridge, UK: Cambridge University Press.

Wertsch, J. V. (2000) Gal'perin's elaboration of Vygotsky. *Human Development* 43(2), 103–106.

Wertsch, J. V. (2005) Making human beings human: Bioecological perspectives on human development. *British Journal of Developmental Psychology* 23(1), 143–151.

Wertsch, J. V., Del Rio, P. and Alvarez, A. (1995) *Sociocultural Studies of Mind*. Cambridge, UK: Cambridge University Press.

Wertsch, J. V., McNamee, G. D., McLane, J. B. and Budwid, N. A. (1980) The adult–child dyad as a problem-solving system. *Child Development* 51, 1215–1221.

Wertsch, J. V. and Sammarco, J. G. (1985) Social precursors to individual cognitive functioning: the problem of units of analysis. In R. A. Hinde, A.-N. Perret-Clermont and J. Stevenson-Hinde (eds), *Social Relationships and Cognitive Development*. Oxford, UK: Clarendon Press.

Wertsch, J. V. and Stone, C. A. (1985) The concept of internalisation in Vygotsky's account of the genesis of higher mental functions. In J. V. Wertsch (ed.), *Culture, Communication and Cognition*. Cambridge, UK: Cambridge University Press.

Wetherford, M. J. and Cohen, L. B. (1973) Developmental changes in infant visual preferences for novelty and familiarity. *Child Development* 44, 416–424.

Wheeler, M. A., Stuss, D. T. and Tulving, E. (1997) Toward a theory of episodic memory: the frontal lobes and autonoetic consciousness. *Psychological Bulletin* 121, 331–354.

Whitaker-Azmitia, P. M. (2001) Serotonin and brain development: role in human developmental disorders. *Brain Research Bulletin* 56(5), 479–485.

White, K. R. (1982) The relation between socioeconomic status and academic achievement. *Psychological Bulletin* 91, 461–488.

Whitehurst, C. J., Falco, F. L., Lonigan, C. J., Fischel, J. E., De Baryshe, B. D., Valdez-Menchaca, M. C. and Caulfield, M. (1988) Accelerating language development through picture book reading. *Developmental Psychology* 24(4), 552–559.

Whitehurst, G. J. and Lonigan, C. J. (2002) Emergent literacy: development from pre-readers to readers. In S. B. Neuman and D. K. Dickinson (eds), *Handbook of Early Literacy Research*. New York: Guilford.

Whittaker, S. (1983) *Memory development in 3 to 6 year-olds: learning how to learn*. Unpublished PhD thesis, University of St Andrews, St Andrews, UK.

Widdowson, E. M. (1951) Mental contentment and physical growth. *The Lancet*, i, 16 June, 1316–1318.

Wiley, A. R., Rose, A. J., Burger, L. K. and Miller, P. J. (1998) Constructing autonomous selves through narrative practices: a comparative study of working-class and middle-class families. *Child Development* 69, 833–847.

Wilkening, F., Levin, I. and Druyan, S. (1987) Children's counting strategies for time quantification and integration. *Developmental Psychology* 23, 823–831.

Wilkinson, J. (1988) Context effects in children's memory. In M. M. Gruneberg, P. E. Morris and R. N. Sykes (eds), *Practical Aspects of Memory: Current Research and Issues*, vol. 1. Chichester, UK: Wiley.

Willats, J. (1977) How children learn to draw realistic pictures. *Quarterly Journal of Experimental Psychology* 29, 367–382.

Williams, J. M., Watts, F. N., Macleod, G. and Mathews, A. (1988) *Cognitive Psychology and Emotional Disorders*. Chichester, UK: Wiley.

Williams, M. (1989) Vygotsky's social theory of mind. *Harvard Educational Review* 59(1), 108–127.

Williams, M. and Rask, H. (2003) Literacy through play: how families with able children support their literacy development. *Early Child Development and Care* 173(5), 527–533.

Wilson, C. and Nettelbeck, T. (1986) Inspection time and the mental age deviation hypothesis. *Personality and Individual Differences* 7, 669–675.

Wilson, C., Nettelbeck, T., Turnbull, C. and Young, R. (1992) IT, IQ and age: a comparison of developmental functions. *British Journal of Developmental Psychology* 10, 179–188.

Wilson, D., Esterman, A., Lewis, M., Roder, D. and Calder, I. (1986) Children's blood lead levels in the lead smelting town of Port Pirie, South Australia. *Archives of Environmental Medicine* 41(4), 245–250.

Wilson, R. S. (1983) The Louisville twin study: developmental synchronies in behaviour. *Child Development* 54, 298–316.

Wimmer, H. (1980) Children's understanding of stories: assimilation by a general schema for actions or coordination of temporal relations? In F. Wilkening, J. Becker and T. Trabasso (eds), *Information Integration by Children*. Hillsdale, NJ: Lawrence Erlbaum Associates, Inc.

Wimmer, H. and Hart, M. (1991) The Cartesian view and the theory view of mind: developmental evidence from understanding false belief in self and other. *British Journal of Developmental Psychology* 9, 125–138.

Wimmer, H. and Perner, J. (1983) Beliefs about beliefs: representation and constraining function of wrong beliefs in young children's understanding of deception. *Cognition* 13, 103–128.

Wimmer, H., Hogrefe, G.-J. and Perner, J. (1988) Children's understanding of informational access as source of knowledge. *Child Development* 59, 386–396.

Wimmer, H., Landerl, K. and Schneider, W. (1994) The role of rhyme awareness in learning to read a regular orthography. *British Journal of Developmental Psychology* 12, 469–484.

Winegar, L. T. (ed.) (1989) *Social Interaction and the Development of Children's Understanding*. Norwood, NJ: Ablex.

Winer, G. A., Cottrell, J. E., Mott, T., Cohen, M. and Fournier, J. (2001) Are children more accurate than adults? Spontaneous use of metaphor by children and adults. *Journal of Psycholinguistic Research* 30(5), 485–496.

Winick, M. (1976) *Malnutrition and Brain Development*. Oxford, UK: Oxford University Press.

Winner, E., Rosensteil, A. K. and Gardner, H. (1976) The development of metaphoric understanding. *Developmental Psychology* 12, 289–297.

Winograd, T. (1972) Understanding natural language. *Cognitive Psychology* 3, 1–191.

Witkin, H. A. (1977) *Cognitive Styles in Personal and Cultural Adaptation*. Worcester, MA: Clark University Press.

Witkin, H. A. and Goodenough, D. R. (1981) *Cognitive Styles: Essence and Origins*. New York: International Universities Press.

Witkin, H. A., Goodenough, D. R. and Oltman, P. K. (1979) Psychological differentiation: current status. *Journal of Personality and Social Psychology* 37, 1127–1145.

Wittgenstein, L. (1976) *Philosophical Investigations*. Oxford, UK: Blackwell.

Wohlwill, J. F. (1973) *The Study of Behavioral Development*. New York: Academic Press.

Wolters, G., Beishuizen, M., Broers, G. and Knoppert, W. (1990) Mental arithmetic: effects of calculation procedure and problem difficulty on solution latency. *Journal of Experimental Child Psychology* 49, 20–30.

Woo, S. L. C. (1991) Molecular genetic analysis of phenylketonuria and mental retardation. In P. R. McHugh and V. A. McKusick (eds), *Genes, Brain and Behaviour*. New York: Raven Press.

Wood, D. J. (1980) Teaching the young child: some relationships between social interaction, language and thought. In D. R. Olson (ed.), *The Social Foundations of Language and Thought*. New York: Norton.

Wood, D. J. (1981) *Working with Underfives*. London: Grant McIntyre.

Wood, D. J. (1998) *How Children Think and Learn: The Social Contexts of Cognitive Development*, 2nd edn. Oxford, UK: Blackwell.

Wood, D. J., Bruner, J. S. and Ross, G. (1976) The role of tutoring in problem solving. *Journal of Child Psychology and Psychiatry* 17(2), 89–100.

Wood, D. J. and Middleton, D. J. (1975) A study of assisted problem solving. *British Journal of Psychology* 66, 181–191.

Wood, D. J., Wood, H. A. and Middleton, D. J. (1978) An experimental evaluation of four face-to-face teaching strategies. *International Journal of Behavioural Development* 1, 131–147.

Woodhead, M. (1985) Pre-school education has long-term effects: but can they be generalised? *Oxford Review of Education* 11, 133–155.

Woodhead, M. (1988) When psychology informs public policy: the case of early chilhood intervention. *American Psychologist* 43, 443–454.

Woodward, A. L. and Markman, E. M. (1998) Early word learning. In D. Kuhn and R. S. Siegler (eds), *Handbook of Child Psychology, vol. 2, Cognition, Perception and Language*. New York: Wiley.

Woolley, J. D. (1995) The fictional mind: young children's understanding of imagination, pretense and dreams. *Developmental Review* 15, 172–211.

Woolley, J. D. (1997) Thinking about fantasy: are children fundamentally different thinkers and believers from adults? *Child Development* 68(6), 991–1011.

Woolley, J. D., Boerger, E. and Markman, A. B. (2004) A visit from the Candy

Witch: factors influencing children's belief in a novel fantastical being. *Developmental Science* 7(4). 456–468.

Woolley, J. D. and Phelps, K. E. (1994) Young children's practical reasoning about imagination. *British Journal of Developmental Psychology* 12, 53–67.

Woolley, J. D., Phelps, K. E., Davis, D. L. and Mandell, D. J. (1999) Where theories of mind meet magic: the development of children's beliefs about wishing. *Child Development* 70, 571–587.

Wozniak, R. H. (1987) Developmental method, zones of development, and theories of the environment. In L. S. Liben (ed.), *Development and Learning*. Hillsdale, NJ: Lawrence Erlbaum Associates, Inc.

Wren, T. and Mendoza, C. (2004) Cultural identity and personal identity: philosophical reflections on the identity discourse of social psychology. In D. Lapsley and D. Narvaez (eds), *Moral Development, Self, and Identity*. Mahwah, NJ: Lawrence Erlbaum Associates, Inc.

Wright, J. C., Huston, A. C., Murphy, K. C., St Peters, M., Pinon, M., Scantlin, R. and Kotler, J. (2001) The relations of early television viewing to school readiness and vocabulary of children from low-income families: the Early Window project. *Child Development* 72, 1347–1366.

Wynn, K. (1992) Children's acquisition of the number words and the counting system. *Cognitive Psychology* 24, 220–251.

Wynn, K. (1998) Numerical competence in infants. In C. Donlan (ed.), *The Development of Mathematical Skills*. Hove, UK: Psychology Press.

Wynn, K. (2000) Findings of addition and subtraction in infants are robust and consistent: Reply to Wakely, Rivera, and Langer. *Child Development* 71, 1535–1536.

Yang-Feng, T. L. (1991) The chromosome: its anatomy, and its aberrations. In P. R. McHugh and V. A. McKusick (eds), *Genes, Brain and Behavior*. New York: Raven Press.

Yaniv, I. and Shatz, M. (1988) Children's understanding of perceptibility. In J. W. Astington, P. L. Harris and D. R. Olson (eds), *Developing Theories of Mind*. Cambridge, UK: Cambridge University Press.

Yates, G. C. R., Yates, S. M. and Beasley, C. J. (1987) Young children's knowledge of strategies in delay of gratification. *Merrill-Palmer Quarterly* 33, 159–169.

Yoshinaga-Itano, C., Sedey, A., Coulter, D. and Mehl, A. (1998) Language of early- and later-identified children with hearing loss. *Pediatrics* 102, 1161–1171.

Young, J. Z. (1978) *Programs of the Brain*. Oxford, UK: Oxford University Press.

Young, J. Z. (1985) What's in a brain? In C. W. Coen (ed.), *Functions of the Brain*. Oxford, UK: Clarendon Press.

Young, J. Z. (1987) *Philosophy and the Brain*. Oxford, UK: Oxford University Press.

Yuill, N. and Perner, J. (1988) Intentionality and knowledge in children's judgment of actor's responsibility and recipient's emotional reaction. *Developmental Psychology* 24(3), 358–365.

Yule, W., Gold, R. D. and Busch, C. (1981) Long-term predictive validity of the WPPSI: an 11-year follow-up study. *Personality and Individual Differences* 3, 65–71.

Yule, W. and Rutter, M. (1985) Reading and other learning difficulties. In M. Rutter and L. Hersov (eds), *Child and Adolescent Psychiatry: Modern Approaches*. Oxford, UK: Blackwell.

Yussen, S. R. (ed.) (1985a) *The Growth of Reflection in Children*. New York: Academic Press.

Yussen, S. R. (1985b) The role of metacognition in contemporary theories of cognitive development. In D. L. Forrest-Pressley, G. E. MacKinnon and G. T. Waller (eds), *Metacognition, Cognition and Human Performance*. Orlando, FL: Academic Press.

Yussen, S. R. and Levy, V. M. (1975) Developmental change in predicting one's own span of short-term memory. *Journal of Experimental Child Psychology* 19, 502–508.

Yussen, S. R., Mathews, S. R., Buss, R. R. and Kane, P. T. (1980) Developmental change in judging important and critical elements of stories. *Developmental Psychology* 16, 213–219.

Zabrucky, K. and Ratner, H. H. (1986) Children's comprehension monitoring and recall of inconsistent stories. *Child Development* 57, 1401–1418.

Zahn-Waxler, C., Cummings, E. M., Iannotti, R. M. and Radke-Yarrow, M. (1984) Young offspring of depressed parents: a population at risk for affective problems. In D. Cicchetti and K. Schneider-Rosen (eds), *New Directions for Child Development: Childhood Depression*. San Francisco: Jossey-Bass.

Zahn-Waxler, C. and Kochanska, G. (1990) The origins of guilt. In R. A. Thompson (ed.), Socioemotional development. *Nebraska Symposium on Motivation*, 1988, vol. 36. Lincoln: University of Nebraska Press.

Zahn-Waxler, C., Radke-Yarrow, M. and King, R. A. (1979) Child rearing and children's prosocial dispositions towards victims of distress. *Child Development* 50, 319–330.

Zajonc, R. B. (1983) Validating the confluence model. *Psychological Bulletin* 93, 457–480.

Zajonc, R. B. and Marcus G. B. (1975) Birth order and intellectual development. *Psychological Review* 82, 74–88.

Zajonc, R. B. and Mullallay, P. R. (1997) Birth order: reconciling conflicting effects. *American Psychologist* 52, 685–699.

Zaremba, J. (1985) Recent medical research. In D. Lane and B. Stratford (eds), *Current Approaches to Down's Syndrome*. London: Holt, Rinehart & Winston.

Zatorre, R. (2005) Music, the food of neuroscience? *Nature* 434, 312–315.

Zeanah, C. H., Nelson, C. A., Fox, N. A., Smyke, A. T., Marshall, P., Parker, S. W. and Koga, S. (2003) Designing research to study the effects of institutionalization on brain and behavioral development: the Bucharest Early Intervention Project. *Development and Psychopathology* 15(4), 885–907.

Zelazo, P., Muller, U., Frye, D. and Marcovitch, S. (2003) The development of executive function in early childhood. *Monographs of the Society for Research in Child Development* 68(3), serial no. 274.

Zelazo, P. D. (2004) The development of conscious control in childhood. *Trends in Cognitive Sciences* 8(1), 12–17.

Zelniker, T. and Jeffrey, W. E. (1976) Reflective and impulsive children: strategies of information-processing underlying differences in problem-solving. *Monographs of the Society for Research in Child Development* 41(5), serial no. 168.

Zelniker, T. and Jeffrey, W. E. (1979) Attention and cognitive style in children. In G. A. Hale and M. Lewis (eds), *Attention and Cognitive Development*. New York: Plenum Press.

Zhang, H. and Zhou, Y. (2003) The teaching of mathematics in Chinese elementary schools. *International Journal of Psychology* 38(5), 286–298.

Zhou, X. and Wang, B. (2004) Preschool children's written representation and understanding of written number symbols. *Early Child Development and Care* 174(3), 253–266.

Zigler, E. and Muenchow, S. (1992) *Head Start: The Inside Story of America's Most Successful Educational Experiment*. New York: Basic Books.

Zigler, E. and Styfco, S. (eds) (1993) *Head Start and Beyond: A National Plan for Extended Childhood Intervention*. New Haven, CT: Yale University Press.

Zigler, E. and Valentine, J. (1979) *Project Head Start: A Legacy of the War on Poverty*. New York: Free Press.

Zinchenko, V. P. (1985) Vygotsky's ideas about units for the analysis of mind. In J. V. Wertsch (ed.), *Culture, Communication and Cognition*, Cambridge, UK: Cambridge University Press.

Zingg, R. M. (1940) Feral man and extreme cases of isolation. *American Journal of Psychology* 53, 487–517.

Zipes, J. (1983) *Fairytales and the Art of Subversion*. London: Heinemann.

Zukrow-Goldring, P. G. (1995) Sibling caregiving. In M. H. Bornstein (ed.), *Handbook of Parenting, vol. 3, Status and Social Conditions of Parenting*. Mahwah, NJ: Lawrence Erlbaum Associates, Inc.

Zurer Pearson, B. (1990) The comprehension of metaphor by preschool children. *Journal of Child Language* 17, 185–204.

Name index

Subject index